Skater's Edge

SOURCEBOOK

ICE SKATING RESOURCE GUIDE

BY ALICE BERMAN

Published by *Skater's Edge*, Box 500, Kensington, MD 20895

In memory of Rachel Leda Berman Janse, whose radiant presence we miss more than words can express.

Cover photo: 1994 Olympic Silver Medalists Maia Usova and Alexander Zhulin. Photo by Alice Berman.

Cover design by Joel and Alice Berman.

Skater's Edge Sourcebook, First Edition

Copyright © 1995 by Alice Berman, *Skater's Edge*.

All rights reserved, including the right to reproduce this book or portions thereof in any form. No part of this book may be used or reproduced in any manner whatsoever without written permission of the publisher exccpt in the case of brief quotations embodied in critical articles and reviews. Printed in the United States of America by Port City Press.

Published by *Skater's Edge*, Box 500, Kensington, MD 20895; Phone/Fax: (301) 946-1971.

Library of Congress Cataloging-in-Publication Data:

Berman, Alice

Skater's Edge Sourcebook / Alice Berman; photography by Alice Berman.

First edition.
   p.   cm.

ISBN 0-9643027-0-5

1. Skating. 2. Sports   I. Berman, Alice   II. Title

Library of Congress Catalog Card Number: 94-93861

This book is available at bulk discount prices for sale as a fundraiser for appropriate skating clubs. Contact the publisher for details.

Appreciation

This book is the result of countless hours of research and hard work on the part of many people. It would not have been possible without the continuous love and support of my husband Joel, our daughter Ilana, my mother, Rose Bailey, and the rest of our family—Ariana, Mara, and David Berman, and Bud, Mike, and Ben Janse. I thank them with all my heart.

I would like to express my gratitude to the following people
for their part in making this book happen:

George Arnaoutis	Jaya Kanal
Rose Bailey	Joe Kershasky
Ilana Berman	Kristin Matta
Joel Berman	Bryce McGowan
Irma Burke	Cecily Morrow
Dick Button	Marc Nelson
Carrie Casey	Doris Penndorf
William Casey	Brian Petrovek
John Christie	Maggie Range
Brenda Chu	Norman Reid
Mike Cunningham	Jirina Ribbens
Beth Davis	Carol Rossignol
Barbara Feinman	Carole Shulman
Jonathan Fishbein	Ron Sing
Hannah Grisar	Linda Stelley
Orrin Getz	Mike Subelsky
Pierre Henry	Holly Townsend
Brooke Higdon	Jordan Young
Steve Hoar	Joanna Wlodawer

Thanks also to the thousands of people who took the time to answer our questions as we were compiling the data for this first edition of the *Skater's Edge SOURCEBOOK*.

Key to Photos

Oksana Baiul and Viktor Petrenko	258
Nicole Bobek	260
Brian Boitano	14
Dick Button	69, 117
Robin Cousins	19
Todd Eldredge	12
Ice Theatre of New York	119
Don Jackson	61
Nancy Kerrigan	128
Jenni Meno and Todd Sand	260
Cecily Morrow	48
Ludmila and Oleg Protopopov	70
Elizabeth Punsalan and Jerod Swallow	58
Renee Roca and Gorsha Sur	260
Jayne Torvill and Christopher Dean	27
Calla Urbanski and Rocky Marval	260
Barbara Underhill and Paul Martini	35
Maia Usova and Alexandr Zhulin	Cover
Paul Wylie	249
Kristi Yamaguchi	16, 31

Contents

Soaring Without Wings 7
Associations and Organizations 9
    Choosing a Pro 12
Books, Books, Books (Listed by author's name) 17
    Books by Title (Cross Reference) 29
    Books by Category (Cross Reference) 33
Boots and Blades 37
    Guide to Fitting Skates 37
    Skate Boots 39
    Guide to Blades 45
    Blades: Makes and Models 47
    Lacing Up 49
Champions: U.S. Nationals, Worlds, Olympics 51
    U.S. National Figure Skating Championships 51
    World Championships 59
    Olympic Winter Games 68
Companies and Organizations 71
    Companies by Categories (Cross Reference) 109
Fan Mail and Letters 127
Federations 129
Rinks, Rinks, Rinks 135
    Finding Rinks in Canada 219
    Rinks: Cross Reference by State and City 221
    Rinks: Cross Reference by Name 233
    Rinks Affiliated with Colleges or Universities
        Listed by State 245
        Listed by School Affiliation 248
Skater's Marketplace 106
Summer Skating Schools 251
Training Centers: Where Top Skaters Train 257
Videos, Videos, Videos 261
Advertiser Index 269

ILLUSTRATION BY WILLIAM CASEY

Soaring Without Wings

You're holding in your hands the first-ever comprehensive resource book created for delirious lovers of ice skating.

It hurts to have been born without wings, but soaring across the ice with the wind in your hair—aah! There's nothing like it.

You'll love our listings of Books, Videos, Magazines, Rinks, Summer Schools, and Training Centers. For information on skating equipment, turn to the chapter on Boots and Blades.

And don't miss the Champions section, which lists all the winners of U.S. Nationals, Worlds and Olympics since 1914. Maybe some day your name will be added to the list!

So stroke on!

Alice Berman, Publisher

Beauty, grace, power and athleticism all combine to form one of the most dazzling sports in the Olympic Winter Games — figure skating. No other sport requires so many diverse talents; talents which take years and years of intense work and dedication to develop.

The Skaters you see competing here today have devoted hours of hard work in their training in pursuit of their dreams of becoming world-class figure skaters. As potential members of the U.S. Team, they have reached the critical point at which they have the chance to turn their dreams into realities. But they cannot do it on their own. They need your help.

U.S. Skaters are currently facing their toughest challenge ever in the form of escalating training costs. Despite gruelling training schedules, many skaters take on full-time jobs to ease the financial burdens, while parents sometimes take on second and even third jobs to keep their children's dreams alive.

The Competitive Skaters Assistance Program of the USFSA Memorial Fund provides the financial assistance that is so urgently needed by these talented athletes. You can help by filling out the form below to make a tax-deductible gift to the Competitive Skaters Assistance Program of the USFSA Memorial Fund. Established in 1961, for over 30 years, the Memorial Fund has assisted literally thousands of competitive skaters *including every U.S. Olympic team member.*

All the talent and determination in the world won't get our skaters to the Olympic Games. They also need funding. With your support, you can help keep the dreams alive for some of our national competitors. You can make a difference.

THE USFSA MEMORIAL FUND
20 First Street, Colorado Springs, Colorado 80906

Enclosed is $_____ for <u>one</u> of the following:

(1) _____ An unrestricted gift to the USFSA Memorial Fund, and its Competitive Skaters Assistance Program.

(2) _____ A gift IN MEMORY OF _____
    Name and Address of Relative _____

(3) _____ A gift IN HONOR OF _____
    Residing at _____

(4) _____ A restricted gift to the USFSA Memorial Fund for such worthy skater or skaters as the Board of
    Directors of the _____ Skating Club may select.
    (While the Memorial Fund will attempt to honor your request, the USFSA reserves the right to exercise discretion, authority and responsibility over restricted funds to assure that they are used to further the exempt purposes of the USFSA and the Memorial Fund and are used in support of skaters who satisfy eligibility criteria to receive benefits.)

NAME:_____
ADDRESS: _____

Please make checks payable to USFSA Memorial Fund and mail to the Fund at the above address.
(Contributions to the USFSA Memorial Fund are tax deductible as charitable contributions.)

Associations and Organizations

Adult Skater's Forum
Contact: Joe Kaplenk
173 Norman Way
Boilingbrook, IL 60440
(708) 739-0992
Serves as an advocacy group for adult skaters, promotes and monitors the visibility and opportunities of adult skaters in figure, freestyle, dance, and pairs ice skating. Additional contact: Sue Chapman, (219) 787-8911.

Amateur Skating Union of America
Contact: Shirley Yates, Executive Secretary
1033 Shady Lane
Glen Ellyn, IL 60137
(708) 790-3230
Founded: 1927. Members are individuals interested in promotion, development, and conduct of ice speed skating competition. Competitors range in age from six to 60 years. Conducts seminars and training programs on a local basis; compiles statistics; maintains biographical archives and Speed Skating Hall of Fame in Newburgh, NY.

Association of the International Winter Sports Federations
Contact: Gian Franco Kasper, Secretary General
Bolchstrasse 2
CH-3653 Oberhofen, Switzerland
33 446161
Serves as umbrella organization for International Bobsleigh and Tobogganing Federation, International Ice Hockey Federation, International Luge Federation, International Skating Union, International Ski Federation, and International Union for Modern Pentathlon and Biathlon.

Canadian Figure Skating Association (CFSA)
Contact: David M. Dore, General Director
1600 James Naismith Drive
Suite 403
Gloucester, Ontario, K1B 5N4 Canada
(613) 748-5635
FAX: (613) 748-5718
The governing body of figure skating for Canada (CAN), with member clubs, skaters and pros. Offers extensive training and certification program for coaches. Figure skating member of the International Skating Union representing Canada.

Cleveland Coaches Council
Contact: Barbara Fitzgerald Mertik, President
P.O. Box 34173
Parma, OH 44134
(216) 546-9152
Founded: 1993. Professional coaches organization for communication and education in the Cleveland area.

Figure Skating Historical Society, Inc.
Contact: Jilliaine Eicher, President
PO Box 621
Chilmark, MA 02535
(508) 645-3063
FAX: (508) 645-2897
Founded: 1993. Dedicated to the study, promotion and preservation of figure skating. The Society's quarterly journal presents historical research, translation of texts, and projects conducted by members which further the appreciation of figure skating. A core resource of the Society is a database of skating information including over 2500 articles of periodical literature, cross-indexed by author and subject.

Ice Skating Institute of America (ISIA)
Contact: Justine Townsend Smith, Executive Director
355 West Dundee
Buffalo Grove, IL 60089
(708) 808-7528
FAX: (708) 808-8329
Since 1959, ISIA has offered rink management programs, conferences, trade shows, and seminars. Internationally-recognized revenue-producing recreational ice-skater programs for hockey, freestyle and figures for every age and ability level.

International Gay Figure Skating Union
Contact: Laura Moore or Arthur Luiz, Co-Presidents
P.O. Box 1101
New York, NY 10113
(212) 255-0559; (212) 691-1690
FAX: (212) 691-1690
Founded: 1992. The IGFSU is dedicated to promoting a safe and supportive environment for all skaters regardless of sexual orientation. Organizers and promoters of gay skating events including the Gay Games.

International In-Line Skating Association
Contact: Henry Zuver, Executive Director
P.O. Box 15482
Atlanta, GA 30333
(404) 728-9707
FAX: (404) 728-9866
Founded: 1991. Work with municipalities to expand access to skating arenas. Run an International Instructor Certification Program. Sanction hockey leagues and competitive events.

(Continued on next page)

International Skating Union (ISU)
Contact: Beat Hasler, General Secretary
Promenade 73, Postfach
CH-7270, Davos Platz, Switzerland
(081) 43 75 77
FAX: (081) 43 66 71
Founded: 1892. The umbrella organization and governing body for ice skating world-wide. Countries wishing to compete in the Olympics must be members of the ISU. All rules governing Olympic skating competitions are set by the ISU. The ISU also sells CDs of ice dance music; write for information.

Laura Stamm International Power Skating System
Contact: Bryce Leavitt McGowan, Director of Marketing/P.R.
205 Lincoln Place
Tuckahoe, NY 10707
(914) 961-7994; (800) 484-7303 x1886
FAX: (914) 961-0337
Laura Stamm Int'l Power Skating System teaches technique training for hockey skating skills. We reach an estimated 8000 hockey players a year and teach in 26 states in the U.S. Stamm has 25 years of experience teaching and coaching professional teams and players, plus amateurs. We offer clinics, workshops and summer schools for beginners up through college and professional players. Also offers power skating book and video.

Lenzi Foundation, The
Contact: Jean Lenzi, President
4228 1/2 River Road, NW
Suite A
Washington, DC 20016
(202) 363-6503
Founded: 1992. Four long-time skating fans formed The Lenzi Foundation to identify and support young U.S. figure skaters. Its mission is to become a viable force in skating, raising and giving away funds to eligible skaters to improve the quality of U.S. skating and ensure that promising young skaters are not lost. While the Foundation's primary focus is on pairs and dance, skaters from all disciplines will benefit.

Mid Atlantic Arena Managers Association
Contact: Robert Mock, Director
505 Larimer, #7
Turtle Creek, PA 15145
(412) 823-6642
Voluntary arena managers association covering Pennsylvania, eastern Ohio and West Virginia.

National Ice Skating Association of UK Limited (NISA)
Contact: James Courtney, President
15-27 Gee Street
London, ECIV 3RE Great Britain
(71) 253 3824/(71) 253 0910
FAX: (71) 490 2589
Member of the ISU representing Great Britain (GRB). The National Governing body for speed, figure, precision, dance and recreational skating. 3700 members.

National Ice Theatre of Canada
Contact: Sandra Shewchuk, Executive Director
10022-103 Street
Edmonton, Alberta, T5J 0X2 Canada
(403) 421-8879
FAX: (403) 426-1049
Founded: 1992. The National Ice Theatre of Canada (NITC), an Edmonton based, not-for-profit foundation, is dedicated through education and performance to nuturing and encouraging theatre on ice as a performing art. An innovative and exciting new art form, ice theatre combines the competitive sport of figure skating with the dynamic and dramatic world of theatre.

New England Ice Skating Managers Association
Contact: Steve Hoar, Facility Director
Hayden Recreation Centre, Inc.
24 Lincoln Street
Lexington, MA 02173
(617) 862-5575
FAX: (617) 674-2946
Founded: 1974. NEISMA has played an active role in supporting the ice rink industry and extending communication between the many rinks in New England for over 20 years.

Ontario Recreational Facilities Association, Inc. (ORFA)
Contact: John Milton, Executve Director
1185 Eglinton Avenue E
North York, Ontario, P4P 1C1 Canada
(416) 495-4200
FAX: (416) 495-4329
Founded: 1947. Refrigeration and Ice-Making manual. Professional development training opportunities in all aspects of facility operation, i.e. refrigeration, concession management, building maintenance, energy conservation, legal awareness, etc.

Pro Skating European Association
Contact: Angel Philippe, President
116 Avenue Charles de Gaulle
Neuilly/Seine, 92250 France
011-33-1-6767 8600
FAX: 011-33-1-6767 8600
Founded: 1991. Specialize in organizing skating events (professional competitions, galas, ice shows) in Europe. Plans to organize a tour in Germany, Lyon, and England in 1995.

Professional Skaters Guild of America (PSGA)
Contact: Carole Shulman, Executive Director
P.O. Box 5904
Rochester, MN 55403
(507) 281-5122
FAX: (507) 281-5491
National association for professional skaters and coaches. Publishes Professional Skater magazine, holds annual educational conferences and offers free fall seminars.

Skating Association for the Blind and Handicapped (SABAH)
Contact: Elizabeth M. O'Donnell, President and Founder
c/o Kaufmann's
1255 Niagara Falls Blvd
Buffalo, NY 14226
(716) 833-2994
FAX: (716) 833-2997
Founded: 1977. Provides skating instruction for people with mental, physical or emotional challenges. Founded in 1977. Currently serves over 750 people annually. Operates at five rinks in the western New York area.

Special Olympics International

Contact: Brian McMonagle, Sport Department
1325 G Street, NW
Suite 500
Washington, DC 20005 USA
(202) 628-3630
FAX: (202) 824-0200
Founded: 1968. Created by the Joseph P. Kennedy Jr. Foundation to promote physical fitness, sports training, and athletic competition for mentally retarded children and adults. Seeks to contribute to the physical, social, and psychological development of the mentally retarded. Participants range in age from 8 years to adult and compete in track and field, swimming, gymnastics, bowling, ice skating, basketball, and other sports.

U.S. Amateur Confederation of Roller Skating

Contact: George Pickard, Executive Director
P. O. Box 6579
Lincoln, NE 68506
(402) 483-7551
FAX: (402) 483-1465
Founded: 1973. Members are amateur artistic roller skaters. Serves as governing body for competitive roller skating in the U.S. Develops rules and requirements; trains and certifies judges and officials; represents U.S. skaters at international conferences. Conducts educational seminars for skaters and coaches. Sponsors championship competitions of all sizes; qualifies and trains skaters; bestows awards. Maintains museum, hall of fame, and rule book library.

U.S. Figure Skating Association (USFSA)

Contact: Jerry Lace, Executive Director
20 First Street
Colorado Sprngs, CO 80906
(719) 635-5200
FAX: (719) 635-9548
Figure skating member of the ISU representing the USA. The USFSA is the governing body for amateur figure skating on ice in the U.S. Since 1921, the USFSA has directed and encouraged the development of figure skating skills instruction and supervised the competitive aspects of the sport. Its national, world, and Olympic champions have made major contributions to figure skating and established outstanding international records and reputations. The USFSA has a membership of over 120,000 athletes and supporters; membership is open to anyone.

U.S. International Speed Skating Association

Contact: Chris Mills, Secretary
P.O. Box 16157
Rocky River, OH 44116 USA
(216) 899-0128
FAX: (216) 899-0109
Speed skating member of the ISU representing the United States (USA). Members are individuals interested in international speed skating. Promotes the metric or Olympic style of speed skating in the U.S. and helps U.S. skaters in international competitions, including the Olympic games. Conducts weekend seminars and summer camps. Sponsors competitions to select national champions, world competitors, and Olympic team members.

U.S. Olympic Committee (USOC)

Contact: Bob Condron, Public Relations
One Olympic Plaza
Colorado Springs, CO 80909
(719) 578-4529
FAX: (719) 578-4677

United States Barrel Jumping Association

Contact: Bennett Sipes, President
950 Wolverine Drive
Walled Lake, MI 48088 USA
(810) 624-0066
Founded: 1977. Members are competitors and coaches in the sport of barrel jumping while on ice skates or roller skates. Barrels are lined up on the ground in a straight line, side to side, and the object is to jump over as many barrels as possible without touching them.

USA Hockey, Inc.

Contact: Brian S. Petrovek, Assistant Executive Director
4965 North 30th Street
Colorado Springs, CO 80919
(719) 599-5500
FAX: (719) 599-5899
Founded: 1937. The national governing body for the sport of ice hockey in the U.S. Its mission is to promote the growth of ice hockey and to provide the best possible experience for all participants in the United States by encouraging, developing, advancing and adminstering the sport. Publishes American Hockey Magazine. Has formed new division, USA Hockey InLine for in-line players.

Wisconsin Ice Arena Management Association (WIAMA)

Contact: Joe Kershasky, Secretary/Treasurer
4001 S. 20th Street
Milwaukee, WI 53221
(414) 281-6289
FAX: (414) 282-4821
Founded: 1991. A professional association of arena and associated personnel, dedicated to the goal of professionalizing the industry by sharing ideas and innovative techniques through newsletters, membership meetings and seminars. Stresses a close working relationship between all types of industry personnel, from maintenance to management to suppliers.

Turn the page for an extensive article on **CHOOSING A PRO**, reprinted with permission from the Nov/Dec 1994 issue of *Skater's Edge*.

Choosing a Pro

BY ALICE BERMAN
PUBLISHER

Finding the right teacher is a crucial part of learning to skate. Many factors are involved, including individual personalities, learning styles, experience, and technical know-how. Many skaters start out with group classes and then move on to private lessons from there. The direction you take depends on what your goals are and what you want to get out of your skating.

LIST YOUR GOALS

"First you need to write down a list of things—or at least have one in your mind—indicating what you are looking for in a coach," says **Caroline Silby**, sports psychologist and former competitive skater. "Ask, 'What do I want this coach to do for me technically? What do I want this coach to do for me emotionally?'... Your list might include the technical aspects you want to learn, how much ice time you want, or how much coaching time you want."

"One of the biggest problems with finding coaches is that people don't make their expectations clear up front, so as to avoid a lot of problems later on," continues Silby. "Most coaches, when you ask 'What is your philosophy of coaching?' will give you the information you need."

According to Silby, people often hire a coach based on reputation, which may mean that coach has great technical knowledge and is a great motivator for certain students.

Todd Eldredge with long-time coach Richard Callaghan.

"But you want to make sure that coach is going to match *your* needs," she says. There are coaches who yell a lot, others who are very supportive, and still others who combine the two styles. "Go into the rink and see that coach in action," she suggests. "How does the coach respond to problems and obstacles? Would that be a good way for you? Do you think you would respond well to the way the coach is handling the situation?"

Another thing to think about is whether the technique being taught is compatible with what you hope to achieve. Do you like the way a particular coach's skaters look on the ice? Is their posture good? Do they have power and flow in their stroking? Do the skaters truly *bend* in the knees and ankles? Is the free leg extended, toes pointed? Is there good contact with the ice? Do jumps have height and distance? Are spins centered with good body alignment? Since all teachers have skaters of varying levels and ability, you'll have to watch a number of students to make a fair evaluation.

DIFFERENT LEARNING STYLES

An important part of finding the right teacher has to do with how you learn. "There are basically three types of learning styles," says Silby. "There's your *visual* learner, your *auditory or verbal* learner, and your *kinesthetic* learner." Most adults are a combination of learning styles because they have adapted to different teaching situations over the years. Parents of a young skater can watch their child's behavior to see which style dominates.

"A *visual learner* is someone who gets side-tracked by looking at other things," says Silby. They *see* things around them; what they pay attention to are the things they can *look* at. "A *kinesthetic learner* tends to wander off and *touch* things." For instance, if you're out shopping, he or she goes through the racks and touches all the clothes. "An *auditory (verbal) learner* is someone who is always talking to other kids." If you're out shopping, this person may stop and start talking to people he or she doesn't know.

At the rink, the *visual learner* tends to watch other skaters. Coaches often say "they don't pay attention to me because they are distracted by what goes on around

PHOTOS BY ALICE BERMAN

them," comments Silby. These people do well with a written list of goals. "Keeping a notebook with information and corrections is good because they can look at it, and read it—they can see it written down." Videotape also works well, but the teacher needs to show the student what to focus on.

"A *kinesthetic learner* is not going to benefit at all from reading something. These are the people who say 'I can remember their face, but I just can't remember their name,'" says Silby. "Kinesthetic learners remember what they *did*, rather than what they were told. ... They learn through how they *feel*." To reach such a learner, the coach might need to actually put the skater's body in the correct position or move it through the right motions. Walking through things off the ice is also good for this type of learner. "These skaters need a lot of repetition, probably more than other learning styles would use. ... They need to do more to really learn what it *feels* like."

The *auditory or verbal learner* can usually listen once and follow directions. "They like listening to things, like music, or being read to," observes Silby. "They like to sing, and they usually problem-solve by talking." On the ice, the coach needs to talk a lot, as does the skater. Not only should the coach explain the mistake to such a learner, the skater should repeat it back to the coach for better understanding.

Once you've figured out what kind of learning style works best for you, you'll be better prepared to find a teacher who can reach you most effectively. The next step is to find out about the different kinds of qualifications a pro can have.

TRAINING AND CREDENTIALS

The **Professional Skaters Guild of America** (PSGA) is the only organization in the U.S. that offers teaching credentials to skating pros. According to **Carole Shulman**, Executive Director, the PSGA has three programs: (1) a certification program run through the University of Delaware (UDE); (2) an apprenticeship program where coaches can apprentice with master-rated coaches; and (3) a rating system, which ranges from a certified instructor to a master-rated coach in the skating disciplines (figures and freestyle, dance, pairs, group instruction, precision, choreography and style). As part of its offerings, the PSGA holds an annual educational conference (ratings exams are given) and offers free training seminars across the country every fall.

The four-day UDE program, "is really the entry for coaches," says Shulman. "What we would like to eventually see happen is that no skater can become a coach without having some basic coach's training. Eventually we'd like to see all skating coaches go through at least a two- to four-week course before they begin to teach."

In order to receive accreditation at the Delaware program, a pro must have 30 hours of classroom training and pass an intensive written exam. Once accredited, he or she can sign up for the apprenticeship program. After the apprenticeship is completed (the PSGA suggests a minimum of 20 hours), the next step is to start the ratings process. One year of coaching experience is required before a pro can take any of the ratings exams. And, regardless of prior experience, all coaches must start at the beginning and proceed through each level to reach the master-rating exam.

"Ratings are not required," says Shulman, "and yet one-third of our members are now rated. And eighty percent more are getting ratings today than three years ago. ... Many skating clubs are saying, 'We're looking for a PSGA member and a PSGA-rated coach.' We are pleased that clubs are inserting this requirement into their policies and seeing that it is enforced."

Obviously, not all coaches are starting from the same point. A recreational skater interested in beginning a basic instructional

ASSOCIATIONS

Canadian Figure Skating Association (CFSA)
1600 James Naismith Drive
Gloucester, Ontario, K1B 5N4
CANADA
(613) 748-5635; Fax (613) 748-5718

CFSA coaches are issued a membership card that includes their CFSA test qualifications and a CAC passport card with their NCCP certification levels.

Ice Skating Institute of America (ISIA)
355 West Dundee Road
Buffalo Grove, IL 60089
(708) 808-SKAT; Fax (708) 808-8FAX

The ISIA does not verify test levels and competitive records of skaters or coaches. They can verify whether someone is an ISIA associate member.

Professional Skaters Guild of America (PSGA)
P.O. Box 5904
Rochester, MN 55903
(507) 281-5122; Fax (507) 281-5491

The PSGA can verify the credentials of its members and, in many cases, provide information about the achievement level of the coach's students.

U. S. Figure Skating Association (USFSA)
20 First Street
Colorado Springs, CO 80906
(719) 635-5200; Fax (719) 635-9548

The USFSA can verify the test level and competitive record of coaches who have come up through the USFSA ranks.

Brian Boitano has worked with coach Linda Leaver from the beginning.

program in a rural area might require a longer apprenticeship than a former national competitor. "But there are some basic skills that even a national competitor needs to learn. He or she may indeed know how to do all the international dances or triple jumps," says Shulman, "but to go back and teach a basic outside edge is sometimes very difficult."

Does a person have to skate well to become a pro? Not necessarily. "We've had some great coaches who weren't great skaters," says **Bob Mock**, Chairman of the Coaches Committee of the **U.S. Figure Skating Association** (USFSA), and also Vice President of the PSGA. "Maybe they were great scientists more than great skaters, and they were able to take that base knowledge and apply it to skating and come up with wonderful skating techniques. I think Gus Lussi was one of those, a great visionary." [Lussi became fascinated by the relationship between physics and skating, and went on to devise innovative spinning and jumping techniques that took advantage of his observations. See *Lussi Spins*, Nov/Dec '92 and *Lussi Spins II*, Jan/Feb '94 issues of *Skater's Edge*.]

"I think that if you're able to study the sport and continue your education, that would be the mark of a good coach," says Mock. "Being aggressive in your attempt to gain more knowledge" is important. "There's nothing that takes the place of being there and doing it. You get backstage, ask a lot of questions, make a lot of phone calls, and you learn the business. It's just like any other sport or any other business."

The USFSA is the governing body of figure skating in the U.S. Skaters eventually hoping to skate in international and Olympic competitions must progress through USFSA tests and qualifying competitions. According to **Bob Crowley**, Executive Business Director, the USFSA does not certify coaches, or require that coaches be certified. "The association doesn't have an official position on what level of accomplishment the skater should have had or should have attained before becoming a coach." He personally believes a coach should have some kind of skating experience. "I think they have to have, at a minimum, significant skating background to understand edges, how edges work against the ice, and the basics of skating. Each member club is responsible for selecting the coaches that fit their needs."

The **Ice Skating Institute of America** (ISIA) focuses on the needs of recreational skaters. While the ISIA does not have a certification program for teachers, it has recently instituted a certification program for its judges (who are also teachers). "With respect to training, we hold an annual education conference where we have all kinds of seminars in professionalism and ethics, teaching techniques" and so forth, says **Mary Hutchinson**, the Instructors Section Representative to the ISIA Board of Directors. "We do not certify our teachers in terms of teaching ability," but, since they also judge the ISIA competitions, the instructors "play dual roles and they have to stay educated and be trained in both fields of our sport, judging and teaching."

When training new teachers, explains Hutchinson, the ISIA starts "with learning how to break things down ... to give people a way to understand not only what is happening to them in terms of feeling, but the actual physics of putting together a maneuver."

While she personally believes that someone who is going to teach skating should have skated themselves, Hutchinson doesn't necessarily mean they had to skate as a child. "I have two teachers on my staff right now who started as adults and worked really hard ... and then went through an apprenticeship program with me. They're both school teachers, so they come with a real ability in terms of teaching. They are two of my better teachers."

Hutchinson does think that pros who coach kids in competition have an advantage if they competed themselves. "If you can say to kids, 'I've been there, I know what you are going through,' especially since so much of our game is mental. ... I think to have competitive experience is a plus."

The Canadian system is very different from the U.S. The **Canadian Figure Skating Association (CFSA)** is the national figure skating body for Canada. The CFSA subscribes to the National Coaching Certification Program (NCCP), a five-level educational program for coaches at all levels in over 60 sports. Each level covers three components of coaching: theory, technical and practical. Levels 1-3 are designed to certify coaches as competent teachers for school, community and club programs. Levels 4 and 5 prepare coaches for leadership roles in national and international sports. In order to coach a skater representing Canada at the 1998 Olympics, for instance, a coach will have to be Level 4 certified.

Before anyone can teach figure skating in Canada, he or she must complete the *Level I Theory* component, a 14-hour course that is the same for all NCCP coaches. In addition, a skating coach must complete the *Level 1 Figure Skating Technical* component, be 18 years or older, and hold a valid first-aid certificate. Once a new coach starts to teach, he or she must complete the remaining *Level I Practical* component within two years to become *Level I Certified*, or cease teaching at CFSA clubs and schools. The technical and practical components in figure skating are developed and administered by the CFSA.

FINDING THE IDEAL PRO
"My concept of the ideal pro," says **Carol Rossignol**, Coaching Coordinator of the CFSA, "is one who is interested in the skater's development as a person as well as a skater. I think the maturity level of the coach is important. I certainly would speak to them on what their fee guidelines are, and what their billing practice is." Other things to ask about: meetings between skater [or parents] and coach, the number of lessons the coach would recommend for the level of the skater, and how long he or she has been coaching. Another good indicator of coaching ability is what level of skaters have been produced, such as what tests the students have passed.

Most of the people interviewed for this article felt it was best to try out several different coaches before making a decision. "I always recommend that they go to an instructor and arrange two lessons, and they should be very clear that they just

---

THINGS TO THINK ABOUT

Certain words and phrases were mentioned frequently throughout the interviews for this article. Following is a list of key things to look for when considering a pro:
- Is there ongoing two-way communication?
- Can s/he explain things in a way you can understand?
- Is s/he flexible in teaching styles? Able to adapt to the student's learning style?
- Is there mutual respect? mutual trust?
- Do you have a good working relationship?
- Is s/he able to inspire and motivate you?
- Is s/he interested in your development as a person?
- Does s/he attend seminars/ workshops to stay current?
- Do you like the way his or her students look on the ice?
- Is this person a good role model?

POSSIBLE QUESTIONS TO ASK
(1) How long have you been teaching? Where? Who have you coached? Is it possible for me to talk with former/current students or parents of students? What kind of successes have your students had?
(2) What kind of training do you have as a skater? What test level did you reach? Did you compete? Up to what level (local, regional, national)?
(3) What kind of training do you have as a coach? Do you belong to any associations? Do you attend professional conferences, seminars or workshops? Are you certified or rated?
(4) May I watch you teach? (Look for enthusiasm, patience, communication skills, quality of information, humor, personality, mutual respect, flexibility, teaching style.)
(5) Can you explain your coaching philosophy? What are your goals for a skater? Do you have regular planning sessions or discussions with your skaters? (Or parents of young skaters?)
(6) What are your fees? On what basis do you charge (per lesson, weekly, monthly, etc.)?
(7) Would you consider a trial period before I make a commitment? Is there a minimum trial period you would prefer?
(8) How often would you suggest lessons? How would they be scheduled? How is the ice time arranged?
(9) Do you sometimes have your skaters work with other coaches for special needs? (e.g., spin coach, jump or harness coach, choreographer, etc.) How is that arranged?
(10) Is the rink where you teach known for any specialty that might influence the direction of my skating? (e.g., freestyle, pairs, dance, precision teams)?

want two lessons," says **Patricia Feeney**, Chairman of the [Judges] Certification Committee for the ISIA. "And then take those lessons and make a judgement as far as: 'Is this the person who is interested in my individual growth?' ... One of the problems we confront daily is the person who comes through the door and has [or is] a beginner skater and wants the top coach in the facility. The top coach in the facility hasn't taught that level in eight years. That skater is better off to go with a lower level coach who's experienced at teaching that level."

"I am always astounded at how often people don't spend enough time asking questions of the teacher before they commit either their own time or their child's time, and certainly their money," says Hutchinson. She suggests first taking time to talk to the teacher and then take a few lessons. "Do they break things down enough that you can understand them? Do you relate on the ice? Do you feel motivated? Do you think this person is excited to be on the ice with you? Do you get the feeling they love what they are doing, and want to help you and further you?"

WHAT TO LOOK FOR

"The first thing I looked for was the personality of the coach, whether it matched the personality of my daughter," says **Carol Yamaguchi**, Kristi's mother and Chairperson of the USFSA Parents Committee, "because my daughter was really very shy ... Anyone who would be too overpowering for her as her first coach might have discouraged her. It's no use having a high-test, high-powered coach if they're not sensitive to your child's particular needs."

Kristi started with ISIA group lessons after Dorothy Hamill won the Olympics. Carol watched the different teachers and picked Kristi's first coach on the basis of whether she thought the personalities would mesh. They had to make a change when Kristi decided (at the age of nine) she wanted to be a national skater. Her first pro couldn't take her past the second USFSA test, so they began looking for a coach who had been fairly successful on a national level. Kristi attended a camp and tried out different teachers, and then

Kristi Yamaguchi and Christy Ness

decided to study with Christy Kjarsgaard Ness, who worked with her all the way through her 1992 Olympic Gold Medal and beyond.

"She (Christy) took an overall view of their [the skaters'] bigger picture," says Carol. "It was a total commitment on her part, to develop her skaters to the best of her ability. She didn't expect each one to become a national competitor, but she put her 100 percent into the total picture, which included school, off-ice training, eating habits. I think these things carry over into later life, not just for skating."

"My concept of an ideal pro," says Hutchinson, is someone who loves their work, loves the sport, and who maintains a high level of credibility by staying educated. "It's also a person who can look at themselves as a human being and know they are fallible and will make mistakes, but is capable of owning up to it and then making it better." In addition, there has to be a good feel for communication with people of all ages, and an ability to modify the teaching approach depending on the kind of students.

CHANGING PROS

For a variety of reasons, there may come a time when it's necessary to find a new teacher. Perhaps the skater is no longer making progress or the student-teacher relationship is no longer effective. Maybe the skater needs to move to a higher level coach to continue up the competitive ladder, or even relocate to a larger training center in another city. For whatever reason the change needs to be made, efforts should be made to discuss the matter in a diplomatic and considerate fashion.

"If your personality types aren't mixing, then perhaps you need to go to the coach and say, 'Look, I don't feel like we can continue this relationship. What do you suggest I do? Are there alternatives, do you have someone you can recommend?'" says Mock. Rossignol feels it's important to notify the coach privately, in a discreet and courteous manner, and also to settle outstanding bills before seeking out a new coach.

"The hardest time comes when a skater says, 'I need to move on to somebody else,' and not to take it personally," comments Hutchinson. When this situation happens among her staff, "I make sure the parents [or skater] and teacher have sat down and discussed the reasons why. ... The worst time is if the student suddenly gets out on the ice and is taking a lesson with another teacher, and the regular teacher doesn't know any of this has taken place."

As with almost any situation, time spent asking questions and comparing opportunities should pay off in the long run with fewer frustrations and less time and money wasted. A coach who can inspire you to learn more and meet or surpass your skating goals is a special person indeed. ■

Books, Books, Books

An extensive search of numerous libraries, computer databases, and individual collections has yielded an astounding total of 347 skating books published in English since the late 1700s. This massive compilation of skating literature is largely due to the efforts of a few hard-working volunteers: **John Christie** of Glasgow, Scotland, **Pierre Henry** of Quebec, Canada, and **Brooke Higdon** of Washington, DC. They spent many hours reading, researching, and comparing lists.

Grateful appreciation also goes to **Beth Davis**, Curator of the U.S. Figure Skating Museum; **Robert Worsfold** and **Catherine Armstrong** of Glasgow, Scotland; **Doris Penndorf**; the **New York Public Library for the Performing Arts Dance Collection**; the **British Library** in London; the **Mitchell Library** in Glasgow; and the **Library of Congress** (just to name a few). Thanks also go to **Hannah Grisar** for her help with data entry, and **Jaya Kanal** for help with converting the database into a publishable format!

The books are listed in *alphabetical order by the author's last name*. Later in the section, there is a *cross-reference in order by book title*, and then listings organized by type of book (e.g., historical, technical, autobiographical) whenever possible. Some of the listings are incomplete; information on many books is scant. If you own or have access to any of the titles included, or you know of any books we have not listed, we invite you to send us details for inclusion in a later edition of *Skater's Edge Sourcebook*.

BOOKS: BY AUTHOR

Aaseng, Nathan. *Eric Heiden: Winner In Gold*. Lerner Publications, Minneapolis, 1980.

Adams, Douglas. *Skating*. George Bell & Sons, London, 1890. *Notes:* Also published by Frederick Stokes, New York 1890.

Addleman, Frank G. *The Winning Edge: Nutrition for Athletic Fitness and Performance*. Prentice-Hall, Englewood Cliffs, NJ, 1984.

Anders, Fred. *Ice Palaces*. Abbeville Press, New York, 1983. *Additional Author(s):* Ann Agranoff.

Anderson, Bob. *Stretching for Everyday Fitness & for Running, Tennis, Raquetball, Cycling, Swimming, etc.* Shelter Publications, Bolinas, CA, 1980. ISBN: 0-936070-01-3.

Anderson, George. *The Art of Skating*. Thomas Murray & Son, Glasgow, 1852. *Latest Edition:* 1880. *Notes:* Author was vice-president of the Crystal Palace Skating Club (CYCLOS), and president of the Glasgow Skating Club. Second and third editions published in 1868, 1873. Each new edition was slightly enlarged with additional 'Figures never previously described.'

Arnold, Richard. *Better Ice Skating*. Kaye & Ward Ltd., London, 1976. ISBN: 0-7182-1442-0. *Notes:* 96 pp.

Arnold, Richard. *Better Sport Skating: The Key to Improved Performance*. Kaye & Ward Ltd., London, 1982. ISBN: 0-7182-1468-4.

Arnold, Richard. *Dancing On Skates*. St. Martin's Press, New York, 1985. *Notes:* Also published in U.K. by David & Charles Ltd. 1985. ISBN: 0-7153-8678-6.

Arnold, Richard. *Ice Skating Made Easy*. Coles Publishing Co., Toronto, 1979. *Notes:* 96 pp.

Arnold, Richard. *Let's Go Ice Skating*. ELM Publications, Kings Ripton Cambs, U.K., 1987. ISBN: 0946-139-26-1.

Baier, Maxie and Ernst. *Maxie & Ernst Baier*. Otto Pannes, Dusseldorf, 1951.

Bailey, Donna. *Skating*. Raintree Steck-Vaughn Publishers, Madison, NJ, 1990. ISBN: 0-8114-4715-4. *Notes:* Introduction to skating for children. ISBN (library edition) 0-8114-2854-0.

Baillie, Major George. *Figure Skating Simplified*. Silwyn & Blount Ltd., London, 1910. *Latest Edition:* 1922. *Notes:* 63 pp.

Barber, Karen. *Spice on Ice*. Sidgwick and Jackson Ltd., London, 1985. *Additional Author(s):* Nicky Slater, Sandra Stevenson. ISBN: 0-283-99245-X. *Notes:* 216 pp. The story of Britain's ice dance champions. Forward by Robin Cousins.

Barrett, Norman. *Ice Sports*. Franklin Watts, London, 1988. ISBN: 0-863-13684-2.

Bass, Howard. *Ice Skating*. Rand McNally, Chicago, 1980. *Latest Edition:* 1992. *Notes:* 45 pp. Also published by Hamlyn Publishing Group Ltd in London. 1988 and subsequent editions published by King Fisher Books under the title *The Superbook of Ice Skating*, ISBN 0-86272-375-2.

Bass, Howard. *Ice Skating For Pleasure.* Gage Publishing, Toronto, 1979. *Notes:* 86 pp.

Bass, Howard. *International Encyclopedia of Winter Sports.* Pelham Books Ltd., London, 1971.

Bass, Howard. *Let's Go Skating.* Stanley Paul & Co Ltd., London, 1974. ISBN: 0-09-121050-X. *Notes:* 176 pp.

Bass, Howard. *Skating: Elegance On Ice.* Marshall Cavendish Books Ltd., London, 1980. ISBN: 0-85685-858-7. *Notes:* 96 pp.

Bass, Howard. *Tackle Skating.* Stanley Paul & Co., London, 1978. ISBN: 0-091337-40-2. *Notes:* 144 pp. Basic steps, spins, jumps, and pairs skating.

Bass, Howard. *The Love of Ice Skating and Speed Skating.* Octopus Books Ltd., London, 1980. ISBN: 0-7064-1203-6. *Notes:* 98 pp. Also published by Crescent Books, New York, and Mandarin Publishers Ltd., Hong Kong. Forward by Robin Cousins.

Bass, Howard. *This Skating Age.* Stanley Paul & Co Ltd., London, 1958.

Bass, Howard. *Winter Sports.* Stanley Paul & Co., London, 1966. *Notes:* Also published by A. S. Barnes & Co., New York, 1966.

Bauer, Tony. *Off-Ice Training Manual.* Canadian Figure Skating Association (CFSA), Gloucester, ON. *Additional Author(s):* Jim Parker. *Notes:* 72 pp. Develops strength, power, flexibility, coordination and endurance. Aimed at coaches.

Beddoes, D. *Skating.* Colban of Canada, 1976. *Additional Author(s):* M. O'Bryan. *Notes:* 96 pp.

Benson, E. F. *Winter Sports in Switzerland.* Gold, Mead, & Co., New York. *Notes:* Illustrations by C. Fleming Williams.

Benson, Edward Frederick. *English Figure Skating.* George Bell & Sons, London, 1908. *Notes:* 261pp. 'A guide to the theory and practice of skating in the English style.' With a set of practice cards which were reprinted separately in 1909.

Berman, Alice. *Skater's Edge Sourcebook.* Skater's Edge, Kensington, MD, 1995. ISBN: 0-9643027-0-5. *Notes:* Extensive resource book with listings of more than 850 ice rinks (facilities, programs, months open), 300+ skating books, 100+ skating videos, and 350+ companies doing business related to ice skating (apparel, equipment, boots, blades, rink builders/suppliers, etc.). *Skater's Edge*, Box 500, Kensington, MD 20895.

Bird, Dennis L. *Know the Game Series: Ice Skating.* A & C Black, London, 1985. ISBN: 0-7136-5502-X. *Notes:* Written in collaboration with the National Skating Association of Great Britain. This author also published under the name 'John Noel'.

Bird, Dennis L. *Our Skating Heritage.* National Skating Association of Great Britain, London, 1979. *Notes:* A centenary history of the National Skating Association of Great Britain 1879-1979.

Bloom, Alan. *The Skaters of the Fens.* Hiffer & Sons Ltd., Cambridge, 1958.

Blundun, Georges. *The Yankee Polka, Ravensburger Waltz, & Tango Romantica.* Canadian Figure Skating Association, Glouchester, ON, 1976. *Notes:* 16 pp.

Boeckl, Wilhelm R. *How to Judge Figure Skating.* New York, 1940.

Boeckl, Wilhelm R. *Willy Boeckl on Figure Skating.* Moore Press, Inc., New York, 1937. *Notes:* 212 pp. School figures, free skating, pairs, fours, dancing, and skating in carnivals. Filled with old photos, woodcuts, plus instructional drawings.

Bolstad, Helen Cambria. *Golden Skates: The Story of Carol Heiss: Teen-Age Champion.* 1958.

Bompa, Tudor. *Off-Ice Training for Figure Skaters.* York University Press, Toronto, 1974. *Additional Author(s):* Tamara Bompa. *Notes:* 84 pp. Pair and dance seminar. Series of off-ice exercises for pairs.

Bouchard, S. H. *Sports Star: Dorothy Hamill.* Harcourt Brace Jovanovich, New York, 1978. ISBN: 0-15278-014-9. *Notes:* 62 pp. A children's story book.

Boy Scouts of America. *Cub Scout Sports: Skating.* Boy Scouts of America, Irving, 1986. ISBN: 0-8395-4083-3.

Boy Scouts of America. *Skating.* Boy Scouts of America, Irving, 1983. ISBN: 0-8395-3250-4.

Bozska, Ilona. *Who Will Win: The Gold Skate.* 1976.

Broadbent, Sidney. *A New Approach to Skating Terminology.* ICEskate Conditioning Equipment, Littleton, CO, 1964.

Broadbent, Sidney. *Skateology.* ICEskate Conditioning Equipment, Littleton, CO, 1985. *Notes:* Technical manual re skates, skate sharpening, etc.

Brokaw, Irving. *The Art of Skating.* Litchworth of Arden Press, London, 1910. *Latest Edition:* 1928. *Notes:* 1913, 1915, 1917, 1921, 1927, 1928 editions published by American Sports Publishers, New York. 1926 edition published by Charles Scribner & Sons, New York. 253 pp.

Brokhin, Yuri. *The Big Red Machine: The Rise and Fall of Soviet Olympic Champions.* Random House, New York, 1977.

Brown, Nigel. *Ice Skating: A History.* A.S. Barnes and Co., New York, 1959. *Notes:* 220 pp. Also published in London by Nicholas Kaye Ltd. From the first bone skates, to the introduction of skating in England, to the first ice dance championships in 1952. Filled with old photos and woodcuts.

Browne, George. *A Handbook of Figure Skating.* Barney & Berry, Springfield, MA, 1910. *Latest Edition:* 1913. *Notes:* Over 600 diagrams. Includes supplement 'The International Style of Figure Skating . . . Chiefly After the Exposition by Gilbert Fuchs.' 1913 edtion revised and enlarged to 223 pp. from 160 pp. in 1900.

Browne, George. *Skating Primer.* Barney & Berry, Springfield, MA, 1912. *Notes:* Small pocket book.

Browning, Kurt. *Forcing the Edge.* Harper Collins Publishers Ltd.,

Toronto, 1991. *Additional Author(s):* Neil Stevens. ISBN: 0-00215843-4. *Notes:* 94 pp.

Buck, Ray. *Tiffany Chin, A Dream On Ice.* Children's Press, Chicago, 1986.

Burakoff, Alexis. *On The Ice.* Hare & Hatter Books, W. Newton, MA, 1994. *Latest Edition:* 1994. ISBN: 0-9640792-0-8. *Notes:* Edited by Pamela Econoply & Suzanne Burakoff. Children's book; non-fiction interview.

Burka, Ellen. *Figure Skating.* Collier-Macmillan Canada Ltd., Ontario, 1974. *Notes:* 132 pp. Figures, basic steps, jumps, and off-ice exercises. Illustrated with diagrams and action photos.

Butterworth, Carol. *Step by Step Ice Skating Guide.* The Leahy Press, Montpelier, VT, 1978. *Additional Author(s):* Rosemary Cloran. *Notes:* Basic steps and jumps. 80 pp.

Button, Dick. *Dick Button on Skates.* Prentice-Hall, Englewood Cliffs, NJ, 1955. *Notes:* Also published by Peter Davies, London 1956.

Button, Dick. *Instant Skating.* Grossett & Dunlap, New York, 1964. *Notes:* Getting started, the right equipment, crossovers, figures, free skating. Includes photographs, diagrams, and woodcuts. 58 pp.

CFSA. *Depth Jumps: Training for Figure Skaters.* Canadian Figure Skating Association, Gloucester, ON. *Notes:* 20 pp. Off-ice jump exercises.

CFSA. *From Boots to Blades.* Canadian Figure Skating Association, Gloucester, ON. *Notes:* Information booklet for parents or new skaters on proper equipment (selection and fit), and beginner skating skills.

CFSA. *Ice Show Manual.* Canadian Figure Skating Association, Gloucester, ON, 1988. *Notes:* 226 pp. Information about planning and preparation for an ice show.

CFSA. *Parent's Guide to Test and Competitive Skating.* Canadian Figure Skating Association, Gloucester, ON, 1994. ISBN: 1-895761-19-0. *Notes:* 45 pp. Introduction to CFSA programs, basic types of skating, equipment and clothing, finding a pro, etc. Includes resource list of books, videos, cassette tapes.

CFSA. *Reflections on the CFSA.* Canadian Figure Skating Association, Gloucester, ON. *Notes:* 200 pp. A History of the CFSA, 1887-1990.

Chaikovsky, Anatoly. *Figures On Ice.* Progress Publishers, Moscow, 1978. *Notes:* 100 black and white and color photos of international stars. Special sections feature the Protopopovs and Rodnina/Zaitsev. Photos by Mstislav Botashev.

Chapman, Joseph. *Fifty Years of Skating (1886-1936).* The Palms Publishers, Coconut Grove, FL, 1944. *Notes:* 52 pp.

Charlotte. *Hippodrome Skating Book.* Hippodrome Skating Club, New York, 1916. *Notes:* 93 pp. 'Practical, illustrated lessons in the art of figure skating as exemplified by Charlotte, greatest woman skater in the world.'

Chubrik, Rimma. *Figure Skating: Pages of History.* Platoro Press, Columbus, OH, 1994. ISBN: 1-882849-02-7. *Notes:* Revised and expanded edition of 1992 chronicle of Russian skating. Includes coverage of 1994 Olympic champions. Translated by Ginger Harmon.

Clark, Nancy. *Nancy Clark's Sports Nutrition Guidebook.* Leisure Press, Champaign, IL, 1990. ISBN: 0-88011-326-X. *Notes:* 323 pp. Daily training diet, sports nutrition basics, weight control, eating disorders, recipes, and resources.

Clay, Thomas. *Instructions on the Art of Skating,* Leeds, U.K., 1828.

Cleaver, Reginald. *A Winter Sports Book.* A & C Black, London, 1911.

Cobb, Humphry H. *Figure Skating in the English Style.* Eveleigh Nash, London, 1913. *Notes:* 253 pp.

Copley-Graves, Lynn. *Figure Skating History: The Evolution of Dance on Ice.* Platoro Press, Columbus, 1992. ISBN: 0-9631758-1-5. *Notes:* 415 pp. Ice dance history from its beginnings to the 1992 Olympics. Hundreds of photos and illustrations.

Cousins, Robin. *Skateaway.* Stanley Paul & Co Ltd., London, 1984. *Additional Author(s):* David Foot. ISBN: 0-09-153850-5. *Notes:* Photos by Stuart Sadd. Paperback edtion ISBN 0-09-153851-3.

Cousins, Robin. *Skating For Gold.* Stanley Paul & Co Ltd., London, 1980. *Latest Edition:* 1981. *Additional Author(s):* Howard Bass. ISBN: 0-09-143300-2. *Notes:* The story of Robin Cousins. Paperback edition published in 1981 by Sphere Books, London.

1980 Olympic Gold Medalist Robin Cousins

PHOTO BY ALICE BERMAN

ISBN 0-7221-2636-0.

Cranston, Toller. *A Ram on the Rampage.* Gage Educational Publishing Co., Toronto, 1977.

Craven. *Walker's Manly Exercises,* London, 1855. *Notes:* Includes section on figure skating.

Crawley, A. E. *Skating.* Methuen & Co Ltd., London, 1920.

Cruikshank, James A. *Figure Skating for Women.* American Sports Publishers, New York, 1917. *Latest Edition:* 1921.

Cruikshank, James A. *Winter Sports.* American Sports Publishers, New York.

Cummings, Diane. *Figure Skating As A Hobby.* Harper & Brothers, New York, 1938. *Notes:* 132 pp.

Curry, Manfred. *The Beauty of Skating.* Scribner & Sons, New York, 1935.

Dean, Heather. *The Winter Book for Girls.* Burke, London, 1956.

Dedic, Joseph. *Single Figure Skating: For Beginners and Champions.* International Skating Union/Olympia, Prague, 1974. *Latest Edition:* 1982. *Notes:* 1982 edition is a revised and enlarged version of 1974 publication. Technical training manual recommended for coaches, judges and senior skaters. Available from the Canadian Figure Skating Association.

Deerfield, Robert L. *The Ancient Art of Skating.* Deerfield Academy, 1957.

DeLeeuw, Dianne. *Figure Skating.* Atheneum, New York, 1978. *Additional Author(s):* Steve Lehrman. *Notes:* 168 pp.

DeMore, Charles A. *The Relationship of Music to Ice Dancing,* Cleveland, OH, 1964.

Dench, Robert. *Pair Skating and Dancing on Ice.* Prentice-Hall, New York, 1943. *Additional Author(s):* Rosemary Stewart.

Diagram Group. *Enjoying Skating.* Stoeger Publishing Co., South Hackensack, NJ, 1978. ISBN: 0-88317-101-5. *Notes:* 160 pp. Also published by Paddington Press in London. Basic guide to all types of skating on and off the ice. Includes 1500 step-by-step drawings.

Dickmeyer, Lowell A. *Ice Skating Is For Me.* Lerner Publications Co., Minneapolis, 1980. *Additional Author(s):* Lin Roberts. ISBN: 0-8225-1088-X. *Notes:* 47 pp. An introduction to ice skating for children.

Dodge, Mary Mapes. *Hans Brinker or The Silver Skates.* Penguin Puffin Classics, London/New York, 1865. *Latest Edition:* 1985. ISBN: 0-14-035042-X. *Notes:* The most frequently re-published skating story for children. Availalble in many editions, current paper edition listed above.

Dolan, Edward F. *Complete Beginner's Guide to Ice Skating.* Doubleday and Co., Garden City, NY, 1974. *Notes:* 157 pp.

Dolan, Edward F. *Dorothy Hamill, Olympic Skating Champion.* Doubleday and Co., Garden City, NY, 1979. *Notes:* 95 pages.

Donahue, Shiobhan. *Kristi Yamaguchi: Artist on Ice.* Lerner Publications Co., Minneapolis, 1993. ISBN: 0-8225-0522-3.

Dorsey, Frances. *Creative Ice Skating: Ice Dancing, Freestyle, & Pair Skating.* Contemporary Books, Inc., Chicago, 1980. *Additional Author(s):* Wendy Williams. ISBN: 0-8092-7107-9. *Notes:* 86 pp. Paperback ISBN: 0-8092-7106-0.

du Bief, Jacqueline. *Thin Ice.* Cassell & Co Ltd., London, 1956.

Duff-Taylor, Captain S. *Elements of Skating,* 1933.

Duff-Taylor, Captain S. *Skating.* Seeley Service & Co Ltd., London, 1935. *Latest Edition:* 1937.

Dyer, Lorna. *Ice Dancing Illustrated.* Moore Publications, Inc., Bellevue, WA, 1980.

Emery, ed, David. *Who's Who in International Winter Sports.* Sphere Books Ltd., London, 1983. ISBN: 0-7221-3322-7.

F., H. D. *The Figure Skating Ready Reckoner,* 1865. *Notes:* In the collection of the British Library, London.

Fassi, Carlo. *Figure Skating With Carlo Fassi.* Charles Scribner's Sons, New York, 1980. *Latest Edition:* 1981. *Additional Author(s):* Gregory Smith. ISBN: 0-684-17644-0. *Notes:* Basic to advanced technique, and advice from this famous coach. Illustrations by Walt Spitzmiller. 1981 edition published by Robert Hale Ltd., London, ISBN 0-7091-8825-0.

Faulkner, Margaret. *I Skate.* Little, Brown & Co., Boston, 1979. *Notes:* 154 pp.

Featherstone, Donald F. *Sports Injuries Manual for Trainers and Coaches.* Philosophical Library, Inc., New York, 1956.

Fitness & Amateur Sport Directorate, Canada. *Figure Skating.* R. Duhamel (Queen's Printer), Ottawa, 1963.

Fitzgerald, Julian T. *Ice King—General Skating Information.* Alfreds, 1922.

Foley, John. *Blades Are Necessary,* 1970. *Additional Author(s):* Carol Foley.

Ford, Joan E. *Skate Like the Wind.* Gage Educational Publishing Co., Toronto, 1983. *Notes:* 128 pp. The Lindy Bernard story for young readers.

Foster, Fred M. *Bibliography of Skating,* 1898.

Foundation for International Ice Skating Advancement. *International Winter Sports Directory.* Foundation for Int'l Ice Skating Advancement, Palm Desert, CA, 1988. ISBN: 0-944925-00-6. *Notes:* Information on winter sports and facility locations in U.S., Canada, and the world.

Foxe, Arthur N. *Nocturne,* 1975.

Foxe, Arthur N. *Skating For Everyone,* 1966.

Gale, Ivy. *Skating On Ice: A Basis for Ice Dancing.* New Arts Publisher's Guild, London, 1950. *Notes:* 102 pp.

Geddes, Stephanie Papp. *Brian Orser.* Fitzhenry & Whiteside, Markham, ON, 1988.

Glasser, Marian S. *Come Skate With Me*. Jean Stoneback Publishing Co., 1985.

Gilder, Jean. *Tom Badger Goes Skating*. The Medici Society, Ltd., London, 1977. ISBN: 85503 040 2. *Notes:* Ages 6 and up. Carpenter makes skates for Tom (the badger) and other woodland animals. 24 pp. Color illustrations.

Goodfellow, Arthur R. *The Skating Scene*, 1981.

Goodfellow, Arthur R. *The Wonderful World of Skates*. ISIA, Wilmette, IL, 1972. *Notes:* 80 pp. The Ice Skating Institute of America (ISIA) is now located in Buffalo Grove, IL.

Goodfellow, Arthur R. *World Ice Skating Guide*, Boston.

Goodman, Albert. *Fen Skating*. Sampson, Low, Marston Searlon, Rivington, 1882. *Additional Author(s):* Neville Goodman.

Goodridge, Arthur. *Cambridge Skating Club, 1898-1948*.

Greenspan, Emily. *Little Winners— Inside the World of the Child Sports Star*. Little, Brown & Co., Boston/Toronto, 1983. *Notes:* The first chapter is devoted to Lisa-Marie Allen. Various other skaters mentioned throughout, including Elaine Zayak.

Grisogano, Vivian. *Children and Sport: Fitness, Injuries, and Diet*. John Murray Publishers, London, 1991. ISBN: 0-7195-4908-6.

Gross, George. *Donald Jackson: King of Blades*. Queen City Publishing Ltd., Toronto, 1977. ISBN: 0-9690508-1-X. *Notes:* 158 pp. Biography, technique and pictures of this world champion, who was the first to land the triple Lutz in international competition.

Gyger, W. J. *Wintersport*, 1925.

Haas, Robert. *Eat to Win: The Sports Nutrition Bible*. New American Library, New York, 1983. *Latest Edition:* 1985. ISBN: 0-451-15509-2. *Notes:* There are many books currently available on sports nutrition. This is one of the more popular titles.

Hadley, Arthur. *Figures of the Second Class Test*. Arthur Hadley, 1910.

Hall, R. E. *Champions All*. Frederick Muller Ltd., London, 1938. *Additional Author(s):* T. D. Richardson. *Notes:* Camera studies by E. R. Hall, with notes and introduction by T. D. Richardson.

Hamill, Dorothy. *Dorothy Hamill: On And Off The Ice*. Alfred A. Knopf, New York, 1983.

Haney, Lynn. *Skaters: Profile Of A Pair*. G. P. Putnam's Sons, New York, 1983.

Harris, Ricky. *Choreography & Style for Ice Skaters*. St. Martin's Press, New York, 1980. *Latest Edition:* 1991. ISBN: 0-312-13388-X. *Notes:* Creating a personal skating style, and how to design your skating programs from beginning to end. Paperback ISBN: 0-312-05401-7.

Health and Welfare Canada. *Figure Skating for Everyone Manual*. Health and Welfare Canada; Crown, 1974. *Notes:* Basic steps, pairs, dancing, figures and free skating.

Heathcote, J. M. *Skating*. Longmans & Co., London, 1892. *Latest Edition:* 1902. *Additional Author(s):* C. G. Tebbutt, T. Maxwell Withan. *Notes:* Figure Skating by T. Maxwell Witham, with contributions on Curling (Rev. John Kerr), Tobogganing (Ormand Hake), Ice-Sailing (H. A. Buck), Bandy (C. G. Tebbutt). Illustrated by Charles Whymper and Captain R. M. Alexander. Also published by Spottswoode and Co., London. 470 pp.

Hedges, Sid G. *Ice and Roller Skating*, London, 1928. *Notes:* 64 pp. This book is number 19 in the series Warnes Recreation Books.

Hedges, Sid G. *Ice-Rink Skating*. C Arthur Pearson Ltd., London, 1932. *Notes:* 123 pp. Illustrated by Dorothy Miller.

Heller, ed., Mark. *The Illustrated Encyclopedia of Ice Skating*. Paddington Press, New York, 1979. ISBN: 0-448-22427-5. *Notes:* 223 pp. Extensive overview of all ice sports.

You are reading the one and only *Skater's Edge Sourcebook*.

If you don't own a copy, you can order it from the publisher for $44.95 in U.S. dollars ($39.95 plus $5 shipping in the U.S.)

Contact:
Skater's Edge
Box 500
Kensington,
MD 20895
Phone/Fax:
301-946-1971

Books and photos of skaters!
No extra postage charge!
Package discounts!

Books: discount $5/3; $10/6

Figure Skating History: The Evolution of Dance on Ice — $35
♦ 400+ packed pages by Lynn Copley-Graves with photos, illus.
♦ Worldwide perspective, sales to date in 18 countries

Ice Skating Fundamentals, by Marilyn Grace House — $25 *Fundamentals*
♦ Illustrations, photos, basics for learners

Get the Edge: Sport Psychology for Figure Skaters — $30
♦ Set goals, control nerves, self-arouse, relax, image
♦ Used by skaters, coaches, parents – it works! *Sport Psychology*

How Sport Psychology Can Make You Champion — $18
♦ Overcome mental mistakes, turn stress into strength, psych up

Symphony on Ice: The Protopopovs, transl. biography — $12
♦ Insights into thinking, training of 1964, '68 Olympic Champs

Patterns of Russian Ice Dance, transl. by Y. Tchaikovskaya — $18
♦ On free dance composition and choreography

The Key to Rhythmic Ice Dancing, Muriel Kay, 3rd printing — $20
♦ Muriel Kay's lessons on 21 compulsory dances Pre through Gold

Origins of Ice Dance Music, Muriel Kay, 2nd ed., 11 rhythms — $12
♦ Learn character of music used in compulsory, original, free dances

Compulsory Pattern Manual, all ISU dances with overlays — $42
♦ See man's and woman's dance patterns relative to each other

Complete Manual of Ice Dance Patterns, by Jeff Lerner — $35
♦ 400+ pp., 152 huge, easy-to-read patterns, footwork ideas

Soviet Secrets: Off-Ice Training Methods, T. Moskvina (in publ.)

Photos of skaters – Send names!
Multi-photo discounts. Send for approval packets.

Books: send check (non-US send int'l postal MO/check with New York branch):
Platoro Press • 4481 Floyd Drive • Columbus, OH 43232 • Tel. 614/837-0003

Henie, Sonja. *Wings On My Feet.* Hurst & Blackett Ltd., New York, 1940. *Latest Edition:* 1955. *Notes:* 1955 edition published by Prentice-Hall, New York.

Henry, William M. *An Approved History of The Olympic Games.* G. P. Putnam's & Sons, New York, 1948.

Hewitt, Foster. *Down The Ice.* Reginald Saunders, Toronto, 1934.

Hilgers, Laura. *Great Skates.* Little, Brown & Co., Boston, 1991.

Hilton, Christopher. *Torvill and Dean: The Full Story.* Oxford Illustrated Press, Haynes Publishing, Somerset, U.K., 1994. ISBN: 1-85509-238-7.

Hogshead, Nancy. *Asthma & Exercise.* Henry Holt and Company, New York, 1990. *Additional Author(s):* Gerald S. Couzens. ISBN: 0-8050-0878-0. *Notes:* 239 pp; A practical guide to coping with exercise induced asthma (EIA). (No direct link to ice skating and EIA.)

Hollander, Phyllis. *American Women in Sports.* Grossett and Dunlap, New York, 1972.

Horne, Pere. *Ice Skating.* Museum Press, London, 1968. *Notes:* 90 pp.

House, Eliot. *An Evening With Champions.* Harvard University Press, 1982.

House, Marilyn G. *Ice Skating Fundamentals.* Kendall/Hunt Publishing Co., Dubuque, 1983. ISBN: 0-8403-2906-7. *Notes:* Basic instruction up to beginning jumps. Includes tests for each chapter on three skill levels. Convenient coil binding.

Hugen, Otto. *The Technique of Skating.* Cassell & Co Ltd., London, 1973. *Latest Edition:* 1977. *Additional Author(s):* Jack Gerschwiler. ISBN: 0-304-29541-8.

Isely, Kenny. *The Skater's Manual.* Icetrea Inc, Wichita, 1978. *Latest Edition:* 1989.

ISIA. *Buying Ice Skates.* ISIA, Buffalo Grove, IL.

ISIA. *Competitors Handbook.* ISIA, Buffalo Grove, IL, 1994. *Notes:* Lists performance and eligibility rules of all ISIA competitive events.

ISIA. *Facility Operations Manual.* ISIA, Buffalo Grove, IL. *Notes:* A guide to job descriptions, policy guidelines, safety checklists, and more.

ISIA. *For Members Only: ISIA Annual Membership Directory.* ISIA, Buffalo Grove, IL. *Notes:* Lists all ISIA Board Members, Administrative Members, Associate Members, Builder/Suppliers, & Retail Merchant Members. Published on an annual basis.

ISIA. *Group Skating Manual.* ISIA, Buffalo Grove, IL. *Notes:* Includes information on forming a precision team, diagrams of formations, and rehearsal guidelines.

ISIA. *Instructor Manual.* ISIA, Buffalo Grove, IL. *Notes:* Tips on teaching lessons, beginners, precision teams, etc.

ISIA. *ISIA Boy Scout and Girl Scout Program.* ISIA, Buffalo Grove, IL. *Notes:* Suggested ice skating requirements and activities for Boy Scout and Girl Scout badge programs.

ISIA. *ISIA Games Book.* ISIA, Buffalo Grove, IL.

ISIA. *ISIA Judges Manual.* ISIA, Buffalo Grove, IL, 1993. *Notes:* Includes referee responsibilities, tips on judging, scoring, and more.

ISIA. *ISIA Manager's Manual.* ISIA, Buffalo Grove, IL. *Notes:* How to implement the ISIA Recreational Ice Skater Test Program and Group Lesson Program. Tips on scheduling lessons, marketing, liability, and advertising.

ISIA. *ISIA Recreational Ice Skater Team Competition Standards.* ISIA, Buffalo Grove, IL, 1991. *Notes:* How to set up, host, and run an ISIA competition.

ISIA. *ISIA Special Skater Test Standards.* ISIA, Buffalo Grove, IL. *Notes:* Description of the ISIA Learn-to-Skate program developed for skaters with physical or mental challenges.

ISIA. *Rink Guard Training Manual.* ISIA, Buffalo Grove, IL. *Notes:* Includes sample guidelines and a written examination.

ISIA. *Rink Responsibilities and Liabilities.* ISIA, Buffalo Grove, IL. *Notes:* Includes safe rink practices, litigation information, sample licenses, contracts, and agreements.

ISIA. *Skating Director Manual.* ISIA, Buffalo Grove, IL. *Notes:* Tips for skating school staff management.

ISU. *ISU Office Holders Through The Years.* International Skating Union, Davos-Platz, Switzerland.

ISU. *Results 1968-1991: Figure Skating Championships.* International Skating Union, Davos-Platz, 1992.

ISU. *Seventy Five Years of European and World's Championships in Figure Skating.* International Skating Union, Davos-Platz, 1968. *Notes:* Complete results of figure skating from 1892-1967.

ISU. *The Olympic Games.* International Skating Union, Davos-Platz, 1968. *Notes:* Results in figure skating from 1908, 1920, 1924-1968. Results in speed skating from 1924-1968.

Jelinek, Henry. *On Thin Ice.* Prentice-Hall, New York, 1965. *Additional Author(s):* Ann Pinchot. *Notes:* Also published by Paperjacks, Markham, Ontario. 107 pages.

Jessup, Elon. *Snow and Ice Sports.* J. M. Dent & Sons Ltd., London, 1923.

Jomland, Einar. *How To Improve Your Ice Skating. Additional Author(s):* Kirby, Priestley, Waldo.

Jomland, Einar. *Inside Ice Skating.* Contemporary Books, Chicago, 1978. *Additional Author(s):* Fitzgerald.

Jomland, Einar. *Introduction To Ice Skating,* 1973. *Additional Author(s):* Kirby, Priestley, Waldo.

Jomland, Einar. *Skating On Ice,* 1963. *Additional Author(s):* Kirby, Priestley, Waldo.

Jones, Captain. *A Treatise on Skating.* J. Walker & Rickman, London, 1792. *Latest Edition:* 1797. *Notes:* One of the oldest skating books we found, thanks to John Christie of Glasgow,

Scotland. Illustrated with charming woodcuts. Located in the collection of the Mitchell Library in Glasgow.

Jones, Ernest. *The Elements of Figure Skating.* Methuen & Co Ltd., London, 1931. *Latest Edition:* 1952. *Notes:* 1952 revised and enlarged edition published by George Allen & Unwin Ltd., London. 1931 edition 142 pp., 1952 edition 312 pp.

Joyner, Stephen C. *The Complete Guide & Resource to In-Line Skating.* Betterway Books, Cincinnati, OH, 1993. ISBN: 1-55870-289-X. *Notes:* 176 pp. Origins of in-line skating, equipment, strength and flexibility, techniques, injuries, safety. Appendix includes resource guide.

Kalb, Jonah. *The Easy Ice Skating Book.* Houghton Mifflin, Boston, 1981. *Notes:* 63 pp.

Kamper, Erich. *Encyclopedia of the Olympic Winter Games.* Union Verlag, Stuttgart, 1964. *Notes:* Multilingual text.

Kay, Muriel. *Origins of Ice Dance Music.* Plataro Press, Columbus, 1979. *Latest Edition:* 1992. ISBN: 0-9631758-6-6. *Notes:* The history and character of eleven social dances. Pamphlet format.

Kay, Muriel. *The Key to Rhythmic Ice Dancing.* Plataro Press, Columbus, OH, 1958. *Latest Edition:* 1992. ISBN: 0-9631758-5-8. *Notes:* Includes charts and patterns for twenty-one ice dances. Detailed step-by-step guidance for each dance.

Kayes, Trevor John. *Ice Skating in the East Midlands.* East Midlands Sports Council, Nottingham, U.K., 1975. ISBN: 0-90516-301-X.

Kent, Colonel H. Vaughn. *Combined Figure and Ice Skating.* Hutchinson and Company, London, 1929. *Latest Edition:* 1933.

Kent, Colonel H. Vaughn. *Dancing on Ice: How to Skate the Lancers.* R. Ward & Sons, Newcastle-Upon-Tyne, U.K., 1910.

Kirby, Michael. *Ice Skating*, 1968.

Kirby, Michael. *The Young Sportsman's*

Skating figure from Capt. Jones' Treatise, published in 1792.

Guide to Ice Skating. Thomas Nelson and Sons, New York, 1962. *Notes:* 96 pp. Published in the series 'Young Sportsman's Library.'

Knesworth, Vincent. *Winter Sports.* Seeley Service and Co., London. *Additional Author(s):* Captain S. Duff-Taylor.

Kraus, M.D., Hans. *The Sports Injury Handbook: An Athlete's Guide to Causes, Prevention, and Treatment.* Nick Lyons Books, New York, 1981. ISBN: 0-399-50861-9.

Krementz, Jill. *A Very Young Skater.* Alfred A. Knopf, New York, 1979. ISBN: 0-394-50833-5. *Notes:* Children's picture book. The story of Katharine Healy.

Law, Ernest. *Valsing on Ice.* Hugh Rees Ltd., London, 1908. *Latest Edition:* 1925. *Notes:* 62 pp. 'Valsing on ice described and analyzed . . . together with the rules & regulations for competitions adopted by Princes Skating Club.' Illustrated. 1925 edition published by G. Bell and Sons Ltd.

Laws, Kenneth. *Physics, Dance, And the Pas de Deux.* Schirmer Books, New York, 1994. *Additional Author(s):* Cynthia Harvey. ISBN: 0-02-871326-5. *Notes:* An expanded edition of Laws' 1984 The Physics of Dance. Includes new sections on figure skating and ice dancing. 227pp. Companion video available: ISBN 0-02-871327-3. Also packaged together: ISBN 0-02-871329-X.

Lerner, Jeff R. *Complete Manual of Compulsory Ice Dances.* Lexicon Ventures, Ltd., Vancouver, B.C., 1994. ISBN: 0-9696538-2-4. *Notes:* 104 pages. Includes steps and patterns for 32 compulsory dances. Man's steps printed in black on white paper; woman's steps printed in red on clear overlay. Each partner's pattern can be studied separately and with patterns juxtaposed. Available from Lexicon Ventures, 1685 West 61st Ave, Vancouver, B.C., Canada V6P 2C2.

Lerner, Jeff R. *The Complete Manual of Ice Dance Patterns.* Lexicon Ventures Ltd., Vancouver, 1992. ISBN: 0-9696538-0-8. *Notes:* 402 pp. 152 dances charted by steps and shown in pattern. Includes complete indexes and descriptions of steps. Illustrations by Sarah Mousseaux.

Lewis, Frederic. *Modern Skating.* Reilly and Co., Chicago, 1938.

Lewis, John F. *Skating and the Philadelphia Club*, Philadelphia, 1895.

Lindsay, Sally. *Figure Skating.* Rand McNally and Co., Chicago, 1963.

Litsky, Frank. *Winners On The Ice.* Picture Life Books, New York, 1970. *Notes:* A book for children.

Lowther, Henry C. *English Skating in Three Parts.* Horace Cox, London, 1900-02. *Notes:* Part I: Edges and Striking, 66 pp., 1902; Part II: Principles of Skating Turns, 52 pp., 1900; Part III: Combined Figure Skating, 92 pp., 1902. Published separately, and together in a cardboard slipcase.

Lunn, Arnold. *Winter Sports*, London, 1930. *Additional Author(s):* Humphrey Cobb.

Lunn, Brian. *Letters to Young Winter*

Sportsmen. Unwin Bros., Ltd., London, 1927.

Lussi, Gustave. *Championship Figure Skating*. A S Barnes and Co., New York, 1951. *Latest Edition:* 1952. *Additional Author(s):* Maurice Richards. *Notes:* 142 pp. Expert guidance from this famous coach of champions.

Lynch, Thomas. *Skating With Heather Grace.* Alfred A. Knopf, New York, 1987. ISBN: 0-394-55480-9. *Notes:* Paperback ISBN: 0-394-74756-9.

Lynn, Janet. *Peace And Love.* Creative House, Carol Stream, IL, 1973. *Additional Author(s):* Dean Merrill.

Lytton, Neville. *Winter Sports*, London, 1930.

MacLean, John S. *Figure Skating For Beginners.* Publishers Ltd., Toronto, 1940. *Notes:* 79 pp. School figures, dancing, free skating.

MacLean, Norman. *Ice Skating Basics.* Prentice-Hall, Englewood Cliffs, NJ, 1984. ISBN: 0-13-448762-1. *Notes:* Illustrations by Bill Gow.

Magnussen, Karen. *Karen.* Collier-Macmillan Canada Ltd., Toronto, 1973. *Additional Author(s):* Jeff Cross. *Notes:* The life story of Karen Magnussen.

Maier, Monika. *How to Succeed at Skating.* Orbis, London, 1982. ISBN: 0-85613-433-3. *Notes:* 127 pp. Translated from German by Beverly Worthington. Also published by Sterling Publishing Co., New York.

Manley, Elizabeth. *Thumbs Up—The Elizabeth Manley Story.* Macmillan of Canada, Toronto, 1990. *Additional Author(s):* Elva Clairmont Oglanby. ISBN: 0-7715-9101-2. *Notes:* 224 pages.

Martin, John. *In-Line Skating: Extreme Blading.* Capstone Press, Mankato, MN, 1994. ISBN: 1-56065-202-0. *Notes:* 48 pp.

Meagher, George A. *Figure and Fancy Skating.* Bliss, Sands and Foster, London, 1895. *Notes:* 160 pp. Preface by Frederick Arthur Stanley, the sixteenth Earl of Derby. Contains over 150 diagrams, etc.

Meagher, George A. *Guide to Artistic Skating*, London, 1919.

Meagher, George A. *Lesson In Skating.* Georges N. Morang and Company Ltd., Toronto, 1900. *Notes:* 94 pages.

Menzius, John. *The Skaters Monitor, Instructor & Evening Companion*, 1846.

Merriam, Robert. *The Ancient Art of Skating.* Robert L. Merriam, Conway, 1957. ISBN: 0-686-33162-1.

Meyer, Bror. *Skating With Bror Meyer.* Doubleday, Page & Co., New York, 1921.

Millard, Clive. *Ice Sports.* Wayland, Hove, 1980. *Additional Author(s):* Susan Crimp. ISBN: 0-853-40788-6. *Notes:* Color photos by All-Sport Limited.

Miller, Elizabeth L. *Get Rolling: The Beginner's Guide to In-Line Skating.* Pix & Pts, Union City, CA, 1992. ISBN: 0-9632196-2-6. *Notes:* 128 pp.

Mirkin, M.D., Gabe. *The Sports Medicine Book.* Little, Brown and Co., Boston, 1978. *Additional Author(s):* Marshall Hoffman. ISBN: 0-316-57434-1. *Notes:* Paperback ISBN: 0-316-57436-8.

Money, Keith. *John Curry.* Michael Joseph Ltd., London, 1978. ISBN: 0-7181-1653-4. *Notes:* Stunning photographs document Curry's 'Theatre of Skating.' Accompanying text by John Curry. Also published in New York by Alfred A. Knopf.

Monier-Williams, Montagu S. F. *Combined Figure Skating.* Horace Cox, London, 1883. *Additional Author(s):* Stanley F. Monier-Williams. *Notes:* 208 pp. '. . . being a collection of all the known combined figures, systematically arranged and illustrated.'

Monier-Williams, Montagu S. F. *Figure Skating.* A. A. Innes & Co., London, 1898. *Additional Author(s):* Stanley F. Monier-Williams.

Monier-Williams, Montagu S. F. *Figure Skating: Simple and Combined.* Macmillan and Co., New York, 1892. *Additional Author(s):* Stanley F. Monier-Williams and Winter Randell Pidgeon. *Notes:* Illustrations by Ronald Gray.

Moore, Cay. *She Skated into our Hearts.* McClelland and Stewart, Toronto, 1948. *Notes:* 117 pp. The story of Barbara Ann Scott.

Moskvina, Tamara. *Pair Skating as Sport and Art.* International Skating Union, Davos-Platz, 1987. *Latest Edition:* 1993. *Additional Author(s):* Igor Moskvin. *Notes:* 63 pp. Originally published in Lenengrad, 1987. Analysis of specific pairs' programs for use by coaches as well as by skaters.

Moskvina, Tamara. *Secrets of the Soviet Skaters: Off-Ice Training Methods.* Platoro Press, Columbus, OH, 1995. ISBN: 1-882849-03-5. *Notes:* Off-ice exercises and training methods to develop strength and flexibility for pairs as well as single skaters. First time in print. Translated by Ginger Harmon.

Mulier, W. *Winter Sport From the Library of Queen Emma*, Haarlem, Netherlands, 1893.

Muller, George. *Original Skate Dances*, 1952. *Additional Author(s):* Elizabeth Muller.

Munshower, Suzanne L. *Eric Heiden: America's Olympic Golden Boy.* Grossett and Dunlap, New York, 1980.

Musselwhite, Robert. *Poetry On Ice*, 1974.

National Skating Association, Great Britain. *Ice Figure Manual.* National Skating Association of Great Britain, London, 1972. *Notes:* 82 pp.

National Skating Association, Great Britain. *Skating: Ice and Roller.* E. P. Publishing, E. Ardsley, W. York, U.K.

NCCP/CFSA. *National Coaching Certification Program (NCCP) Manuals.* Canadian Figure Skating Association, Gloucester, ON. *Notes:* NCCP Levels I, II & III Technical Manuals. Singles Manual. Precision Manual. Ice Dancing Manual. Figures Manual. Free Skating Manual. Ice Show Manual, Judges Handbooks.

Nicholson, Howard. *Nicholson on Figure Skating*. John Lane, London, 1934. *Notes:* 130 pp.

Noel, John. *Figure Skating for Beginners*. Thomas Nelson and Sons, London, 1964. *Notes:* 126 pp. 'John Noel' is a pseudonym for Dennis Leslie Bird.

Noyes, Tina. *I Can Teach You To Figure Skate*. Hawthorn Books, New York, 1973. *Additional Author(s):* Freda Alexander. ISBN: 0-8015-3912-9. *Notes:* 178 pages.

Ogilvie, Robert. *Basic Ice Skating Skills*. J. B. Lippincott, Philadelphia, 1968. *Latest Edition:* 1973. ISBN: 0-397-00518-0. *Notes:* Paperback ISBN: 0-397-00519-9; 1973 edition published in the U.K. by A & C Black Ltd., London, ISBN 0-7136-1358-0. 176 pp. Official handbook prepared for the USFSA in 1968.

Ogilvie, Robert. *Competitive Figure Skating*. Harper & Row, New York/London, 1985.

Ogilvie, Robert. *Handbook of New Era Figures*. Professional Skaters Guild of America (PSGA), Rochester, MN, 1993. *Notes:* Detailed description of PSGA alternatives to USFSA figures.

Ogilvie, Robert. *The Parent's Guide to Competitive Figure Skating: How to Start Your Child on the Way to the Top*. HarperCollins Publishers, Inc, New York, 1985. ISBN: 0-06-015357-1.

Oglanby, Elva. *Toller*. Gage Publishing Ltd., Tornonto, 1975. *Additional Author(s):* Toller Cranston. *Notes:* 132 pp. The Toller Cranston story.

Oppelt, Kurt. *Oppelt Standard Method of Therapeutic & Recreational Ice Skating*, 1974.

Orlick, Terry. *Psyching for Sport: Mental Training for Athletes*. Leisure Press/Human Kinetics, Champaign, IL, 1986. ISBN: 0-8801-273-5.

Orser, Brian. *Orser: A Life On Skates*. Key Porter Books Ltd., Toronto, 1988. *Additional Author(s):* Steve Milton. *Notes:* 214 pp.

Owen, Maribel Vinson. *The Fun of Figure Skating: A Primer of the Art-Sport*. Arthur Baker Ltd., London, 1960. *Notes:* 167 pp. Printed in USA by Harper Brothers, New York 1960. Illustrations by Robert Riger.

Palmer, Shawna L. *Get the Edge: Sport Psychology for Figure Skaters*. The Sport Consulting Center, Burnaby, B. C., 1993. *Notes:* 163 pp. Step-by-step mental preparation for competition. How to improve concentration, increase confidence, and evaluate your performance.

Parker, Robert. *Carol Heiss, Olympic Queen*. Doubleday and Co., New York, 1961.

Peterson, Gunnar. *The Book of Outdoor Winter Activities*. Association Press, New York, 1962. *Additional Author(s):* Harry Edgren.

Petkevich, John Misha. *Skater's Handbook*. Charles Scribner's Sons, New York, 1984. *Notes:* 210 pages.

Petkevich, John Misha.. *Sports Illustrated Figure Skating: Championship Techniques*. Sports Illustrated Winner's Circle Books, New York, 1988. ISBN: 0-452-26209-7. *Notes:* 288 pp. Equipment, terminology, body positions, gliding, stroking, pushs, edges, turns, stopping, spinning, and jumping. Jumps demonstrated by Brian Boitano. Photos by Heinz Kluetmeier.

Phillips, Betty Lou. *The Picture Story of Dorothy Hamill*. J. Messner, New York, 1978. *Latest Edition:* 1979. *Notes:* 63 pp.

Phillips, D. *Ice Skating: Form, Fitness and Speed*. Troll Associates, New York, 1974. *Notes:* 32 pp.

Phillips, George D. *Figure Skating*, 1897.

Phillips, Meredith. *Death Spiral*. Perseverance Press, Menlo Park, CA.

Price, Phyllis. *Circling to The Top*. Merlin, Branunton, Devon, U.K., 1984. *Notes:* 31 pp.

Proctor, Marian. *Figure Skating*. Brown, Dubuque, IA, 1969. *Notes:* 70 pp.

The first complete MENTAL TRAINING book written specifically for figure skating

Pre Competition
- Goal Setting
- Improving Concentration
- Mental Practice for Figures
- Relaxation & Imagery
- Monitoring Performance
- Competition Simulation

Competition
- Maintaining Confidence
- Applying Skills & Strategies
- Controlling Arousal & Focus

Post Competition
- Evaluation Form
- Trying Too Hard
- Avoiding Burn-Out

Get The Edge: Sport Psychology for Figure Skating
Shawna L. Palmer, M.A.

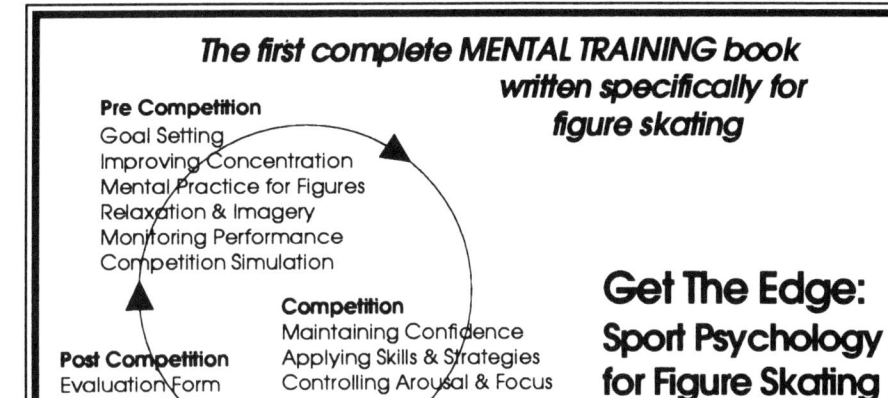

Get the Edge gives skaters and coaches the psychological skills they need to compete and train successfully. The above topics are covered in an easy-to-understand instructive style including dozens of self evaluation forms, charts, and exercises for both on and off the ice. The book emphasizes personal goals and achievement and has been found by many skaters and coaches to be both practical and effective.

TO ORDER Send $28.00 + $3.00 shipping (in Canada add GST) to:
The Sport Consulting Centre
P.O. Box 54135 - 1562 Lonsdale Avenue
North Vancouver, B.C. Canada V7M 3L5
Telephone/Fax (604) 987-8488

1993 ♦ Paper ♦ 170pp ♦ ISBN 0-9698630-0-4

Putnam, Harold. *Skating.* AS Barnes and Co., New York, 1939. *Additional Author(s):* Dwight Parkinson.

Quinn, Robert. *Figure Skating Pins.* Quin-Tel Productions, Larchmont, 1987. *Additional Author(s):* Nancy Quinn. ISBN: 0-9618349-1-9.

Radspinner, William Ambrose. *Skating and Skate Dancing.* W. A. Radspinner, New York, 1950.

Rankine, Yve M. *Winter Sports Do's and Don'ts*, London, 1925.

Rappelfeld, Joel. *The Complete Blader.* St. Martin's Press, New York, 1992. ISBN: 0-312-06936-7. *Notes:* 144 pp. A guide to in-line skating.

Rawson, Perry B. *Skate Dance Diagrams.*

Readhead, Monty. *Ice Dancing.* Peter Davies Ltd., London, 1939. *Latest Edition:* 1968. *Notes:* 1968 edition published by Pelham Books, London.

Renick, M. R. *Skating Today*, 1945.

Richardson, Thomas D. *Ice Rink Skating.* C Arthur Pearson Ltd., London, 1936. *Latest Edition:* 1949. *Notes:* 111 pp. 1949 edition published by Empire Press, Norwich, U.K.

Richardson, Thomas D. *Ice Skating.* BT Botsford, London, 1956. *Notes:* 127 pp.

Richardson, Thomas D. *Modern Figure Skating.* Methuen & Co Ltd., London, 1930. *Latest Edition:* 1980. *Notes:* 200 pp. 1980 edition published by Gordon Press, New York. ISBN 0-8490-3126-5.

Richardson, Thomas D. *Skating.* Burke Publishing Ltd., London, 1959. *Latest Edition:* 1964.

Richardson, Thomas D. *Skating With T. D. Richardson.* Sir Isaac Pitman & Sons Ltd., London, 1952. *Notes:* 144 pp.

Richardson, Thomas D. *The Art of Figure Skating.* Nicholas Kaye Ltd., London, 1962. *Notes:* 158 pp. Also published by A.S. Barnes & Co., New York 1962.

Richardson, Thomas D. *The Complete Figure Skater.* Methuen & Co. Ltd., London, 1948. *Notes:* 213 pp.

Richardson, Thomas D. *The Girls' Book of Skating.* Burke, London, 1959.

Richardson, Thomas D. *Your Book of Skating.* Faber & Faber Ltd., London, 1963.

Ritter, MD, Merrill A. *Your Injury: A Common Sense Guide to Sports Injuries.* Brown & Benchmark, Madison, WI, 1987. *Latest Edition:* 1994. *Additional Author(s):* Marjorie J. Albohm. ISBN: 0-697-14824-6. *Notes:* 190 pp. 1994 edition published by Masterspress, Indianapolis. ISBN 1-57028-011-8.

Rubenstein, Louis. *Skating in Canada*, London, 1880.

Ryan, M. *Figure Skating.* Franklin Watts, New York, 1987.

Salvesen, Charles E. *The Foundation of Skating.* The Moray Press, Edinburgh, 1932.

Sanderson, L. B. *Evaluation of Errors in Figures.* United States Figure Skating Association, Colorado Springs, 1976. *Notes:* 142 pp.

Schaefer, Karl. *Living Pictures of My 1937 Figure Skating*, Vienna, 1937. *Notes:* Booklet and 24 mini frame-by-frame flip pictures illustrating 24 compulsory figures.

Schneider, Max. *Winter Sports*, Leipzig, 1894.

Scholich, Manfred. *Circuit Training for all Athletes: Methodology of Effective Fitness Training.* Sports Book Publishers, Toronto, 1992.

Schumacher, Alice Clink. *Linda Lane, Figure Skater.* Alice Clink Schumacher, 1969.

Scott, Barbara Ann. *Skate With Me.* Doubleday and Company, New York, 1980. *Notes:* 159 pp.

Scott, Barbara Ann. *Skating for Beginners.* Alfred A. Knopf, New York, 1953. *Additional Author(s):* Michael Kirby.

Sheffield, Robert. *The Ice Skating Book.* Universe Books, New York, 1980. *Additional Author(s):* Richard Woodward. ISBN: 0-87663-276-2. *Notes:* 96 pp. Paperback ISBN: 0-87663-920-1.

Shelley, Patricia A. *The Figure Skating Film: A Thesis.* Brigham Young University, 1980.

Shelukin, Anatoly A. *Symphony On Ice: The Protopopovs.* Platoro Press, Columbus, 1993. ISBN: 0-9631758-9-0. *Notes:* The story of Oleg Protopopov and Ludmila Belousova Protopopov. Translated from Russian by Beatrice Yusem.

Shuffle, Ted. *Holiday on Ice: The First Fifty Years.* Arena International Bookings BV, Netherlands, 1994. ISBN: 90-802064-1-5. *Notes:* Arena Int'l Bookings BV, P.O. Box 9048, NL-1006AA, Amsterdam, the Netherlands.

Silva, Alphonse. *Ice Skating and Dancing*, 1929.

Smith, Beverley. *Figure Skating: A Celebration.* McClelland & Stewart, Toronto, 1994. ISBN: 0-7710-2819-9. *Notes:* 256 pp. History of competitive skating up to the 1994 World Championship. Many photos of past and current champions. Separate overviews of each of the four competitive categories, as well as an analysis of the controversial element of judging. Introduction by Elvis Stojko.

Smith, M. *Dorothy Hamill.* Creative Education, Mankato, MN, 1977. *Notes:* 31 pp.

Soanes, Sidney. *Ice Dancing: A Manual for Judges and Skaters.* Queen City Publishing, Toronto, 1976. *Notes:* 148 pp. CFSA and USFSA ice dancing manual. Explains and illustrates terminology, general judging principles, music and dance tests, plus section of study for musical rhythms.

Speidel, J. *Movements of the Body for Figure Skating*, 1982.

Stamm, Laura. *Power Skating.* Leisure Press: Human Kinetics, Champaign, IL, 1982. *Latest Edition:* 1989. ISBN: 0-88011-331-6. *Notes:* 243 pp. A complete survey of hockey skating techniques, with drills and exercises to develop agility and power in skating.

Stanbrook, Audrey Kaxton. *Someone Like Me*. Jarrolds, 1963.

Starbuck Bradshaw, JoJo. *JoJo Starbuck*. Acton House, Rolling Meadow, IL, 1978. *Additional Author(s)*: Nina Ball.

Stark-Slapnik, Nina. *Figure It Out: Think Your Way to Skating Great Figures*. Professional Skater's Guild of America (PSGA), Rochester, MN, 1986. ISBN: 0-9616977-0-9. *Notes*: Instruction manual and workbook for figures. Introduction by Robin Cousins. Illustrated by Cheryl Onesky.

Steere, Michael. *Scott Hamilton: A Behind-the-Scenes Look*. Saint Martin's Press, New York, 1985. ISBN: 0-312-70449-6. *Notes*: 347 pp. Complete title is Scott Hamilton: A Behind-the-Scenes Look at the Life & Competitive Times of America's Favorite Figure Skater.

Steere, Michael. *Skating for Gold: The Intimate Life Story of Scott Hamilton*. Saint Martin's Press, New York, 1985. ISBN: 0-312-72760-7.

Stephenson, Lois. *A History and Annotated Bibliography of Skating Costumes*. Bayberry Hill Press, Meridan, CT, 1970. *Additional Author(s)*: Richard Stephenson. *Notes*: Limited edition press run of 300.

Stephenson, Richard Montgomery. *The Ice Skater's Bible*. Doubleday and Co., Garden City, NY, 1982. *Additional Author(s)*: Theodore G. Clarke. *Notes*: 131 pp.

Stevenson, Sandra. *The BBC Book of Skating*. British Broadcasting Corporation, London, 1984. ISBN: 0-563-20223-8. *Notes*: 160 pp.

Stock, Clarence Sidney D'Este. *The Figure Skate*. A. Stace & Sons, Folkestone, U.K., 1954. *Notes*: 32 pp. 'Research into dimensions and their effects upon performance, with a consideration of penetrations into the ice and pressure upon it.' With illustrations.

Strait, Raymond. *Queen of Ice, Queen of Shadows*. Stein and Day Publishers, New York, 1985. *Additional Author(s)*: Leif Henie. *Notes*: 339 pp. The Sonja Henie story.

Sullivan, George. *Better Ice Skating for Boys and Girls*. Dodd, Mead & Co., 1976. *Notes*: 64 pages.

Swift, Frank. *The Skater's Text Book*. Gray and Green, New York, 1868. *Additional Author(s)*: Marvin R. Clark.

Syers, Edgar Wood. *Figure Skating*. Mitchell's, Manchester, U.K., 1912. *Notes*: Includes a catalogue of blades manufactured by Francis Wood & Son, Thorpe Works, Henry Street, Sheffield.

Syers, Edgar Wood. *The Art of Skating—International Style*, 1913. *Additional Author(s)*: Madge Syers.

Syers, Edgar Wood. *The Book of Winter Sports*. Edward Arnold, London, 1908.

Syers, Edgar Wood. *The Poetry of Skating*. Watts and Co, London, 1905.

Taylor, Alex. *Ice Skating*. A & C Black, London, 1994. ISBN: 0-713-63743-9.

Taylor, Alex. *Let's Go Skating*. Transworld Publishers Ltd., London, 1991. ISBN: 1-85225-128-X.

Tchaikovskaya, Yelena. *Patterns of Russian Ice Dance*. Plataro Press, Columbus, OH, 1994. ISBN: 1-882849-01-9. *Notes*: Coach of 1976 Olympic champions and current head coach of the Russian team, Tchaikovskaya relates her choreographic methods and many anecdotes from her experience. Originally published in 1976. Translated by Beatrice Yusem.

Tebbutt, C. G. *Skating*. Alcock's Oval Series, London, 1893. *Latest Edition*: 1927. *Additional Author(s)*: A. Read, A. Tebbutt. *Notes*: In three parts : Speed Skating by C.G. Tebbutt; Figure Skating by A. Read; and Bandy by A. Tebbutt. With illustrations.

Terauds, J. *Science in Skiing, Skating and Hockey*. Academic Publishers, Del Mar, CA, 1979. *Additional Author(s)*: H. J. Gros. *Notes*: 205 pp.

Thompson, Norcliffe G. *Combined Hand-in-Hand Figure Skating*. Longmans, Green & Co., London, 1904. *Additional Author(s)*: Laura Cannan & Viscount Doneraile.

Tomlins, Peggy. *Freddie Tomlins: His Life On Skates*. New Arts Publishers, London.

Torvill, Jayne. *Fire on Ice—Torvill and Dean*. Weidenfeld & Nicolson Ltd., London, 1994. *Additional Author(s)*: Christopher Dean with Neil Wilson. ISBN: 0-297-833-863. *Notes*: Photographs by Bob Martin.

Torvill, Jayne. *Torvill & Dean*. David & Charles Ltd., Newton Abbot, U.K., 1983. *Latest Edition*: 1984. *Additional Author(s)*: Christopher Dean with John Hennessy. ISBN: 0-7153-

1984 Olympic Ice Dance Champions Jayne Torvill and Christopher Dean

PHOTO BY ALICE BERMAN

8476-7. *Notes:* 208 pp. Paperback ISBN 0-7153-8622-0.

Trenary, Jill. *The Day I Skated for the Gold.* Simon and Schuster Books For Young Readers, New York, 1989. *Additional Author(s):* Dale Mitch. ISBN: 0-671-68315-2. *Notes:* Alternate title: Jill Trenary: The Time of My Life.

Turner, Roger F. *Edges.* Mill Pond Press, 1973. *Notes:* 116 pages.

Unknown. *Great Skaters Coloring Book.* Variety Arts, New York, 1991. ISBN: 0-937180-07-6. *Notes:* A children's coloring book with biographies of Sonja Henie, Salchow and others.

Unknown. *Irina Rodnina: Her Life For Skating. Notes:* This book has recently (1994) been available in the U.K. from Skate Magazine.

Unknown. *Skaters Textbook,* 1883. *Notes:* In the collection of the U.S. Figure Skating Museum, Colorado Springs.

USFSA. *Skating Through The Years.* U.S. Figure Skating Association, 1942. *Notes:* 66 pp. Photographs of U.S. champions.

Van der Weyden, Erik. *Dancing On Ice.* Grunberg, New York, 1950. *Latest Edition:* 1951. *Notes:* 1951 edition published by C. Arthur Pearson Ltd., London.

Van der Weyden, Erik. *Instructions to Young Skaters.* Museum Press Ltd., London, 1957.

Van Steenwyck, Elizabeth. *Dorothy Hamill Olympic Champion.*

Van Steenwyck, Elizabeth. *Peggy Fleming: Cameo Of A Champion.* McGraw Hill, New York, 1978. *Notes:* 132 pp.

Van Steenwyck, Elizabeth. *Stars On Ice.* Dodd, Mead and Company, New York, 1980.

Van Steenwyck, Elizabeth. *Women in Sports: Figure Skating.* Harvey House, New York, 1976. *Notes:* 78 pp.

Vandervell, H. E. *A System of Figure Skating.* Macmillan & Co., London, 1869. *Latest Edition:* 1993. *Additional Author(s):* T. Maxwell Witham. ISBN: 0-87566-710 -X. *Notes:* 1983 & 1993 editions published by Albert SaiFer Publishing, Wachtung NJ. 1993 edition ISBN 0-685-66854-1.

Vandervell, H. E. *The Figure Skate.* Straker Brothers, London, 1901. *Notes:* 72 pp. 'Research into the form of blade best adapted to curvilinear skating.' With illustrations.

Vinson, Maribel Y. *Advanced Figure Skating.* McGraw Hill, New York/London, 1940. *Notes:* 292 pp.

Vinson, Maribel Y. *Primer of Figure Skating.* McGraw Hill, New York/London, 1938. *Notes:* 182 pp.

Von Gassner, Paul. *Figure and Dance Skating.* A&S Publishing Co., New York, 1949. *Notes:* 190 pp.

Wade, A.C.A. *The Skater's Cavalcade—Fifty Years of Skating,* 1930.

Wallechnisky, David. *The Complete Book Of The Olympics.* Viking Press, New York, 1983.

Whedon, Julia. *The Fine Art of Ice Skating: An Illustrated History & Portfolio of Stars.* Harry N. Abrams, New York, 1988. ISBN: 0-8109-1127-2. *Notes:* 127 pp. Illustrated history of skating, with old photos and woodcuts, plus full-page color photos of many top skaters through 1988. Second hardcover edition ISBN 0-318-37454-4.

White, Harold. *Figure Skating Techniques.* George Routledge & Sons Ltd., London, 1933. *Notes:* 110 pp.

White, W. Dustin. *The Book of Winter Sports.* Houghton Mifflin, Boston, 1925.

IN THE WORKS

Christine Brennan has taken leave from the *Washington Post* to write a behind-the-scenes book after following the 1994-95 skating season. From Scribner's, early '96. **Steve Woodward** has left *USA Today* and is co-authoring a book with **Nancy Kerrigan** aimed at children. *Publisher:* Disney's Hyperion Books for Children.

Winter, Ginny L. *Skating Book.* Astor-Honor, New York, 1963. ISBN: 0-8392-3035-4.

Witham, T. Maxwell. *Skating.* Little Brown Co., Boston, 1892. *Latest Edition:* 1894. *Notes:* 1894 edition published by Longman's, Green and Co., London.

Wohlrath, Thomas. *Winter Sport,* Stuttgart, 1910.

Wolter, Carlo. *Figure Skating.* Franklin Watts, London/New York, 1977. ISBN: 0-531-00396-5.

Wood, George. *Combined Figure Skating.* F. E. Robinson, London, 1899. *Notes:* 166 pp.

Wood, The Rev. J. G. *Skating And Sliding.* George Routledge & Sons Ltd., London, 1872.

Wood, Tim. *Ice Skating.* Franklin Watts, London/New York, 1990. ISBN: 0-531-14051-2. *Notes:* Introduction to skating for children; photographs by Chris Fairclough. Also pulished by Franklin Watts, New York.

Wright, Benjamin T. *Skating Around the World 1892-1992.* International Skating Union, Davos-Platz, 1992. *Notes:* The one hundredth anniversary history of the International Skating Union.

Yglesias, H. R. *Figure Skating.* George Routledge & Sons Ltd., London, 1905. *Latest Edition:* 1908. *Notes:* Second edition rewritten and enlarged 1913.

Yglesias, H. R. *Notes on Judging Figure Skating.* Richmond, Surrey Figure Skating Club, Richmond, U.K., 1932. *Notes:* 11 pp. with diagrams.

Young, David. *The Golden Age of Canadian Figure Skating.* Summerhill Press Ltd., Toronto, 1984. *Notes:* 200 pp., 24 pp. of plates. Includes index. History of Canadian figure skating from beginning to 1984.

Young, Stephanie. *Peggy Fleming: Portrait Of An Ice Skater.* Avon, New York, 1984. *Additional Author(s):* B. Curtis. *Notes:* 159 pp. The basics of figure skating explained for young people, with photographs of Peggy Fleming.

Cross Reference: Books by Title

For ease of finding books where the author is unknown, the books are listed in alphabetical order by title. For more details on individual books, use the author's name to locate the longer listing in the previous section.

A Handbook of Figure Skating. George Browne. 1910.

A History and Annotated Bibliography of Skating Costumes. Lois Stephenson. 1970.

A New Approach to Skating Terminology. Sidney Broadbent. 1964.

A Ram on the Rampage. Toller Cranston. 1977.

A System of Figure Skating. H. E. Vandervell. 1869.

A Treatise on Skating. Captain Jones. 1792.

A Very Young Skater. Jill Krementz. 1979.

A Winter Sports Book. Reginald Cleaver. 1911.

Advanced Figure Skating. Maribel Y. Vinson. 1940.

American Women in Sports. Phyllis Hollander. 1972.

An Approved History of The Olympic Games. William M. Henry. 1948.

An Evening With Champions. Eliot House. 1982.

Asthma & Exercise. Nancy Hogshead. 1990.

Basic Ice Skating Skills. Robert Ogilvie. 1968.

Better Ice Skating. Richard Arnold. 1976.

Better Ice Skating for Boys and Girls. George Sullivan. 1976.

Better Sport Skating: The Key to Improved Performance. Richard Arnold. 1982.

Bibliography of Skating. Fred M. Foster. 1898.

Blades Are Necessary. John Foley. 1970.

Brian Orser. Stephanie Papp Geddes. 1988.

Buying Ice Skates. ISIA.

Cambridge Skating Club, 1898-1948. Arthur Goodridge.

Carol Heiss, Olympic Queen. Robert Parker. 1961.

Champions All. R. E. Hall. 1938.

Championship Figure Skating. Gustave Lussi. 1951.

Children and Sport: Fitness, Injuries, and Diet. Vivian Grisogano. 1991.

Choreography & Style for Ice Skaters. Ricky Harris. 1980.

Circling to The Top. Phyllis Price. 1984.

Circuit Training for all Athletes: Methodology of Effective Fitness Training. Manfred Scholich. 1992.

Combined Figure and Ice Skating. Colonel H. Vaughn Kent. 1929.

Combined Figure Skating. Montagu S. F. Monier-Williams. 1883.

Combined Figure Skating. George Wood. 1899.

Combined Hand-in-Hand Figure Skating. Norcliffe G. Thompson. 1904.

Come Skate With Me. Marian S. Glasser. 1985.

Competitive Figure Skating. Robert Ogilvie. 1985.

Competitors Handbook. ISIA. 1994.

Complete Beginner's Guide to Ice Skating. Edward F. Dolan. 1974.

Complete Manual of Compulsory Ice Dances. Jeff R. Lerner. 1994.

Creative Ice Skating: Ice Dancing, Freestyle, & Pair Skating. Frances Dorsey. 1980.

Cub Scout Sports: Skating. Boy Scouts of America. 1986.

Dancing On Ice. Erik Van der Weyden. 1950.

Dancing on Ice: How to Skate the Lancers. Colonel H. Vaughn Kent. 1910.

Dancing On Skates. Richard Arnold. 1985.

Death Spiral. Meredith Phillips.

Depth Jumps: Training for Figure Skaters. CFSA.

Dick Button on Skates. Dick Button. 1955.

Donald Jackson: King of Blades. George Gross. 1977.

Dorothy Hamill. M. Smith. 1977.

Dorothy Hamill Olympic Champion. Elizabeth Van Steenwyck.

Dorothy Hamill, Olympic Skating Champion. Edward F. Dolan. 1979.

Dorothy Hamill: On And Off The Ice. Dorothy Hamill. 1983.

Down The Ice. Foster Hewitt. 1934.

Eat to Win: The Sports Nutrition Bible. Robert Haas. 1983.

Edges. Roger F. Turner. 1973.

Elements of Skating. Captain S. Duff-Taylor. 1933.

Encyclopedia of the Olympic Winter Games. Erich Kamper. 1964.

English Figure Skating. Edward Frederick Benson. 1908.

English Skating in Three Parts. Henry C. Lowther. 1900-02.

Enjoying Skating. Diagram Group. 1978.

Eric Heiden: America's Olympic Golden Boy. Suzanne L. Munshower. 1980.

Eric Heiden: Winner In Gold. Nathan Aaseng. 1980.

Evaluation of Errors in Figures. L. B. Sanderson. 1976.

Facility Operations Manual. ISIA.

Fen Skating. Albert Goodman. 1882.

Fifty Years of Skating (1886-1936). Joseph Chapman. 1944.
Figure and Dance Skating. Paul Von Gassner. 1949.
Figure and Fancy Skating. George A. Meagher. 1895.
Figure It Out: Think Your Way to Skating Great Figures. Nina Stark-Slapnik. 1986.
Figure Skating. H. R. Yglesias. 1905.
Figure Skating. Edgar Wood Syers. 1912.
Figure Skating. Ellen Burka. 1974.
Figure Skating. Sally Lindsay. 1963.
Figure Skating. Carlo Wolter. 1977.
Figure Skating. Dianne DeLeeuw. 1978.
Figure Skating. George D. Phillips. 1897.
Figure Skating.. Marian Proctor. 1969.
Figure Skating. Fitness & Amateur Sport Directorate, Canada. 1963.
Figure Skating. M. Ryan. 1987.
Figure Skating. Montagu S. F. Monier-Williams. 1898.
Figure Skating: A Celebration. Beverley Smith. 1994.
Figure Skating As A Hobby. Diane Cummings. 1938.
Figure Skating for Beginners. John Noel. 1964.
Figure Skating For Beginners. John S. MacLean. 1940.
Figure Skating for Everyone. Manual. Health and Welfare Canada. 1974.
Figure Skating for Women. James A. Cruikshank. 1917.
Figure Skating History: The Evolution of Dance on Ice. Lynn Copley-Graves. 1992.
Figure Skating in the English Style. Humphry H. Cobb. 1913.
Figure Skating: Pages of History. Rimma Chubrik. 1994.
Figure Skating Pins. Robert Quinn. 1987.
Figure Skating: Simple and Combined. Montagu S. F. Monier-Williams. 1892.
Figure Skating Simplified. Major George Baillie. 1910.
Figure Skating Techniques. Harold White. 1933.
Figure Skating With Carlo Fassi. Carlo Fassi. 1980.
Figures of the Second Class Test. Arthur Hadley. 1910.
Figures On Ice. Anatoly Chaikovsky. 1978.
Fire on Ice—Torvill and Dean. Jayne Torvill. 1994.
For Members Only: ISIA Annual Membership Directory. ISIA.
Forcing the Edge. Kurt Browning. 1991.
Freddie Tomlins: His Life On Skates. Peggy Tomlins.
From Boots to Blades. CFSA.

Get Rolling: The Beginner's Guide to In-Line Skating. Elizabeth L. Miller. 1992.
Get the Edge: Sport Psychology for Figure Skaters. Shawna L. Palmer. 1993.
Golden Skates: The Story of Carol Heiss—Teen-Age Champion. Helen Cambria Bolstad. 1958.
Great Skaters Coloring Book. Unknown. 1991.
Great Skates. Laura Hilgers. 1991.

Group Skating Manual. ISIA.
Guide to Artistic Skating. George A. Meagher. 1919.

Handbook of New Era Figures. Robert Ogilvie. 1993.
Hans Brinker or The Silver Skates. Mary Mapes Dodge. 1865.
Hippodrome Skating Book. Charlotte. 1916.
Holiday on Ice: The First Fifty Years. Ted Shuffle. 1994.
How To Improve Your Ice Skating. Einar Jomland.
How to Judge Figure Skating. Wilhelm R. Boeckl. 1940.
How to Succeed at Skating. Monika Maier. 1982.

I Can Teach You To Figure Skate. Tina Noyes. 1973.
I Skate. Margaret Faulkner. 1979.
Ice and Roller Skating. Sid G. Hedges. 1928.
Ice Dancing. Monty Readhead. 1939.
Ice Dancing: A Manual for Judges and Skaters. Sidney Soanes. 1976.
Ice Dancing Illustrated. Lorna Dyer. 1980.
Ice Figure Manual. National Skating Association, Great Britain. 1972.
Ice King—General Skating Information. Julian T. Fitzgerald. 1922.
Ice Palaces. Fred Anders. 1983.
Ice Rink Skating. Thomas D. Richardson. 1936.
Ice Show Manual. CFSA. 1988.
Ice Skating. Howard Bass. 1980.
Ice Skating. Tim Wood. 1990.
Ice Skating. Alex Taylor. 1994.
Ice Skating. Pere Horne. 1968.
Ice Skating. Michael Kirby. 1968.
Ice Skating. Thomas D. Richardson. 1956.
Ice Skating: A History. Nigel Brown. 1959.
Ice Skating and Dancing. Alphonse Silva. 1929.
Ice Skating Basics. Norman MacLean. 1984.
Ice Skating For Pleasure. Howard Bass. 1979.
Ice Skating: Form, Fitness and Speed. D. Phillips. 1974.
Ice Skating Fundamentals. Marilyn G. House. 1983.
Ice Skating in the East Midlands. Trevor John Kayes. 1975.
Ice Skating Is For Me. Lowell A. Dickmeyer. 1980.
Ice Skating Made Easy. Richard Arnold. 1979.
Ice Sports. Norman Barrett. 1988.
Ice Sports. Clive Millard. 1980.
Ice-Rink Skating. Sid G. Hedges. 1932.
In-Line Skating: Extreme Blading. John Martin. 1994.
Inside Ice Skating. Einar Jomland. 1978.
Instant Skating. Dick Button. 1964.
Instructions on the Art of Skating. Thomas Clay. 1828.
Instructions to Young Skaters. Erik Van der Weyden. 1957.
Instructor Manual. ISIA.

International Encyclopedia of Winter Sports. Howard Bass. 1971.
Introduction To Ice Skating. Einar Jomland. 1973.
Irina Rodnina: Her Life For Skating. Unknown.
ISIA Boy Scout and Girl Scout Program. ISIA.
ISIA Games Book. ISIA.
ISIA Judges Manual. ISIA. 1993.
ISIA Manager's Manual. ISIA.
ISIA Recreational Ice Skater Team Competition Standards. ISIA. 1991.
ISIA Special Skater Test Standards. ISIA.
ISU Office Holders Through The Years. ISU.

John Curry. Keith Money. 1978.
JoJo Starbuck. JoJo Starbuck Bradshaw. 1978.

Karen. Karen Magnussen. 1973.
Know the Game Series—Ice Skating. Dennis L. Bird. 1985.
Kristi Yamaguchi: Artist on Ice. Shiobhan Donahue. 1993.

Lesson In Skating. George A. Meagher. 1900.
Let's Go Ice Skating. Richard Arnold. 1987.
Let's Go Skating. Howard Bass. 1974.
Let's Go Skating. Alex Taylor. 1991.
Letters to Young Winter Sportsmen. Brian Lunn. 1927.
Linda Lane, Figure Skater. Alice Clink Schumacher. 1969.
Little Winners—Inside the World of the Child Sports Star. Emily Greenspan. 1983.
Living Pictures of My 1937 Figure Skating. Karl Schaefer. 1937.

Maxie & Ernst Baier. Maxie and Ernst Baier. 1951.
Modern Figure Skating. Thomas D. Richardson. 1930.
Modern Skating. Frederic Lewis. 1938.
Movements of the Body for Figure Skating. J. Speidel. 1982.

Nancy Clark's Sports Nutrition Guidebook. Nancy Clark. 1990.
National Coaching Certification Program (NCCP) Manuals. NCCP/CFSA.
Nicholson on Figure Skating. Howard Nicholson. 1934.
Nocturne. Arthur N. Foxe. 1975.
Notes on Judging Figure Skating. H. R. Yglesias. 1932.

Off-Ice Training for Figure Skaters. Tudor Bompa. 1974.
Off-Ice Training Manual. Tony Bauer.
On The Ice. Alexis Burakoff. 1994.
On Thin Ice. Henry Jelinek. 1965.
Oppelt Standard Method of Therapeutic & Recreational Ice Skating. Kurt Oppelt. 1974.
Original Skate Dances. George Muller. 1952.

1992 Olympic Gold Medalist Kristi Yamaguchi

Origins of Ice Dance Music. Muriel Kay. 1979.
Orser: A Life On Skates. Brian Orser. 1988.
Our Skating Heritage. Dennis L. Bird. 1979.

Pair Skating and Dancing on Ice. Robert Dench. 1943.
Pair Skating as Sport and Art. Tamara Moskvina. 1987.
Parent's Guide to Test and Competitive Skating. CFSA. 1994.
Patterns of Russian Ice Dance. Yelena Tchaikovskaya. 1994.
Peace And Love. Janet Lynn. 1973.
Peggy Fleming: Cameo Of A Champion. Elizabeth Van Steenwyck. 1978.
Peggy Fleming: Portrait Of An Ice Skater. Stephanie Young. 1984.
Physics, Dance, And the Pas de Deux. Kenneth Laws. 1994.
Poetry On Ice. Robert Musselwhite. 1974.
Power Skating. Laura Stamm. 1982.
Primer of Figure Skating. Maribel Y. Vinson. 1938.
Psyching for Sport: Mental Training for Athletes. Terry Orlick. 1986.

Queen of Ice, Queen of Shadows. Raymond Strait. 1985.

Reflections on the CFSA. CFSA.
Results 1968-1991: Figure Skating Championships. ISU. 1992.
Rink Guard Training Manual. ISIA.
Rink Responsibilities and Liabilities. ISIA.

Science in Skiing, Skating and Hockey. J. Terauds. 1979.
Scott Hamilton: A Behind-the-Scenes Look. Michael Steere. 1985.
Secrets of the Soviet Skaters: Off-Ice Training Methods. Tamara Moskvina. 1995.
Seventy Five Years of European and World's Championships in Figure Skating. ISU. 1968.
She Skated into our Hearts. Cay Moore. 1948.

PHOTO BY ALICE BERMAN

Single Figure Skating: For Beginners and Champions. Joseph Dedic. 1974.

Skate Dance Diagrams. Perry B. Rawson.

Skate Like the Wind. Joan E. Ford. 1983.

Skate With Me. Barbara Ann Scott. 1980.

Skateaway. Robin Cousins. 1984.

Skateology. Sidney Broadbent. 1985.

Skater's Edge Sourcebook. Alice Berman. 1995.

Skater's Handbook. John Misha Petkevich. 1984.

Skaters: Profile Of A Pair. Lynn Haney. 1983.

Skaters Textbook. Unknown. 1883.

Skating. Captain S. Duff-Taylor. 1935.

Skating. Donna Bailey. 1990.

Skating. Boy Scouts of America. 1983.

Skating. A. E. Crawley. 1920.

Skating. Harold Putnam. 1939.

Skating. C. G. Tebbutt. 1893.

Skating. J. M. Heathcote. 1892.

Skating. Douglas Adams. 1890.

Skating. Thomas D. Richardson. 1959.

Skating. T. Maxwell Witham. 1892.

Skating. D. Beddoes. 1976.

Skating and Skate Dancing. William Ambrose Radspinner. 1950.

Skating And Sliding. The Rev. J. G. Wood. 1872.

Skating and the Philadelphia Club. John F. Lewis. 1895.

Skating Around the World 1892-1992. Benjamin T. Wright. 1992.

Skating Book. Ginny L. Winter. 1963.

Skating Director Manual. ISIA.

Skating: Elegance On Ice. Howard Bass. 1980.

Skating for Beginners. Barbara Ann Scott. 1953.

Skating For Everyone. Arthur N. Foxe. 1966.

Skating For Gold. Robin Cousins. 1980.

Skating for Gold: The Intimate Life Story of Scott Hamilton. Michael Steere. 1985.

Skating: Ice and Roller. National Skating Association, Great Britain.

Skating in Canada. Louis Rubenstein. 1880.

Skating On Ice. Einar Jomland. 1963.

Skating On Ice: A Basis for Ice Dancing. Ivy Gale. 1950.

Skating Primer. George Browne. 1912.

Skating Through The Years. USFSA. 1942.

Skating Today. M. R. Renick. 1945.

Skating With Bror Meyer. Bror Meyer. 1921.

Skating With Heather Grace. Thomas Lynch. 1987.

Skating With T. D. Richardson. Thomas D. Richardson. 1952.

Snow and Ice Sports. Elon Jessup. 1923.

Someone Like Me. Audrey Kaxton Stanbrook. 1963.

Spice on Ice. Karen Barber. 1985.

Sports Illustrated Figure Skating: Championship Techniques. John Misha Petkevich. 1988.

Sports Injuries Manual for Trainers and Coaches. Donald F. Featherstone. 1956.

Sports Star: Dorothy Hamill. S. H. Bouchard. 1978.

Stars On Ice. Elizabeth Van Steenwyck. 1980.

Step by Step Ice Skating Guide. Carol Butterworth. 1978.

Stretching for Everyday Fitness & for Running, Tennis, Raquetball, Cycling, Swimming, etc. Bob Anderson. 1980.

Symphony On Ice: The Protopopovs. Anatoly A. Shelukin. 1993.

Tackle Skating. Howard Bass. 1978.

The Ancient Art of Skating. Robert Merriam. 1957.

The Ancient Art of Skating. Robert L. Deerfield. 1957.

The Art of Figure Skating. Thomas D. Richardson. 1962.

The Art of Skating. George Anderson. 1852.

The Art of Skating. Irving Brokaw. 1910.

The Art of Skating—International Style. Edgar Wood Syers. 1913.

The BBC Book of Skating. Sandra Stevenson. 1984.

The Beauty of Skating. Manfred Curry. 1935.

The Big Red Machine: The Rise and Fall of Soviet Olympic Champions. Yuri Brokhin. 1977.

The Book of Outdoor Winter Activities. Gunnar Peterson. 1962.

The Book of Winter Sports. Edgar Wood Syers. 1908.

The Book of Winter Sports. W. Dustin White. 1925.

The Complete Blader. Joel Rappelfeld. 1992.

The Complete Book Of The Olympics. David Wallechinsky. 1983.

The Complete Figure Skater. Thomas D. Richardson. 1948.

The Complete Guide & Resource to In-Line Skating. Stephen C. Joyner. 1993.

The Complete Manual of Ice Dance Patterns. Jeff R. Lerner. 1992.

The Day I Skated for the Gold. Jill Trenary. 1989.

The Easy Ice Skating Book. Jonah Kalb. 1981.

The Elements of Figure Skating. Ernest Jones. 1931.

The Figure Skate. Clarence Sidney D'Este Stock. 1954.

The Figure Skate. H. E. Vandervell. 1901.

The Figure Skating Film: A Thesis. Patricia A. Shelley. 1980.

The Figure Skating Ready Reckoner. H. D. F. 1865.

The Fine Art of Ice Skating: An Illustrated History & Portfolio of Stars. Julia Whedon. 1988.

The Foundation of Skating. Charles E. Salvesen. 1932.

The Fun of Figure Skating: A Primer of the Art-Sport. Maribel Vinson Owen. 1960.

The Girls' Book of Skating. Thomas D. Richardson. 1959.

The Golden Age of Canadian Figure Skating. David Young. 1984.

The Ice Skater's Bible. Richard Montgomery Stephenson. 1982.

The Ice Skating Book. Robert Sheffield. 1980.
The Illustrated Encyclopedia of Ice Skating. Mark Heller, ed. 1979.
The Key to Rhythmic Ice Dancing. Muriel Kay. 1958.
The Love of Ice Skating and Speed Skating. Howard Bass. 1980.
The Olympic Games. ISU. 1968.
The Parent's Guide to Competitive Figure Skating: How to Start Your Child on the Way to the Top. Robert Ogilvie. 1985.
The Picture Story of Dorothy Hamill. Betty Lou Phillips. 1978.
The Poetry of Skating. Edgar Wood Syers. 1905.
The Relationship of Music to Ice Dancing. Charles A. DeMore. 1964.
The Skater's Cavalcade—Fifty Years of Skating. A. C. A. Wade. 1930.
The Skater's Manual. Kenny Isely. 1978.
The Skater's Text Book. Frank Swift. 1868.
The Skaters Monitor, Instructor & Evening Companion. John Menzius. 1846.
The Skaters of the Fens. Alan Bloom. 1958.
The Skating Scene. Arthur R. Goodfellow. 1981.
The Sports Injury Handbook: An Athlete's Guide to Causes, Prevention, and Treatment. Hans Kraus, M.D. 1981.
The Sports Medicine Book. Gabe Mirkin, M.D. 1978.
The Technique of Skating. Otto Hugen. 1973.
The Winning Edge: Nutrition for Athletic Fitness and Performance. Frank G. Addleman. 1984.
The Winter Book for Girls. Heather Dean. 1956.
The Wonderful World of Skates. Arthur R. Goodfellow. 1972.
The Yankee Polka, Ravensburger Waltz, & Tango Romantica. Georges Blundun. 1976.
The Young Sportsman's Guide to Ice Skating. Michael Kirby. 1962.
Thin Ice. Jacqueline du Bief. 1956.
This Skating Age. Howard Bass. 1958.
Thumbs Up—The Elizabeth Manley Story. Elizabeth Manley. 1990.
Tiffany Chin, A Dream On Ice. Ray Buck. 1986.
Toller. Elva Oglanby. 1975.
Torvill and Dean: The Full Story. Christopher Hilton. 1994.
Torvill & Dean. Jayne Torvill. 1983.

Valsing on Ice. Ernest Law. 1908.

Walker's Manly Exercises. Craven. 1855.
Who Will Win—The Gold Skate. Ilona Bozska. 1976.
Who's Who in International Winter Sports. David Emery, ed. 1983.
Willy Boeckl on Figure Skating. Wilhelm R. Boeckl. 1937.
Wings On My Feet. Sonja Henie. 1940.
Winners On The Ice. Frank Litsky. 1970.

Winter Sport. Thomas Wohlrath. 1910.
Winter Sport From the Library of Queen Emma. W. Mulier. 1893.
Winter Sports. Arnold Lunn. 1930.
Winter Sports. Neville Lytton. 1930.
Winter Sports. Howard Bass. 1966.
Winter Sports. James A. Cruikshank.
Winter Sports. Vincent Knesworth.
Winter Sports. Max Schneider. 1894.
Winter Sports Do's and Don'ts. Yve M. Rankine. 1925.
Winter Sports in Switzerland. E. F. Benson.
Wintersport. W. J. Gyger. 1925.
Women in Sports: Figure Skating. Elizabeth Van Steenwyck. 1976.
World Ice Skating Guide. Arthur R. Goodfellow.

Your Book of Skating. Thomas D. Richardson. 1963.
Your Injury: A Common Sense Guide to Sports Injuries. Merrill A. Ritter, MD. 1987.

Cross Reference: Books by Category

Following are listings of some of the books by categories, where categories are known or fairly evident from the book's title. Not all the books in the primary listing section are included below. For more details on individual titles, locate the book by the author's name in the longer primary listings.

BIOGRAPHY/AUTOBIOGRAPHY

Aaseng, Nathan. *Eric Heiden: Winner In Gold.* 1980.
Barber, Karen. *Spice on Ice.* 1985.
Bolstad, Helen Cambria. *Golden Skates: The Story of Carol Heiss—Teen-Age Champion.* 1958.
Bouchard, S. H. *Sports Star: Dorothy Hamill.* 1978.
Browning, Kurt. *Forcing the Edge.* 1991.
Buck, Ray. *Tiffany Chin, A Dream On Ice.* 1986.
Button, Dick. *Dick Button on Skates.* 1955.
Cousins, Robin. *Skating For Gold.* 1980.
Cranston, Toller. *A Ram on the Rampage.* 1977.
Dolan, Edward F. *Dorothy Hamill, Olympic Skating Champion.* 1979.
Donahue, Shiobhan. *Kristi Yamaguchi: Artist on Ice.* 1993.
du Bief, Jacqueline. *Thin Ice.* 1956.
Emery, ed, David. *Who's Who in International Winter Sports.* 1983.
Ford, Joan E. *Skate Like the Wind.* 1983.
Geddes, Stephanie Papp. *Brian Orser.* 1988.
Greenspan, Emily. *Little Winners—Inside the World of the Child Sports Star.* 1983.
Gross, George. *Donald Jackson: King of Blades.* 1977.
Hamill, Dorothy. *Dorothy Hamill: On And Off The Ice.* 1983.
Henie, Sonja. *Wings On My Feet.* 1940.

Hilton, Christopher. *Torvill and Dean: The Full Story.* 1994.
Lynn, Janet. *Peace And Love.* 1973.
Magnussen, Karen. *Karen.* 1973.
Manley, Elizabeth. *Thumbs Up—The Elizabeth Manley Story.* 1990.
Money, Keith. *John Curry.* 1978.
Moore, Cay. *She Skated into our Hearts.* 1948.
Munshower, Suzanne L. *Eric Heiden: America's Olympic Golden Boy.* 1980.
Oglanby, Elva. *Toller.* 1975.
Orser, Brian. *Orser: A Life On Skates.* 1988.
Parker, Robert. *Carol Heiss, Olympic Queen.* 1961.
Phillips, Betty Lou. *The Picture Story of Dorothy Hamill.* 1978.
Schumacher, Alice Clink. *Linda Lane, Figure Skater.* 1969.
Shelukin, Anatoly A. *Symphony On Ice: The Protopopovs.* 1993.
Stanbrook, Audrey Kaxton. *Someone Like Me.* 1963.
Starbuck Bradshaw, JoJo. *JoJo Starbuck.* 1978.
Steere, Michael. *Scott Hamilton: A Behind-the-Scenes Look.* 1985.
Steere, Michael. *Skating for Gold: The Intimate Life Story of Scott Hamilton.* 1985.
Strait, Raymond. *Queen of Ice, Queen of Shadows.* 1985.
Tomlins, Peggy. *Freddie Tomlins: His Life On Skates.*
Torvill, Jayne. *Fire on Ice—Torvill and Dean.* 1994.
Torvill, Jayne. *Torvill & Dean.* 1983.
Trenary, Jill. *The Day I Skated for the Gold.* 1989.
Unknown. *Irina Rodnina: Her Life For Skating.*
Van Steenwyck, Elizabeth. *Dorothy Hamill Olympic Champion.*
Van Steenwyck, Elizabeth. *Peggy Fleming: Cameo Of A Champion.* 1978.
Van Steenwyck, Elizabeth. *Women in Sports: Figure Skating.* 1976.

BOOKS: HISTORICAL

Bird, Dennis L. *Our Skating Heritage.* 1979.
Brokhin, Yuri. *The Big Red Machine: The Rise and Fall of Soviet Olympic Champions.* 1977.
Brown, Nigel. *Ice Skating: A History.* 1959.
CFSA. *Reflections on the CFSA.*
Chapman, Joseph. *Fifty Years of Skating (1886-1936).* 1944.
Copley-Graves, Lynn. *Figure Skating History: The Evolution of Dance on Ice.* 1992.
Deerfield, Robert L. *The Ancient Art of Skating.* 1957.
Foster, Fred M. *Bibliography of Skating.* 1898.
Goodfellow, Arthur R. *The Wonderful World of Skates.* 1972.
Henry, William M. *An Approved History of The Olympic Games.* 1948.
Hollander, Phyllis. *American Women in Sports.* 1972.
ISU. *ISU Office Holders Through The Years.*
ISU. *Results 1968-1991: Figure Skating Championships.* 1992.
ISU. *Seventy Five Years of European and World's Championships in Figure Skating.* 1968.
ISU. *The Olympic Games.* 1968.
Kamper, Erich. *Encyclopedia of the Olympic Winter Games.* 1964.
Kay, Muriel. *Origins of Ice Dance Music.* 1979.
Lewis, John F. *Skating and the Philadelphia Club.* 1895.
Merriam, Robert. *The Ancient Art of Skating.* 1957.
Mulier, W. *Winter Sport From the Library of Queen Emma.* 1893.
Shuffle, Ted. *Holiday on Ice: The First Fifty Years.* 1994.
Smith, Beverley. *Figure Skating: A Celebration.* 1994.
Stephenson, Lois. *A History and Annotated Bibliography of Skating Costumes.* 1970.
Wade, A. C. A. *The Skater's Cavalcade—Fifty Years of Skating.* 1930.
Wallechnisky, David. *The Complete Book Of The Olympics.* 1983.
Wright, Benjamin T. *Skating Around the World 1892-1992.* 1992.
Young, David. *The Golden Age of Canadian Figure Skating.* 1984.
USFSA. *Skating Through The Years.* 1942.
Whedon, Julia. *The Fine Art of Ice Skating: An Illustrated History & Portfolio of Stars.* 1988.

BOOKS: INSTRUCTIONAL/TECHNICAL

Anderson, George. *The Art of Skating.* 1852.
Arnold, Richard. *Better Ice Skating.* 1976.
Arnold, Richard. *Better Sport Skating: The Key to Improved Performance.* 1982.
Arnold, Richard. *Dancing On Skates.* 1985.
Arnold, Richard. *Ice Skating Made Easy.* 1979.
Arnold, Richard. *Let's Go Ice Skating.* 1987.
Bailey, Donna. *Skating.* 1990.
Baillie, Major George. *Figure Skating Simplified.* 1910.
Bass, Howard. *Let's Go Skating.* 1974.
Bass, Howard. *Tackle Skating.* 1978.
Bauer, Tony. *Off-Ice Training Manual.*
Benson, Edward Frederick. *English Figure Skating.* 1908.
Blundun, Georges. *The Yankee Polka, Ravensburger Waltz, & Tango Romantica.* 1976.
Boeckl, Wilhelm R. *How to Judge Figure Skating.* 1940.
Boeckl, Wilhelm R. *Willy Boeckl on Figure Skating.* 1937.
Bompa, Tudor. *Off-Ice Training for Figure Skaters.* 1974.
Boy Scouts of America. *Cub Scout Sports: Skating.* 1986.
Boy Scouts of America. *Skating.* 1983.
Broadbent, Sidney. *Skateology.* 1985.
Browne, George. *A Handbook of Figure Skating.* 1910.
Burka, Ellen. *Figure Skating.* 1974.
Butterworth, Carol. *Step by Step Ice Skating Guide.* 1978.
Button, Dick. *Instant Skating.* 1964.
CFSA. *Depth Jumps: Training for Figure Skaters.*
CFSA. *From Boots to Blades.*
CFSA. *Ice Show Manual.* 1988.
CFSA. *Parent's Guide to Test and Competitive Skating.* 1994.
Charlotte. *Hippodrome Skating Book.* 1916.
Clay, Thomas. *Instructions on the Art of Skating.* 1828.
Cousins, Robin. *Skateaway.* 1984.
Cummings, Diane. *Figure Skating As A Hobby.* 1938.

Dedic, Joseph. *Single Figure Skating: For Beginners and Champions.* 1974.
Dench, Robert. *Pair Skating and Dancing on Ice.* 1943.
Diagram Group. *Enjoying Skating.* 1978.
Dickmeyer, Lowell A. *Ice Skating Is For Me.* 1980.
Dolan, Edward F. *Complete Beginner's Guide to Ice Skating.* 1974.
Duff-Taylor, Captain S. *Elements of Skating.* 1933.
Duff-Taylor, Captain S. *Skating.* 1935.
Dyer, Lorna. *Ice Dancing Illustrated.* 1980.
Fassi, Carlo. *Figure Skating With Carlo Fassi.* 1980.
Fitzgerald, Julian T. *Ice King—General Skating Information.* 1922.
Gale, Ivy. *Skating On Ice: A Basis for Ice Dancing.* 1950.
Hadley, Arthur. *Figures of the Second Class Test.* 1910.
Harris, Ricky. *Choreography & Style for Ice Skaters.* 1980.
Health and Welfare Canada. *Figure Skating for Everyone Manual.* 1974.
Hedges, Sid G. *Ice-Rink Skating.* 1932.
Horne, Pere. *Ice Skating.* 1968.
House, Marilyn G. *Ice Skating Fundamentals.* 1983.
Hugen, Otto. *The Technique of Skating.* 1973.
Isely, Kenny. *The Skater's Manual.* 1978.
ISIA. *Group Skating Manual.*
ISIA. *Instructor Manual.*
ISIA. *ISIA Special Skater Test Standards.*
Jomland, Einar. *How To Improve Your Ice Skating.*
Jomland, Einar. *Introduction To Ice Skating.* 1973.
Jomland, Einar. *Skating On Ice.* 1963.
Jones, Captain. *A Treatise on Skating.* 1792.
Jones, Ernest. *The Elements of Figure Skating.* 1931.
Kalb, Jonah. *The Easy Ice Skating Book.* 1981.
Kay, Muriel. *The Key to Rhythmic Ice Dancing.* 1958.
Kent, Colonel H. Vaughn. *Combined Figure and Ice Skating.* 1929.
Kent, Colonel H. Vaughn. *Dancing on Ice: How to Skate the Lancers.* 1910.
Law, Ernest. *Valsing on Ice.* 1908.
Lerner, Jeff R. *Complete Manual of Compulsory Ice Dances.* 1994.
Lerner, Jeff R. *The Complete Manual of Ice Dance Patterns.* 1992.
Lowther, Henry C. *English Skating in Three Parts.* 1900-02.
Lussi, Gustave. *Championship Figure Skating.* 1951.
Maclean, John S. *Figure Skating For Beginners.* 1940.
MacLean, Norman. *Ice Skating Basics.* 1984.
Maier, Monika. *How to Succeed at Skating.* 1982.
Meagher, George A. *Figure and Fancy Skating.* 1895.
Meagher, George A. *Guide to Artistic Skating.* 1919.
Meagher, George A. *Lesson In Skating.* 1900.
Menzius, John. *The Skaters Monitor, Instructor & Evening Companion.* 1846.
Meyer, Bror. *Skating With Bror Meyer.* 1921.
Monier-Williams, Montagu S. F. *Combined Figure Skating.* 1883.
Monier-Williams, Montagu S. F. *Figure Skating.* 1898.
Monier-Williams, Montagu S. F. *Figure Skating: Simple and Combined.* 1892.

1984 World Champions Barbara Underhill & Paul Martini

Moskvina, Tamara. *Pair Skating as Sport and Art.* 1987.
Moskvina, Tamara. *Secrets of the Soviet Skaters: Off-Ice Training Methods.* 1995.
NCCP/CFSA. *National Coaching Certification Program (NCCP) Manuals.*
Nicholson, Howard. *Nicholson on Figure Skating.* 1934.
Noel, John. *Figure Skating for Beginners.* 1964.
Noyes, Tina. *I Can Teach You To Figure Skate.* 1973.
Ogilvie, Robert. *Basic Ice Skating Skills.* 1968.
Ogilvie, Robert. *Handbook of New Era Figures.* 1993.
Ogilvie, Robert. *The Parent's Guide to Competitive Figure Skating: How to Start Your Child on the Way to the Top.* 1985.
Oppelt, Kurt. *Oppelt Standard Method of Therapeutic & Recreational Ice Skating.* 1974.
Owen, Maribel Vinson. *The Fun of Figure Skating: A Primer of the Art-Sport.* 1960.
Petkevich, John Misha. *Skater's Handbook.* 1984.
Petkevich, John Misha. *Sports Illustrated Figure Skating: Championship Techniques.* 1988.
Phillips, D. *Ice Skating: Form, Fitness and Speed.* 1974.
Rawson, Perry B. *Skate Dance Diagrams.*
Readhead, Monty. *Ice Dancing.* 1939.
Richardson, Thomas D. *Ice Rink Skating.* 1936.
Richardson, Thomas D. *Modern Figure Skating.* 1930.
Richardson, Thomas D. *Skating With T. D. Richardson.* 1952.
Richardson, Thomas D. *The Art of Figure Skating.* 1962.
Richardson, Thomas D. *The Complete Figure Skater.* 1948.
Richardson, Thomas D. *The Girls' Book of Skating.* 1959.
Salvesen, Charles E. *The Foundation of Skating.* 1932.
Sanderson, L. B. *Evaluation of Errors in Figures.* 1976.
Schaefer, Karl. *Living Pictures of My 1937 Figure Skating.* 1937.
Scott, Barbara Ann. *Skating for Beginners.* 1953.
Soanes, Sidney. *Ice Dancing: A Manual for Judges and Skaters.* 1976.
Speidel, J. *Movements of the Body for Figure Skating.* 1982.
Stamm, Laura. *Power Skating.* 1982.
Stark-Slapnik, Nina. *Figure It Out: Think Your Way to Skating Great Figures.* 1986.
Stock, Clarence Sidney D'Este. *The Figure Skate.* 1954.
Sullivan, George. *Better Ice Skating for Boys and Girls.* 1976.
Swift, Frank. *The Skater's Text Book.* 1868.

PHOTO BY ALICE BERMAN

Skater's Edge

is the world's leading publication with how-to articles by top coaches and pros. Authors include **Robin Cousins, Don Jackson, Natalia Dubova,** and many others. Five issues per year. Back issues available. To order, check boxes and send name, address, and phone number with payment to: *Skater's Edge*, Box 500, Dept. SB, Kensington, MD 20895; (301) 946-1971.

To subscribe:[1]	one year	two years
United States	❑ $18[2]	❑ $33[2]
Canada	❑ $25/USD[3]	❑ $45/USD[3]
Europe/Japan	❑ $30/USD[4]	❑ $55/USD[4]

[1]Prices in 1994-95; may change. [2]MD RESIDENTS add 5% sales tax. [3]Or current Canadian equivalent. [4]Foreign checks or money orders payable on U.S. banks in U.S. dollars; int'l bank or postal orders accepted.

~BACK ISSUES AVAILABLE~

Every issue of *Skater's Edge* is packed with timeless how-to articles and skating tips. Order the issues you've missed!
In U.S.—$4 each (5/$18; 10/$33; 15/$50).
Canada—$5/USD each (10 for $45/USD; 15 for $68/USD).
Europe—$6/USD each (10 for $55/USD; 15 for $83/USD).
Note: MD residents add 5% sales tax. Prices are 1994-95.

- ❑ S/O '91 — *Leg Power* by Ron Ludington / *Guide to Fitting Skates* with Mike Cunningham
- ❑ N/D '91 — *Overcoming Fear* by Caroline Silby / *Stretching for Flexibility* with Sharon Jordan
- ❑ J/F '92 — *Smooth Moves* by Tim Murphy / *Connecting Moves* (footwork) by Tim Murphy / *Skate Mirror Images* by Robin Cousins
- ❑ M/A '92 — *Edges!!* by Peter Dunfield / *Skating Vacations* by Julia Ridgely
- ❑ Sum '92 — *Roller Blading* by Nick Perna / *Summer Training* by Kim Goss
- ❑ S/O '92 — *Music and Skating* by Robin Cousins / *Skate Boots* by Alice Berman
- ❑ N/D '92 — *Lussi Spins* by Cecily A. Morrow / *Skating Videos* by Maggie Range
- ❑ J/F '93 — *Stroking* by Natalia Dubova / *My Trademark Slide Spiral* by Robin Cousins
- ❑ M/A '93 — *Figures With a New Twist* by Debi Leeming / *Summer Skating Schools* by Julia Ridgely
- ❑ Sum '93 — *Plié Power* by Rob McBrien / *Thoughts on Plié Power* by Alice Berman
- ❑ S/O '93 — *Jumping* by Don Jackson / *Farewell to Mr. Gustave Lussi* by Dick Button
- ❑ N/D '93 — *Edgework!* by Natalia Dubova / *Guide to Blades* by Alice Berman
- ❑ J/F '94 — *Lussi Spins II* by Cecily Morrow / *The Protopopov Spirals* with the Protopopovs
- ❑ M/A '94 — *Warming Up, Cooling Down* by Carl Poe / *Ice Capades Master Class* with Nathan Birch / *Think Straight Lines* by Robin Cousins
- ❑ Sum '94 — *Power Stroking* by Audrey Weisiger / *Lacing Up* by Cecily Morrow

---

Syers, Edgar Wood. *Figure Skating.* 1912.
Syers, Edgar Wood. *The Art of Skating—International Style.* 1913.
Taylor, Alex. *Let's Go Skating.* 1991.
Tebbutt, C. G. *Skating.* 1893.
Thompson, Norcliffe G. *Combined Hand-in-Hand Figure Skating.* 1904.
Tchaikovskaya, Yelena. *Patterns of Russian Ice Dance.* 1994.
Turner, Roger F. *Edges.* 1973.
Van der Weyden, Erik. *Instructions to Young Skaters.* 1957.
Vandervell, H. E. *A System of Figure Skating.* 1869.
Vandervell, H. E. *The Figure Skate.* 1901.
Vinson, Maribel Y. *Advanced Figure Skating.* 1940.
Vinson, Maribel Y. *Primer of Figure Skating.* 1938.
Von Gassner, Paul. *Figure and Dance Skating.* 1949.
White, Harold. *Figure Skating Techniques.* 1933.
Wood, Tim. *Ice Skating.* 1990.
Yglesias, H. R. *Figure Skating.* 1905.
Young, Stephanie. *Peggy Fleming: Portrait Of An Ice Skater.* 1984.

BOOKS: NUTRITION/FITNESS

There are far more books on this subject than are included here; we've listed some that may be used as guidelines for locating more books on this topic.

Addleman, Frank G. *The Winning Edge: Nutrition for Athletic Fitness and Performance.* 1984.
Clark, Nancy. *Nancy Clark's Sports Nutrition Guidebook.* 1990.
Grisogano, Vivian. *Children and Sport: Fitness, Injuries, and Diet.* 1991.
Haas, Robert. *Eat to Win: The Sports Nutrition Bible.* 1983.
Scholich, Manfred. *Circuit Training for all Athletes: Methodology of Effective Fitness Training.* 1992.

BOOKS: SPORTS MEDICINE/PSYCHOLOGY

There are far more books on this subject than are included here; we've listed some that are specific to ice skating or that may be used as guidelines for locating more books on this topic.

Anderson, Bob. *Stretching for Everyday Fitness & for Running, Tennis, Raquetball, Cycling, Swimming, etc.* 1980.
Featherstone, Donald F. *Sports Injuries Manual for Trainers and Coaches.* 1956.
Hogshead, Nancy. *Asthma & Exercise.* 1990.
Kraus, M.D., Hans. *The Sports Injury Handbook; An Athlete's Guide to Causes, Prevention, and Treatment.* 1981.
Mirkin, M.D., Gabe. *The Sports Medicine Book.* 1978.
Orlick, Terry. *Psyching for Sport: Mental Training for Athletes.* 1986.
Ritter, MD, Merrill A. *Your Injury: A Common Sense Guide to Sports Injuries.* 1987.
Palmer, Shawna L. *Get the Edge: Sport Psychology for Figure Skaters.* 1993.

Guide to Fitting Skates

BY ALICE BERMAN

Skates that don't fit do more than give you blisters. If they're too big, for instance, they can make you trip. And you instinctively try to keep your feet from moving around by curling up your toes.

"It's like trying to hang onto a tree limb with your fingers," says **Mike Cunningham**, owner of *Skater's Paradise* in Alexandria, VA. "You grab hold of the bottom of the boot with your toes, and it creates a tremendous amount of tension through all the muscles in your feet. If you're not used to doing that—and even if you are—it's eventually going to wear you out."

FITTING BASICS

There are a few basics that can help you find the right size skates, whether you're renting or buying. First, your feet should *not* move around inside the boots, especially your heel. Your heel should be as far back into the boot as possible, and should feel snug.

Another important factor is support. Skates that lack adequate support can't hold you up; you wind up using a lot of your muscle power just to stay upright.

To determine if a pair of skates offers good support, pick up one of the skates and hold it by the top of the boot. Turn it sideways in the air, so the boot and blade are horizontal. (See the *Flop Test.*)

The boot should be strong enough to stay straight and support the weight of the blade. If the bottom flops down to form a 90 degree angle, the boots are too weak to support you. Try another pair. (If these are *new* skates you're looking at, forget it!)

RENTING SKATES

Lots of people find it convenient to rent skates at the rink. While rental skates are not always the best, they can suffice if you know what to look for.

Rental skates can be made out of plastic or out of leather. Since they're designed to fit everyone, they don't fit anyone precisely. Most rinks offer skates in whole sizes (with medium widths); some also have half-sizes available.

When renting skates, be aware that your skate size is not the same as your shoe size. For adults, leather rental skates generally fit one to one-and-a-half sizes smaller than your dress shoe size. For instance, if you wear an 8-1/2 women's shoe, start out by trying on a size 7 or 7-1/2 in rental skates.

Children's sizes are different. Kids who wear small shoe sizes (10, 11, or 12) might need skates in a slightly larger size. For medium-sizes (13, 1, 2, 3), skate sizes are pretty similar to shoe sizes.

Keep trying on skates until you find a pair that fits. The boots should feel snug, but your toes shouldn't be crushed. The closer the fit, the more control you'll have. You should wear thin socks or tights; heavy socks take up space and force you into a larger skate than you need.

If the leather boots are in good condition, they should provide adequate support. If the leather collapses, ask for another pair. If you can't find a decent leather pair that fits, try the plastic ones (the sizes may be different).

Plastic boots are designed especially for rental purposes; they are more durable and last longer than leather skates. That's important to a high-traffic rink that has to replace a third of its rental skates every year.

LACING UP

How skates look when they're laced up can offer a clue to how well they fit. When properly laced, there should be an inch or an inch-and-a-half of space between the sides holding the laces. If the boot wrinkles up around the first and second lace, then it's too wide for your foot.

Once you've found the right size, make a note of it, along with the inventory number on the rental skates. Then you'll be able to ask for the same pair each time, sparing yourself the grief of going through this process every time you rent skates!

When you're ready to lace up, tap your heel back into the boot as far as possible. Make sure you keep your foot and the boot in an upright position as you tighten the laces. (If you roll your foot sideways while lacing, that's how it will be set in the boot for skating.) When you get to the top two hooks, lean forward slightly to allow extra space at the top of the boot (just enough to fit in two fingers side-by-side in the back). It usually takes more than once to get the boots laced up properly, so just keep trying till they're comfortable and snug.

FITTING NEW SKATES

If you've really gotten into ice skating, it won't take long before you'll want to buy your own skates. You may find it's difficult or impossible to do what your teacher is asking you to do if the rental skates lack support or good, sharp edges.

"Cheap skates that lack support are basically a waste of money," says Cunningham. "There's no point in trying to do even basic lessons in skates that don't fit you right or don't provide you with the kind of support you need."

The best way to find out where to go to buy skates is to ask your teacher and several serious skaters. In some cases, the pros are under considerable pressure from management to recommend only the shop at the rink where they teach. While some rinks have excellent pro shops, that's not always the case. It pays to ask around.

When being fitted for new skates, wear thin socks or tights for the best fit. At the shop, make sure you are fitted by an experienced salesperson who knows a lot about ice skates. Your feet should be measured with a device calibrated for skate sizes.

One common measuring tool is the Brannock Device, which is like the gadget used in shoe stores. Special Brannock Devices are calibrated for fitting ski boots, hockey skates, and figure skates. In addition, some skate manufacturers produce their own fitting devices.

After your feet are measured, you should be asked about what kind of skating you do, how often you skate, and other questions that will help determine what kind of boots and blades you'll need.

"I use the measuring device only as an indication of where to start from a fitting standpoint," explains Cunningham. "Often I'll take the insoles out of the boots and check it against the person's foot to see how it lines up. I check to see if the heel is where it ought to be, and if the ball of the foot hits the right spot. I also look to see if there's enough room around the toes."

According to Cunningham, two measurements are critical when fitting skates: (1) the width of the boot at the heel, and (2) the length of the boot at the ball of the foot. "The heel has the *counter* around it, which is that hard, immovable piece of leather or fiber material that actually forms the shape of the heel and the arch," he explains. "And that basically has to fit.

"The position of the ball of the foot in the boot determines whether your arch is where it should be. Your arch has a tendency to center itself. So if your skates are a size too long, then eventually the ball of your foot is going to wind up where it ought to be—but your heel is going to be pulled out of the back of the boot."

New skates should feel snug in the heel, and the ball of the foot should be at the widest part of the boot. There should be good contact between the side of the boot and the foot, and no wrinkling or distortion around the toes.

MAKING ADJUSTMENTS

If a particular spot hurts, adjustments can usually be made to accommodate bunions, corns, or little bones that stick out. But new skates should *not* feel comfortable. "If they feel really good when they're new," comments Cunningham, "they are too big. They are going to stretch out—a lot. . . We worry a whole lot more about skates being too loose than too tight. Too tight you can usually fix; too loose you can't do a whole lot with."

If you're thinking about buying used skates, use the flop test to check for support. If the boots are weak and broken down, don't waste your money. Check the blades for nicks and severe rust. If you can't tell, ask a pro or someone you trust to evaluate the skates for you.

Ice skating is a lot of fun—and a true challenge for those who want to master the sport. Good equipment directly affects your ability to skate. Whether you rent or buy, it's wise to take the time to find skates that fit well and offer good support. ∎

THE FLOP TEST

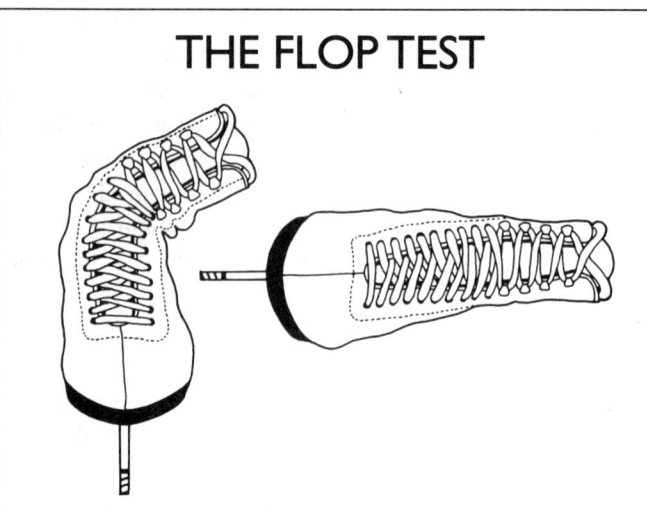

Hold one of the skates by the top of the boot. Turn it sideways so the boot and blade are horizontal to the ground. If the bottom flops down to form a 90 degree angle, the boots are too weak to support you.

Skate Boots

Buying new skate boots is almost always a challenge. (As is breaking them in!) Whether this is your first or umpteenth pair, you still have to determine which boots are best for you. Factors that should be considered include *age, size (height and weight), type and level of skating, amount of time spent skating, and size and shape of foot.*

Many makes and models of boots are available, ranging from fairly inexpensive to very expensive. Some of the least expensive models come with blades already attached, and are designed for the occasional skater or someone first trying the sport. Make sure the boots are strong enough to offer adequate support (see *The Flop Test,* left). Most boots and blades are purchasely separately, and the blade must be mounted by a knowledgeable person (see *Guide to Blades,* page 45). The boots described here represent the upper line of each maker. Stock boots are manufactured in predetermined sizes, while custom boots are cut specifically to fit your feet.

How the boots are cut and fit will vary among manufacturers, says Mike Cunningham of *Skater's Paradise* in Alexandria, VA. Some boots, such as SP-Teri, Klingbeil, Rose, and Risport, have wider toe boxes. Others, such as WIFA and Risport, have European-style higher heels. The arches are highest in Harlick and SP-Teri boots, and lower in Riedells. Try on as many different makes as possible.

If you've bought boots before and you haven't had problems with the fit or your feet, there's no reason to change manufacturers, says Cunningham, although you may want to move up to higher level boots as your skating progresses. Problems that warrant making a change include heel spurs, corns, bunions, arch problems, and poor fit. If you can't find comfortable stock boots, consider having boots custom-made. Other problems, such as feet that turn in or out, can often be corrected with orthotics.

Following is a list of some of today's major boot manufacturers, with suggested retail prices (as of December 1994). Prices vary by region and retailer. For details on how boots should fit, read *Guide to Fitting Skates* (page 37) reprinted from the premiere issue of *Skater's Edge* (Sept/Oct 1991).

HARLICK AND COMPANY
893 American Street
San Carlos, CA 94070
(415) 593-2093
FAX: (415) 593-9704

Sizing: Adults, sizes 3 thru 11, widths B thru AAAA; Junior models, sizes 9 to 2 1/2, and common widths; Jr. models come with lower heels and flatter arches; 10% restocking charge on returned boots ordered by size. Sizes 12 to 16 & widths C, D & E are special order; not returnable. Stock boots are made of elk leather, have strong counters, and brass hooks. Minimum deposit $75.

Finalist (stock)
Strongest stock boot; three-piece construction; double duo-bond reinforced ankle areas; split-leather lining; achilles tendon pads; ankle-hugger padding; designed for double and triple jumps.
Ladies white and Mens black: $360
Jr. Ladies white; Mens black: $320

High Tester (white)
Gold Tester (black) (stock)
Strong stock boot; three-piece construction; duo-bond reinforced ankle areas; split-leather lining; achilles tendon pads; ankle-hugger padding; designed for double and triple jumps.
Ladies white and Mens black: $320
Jr. Ladies white; Mens black: $280

Competitor (stock)
Medium strength boot; two-piece construction; soft leather linings; ankle-hugger padding; reinforced ankle area; designed for figures and single jumps.
Ladies white; Mens black: $295
Jr. Ladies white; Mens black: $260

Classic (stock)
Soft, flexible boot; two-piece construction; soft, split-leather lining; achilles tendon pads; for figures.
Ladies white; Mens black: $290
Jr. Ladies white; Mens black: $255

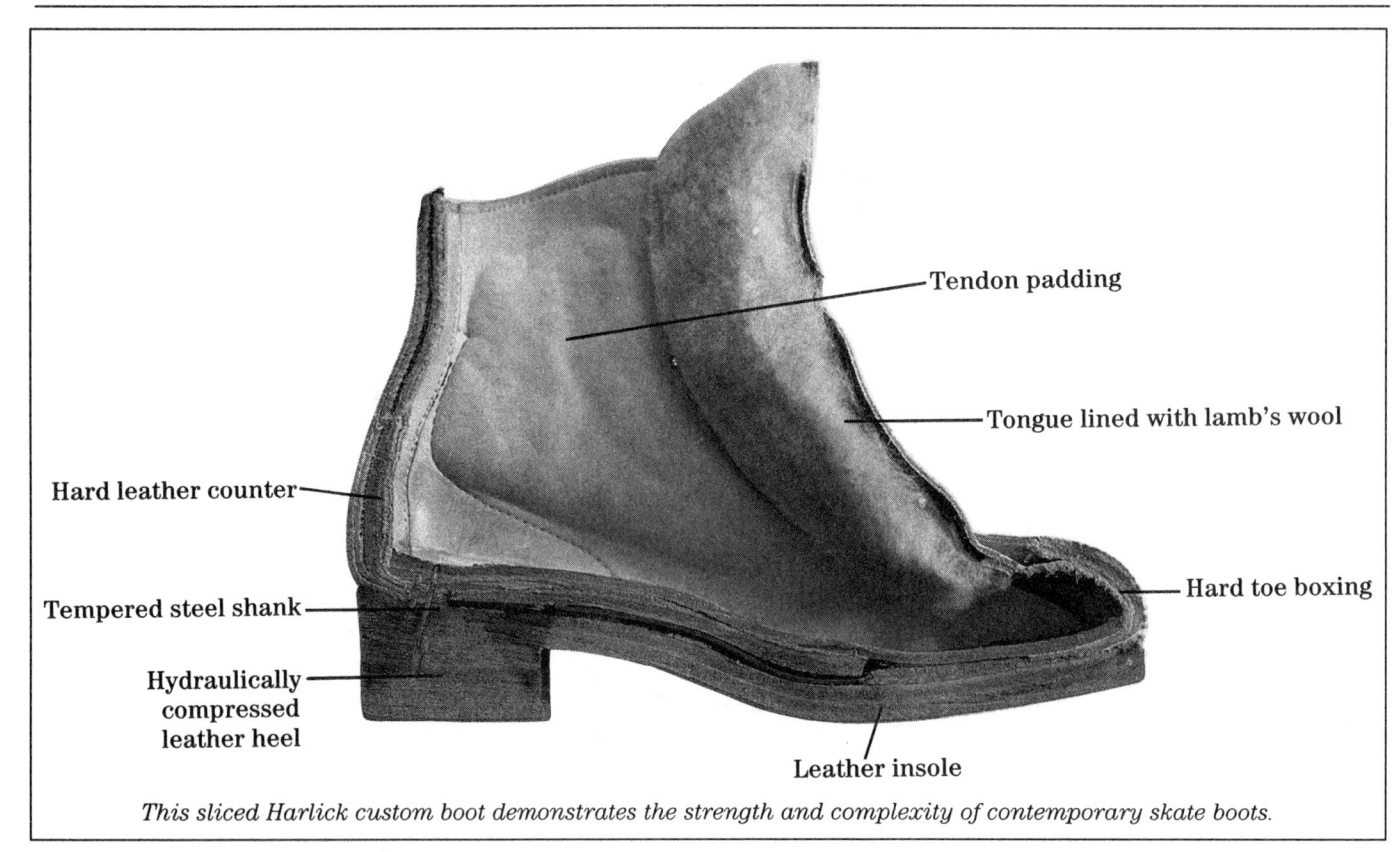

This sliced Harlick custom boot demonstrates the strength and complexity of contemporary skate boots.

Labels on boot: Tendon padding; Tongue lined with lamb's wool; Hard toe boxing; Leather insole; Hydraulically compressed leather heel; Tempered steel shank; Hard leather counter.

Special options on stock boots: orthopedic arch mold kit ($50); orthopedic arches ($65-$75); growth insoles ($15); inside wedges ($40; for flat feet with inward rotating ankles); lambs wool tongues ($20); special height heels ($20); double rubber tongues ($20); natural soles/heels ($25); tan elk uppers ($30). Expedite service: $45.

Custom Boots

Triple-stitched backstay; soft leather linings; hard leather counters; supportive tendon padding; hard toe boxing; tempered steel shanks; leather insole; heel huggers (padding around the ankles that helps hold the heels down) and orthotics are available. Custom orders require $200 deposit; not refundable once leather is cut. Expedite service: $45.
Elk uppers, deluxe lining & tendon pads: Ladies/Mens: $395; Jrs: $350
Elk, deluxe lining & heel huggers: Ladies/Mens: $425; Jrs: $380

Special options on custom boots: lightweight construction (20% lighter): $50; quadrabond strength (strongest): $40; double duo-bond strength (very strong): $30; duo-bond strength (medium): $20; Dance Back Stay (rolled lining on top edge of boot back for greater flexibility): $25; Scallops at instep for greater flexibility: $25; Lambs wool tongues: $20; wool and rubber tongues: $35. Also asymetrical quarters, foot molds, orthotics, special arches, inside wedge balance correction, split-leather lining. Write for details.

JACKSON BOOTS

Distributor: Tournament Sports
145 Northfield Drive
Waterloo, Ontario
N2L 5J3 Canada
(519) 888-6500
FAX: (519) 888-6540
A line of boots designed by and named for 1962 World Champion Donald Jackson: "quality boots for the beginning skater." All Jackson skates are pre-fitted with MK blades manufactured for Jackson boots; top models can be ordered without blades.

Sizes: Ladies 4-10, full & half; Juniors 11 - 3 1/2 full & half; Tots 8-10, Youth. Prices ranges roughly from $80 to $125 in the U.S.

DJ 1100 - Competitor II

Premium full-grade leather uppers with padded split-leather lining; double-leather outsole; fitted with Jackson Mark V chrome blade. Good for adult or serious badge-level skaters. Also available as boot only. Ladies, Juniors.

DJ 900 - Junior Competitor

Full-grain leather uppers, padded split-leather lining, black leather outsole; fitted with Jackson Mark IV chrome blade, custom made by MK blades. For adult and badge-level skaters. Also available as boot only. Ladies, Juniors, Tots.

DJ 700 - Novice II

Full-grain leather upper, split-leather lining, full padding, composition outsole; fitted with Jackson Mark III chrome-plated blade (MK). Ladies, Juniors.

DJ 400 - Artistic
Recreational skate; leather uppers, split leather lining, ankle padding. PVC unitsole fitted with chromed-plated Jackson Mark II blade. Ladies, Juniors, Tots.

KLINGBEIL SHOE LABS, INC.
145-01 Jamaica Avenue
Jamaica, NY 11435
(718) 297-6864; FAX: (718) 658-2396

Klingbeil is a family-owned and operated business that has been making custom boots for over forty years. Each pair of boots is based on the skater's foot measurements, height and weight, hours per week spent skating, test level, and skating purpose. Features include special four-hook design, coated leather to reduce scuffing, and padded tongues and uppers to promote comfort. Any color combination and strength made. Delivery takes 4-5 weeks.
Children: $385; Adults: $410

JOHN KNEBLI, LTD
32 Camden Street
Toronto, Canada, M5V 1V1
(416) 368-5565
Family owned and operated business that has manufactured custom boots for 48 years.

OBERHAMER, INC.
11975 Portland Ave South, Suite 122
Burnsville, MN 55337
(612) 890-1657; FAX: (612) 890-0511

All models feature narrow heel, proper arch height and length, and ample toe room. Half-sizes available in most boots.

World Class (stock)
Extra-extra-firm boot with top-grain leather upper; velvet tannage leather lining; airfoam tendon and ankle pads; high, long counters; steel arches; leather insoles, midsoles, and outsoles; sponge tongue lining.
Womens white, 4-11, AA-C: $240
Mens black, 5-13, N, M, W: $240

Gold (stock)
Extra-firm boot; same features as World Class with slight reduction in firmness.
Womens white, 4-11, AA-C: $188
Mens black, 5-13, N, M, W: $188
Childrens sizes: $157

Silver (stock)
Less firm than Gold; top-grain leather upper; leather lining with fossprene and cloth reinforcement; long firm counters; air foam tendon pads; sponge tongue lining; thick leather soles.
Womens white, 4-11, AA-C: $157
Mens black, 5-14, N, M, W: $157
Girls white, 12-4, N, M, W: $125
Boys black, 12-4, N, M, W: $125

Supreme Custom
Hand-crafted based on skater's measurements; full-grain leather lining; oak tanned leather innersoles, midsoles and outersoles; choose medium firm, firm, or extra-firm upper reinforcement; choose lamb's

BOOTS & BLADES

Skater's Paradise

Harlick ★ Riedell ★ SP-Teri
John Wilson ★ MK

1602 Belle View Blvd.
Alexandria, Virginia 22307
(703) 660-6525

Skater's Paradise of Delaware, Inc.
C/0 University of Delaware Ice Arena
547 South College Avenue
Newark, Delaware 19716
(302) 738-2999

Super Discount Prices...
- Boots
- Blades
- Dresses
- Scribes
- Bags

...and more!

CLUB SKATE

Call Today for a Free Catalog!

(800) CLUB-SK8
(800) 258-2758

wool or sponge rubber tongue lining. Minimum deposit of 50%; non-refundable after work has begun.
Womens white, Mens black: $445
Girls white, Boys black: $385

RIEDELL SHOES, INC.
122 Cannon River Avenue
Industrial Park
Red Wing, MN 55066
(612) 388-8251; FAX: (612) 388-8616

Beige uppers available in all boots; allow 4 to 6 weeks. TS Fit System is a padding system that is activated by the skater's body temperature. Available sizes vary with boots; see individual descriptions below.

Comp 925 (stock)
Strongest stock boot; extra leather reinforcing in ankle; Flolite and TS padding; water-repellant uppers; moisture-resistant leather linings; metal eyelets at instep; natural finish soles and heels; contoured tongue design, 1/2" foam tongue lining; for advanced competitive freestyle.
Ladies white, 4-10 AA,A,B,C: $349
Mens blk, 4-13 med, narrow: $349

Royal 900 (stock)
Best-selling freestyle and dance boot; firm temper water-repellant leather uppers; orthopedic-grade leather linings; TS padding; foam tendon pads; strong stud hooks; contour molded footbed; natural finish sole and heel edges.
Ladies white, 3-10, 3A, 2A, A, B, C: $315
Mens black, 4-13, Med, Nar: $315
Girls white, 13-4, Med, Nar: $230
Boys black, 13-4 Medium: $230

Gold Star 375 (stock)
Medium-temper leather uppers; tan split-leather linings; TS padding; foam tendon pads; strong stud hooks; contoured tongue design; 1/2" foam tongue lining; contoured molded footbed; natural finish sole & heel.
Ladies, 3-10,3A,2A,A,B,C: $274
Mens black, 4-13 N, Med, W: $274
Girls white, 11-4 N, Med: $202
Boys black, 11-4 Med: $202

Silver Star 355 (stock)
Medium-temper leather uppers; gray top-grain leather linings; TS padding; foam tendon pads; 1/4" foam tongue linings; contoured molded footbed; natural finish sole and heel edges; for intermediate freestyle skaters.
Ladies white, 4-10 AA, A,B,C: $230
Mens black 4-13 Med: $230
Girls white, 9-4, Nar, Med: $175
Boys, black 9-4 Medium: $175

Custom Boots
Hand-cut, hand-lasted; made to individual specifications; allowances for arches, heel spurs, toe room, etc; choose from variety of leather colors, leather temper, ankle firmness, heel heights, lining material and more. Includes Flolite and TS padding. Options include scallop cut, allowances for orthotics, choice of tongue linings. Allow 6-8 weeks.
Mens and Ladies: $520
Juniors: $422

RISPORT (made in Italy)
U.S. distributors include:
Centre Sports, 29158 U.S. Highway 19 North, Clearwater, FL 34621. (813) 787-0423; FAX: (813) 786-5711.
Danco Sports, Inc., 4111 Stephenie Dr, Bldg. 14, Cortland, IL 60112; Phone/FAX: (815) 756-7692.
Tomy's Skater Shop, Northampton Business Center, 1209 Baker Road, Suite 512, Virginia Beach, VA; (800) 955-TOMY; (804) 464-1464 or -0468; FAX: (804) 464-1157.
Westwood Sports, 9601 Garfield Ave South, Bloomington, MN 55420; (800) 877-6304; (612) 881-2222; FAX: (612) 881-1707.
Models include Elite and Elite Super, Diamant and Diamant Super, Cristallo and Cristallo Super, Star, and Laser. Prices range from $273 to $356. Contact distributors for details.

ROSE CUSTOM BOOT, LTD.
P.O. Box 21057
Holiday Postal Outlet
Cambridge, Ontario
Canada N3C 4B1
(519) 622-3340

Rose Custom Boot is a family-owned and operated business offering both stock and custom boots in adult and junior sizes. Stock boots available in white only; custom boots available in white, black, and beige. Custom fit based on foot measurements sitting and standing, type and level of skating, hours spent skating per week, and customer preference for strength and stiffness. Can make or allow space for prescription orthotics.

Prices given are in Canadian dollars; U.S. prices vary with exchange rate and import taxes. Customer pays shipping.

Junior boot: $269; *Stock boot:* $369
Conventional custom: $389
Top Line Centurian custom: $409

SK SPORT SHOES, LTD..
280 Donlands Avenue
Toronto, Ontario
M4J 3R4 Canada
(416) 465-2784; FAX: (416) 465-7802

Popular line of hand-made boots manufactured in Canada for 25 years. Victorian model is lightweight, has scalloped uppers for flexibility, plus thick ankle padding. Write or call for more information.

SP-TERI COMPANY, INC.
436 North Canal Street, #1
South San Francisco, CA 94080;
415-871-1715; FAX: 415-871-9062

Sizing: Adult Ladies: 3 1/2 to 10 1/2; Adult Mens: 3 1/2 to 12; Junior: Boys & Girls: 11 to 3. Width Range: A, AA (Average); B, C, D (Wide); 3A, 4A, 5A (narrow). *Note:* 5A, C, & D widths are special order and not returnable.

All girls and ladies boots come with natural soles unless otherwise specified. Stock boots: 4-6 weeks; Custom: 6-8 wks.

Advantage Boot (stock)
Stiffest stock boot; perspiration-resistant leather lining; stiff counter; ankle padding with poron cushion; rolled/formed tongue; cushioned insole for arch support; designed for triple jumps.
Ladies white and Mens black: $378

Super Teri-Deluxe (stock)
Extra reinforced ankle area; smooth orthopedic lining ankle padding and 3/4" heel huggers; designed for double jumps.
Ladies beige: $355 (specify beige);
Ladies white and Mens black: $327

Super-Teri (stock)
Reinforced ankle for medium support; firm suede lining; ankle padding and heel huggers; designed for single jumps.
Ladies white and Mens black: $280
Girls white and Boys black: $245

Pro-Teri (stock)
Semi-firm boot; suede lining; ankle padding; heel huggers; designed for figures/beginner freestyle.
Ladies white and Mens black: $245
Girls white and Boys black: $227

Custom Boots
All-leather uppers, counters, soles and heels. Hand-lasted; includes orthopedic lining, foam ankle padding with 3/4" tendon pads; orthotic allowance/custom insole as needed; varied stiffness (soft to XXX stiff);

Harlick SKATING BOOTS

Committed to the Tradition of Excellence

National, World and Olympic Gold Medalist *Kristi Yamaguchi* achieved all her skating triumphs in *Harlick Boots.*

WE ACCEPT MASTERCARD/VISA

Create some magic in Harlick boots!
Kristi Yamaguchi

PHOTO BY DINO RICCI

Please call for the location of your nearest dealer or instructions for ordering direct:
Harlick & Company • 893 American Street • San Carlos, CA 94070 • (415) 593-2093

allowance for spurs/bunions; scallop-cut upper for dance; asymmetrical uppers as needed; beige leather add $35. Expedite service: $55.
Ladies or Mens, 3 1/2 thru 13: $455
Jr. black or white, 11 thru 3: $378

Special Features Available
Stock boots available in combination ball and heel widths (e.g., AA heel & A ball); max one-width difference: $30; sheepskin wool tongues: $25; 1/2 sponge & 1/2 wool tongues: $25; custom insole for pronation correction: $40; heel-arch wedge: $5 to $15; growth innersoles: $10; clear lacquer or wax finish on natural soles: $25.

WIFA (made in Austria)
Can Alpine Agencies, Ltd.
1314 S.W. Marine Drive
Vancouver, B.C.
Canada V6P 5Z6
(604) 266-4490
FAX: (604) 266-5470

While relatively unknown in the U.S., WIFA is a popular boot among Canadian and European skaters. WIFA boots have been worn by Kurt Browning, Tracy Wilson, and Torvill & Dean. In the 1994 Olympics, WIFA boots were worn by the first four places in dance: Gritschuk & Platov, Usova & Zhulin, Torvill & Dean, and Rahkamo & Kokko.

WIFA skates feature strong leather uppers; leather lining; layers of reinforcement; tendon padding; padded tongue; orthopedic arch support; steel shank; leather insole; double-leather sole; contoured leather counters; laminated leather heel. WIFA has a complete line of models ranging from beginner to their top boot, *Diamond*, used by champions. ■

Note: This article was revised and reprinted with permission from the Sept/Oct '92 issue of *Skater's Edge*, Box 500, Kensington, MD 20895.

NATURAL SOLES

Many of today's manufacturers offer soles and heels with the popular "natural" look. It's important to make sure this type of finish is protected against moisture.

Most experts recommend using a hot wax treatment instead of a shellac-type finish to seal the leather. A hard shellac finish can crack and allow moisture to penetrate and cause damage. Once under the finish, the water can't escape. Any previous shellac finish must be removed before applying a hot wax treatment.

Want to know more about skating? Subscribe to *Skater's Edge*, Box 500, Kensington, MD 20895. Phone/FAX: (301) 946-1971. Free brochure.

GLOSSARY

Asymmetrical uppers: the leather uppers are shaped unevenly to accommodate the differences between ankle bones.

Counter: the hard, immovable piece of leather that actually forms the shape of the heel and the arch.

Flolite: heat-sensitive, gel-like padding that conforms to shape of the foot.

Heel huggers: pads built into boots around the heel and/or the ankle area to help hold the heel in place.

Last: wooden or plastic model of foot used for making boots; customized to measurements by adding bits of leather where needed.

Orthotic: custom device made to fit inside shoe/boot to correct foot problems.

Tendon padding: large pads built into boots in the area of the achilles tendon to help keep the heel in place.

Three-piece construction: three layers of leather used for stiffness and support.

TS Fit System: Riedell padding system that is activated by the skater's body temperature.

Guide to Blades

BY ALICE BERMAN

Blades . . . one of the great mysteries of skating. Which make is best for you and why? There are so many choices!

This article presents information about the different models of blades available; no attempt is made to "rate" them. As with buying skate boots, it's wise to talk with professionals, experienced salespeople, and avid skaters.

TYPES OF BLADES

Different blades are designed for specific uses, depending on the type of skating in question. The most common categories are dance, figures, and freestyle/all-purpose. Because all-purpose blades are based on freestyle designs; we've grouped them together. There are also blades for hockey and speed skating, which are beyond the scope of this article.

Blade designs and prices vary widely within each category. Elements that can differ include: size and placement of toe picks; degree of curvature of rocker; depth of hollow; length of blade from front to back; and width of blade. In addition, the blade may be tapered from front to back; and the sides of the blade can remain parallel from top to bottom or be side-honed. (See *Glossary.*)

Freestyle blades generally have more accessible toe picks than dance or figure blades. The top toe pick is used to assist in toe jumps. The bottom tooth is the last thing to leave the ice and the first thing to make contact with the ice when landing jumps; it is also used to help set spins.

Most dance blades have smaller or more recessed toe picks. In addition, the blades are often shorter to prevent stepping on the heel during mohawks and choctaws. Some dance blades are thinner for faster run and greater lean; these are sharpened with a deeper hollow to achieve the same cutting angle as the wider blades.

Figure blades are similar in length to freestyle blades, but have smaller toe picks—or none at all, a point that is controversial. Figure blades are sharpened with a much shallower hollow to prevent the edges from sinking too deeply into the ice.

Robert Ogilvie, author of *The Ogilvie-Gutzman Blade Gauges and Basic Principles of Sharpening*[1] prefers to use a very shallow hollow for figures: a radius of 4$^{5/16}$" (11 cm). The advantage of such a flat hollow, according to Ogilvie, is that "it lifts you further off the ice [the edges of a shallow grind don't sink as deep into the ice], so the chances of getting flats or changes are less. And, because you are lifted somewhat more, the blade is much more maneuverable. However, if your positions are not 100% correct or nearly so, you might skid."

SHARPENING BLADES

"To a certain extent, the depth of hollow is dictated by the type of skater, the size of the skater, and the kind of ice you're skating on," says **Mike Cunningham** of Skater's Paradise in Alexandria, VA. "Harder ice requires a deeper hollow and sharper edges for whatever discipline you're doing. With softer ice, you generally want a little shallower grind because the blades have a tendency to sink deeper into the ice and grab."

When a blade is sharpened, the hollow is ground by a disk-shaped stone that spins around at high speed. The rim, or face, of the stone curves outward. A diamond dressing tool can be used to adjust the face of the stone, giving it a deeper or flatter curve as needed to produce the desired hollow. The depth of hollow is actually an arc from an imaginary circle, which is measured by the length of its radius. A circle with a smaller radius forms a deeper curve—and therefore creates a deeper hollow—than a circle with a larger radius.

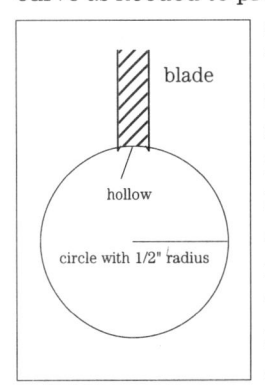

Most blades are manufactured

The curved face of the grinding stone is adjusted to produce the desired depth of hollow in a blade.

with a specific factory hollow, but the individual skater is not restricted to that grind. Ogilvie prefers 5/8" radius for freestyle grind; Cunningham uses 1/2" to 5/8". Dance grinds may range from 1/2" to 7/16" for regular-width blades to 5/16" for the narrower blades. Patch grinds range from 1 1/2" to over 4". For skaters who use the same blade for patch and free, Ogilvie and Cunningham use a 3/4" hollow.

Once you find a depth of hollow that suits you, make a note of the grind (or radius) so you can request it in the future. It's wise to have your blades sharpened consistently so you aren't constantly fighting edges that are dull and then suddenly too sharp.

MOUNTING BLADES

Determining the final position of each blade begins with a test-mount, using slotted holes that allow for minor adjustments. According to Cunningham, the basic starting position should be between the big toe and the toe next to it, and roughly in the center of the heel. Adjustments are made from there--after the skates are tried out on the ice--depending on the skater's anatomy and preferences.

Improper mounting of blades is one of former national dance champion **Jim Sladky**'s pet peeves. "Everybody puts them in the middle of the boot," says Sladky. "That isn't where you balance. . . If you stood on a knife edge [or the thin side of a two-by-four] in bare feet like a high-wire artist, where would you balance without having to use a lot of muscle control to keep yourself upright, and without pronating or supinating to any degree?" he asks. "Maybe at the center of the heel, maybe a tad inside the center of the heel, and almost where the space is between your big toe and your first toe, rather than down the middle."

If the blade is mounted correctly,

---

[1]Booklet $4.75; with gauges, $45. Write: Ogilvie-Gutzman Blade Gauges, 617 8th Ave, Box 267, Ironton, MN 56455.

GLOSSARY

- *Chrome-relief line:* The line below which the chrome-plating (which prevents the blade from tarnishing) has been removed to allow for sharpening.

- *Co-Planar blades:* Blades designed so the heel and sole plate form a totally flat line; used in conjunction with special boots made with a flat sole so both mounting surfaces are in the same plane. Blades manufactured by MK; boots by Harlick, Klingbeil, and S-P Teri.

- *Counter-bore hole:* Tapered holes that are wider at the top than at the bottom; used with counter-sunk screws.

- *Depth of hollow:* The depth of the curve ground into the length of the blade by the grinding stone during sharpening. Measured in terms of radius of circle.

- *Hollow:* The curved space that runs down the center of the length of the blade, between the inside and outside edges. If it is missing, the blade will skid.

- *Parallel:* The two sides of the blade remain parallel to each other throughout the height of the blade; not side-honed.

- *Rocker:* The curvature of the blade from front to back (similar to the rocker on a rocking chair). Also called the *rocker radius*. A circle with a larger radius forms a flatter curve (and thus a flatter blade) than a circle with a smaller radius.

- *Radius:* The radius is the measurement taken from the center to the boundary of a circle (or half the width of the circle). The larger the radius, the larger the circle, and the flatter the curve formed by the outside boundary of the circle.

- *Side-honed:* The lower portion of the blade (below the chrome-relief line) is tapered from top to bottom, theoretically making sharper edges possible. Because the sides of the blade are no longer parallel, precise sharpening can be difficult.

- *Sharpening:* Restoring the hollow and sharpening the edges by grinding the blade against a sharpening stone.

- *Tapered:* The width of the blade is tapered, or becomes narrower, from front to back; designed to increase maneuverability and control in figures.

---

you should be able to "skate on a flat in a straight line without having your blade pull you in one direction or the other," says Cunningham, "and to be able to do edges on both feet without having to force an edge: inside and outside, forward and backward." If the blades *and* the boots are new, the boots need to be broken in first (skated in for roughly six to eight hours) before you can really tell if the blade is set properly. And edges that aren't level can feel the same as a blade that is out of position, so bad sharpening can complicate matters.

Cunningham strongly advises skaters not to jump while the blades are test-mounted, as this can cause the blades to shift and warp. Once you've found the right position, your blades should be mounted permanently; this involves putting more screws into the non-slotted holes. A few things to keep in mind: (1) if the blades are warped or bowed, they should be straightened first; and (2) the screws should be put in vertically, with the screw centered on the top, not the bottom, of the tapered counter-bore holes. ■

BLADE MANUFACTURERS

Wilson Blades:
John Wilson, Marsden Bros & Co.
71 Greystock Street
Sheffield, S4 7WA, England
Tel: (0742) 440238; Fax: (0742) 729330

Mitchel & King Skates, Ltd. (MK Blades)
818/819 Leigh Road
Slough, Berkshire, SL1 4SA, England
Tel: (0753) 528444; Fax: (0753) 528446

Information on Co-Planar Blades:
IceSkate Conditioning Equipment
5265 W. Quarles Drive
Littleton, CO 80123
(303) 979-3800

~ SKATER'S EDGE SOURCEBOOK ~

Blades: Makes and Models

Blade Model	Mfg	Use	Rocker Radius	Factory Hollow	Notes	Suggested Retail Price*
Coronation Dance	Wilson	Dance	7 ft	3/8" radius	Based on Coronation Ace, but with shorter heel	$167
Dance 99	Wilson	Dance	8 ft	3/8" radius	Based on Pattern 99; bottom toe pick smaller; available as blade inset for Pattern 88 fittings: $145	$240
MK Dance	MK	Dance	7 ft	5/16" radius	Parallel; narrower width; short heel; domed pick	$349
Silver Dance	MK	Dance	7 ft	7/16" radius	Based on MK Dance; full-width blade; short heel	$168
Super Dance 99	Wilson	Dance	8 ft	3/8" radius	Based on Pattern 99; thinner; parallel sides; shorter heel; smaller toe picks; as Pattern 88 blade inset: $253	$338
Wilson Dance	Wilson	Dance	7 ft	3/8" radius	No longer manufactured; some shops may still have in stock	
Comet Test	Wilson	Figures	8 ft 6 in	1" radius	Matched for use with Coronation Comet; polished hollow	$167
Gold Test	MK	Figures	7 ft	1" radius	Contoured radius to toe pick; side-honed; special hollow grinding	$338
Pattern 88	Wilson	Figures	7 ft.	1" radius	Available as one-piece blades or as set of sole and heel plates; see Pattern 88 Fittings	$415
Pattern 88 Fittings	Wilson	Figures	7 ft	1" radius	Blades can be detached from sole and heel plates and changed; fittings alone: $290; Dance 88 inset: $217	$502/set
Silver Test	MK	Figures	7 ft	1&1/2" radius	Parallel; contoured radius; shallow ground edge; based on MK Professional Blade	$188
Wilson Figure	Wilson	Figures	8 ft	1" radius	Small pyramid tooth	$323
Club 2000	MK	Freestyle & all-purpose	7 ft	3/8" radius	Starter freestyle blade	$35
Coronation Ace	Wilson	Freestyle & all-purpose	7 ft	3/8" radius	Starter blade with cross-milled teeth; parallel sides	$157
Coronation Comet	Wilson	Freestyle	8 ft 6 in	3/8" radius	Developed from Coronation Ace, but with flatter radius	$167
Four Aces	Wilson	Freestyle	7 ft	3/8" radius	Middle-range freestyle blade; not stocked much in the U.S.	$238
Gold Seal	Wilson	Freestyle	8 ft	1/2" radius	Higher stanchion; hollow ground; tapered; side-honed edges	$462
Gold Star	MK	Freestyle	7 ft	7/16" radius	Side-honed and tapered; larged hardened toe picks; available in chrome or gold plate	$375 (gold, $510)
Majestic	Wilson	All-purpose	6 ft	3/8" radius	General-purpose blade with spinning tooth; parallel	$102
Mercurio	Wilson	All-purpose	6 ft	3/8" radius	Cheaper general-purpose blade with spinning tooth; nickel & chrome plated	$77
Pattern 99	Wilson	Freestyle	8 ft	3/8" radius	Flatter radius; based on original design by Gustave Lussi; parallel edges	$338
Phantom	MK	Freestyle & all-purpose	7 ft	7/16" radius	Tapered; side-honed edges; large jumping picks	$320
Phantom Special	MK	Freestyle	7 ft	7/16" radius	Parallel sides with dovetail	$365
Professional	MK	Freestyle & all-purpose	7 ft	7/16" radius	Parallel sides; cross-cut toe picks; polished hollow	$152
Rinkmaster	MK	All-purpose	7 ft	1/2" radius	Beginner and rental blade; nickel-plated	$35
Select Classic	MK	Freestyle & all-purpose	7 ft	7/16" radius	Parallel sides; similar to Vantage with smaller toe picks	$115
Single Star	MK	All-purpose	7 ft	1/2" radius	Parallel; two large toe picks; beginning freestyle	$93
Vantage	MK	Freestyle	7 ft	7/16" radius	Parallel; edges hardened to 5/16"; based on MK Phantom; large top toe pick	$255

*Note: Prices may vary by region and distributor. These prices were current as of December 1994. Revised and reprinted with permission from the Nov/Dec '93 issue of *Skater's Edge*.

BOOTS & BLADES

Cecily Alexandra Morrow, creator and producer of the Lussi Technical Videos.

Lacing Up

BY CECILY MORROW

I began skating at four and soon, with great pride, was doing up my own skates—very quickly. Like many young competitors, rushing from school, eager to be on time, I developed a "yank and run" method of lacing.

At eleven, I went to Lake Placid to study with **Gustave Lussi**.[1] There I stood, the first day, trembling before the famous coach. He looks me in the eye, looks down at my skates, then gestures with that peculiarly eloquent left hand of his, and tells me he's going to teach me how to lace my skates. We sit in the stands. There he painstakingly made clear what I should do.

Since then, it has become increasingly clear to me that careful lacing—and an ongoing, personal study of what works best for you, your skating, your boots—enhances performance and prolongs the boots' useful lifetime. Hasty, un-studied lacing can cause premature breakdown of boots; they may develop sharp, digging creases at the ankle instead of nicely conforming layers of leather that permit the ankle to flex fully while maintaining good foot support. New boots, especially good custom-made ones, acquire contours in the stretchable leather as they are broken in, "habits" that actually result from the lacing process. It's worth the time to train your boots from the beginning.

LACING BASICS

First, loosen the laces evenly *all the way* to the bottom, and pull the tongue completely up. Now insert and position the foot directly under the knee, with lower leg perpendicular to the floor, heel pressed against the back of the boot. Make sure the tongue is extended completely (give it a gentle pull), then try to secure it straight up and down. Tongues, given a chance, take on a life of their own; they can twist over time, causing pinching and abrasion. (I pull the uppermost laces snug before proceeding; others reduce lace slackness up to the ankle before lacing, just enough to restrain the errant tongue.)

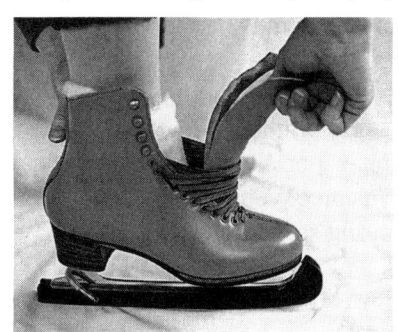

Heel back; tongue up

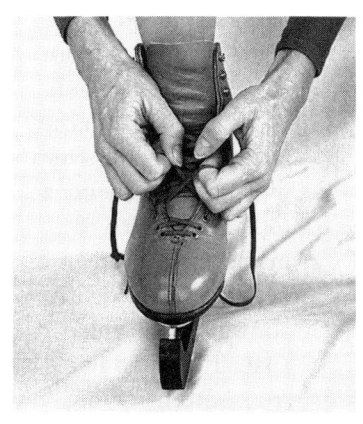

Tighten lower laces

Finger secures lace

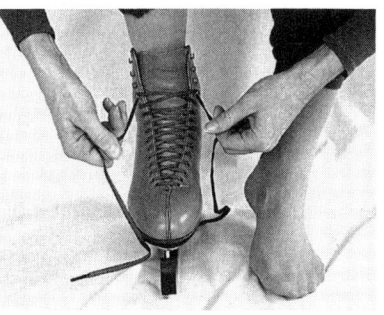

Laces over hooks; under & across

Starting with the second or third set of laces from the bottom, begin to pull the laces tightly, one pair at a time, so the boot closes well over the front of your foot. Depending upon boot design and your anatomy, you'll feel comfortable with a certain precise tension of lacing throughout the foot. Awareness of this and constant attention to the lacing process will pay off.

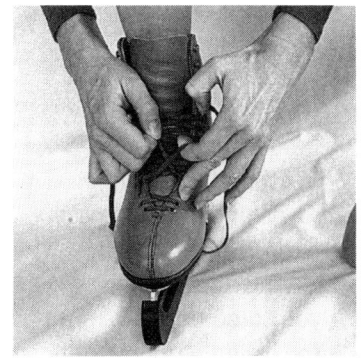

To ensure a snug, gripping fit up to the ankle, I place one finger over the grommet which holds the lace I've just tightened. This prevents loosening of laces while I'm shifting the other hand to grab and pull taut the next lace. (Some place a finger or thumb firmly over the "x" formed by the already tightened laces; experiment to find what works best.) It's important not to let the laces slip: your foot bones, tendons, ligaments, and muscles need the correct support to perform this peculiar thing we do on the ice—balancing over a thin steel blade.

Now, having laced upward to the ankle joint (firmly, so you are not able to squeeze a finger under the crossed laces already tightened), hold the laces taut and cross them, lifting *over* the first hooks, then down, then cross again, and secure the second hook lacing over the top, and so on in a downward motion. Mr. Lussi explained how this held the laces better, prevented slippage, and

---

[1] Coach of many champions. See *Lussi Spins* (Nov/Dec '92) and *Lussi Spins II* (Jan/Feb '94) by Cecily Morrow.

PHOTOS BY ALICE BERMAN

offered more support than the under/over method, because more tongue surface was covered (thus preventing bulges and creases from developing in the leather, which eventually cause pressure, then pain on the front tendon).

Shift foot back; flex ankle

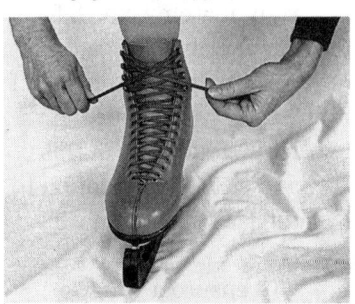

Secure extra laces

Before lacing the hooks above the ankle bones, shift your foot back slightly so your ankle assumes a more flexed position. Then, without pulling on the laces, just cross (over to under) up to the boot top. If extra lace remains, cross it down over the hooks neatly, starting at the ankle (usually second hook from bottom), tying bow at the bottom hooks.

Not done yet . . . loose loops and lace ends can cause accidents. Take the bow loops, place them around the nearest hooks, pull gently, then secure ends under lace crossings or between tongue and boot (hard tips facing out).

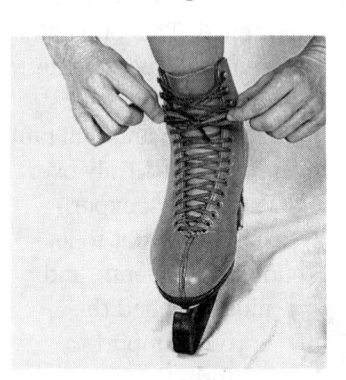

And now, and always, as you stand up, make sure the lacing permits your ankles to flex forward freely. Ideally, skaters' knees should be able to position several inches in front of the toes, allowing significant knee and ankle adjustment. Generally, when skates are laced effectively, there should be, with ankle flexed, enough room to stick a finger between the back of the boot and your leg.

Secure bow loops over hooks

Room to flex ankle

The goal of proper lacing is to achieve maximum, instantaneous control over body stance and the blades' subtle course over the ice. Nuances of foot and ankle motions must be communicated deftly in skating, instant to instant. I like to think of my skates as being akin to an extremely responsive sports car, with no "play" in the steering. The looser the boot, the more removed your foot is from boot support, providing less contact and control over what you are doing.

Above all, I suggest that skaters not ignore signals from foot and ankle. If it hurts or doesn't feel right, spend time relacing and adjusting, especially with new boots. On ice, skates are an extension of your whole body, an essential instrument requiring sensitive tuning to your own needs.

Don't just "yank and run!" ■

Cecily A. Morrow is producer of the video series *Systematic Figure Skating: The Spin and Jump Techniques of Gustave Lussi.* She has recently co-produced a video with her mother, Cecily H. Morrow, called *Ice Skating for Everyone: Beginner's Guide to a Lifetime Sport.*

Reprinted with permission from the Summer 1994 issue of *Skater's Edge*, Box 500, Kensington, MD 20895.

FOOT PROBLEMS?

What if, despite getting the best skates you can and lacing up with care, you experience foot problems, such as blisters and lumps? If it's serious and persists (a bone spur, for example), see your doctor. But *prevention* of abrasion and further pressure on delicate tissues is up to you.

Thin moleskin, bought in sheets and cut to size (rounding corners), usually provides sufficient protection when placed on a skin area that is rubbing and reddening; the boots will eventually stretch and conform. If you've worked up a blister, put a dab of ointment on it, then cover with a moleskin patch. This works better than a bandaid, which can become displaced and cause worse problems.

For corns or lumps, I recommend placing an appropriate size of "cushion" around the offending area. Small foam cushions with the middles cut out relieve pressure by lifting the leather off the skin surface (a solid pad only puts more pressure it). New, encapsulated gel cushions may work even better; ballet dancers are using them in toe shoes, and I'm experimenting. Then there's lamb's wool for real tenderfoots like me—I have bony, enlarged ankles and fragile skin. I wrap a thick layer of lamb's wool around my ankles, holding the two ends at the back, so it stays in place while I lower my foot into the boot.

Champions: U.S. Nationals, Worlds, Olympics

U.S. FIGURE SKATING CHAMPIONSHIPS

MEN'S SINGLES

	GOLD	SILVER	BRONZE
1914 New Haven, CT	Norman M. Scott	Edward Howland	Nathaniel Niles
1915-1917	No Competition		
1918 New York, NY	Nathaniel Niles	Karl Engel	Edward Howland
1919	No Competition		
1920 New York, NY	Sherwin Badger	Nathaniel Niles	Petros Wahlman
1921 Philadelphia, PA	Sherwin Badger	Nathaniel Niles	Edward Howland
1922 Boston, MA	Sherwin Badger	Nathaniel Niles	—
1923 New Haven, CT	Sherwin Badger	Chris Christenson	Julius Nelson
1924 Philadelphia, PA	Sherwin Badger	Nathaniel Niles	Chris Christenson
1925 New York, NY	Nathaniel Niles	George Braakman	Carl Engel
1926 Boston, MA	Chris Christenson	Nathaniel Niles	Ferrier Martin
1927 New York, NY	Nathaniel Niles	Roger Turner	George Braakman
1928 New Haven, CT	Roger Turner	Fredrick Goodridge	W. Langer
1929 New York, NY	Roger Turner	Fredrick Goodridge	J. Lester Madden
1930 Providence, RI	Roger Turner	J. Lester Madden	George Hill
1931 Boston, MA	Roger Turner	J. Lester Madden	George Hill
1932 New York, NY	Roger Turner	J. Lester Madden	G. Borden
1933 New Haven, CT	Roger Turner	J. Lester Madden	Robin Lee
1934 Philadelphia, PA	Roger Turner	Robin Lee	George Hill
1935 New Haven, CT	Robin Lee	Roger Turner	J. Lester Madden
1936 New York, NY	Robin Lee	Erle Reiter	George Hill
1937 Chicago, IL	Robin Lee	Erle Reiter	William Nagle
1938 Philadelphia, PA	Robin Lee	Erle Reiter	Ollie Haupt, Jr.
1939 St. Paul, MN	Robin Lee	Ollie Haupt, Jr.	Eugene Turner

MEN	GOLD	SILVER	BRONZE
1940 Cleveland, OH	Eugene Turner	Ollie Haupt, Jr.	Skippy Baxter
1941 Boston, MA	Eugene Turner	Arthur Vaughn	William Nagle
1942 Chicago, IL	Bobby Specht	William Grimditch	Arthur Vaughn
1943 New York, NY	Arthur Vaughn	Arthur Preusch	William Nagle
1944-45	No Competition		
1946 Chicago, IL	Richard Button	James Lochead	John Tuckerman
1947 Berkeley, CA	Richard Button	John Lettengarver	James Grogan
1948 Colo. Springs, CO	Richard Button	James Grogan	John Lettengarver
1949 Colo. Springs, CO	Richard Button	James Grogan	Hayes A. Jenkins
1950 Washington, D. C.	Richard Button	Hayes A. Jenkins	Richard Dwyer
1951 Seattle, WA	Richard Button	James Grogan	Hayes A. Jenkins
1952 Colo. Springs, CO	Richard Button	James Grogan	Hayes A. Jenkins
1953 Hershey, PA	Hayes A. Jenkins	Ronald Robertson	Dudley Richards
1954 Los Angeles, CA	Hayes A. Jenkins	David Jenkins	Ronald Robertson
1955 Colo. Springs, CO	Hayes A. Jenkins	David Jenkins	Hugh Graham
1956 Philadelphia, PA	Hayes A. Jenkins	Ronald Robertson	David Jenkins
1957 Berkeley, CA	David Jenkins	Tim Brown	Tom Moore
1958 Minneapolis, MN	David Jenkins	Tim Brown	Tom Moore
1959 Rochester, NY	David Jenkins	Tim Brown	Robert Brewer
1960 Seattle, WA	David Jenkins	Tim Brown	Robert Brewer
1961 Colo. Springs, CO	Bradley Lord	Gregory Kelley	Tim Brown
1962 Boston, MA	Monty Hoyt	Scott Allen	David Edwards
1963 Long Beach, CA	Thomas Litz	Scott Allen	Monty Hoyt
1964 Cleveland, OH	Scott Allen	Thomas Litz	Monty Hoyt

CHAMPIONS

U.S. NATIONALS

51

SKATER'S EDGE SOURCEBOOK

MEN	GOLD	SILVER	BRONZE
1965 Lake Placid, NY	Gary Visconti	Scott Allen	Tim Wood
1966 Berkeley, CA	Scott Allen	Gary Visconti	Billy Chapel
1967 Omaha, NE	Gary Visconti	Scott Allen	Tim Wood
1968 Philadelphia, PA	Tim Wood	Gary Visconti	J. Misha Petkevich
1969 Seattle, WA	Tim Wood	J. Misha Petkevich	Gary Visconti
1970 Tulsa, OK	Tim Wood	J. Misha Petkevich	Kenneth Shelley
1971 Buffalo, NY	J. Misha Petkevich	Kenneth Shelley	Gordon McKellen
1972 Long Beach, CA	Kenneth Shelley	J. Misha Petkevich	Gordon McKellen
1973 Minneapolis, MN	Gordon McKellen	Robert Bradshaw	David Santee
1974 Providence, RI	Gordon McKellen	Terry Kubicka	Charles Tickner
1975 Oakland, CA	Gorden McKellen	Terry Kubicka	Charles Tickner
1976 Colo. Springs, CO	Terry Kubicka	David Santee	Scott Cramer
1977 Hartford, CT	Charles Tickner	Scott Cramer	David Santee
1978 Portland, OR	Charles Tickner	David Santee	Scott Hamilton
1979 Cincinnati, OH	Charles Tickner	Scott Cramer	David Santee
1980 Atlanta, GA	Charles Tickner	David Santee	Scott Hamilton
1981 San Diego, CA	Scott Hamilton	David Santee	R. Wagenhoffer
1982 Indianapolis, IN	Scott Hamilton	R. Wagenhoffer	David Santee
1983 Pittsburgh, PA	Scott Hamilton	Brian Boitano	Mark Cockerell
1984 Salt Lake City, UT	Scott Hamilton	Brian Boitano	Mark Cockerell
1985 Kansas City, MO	Brian Boitano	Mark Cockerell	Scott Williams
1986 Long Island, NY	Brian Boitano	Scott Williams	Daniel Doran
1987 Tacoma, WA	Brian Boitano	Chris Bowman	Scott Williams
1988 Denver, CO	Brian Boitano	Paul Wylie	Chris Bowman
1989 Baltimore, MD	Christopher Bowman	Daniel Doran	Paul Wylie
1990 Salt Lake City, UT	Todd Eldredge	Paul Wylie	Mark Mitchell
1991 Minneapolis, MN	Todd Eldredge	Chris Bowman	Paul Wylie
1992 Orlando, FL	Christopher Bowman	Paul Wylie	Mark Mitchell

MEN	GOLD	SILVER	BRONZE
1993 Phoenix, AZ	Scott Davis	Mark Mitchell	Michael Chack
1994 Detroit, MI	Scott Davis	Brian Boitano	Aren Nielsen

U.S. FIGURE SKATING CHAMPIONSHIPS
LADIES' SINGLES

	GOLD	SILVER	BRONZE
1914 New Haven, CT	Theresa Weld	Edith Rotch	R. Townshend
1915-1917	No Competition		
1918 New York, NY	Rosemary Beresford	Theresa Weld	—
1919	No Competition		
1920 New York, NY	Theresa Weld	Martha Brown	Lilian Cramer
1921 Philadelphia, PA	Theresa Blanchard	Lilian Cramer	
1922 Boston, MA	Theresa Blanchard	Beatrix Loughran	—
1923 New Haven, CT	Theresa Blanchard	Beatrix Loughran	Lilian Cramer
1924 Philadelphia, PA	Theresa Blanchard	Rosalie Knapp	—
1925 New York, NY	Beatrix Loughran	Theresa Blanchard	Rosalie Knapp
1926 Boston, MA	Beatrix Loughran	Theresa Blanchard	Maribel Vinson
1927 New York, NY	Beatrix Loughran	Maribel Vinson	Theresa Blanchard
1928 New Haven, CT	Maribel Vinson	Suzanne Davis	-
1929 New York, NY	Maribel Vinson	Edith Secord	Suzanne Davis
1930 Providence, RI	Maribel Vinson	Edith Secord	Suzanne Davis
1931 Boston, MA	Maribel Vinson	Edith Secord	Hulda Berger
1932 New York, NY	Maribel Vinson	Margaret Bennett	Louise Weigel
1933 New Haven, CT	Maribel Vinson	Suzanne Davis	Louise Weigel
1934 Philadelphia, PA	Suzanne Davis	Louise Weigel	Estelle Weigel
1935 New Haven, CT	Maribel Vinson	Suzannne Davis	Louise Weigel
1936 New York, NY	Maribel Vinson	Louise Weigel	Audrey Peppe
1937 Chicago, IL	Maribel Vinson	Polly Blodgett	Katherine Durbrow
1938 Philadelphia, PA	Joan Tozzer	Audrey Peppe	Polly Blodgett
1939 St. Paul, MN	Joan Tozzer	Audrey Peppe	Charlotte Walther
1940 Cleveland, OH	Joan Tozzer	Heddy Stenuf	Jane Vaughn

~ SKATER'S EDGE SOURCEBOOK ~

LADIES	GOLD	SILVER	BRONZE	LADIES	GOLD	SILVER	BRONZE
1941 Boston, MA	Jane Vaughn	Gretchen Merrill	Charlotte Walther	1969 Seattle, WA	Janet Lynn	Julie Holmes	Albertina Noyes
1942 Chicago, IL	Jane Vaughn	Gretchen Merrill	Phebe Tucker	1970 Tulsa, OK	Janet Lynn	Julie Holmes	Dawn Glab
1943 New York, NY	Gretchen Merrill	Dorothy Goos	Janette Ahrens	1971 Buffalo, NY	Janet Lynn	Julie Holmes	Suna Murray
1944 Minneapolis, MN	Gretchen Merrill	Dorothy Goos	Ramona Allen	1972 Long Beach, CA	Janet Lynn	Julie Holmes	Suna Murray
1945 New York, NY	Gretchen Merrill	Janette Ahrens	Madelon Olson	1973 Minneapolis, MN	Janet Lynn	Dorothy Hamill	Juli McKinstry
1946 Chicago, IL	Gretchen Merrill	Janette Ahrens	Madelon Olson	1974 Providence, RI	Dorothy Hamill	Juli McKinstry	Kath Malmberg
1947 Berkeley, CA	Gretchen Merrill	Janette Ahrens	Eileen Seigh	1975 Oakland, CA	Dorothy Hamill	Wendy Burge	Kath Malmberg
1948 Colo. Springs, CO	Gretchen Merrill	Yvonne C. Sherman	Helen Uhl	1976 Colo. Springs, CO	Dorothy Hamill	Linda Fratianne	Wendy Burge
1949 Colo. Springs, CO	Yvonne C. Sherman	Gretchen Merrill	Virginia Baxter	1977 Hartford, CT	Linda Fratianne	Barbie Smith	Wendy Burge
1950 Washington, DC	Yvonne C. Sherman	Sonya Klopfer	Virginia Baxter	1978 Portland, OR	Linda Fratianne	Lisa-Marie Allen	Priscilla Hill
1951 Seattle, WA	Sonya Klopfer	Tenley Albright	Virginia Baxter	1979 Cincinnati, OH	Linda Fratianne	Lisa-Marie Allen	Carrie Rugh
1952 Colo. Springs, CO	Tenley Albright	Frances Dorsey	Helen Geekie	1980 Atlanta, GA	Linda Fratianne	Lisa-Marie Allen	Sandy Lenz
1953 Hershey, PA	Tenley Albright	Carol Heiss	Margaret Graham	1981 San Diego, CA	Elaine Zayak	Priscilla Hill	Lisa-Marie Allen
1954 Los Angeles, CA	Tenley Albright	Carol Heiss	Frances Dorsey	1982 Indianapolis, IN	Rosalynn Sumners	Vikki de Vries	Elaine Zayak
1955 Colo. Springs, CO	Tenley Albright	Carol Heiss	Catherine Machado	1983 Pittsburgh, PA	Rosalynn Sumners	Elaine Zayak	Tiffany Chin
1956 Philadelphia, PA	Tenley Albright	Carol Heiss	Catherine Machado	1984 Salt Lake City, UT	Rosalynn Sumners	Tiffany Chin	Elaine Zayak
1957 Berkeley, CA	Carol Heiss	Joan Schenke	Claralynn Lewis	1985 Kansas City, MO	Tiffany Chin	Debi Thomas	Caryn Kadavy
1958 Minneapolis, MN	Carol Heiss	Carol Wanek	Lynn Finnegan	1986 Long Island, NY	Debi Thomas	Caryn Kadavy	Tiffany Chin
1959 Rochester, NY	Carol Heiss	Nancy Heiss	Barbara Roles	1987 Tacoma, WA	Jill Trenary	Debi Thomas	Caryn Kadavy
1960 Seattle, WA	Carol Heiss	Barbara Roles	Laurence Owen	1988 Denver, CO	Debi Thomas	Jill Trenary	Caryn Kadavy
1961 Colo. Springs, CO	Laurence Owen	S. Westerfeld	Rhode Michelson	1989 Baltimore, MD	Jill Trenary	Kristi Yamaguchi	Tonya Harding
1962 Boston, MA	Barbara Roles	Lorraine Hanlon	Victoria Fisher	1990 Salt Lake City, UT	Jill Trenary	Kristi Yamaguchi	Holly Cook
1963 Long Beach, CA	Lorraine Hanlon	Christine Haigler	Karen Howland	1991 Minneapolis, MN	Tonya Harding	Kristi Yamaguchi	Nancy Kerrigan
1964 Cleveland, OH	Peggy Fleming	Albertina Noyes	Christine Haigler	1992 Orlando, FL	Kristi Yamaguchi	Nancy Kerrigan	Tonya Harding
1965 Lake Placid, NY	Peggy Fleming	Christine Haigler	Albertina Noyes	1993 Phoenix, AZ	Nancy Kerrigan	Lisa Ervin	Tonia Kwiatkowski
1966 Berkeley, CA	Peggy Fleming	Albertina Noyes	Pamela Schneider	1994 Detroit, MI	Tonya Harding*	Michelle Kwan	Nicole Bobek
1967 Omaha, NE	Peggy Fleming	Albertina Noyes	Jennie Walsh				
1968 Philadelphia, PA	Peggy Fleming	Albertina Noyes	Janet Lynn				

*The title was revoked after Harding was linked to the attack that prevented Nancy Kerrigan from competing.

CHAMPIONS

U.S. NATIONALS

U.S. FIGURE SKATING CHAMPIONSHIPS
PAIRS

	GOLD	SILVER	BRONZE
1914 New Haven, CT	Jeanne Chevalier Norman M. Scott	Theresa Weld Nathaniel Niles	Eleanor Crocker Edward Howland
1915-1917	No Competition		
1918 New York, NY	Theresa Weld Nathaniel Niles	Clara Frothingham Sherwin Badger	— —
1919	No Competition		
1920 New York, NY	Theresa Weld Nathaniel Niles	Edith Rotch Sherwin Badger	—
1921 Philadelphia, PA	Theresa Blanchard Nathaniel Niles	Mrs. Ed. Howland Mr. Ed. Howland	C. Frothingham Charles Rotch
1922 Boston, MA	Theresa Blanchard Nathaniel Niles	Mrs. Ed. Howland Mr. Ed. Howland	Edith Rotch Francis Munroe
1923 New Haven, CT	Theresa Blanchard Nathaniel Niles	— —	— —
1924 Philadelphia, PA	Theresa Blanchard Nathaniel Niles	Grace Munstock Joel Liberman	—
1925 New York, NY	Theresa Blanchard Nathaniel Niles	Ada Bauman George Braakman	Grace Munstock Joel Liberman
1926 Boston, MA	Theresa Blanchard Nathaniel Niles	Sydney Good James Greene	Grace Munstock Joel Liberman
1927 New York, NY	Theresa Blanchard Nathaniel Niles	Beatrix Loughran Raymond Harvey	Ada Bauman George Braakman
1928 New Haven, CT	Maribel Vinson Thornton Coolidge	Theresa Blanchard Nathaniel Niles	Ada Bauman George Braakman
1929 New York, NY	Maribel Vinson Thornton Coolidge	Theresa Blanchard Nathaniel Niles	Edith Secord Joseph Savage
1930 Providence, RI	Beatrix Loughran Sherwin Badger	Maribel Vinson George Hill	Edith Secord Joseph Savage
1931 Boston, MA	Beatrix Loughran Sherwin Badger	Maribel Vinson George Hill	Grace Madden J. Lester Madden
1932 New York, NY	Beatrix Loughran Sherwin Badger	Maribel Vinson George Hill	G. Meredith Joseph Savage
1933 New Haven, CT	Maribel Vinson George Hill	Grace Madden J. Lester Madden	G. Meredith Joseph Savage
1934 Philadelphia, PA	Grace Madden J. Lester Madden	Eva Schwerdt William Bruns	—
1935 New Haven, CT	Maribel Vinson George Hill	Grace Madden J. Lester Madden	Eva Schwerdt William Bruns, Jr.
1936 New York, NY	Maribel Vinson George Hill	Polly Blodgett Roger Turner	Majorie Parker Howard Meredith
1937 Chicago, IL	Maribel Vinson George Hill	Grace Madden J. Lester Madden	Joan Tozzer Bernard Fox
1938 Philadelphia, PA	Joan Tozzer Bernard Fox	Grace Madden J. Lester Madden	Ardelle Sanderson Roland Janson
1939 St. Paul, MN	Joan Tozzer Bernard Fox	Annah M. Hall William Hall	Eva Bruns William Bruns
1940 Cleveland, OH	Joan Tozzer Bernard Fox	Heddy Stenuf Skippy Baxter	Eva Bruns William Bruns
1941 Boston, MA	Donna Atwood Eugene Turner	Patricia Vaeth Jack Might	Joan Mitchell Bobby Specht
1942 Chicago, IL	Doris Schubach Walter Noffke	Janette Ahrens Robert Uppgren	Margaret Field Jack Might
1943 New York, NY	Doris Schubach Walter Noffke	Janette Ahrens Robert Uppgren	Dorothy Goos Edward LeMaire
1944 Minneapolis, MN	Doris Schubach Walter Noffke	Janette Ahrens Arthur Preusch	Marcella May James Lochead
1945 New York, NY	Donna J. Pospisil Jean P. Brunet	Ann McGean Michael McGean	Marcella M. Willis James Lochead
1946 Chicago, IL	Donna J. Pospisil Jean P. Brunet	Karol Kennedy Peter Kennedy	Patty Sonnekson Charles Brinkman
1947 Berkeley, CA	Yvonne Sherman Robert Swenning	Karol Kennedy Peter Kennedy	Carolyn Welch Charles Brinkman
1948 Colo. Springs, CO	Karol Kennedy Peter Kennedy	Yvonne Sherman Robert Swenning	Harriet Sutton Lyman Wakefield
1949 Colo. Springs, CO	Karol Kennedy Peter Kennedy	Irene Maguire W. Muehlbronner	Anne Davies Carleton Hoffner
1950 Washington, DC	Karol Kennedy Peter Kennedy	Irene Maguire W. Muehlbronner	Anne Davies Carleton Hoffner
1951 Seattle, WA	Karol Kennedy Peter Kennedy	Janet Gerhauser John Nightingale	Anne Holt Austin Holt
1952 Colo. Springs, CO	Karol Kennedy Peter Kennedy	Janet Gerhauser John Nightingale	— —
1953 Hershey, PA	Carole Ormaca Robin Greiner	Margaret Graham Hugh C. Graham	Kay Servatius Sully Kothman

SKATER'S EDGE SOURCEBOOK

CHAMPIONS — U.S. NATIONALS

PAIRS	GOLD	SILVER	BRONZE
1954 Los Angeles, CA	Carole Ormaca / Robin Greiner	Margaret Graham / Hugh C. Graham	Lucille Ash / Sully Kothman
1955 Colo. Springs, CO	Carole Ormaca / Robin Greiner	Lucille Ash / Sully Kothman	Agnes Tyson / Richard Swenning
1956 Philadelphia, PA	Carole Ormaca / Robin Greiner	Lucille Ash / Sully Kothman	Maribel Owen / Charles Foster
1957 Berkeley, CA	Nancy Rouillard / Ronald Ludington	Mary J. Watson / John Jarmon	Anita Tefkin / James Barlow
1958 Minneapolis, MN	Nancy Ludington / Ronald Ludington	Sheila Wells / Robin Greiner	Maribel Owen / Dudley Richards
1959 Rochester, NY	Nancy Ludington / Ronald Ludington	Gayle Freed / Karl Freed	Maribel Owen / Dudley Richards
1960 Seattle, WA	Nancy Ludington / Ronald Ludington	Maribel Owen / Dudley Richards	Ila Ray Hadley / Ray Hadley, Jr.
1961 Colo. Springs, CO	Maribel Owen / Dudley Richards	Ila Ray Hadley / Ray Hadley, Jr.	Laurie Hickox / William Hickox
1962 Boston, MA	Dorothyann Nelson / Pieter Kollen	Judi Fotheringill / Jerry Fotheringill	Vivian Joseph / Ronald Joseph
1963 Long Beach, CA	Judianne Fotheringill / Jerry Fotheringill	Vivian Joseph / Ronald Joseph	Patti Gustafson / Pieter Kollen
1964 Cleveland, OH	Judianne Fotheringill / Jerry Fotheringill	Vivian Joseph / Ronald Joseph	Cynthia Kauffman / Ronald Kauffman
1965 Lake Placid, NY	Vivian Joseph / Ronald Joseph	Cynthia Kauffman / Ronald Kauffman	Joanne Heckert / Gary Clark
1966 Berkeley, CA	Cynthia Kauffman / Ronald Kauffman	Susan Berens / Roy Wagelein	Page Paulsen / Larry Dusich
1967 Omaha, NE	Cynthia Kauffman / Ronald Kauffman	Susan Berens / Roy Wagelein	Betty Lewis / Richard Gilbert
1968 Philadelphia, PA	Cynthia Kauffman / Ronald Kauffman	Sandi Sweitzer / Roy Wagelein	JoJo Starbuck / Kenneth Shelley
1969 Seattle, WA	Cynthia Kauffman / Ronald Kauffman	JoJo Starbuck / Kenneth Shelley	Melissa Militano / Mark Militano
1970 Tulsa, OK	JoJo Starbuck / Kenneth Shelley	Melissa Militano / Mark Militano	Sheri Thrapp / Larry Dusich
1971 Buffalo, NY	JoJo Starbuck / Kenneth Shelley	Melissa Militano / Mark Militano	Barbara Brown / Doug Berndt
1972 Long Beach, CA	JoJo Starbuck / Kenneth Shelley	Melissa Militano / Mark Militano	Barbara Brown / Doug Berndt
1973 Minneapolis, MN	Melissa Militano / Mark Militano	Gale Fuhrman / Joel Fuhrman	Emily Benenson / Johnny Johns
1974 Providence, RI	Melissa Militano / Johnny Johns	Tai Babilonia / Randy Gardner	Erica Susman / Thomas Huff
1975 Oakland, CA	Melissa Militano / Johnny Johns	Tai Babilonia / Randy Gardner	Emily Benenson / Jack Courtney
1976 Colo. Springs, CO	Tai Babilonia / Randy Gardner	Alice Cook / William Fauver	Emily Benenson / Jack Courtney
1977 Hartford, CT	Tai Babilonia / Randy Gardner	Gail Hamula / Frank Sweiding	Sheryl Franks / Michael Botticelli
1978 Portland, OR	Tai Babilonia / Randy Gardner	Gail Hamula / Frank Sweiding	Sheryl Franks / Michael Botticelli
1979 Cincinnati, OH	Tai Babilonia / Randy Gardner	Vicki Heasley / Robert Wagenhoffer	Sheryl Franks / Michael Botticelli
1980 Atlanta, GA	Tai Babilonia / Randy Gardner	Caitlin Carruthers / Peter Carruthers	Sheryl Franks / Michael Botticelli
1981 San Diego, CA	Caitlin Carruthers / Peter Carruthers	Lea Ann Miller / William Fauver	Beth Flora / Ken Flora
1982 Indianapolis, IN	Caitlin Carruthers / Peter Carruthers	Maria DiDomenico / Burt Lancon	Lea Ann Miller / William Fauver
1983 Pittsburgh, PA	Caitlin Carruthers / Peter Carruthers	Lea Ann Miller / William Fauver	Jill Watson / Burt Lancon
1984 Salt Lake City, UT	Caitlin Carruthers / Peter Carruthers	Lea Ann Miller / William Fauver	Jill Watson / Burt Lancon
1985 Kansas City, MO	Jill Watson / Peter Oppegard	Natalie Seybold / Wayne Seybold	Gillian Wachsman / Todd Waggoner
1986 Long Island, NY	Gillian Wachsman / Todd Waggoner	Jill Watson / Peter Oppegard	Natalie Seybold / Wayne Seybold
1987 Tacoma, WA	Jill Watson / Peter Oppegard	Gillian Wachsman / Todd Waggoner	Katy Keeley / Joseph Mero
1988 Denver, CO	Jill Watson / Peter Oppegard	Gillian Wachsman / Todd Waggoner	Natalie Seybold / Wayne Seybold
1989 Baltimore, MD	Kristi Yamaguchi / Rudi Galindo	Natalie Seybold / Wayne Seybold	Katy Keeley / Joseph Mero
1990 Salt Lake City, UT	Kristi Yamaguchi / Rudi Galindo	Natasha Kuchiki / Todd Sand	Sharon Carz / Doug Williams
1991 Minneapolis, MN	Natasha Kuchiki / Todd Sand	Calla Urbanski / Rocky Marval	Jenni Meno / Scott Wendland

55

~ SKATER'S EDGE SOURCEBOOK ~

PAIRS	GOLD	SILVER	BRONZE
1992	Calla Urbanski	Jenni Meno	Natasha Kuchiki
Orlando, FL	Rocky Marval	Scott Wendland	Todd Sand
1993	Calla Urbanski	Jenni Meno	Karen Courtland
Phoenix, AZ	Rocky Marval	Todd Sand	R. Todd Reynolds
1994	Jenni Meno	Kyoko Ina	Karen Courtland
Detroit, MI	Todd Sand	Jason Dungjen	Todd Reynolds

U.S. FIGURE SKATING CHAMPIONSHIPS
ICE DANCE

	GOLD	SILVER	BRONZE
1914 New Haven, CT			
Waltz	Theresa Weld	Jeanne Chavalier	—
	Nathaniel Niles	Norman Scott	—
1915-1919	No Competition		
1920 New York, NY			
Waltz	Theresa Weld	Rosalie Dunn	—
	Nathaniel Niles	Joel Liberman	—
Fourteen Step	Gertrude C. Porter	Rosalie Dunn	—
	Irving Brokaw	Joel Liberman	—
1921 Philadelphia, PA			
Waltz	Theresa W Blanchard	Clara Frothingham	Virginia Slattery
	Nathaniel Niles	Sherwin Badger	C. J. Cruikshank
Fourteen Step	Theresa W Blanchard	Virginia Slattery	Mrs. Ed.Howland
	Nathaniel Niles	C. J. Cruikshank	Mr. Ed.Howland
			- Tie -
			Clara Frothingham
			Charles Rotch
1922 Boston, MA			
Waltz	Beatrix Loughran	Theresa Blanchard	Mrs. Henry Howe
	Edward Howland	Nathaniel Niles	Mr. Henry Howe
Fourteen Step	Theresa W Blanchard	Mrs. Henry Howe	Ella Snelling
	Nathaniel Niles	Mr. Henry Howe	Sherwin Badger
1923 New Haven, CT			
Waltz	Mrs. Henry Howe	Theresa Blanchard	Rosalie Dunn
	Mr. Henry Howe	Charles Rotch	Petros Wahlman
Fourteen Step	Sydney Goode	Theresa Blanchard	Rosalie Dunn
	James Greene	Nathaniel Niles	Petros Wahlman
1924 Philadelphia, PA			
Waltz	Rosalie Dunn	Sydney Goode	Theresa Blanchard
	Fredrick Gabel	James Greene	Nathaniel Niles
Fourteen Step	Sydney Goode	Theresa Blanchard	Clara Frothingham
	James Greene	Nathaniel Niles	Sherwin Badger
1925 New York, NY			
Waltz	Virginia Slattery	Sydney Goode	Mrs. Henry Howe
	Ferrier Martin	James Greene	Mr. Henry Howe
Fourteen Step	Virginia Slattery	Sydney Goode	Ada Baumann
	Ferrier Martin	James Greene	George Braakman

DANCE	GOLD	SILVER	BRONZE
1926 New York, NY		Rosalie Dunn	Sydney Goode
Waltz	Rosalie Dunn	Sydney Goode	Edna Gutterman
	Joseph Savage	James Greene	Frederick Gabel
Fourteen Step	Sydney Goode	Virginia Slattery	Edna Gutterman
	Joseph Savage	Ferrier Martin	Frederick Gabel
1927 New York, NY			
Waltz	Rosalie Dunn	Virginia S. Martin	Ada Bauman
	Joseph Savage	Ferrier Martin	George Braakman
Fourteen Step	Rosalie Dunn	Ada Baumann	Virginia S. Martin
	Joseph Savage	George Braakman	Ferrier Martin
1928 New Haven, CT			
Waltz	Rosalie Dunn	Elsie Koscheck	Ada B. Kelly
	Joseph Savage	Frederick Gabel	George Braakman
Fourteen Step	Ada Baumann Kelly	Maribel Vinson	Rosalie Dunn
	George Braakman	Lester Madden	Joseph Savage
1929 New York, NY			
Waltz & Original	Edith Secord	Theresa Blanchard	Maribel Vinson
Dance Combined	Joseph Savage	Nathaniel Niles	Lester Madden
1930 Providence, RI			
Waltz	Edith Secord	Virginia Martin	Nettie Prantell
	Joseph Savage	Ferrier Martin	Roy Hunt
Orginal Dance	Clara Frothingham	Edith Secord	Theresa Blanchard
	George Hill	Joseph Savage	Nathaniel Niles
1931 Boston, MA			
Waltz	Edith Secord	Clara Frothingham	—
	Ferrier Martin	Harold Hartshorne	—
Orginal Dance	Theresa Blanchard	Edith Secord	Clara Frothingham
	Nathaniel Niles	Ferrier Martin	George B. Hill
1932 New York, NY			
Waltz	Edith Secord	Nettie Prantell	Clara Frothingham
	Joseph Savage	Roy Hunt	F. Goodridge
Original Dance	Clara Frothingham	Edith Secord	Theresa Blanchard
	George Hill	Joseph Savage	Nathaniel Niles
1933 New Haven, CT			
Waltz	Ilse Twaroschk	Eva Schwerdt	Miss Dutton
	Fred Fleischman	William Burns	Harold Hartshorne
Original Dance	Suzanne Davis	Gertrude Meredith	Grace Madden
	Frederick Goodridge	Joseph Savage	James Madden
1934 Philadelphia, PA			
Waltz	Nettie Prantell	Ise Twaroschk	Eva Schwerdt
	Roy Hunt	Fred Fleischman	William Bruns
Orginal Dance	Suzanne Davis	Grace Madden	Ruth English
	Frederick Goodridge	Joseph Madden	Len Fogassey

SKATER'S EDGE SOURCEBOOK

DANCE	GOLD	SILVER	BRONZE
1935 New Haven, CT Waltz*	Nettie Prantell / Roy Hunt	Ilse Twaroschk / Fred Fleischman	Maribel Vinson / Joseph Savage

Original Dance Competition was an exhibition in 1935 in anticipation of a new dance championship the following year.

DANCE	GOLD	SILVER	BRONZE
1936 Boston, MA	Marjorie Parker / Joseph Savage	Nettie Prantell / Harold Hartshorne	Clara Frothingham / Ashton Parmenter
1937 Chicago, IL	Nettie Prantell / Harold Hartshorne	Marjorie Parker / Joseph Savage	Ardelle Kloss / Roland Jansea
1938 Philadelphia, PA	Nettie Prantel / Harold Hartshorne	Katherine Durbrow / Joseph Savage	Louise W. Atwell / Otto Dallmayr
1939 St. Paul, MN	Sandy MacDonald / Harold Hartshorne	Nettie Prantel / Joseph Savage	Marjorie Parker / George Boltres
1940 Cleveland, OH	Sandy MacDonald / Harold Hartshorne	Nettie Prantel / George Boltres	Vernafay Thysell / Paul Harrington
1941 Boston, MA	Sandy MacDonald / Harold Hartshorne	Elizabeth Kennedy / Eugene Turner	Edith Whetstone / A. L. Richards
1942 Chicago, IL	Edith Whetstone / Alfred Richards	Sandy MacDonald / Harold Hartshorne	Ramona Allen / Herman Torrano
1943 New York, NY	Marcella May / James Lochead	Marjorie P. Smith / Joseph Savage	Nettie Prantel / Harold Hartshorne
1944 Minneapolis, MN	Marcella May / James Lochead	Kathe Mehl / Harold Hartshorne	Mary Anderson / Jack Anderson
1945 New York, NY	Kathe Williams / Robert Swenning	Marcella Willis / James Lochead	Anne Davies / Carleton Hoffner
1946 Chicago, IL	Anne Davies / Carleton Hoffner	Lois Waring / Walter Bainbridge	Carmel Waterbury / Edward Bodel
1947 Berkeley, CA	Lois Waring / Walter Bainbridge	Anne Davies / Carleton Hoffner	Marcella Willis / Frank Davenport
1948 Colo. Springs, CO	Lois Waring / Walter Bainbridge	Anne Davies / Carleton Hoffner	Irene Maguire / Frank Davenport
1949 Colo. Springs, CO	Lois Waring / Walter Bainbridge	Irene Maguire / W. Muehlbronner	Carmel Bodel / Edward Bodel
1950 Washington, DC	Lois Waring / Michael McGean	Irene Maguire / W. Meuhlbronner	Anne Davies / Carleton Hoffner
1951 Seattle, WA	Carmel Bodel / Edward Bodel	Virginia Hoyns / Donald Jacoby	Carol Ann Peters / Daniel Ryan
1952 Colo. Springs, CO	Lois Waring / Michael McGean	Carol Ann Peters / Daniel Ryan	Carmel Bodel / Edward Bodel
1953 Hershey, PA	Carol Ann Peters / Daniel Ryan	Virginia Hoyns / Donald Jacoby	Carmel Bodel / Edward Bodel
1954 Los Angeles, CA	Carmel Bodel / Edward Bodel	Phyllis Forney / Martin Forney	Patsy Riedel / Roland Junso
1955 Colo. Springs, CO	Carmel Bodel / Edward Bodel	Joan Zamboni / Roland Junso	Phyllis Forney / Martin Forney
1956 Philadelphia, PA	Joan Zamboni / Roland Junso	Carmel Bodel / Edward Bodel	Sidney Arnold / Franklin Nelson
1957 Berkeley, CA	Sharon McKenzie / Bert Wright	Andree Anderson / Donald Jacoby	Joan Zamboni / Roland Junso
1958 Minneapolis, MN	Andree Anderson / Donald Jacoby	Claire O'Neil / John Bejshak	Susan Sebo / Tim Brown
1959 Rochester, NY	Andree Jacoby / Donald Jacoby	Margie Ackles / Charles Phillips	Judy Ann Lamar / Ronald Ludington
1960 Seattle, WA	Margie Ackles / Charles Phillips	Marilyn Meeker / Larry Pierce	Yvonne Littlefield / Roger Campbell
1961 Colo. Springs, CO	Dianne Sherbloom / Larry Pierce	Dona Lee Carrier / Roger Campbell	Patricia Dineen / Robert Dineen
1962 Boston, MA	Yvonne Littlefield / Peter Betts	Dorothyann Nelson / Pieter Kollen	Lorna Dyer / King Cole
1963 Long Beach, CA	Sally Schantz / Stanley Urban	Yvonne Littlefield / Peter Betts	Lorna Dyer / John Carrell
1964 Cleveland, OH	Darlene Streich / Charles Fetter	Carol MacSween / Robert Munz	Lorna Dyer / John Carrell
1965 Lake Placid, NY	Kristin Fortune / Dennis Sveum	Lorna Dyer / John Carrell	Susan Urban / Stanley Urban
1966 Berkeley, CA	Kristin Fortune / Dennis Sveum	Lorna Dyer / John Carrell	Susan Urban / Stanley Urban
1967 Omaha, NE	Lorna Dyer / John Carrell	Alma Davenport / Roger Berry	Judy Schwomeyer / James Sladky
1968 Philadelphia, PA	Judy Schwomeyer / James Sladky	Vicki Camper / Eugene Heffron	Debbie Gerken / R. Tiedmeann
1969 Seattle, WA	Judy Schwomeyer / James Sladky	Joan Bitterman / Brad Hislop	Debbie Gerken / R. Tiedemann
1970 Tulsa, OK	Judy Schwomeyer / James Sladky	Anne Millier / Harvey Millier	Debbie Ganson / Brad Hislop
1971 Buffalo, NY	Judy Schwomeyer / James Sladky	Anne Millier / Harvey Millier	Mary Campbell / Johnny Johns

CHAMPIONS — U.S. NATIONALS

~ SKATER'S EDGE SOURCEBOOK ~

DANCE	GOLD	SILVER	BRONZE
1972 Long Beach, CA	Judy Schwomeyer James Sladky	Anne Millier Skip Millier	Mary Campbell Johnny Johns
1973 Minneapolis, MN	Mary Campbell Johnny Johns	Anne Millier Harvey Millier	Jane Pankey Richard Horne
1974 Providence, RI	Colleen O'Connor Jim Millns	Anne Millier Skip Millier	Michell Ford Glenn Patterson
1975 Oakland, CA	Colleen O'Connor Jim Millns	Judi Genovesi Kent Weigle	Michell Ford Glenn Patterson
1976 Colo. Springs, CO	Colleen O'Connor Jim Millns	Judi Genovesi Kent Weigle	Susan Kelley Andrew Stroukoff
1977 Hartford, CT	Judi Genovesi Kent Weigle	Susan Kelley Andrew Stroukoff	Michelle Ford Glenn Patterson
1978 Portland, OR	Stacey Smith John Summers	Carol Fox Richard Dalley	Susan Kelley Andrew Stroukoff
1979 Cincinnati, OH	Stacey Smith John Summers	Carol Fox Richard Dalley	Judy Blumberg Michael Seibert
1980 Atlanta, GA	Stacey Smith John Summers	Judy Blumberg Michael Seibert	Carol Fox Richard Dalley
1981 San Diego, CA	Judy Blumberg Michael Seibert	Carol Fox Richard Dalley	Kim Krohn Barry Hagan
1982 Indianapolis, MN	Judy Blumberg Michael Seibert	Carol Fox Richard Dalley	Elisa Spitz Scott Gregory
1983 Pittsburg, PA	Judy Blumberg Michael Seibert	Elisa Spitz Scott Gregory	Carol Fox Richard Dalley
1984 Salt Lake City, UT	Judy Blumberg Michael Seibert	Carol Fox Richard Dalley	Elisa Spitz Scott Gregory
1985 Kansas City, MO	Judy Blumberg Michael Seibert	Renee Roca Donald Adair	Suzanne Semanick Scott Gregory
1986 Long Island, NY	Renee Roca Donald Adair	Suzanne Semanick Scott Gregory	Lois Luciani Russ Witherby
1987 Tacoma, WA	Suzanne Semanick Scott Gregory	Renee Roca Donald Adair	Susan Wynne Joseph Druar
1988 Denver, CO	Suzanne Semanick Scott Gregory	Susan Wynne Joseph Druar	April Sargent Russ Witherby
1989 Baltimore, MD	Susan Wynne Joseph Druar	April Sargent Russ Witherby	Suzanne Semanick Ron Kravette
1990 Salt Lake City, UT	Susan Wynne Joseph Druar	April Sargent Russ Witherby	Suzanne Semanick Ron Kravette

'94 U.S. Dance Champions Liz Punsalan and Jerod Swallow

DANCE	GOLD	SILVER	BRONZE
1991 Minneapolis, MN	Elizabeth Punsalan Jerod Swallow	April Sargent Russ Witherby	Jeanne Miley Michael Verlich
1992 Orlando, FL	April Sargent Russ Witherby	Rachel Mayer Peter Breen	Elizabeth Punsalan Jerod Swallow
1993 Phoenix, AZ	Renee Roca Gorsha Sur	Susan Wynne Russ Witherby	Elizabeth Punsalan Jerod Swallow
1994 Detroit, MI	Elizabeth Punsalan Jerod Swallow	Susan Wynne Russ Witherby	Amy Webster Ron Kravette

U.S. FIGURE SKATING CHAMPIONSHIPS
FOURS

	GOLD	SILVER	BRONZE
1924 Philadelphia, PA	Clara Hartman Grace Munstock Paul Armitage Joel Liberman	G. Pancoast Mrs. J. Chapman Joseph Chapman Charles Meyers	— — — —
1925 New York, NY	Clara Hartman Grace Munstock Paul Armitage Joel Lieberman	— — — —	— — — —
1926-1933	No Competition		
1934 Philadelphia, PA	Suzanne Davis Theresa Blanchard Frederick Goodridge Richard Hapgood	Valerie Jones Nettie Prantel Roy Hunt Joseph Savage	Hulda Berger E. Harris Arthur Janson Roland Janson
1935 New Haven, CT	Nettie Prantell Ardelle Kloss Joseph Savage Roy Hunt	Suzanne Davis Grace Madden George Hill Fred Goodridge	Mrs Banks Mrs. English W.R. Cady Len Fogassey

PHOTO BY ALICE BERMAN

FOURS

	GOLD	SILVER	BRONZE
1936-1938	No Competition		
1939 St. Paul, MN	Nettie Prantell Marjorie Parker Joseph Savage George Boltres	Mary Dayton Annah M. Hall William Hall William Lukens Jr.	— — — —
1940 Cleveland, OH	Janette Ahrens Mary Louise Premer Robert Uppgren Lyman Wakefield Jr.	Mary Stuart Dalton Annah M. Hall William Lukens Jr. William Hall	— — — —
1941-1944	No Competition		
1945 New York, NY	Jacqueline Dunne Joan Yocum Ed. Van Der Bosch Larry Van Der Bosch	Jane Lemmon Nancy Lemmon Edgar Black Charles Brinkman	Mary Anderson Patricia Ryan Henry Trenkamp Gary Wilson
1946 Chicago, IL	Jacqueline Dunne Joan Yocum Ed. Van Der Bosch Larry Van Der Bosch	Sandra Rittinger Nancy S. Jenkins Hayes Alan Jenkins Garry Wilson	— — — —
1947 Berkeley, CA	Janet Gerhauser Marilyn Thomsen Marlyn Thomsen John Nightingale	Joan Swanston Barbara Torrano Herman Maricich Robert O'Connell	— — — —
1948 Colo. Springs, CO	Janet Gerhauser Marilyn Thomsen Marlyn Thomsen John Nightingale	Ferne Fletcher Anne Davis Carlton C. Hoffner Donald Laws	Kathryn Ehlers Anne Hall James Phillips Jean P. Brunet
1949	No Competition		
1950 Washington, DC	Janet Gerhauser Marilyn Thomsen Marlyn Thomsen John Nightingale	Dorothy Dort Mary Lou King Daniel Ryan Richard Juten	Barbara Davis Elizabeth Jones William Lemmon James Coote
1951-1990	No Competition		
1991 Minneapolis, MN	Elaine Asanakis Calla Urbanski Joel McKeever Rocky Marval	Janis Bosch Laura LaBarca Kenneth Benson Sean Gales	— — — —
1992-1994	No Competition		

WORLD CHAMPIONSHIPS

MEN'S SINGLES

	GOLD	SILVER	BRONZE
1896 St. Petersburg, RUS	Gilbert Fuchs (GER)	Gustav Hugel (AUT)	Georg Sanders (RUS)
1897 Stockholm, SWE	Gustav Hugel (AUT)	Ulrich Salchow (SWE)	Johan Lefstad (NOR)
1898 London, GBR	Henning Grenander (SWE)	Gustav Hugel (AUT)	Gilbert Fuchs (GER)
1899 Davos, SUI	Gustav Hugel (AUT)	Ulrich Salchow (SWE)	Edgar Syers (GBR)
1900 Davos, SUI	Gustav Hugel (AUT)	Ulrich Salchow (SWE)	—
1901 Stockholm, SWE	Ulrich Salchow (SWE)	Gilbert Fuchs (GER)	—
1902 London, GBR	Ulrich Salchow (SWE)	Madge Syers* (GBR)	Martin Gordan (GER)

*1902 marked the first year a woman applied to compete in the World Championships. At that time there was no provision in the rules for such an occurrence and it was not until 1903 that the Congress decided that Ladies should not be permitted to compete at international men's championships. The Ladies event was introduced at the 1906 World Championships.

	GOLD	SILVER	BRONZE
1903 St. Petersburg, RUS	Ulrich Salchow (SWE)	Nicolai Panin (RUS)	Max Bohatsch (AUT)
1904 Berlin, GER	Ulrich Salchow (SWE)	Heinrich Burger (GER)	Martin Gordan (GER)
1905 Stockholm, SWE	Ulrich Salchow (SWE)	Max Bohatsch (AUT)	Per Thoren (SWE)
1906 Munich, GER	Gilbert Fuchs (GER)	Heinrich Burger (GER)	Bror Meyer (SWE)
1907 Vienna, AUT	Ulrich Salchow (SWE)	Max Bohatsch (AUT)	Gilbert Fuchs (GER)
1908 Troppau, CZE	Ulrich Salchow (SWE)	Gilbert Fuchs (GER)	Heinrich Burger (GER)
1909 Stockholm, SWE	Ulrich Salchow (SWE)	Per Thoren (SWE)	Ernest Herz (AUT)
1910 Davos, SUI	Ulrich Salchow (SWE)	Werner Rittberger (GER)	Andor Szende (HUN)
1911 Berlin, GER	Ulrich Salchow (SWE)	Werner Rittberger (GER)	Fritz Kachler (AUT)
1912 Manchester, GBR	Fritz Kachler (AUT)	Werner Rittberger (GER)	Andor Szende (HUN)

SKATER'S EDGE SOURCEBOOK

MEN	GOLD	SILVER	BRONZE
1913 Vienna, AUT	Fritz Kachler (AUT)	Willy Boeckl (AUT)	Andor Szende (HUN)
1914 Helsinki, FIN	Gosta Sandahl (SWE)	Fritz Kachler (AUT)	Willy Boeckl (AUT)
1915-1921	No Championship		
1922 Stockholm, SWE	Gillis Grafstrom (SWE)	Fritz Kachler (AUT)	Willy Boeckl (AUT)
1923 Vienna, AUT	Fritz Kachler (AUT)	Willy Boeckl (AUT)	Gosta Sandahl (SWE)
1924 Manchester, GBR	Gillis Grafstrom (SWE)	Willy Boeckl (AUT)	Ernst Oppacher (AUT)
1925 Vienna, AUT	Willy Boeckl (AUT)	Fritz Kachler (AUT)	Otto Preissecker (AUT)
1926 Berlin, GER	Willy Boeckl (AUT)	Otto Preissecker (AUT)	John Page (GBR)
1927 Davos, SUI	Willy Boeckl (AUT)	Otto Preissecker (AUT)	Karl Schafer (AUT)
1928 Berlin, GER	Willy Boeckl (AUT)	Karl Schafer (AUT)	Hugo Distler (AUT)
1929 London, GBR	Gillis Grafstrom (SWE)	Karl Schafer (AUT)	Ludwig Wrede (AUT)
1930 New York, USA	Karl Schafer (AUT)	Roger Turner (USA)	Georg Gautschi (SUI)
1931 Berlin, GER	Karl Schafer (AUT)	Roger Turner (USA)	Ernst Baier (GER)
1932 Montreal, CAN	Karl Schafer (AUT)	Montgomery Wilson (CAN)	Ernst Baier (GER)
1933 Zurich, SUI	Karl Schafer (AUT)	Ernst Baier (GER)	Markus Nikkanen (FIN)
1934 Stockholm, SWE	Karl Schafer (AUT)	Ernst Baier (GER)	Erich Erdos (AUT)
1935 Budapest, HUN	Karl Schafer (AUT)	Jack Dunn (GBR)	Denes Pataky (HUN)
1936 Paris, FRA	Karl Schafer (AUT)	Graham Sharp (GBR)	Felix Kaspar (AUT)
1937 Vienna, AUT	Felix Kaspar (AUT)	Graham Sharp (GBR)	Elemer Tertak (HUN)
1938 Berlin, GER	Felix Kaspar (AUT)	Graham Sharp (GBR)	Herbert Alward (AUT)
1939 Budapest, HUN	Graham Sharp (GBR)	Freddie Tomlins (GBR)	Horst Faber (GER)
1940-1946	No Championship		
1947 Stockholm, SWE	Hans Gerschwiler (SUI)	Richard Button (USA)	Arthur Apfel (GBR)
1948 Davos, SUI	Richard Button (USA)	Hans Gerschwiler (SUI)	Ede Kiraly (HUN)
1949 Paris, FRA	Richard Button (USA)	Ede Kiraly (HUN)	Edi Rada (AUT)
1950 London, GBR	Richard Button (USA)	Ede Kiraly (HUN)	Hayes Jenkins (USA)
1951 Milan, ITA	Richard Button (USA)	James Grogan (USA)	Helmut Seibt (AUT)
1952 Paris, FRA	Richard Button (USA)	James Grogan (USA)	Hayes Jenkins (USA)
1953 Davos, SUI	Hayes Jenkins (USA)	James Grogan (USA)	Carlo Fassi (ITA)
1954 Oslo, NOR	Hayes Jenkins (USA)	James Grogan (USA)	Alain Giletti (FRA)
1955 Vienna, AUT	Hayes Jenkins (USA)	Ronald Robertson (USA)	David Jenkins (USA)
1956 Garmisch, FRG	Hayes Jenkins (USA)	Ronald Robertson (USA)	David Jenkins (USA)
1957 Colo. Spgs., USA	David Jenkins (USA)	Tim Brown (USA)	Charles Snelling (CAN)
1958 Paris, FRA	David Jenkins (USA)	Tim Brown (USA)	Alain Giletti (FRA)
1959 Colo. Spgs., USA	David Jenkins (USA)	Donald Jackson (CAN)	Tim Brown (USA)
1960 Vancouver, CAN	Alain Giletti (FRA)	Donald Jackson (CAN)	Alain Calmat (FRA)
1961	No Championship		
1962 Prague, CZE	Donald Jackson (CAN)	Karol Divin (CZE)	Alain Calmat (FRA)
1963 Cortina, ITA	Donald McPherson (CAN)	Alain Calmat (FRA)	M. Schnelldorfer (FRG)

SKATER'S EDGE SOURCEBOOK

MEN	GOLD	SILVER	BRONZE
1964 Dortmund, FRG	M. Schnelldorfer (FRG)	Alain Calmat (FRA)	Karol Divin (CZE)
1965 Colo. Spgs., USA	Alain Calmat (FRA)	Scott Allen (USA)	Donald Knight (CAN)
1966 Davos, SUI	Emmerich Danzer (AUT)	Wolfgang Schwarz (AUT)	Gary Visconti (USA)
1967 Vienna, AUT	Emmerich Danzer (AUT)	Wolfgang Schwarz (AUT)	Gary Visconti (USA)
1968 Geneva, SUI	Emmerich Danzer (AUT)	Tim Wood (USA)	Patrick Pera (FRA)
1969 Colo. Spgs., USA	Tim Wood (USA)	Ondrej Nepela (CZE)	Patrick Pera (FRA)
1970 Ljubljana, YUG	Tim Wood (USA)	Ondrej Nepela (CZE)	Gunter Zoller (GDR)
1971 Lyon, FRA	Ondrej Nepela (CZE)	Patrick Pera (FRA)	S. Chetverukhin (URS)
1972 Calgary, CAN	Ondrej Nepela (CZE)	S. Chetverukhin (URS)	Vladimir Kovalev (URS)
1973 Bratislava, CZE	Ondrej Nepela (CZE)	S. Chetverukhin (URS)	Jan Hoffmann (GDR)
1974 Munich, FRG	Jan Hoffmann (GDR)	Sergei Volkov (URS)	Toller Cranston (CAN)
1975 Colo. Spgs., USA	Sergei Volkov (URS)	Vladimir Kovalev (URS)	John Curry (GBR)
1976 Gothenberg, SWE	John Curry (GBR)	Vladimir Kovalev (URS)	Jan Hoffmann (GDR)
1977 Tokyo, JPN	Vladimir Kovalev (URS)	Jan Hoffmann (GDR)	Minoru Sano (JPN)
1978 Ottawa, CAN	Charles Tickner (USA)	Jan Hoffmann (GDR)	Robin Cousins (GBR)
1979 Vienna, AUT	Vladimir Kovalev (URS)	Robin Cousins (GBR)	Jan Hoffmann (GDR)
1980 Dortmund, FRG	Jan Hoffmann (GDR)	Robin Cousins (GBR)	Charles Tickner (USA)
1981 Hartford, USA	Scott Hamilton (USA)	David Santee (USA)	Igor Bobrin (URS)
1982 Copenhagen, DEN	Scott Hamilton (USA)	Norbert Schramm (FRG)	Brian Pockar (CAN)

1962 World Champion Don Jackson landed the first triple Lutz

MEN	GOLD	SILVER	BRONZE
1983 Helsinki, FIN	Scott Hamilton (USA)	Norbert Schramm (FRG)	Brian Orser (CAN)
1984 Ottawa, CAN	Scott Hamilton (USA)	Brian Orser (CAN)	Alexandr Fadeev (URS)
1985 Tokyo, JPN	Alexandr Fadeev (URS)	Brian Orser (CAN)	Brian Boitano (USA)
1986 Geneva, SUI	Brian Boitano (USA)	Brian Orser (CAN)	Alexandr Fadeev (URS)
1987 Cincinnati, USA	Brian Orser (CAN)	Brian Boitano (USA)	Alexandr Fadeev (URS)
1988 Budapest, HUN	Brian Boitano (USA)	Brian Orser (CAN)	Viktor Petrenko (URS)
1989 Paris, FRA	Kurt Browning (CAN)	Chris Bowman (USA)	Grzegorz Filipowski (POL)
1990 Halifax, CAN	Kurt Browning (CAN)	Viktor Petrenko (URS)	Chris Bowman (USA)
1991 Munich, GER	Kurt Browning (CAN)	Viktor Petrenko (URS)	Todd Eldredge (USA)
1992 Oakland, USA	Viktor Petrenko (CIS)	Kurt Browning (CAN)	Elvis Stojko (CAN)
1993 Prague, CZE	Kurt Browning (CAN)	Elvis Stojko (CAN)	Alexei Urmanov (RUS)
1994 Chiba, JPN	Elvis Stojko (CAN)	Philippe Candeloro (FRA)	V. Zagorodniuk (UKR)

CHAMPIONS

WORLDS

PHOTO COURTESY OF CANADIAN FIGURE SKATING ASSOCIATION

WORLD CHAMPIONSHIPS
LADIES' SINGLES

	GOLD	SILVER	BRONZE
1906 Davos, SUI	Madge Syers (GBR)	Jenny Herz (AUT)	Lily Kronberger (HUN)
1907 Vienna, AUT	Madge Syers (GBR)	Jenny Herz (AUT)	Lily Kronberger (HUN)
1908 Troppau, CZE	Lily Kronberger (HUN)	Elsa Rendschmidt (GER)	—
1909 Budapest, HUN	Lily Kronberger (HUN)	—	—
1910 Berlin, GER	Lily Kronberger (HUN)	Elsa Rendschmidt (GER)	—
1911 Vienna, AUT	Lily Kronberger (HUN)	Opika von Horvath (HUN)	Ludowika Eilers (GER)
1912 Davos, SUI	Opika von Horvath (HUN)	D. Greenhough (GBR)	Phyllis Johnson (GBR)
1913 Stockholm, SWE	Opika von Horvath (HUN)	Phyllis Johnson (GBR)	Svea Noren (SWE)
1914 St. Moritz, SUI	Opika von Horvath (HUN)	Angela Hanka (AUT)	Phyllis Johnson (GBR)
1915-1921	No Championship		
1922 Stockhom, SWE	Herma Plank-Szabo (AUT)	Svea Noren (SWE)	Margot Moe (NOR)
1923 Vienna, AUT	Herma Plank-Szabo (AUT)	Gisela Reichmann (AUT)	Svea Noren (SWE)
1924 Oslo, NOR	Herma Plank-Szabo (AUT)	Ellen Brockhofft (GER)	Beatrix Loughran (USA)
1925 Davos, SUI	Herma Jaross-Szabo (AUT)	Ellen Brockhofft (GER)	Elisabeth Bockel (GER)
1926 Stockholm, SWE	Herma Jaross-Szabo (AUT)	Sonja Henie (NOR)	Kathleen Shaw (GBR)
1927 Oslo, NOR	Sonja Henie (NOR)	H. Jaross-Szabo (AUT)	Karen Simensen (NOR)
1928 London, GBR	Sonja Henie (NOR)	Maribel Vinson (USA)	Fritzi Burger (AUT)
1929 Budapest, HUN	Sonja Henie (NOR)	Fritzi Burger (AUT)	Melitta Brunner (AUT)
1930 New York, USA	Sonja Henie (NOR)	Cecil Smith (CAN)	Maribel Vinson (USA)

LADIES	GOLD	SILVER	BRONZE
1931 Berlin, GER	Sonja Henie (NOR)	Hilde Holovsky (AUT)	Fritzi Burger (AUT)
1932 Montreal, CAN	Sonja Henie (NOR)	Fritzi Burger (AUT)	Constance Samuel (CAN)
1933 Stockholm, SWE	Sonja Henie (HUN)	Vivi-Anne Hulten (SWE)	Hilde Holovsky (AUT)
1934 Olso, NOR	Sonja Henie (NOR)	Megan Taylor (GBR)	Liselotte Landbeck (AUT)
1935 Vienna, AUT	Sonja Henie (NOR)	Cecilia Colledge (GBR)	Vivi-Anne Hulten (SWE)
1936 Paris, FRA	Sonja Henie (NOR)	Megan Taylor (GBR)	Vivi-Anne Hulten (SWE)
1937 London, GBR	Cecilia Colledge (GBR)	Megan Taylor (GBR)	Vivi-Anne Hulten (SWE)
1938 Stockholm, SWE	Megan Taylor (GBR)	Cecilia Colledge (GBR)	Hedy Stenuf (USA)
1939 Prague, CZE	Megan Taylor (GBR)	Hedy Stenuf (USA)	Daphne Walker (GBR)
1940-1946	No Championship		
1947 Stockholm, SWE	Barbara Ann Scott (CAN)	Daphne Walter (GBR)	Gretchen Merrill (USA)
1948 Davos, SUI	Barbara Ann Scott (CAN)	Eva Pawlik (AUT)	Jirina Nekolova (CZE)
1949 Paris, FRA	Alena Vrzanova (CZE)	Yvonne Sherman (USA)	Jeannette Altwegg (GBR)
1950 London, GBR	Alena Vrzanova (CZE)	Jeannette Altwegg (GBR)	Yvonne Sherman (USA)
1951 Milan, ITA	Jeannette Altwegg (GBR)	Jacqueline du Bief (FRA)	Sonya Klopfer (USA)
1952 Paris, FRA	Jacqueline du Bief (FRA)	Sonja Klopfer (USA)	Virginia Baxter (USA)
1953 Davos, SUI	Tenley Albright (USA)	Gundi Busch (FRG)	Valda Osborn (GRB)
1954 Oslo, NOR	Gundi Busch (FRG)	Tenley Albright (USA)	Erica Batchelor (GRB)
1955 Vienna, AUT	Tenley Albright (USA)	Carol Heiss (USA)	Hanna Eigel (AUT)

SKATER'S EDGE SOURCEBOOK

CHAMPIONS — WORLDS

LADIES	GOLD	SILVER	BRONZE
1956 Garmisch, FRG	Carol Heiss (USA)	Tenley Albright (USA)	Ingrid Wendl (AUT)
1957 Colo. Spgs., CO	Carol Heiss (USA)	Hanna Eigel (AUT)	Ingrid Wendl (AUT)
1958 Paris, FRA	Carol Heiss (USA)	Ingrid Wendl (AUT)	Hanna Walter (AUT)
1959 Colo. Spgs., CO	Carol Heiss (USA)	Hanna Walter (AUT)	Sjoukje Dijkstra (HOL)
1960 Vancouver, CAN	Carol Heiss (USA)	Sjoukje Dijkstra (HOL)	Barbara Roles (USA)
1961	No Championship		
1962 Prague, CZE	Sjoukje Dijkstra (HOL)	Wendy Griner (CAN)	Regine Heitzer (AUT)
1963 Cortina, ITA	Sjoukje Dijkstra (HOL)	Regine Heitzer (AUT)	Nicole Hassler (FRA)
1964 Dortmund, FRG	Sjoukje Dijkstra (HOL)	Regine Heitzer (AUT)	Petra Burka (CAN)
1965 Colo. Spgs., CO	Petra Burka (CAN)	Regine Heitzer (AUT)	Peggy Fleming (USA)
1966 Davos, SUI	Peggy Fleming (USA)	Gabriele Seyfert (GDR)	Petra Burka (CAN)
1967 Vienna, AUT	Peggy Fleming (USA)	Gabriele Seyfert (GDR)	Hana Maskova (CZE)
1968 Geneva, SUI	Peggy Fleming (USA)	Gabriele Seyfert (GDR)	Hana Maskova (CZE)
1969 Colo. Spgs., CO	Gabriele Seyfert (GDR)	Beatrix Schuba (AUT)	Zsuzsa Almassy (HUN)
1970 Ljubljana, YUG	Gabriele Seyfert (GDR)	Beatrix Schuba (AUT)	Julie Holmes (USA)
1971 Lyon, FRA	Beatrix Schuba (AUT)	Julie Holmes (USA)	Karen Magnussen (CAN)
1972 Calgary, CAN	Beatrix Schuba (AUT)	Karen Magnussen (CAN)	Janet Lynn (USA)
1973 Bratislava, CZE	Karen Magnussen (CAN)	Janet Lynn (USA)	Christine Errath (GDR)
1974 Munich, FRG	Christine Errath (GDR)	Dorothy Hamill (USA)	Dianne de Leeuw (HOL)
1975 Colo. Spgs., CO	Dianne de Leeuw (HOL)	Dorothy Hamill (USA)	Christine Errath (GDR)
1976 Gothenberg, SWE	Dorothy Hamill (USA)	Christine Errath (GDR)	Dianne de Leeuw (HOL)
1977 Tokyo, JPN	Linda Fratianne (USA)	Anett Poetzsch (GDR)	Dagmar Lurz (FRG)
1978 Ottawa, CAN	Anett Poetzsch (GDR)	Linda Fratianne (USA)	Susanna Driano (ITA)
1979 Vienna, AUT	Linda Fratianne (USA)	Anett Poetzsch (GDR)	Emi Watanabe (JPN)
1980 Dortmund, FRG	Anett Poetzsch (GDR)	Dagmar Lurz (FRG)	Linda Fratianne (USA)
1981 Hartford, USA	Denise Biellmann (SUI)	Elaine Zayak (USA)	C Kristofics-Binder (AUT)
1982 Copenhagen, DEN	Elaine Zayak (USA)	Katarina Witt (GDR)	C Kristofics-Binder (AUT)
1983 Helsinki, FIN	Rosalynn Sumners (USA)	Claudia Leistner (FRG)	Elena Vodorezova (URS)
1984 Ottawa, CAN	Katarina Witt (GDR)	Anna Kondrashova (URS)	Elaine Zayak (USA)
1985 Tokyo, JPN	Katarina Witt (GDR)	Kira Ivanova (URS)	Tiffany Chin (USA)
1986 Geneva, SUI	Debi Thomas (USA)	Katarina Witt (GDR)	Tiffany Chin (USA)
1987 Cincinnati, USA	Katarina Witt (GDR)	Debi Thomas (USA)	Caryn Kadavy (USA)
1988 Budapest, HUN	Katarina Witt (GDR)	Elizabeth Manley (CAN)	Debi Thomas (USA)
1989 Paris, FRA	Midori Ito (JPN)	Claudia Leistner (FRG)	Jill Trenary (USA)
1990 Halifax, CAN	Jill Trenary (USA)	Midori Ito (JPN)	Holly Cook (USA)
1991 Munich, GER	Kristi Yamaguchi (USA)	Tonya Harding (USA)	Nancy Kerrigan (USA)
1992 Oakland, USA	Kristi Yamaguchi (USA)	Nancy Kerrigan (USA)	Lu Chen (CHN)
1993 Prague, CZE	Oksana Baiul (UKR)	Surya Bonaly (FRA)	Lu Chen (CHN)
1994 Chiba, JPN	Yuka Sato (JPN)	Surya Bonaly (FRA)	Tanja Szewczenko (GER)

63

WORLD CHAMPIONSHIPS
PAIRS

	GOLD	SILVER	BRONZE
1908 St. Petersbg, RUS	Anna Hubler Heinrich Burger (GER)	Phyllis Johnson James Johnson (GBR)	A. Fischer L. Popowa (RUS)
1909 Stockholm, SWE	Phyllis Johnson James Johnson (GBR)	Valborg Lindahl Nils Rosenius (SWE)	Gertrud Strom Richard Johanson (SWE)
1910 Berlin, GER	Anna Hubler Henrich Burger (GER)	Ludowika Eilers Walter Jakobsson (FIN)	Phyllis Johnson James Johnson (GBR)
1911 Vienna, AUT	Ludowika Eilers Walter Jakobsson (FIN)	—	—
1912 Manchester, GBR	Phyllis Hohnson James Johnson (GBR)	L. Jakobsson Walter Jakobsson (FIN)	Alexia Schoyen Yngvar Bryn (NOR)
1913 Stockholm, SWE	Helen Engelmann Karl Mejstrik (AUT)	L. Jakobsson Walter Jakobosson (FIN)	Christa von Szabo Leo Horwitz (AUT)
1914 St. Moritz, SUI	Ludowika Jakobsson Walter Jakobosson (FIN)	Helen Engelmann Karl Mejstrik (AUT)	Christa von Szabo Leo Horwitz (AUT)
1915-1921	No Championship		
1922 Davos, SUI	Helen Engelmann Alfred Berger (AUT)	L. Jakobsson Walter Jakobsson (FIN)	Margaret Metzner Paul Metzner (GER)
1923 Oslo, NOR	Ludowika Jakobsson Walter Jakobsson (FIN)	Alexia Bryn Yngvar Bryn (NOR)	Elna Henrikson Kajaf Ekstrom (SWE)
1924 Manchester, GBR	Helene Engelmann Alfred Berger (AUT)	Ethel Muckelt John Page (GBR)	Elna Henrikson Kaj af Ekstrom (SWE)
1925 Vienna, AUT	Herma Jaross-Szabo Ludwig Wrede (AUT)	Andree Brunet Pierre Brunet (FRA)	Lilly Scholz Otto Kaiser (AUT)
1926 Berlin, GER	Andree Brunet Pierre Burnet (FRA)	Lilly Scholz Otto Kaiser (AUT)	H. Jaross-Szabo Ludwig Wrede (AUT)
1927 Vienna, AUT	Herma Jaross-Szabo Ludwig Wrede (AUT)	Lilly Scholz Otto Kaiser (AUT)	Else Hoppe Oscar Hoppe (CZE)

PAIRS	GOLD	SILVER	BRONZE
1928 London, GBR	Andree Brunet Pierre Brunet (FRA)	Lilly Scholz Otto Kaiser (AUT)	Melitta Brunner Ludwig Wrede (AUT)
1929 Budapest, HUN	Lilly Scholz Otto Kaiser (AUT)	Melitta Brunner Ludwig Wrede (AUT)	Olga Orgonista Sandor Szalay (HUN)
1930 New York, USA	Andree Brunet Pierre Brunet (FRA)	Melitta Brunner Ludwig Wrede (AUT)	Beatrix Loughran Sherwin Badger (USA)
1931 Berlin, GER	Emilie Rotter Laszlo Szollas (HUN)	Olga Orgonista Sandor Szalay (HUN)	Idi Papez Karl Zwack (AUT)
1932 Montreal, CAN	Andree Brunet Pierre Brunet (FRA)	Emilie Rotter Laszlo Szollas (HUN)	Beatrix Loughran Sherwin Badger (USA)
1933 Stockholm, SWE	Emilie Rotter Laszlo Szollas (HUN)	Idi Papez Karl Zwack (AUT)	Randi Bakke C. Christensen (NOR)
1934 Helsinki, FIN	Emilie Rotter Laszlo Szollas (HUN)	Idi Papez Karl Zwack (AUT)	Maxi Herber Ernest Baier (GER)
1935 Budapest, HUN	Emilie Rotter Laszlo Szollas (HUN)	Ilse Pausin Erich Pausin (AUT)	Lucy Gallo Rezso Dillinger (HUN)
1936 Paris, FRA	Maxi Herber Ernst Baier (GER)	Ilse Pausin Erich Pausin (AUT)	Violet Cliff Leslie Cliff (GBR)
1937 London, GBR	Maxi Herber Ernst Baier (GER)	Ilse Pausin Erich Pausin (AUT)	Violet Cliff Leslie Cliff (GBR)
1938 Berlin, GER	Maxi Herber Ernst Baier (GER)	Ilse Pausin Erich Pausin (AUT)	Inge Koch Gunther Noack (GER)
1939 Budapest, HUN	Maxi Herber Ernst Baier (GER)	Ilse Pausin Erich Pausin (AUT)	Inge Koch Gunther Noack (GER)
1940-1946	No Championship		
1947 Stockholm, SWE	Micheline Lannoy Pierre Baugniet (BEL)	Karol Kennedy Peter Kennedy (USA)	Suzanne Diskeuv Edmond Verbustel (BEL)

~ SKATER'S EDGE SOURCEBOOK ~

PAIRS	GOLD	SILVER	BRONZE	PAIRS	GOLD	SILVER	BRONZE
1948 Davos, SUI	Micheline Lannoy Pierre Baugniet (BEL)	Andrea Kekesy Ede Kiraly (HUN)	Suzanne Morrow W. Diestelmeyer (CAN)	1962 Prague, CZE	Maria Jelinek Otto Jelinek (CAN)	Ludmila Belousova Oleg Protopopov (URS)	Margret Gobl Franz Ningel (FRG)
1949 Paris, FRA	Andrea Kekesy Ede Kiraly (HUN)	Karol Kennedy Peter Kennedy (USA)	Anne Davies Carleton Hoffner (USA)	1963 Cortina, ITA	Marika Kilius Hans Baumler (FRG)	Ludmila Belousova Oleg Protopopov (URS)	Tatiana Zhuk Alexandr Gavrilov (URS)
1950 London, GBR	Karol Kennedy Peter Kennedy (USA)	Jennifer Nicks John Nicks (GBR)	Marianne Nagy Laszlo Nagy (HUN)	1964 Dortmund, FRG	Marika Kilius Hans Baumler (FRG)	Ludmila Belousova Oleg Protopopov (URS)	Debbi Wilkes Guy Revell (CAN)
1951 Milan, ITA	Ria Falk Paul Falk (FRG)	Karol Kennedy Peter Kennedy (USA)	Jennifer Nicks John Nicks (GBR)	1965 Colo. Spgs., USA	Ludmila Belousova Oleg Protopopov (URS)	Vivian Joseph Ronald Joseph (USA)	Tatiana Zhuk Alexandr Gorelik (URS)
1952 Paris, FRA	Ria Falk Paul Falk (FRG)	Karol Kennedy Peter Kennedy (USA)	Jennifer Nicks John Nicks (GBR)	1966 Davos, SUI	Ludmila Belousova Oleg Protopopov (URS)	Tatiana Zhuk Alexandr Gorelik (URS)	Cynthia Kauffman Ronald Kauffman (USA)
1953 Davos, SUI	Jennifer Nicks John Nicks (GBR)	Frances Dafoe Norris Bowden (CAN)	Marianne Nagy Laszlo Nagy (HUN)	1967 Vienna, AUT	Ludmila Belousova Oleg Protopopov (URS)	Margot Glockshuber Wolfgang Danne (FRG)	Cynthia Kauffman Ronald Kauffman (USA)
1954 Oslo, NOR	Frances Dafoe Norris Bowden (CAN)	Silvia Grandjean Michel Grandjean (SUI)	Elisabeth Schwarz Kurt Oppelt (AUT)	1968 Geneva, SUI	Ludmila Belousova Oleg Protopopov (URS)	Tatiana Zhuk Alexandr Gorelik (URS)	Cynthia Kauffman Ronald Kauffman (USA)
1955 Vienna, AUT	Frances Dafoe Norris Bowden (CAN)	Elisabeth Schwarz Kurt Oppelt (AUT)	Marianne Nagy Laszlo Nagy (HUN)	1969 Colo. Spgs., CO	Irina Rodnina Alexsei Ulanov (URS)	Tamara Moskvina Alexsei Mishin (URS)	Ludmila Belousova Oleg Protopopov (URS)
1956 Garmisch, FRG	Elisabeth Schwarz Kurt Oppelt (AUT)	Frances Dafoe Norris Bowden (CAN)	Marika Kilius Franz Ningel (FRG)	1970 Ljubljana, YUG	Irina Rodnina Alexsei Ulanov (URS)	Ludmila Smirnova Andrei Suraikin (URS)	Heidemarie Steiner Heinz Walther (GDR)
1957 Colo. Spgs., CO	Barbara Wagner Robert Paul (CAN)	Marika Kilius Franz Ningel (FRG)	Maria Jelinek Otto Jelinek (CAN)	1971 Lyon, FRA	Irina Rodnina Alexsei Ulanov (URS)	Ludmila Smirnova Andrei Suraikin (URS)	JoJo Starbuck Kenneth Shelley (USA)
1958 Paris, FRA	Barbara Wagner Robert Paul (CAN)	Vera Suchankova Zdenek Dolezal (CZE)	Maria Jelinek Otto Jelinek (CAN)	1972 Calgary, CAN	Irina Rodnina Alexsei Ulanov (URS)	Ludmila Smirnova Andrei Suraikin (URS)	JoJo Starbuck Kenneth Shelley (USA)
1959 Colo. Spgs., CO	Barbara Wagner Robert Paul (CAN)	Marika Kilius Hans Baumler (FRG)	Nancy Ludington Ronald Ludington (USA)	1973 Bratislava, CZE	Irina Rodnina Alexandr Zaitsev (URS)	Ludmila Smirnova Alexsei Ulanov (URS)	Manuela Gross Uwe Kagelmann (GDR)
1960 Vancouver, CAN	Barbara Wagner Robert Paul (CAN)	Maria Jelinek Otto Jelinek (CAN)	Marika Kilius Hans Baumler (FRG)	1974 Munich, FRG	Irina Rodnina Alexandr Zaitsev (URS)	Ludmila Smirnova Alexsei Ulanov (URS)	Romy Kermer Rolf Osterreich (GDR)
1961	No Championship			1975 Colo. Spgs., CO	Irina Rodnina Alexandr Zaitsev (URS)	Romy Kermer Rolf Osterreich (GDR)	Manuela Gross Uwe Kagelmann (GDR)

CHAMPIONS

WORLDS

~ SKATER'S EDGE SOURCEBOOK ~

PAIRS	GOLD	SILVER	BRONZE
1976 Gothenberg, SWE	Irina Rodnina Alexandr Zaitsev (URS)	Romy Kermer Rolf Osterreich (GDR)	Irina Vorobieva Alexandr Vlasov (URS)
1977 Tokyo, JPN	Irina Rodnina Alexandr Zaitsev (URS)	Irina Vorobieva Alexandr Vlasov (URS)	Tai Babilonia Randy Gardner (USA)
1978 Ottawa, CAN	Irina Rodnina Alexandr Zaitsev (URS)	Manuela Mager Uwe Bewersdorff (URS)	Tai Babilonia Randy Gardner (USA)
1979 Vienna, AUT	Tai Babilonia Randy Gardner (USA)	Marina Cherkosova Sergei Shakhrai (URS)	Sabine Baess Tassilo Thierbach (GDR)
1980 Dortmund, FRG	Marina Cherkasova Sergei Shakhrai (URS)	Manuela Mager Uwe Bewersdorff (GDR)	Marina Pestova S. Leonovich (URS)
1981 Hartford, USA	Irina Vorobieva Igor Lisovsky (URS)	Sabine Baess Tassilo Thierbach (GDR)	Christina Riegel Andreas Nischwitz (FRG)
1982 Copenhagen, DEN	Sabine Baess Tassilo Thierbach (GDR)	Marina Pestova Stansilav Leonovich (URS)	Caitlin Carruthers Peter Carruthers (USA)
1983 Helsinki, FIN	Elena Valova Oleg Vasiliev (URS)	Sabine Baess Tassilo Thierbach (GDR)	Barbara Underhill Paul Martini (CAN)
1984 Ottawa, CAN	Barbara Underhill Paul Martini (CAN)	Elena Valova Oleg Vasiliev (URS)	Sabine Baess Tassilo Thierbach (GDR)
1985 Tokyo, JPN	Elena Valova Oleg Vasiliev (URS)	Larisa Selezneva Oleg Makarov (URS)	K. Matousek Lloyd Eisler (CAN)
1986 Geneva, SUI	Ekaterina Gordeeva Sergei Grinkov (URS)	Elena Valova Oleg Vasiliev (URS)	Cynthia Coull Mark Rowsom (CAN)
1987 Cincinnati, USA	Ekaterina Gordeeva Sergei Grinkov (URS)	Elena Valova Oleg Vasiliev (URS)	Jil Watson Peter Oppegard (USA)
1988 Budapest, HUN	Elena Valova Oleg Vasiliev (URS)	Ekaterina Gordeeva Sergei Grinkov (URS)	Larisa Selezneva Oleg Makarov (URS)
1989 Paris, FRA	Ekaterina Gordeeva Sergei Grinkov (URS)	Cindy Landry Lyndon Johnston (CAN)	Elena Bechke Denis Petrov (URS)
1990 Halifax, CAN	Ekaterina Gordeeva Sergei Grinkov (URS)	Isabelle Brasseur Lloyd Eisler (CAN)	N. Mishkutenok Artur Dmitriev (URS)
1991 Munich, GER	Natalia Mishkutenok Artur Dmitriev (URS)	Isbelle Brasseur Lloyd Eisler (CAN)	Natasha Kuchiki Todd Sand (USA)
1992 Oakland, USA	Natalia Mishkutenok Artur Dmitriev (URS)	Radka Kovarikova Rene Novotny (CIS)	Isbelle Brasseur Lloyd Eisler (CAN)
1993 Prague, CZE	Isbelle Brasseur Lloyd Eisler (CAN)	Mandy Wotzel Ingo Steuer (GER)	Evgenia Shishkova Vadim Naumov (RUS)
1994 Chiba, JPN	Evgenia Shishkova Vadim Naumov (RUS)	Isabelle Brasseur Lloyd Eisler (CAN)	Marina Eltsova Andrei Bushkov (RUS)

WORLD CHAMPIONSHIPS
ICE DANCING

	GOLD	SILVER	BRONZE
1952 Paris, FRA	Jean Westwood Lawrence Demmy (GBR)	Joan Dewhirst John Slater (GBR)	Carol Peters Daniel Ryan (USA)
1953 Davos, SUI	Jean Westwood Lawrence Demmy (GBR)	Joan Dewhirst John Slater (GBR)	Carol Peters Daniel Ryan (USA)
1954 Oslo, NOR	Jean Westwood Lawrence Demmy (GBR)	Nesta Davies Paul Thomas (GBR)	Carmel Bodel Edward Bodel (USA)
1955 Vienna, AUT	Jean Westwood Lawrence Demmy (GBR)	Pamala Weight Paul Thomas (GBR)	Barbara Radford R. Lockwood (GBR)
1956 Garmisch, FRG	Pamela Weight Paul Thomas (GBR)	June Markham Courtney Jones (GBR)	Barbara Thompson Gerard Rigby (GBR)
1957 Colo. Spgs., CO	June Markham Courtney Jones (GBR)	Geraldine Fenton William McLachlan (CAN)	Sharon McKenzie Bert Wright (USA)

~ SKATER'S EDGE SOURCEBOOK ~

DANCE	GOLD	SILVER	BRONZE	DANCE	GOLD	SILVER	BRONZE
1958 Paris, FRA	June Markham Courtney Jones (GBR)	Geraldine Fenton William McLachlan (CAN)	Andree Anderson Donald Jacoby (USA)	1973 Bratislava, CZE	Ludmila Pakhomova Aleksandr Gorshkov (URS)	Angelika Buck Erich Buck (FRG)	Hilary Green Glyn Watts (GBR)
1959 Colo. Spgs., CO	Doreen Denny Courtney Jones (GBR)	Andree Anderson Donald Jacoby (USA)	Geraldine Fenton W. McLachlan (CAN)	1974 Munich, FRG	Ludmila Pakhomova Aleksandr Gorshkov (URS)	Hilary Green Glyn Watts (GBR)	Natalia Linichuk G. Karponosov (URS)
1960 Vancouver, CAN	Doreen Denny Courtney Jones (GBR)	Virginia Thompson William McLachlan (CAN)	Christine Guhel Jean Paul Guhel (FRA)	1975 Colo. Spgs., CO	Irina Moiseeva Andrei Minehkov (URS)	Colleen O'Connor Jim Millns (USA)	Hilary Green Glyn Watts (GBR)
1961	No Competition						
1962 Prague, CZE	Eva Romanova Pavel Roman (CZE)	Christine Guhel Jean Paul Guhel (FRA)	Virginia Thompson W. McLachlan (CAN)	1976 Gothenberg, SWE	Ludmila Pakhomova Aleksandr Gorshkov (URS)	Irina Moiseeva Andrei Minenkov (URS)	Colleen O'Connor Jim Millns (USA)
1963 Cortina, ITA	Eva Romanova Pavel Roman (CZE)	Linda Shearman Michael Phillips (GBR)	Paulette Doan Kenneth Ormsby (CAN)	1977 Toyko, JPN	Irina Moiseeva Andrei Minenkov (URS)	Janet Thompson Warren Maxwell (GBR)	Natalia Linichuk G. Karponosov (URS)
1964 Dortmund, FRG	Eva Romanova Pavel Roman (CZE)	Paulette Doan Kenneth Ormsby (CAN)	Janet Sawbridge D. Hickinbottom (GBR)	1978 Ottawa, CAN	Natalia Linichuk Gennadi Karponosov (URS)	Irina Moiseeva Andrei Minekov (URS)	Krisztina Regoeczy Andras Sallay (HUN)
1965 Colo. Spgs., CO	Eva Romanova Pavel Roman (CZE)	Janet Sawbridge David Hickinbottom (GBR)	Lorna Dyer John Carrell (USA)	1979 Vienna, AUT	Natalia Linichuk Gennadi Karponosov (URS)	Krisztina Regoeczy Andras Sallay (HUN)	Irina Moiseeva Andrei Minenkov (URS)
1966 Davos, SUI	Diane Towler Bernard Ford (GBR)	Kristin Fortune Dennis Sveum (USA)	Lorna Dyer John Carrell (USA)	1980 Dortmund, FRG	Krisztina Regoeczy Andras Sallay (HUN)	Natalia Linichuk G. Karponosov (URS)	Irina Moiseeva Andrei Minenkov (URS)
1967 Vienna, AUT	Diane Towler Bernard Ford (GBR)	Lorna Dyer John Carrell (USA)	Yvonne Suddick Malcolm Cannon (GBR)	1981 Hartford, CT	Jayne Torvill Christopher Dean (GBR)	Irina Moiseeva Andrei Minenkov (URS)	N. Bestemianova Andrei Bukin (URS)
1968 Geneva, SUI	Diane Towler Bernard Ford (GBR)	Yvonne Suddick Malcolm Cannon (GBR)	Janet Sawbridge Jon Lane (GBR)	1982 Copenhagen, DEN	Jayne Torvill Christopher Dean (GBR)	N. Bestemianova Andrei Bukin (URS)	Irina Moiseeva Andrei Minenkov (URS)
1969 Colo. Spgs., CO	Diane Towler Bernard Ford (GBR)	L. Pakhomova A. Gorshkov (URS)	Judy Schwomeyer James Sladky (USA)	1983 Helsinki, FIN	Jayne Torvill Christopher Dean (GBR)	N. Bestimianova Andrei Bukin (URS)	Judy Blumberg Michael Seibert (USA)
1970 Ljubljana, YUG	Ludmila Pakhomova Aleksandr Gorshkov (URS)	Judy Schwomeyer James Sladky (USA)	Angelika Buck Erich Buck (FRG)	1984 Ottawa, CAN	Jayne Torvill Christopher Dean (GBR)	N. Bestimianova Andrei Bukin (URS)	Judy Blumberg Michael Seibert (USA)
1971 Lyon, FRA	Ludmila Pakhomova Aleksandr Gorshkov (URS)	Angelika Buck Erich Buck (FRG)	Judy Schwomeyer James Sladky (USA)	1985 Tokyo, JPN	Natalia Bestemianova Andrei Bukin (URS)	Marina Klimova S. Ponomarenko (URS)	Judy Blumberg Michael Seibert (USA)
1972	Ludmila Pakhomova Aleksandr Gorshkov (URS)	Angelika Buck Erich Buck (FRG)	Judy Schwomeyer James Sladky (USA)	1986 Geneva, SUI	Natalia Bestemianova Andrei Bukin (URS)	Marina Klimova S. Ponomarenko (URS)	Tracy Wilson Robert McCall (CAN)

CHAMPIONS

WORLDS

SKATER'S EDGE SOURCEBOOK

DANCE

	GOLD	SILVER	BRONZE
1987 Cincinnati, OH	Natalia Bestemianova Andrei Bukin (URS)	Marina Klimova S. Ponomarenko (URS)	Tracy Wilson Robert McCall (CAN)
1988 Budapest, HUN	Natalia Bestemianova Andrei Bukin (URS)	Marina Klimova S.Ponomarenko (URS)	Tracy Wilson Robert McCall (CAN)
1989 Paris, FRA	Marina Klimova Sergei Ponomarenko (URS)	Maia Usova Alexandr Zhulin (URS)	Isabelle Duchesnay Paul Duchesnay (FRA)
1990 Halifax, CAN	Marina Klimova Sergei Ponomarenko (URS)	Isabelle Duchesnay Paul Duchesnay (FRA)	Maia Usova Alexandr Zhulin (URS)
1991 Munich, GER	Isabelle Duchesnay Paul Duchesnay (FRA)	Marina Klimova S. Ponomarenko (URS)	Maia Usova Alexandr Zhulin (URS)
1992 Oakland, USA	Marina Klimova Sergei Ponomarenko (URS)	Maia Usova Alexandr Zhulin (URS)	Oksana Gritschuk Evgeni Platov (URS)
1993 Prague, CZE	Maia Usova Alexandr Zhulin (RUS)	Oksana Gritschuk Evgeny Platov (RUS)	Anjelika Krylova Vladimir Fedorov (RUS)
1994 Chiba, JPN	Oksana Gritschuk Evgeny Platov (RUS)	Sophie Moniotte Pascal Lavanchy (FRA)	Susanna Rahkamo Petri Kokko (FIN)

OLYMPIC WINTER GAMES
MEN'S SINGLES

	GOLD	SILVER	BRONZE
1908 London, GBR	Ulrich Salchow (SWE)	Richard Johansson (SWE)	Per Thoren (SWE)
1920 Antwerp, BEL	Gillis Grafstom (SWE)	Andreas Krogh (NOR)	Martin Stixrud (NOR)
1924 Chamonix, FRA	Gillis Grafstrom (SWE)	Willy Boeckl (AUT)	Georg Gautschi (SUI)
1928 St. Moritz, SUI	Gillis Grafstrom (SWE)	Willy Boeckl (AUT)	R. van Zeebroeck (BEL)
1932 Lake Placid, NY	Karl Schafer (AUT)	Gillis Grafstrom (SWE)	M. Wilson (CAN)
1936 Garmisch, GER	Karl Schafer (AUT)	Ernst Baier (GER)	Felix Kaspar (AUT)
1940-1944	No Olympic Games		

MEN

	GOLD	SILVER	BRONZE
1948 St. Moritz, SUI	Richard Button (USA)	Hans Gerschwiler (SUI)	Edi Rada (AUT)
1952 Oslo, NOR	Richard Button (USA)	Helmut Seibt (AUT)	James Grogan (USA)
1956 Cortina, ITA	Hayes Jenkins (USA)	Ronald Robertson (USA)	David Jenkins (USA)
1960 Squaw Valley, CA	David Jenkins (USA)	Karol Divin (CZE)	Donald Jackson (CAN)
1964 Innsbruck, AUT	M. Schnelldorfer (FRG)	Alain Calmat (FRA)	Scott Allen (USA)
1968 Grenoble, FRA	Wolfgang Schwarz (AUT)	Tim Wood (USA)	Patrick Pera (FRA)
1972 Sapporo, JPN	Ondrej Nepela (CZE)	S. Chetverukhin (URS)	Patrick Pera (FRA)
1976 Innsbruck, AUT	John Curry (GBR)	Vladimir Kovalev (URS)	Toller Cranston (CAN)
1980 Lake Placid, NY	Robin Cousins (GBR)	Jan Hoffman (GDR)	Charles Tickner (USA)
1984 Sarajevo, YUG	Scott Hamilton (USA)	Brian Orser (CAN)	Jozef Sabovtchik (CZE)
1988 Calgary, CAN	Brian Boitano (USA)	Brian Orser (CAN)	Viktor Petrenko (URS)
1992 Albertville, FRA	Viktor Petrenko (EUN)	Paul Wylie (USA)	Peter Barna (CZE)
1994 Lillehammer, NOR	Alexei Urmanov (RUS)	Elvis Stojko (CAN)	Philippe Candeloro (FRA)

OLYMPIC WINTER GAMES
LADIES' SINGLES

	GOLD	SILVER	BRONZE
1908 London, GBR	Madge Syers (GBR)	Elsa Rendschmidt (GER)	D. Greenhough (GBR)
1920 Antwerp, BEL	Magda Julin-Mauroy (SWE)	Svea Noren (SWE)	Theresa Weld (USA)
1924 Chamonix, FRA	Herma Plank-Szabo (AUT)	Beatrix Loughran (USA)	Ethel Muckelt (GBR)
1928 St. Moritz, SUI	Sonja Henie (NOR)	Fritzi Burger (AUT)	Beatrix Loughran (USA)
1932 Lake Placid, NY	Sonja Henie (NOR)	Fritzi Burger (AUT)	Maribel Vinson (USA)

~ SKATER'S EDGE SOURCEBOOK ~

LADIES	GOLD	SILVER	BRONZE
1936 Garmisch, GER	Sonja Henie (NOR)	Cecilia Colledge (GBR)	Vivi-Anne Hulten (SWE)
1940-1944	No Olympic Games		
1948 St. Moritz, SUI	Barbara Ann Scott (CAN)	Eva Pawlik (AUT)	Jeannette Altwegg (GBR)
1952 Oslo, NOR	Jeannette Altwegg (GBR)	Tenley Albright (USA)	Jacqueline du Bief (FRA)
1956 Cortina, ITA	Tenley Albright (USA)	Carol Heiss (USA)	Ingrid Wendl (AUT)
1960 Squaw Valley, CA	Carol Heiss (USA)	Sjoukje Dijkstra (HOL)	Barbara Roles (USA)
1964 Innsbruck, AUT	Sjoukje Dijkstra (HOL)	Regine Heitzer (AUT)	Petra Burka (CAN)
1968 Grenoble, FRA	Peggy Fleming (USA)	Gabriele Seyfert (GDR)	Hana Maskova (CZE)
1972 Sapporo, JPN	Beatrix Schuba (AUT)	Karen Magnussen (CAN)	Janet Lynn (USA)
1976 Innsbruck, AUT	Dorothy Hamill (USA)	Dianne de Leeuw (HOL)	Christine Errath (GDR)
1980 Lake Placid, NY	Anett Poetzsch (GDR)	Linda Fratianne (USA)	Dagmar Lurz (FRG)
1984 Sarajevo, YUG	Katarina Witt (GDR)	Rosalynn Summers (USA)	Kira Ivanova (URS)
1988 Calgary, CAN	Katarina Witt (GDR)	Elizabeth Manley (CAN)	Debi Thomas (USA)
1992 Albertville, FRA	Kristi Yamaguchi (USA)	Midori Ito (JPN)	Nancy Kerrigan (USA)
1994 Lillehammer, NOR	Oksana Baiul (UKR)	Nancy Kerrigan (USA)	Chen Lu (CHN)

OLYMPIC WINTER GAMES
PAIRS

	GOLD	SILVER	BRONZE
1908 London, GBR	Anna Hubler Heinrich Burger (GER)	Phyllis Johnson James Johnson (GBR)	Madge Syers Edgar Syers (GBR)
1920 Antwerp, BEL	Ludowika Jakobsson Walter Jakobsson (FIN)	Alexia Bryn Yngvar Bryn (NOR)	Phyllis Johnson Basil Williams (GBR)

1948 and 1952 Olympic Champion Richard Button

PAIRS	GOLD	SILVER	BRONZE
1924 Chamonix, FRA	Helene Engelmann Alfred Berger (AUT)	L. Jakobsson Walter Jakobsson (FIN)	Andree Brunet Pierre Brunet (FRA)
1928 St. Moritz, SUI	Andree Brunet Pierre Brunet (FRA)	Lilly Scholz Otto Kaiser (AUT)	Melitta Brunner Ludwig Wrede (AUT)
1932 Lake Placid, USA	Andree Brunet Pierre Brunet (FRA)	Beatrix Loughran Sherwin Badger (USA)	Emilie Rotter Laszlo Szolla (HUN)
1936 Garmisch, GER	Maxie Herber Ernst Baier (GER)	Ilse Pausin Erich Pausin (AUT)	Emilie Rotter Laszlo Szolla (HUN)
1940-1944	No Olympic Games		
1948 St. Moritz, SUI	Micheline Lannoy Pierre Baugniet (BEL)	Andrea Kekesy Ede Kiraly (HUN)	Suzanne Morrow W. Distelmeyer (CAN)
1952 Oslo, NOR	Ria Falk Paul Falk (FRG)	Karol Kennedy Peter Kennedy (USA)	Marianne Nagy Laszlo Nagy (HUN)
1956 Cortina, ITA	Elizabeth Schwarz Kurt Oppelt (AUT)	Frances Dafoe Norris Bowden (CAN)	Marianne Nagy Laszlo Nagy (HUN)
1960 Squaw Valley, CA	Barbara Wagner Robert Paul (CAN)	Marika Kilius Hans Baumler (FRG)	Nancy Ludington Ronald Ludington (USA)

PHOTO COURTESY OF RICHARD BUTTON

*1964 and 1968 Olympic Pairs Champions **Ludmila Belousova** and **Oleg Protopopov** performing the forward inside Life Spiral.*

PAIRS

Year/Location	GOLD	SILVER	BRONZE
1964 Innsbruck, AUT	Ludmila Belousova / Oleg Protopopov (URS)	Marika Kilius* / Hans Baumler* (CAN)	Debbi Wilkes / Guy Revell (USA)

*Proven after the games that they had signed a show contract prior to the games. Silver went to Revell and Wilkes. Bronze went to Ronald and Vivian Joseph, USA.

Year/Location	GOLD	SILVER	BRONZE
1968 Grenoble, FRA	Ludmila Protopopov / Oleg Protopopov (URS)	T. Joukchesternava / Alexandr Gorelik (URS)	M. Glockshuber / Wolfgang Danne (FRG)
1972 Sapporo, JPN	Irina Rodnina / Alexsei Ulanov (URS)	Ludmila Smirnova / Andrei Suraikin (URS)	Manuela Gross / Uwe Kagelmann (GDR)
1976 Innsbruck, AUT	Irina Rodnina / Aleksandr Zaitsev (URS)	Romy Kermer / Rolf Osterreich (GDR)	Manuela Gross / Uwe Kagelmann (GDR)
1980 Lake Placid, NY	Irina Rodnina / Aleksandr Zaitsev (URS)	Marina Cherkosova / Sergei Shakrai (URS)	Manuella Mager / Uwe Bewersdorff (GDR)
1984 Sarajevo, YUG	Elena Valova / Oleg Vassiliev (URS)	Caitlin Carruthers / Peter Carruthers (USA)	Larissa Selezneva / Oleg Makarov (URS)
1988 Calgary, CAN	Ekaterina Gordeeva / Sergei Grinkov (URS)	Elena Valova / Oleg Vasiliev (URS)	Jill Watson / Peter Oppegard (USA)
1992 Albertville, FRA	Natalia Mishkutenok / Artur Dmitriev (EUN)	Elena Bechke / Denis Petrov (EUN)	Isabelle Brasseur / Lloyd Eisler (CAN)
1994 Lillehammer, NOR	Ekaterina Gordeeva / Sergei Grinkov (RUS)	N. Mishkutenok / Artur Dmitriev (RUS)	Isabelle Brasseur / Lloyd Eisler (CAN)

OLYMPIC WINTER GAMES

ICE DANCE

Year/Location	GOLD	SILVER	BRONZE
1976 Innsbruck, AUT	Ludmila Pakhomova / Aleksandr Gorshkov (URS)	Irina Moiseeva / Andrei Minenkov (URS)	Colleen O'Connor / Jim Millns (USA)
1980 Lake Placid, USA	Natalia Lininchuk / Gennadi Karponosov (URS)	Krisztina Regoczy / Andras Sallay (HUN)	Irina Moiseeva / Andrei Minenkov (URS)
1984 Sarajevo, YUG	Jayne Torvill / Christopher Dean (GBR)	N. Bestemianova / Andrei Bukin (URS)	Marina Klimova / S. Ponomarenko (URS)
1988 Calgary, CAN	Natalia Bestemianova / Andrei Bukin (URS)	Marina Klimova / S. Ponomarenko (URS)	Tracy Wilson / Robert McCall (CAN)
1992 Albertville, FRA	Marina Klimova / Sergei Ponomarenko (EUN)	Isabelle Duchesnay / Paul Duchesnay (FRA)	Maia Usova / Alexandr Zhulin (EUN)
1994 Lillehammer, NOR	Oksana Gritschuk / Evgeni Platov (RUS)	Maia Usova / Alexandr Zhulin (RUS)	Jayne Torvill / Christopher Dean (GRB)

Grateful appreciation goes to the United States Figure Skating Association (USFSA) for compiling the competition results used in this chapter, and for granting us permission to use the information.

PHOTO COURTESY OF THE PROTOPOPOVS

Companies and Organizations

Following are detailed listings of the many companies and individuals who do business related to ice skating. They are listed here in alphabetical order. In the *Companies by Categories* section, the companies are sorted by the types of services they provide, with shorter listings that include names and phone numbers.

A.J. Nichols
Contact: A.J. Nichols, Artist
1635 North Belmont Street
Manchester, NH 03104-2720
(603) 669-6243
A practicing artist and high school art instructor for 20 years. A.J. Nichols has created a whimsical (limited first edition) print: *From Dreams Come Champions* (actual size 14 x 18 inches). Ready for framing - numbered and signed (autographed if requested).

ABC Sports
47 West 66th Street, 13th Floor
New York, NY 10023
(212) 456-7777

Adult Skaters Forum
Contact: Joe Kaplenk
173 Norman Way
Boilingbrook, IL 60440
(708) 739-0992
Serves as an advocacy group for adult skaters, promotes and monitors the visibility and opportunities of adult skaters in figures, freestyle, dance, and pairs ice skating. Additional contact: Sue Chapman, (219) 787-8911.

Akst & Akst
Contact: George Akst, Partner
40 West 57th Street, 33rd Floor
New York, NY 10019
(212) 581-9010
FAX: (212) 765-6370
Founded: 1977. U.S. Immigration: temporary and permanent work; VISAS (green cards) for professional skaters and coaches; filings in all 50 states and at all American consulates.

Alleisure Corporation
Contact: Stuart Bernstein, President
6 St. Lawrence Way
Marlboro, NJ 07746
(908) 972-1235; FAX: (908) 972-1262
Founded: 1982. Soffadias rental skates. Rental figure and hockey skates in pvc; full leather lining injected into pvc. MK Rinkmaster blades.

Allied Specialty Insurance
Contact: Dean Smith, Vice President
10451 Gulf Boulevard
Treasure Island, FL 33706
(813) 237-3355
FAX: (813) 367-1407
Founded: 1983. Customized policies including coverage for ice hockey leagues, tournaments, participants' liability, and ice skating competitions. Competitive rates; 24-hr. claims service.

American Locker Security Systems
Contact: David L. Henderson, Vice President/General Manager
15 West Second Street, P.O. Box 489
Jamestown, NY 14702-0489
(800) 828-9118; FAX: (716) 664-2949
Founded: 1931. Security lockers in a wide variety of styles including: seven door configurations, sixteen color options and select-o-matic coin/key locks. Supported by a national service center.

American Skating World
Contact: H. Kermit Jackson
1816 Brownsville Road
Pittsburgh, PA 15210-3908
(412) 885-7600; FAX: (412) 885-7617
Founded: 1981. *American Skating World* is a monthly tabloid-format newspaper that focuses on recreational, eligible, and professional figure skating in the U.S. and abroad. Includes competition results, reviews, profiles, industry and club news, lively debate, and more.

American Video Productions
Contact: Jim Hinte, President
633 North Mildred, Suite A
Tacoma, WA 98406
(206) 564-4454; FAX: (206) 564-8731
Founded: 1984. American Video Productions has captured thousands of skaters in competition over the past 11 years, including the West Coast Championships. In addition to recording the skaters individually on ice, we include a montage of the event set to music. A great personal touch.

Anderson Ice Rinks, Inc.
Contact: Joel Anderson, President
1900 Oakcrest Avenue
Suite #3
Roseville, MN 55113
(612) 633-7363; FAX: (612) 633-7472
Founded: 1992. Anderson Ice Rinks assembles and installs ice rink refrigeration systems. We can do complete system design and installation, and offer complete after-installation service. We also sell all ice rink-associated supplies.

Annie's Edges
Contact: Anne E. Schelter, Proprietor
Box 18
Freelton, Ontario, L0R 1K0 Canada
(905) 659-7402
Founded: 1988. *Annie's Edges* is the name of a stroking class skated on a series of simple ice patterns. Each pattern is named for its rhythm, which is supplied by an audio cassette of percussion instruments. There are variations of edges and turns for each pattern, which are laid out in a logical progression from simple to difficult making *Annie's Edges* suitable for skaters young and old from beginner to advanced.

Arena Contractors & Equipment, Inc.
Contact: Scott Herrick, Marketing Manager
5118 130th Street North
White Bear Lake, MN 55110
(612) 653-4444; FAX: (612) 653-4436
Founded: 1993. We provide flooring, refrigeration parts, goal frame packages, and accessories for ice rinks. We also manufacture top-of-the-line dasher systems. 1-800-328-6808.

Artistry In Motion
Contact: Paula Wagener, Owner
191 Preston Place
Dallas, GA 30132
(404) 443-0872; FAX: (404) 445-1156
Founded: 1993. Workshops cover on-ice choreography and style class, and off-ice training program (ballet, jazz, stretching, conditioning). Will travel to rinks to set up and implement programs. Also freelance choreography and workshops.

ASCAP
Contact: Patrick Collins, Director of General Licensing
One Lincoln Plaza
New York, NY 10023
(212) 621-6400
FAX: (212) 873-3133
Founded: 1914. ASCAP (American Society of Composers, Authors & Publishers) is the oldest and foremost music-performance rights licensing association, offering easy legal access to the world's greatest repertoire of copyrighted music of every variety.

Ashworth Associates
Contact: Douglas Ashworth, President
753 East Washington Street
North Attleboro, MA 02760
(508) 695-1900
FAX: (508) 695-0377
Founded: 1965. Emblematic Jewelry, Club and competition pins, competition medals, specialty items depicting club or team logos.

Axel & Lutz Outfitters
Contact: Linda Khezami, Owner
P.O. Box 14562
Chicago, IL 60614-0562
Founded: 1993. Axel & Lutz Skating Outfitters has created a line of apparel designed especially for figure skaters, with heavyweight construction and an innovative style with a clean line. Free color brochure available. Dealer inquiries are welcome.

B & G Skate Supply
Contact: Barbara Johnson, Owner
1341 W. Holt Blvd.
Ontario, CA 91762
(909) 460-6606
FAX: (909) 460-6605
Founded: 1992. Boots: SP-Teri, Harlick, Riedell, Don Jackson. Blades: MK, Wilson. Videos, books, music, clothes.

B.K. Mechanicals, Inc.
Contact: John Krupinski, General Manager
24 Hagerty Blvd., Suite 13
Westchester, PA 19382
(610) 692-7965
FAX: (610) 692-5552
Founded: 1983. Design and installation of rink floors, refrigeration, dehumidifiers, and dasher boards. Rental equipment service. (Computer system for demand loads). Retrofitting existing facility.

Bay State Ice Skating School
Contact: Carol Butterworth, VP/Treasurer
395 Totten Pond Road #203
Waltham, MA 02154
(617) 290-0556
FAX: (617) 890-1799
Founded: 1974. Ice skating lessons to children and adults at seventeen greater-Boston rinks. Beginner, intermediate and advanced skills are taught by professional instructors to students wearing figure or hockey skates. Weekday, weekend and evening classes available.

Beads, Etc.
Contact: Gerrie Ball, Owner
310 Juniper Street
Brea, CA 92621
(714) 529-1474
Founded: 1976. Austrian crystal: margaritas, lochrosens, tear-drops, rhinestone chain etc. Sequins: regular, prism and zodiac. Also bugle beads, silver-lined rocailles and pearls. Visa/MC.

Becker Arena Products
Contact: Jim Becker
5448 Cottonwood Lane SE
Prior Lake, MN 55372
(612) 440-8655; 800-234-5522
FAX: (612) 440-8656
Supplier of the Olympia Ice Resurfacer, hockey board systems and hardware, ice maintainence and marking supplies, protective flooring, rental skates and skate sharpeners, goals, nets, padding and more.

Bezic, Sandra
c/o IMG Canada
One St. Clair Avenue East, #700
Toronto, Ontario, M4T 2V7 Canada
(416) 960-5312
FAX: (416) 960-0564
High level choreographer and consultant for top skaters.

Birch Hill Designs/ Kai-Lei On Ice
Contact: Karen Begins, Owner
RD 3, Box 3365
Vergennes, VT 05491
(802) 475-2327
FAX: (802) 475-2320
Founded: 1981. Practice dresses, skirt and leg sets, competition dresses, warm-up jackets, boot covers and scrunchies to match all clothing; Danskin tights.

Black (Dave) Photography
Contact: Dave Black, Photographer
2 Red Rock Avenue
Colorado Springs, CO 80904
(719) 636-3510
Photographs National Championships and Olympic Games. Also feature work for *Sports Illustrated* and *Newsweek*.

Blade and Roller Fashions
Contact: Stephen Kanter, C.E.O
99 Moody Street
Waltham, MA 02154
(617) 899-2830
Founded: 1975. Blade and Roller Fashions is a designer and manufacturer of skating apparel. We offer ready-made competition, practice, and team outfits, and can also custom design or manufacture outfits for you. Manufacturer and distributor of SK-UNKR skating skirts.

Blades on Ice
Contact: Gerri Walbert, Editor
7040 North Mona Lisa Road
Tucson, AZ 85741-2633
(602) 575-1747; FAX: (602) 575-1484
Founded: 1990. Bi-monthly color news

magazine with full-page glossy photos, reports on national and international skating events and competitions, profiles of skaters, some historical articles, plus news, tours, events, etc.

Boitano (Brian) Enterprises
Contact: Linda Leaver, General Manager
101 First Street, Suite 370
Los Altos, CA 94024 USA
(415) 948-2478
Please contact regarding services of Brian Boitano.

Bonestroo, Rosene, Anderlik & Associates
Contact: Dave Loskota, Associate Principal
2335 West Highway 36
St. Paul, MN 55113
(612) 636-4600
FAX: (612) 636-1311
Founded: 1956. 150-member consulting firm of architects and engineers who plan, design, and oversee the construction of ice arenas, including refrigeration systems and ice floors. Past projects include new arenas and renovation of existing arenas or equipment in 16 states from coast to coast; firm specializes in community-sized arenas. Member of ISIA; MN and WI Arena Managers Associations. One phone consultation without charge.

Boston Hockey Company
161 Portland Avenue
Dover, NH 03820
(603) 742-4333
FAX: (603) 742-9311
A catalogue company which will special-order figure skating boots and blades. Affiliated with Philbrick Sports. 1-800-FACE OFF.

Boston Skater
Contact: Ann McKenna
1240 Soldiers Field Road
Brighton, MA 02135
(617) 789-3650
Located in the same building as the Skating Club of Boston Ice Rink. Full line of skating apparel for women: sweaters, dresses, competition dresses, gift items.

Bramwell (Patricia) Sports Psychology
Contact: Patricia Bramwell, Counselor
136 138th Street
Belle Harbor, NY 11694
(718) 474-6850
Founded: 1986. Performance enhancement counseling. In her practice of sports pyschology, Patricia Bramwell helps skaters, coaches, and parents make decisions, perform the way they want to perform, and fully use practice time.

Bryan Sports Events
Contact: Joan Burns, Skating Desk
400 South El Camino Real #1550
San Mateo, CA 94402
(415) 579-0455; FAX: (415) 579-0811
Founded: 1949.

BSH Video
Contact: Barry 'Hoagie' Hogenauer
318 Old Evarts Lane
Mystic, CT 06355
(610) 399-0578
FAX: (203) 536-3221
Founded: 1989. Freelance camera (video) and video crews; Northeast U.S.

BEFORE YOUR SKATER'S SKILL IS SHOWN ON THE ICE, START BELOW THE SURFACE — WITH THE SKILL OF ANDERSON ICE RINKS.

Ice rink refrigeration systems that run as smoothly as the surface that carries your athletes...

FOR YOUR ICE RINK, ANDERSON ICE RINKS.
(612) 633-7363
FAX (612) 633-7472

ANDERSON ICE RINKS, INC.

Buck's Skater's Blade Collectibles
Contact: Joe Mendiola, Owner
774 Anderson Avenue
Akron, OH 44306
(216) 724-8972
Founded: 1992. Serves the skating world's memorabilia needs through our bi-monthly illustrated catalog. Features trading cards, books, magazines, show programs, competition programs, posters, pins and other memorabilia dating from the 1940s to present. Always willing to buy or trade for desired items. Send list of items you are offering for more information. We help make your cherished skating memories come alive.

Burley's Rink Supply, Inc.
Contact: John Burley, V.P. Sales
    Engineering
#115 School Street, P.O. Box 250
Salix, PA 15952-0250
(814) 487-7666
FAX: (814) 487-5566
Founded: 1983. Designer, manufacturer/distributor and installer of Turn-Key ice rink systems. Includes state-of-the-art rink piping systems, rebate awarded refrigeration packages, dehumidification, steel-framed ice rink and 'new' steel framed Dek Hockey dasher boards. Also ice edgers, hockey frames and many miscellaneous rink-related items to run and maintain your rink.

Butt (Ingrid) Photography
Contact: Ingrid Butt, Photographer
c/o *Blades on Ice*
7040 North Mona Lisa Road
Tucson, AZ 85741-2633
Freelance photographer for *Blades on Ice* and other skating publications. No sales to general public.

Cag One Skate Sharpeners, Inc.
Contact: Alvar Ohlsson, President/
    Owner
1 Hubbard Drive
White Plains, NY 10605
(914) 949-3120
FAX: (914) 949-3132
Founded: 1989. Robotic skatesharpeners generating consistent high-quality sharpening and profiling/rockering. Cuts costs, no labor, ideal for hockey stores and pro shops at rinks.

Can Alpine Agencies, Ltd.
Contact: Hellmut May, President
1314 S.W. Marine Drive
Vancouver, B.C., V6P 5Z6 Canada
(604) 266-4490
FAX: (604) 266-5470
Founded: 1969. Distributor for WIFA, high quality skating boots made in Austria and used by world champions: Kurt Browning, Torvill & Dean, Usova & Zhulin, Klimova & Ponomarenko, Mishkuteniok & Dmitriev, etc. Complete range from beginner to champion.

Canada West Skating International, Ltd.
Contact: Jan Glerup, President
6613 Norcross Road, R.R. # 4
Duncan, B.C., V9L 3W8 Canada
(604) 748-6619
FAX: (604) 748-1000
Founded: 1990. On- and off-ice Pro-Motion jumping harness. Completely portable, sold world-wide. Demonstration video available on request.

Canadian Figure Skating Association (CFSA)
Contact: David M. Dore, General
    Director
1600 James Naismith Drive, Suite 403
Gloucester, Ontario, K1B 5N4 Canada
(613) 748-5635
FAX: (613) 748-5718
The governing body of figure skating for Canada (CAN), with member clubs, skaters and pros. Offers extensive training and certification program for coaches. Figure skating member of the International Skating Union representing Canada.

Candid Productions, Inc.
Contact: Dick Button, President
250 West 57th Street, #1818
New York, NY 10107
(212) 581-9450
FAX: (212) 581-9373
Events: World Professional Figure Skating Championships (since 1980); Challenge of Champions (since 1985); The Superstars (since 1973); HBO specials and various network TV specials.

CanStar Sports
Contact: Cliff Penke, U.S. Sales Manager
50 Jonergin Drive
Swanton, VT 05488
(802) 868-2711
FAX: (802) 868-4713
Bauer and Cooper ice skates and equipment: Mega, Daoust, and Bauer in-lines. Licensed apparel for International Hockey League, Roller Hockey International. In-line skating accessories and protective equipment.

Capezio/Ballet Makers, Inc.
One Campus Road
Totowa, NJ 07512
(201) 595-9000
FAX: (201) 595-9120
Founded: 1887. Capezio dance wear. Consumer Information Hotline 1-800-234-4858.

Cartan Tours, Inc.
Contact: Don Williams, Vice President
1344 Parkview Avenue, Suite 210
Manhattan Beach, CA 90266
(800) 874-1996; (310) 546-9662
FAX: (310) 546-8433
Founded: 1899. Travel packages: 1995 World Figure Skating Championships (hotel, airfare, Gold category tickets, USFSA skater host, sightseeing); Olympic Games travel programs.

Cartier Insurance Agency
Contact: Rob Pavlatos, Hockey Insurance
    Specialist
2701 W. Superior Street
Duluth, MN 55806
(800) 756-3346; (218) 727-5992
FAX: (218) 727-8501
Founded: 1978. Writes an innovative Ice Arena Insurance package, as well as coverage for hockey leagues, teams, tournaments, and schools.

CBS Sports
51 West 52nd Street, 25th Floor
New York, NY 10019
(212) 975-4321
FAX: (212) 975-4074

Chelsea Piers Sports & Entertainment Complex
Pier 62, Chelsea Piers
New York, NY 10011
(212) 336-6666
Owners of the new Sky Rink at Chelsea Piers (opening summer '95). The new Sky Rink will have two Olympic-sized rinks, plus seating for 1,600 spectators and facilities to televise events. The twin

rinks will be part of the Chelsea Piers Project, a massive sports and entertainment complex on Manhattan's Hudson River waterfront.

Cimco Refrigeration
Contact: Steven McLeod, President
65 Villiers Street
Toronto, Ontario, M5A 3S1 Canada
(416) 465-7581
FAX: (416) 465-7530
Founded: 1913. Cimco designs, engineers, manufactures, installs, and services ice rink systems. Over 4,000 installations!

Classic Cassettes
Contact: Bob Lambert, President
4720 West Jennifer, Suite 107
Fresno, CA 93722
(800) 678-1127
FAX: (209) 276-8632
Founded: 1988. Classic Cassettes manufactures blank audio and blank video cassettes in bulk. We use top of the line, professional tape to ensure premium sound quality. As short as five minutes, as long as five hours.

Cleveland Coaches Council
Contact: Barbara Fitzgerald Mertik, President
P.O. Box 34173
Parma, OH 44134
(216) 546-9152
Founded: 1993. Professional coaches organization for communication and education in Cleveland area.

Club Skate
Contact: Sharene Eble, Owner
4967 Newport Avenue
Newport Mall, #10
San Diego, CA 92107
(619) 965-7447; (800) CLUB SK8
FAX: (619) 589-4076
Founded: 1993. We are a skate shop specializing in top-quality products at discount prices. We sell boots, blades, dresses, scribes, bags, jewelry, books, videos, sweatshirts and T-shirts. Call for a free catalog.

Coastal A.V., Inc.
Contact: Kent Sponseller, President
700 Washington Street, Suite 2
New Castle, DE 19720
(302) 322-7775
FAX: (302) 322-7793
Founded: 1993. Coastal A.V. Inc. is a full service audio and video company. We specialize in the design, sales, installation and service of complete audio and video systems. We also carry a full line of peripheral equipment for old and new systems.

Creative Pins by Lynne
Swarovski Crystal Pins

Coach $9.95
The Blade $34.95
All Others $19.95
($1.95 S & H)

Call or Write:

Lynne Voepel Gaudette
6 Country Drive
Greenville, RI 02828
401-949-3665

Allow 3-4 Weeks
Custom Available
Send for Free Brochure

➤ Sharpens perfectly every time - AUTOMATICALLY!
➤ Computerized grinding machine memorizes different players blade profiles
➤ Exhaust system included

**GREAT REVENUE SOURCE FOR STORES & ARENAS
EXCELLENT FOR PLAYER & TEAM USE
EASILY TRANSPORTABLE
LIGHTWEIGHT & COMPACT**

(weighs only 25 kilos /55 lbs)

*REGULAR SHARPENING CARTRIDGE INCLUDED

**RETAILER INQUIRIES
ENCOURAGED!**

FOR FURTHER INFORMATION:
CAG ONE

Canada: CAG ONE SKATE SHARPENER INC.
2266 Kingston Rd., Scarborough, ON M1N 1T9
Tel: (416) 266-6263 Fax: (416) 266-3009

USA: CAG ONE SKATE SHARPENER INC.
1 Hubbard Dr., White Plains N.Y. 10605
Tel: (914) 949-3120 Fax: (914) 949-3132

Coffey & Associates
Contact: Michelle Coffey, Videographer
160 S.W. Meadow Drive
Beaverton, OR 97006
(503) 644-0761
FAX: (503) 644-1423
Founded: 1982. Videotape ice-skating competitions in Oregon, Idaho and Washington states. Industrial video, theatre productions.

Colonial Travel
Contact: Maria Scerrato, President
784 Farmington Avenue
Farmington, CT 06032
(203) 677-0875; FAX: (203) 678-9716
Founded: 1978. Deluxe travel packages for skating events at affordable prices.

Competitor's Closet
Contact: Angela Fusco, Owner
2362 W. Shore Road
Warwick, RI 02886
(401) 737-7447
Founded: 1994. Specializing in skating apparel, accessories, and gift items. Also available for mail order is a complete line of beautiful skating T-shirts and sweatshirts with four different skating themes to choose from: freestyle girl, triple-axel boy, pairs and ice dancers. Manufacturer of silk-screened T-shirts and sweats with skaters on them.

Cooke's Pro Skate Shop
Contact: Scott Cooke, President/Owner
250 Middlesex Avenue
Wilmington, MA 01887
(508) 657-4087; FAX: (508) 988-0000
Founded: 1960. We deal with maintenance, marketing, and manufacturing of top quality figure skating boots and hockey equipment.

Cosmos Software
Contact: Gary Garbin, Director, Applications Development
29735 Nova Woods Drive
Farmington Hills, MI 48331-1996
(810) 661-5881
Founded: 1992. Existing or custom unique software for the P.C. (business or personal). Current offerings include the 'when' scheduling system, 'skaters' and 'teams.' Personal assistance and lifetime support included with each program. Easy-to-use, comprehensive, time-saving and 30-day free trial.

Cottam, Kevin
c/o King Arthur Productions, Inc.
P.O. Box 93508, Nelson Park
Vancouver, British Columbia
V6E 4L7 Canada
(604) 592-6389
Founder and Artistic Director of the National Ice Theatre of Canada. Choreographs ice theatre productions and does high level choreography for individual skaters. Also directs choreography and drama for TV and film.

Cousins, Robin
Contact: Robin Cousins, Choreographer
c/o Lee Mimms, Mimms & Associates
2644 East Chevy Chase Drive
Glendale, CA 91206
(818) 246-5601
FAX: (818) 246-5605
High level choreography and consulting.

Covermaster
Contact: Bob Curry, President
100 Westmore Drive, Unit 11-D
Rexdale, Ontario, M9V 5C3 Canada
(800) 387-5808; (416) 745-1811
FAX: (416) 742-6837
Founded: 1969. Homasote ice deck panels 4 ft. x 8 ft. x 1 in. or 1 1/2 in. thickness. The panels convert ice surfaces into multi-purpose surfaces for holding alternate events, such as trade shows, concerts, conventions, or other sporting events.

Cranston, Toller
Contact: Paul LaPointe
Thompson and LaPointe
105 Thursfield Crescent
Toronto, Ontario, M4G 2N4 Canada
(416) 467-9864
FAX: (416) 467-0256
High-level choreography and consulting.

Creations By Anne-Marie
Contact: Anne-Marie Gamache, Owner
P.O. Box 1473
Manchester, NH 03105-1473
(603) 645-1052
Founded: 1993. Competition costumes for men, women, pair skaters and ice dancers. Exclusive, original designs offered through catalog. Clients can also create with exclusive 'Design your own' program. Costumes made to measure, individually sized and proportioned to client. Outfitters for teams and shows.

Creative Pack Works
Contact: Patty Martin, President
P.O. Box 217
Salinas, CA 93902
(408) 753-6995
Founded: 1985. Custom ice-skating equipment bags designed by a skater in a multitude of color choices, with exclusive embroidered skater designs and monograming. Skate bags, garment bags, back packs, tote bags, scribe cases, towels and sweatshirts. Products feature heavy-duty zippers, adjustable shoulder straps, foam padding and corduroy lining. Some styles with dividers to form separate skate compartments.

Creative Pins By Lynne
Contact: Lynne Voepel-Gaudette, President
6 Country Drive
Greenville, RI 02828
(401) 949-3665
FAX: (401) 726-9688
Founded: 1993. A manufacturer of Swarovski Crystal custom-designed pins. Hand-crafted logos, custom names, and symbols (i.e. skating figures, 'skating mom') are available.

Crown Trophy
Contact: E. Weisenfeld, Ad Director
One Odell Plaza
Yonkers, NY 10701
(914) 963-0005
FAX: (914) 963-0181
Crown Trophy is a manufacturer of quality skating awards including trophies, plaques, and medallions. Low prices, rush delivery, free engraving and free shipping for trophies. Call for a free catalog 1-800-227-1557.

Crystalplex, Division of Laird
Contact: Matt Broughton, Sales Manager
7100 Torbram Road
Mississauga, Ontario, L5T 4B5 Canada
(905) 673-8072; (800) 665-7494
FAX: (905) 673-2696
Dasher-board systems, dasher boards, components, gates and hardware, arena accessories, sports surfaces, facility products. 4,000 ProLine demountable system; 3,000 aluminum prefabricated system; 2,500 steel prefabricated; 2,000 steel permanent system; 1,000 do-it-yourself system.

Cutting Edge Sports Sciences
Contact: Dyke Naughton, Head Coach
189 Old Loudon Road
Latham, NY 12110
(518) 785-8096
Founded: 1991. Speed, strength and facility coach. Explosive speed and power developers.

D & F Group
Contact: Stephan Disson, President
5301 Wisconsin Avenue, NW
Suite 325
Washington, DC 20015
(202) 364-8500
FAX: (202) 364-8500
Founded: 1989. A corporate sponsorship agency advising companies with respect to their event marketing activities. Introduced many clients to sponsorship opportunities in figure skating.

D's Fashion Accents, Inc.
Contact: Deborah Farris, President/ Owner
8420 Ulmerton Road #400
Largo, FL 34641
(800) 821-1603; (813) 532-6855
Founded: 1989. Retail/wholesale supplier of sequin appliques, rhinestones, fabric, any type of costume trimmings for the skater's outfit. Custom dresses made from mail-in measurements (in conjunction with local seamstresses). Also, custom-designed skating-jewelry line available in rhinestones, gold-plated, 14kt gold or sterling silver.

Damschroder Skate Sales
Contact: Jerry Damschroder, Owner-President
13227 Saticoy Street
North Hollywood, CA 91605
(818) 982-9090
FAX: (818) 982-9355
Distributor only; no retail boots, blades, dresses or accessories.

Dante Cozzi Sports
Contact: Dante Cozzi, President
2600 Newbridge Road
Bellmore, NY 11710
(516) 783-0215
FAX: (516) 783-2964
Founded: 1975. Specializing in: figure skating boots, blades, sharpenings, and hockey equipment, sharpening and repair.

Dectron, Inc.
Contact: Eglal Homsy, Marketing Supervisor
P.O. Box 2076
South Burlington, VT 05407-9988
(802) 862-8342
FAX: (514) 334-9184
Founded: 1977. Dectron is the manufacturer of the DRY-O-TRON energy recycling mechanical dehumidification systems. Dectron produces a wide range of products for commercial and industrial applications such as ice rinks, curling rinks, indoor swimming pools, factories, warehouses, hospitals, water treatment plants, supermarkets and any application where humidity control is critical.

Del Arbour Designs
Contact: Del Arbour, Founder
20 Commerce Park Road
Milford, CT 06460
(203) 882-8501
FAX: (203) 882-8503
Distinctive skatewear from beginner to

Coastal A•V Inc.
when sight and sound are important

700 Washington Street,
Suite #2
New Castle, DE 19720

302-322-7775

Corporate

System Design

Upgrades

Sales & Service

Free Consultation

Not Local?
Call 1-800-427-2029

• **Your Audio-Visual Specialists** •

Olympic. Del Arbour Designs produces high style, top quality, long lasting skatewear for practice, competitions, tests and shows. Original design custom skatewear by appointment in our Milford, CT showroom or via FAX. Complete catalog of ready-to-wear skatewear, outerwear and accessories for men, women and children.

Devon Management Group, Inc.
Contact: Chip Connell, President
P.O. Box 182
Little Silver, NJ 07739
(908) 530-2677
FAX: (908) 530-2680
Founded: 1989. The Devon Management Group, Inc. provides management consulting services to the figure-skating community. Expertise encompasses strategic planning, feasibility studies, market analysis, membership building and organizational change management. Working with client boards, trustees, patrons, and senior management, we are able to implement our recommendations efficiently and effectively.

Diamond Connection
Contact: Steven C. Graus, President
6740 E. 10 Mile Road
Center Line, MI 48015
(810) 759-2520
FAX: (810) 759-5850
Founded: 1985. The Diamond Connection is a full-service collectibles business. We carry all major sports collectibles including hockey, baseball, football, and basketball figurines. Ice skating figurines include Kristi Yamaguchi. Autographs also available.

Dorothy Hamill Entertainment
Contact: Julie Patterson, Director of Skating
15021 74th Street
Scottsdale, AZ 85260
(602) 996-1976
FAX: (602) 596-7906
Founded: 1993. Dorothy Hamill's Ice Capades with live 70-city tour. Also, catalogue/mail order, skating apparel and Ice Capades collectible merchandise. Director of Merchandise: Ken Beigel. For audition information, please write the Ice Capades at above address.

Dreams on Ice
Contact: Sandy Mulhern
P.O. Box 3421
Amerillo, TX 79116
(806) 352-7877
Skating clothing and apparel: Danskin and Mondor; custom crystal and silver jewelry.

Dupliskate Jonah Ltd.
Contact: John P. Lanfer, President
1610 De Beauharnois
Montreal, Quebec, H4N 1J5 Canada
(514) 382-1140
FAX: (514) 382-8249
Founded: 1978. Manufacturer and distributor of Dupliskate automatic and manual skate-sharpening machines and Dupliskate accessories.

Duxbury Travel Service, Inc.
Contact: Hal Gates, Vice President
P.O. Box 3, Snug Harbor
Duxbury, MA 02331
(617) 934-5633
FAX: (617) 934-5739
Founded: 1957. Travel to sporting events including Olympics and Worlds. Special interest tours. Worldwide golf arrangements and private tours for organizations.

Eastern Ice Sports
Contact: Russ Depack, Manager
250 Hobart Avenue
Summit, NJ 07901
(908) 277-6688
FAX: (908) 277-3957
Founded: 1980. Boots: SP-Teri, CCM, Jackson, Harlick, Riedell. Blades: MK, Wilson. Hockey gear: Cooper, Douglas, Easton. Clothing.

Edge Specialties, Inc.
Contact: Jeff Haiskanen, Sales Manager
P.O. Box 575
Alexandria, MN 56308
(800) 827-3343
FAX: (612) 762-5213
Manufacturer of the Pro-Filer, a hand-held skate-sharpener.

Eight-Mate Skating Products Co.
Contact: Nicolas Perna, President
10213 Bens Way
Manassas, VA 22110
(703) 369-6902; FAX: (703) 369-6902
Founded: 1988. The 8-Mate Scribe Attattchment is a marker-holding device for an ice scribe that allows you to mark the ice with a wide, highly visible ink line for patch sessions, etc.

Enchantment On Ice, Inc.
Contact: Alycia Walker-Gaynor, President
309 Aragona Boulevard, Suite 116
Virginia Beach, VA 23462
(804) 490-0676
FAX: (804) 490-0689
Founded: 1994. Figure skaters' 'specialty shop,' with gifts by Icicles, an Enchantment custom apparel and accessory line, custom gift boxes made for all occasions, stuffed animals, jewelry, and much more. We carry Riedell, SP-Teri, Harlick, Kold Cuts Design and Design Your Line apparel. For custom gifts, allow 4-6 weeks delivery.

Engelhard - ICC
Contact: Robert Mitro, President
441 N. Fifth Street, Suite 102
Philadelphia, PA 19123
(215) 625-0700; FAX: (215) 592-8299
Founded: 1984. Refrigeration machinery of all types and sizes.

Etch Design Industries
Contact: Lois Hill
1181 Tidewood Drive
Bethel Park, PA 15102
(412) 221-4782; FAX: (412) 833-2184
Founded: 1993. Etched vases and souvenirs. Will custom-make any etch design.

Figure 8 Boutique Ltd.
Contact: Jasmin Simard, President
1408 Bank Street
Ottawa, Ontario, K1H 7Y9 Canada
(613) 731-4007; FAX: (613) 736-7747
Founded: 1974. Retail store carries figure (Risport, Riedell, WIFA, SP Teri, Wilson, MK), hockey, recreational, speed, and in-line skates and accessories. Specialize in fitting boot properly for level of skating achieved. Wholesale distributors of boots, blades, speedskates and equipment to 280 Canadian stores.

Figure Mates
Contact: Margaret Johnson
P.O. Box 218
East Hanover, NJ 07936-0218
(201) 386-9314

Founded: 1978. Manufactures skating apparel.

Figure Skating Boutique
Contact: Laura Hallis, Manager
6174 Young Street
Willowdale, Ontario, M2M 3X1 Canada
(416) 225-1377; (416) 225-1390
FAX: (416) 225-3071
Skate shop carrying large selection of boots, blades, skating apparel, etc. Retail and wholesale divisions. Also mail-order.

Figure Skating Historical Society, Inc.
Contact: Jilliaine Eicher, President
P.O. Box 621
Chilmark, MA 02535 USA
(508) 645-3063
FAX: (508) 645-2897
Founded: 1993. Dedicated to the study, promotion and preservation of figure skating. The Society's quarterly journal presents historical research, translation of texts, and projects conducted by members which further the appreciation of figure skating. A core resource of the Society is a database of skating information including over 2500 articles of periodical literature, cross-indexed by author and subject.

Figures on Ice
Contact: Christine Smith, Owner
P.O. Box 4264
Manchester, NH 03108
(603) 644-4521
FAX: (603) 644-1412
Founded: 1993. Catalog offering ice and roller skating apparel from practice dresses to one-of-a-kind dresses; also offers many accessories and gifts.

Fingertips to Toepicks
Contact: Darlene Vento, Owner
10 Knight Street
Norwalk, CT 06850
(203) 838-1203
Founded: 1990. Blades: MK, Wilson. Boots: Riedell, Harlick.

First Movement Music, Co.
Contact: Dana Ashworth, Composer
19R Granite Street
Somerville, MA 02143
(617) 623-0998
Founded: 1992. We will write the skaters' music according to their specifications. Our goal is to make music more of an integral part of the skater's personality on the ice. All music will be exclusively licensed to the person it is written for.

First Place Designs
Contact: Jackie McCarthy, Owner
1995 Castille Drive
Palm Harbor, FL 34683
(813) 784-6418
Founded: 1987. Skating jewelry - 14 kt gold and sterling-silver custom quality designs of charms, name-blades, scribes, charm rings, holders, test numbers, etc. Also unique designs of skating dresses and embroidered sweatshirts.

Flex-Ice, Inc.
Contact: Kevin Kossi, President
250 W. 57th Street #1818
New York, NY 10107
(212) 581-9450; FAX: (212) 581-9373
The Flex-Ice portable ice rink system rolls out over virtually any level surface to create a mirror-like sheet of ice in

Walt Disney's WORLD ON ICE
Produced by KENNETH FELD

COME JOIN THE WORLD'S GREATEST SKATERS!

Auditions for **males** and **females** for the U.S. and international editions of **Walt Disney's World On Ice** are held in conjunction with an engagement in a city near you. If you are looking for a great opportunity, please send your resume and photo with phone number to:

Judy Thomas,
Artistic Talent Coordinator
Walt Disney's World On Ice
8607 Westwood Center Drive
Vienna, VA 22182

© Disney • © 1994 Ice Follies and Holiday On Ice, Inc.

Enchantment On Ice

The finest specialty shop for figure and roller skaters, featuring:
- Gifts and apparel by *Icicles*
- *Ice Crystals* custom apparel & accessories
- Custom-filled gift boxes
- Skating art by Frank Fuller
- Stuffed skating animals
- Custom and stock jewelry
- Skate Spinner; Skating videos

and much more . . .

Plus Riedell, SP-Teri, and Harlick boots; MK and Wilson blades; Kold Cuts Design-Your-Line Apparel. Custom orders take 4-6 weeks. **Fast, personalized service.**

Enchantment On Ice, Inc.
(804) 490-0676; FAX: (804) 490-0689
309 Aragona Boulevard, Suite 116
Virginia Beach, VA 23462

COMPANIES

Silly Skating — The Game

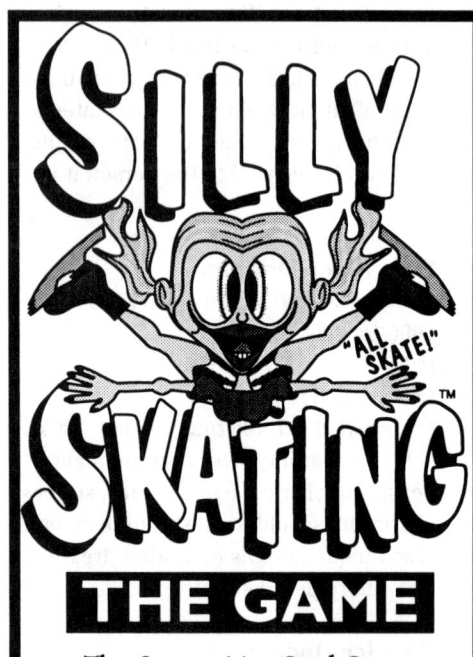

The Competitive Card Game Created by Skaters for Skaters.

ONLY $9.95
includes shipping & handling

FOY TOYS
3275 E. Patrick Lane • Las Vegas, NV 89120
702-454-3300

---

under 24 hours. The most frequent applications for Flex-Ice are temporary public ice skating venues used to create a major winter attraction and a revenue stream. Flex-Ice was designed for portability and reliability; easily transported by truck, rail or air.

Foy Toys
Contact: Teresa Foy
3275 East Patrick Lane
Las Vegas, NV 89120
(702) 454-3500
'Silly Skating' card game designed to entertain while it teaches.

Free Style Designs
Contact: Susan Smith-Habelow, Owner/Designer
One Echo Lane
Woodside, CA 94062-4801
(415) 851-3233
FAX: (415) 851-7306
Founded: 1991. Custom skating apparel for freestyle skaters and ice dancers designed by sportswear designer with over 20 years experience as a fashion designer and production patternmaker. Includes: protective tights, helmets, dresses, chiffon dance skirts, separates; men's and boy's trousers and custom shirts. Adult and children sizes.

Futerman & Futerman
Contact: Ed Futerman, Esquire
2 Saint Claire Ave. East, 15th Floor
Toronto, Ontario, M4T 2R1 Canada
(416) 925-4100
FAX: (416) 323-9132
Represents Elvis Stojko and Uschi Keszler.

Garde Sportswear
Contact: Lois Gardner, President
3003-4 Forest Laneway
Willowdale, Ontario, M2N 5X8 Canada
(416) 225-3391
FAX: (416) 225-3391
GardeTard Protective Wear reduces impact injuries; provides protection for the tailbone, hips, thighs, sitting-bones, knees, elbows, and hands. Unitards, leggings, shorts, briefs, fingermitts in many colors, sizes, styles (stock and custom); pliable pads are removable, light-weight, and air-vented.

Gardner, Randy
c/o MARCO Entertainment
73271 Riata Trail
Palm Desert, CA 92260
(619) 776-5500
FAX: (619) 776-5575
High level choreography for individual skaters and ice shows.

Giant On Ice, Inc.
Contact: Peter Bylsma, Director of Marketing
517 North Robertson Blvd., Suite 2
Los Angeles, CA 90048
310-278-5114
FAX: 310-278-5795
Founded: 1994. Producer of family ice shows, including *Nutcracker On Ice* and Warner Brothers Family Entertainment On Ice.

Global Information Systems
Contact: Tim Zagorc, Marketing Representative
5405 Cypress Center Drive, Suite 100
Tampa, FL 33609
(813) 289-3611
FAX: (813) 289-3072
Founded: 1980. GIS installs and supports the Admits Admission Ticketing System. Admits provides rinks with computerized admissions, printing tickets, wristbands, or receipts at point-of-sale. Complete mailing-list capabilities, demographic data capture, and reporting are included.

Global Sports
Contact: Laurence Chase
575 Washington Street
Wellesley, MA 02181
(617) 237-7678
FAX: (617) 431-1946
Travel packages to the World Figure Skating Championships and Olympic Winter Games.

Gold Edge
Contact: Dan Tousignant, Sales Manager
9601 Garfield Avenue South
Bloomington, MN 55420
(612) 881-2222; (800) 877-6304
FAX: (612) 881-1707
Founded: 1989. Risport, Don Jackson, Riedell, SP-Teri boots. Wilson, MK blades. Perfect scribe. Complete line of figure skates and apparel. Wholesale.

Great Island Knits
Contact: Elisa Smith
2285 Cundy's Harbor Road
Brunswick, ME 04011
(800) 421-9538
Hand-loomed competition sweaters (your design or ours); knitted patch sets, includes zippered leggings; practice sweaters; club sweaters.

Green & Spiegel
Contact: Mendel M. Green, Senior Partner
121 King Street West, Suite 2200
Toronto, Ontario, M5H 3T9 Canada
(416) 862-7880; FAX: (416) 862-1698
We provide assistance to foreign skaters who require immigrant visas to come to Canada for temporary or permanent purposes.

Hare & Hatter Books, Inc.
Contact: Susan Weindling, President
15 Wykeham Road
W. Newton, MA 02165
(617) 928-0906

Founded: 1994. Publisher of *On the Ice: Kids Views and Interviews with Famous (and not so famous) Skaters*. Other books slated for publication. Contact company for more information.

Harlick & Company, Inc.
Contact: Sam Swartz, CFO
893 American Street
San Carlos, CA 94070
(415) 593-2093; FAX: (415) 593-9704
Founded: 1935. Harlick manufactures both stock and custom boots. Custom boots are comfortable and supportive, with a wide variety of features and options. Stock boots provide exceptional quality, and incorporate many of the features found in Harlick custom boots. Worn by such champions as Kristi Yamaguchi and Brian Boitano.

Harris (Ricky) - Choreography and Style
c/o PSGA
P.O. Box 5904
Rochester, MN 55903
(509) 281-5122
High-level choreography and consulting. Author of *Choreography and Style for Ice Skaters*.

Have the Mental Edge
Contact: Marilyn Norcross, Mental Trainer
1032 49th Avenue
Greeley, CO 80634
(303) 353-1098
Certified practitioner of Neuro-Linguistic Programming (NLP). Workshops focus on increasing self-confidence, motivation, self-esteem, communication, and enhancing skills. Work with parents in communication: how to be a good competitive skating parent.

Henie Onstead Art Center
Contact: Reidar Borjeson, Consultant
1311 Hovikodden, Norway
(47) 67 543050; FAX: 67 543270
Founded: 1968. Henie Onstad Art Center is Norway's largest museum of international modern art. It was founded by the Norwegian Champion and Olympic Gold Medalist Sonja Henie. The museum exhibits her trophies and medals and has an extensive archive of background information, as well as films, photographs, letters, etc.

Highland Sports Center
Contact: Rick Stewart, Owner
18005 Aurora Avenue NE
Seattle, WA 98133
(206) 546-2431
FAX: (206) 546-3130
Boots: Harlick, SP-Teri, Riedell. Blades: MK, Wilson. Hockey equipment: Bauer, Canadian, Slack, CCM, Cooper.

FREE STYLE DESIGNS

Protective Skating Tights
Apparel & Helmets

▼

Mens and Boys
Skating Trousers & Shirts

▼

Skating Dresses
Separates
Dance Skirts

For Free Brochure:
FREE STYLE DESIGNS
Department SE
1 Echo Lane, Woodside
California, 94062-4801

▼

Tel.: (415) 851-3233
Fax: (415) 851-7306

Hodges Badge Company, Inc.
Contact: Wadson Eden, Sales Manager
42 Valley Road
Middletown, RI 02842
(401) 847-2000; (800) 556-2440
FAX: (800) 292-7377
Founded: 1920. Hodges Badge Co. is a family-operated business that has been providing top quality awards for 75 years. We can put your logo on a ribbon or medal award and deliver to you within three weeks. We manufacture medals, rosettes, badges, buttons, stickers and certificates.

Hurd Video
Contact: John Hurd
3019 Croyden Bay
Costa Mesa, CA 92626
(714) 546-4085
Videos of skating competitions and shows. ISIA District Championships and 1991 ISIA Nationals

Ice Age
Contact: Michiko Carlson, Owner
55 W. 59th Street #2G
Westmont, IL 60559
(708) 968-7921; (708) 988-3825
Founded: 1993. Mail-order representation of quality accessories, including protective tights, Tracer scribes and skate sweaters (Great Island Knits).

Ice Age Magazine
Contact: Alan Price, Commercial Director
Denbigh House, Denbigh Road,
Bletchley, Milton Keynes, Bucks,
MK11YP England
09-08-366-161
FAX: 09-08-371-751
Founded: 1994. *Ice Age* is a glossy, monthly magazine published in the U.K. covering many disciplines of ice skating (figure, dance, precision, recreational), together with news and features from the U.K., Europe and the international scene. Available on subscription from: Wise Owl Worldwide Publications, 4314 West 238th St., Torrance, CA 90506-4505. Phone: (310) 375-6258; FAX: (310) 375-0548

Ice Castles International Training Center
Contact: Judith Light, Vice President/General Manager
P.O. Box 939
480 Cottage Grove Road
Lake Arrowhead, CA 92352
(909) 337-0802; FAX: (909) 337-8949
Founded: 1981. Training center with two 85' x 185' rinks (one private and one public). A cooperative public school district providing individualized schedules. Supervised 80-bed dormitory, 24 cottages, lodge with chef, 40' x 50' dance pavilion. Complete gym, swimming pool, and jacuzzi.

Ice Chalets, Inc.
1640 S. Sepulveda Blvd., Suite 318
Los Angeles, CA 90025
(310) 575-4466; FAX: (310) 575-4388
Founded: 1968. Ice skating equipment and accessories. Own and operate ice skating facilities nationwide.

Ice Command
Contact: Cecily Morrow
207 Earle Avenue
Easton, MD 21601
(410) 820-5614
Cecily Morrow has initiated an instructional series for begining skaters, *Ice Skating for Everyone: The Beginner's Guide to a Lifetime Sport*. Volume 1 shows a family learning to skate - from first steps on ice, forward and backward skating, through forward crossovers. Other volumes assists viewer with one-foot turns, backward crossovers, and elementry freestyle maneuvers. Ice Command also presents *Stroking Exercises on Ice: The Dance Training Methods of Natalia Dubova*, video instruction in the universally beneficial stroking exercises with the Russian Olympic dance coach.

Ice Command Workshops
Contact: Cecily Morrow
207 Earle Avenue
Easton, MD 21601
(410) 820-5614
Under direction of Cecily Morrow, workshops offer three inter-related options tailored to rink/club/professional needs, for skaters of any level or interest: 1) Gustave Lussi Method, for spins and jumps (see Lussi Technical Video); 2) Ice Energy, edge/turn exercises, dance and music oriented; 3) Group freestyle training intensifies, organizes skater's practice sessions in patterned sequences.

Ice Follies/Holiday on Ice
6150 Porter Road
Sarasota, FL 344240
(813) 377-4210
FAX: (813) 378-4591
Founded: 1979. Two of the oldest names in ice show history. Operational end of Walt Disney's World on Ice. See also *Walt Disney's World on Ice.*

Ice House, The
Contact: Glen Kennis, President
473 Washington Street
Wellesley, MA 02181
(617) 237-6707
FAX: (617) 237-9609
Founded: 1978. Riedell, SP-Teri, Harlick, Klingbeil. Catalogue available during Olympic years. Also carries skating apparel; full service store.

Ice Magic
Contact: Barbara Buchleitner, Owner
Division of MD Sporting Goods
1029 Benfield Boulevard
Millersville, MD 21108
(410) 987-5189; FAX: (410) 987-4104
Carries skating apparel (including sweaters and suits), accessories and novelties. Call for catalogue.

Ice Pics
Contact: Sue Pon, Photographer
238 Roosevelt Way
San Francisco, CA 94114
(415) 626-5289
Freelance skating photographer.

Ice Pro - C.W. Davis Supply, Inc.
Contact: Jim Hartnett, Vice President
15 Dwight Park Drive
Syracuse, NY 13209
(315) 453-2056; FAX: (315) 453-3852
Founded: 1924. Design, construct, and reconstruct ice rinks and ice rink equipment. We offer a full line of rink accessories, evaluation of existing rink equipment, seasonal start-up and shutdown. We schedule preventive maintenance programs.

Ice Rink Engineering
Contact: Jim Durham, Owner
1727 E Saluda Lake Road
Greenville, SC 29611
(803) 232-2591
FAX: (803) 246-4355
Sales and installation of ice rinks.

Ice Skate Conditioning Equipment Co.
Contact: Sidney Broadbent, President
5265 W. Quarles Drive
Littleton, CO 80123
(303) 979-3800
FAX: (303) 979-3800
Founded: 1975. (1) CoPlanar Skateblades: Conquest, Concord, Control, Professional-CP and Gold Quest. (2) The ICEskate Sharpener, Edge squareness, rocker radius, and ROH gages and little edger. (3) Skateology Manual and Skateologist Newsletter. (4) Power Boot Stretcher - 'The Conformer.' Our CoPlanar Concept results from research supported by the US Olympic Committee and several skate and boot manufacturers. We have eliminated disadvantageous walking boot features and provided a design based on sound engineering principles for improved comfort, performance, mounting precision and quality control. Our ICEskate Sharpener provides precision edges, and our Skateology manual remains a great source of information for Sharpeners.

Ice Skater's Edge
Contact: Bill Ross, Owner
6 Freeborn Street
Warwick, RI 02886
(401) 732-5252
FAX: (401) 738-4531
Founded: 1991. Jewelry, pictures, lease skates (200 pairs). Boots: Riedell, Harlick, SP-Teri, Risport, Jackson. Blades: Wilson, MK. Clothing: Danskin, Uncior, Kai Lei. Accessories: bags, polish. Hockey: everything.

Ice Skating Down Under
P.O. Box 567
Archerfield
Queenland, 4108 Australia
ISU official-member journal of Australian Skating Federation.

Ice Skating Institute of America (ISIA)
Contact: Justine Townsend Smith, Executive Director
355 West Dundee
Buffalo Grove, IL 60089
(708) 808-7528
FAX: (708) 808-8329
Since 1959, ISIA has offered rink management programs, conferences, trade shows, and seminars. Internationally-recognized revenue-producing recreational ice-skater programs for hockey, freestyle and figures for every age and ability level.

Ice Sports
Contact: Robyn Levin, President
4601 N. Federal Highway
Pompano Beach, FL 33064 USA
(305) 943-1437
FAX: (305) 781-1966
Founded: 1990. Ice skates, hockey equipment, figure-skating merchandise, jewelry, and NHS licensed products.

Ice Systems of America, Inc.
Contact: Bob & Don May, Owners
5918 E. County Line Road
Highlands Ranch, CO 80126-3918
(303) 220-1444
FAX: (303) 220-0455
Founded: 1983. Consultants, designers, builders, installers for all refrigerated ice surfaces, including full turn-key construction services. Distributors of ICEMAT, HEATMAT, dasher boards, and prepackaged chiller units. Specialize in all types of ice surfaces, permanent or portable, with over 200 previous installations. Supply rental ice rinks of all sizes.

Ice Theatre of New York, Inc.
c/o Sky Rink
450 West 33rd Street
New York, NY 10001
(212) 239-4320; FAX: (212) 239-4327
Founded: 1984. America's first artistic skating company with an acclaimed repertory of ensemble works by dance and skating choreographers including

---

IMPACT WEAR™ by Hôljen inc.

Impactwear is made with a light high-tech padding that is unparalleled in it's shock absorbing capability. The tights and shorts have this special padding in the hip and tailbone areas.

Protective Skating Accessories
- Compression shorts
- Protective tights
- Individual placement pads

Don't Hit The Ice Without It!™

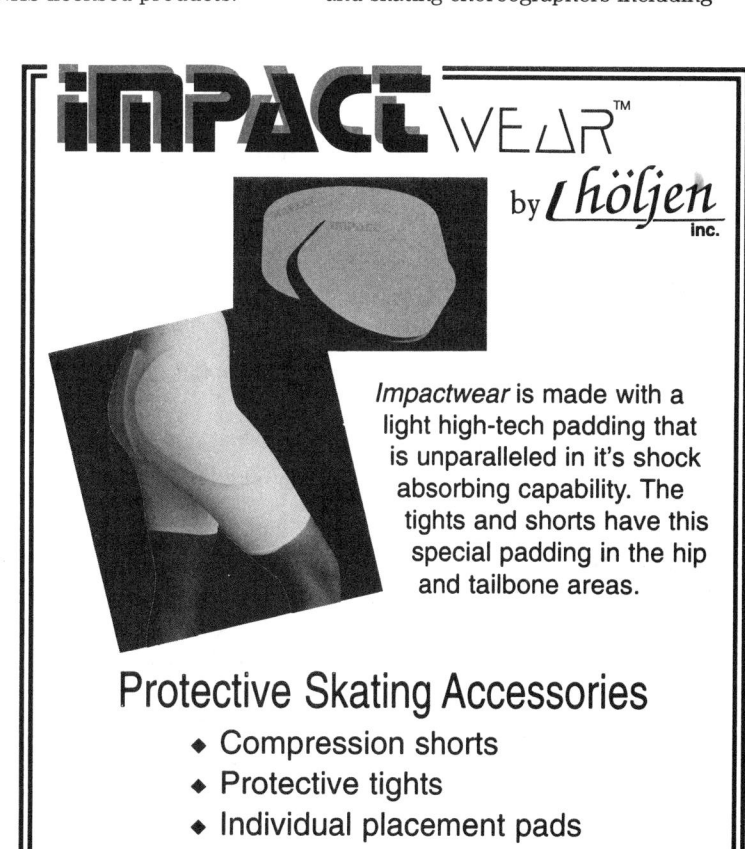

For orders/information call (303) 223-8576, or FAX (303) 223-2753. Please have waist and hip sizes available. Allow 2-3 weeks for delivery. Pro Shop inquiries welcome. ©1991 Holjen, Inc., all rights reserved, patent pending. Holjen, Inc., 749 South Lemay Ave., Suite A3-210, Fort Collins, CO 80524.

Laura Dean, Ann Carlson, Moira North, and Rob McBrien. Available for booking performances, residencies, lecture/demonstrations and workshops. Offers summer intensive in affiliation with Sky Rink, NYC. Supported in part by National Endowment for the Arts.

Ice Top International Inc.
Contact: Beat Aschmann, President
1433 Emerson Way
North Vancouver, B.C., V7H 2B9 Canada
(604) 924-1858
FAX: (604) 924-1878
Founded: 1992. Ice Top is a product used to raise the brine temperature of ice. The ice does not have to be kept as cold; this saves compressor-time, energy and reduces energy costs.

Ignel Associates
Contact: Alina Sivorinovsky, Book Divison
3025 21st Avenue
San Francisco, CA 94132
(415) 681-5088
FAX: (415) 681-5088
Book: *As the Toe Picks: The Skating Lover's Ultimate Trivia Challenge.*

Impact Wear by Holjen, Inc.
Contact: Paul & Heidi Thibert
749 South Lemay Ave., Suite A3-210
Fort Collins, CO 80524
(303) 223-8576
FAX: (303) 223-2753
Founded: 1989. Protective skate wear, padded lycra shorts and tights. Individual pads for hips, knee, palms, and inside boots (Ankle Donuts).

Independent Consulting Engineers, Inc.
Contact: Bradford A. Lemberg, President/Owner
80 W. County Road C, Suite 801
St. Paul, MN 55117
(612) 482-9313; FAX: (612) 482-9558
Founded: 1989. I.C.E. does consulting and designing of ice rinks and arenas across the country. Twenty-five years of arena experience.

INGA Creations Inc.
Contact: Susie Holler, Owner
1456 San Lorenzo Road
Palm Springs, CA 92264
(619) 327-6075
FAX: (619) 327-6075
Founded: 1977. Manufacturer of ice and roller skating outfits, plus outfits for gymnastic and aerobic use. We have been manufacturing top quality products for the last 20 years.

International Figure Skating Magazine
Contact: Mark Lund, Publisher
55 Ideal Road
Worcester, MA 01604
(508) 756-2595
FAX: (508) 792-5981
Founded: 1993. Parent company: Paragraph Communications, Inc. International Figure Skating is a mass-marketed international news magazine published six times a year. Each issue provides news and insight from all segments of the sport. Sold on newsstands in both the U.S. and Canada.

International Gay Figure Skating Union
Contact: Laura Moore, Arthur Luiz, Co-Presidents
P.O. Box 1101
New York, NY 10113
(212) 255-0559; (212) 691-1690
FAX: (212) 691-1690
Founded: 1992. The IGFSU is dedicated to promoting a safe and supportive environment for all skaters regardless of sexual orientation. Organizers and promoters of gay skating events including the Gay Games.

International Ice Rink Consultants
Contact: Henry J. Coupe, Jr. P.E., President
469 Centerville Road, Suite 201
Warwick, RI 02886-4357
(401) 737-8689; FAX: (401) 737-8696
Ice systems designed by registered professional engineers.

International In-Line Skating Association
Contact: Henry Zuver, Exec. Director
P.O. Box 15482
Atlanta, GA 30333 USA
(404) 728-9707; FAX: (404) 728-9866
Founded: 1991. Work with municipalities to expand access to skating arenas. Run an International Instructor Certification Program. Sanction hockey leagues and competitive events.

International Management Group (IMG) New York
Contact: Byron Allen, Vice President
22 East 71st Street
New York, NY 10021 USA
(212) 772-8900; FAX: (212) 772-2617
Management group representing numerous skaters and the Discover Card *Stars on Ice* Tour.

International Management Group (IMG) Canada
Contact: Kevin Albrecht
One St. Clair Avenue East, #700
Toronto, Ontario, M4T 2V7 Canada
(416) 960-5312
FAX: (416) 960-0564
Management group representing numerous skaters.

International Skating Union (ISU)
Contact: Beat Hasler, General Secretary
Promenade 73, Postfach
CH-7270, Davos Platz, Switzerland
(081) 43 75 77; FAX: (081) 43 66 71
Founded: 1892. The umbrella organization and governing body for ice skating world-wide. Countries wishing to compete in the Olympics must be members of the ISU. All rules governing Olympic skating competitions are set by the ISU. The ISU also sells CDs of ice dance music; write for information.

International Winter Sports Museum
Contact: David Heim, President
P.O. Box 1932, 130 Main Street
Lake Placid, NY 12946
(518) 523-4100; FAX: (518) 523-3470
Founded: 1994. An interactive winter-sports museum focusing on figure skating, ice hockey, speed skating, bobsled, luge, ski jumping, alpine skiing and biathalon. Features an in-house theater and a virtual-reality bobsled simulator.

ISIA Newsletter
Contact: Editor
ISIA, 355 West Dundee Road
Buffalo Grove, IL 60089-3500
(708) 808-7528; FAX: (708) 808-8329
Published six times a year, the ISIA Newsletter features information for the ice-skating industry, including rink owners/managers, instructors, etc. Topics include blade-sharpening,

management, maintenance, ISIA competitions and shows, builders/suppliers directory, and industry news. Sent to associate, administrative, and builder/supplier members.

ISIS Entertainment
Contact: Leslie Robinson, President
P.O. Box 35793
Los Angeles, CA 90035
(213) 935-3660
FAX: (213) 935-6953
Founded: 1993. Ice show production company, touring ice shows, TV, video, film community workshops and seminars focusing on minority artists and skaters.

ISU Hoffman Insurance Services
Contact: Gilbert Lincoln
200 Linden Street, P.O. Box 9002
Wellseley, MA 02181-9002
(800) 277-6052; FAX: (617) 235-6665
ISU Hoffman Insurance Services, Inc. offers an insurance program designed to meet the unique needs of ice-rink operators nationwide. The program is underwritten by CIGMA Property and Casualty Companies and includes customized coverage, less control and claims services.

It's a Laurie! Original
Contact: Laurie Hill, Owner
12235 Garden Lake Circle
Odessa, FL 33556
(813) 920-3757
Founded: 1988. Specialist in design and production of custom-made competition costumes. By appointment only. Portable phone (813) 460-3615.

J&R Skates
Contact: Joyce Edmonds, Owner
14 Jordan Street
Skaneatles, NY 13152
(315) 685-1048; FAX: (315) 685-7343
Founded: 1982. Blades: Wilson, MK. Boots: Harlick, Riedell. Clothing: Danskin.

JAMA & Friends Skate
Contact: Jay & Amy Slatus, Owner
7 Browning Drive
Livingston, NJ 07039
(201) 992-7491
Founded: 1994. JAMA & Friends, a summer sleep-away camp for figure skaters, includes patch, freestyle, dance and *Moves in the Field* daily. Off-ice activities include conditioning, dance, lectures, swimming, tennis, sightseeing, shopping and movies. Skaters live in local college dorms. PSGA-rated professionals.

Jazz on Ice
Contact: G. Webster Smith
c/o WOJM & Associates
P.O. Box 19392-A
Los Angeles, CA 90019
(213) 936-2584
FAX: (213) 934-9571
Founded: 1987. Workshops involving dance, jazz, and skating. Also offers workshops for dancers called *Jazzin' w' Rhythm.*

Jefferson Pilot Sports
Contact: Michael Burg, Exec. Director
    Program Planning
One Julian Price Place
Charlotte, NC 28208
(704) 374-3636; FAX: (704) 374-3859
Promotion and public relations.

Jerry's Pro Shop
Contact: Glen Busch, Manager
3900 Owl Drive
Rolling Meadows, IL 60008
(708) 398-7446; FAX: (708) 398-7452
Blades: MK, Wilson. Boots: Riedell, Risport, Jackson, Harlick. Clothing: Danskin. Accessories: hockey and figure-skating equipment. Collectibles: pins, dolls.

Jerry's Skating World
Contact: Jerry Zawadzki
520 Hood Road
Markham, Ontario, L3R 3K9 Canada
(905) 477-1172
FAX: (905) 477-8859
Carries boots, blade, skating apparel and equipment. Write for free catalogue.

Jet Ice Paints Limited
Contact: Dave Loverock, National Sales
    Manager
359 Enford Road, Unit 2
Richmond Hill, Ontario, L4C 3G2 Canada
(905) 883-4204
FAX: (905) 770-3071
Founded: 1979. Manufacturer of high quality ice paints including white, red, blue, and 1,000 special colors. Supplier of paper pounce logo stencils for anniversaries or clubs for on-ice advertising.

Joe's Skate Service
Contact: P. Joseph De Lio, Owner
South Suburban Ice Arena
6580 S. Vine Street
Littleton, CO 80121
(303) 798-7881; FAX: (303) 980-0356
Founded: 1972. World Class Sharpening: patch, freestyle and dance available through mail; 24 hour turn around. Four Olympic, ten World and many National Champions. Also, Skate Technician Training available. Seminar information available from above address.

Jumpometer Co.
Contact: Allan W. Lee, Owner
265 Lawlor Street, P.O. Box 318
Haileybury, Ontario, P0J 1K0 Canada
(705) 672-5455; FAX: (705) 672-5867
Founded: 1994. The Jumpometer is a portable instrument for use on the ice surface to indicate how high a skater can jump. The meter sets targets and signals immediate results for a skater's effort on each jump. Easy to set up and use. Enhances jump practice.

K & K Insurance Group, Inc.
Contact: Angie Poulos, V.P., Corporate
    Communications
1712 Magnavox Way
Fort Wayne, IN 46804
(219) 459-5663; FAX: (219) 459-5967
Founded: 1952. K & K Insurance provides sport, leisure and entertainment insurance, and offers comprehensive insurance packages to ice skating rinks. Coverages include (but are not limited to) general liability including participant liability, excess liability, property and auto coverages.

K-Tee Enterprises
Contact: Katherine Monnier, Owner/CEO
P.O. Box 1063
Kenwood, CA 95452
(707) 539-6351
Founded: 1989. K-Tee carries easy zip-front boot covers, hand, foot and body warmers. Also body wraps of various sizes. The sports muff fastens about the waist and can be used as a cozy cushion-fanny warmer on those cold bleachers. Light-weight, colorful skate bags make air, train or bus travel a snap, with beaucoup pockets for tapes, laces, gloves and all that necessary stuff.

Karleen Insurance Agency
Contact: Kathleen O'Connell, Vice President
1931 North Meacham Road #350
Schaumburg, IL 60173
(708) 303-5070; FAX: (708) 303-5072
Founded: 1989. Karleen Insurance is an independent insurance agency that serves the Ice Skating Institute of America (ISIA), providing the liability insurance for the Associate Members and the accident insurance for the individual members. Karleen represents several insurance carriers; specialty is business insurance.

Kast, Nancy L.
Contact: Nancy Kast, Photographer
743 W. Princeton Avenue
Fresno, CA 93705
(209) 227-0783
Freelance skating photographer.

Kathy Barron
Contact: Kathy Barron, Owner
2 Joseph Drive
Simsbury, CT 06070
(203) 658-4688
Founded: 1992. Hand-decorated skating apparel, gifts and accessories. Complete matching outfits. Wide assortment of colors, fabrics, and decorations, as well as custom-made apparel and accessories. Cookbook for skaters. Mens and boys skating trousers and shirts. Personalized gifts for skaters. Solids, velvets, and foil fabrics available, too.

Kawahara, Sarah
Contact: Manager
c/o P.C.K. Enterprises, Inc.
41-865 Boardwalk, Suite 211
Palm Desert, CA 92211
(619) 341-5174; FAX: (614) 341-5176
High-level choreographer and consultant for top skaters, including Scott Hamilton.

Keith's Precision Skate Sharpening
Contact: Keith Galgot, Owner
88 Spruce Street
Watertown, MA 02172
(617) 924-4518
Founded: 1954. Sharpening figure skates and mounting blades. Keith is a professional skater who understands the importance of skating on freshly sharpened blades.

Keszler, Uschi
Contact: Uschi Keszler, Choreographer
c/o Futerman & Futerman
2 Saint Claire Ave East, 15th Floor
Toronto, Ontario, M4T 2R1 Canada
(416) 925-4100; FAX: (416) 323-9132
Personal style development and high-level choreography for top skaters, including Brian Orser, Elvis Stojko, Brasseur & Eisler, Bourne & Kraatz, Tanya Szewczenko, and others. Specializes in self-expression. Creator of Hydroblading.

Keystone Resort
Contact: Thomas Davidson, Manager of Recreation
P.O. Box 38
Keystone, CO 80435
(303) 468-4208; FAX: (303) 468-4024
Founded: 1970. Day and evening ice skating at Keystone Resort, located 75 miles west of Denver, CO. Keystone Village ice surface is one of the largest in the country. Restaurants and a variety of shops surround this frozen five-acre lake. Skate, sled, and hockey stick rentals available, as well as lessons. Open daily in the winter (late Nov. - mid March) from 10:00 a.m. - 10:00 p.m. For more information call 1-800-354-4FUN.

Klingbeil Shoe Labs, Inc
Contact: Donald Klingbeil, Vice-President
145-01 Jamaica Avenue
Jamaica, NY 11435
(718) 297-6864; FAX: (718) 658-2396
Founded: 1950. Manufactures and sells Klingbeil line of custom skate boots.

Knebli, John Ltd.
Contact: John Knebli, President
32 Camden Street
Toronto, Ontario, M5V 1V1 Canada
(416) 368-5565
Founded: 1946. Skating boots to order. Family business for 48 years. Known throughout the world.

L.E.A. Sports
Contact: Bonnie Epstein
1100 Johnson Ferry Road, Suite 250
Marietta, GA 30068
(404) 565-9536
FAX: (404) 565-9329
Design and make custom skating clothing.

Lake Placid 1932 & 1980 Winter Olympic Museum
Contact: Jacqueline Baker, Museum Director
Olympic Center
Lake Placid, NY 12946
(518) 523-1655 x.263
FAX: (518) 523-9275
Founded: 1994. The museum exhibits include highlights of the Lake Placid Winter Olympic Games, sports equipment, photographs, and Olympic memorabilia.

Lake Placid International School of Ice Dancing
Contact: Natalia Dubova
ORDA, Olympic Center
Lake Placid, NY 12946
(518) 523-1655; FAX: (518) 523-9275
Founded: 1993. Top level training center for ice dance, including Russian teams such as Usova & Zhulin.

Lar Lubovitch Dance Company
Contact: Richard Caples, Executive Director
15 W. 18th Street
New York, NY 10011
(212) 242-0633
FAX: (212) 691-8315
Founded: 1968. Lar Lubovitch has made a notable contribution to the advancement of choreography in the field of ice-dancing. He has created dances for Olympic gold medalists John Curry, Peggy Fleming and Dorothy Hamill and has choreographed a full-length ice-dancing version of *The Sleeping Beauty*, as well as an hour-long TV show called *The Planets*.

Laura Stamm International Power Skating System
Contact: Bryce Leavitt McGowan, Director of Marketing/ P.R.
205 Lincoln Place
Tuckahoe, NY 10707
(914) 961-7994; (800) 484-7303 x 1886
FAX: (914) 961-0337
Laura Stamm Int'l Power Skating System teaches technique training for hockey skating skills. We reach an estimated 8,000 hockey players a year and teach in 26 states in the U.S. Stamm has 25 years of experience teaching and coaching professional teams and players, plus amateurs. We offer clinics, workshops

and summer schools for beginners up through college and professional players. Also offers power skating book & video.

Le Patinage Suisse
Avenue du Tribunal - Federal 38
CH -1005, Lausanne, Switzerland
ISU official member journal of the Swiss skating federation.

Leclair Arena Equipment Ltd.
Contact: Cary Miller, President
185 Van Horne Avenue
Montreal, Quebec, H2T 2J2 Canada
(514) 277-1186; FAX: (514) 277-3277
Founded: 1970. Distributors of Olympic ice resurfacers with zero emissions and the capability of maintaining zero emissions; distributors of other arena products.

Ledin Photo & Video
Contact: Noel & Alice Ledin, Owner
22495 Madison
St. Clair Shores, MI 48081
(810) 778-8971
Founded: 1965. Videotapes primarily local competitions. Has videos of 1989, 1990, 1992, 1994 Skate America, plus 1991, 1992, 1994 National Championships. Scheduled to videotape 1995 U.S. Nationals in Providence, RI.

Lenzi Foundation, The
Contact: Jean Lenzi, President
4228 1/2 River Road, NW, Suite A
Washington, DC 20016
(202) 363-6503
Founded: 1992. Four long-time skating fans formed The Lenzi Foundation to identify and support young U.S. figure skaters. Its mission is to become a viable force in skating, raising and giving away funds to eligible skaters to improve the quality of U.S. skating and ensure that promising young skaters are not lost. While the Foundation's primary focus is on pairs and dance, skaters from all disciplines will benefit.

Leo's Dancewear, Inc.
Contact: Kari Shannon, Marketing Assistant
1900 N. Narraganset Avenue
Chicago, IL 60639
(312) 889-7700; FAX: (312) 889-7593
Founded: 1924. Leo's manufactures skatewear including dresses, tights, skirts and leggings. They have been designed in cooperation with skaters and coaches to incorporate functional features like Velcro-closure leggings.

Lesnik Public Relations
Contact: Michael Myers, Vice President
455 North Cityfront Plaza Dr., 15th Floor
Chicago, IL 60611
(312) 755-3500; FAX: (312) 755-0276
Does public relations and promotion for the World Professional Figure Skating Championships (in Landover, MD), and the Challenge of Champions.

Lexicon Ventures Limited
Contact: Jeff Lerner, President
1685 West 61st Avenue
Vancouver, B.C., V6P 2C2 Canada
(604) 261-0371; FAX: (604) 266-7998
Two books, by Jeff R. Lerner, *The Compete Manual of Ice Dance Patterns*, a collection of 152 unusual dances with compulsories and *The Complete Manual of Compulsory Ice Dances* which includes 32 different test dances and four new ISU dances. The latter is unique in that the man's pattern is overlain by the lady's transparent pattern in red, clearly showing tracking techniques. Both include lists of steps, dance positions, turns, glossary. Laminated covers and 8 1/2" x 11" format.

Linichuk, Natalia
Contact: Natalia Linichuk
c/o University of DE Ice Skating Science Development Center
Blue Arena
Newark, DE 19716
(302) 831-2868
Coach and manager for Oksana Gritshuk and Evgeni Platov (1994 Olympic Dance Champions).

Lubin's Skate Supply, Inc.
Contact: Brian Armbruster, Vice-President
9 State Street
Nashua, NH 03063
(603) 886-5777
FAX: (603) 883-6270
Founded: 1955. Riedell boots, MK blades, Wilson blades, Fleming Gray skate sharpeners, Jerry's scribes. Wholesale distributor to rinks, pro shops, skate shops and sporting goods stores.

Lucas (Pam) Photography
Contact: Pam Lucas, Photographer
c/o *Blades on Ice*
7040 North Mona Lisa Road
Tucson, AZ 85741-2633
Freelance photographer for *Blades on Ice* and other skating publications. No sales to general public.

Lucky S Action Fashion
Contact: Sheri Hull, Owner
508 N. San Jose Street
Stockton, CA 95203
(800) 735-0458
FAX: (209) 946-0467
Founded: 1980. Skatewear and dancewear for women and girls. We manufacture, wholesale and distribute skatewear to sport shops and retail stores. Lucky S has been supplying sport shops with skate dresses, skirts, lycra tights, pony tail holders and boot covers for 14 years. We also produce costumes for skate, dance, and drill teams.

Luistelija
Radoikatu 20, Box 27
FIN-00240, Helsinki, Finland
ISU official-member journal of the Finnish Speed-Skating Federation.

Lussi Technical Video
Contact: Cecily A. Morrow, Producer
207 Earle Avenue
Easton, MD 21601
(410) 820-6125
A four-volume series, *Systematic Figure Skating: The Spin and Jump Techniques of Gustave Lussi*, demonstrates step-by-step the methods developed by the world-renowned coach whose techniques form the foundation of today's freeskating. Produced by Cecily Morrow, hosted by Dick Button, and directed by Doug Wilson, the videos show Mr. Lussi instructing Paul Wylie and other skaters.

Lynch's
Contact: Susan Lynch, Advertising Manager
939 Howard
Dearborn, MI 48124
(313) 565-3425; (800) 24-LYNCH
FAX: (313) 565-0590
Skate dresses, skate sweaters, skate laces, soakers, blade covers, tights, fabrics, sequins, rhinestones, sequin

appliques, hats, boot covers, legwarmers and skate skirts. We offer an 800-number for orders.

Lyteman Inc.
Contact: Ferd L. Manning, President
26 Shaker Ridge Drive
Canaan, NY 12029-9712
(518) 781-4300
FAX: (518) 781-4300
Founded: 1968. A full-service lighting organization, New-York based, with national and international clients. Theatrical and television lighting is our specialty. Highly experienced with ice skating competitions and shows.

M&M Trims
Contact: Myra Ward, Partner
91 South Main Street
Wilkes Barre, PA 18701
(717) 825-7305
FAX: (717) 825-7463
Do all kinds of trims for costumes, wholesale to anyone. Skating pins.

Maestro Editing Service
Contact: Mikchail A. Zverev, Maestro
367 Windsor Highway Unit 200
New Windsor, NY 12553
(914) 691-7026
Founded: 1992. Custom editing. Music research, Large collection of pre-edited cuts one to three minutes in length. Free catalog.

Magic of Style
Contact: Ann-Margreth Frei, Owner/
    Director
P.O. Box 2676
Vail, CO 81658
(303) 926-3345; FAX: (303) 926-5176
Founded: 1991. The Magic of Style video series consists of three volumes; Volume I: Thirty-eight exercises to help develop artistry, and the winning look of skating champions. Volume II: Flexibility/Strength for the skating athlete with 25 variations in spirals, extensions, butterflies and supersplit jump techniques, stretch and tone-up. Volume III: Develop easy to intricate footwork, connecting steps, and *Moves in the Field*.

Manhattan Library of Dance Skating Music
Contact: Christian Orlov
163 Amsterdam Avenue, Suite 348
New York, NY 10023
(212) 873-2307
FAX: (212) 873-2307
Founded: 1990. Exclusive music and program dance tapes for the compulsory ice dances.

Marc Evon Enterprises
Contact: Marc Evon, Owner
5325 Outer Drive, Units 3 & 4
Windsor, Ontario, N9A 6J3 Canada
(519) 737-7659
FAX: (519) 737-7052
Founded: 1980. Manufactures skate guards.

Marc Nelson Ice Development
Contact: Marc Nelson, President
150 North Broadway
White Plains, NY 10603 USA
(914) 428-4976
Founded: 1980. General consultant and independent contractor to the ice skating industry. Universal ice skating development and training systems. Ice skating industry research and development. Iceplay News and information services.

MARCO Entertainment: Michael A. Rosenburg Management
Contact: Michael and Nancy Rosenberg
73271 Riata Trail
Palm Desert, CA 92260
(619) 776-5500; FAX: (619) 776-5575
Founded: 1977. Personal manager to 36 Olympic, World and National Champions; Produces World Cup Figure Skating Champions Tour; also produces skating television specials and movies; including *The Tai Babilonia Story* on ABC and *The Oksana Baiul Story* on CBS.

Maximum Edges
Contact: Doug Trudell, Marketing
1932 Ambassador Drive
Windsor, Ontario, N9C 3R3
(519) 969-7575; FAX: (519) 969-3199
Founded: 1992. Sharpen skates to ensure that edges are square, smooth, and safe. Also provide kit (tools and process) to pros and skaters to check the sharpenings on their blades after they have been sharpened. Hone and glaze provided to ensure a smoother edge.

McBrien, Rob
Contact: Rob McBrien, Choreographer
c/o Ice Theatre of New York, Sky Rink
450 West 33rd Street
New York, NY 10001
(212) 239-4320; FAX: (212) 239-4327
Choreographer for amateur competitors since 1972. Former Ensemble Director for John Curry Skating Company. As Artistic Director of Ice Theatre, choreographed over twenty works of acclaimed ensemble artistic skating. Professional competitive works for Blumberg & Seibert, Blumberg & Yorke, Starbuck & Shelley, and Katherine Healy. Personal coach to John Curry, 1982-1990.

Mentor Marketing & Management
Contact: Jeanne Martin, President
Suite 810, 202 S. Michigan Street
Society Bank Building
South Bend, IN 46601
(219) 233-9601
FAX: (219) 233-9484
Founded: 1982. Established to identify opportunities and advance the career development of skaters in the U.S. and around the world by providing individually tailored services designed to address the needs and potential of each client. Services include career management, contract negotiation, endorsement, targeting and solicitation, publicity and public relations, plus event development and implementation, with a strong focus on personal attention and consultation.

Michellene-Apparel
Contact: Darlene R. McDonough, Owner
1709 Ludington Street
Escanada, MI 49829
(906) 786-8032; (800) 786-8033
FAX: (906) 786-8032
Manufacturers - skating apparel: sweaters (warm-up, club, and custom beaded with angora); knitted zip-off pants; practice, precision and custom competition dresses. Full bodysuits for cross-country skiing and speed skating. Skating, skiing sweatshirts, turtlenecks. Fabric, trim and beading. Boots, blades and other accessories. Mondor, Gilda Marx, and Bloch tights.

Mid Atlantic Arena Managers Association
Contact: Robert Mock, Director
505 Larimer, #7
Turtle Creek, PA 15145
(412) 823-6642
Voluntary arena managers association covering Pennsylvania, eastern Ohio and West Virginia.

Midwest Skate Company
Contact: Louis Armbruster, Owner
24370 Indoplex Circle
P.O. Box 87
Farmington Hills, MI 48335
(800) 521-0185
FAX: (810) 477-9550
Wholesale distributor to skate shops, sporting-goods stores, ice arenas and roller skating rinks. Riedell, Suregrip (in-line frames), Wilson and MK. Also carry Up In the Air Products, Jerry's Skating World, Unicorn Sports, and Danskin products.

Mimms (Lee S.) & Associates
Contact: Lee Mimms
2644 East Chevy Chase Drive
Glendale, CA 91206
(818) 246-5601; FAX: (818) 246-5605
Manager for 1980 Olympic Champion Robin Cousins and other Broadway, film, and television personalities.

Mitchel & King (MK) Skates Ltd.
Contact: David Whitworth, Managing Director
818/819 Leigh Road
Slough, Berkshire, SL1 4SA England
07-53-528-444
FAX: 07-53-528-446
Founded: 1945. Manufactures the MK line of skate blades.

Mitchell Rubber Products
Contact: Rachelle Mathias, National Sales Manager
491 Wilson Way
City of Industry, CA 91744
(800) 453-7526
FAX: (818) 968-2026
Founded: 1968. Off-ice tile lock is a high quality resilient surfacing for ice rinks. Call for specification sheets, color samples or more information.

Mittan (J. Barry) Photography
Contact: Barry Mittan, Owner
11398 Buck Lake Road
Tallahasse, FL 32311-8648
(800) 758-7318
FAX: (904) 877-2569
Founded: 1968. Professional and amateur skating photography, especially fast-action, photo-layouts, computer photo-scanning, posters, etc.

Moletec Corporation
Contact: Charles A. Snyder, Engineer-Consultant
1701 Holt Road NE
Tuscaloosa, AL 35404
(800) 638-3219; (205) 553-9686
FAX: (205) 553-9726
Founded: 1992. Moletec's Frigaid is a patented oil additive developed for refrigeration compressors; forms a boundary film on metal parts, increases lubricity 1500%, accelerates heat transfer throughout the system, extends equipment life and reduces power usage.

Mondor
Contact: Juteau Christian, Vice-President, Sales
785 Mercier Street
Iberville, Quebec, J2X 3S2 Canada
(514) 347-5321; FAX: (514) 347-5811
Founded: 1955. Mondor tights, figure skating dresses, and Monsport hockey jerseys, socks, underwear and protective gear.

Morris (William) Agency
Contact: Michael Carlisle, Vice-President
1350 Avenue of the Americas
New York, NY 10019
(212) 586-5100; FAX: (212) 246-3583
Founded: 1898. Talent and literary agency. Serve as agents for Oksana Baiul, Viktor Petrenko, Galina Zmievskaya (coach), and Dorothy Hamill.

Moskvina School of Ice Skating
Contact: Zoe Thompson
Stevenhage Ice Bowl
Roaring Meg Retail Estate
London Road
Stevenhage, Herts, SG1 1XH England
011-44-438-747647
FAX: 011-44-438-740051
Skating school and training center primarily for Russian skaters; founded by renowned pairs coach Tamara Moskvina.

Mother Goose Imagines (MGI)
Contact: Barbara Smith, Partner
147 Fairway Drive
Coventry, RI 02816
(401) 828-6627; FAX: (401) 272-2560
Founded: 1993. Rhinestone pins; sterling-silver pins; laminated pins made of original, uncanceled stamps (last from '92 Olympics); skaters & hockey players.

Murray Sandler Skate & Rink Supply
Contact: Murray Sandler, President
60 Concord Avenue, P.O. Box 301
Belmont, MA 02178
(617) 484-5100; FAX: (617)489-5232
Founded: 1977. Distributors of the finest lines of rink related supplies and equipment along with boots, blades, and complete lines of hockey equipment. Dealer inquiries only.

Risport Klingbeil Riedell SP-Teri Bisland Sportswear Pat Hudson Originals Eva Schmidt Unicorn

The Outside Edge

Send For Your Free Catalog:
370 Deerpath Drive
Winthrop Harbor, IL 60096 U.S.A.
Illinois (708) 746-3655   1-800-Skate93

MK Blades Co-Planer Wilson Blades Harlick

Silver Lining Danskin Gilde Marx Up in the Air

Jewelry Collector Pins Collectibles Sweaters Gloves Guards Books Videos Artwork Enesco

Museum of Television and Radio
25 West 52nd Street
New York, NY 10019
(212) 621-6800; FAX: (212) 621-6715
Founded: 1975. The museum has a lot of skating footage (both old and new), including all the Olympic footage. Seventy years of television and radio history.

National Audio
Contact: Kim Clark, Owner
231 W. Olive Avenue, Suite A
Burbank, CA 91502
(800) 777-3838
Founded: 1982. Short blank cassettes for freestyle programs.

National Ice Skating Association of UK Limited (NISA)
Contact: James Courtney, President
15-27 Gee Street
London, ECIV 3RE Great Britain
(71) 253 3824/(71) 253 0910
FAX: (71) 490 2589
Member of the ISU representing Great Britain (GRB). The National Governing body for speed, figure, precision, dance and recreational skating. 3700 members.

National Ice Skating Centers, Inc.
Contact: Peter Burrows, President
192 Heron Lane
Manhasset, NY 11030
(516) 484-0040
FAX: (516) 484-8470
Founded: 1992. Directed by Peter Burrows, Kerry Leitch, and Ron Ludington. Offers consulting in: specially tailored computer program, layout of school office, staffing of office, bookkeeping system, lesson ticket system, class card procedure, admission ticket system, private lesson ticket system, pro shop pricing, computerized inventory, staffing, stocking, setting up skate rental, and skating programs. Our own school offers PSGA and National Ice Skating Center-trained professional teaching staff, recreational to competitive levels. USFSA and ISIA group classes as well.

National Ice Theatre of Canada
Contact: Sandra Shewchuk, Executive Director
10022-103 Street
Edmonton, Alberta, T5J 0X2 Canada
(403) 421-8879; FAX: (403) 426-1049
Founded: 1992. The National Ice Theatre of Canada (NITC), an Edmonton based, not-for-profit foundation, is dedicated through education and performance to nuturing and encouraging theatre on ice as a performing art. An innovative and exciting new art form, ice theatre combines the competitive sport of figure skating with the dynamic and dramatic world of theatre.

National Skate Distributors
3852 S. 66th Street
(206) 473-3636
FAX: (206) 473-3791
Founded: 1970. Wholesale suppliers of ice skates and accessories, including Riedell shoes, MK blades, Wilson blades, Bont Shoes and Zandstra blades.

National Skate Locker
Contact: Jim Hambas, Vice President
2600 E. Katella
Anaheim, CA 92806
(714) 935-9500
FAX: (714) 935-2494
Founded: 1990. Boots: Harlick, Riedell, SP-Teri, Klingbeil. Blades: MK, Wilson. Clothing: jerseys, Danskin, Unicorn, Mondor, Up-in-the-Air, LC Designs. Full-service skate shop.

National Sports Academy
Contact: David Wenn, Head of School
12 Lake Placid Club Drive
Lake Placid, NY 12946
(518) 523-3460; FAX: (518) 523-3488
Founded: 1979. An independent preparatory academy offering top-level academic and athletic programs to winter-sports athletes. Openings for 8th to 12th graders; offers traditional nine-month session along with a winter-term program.

NBC Sports
30 Rockefeller Plaza
New York, NY 10020
(212) 664-4444
FAX: (212) 664-3602

Neon I
Contact: Don Merrell
216 E. 5th Street
San Dimas, CA 91773
(909) 592-2492
Don Merrell is a glass artist who creates glass trophies, awards and jewelry.

NESSI: New England Sports Sales, Inc.
Contact: Charles Gualtieri, President
22 Prospect Street Unit 6
Woburn, MA 01801
(800) 878-4648
FAX: (617) 932-6695
Founded: 1984. Blademaster/Custom Radius skate sharpening machines, riveters, and contour systems. The only skate sharpening machine used by every national hockey league team in North America.

New England Figure Skating Camp
Contact: Werner Rothchild, Skating Director
14 Joyce Lane
Woodbury, NY 11797
(516) 364-8050
Founded: 1970. Summer Camp location: Route 2, Contoocook, NH 03229; (603) 746-3195. New England Hockey and Figure Skating camp is a summer-resident camp for boys and girls. The camp aims to provide each camper (beginner - advanced) with an individualized program to suit his/her needs. The camp includes many land and water sports and is accredited by the American Camping Association.

New England Ice Skating Managers Association
Contact: Steve Hoar, Facility Director
Hayden Recreation Centre, Inc.
24 Lincoln Street
Lexington, MA 02173
(617) 862-5575
FAX: (617) 674-2946
Founded: 1974. NEISMA has played an active role in supporting the ice rink industry and extending communication between the many rinks in New England for over 20 years.

Newton Video Photography
Contact: Jim & Shelley Newton, Videographer/ Photographer
114 Indian Wells Lane
Colorado Springs, CO 80919
(719) 599-0954
Founded: 1993. Production videos; stills and action shots; portraits.

Next Ice Age
Contact: Nathan Birch, Artistic Director
P.O. Box 65127
Baltimore, MD 65127
(410) 685-4977
FAX: (410) 435-5774
Performance troupe co-founded by Tim Murphy and Nathan Birch. Tim Murphy is Skating Director and Choreographer for Dorothy Hamill's Ice Capades. Nathan Birch, who was the first skating choreographer to receive a grant from the National Endowment for the Arts, is Associate Skating Director/Choreographer for DHI's Ice Capades.

Northwest Designs Ink
Contact: Ben Smith, President
12870 NE 15th Place
Bellevue, WA 98005
(800) 925-9327
FAX: (206) 455-5778
Founded: 1983. We provide T-shirts and sweatshirts for skating competition. We also have a skating catalogue of sayings, designs, and miscellaneous items for skaters.

Oberhamer, Inc.
Contact: Kent Orwoll, President
11975 Portland Ave. South, Suite #122
Burnsville, MN 55337
(612) 890-1657
FAX: (612) 890-0511
Founded: 1989. Manufactures figure boots, speed boots, and in-line speed boots. Custom boots also. Blade sales, sharpening, mounting, boot maintenance, accessories, clothing, laces. Best in-line speed boot on the market.

Ogilvie-Gutzman Blade Gauges
Contact: Alan Gutzman
617 8th Avenue, Box 267
Ironton, MN 56455
The Ogilvie-Gutzman Blade Gauges consist of a set of four metal disks plus an edge level tester; set comes with a 32-page manual (by Robert Ogilvie) that shows how to use the gauges and describes the effects of different hollows.

Ontario Recreational Facilities Association, Inc. (ORFA)
Contact: John Milton, Executve Director
1185 Eglinton Avenue E
North York, Ontario, P4P 1C1 Canada
(416) 495-4200
FAX: (416) 495-4329
Founded: 1947. Refrigeration and Ice-Making manual. Professional development training opportunities in all aspects of facility operation, i.e. refrigeration, concession management, building maintenance, energy conservation, legal awareness, etc.

Outside Edge
P.O. Box 4192
Pretoria, 0001 South Africa
ISU official-member journal of South African Skating Federation.

Outside Edge
Contact: Connie Anderson, President
370 Deerpath Drive
Winthrop Harbor, IL 60096
(800) SKATE 93
FAX: (708) 746-3655
Founded: 1991. The Outside Edge Catalogue contains a complete line of major boot and blade products, equipment and accessories, 12 skating apparel lines and fine jewelry. Also collector pins, artwork, dolls, toys, books and videos, collectables, and other gift and holiday items. Equipment and fashion consultants are available. In addition to catologue sales, The Outside Edge exhibits at most major USFSA and ISIA competitions where vendors are present.

P.H.D. Products
Contact: Wendy Pittman, Owner, P.H.D.
3630 Citadel Drive North
Colorado Springs, CO 80909
(719) 591-4425
Founded: 1994. Instructional in-line skating videos by professional figure skater Scott Cramer.

Path Editions
Contact: Igor Mojes
1644 Bayview Avenue, Suite 1922
Toronto, Ontario, M4G 3C2 Canada
(416) 423-2271
Founded: 1992. Publish skating pictures and art work. Figure skating note cards for all occasions from the scenes of original oil paintings by Igor Mojzes. Box of 12 cards.

National Ice Skating Centers Inc.

Peter Burrows
United States National, International, World and Olympic Coach

Kerry Leitch
Canadian National, International, World and Olympic Coach

Ron Ludington
United States National, International, World and Olympic Coach

Offering a balanced program encompassing public and recreational instruction. Hockey and competitive figure skating.

Skating School Operations include: Specially tailored computerized program; layout of skating school office; staffing office with qualified personnel; bookkeeping system; lesson ticket system; class card procedure; admission ticket system; private lesson ticket system.
Teaching Staff: All professionals certified by PSGA. Group instruction programs: ISIA and USFSA.
Pro Shop: Correct square footage; stocking equipment; pricing structure; computerized inventory; staffing.
Skate Rental: Square footage; traffic flow; equipment; staffing; fees.
Additional Services: Set up of skating school, pro shop, and/or skate rental; personal monthly supervision; franchising available.

192 Heron Lane, Manhasset, NY 11030
(516) 484-0040; Fax: (516) 484-8470

Patinage Magazine
Contact: Vincent Guerrier, Publication Director
39 Boulevarde de la Marne
F-76000, Rouen, FRANCE
(16) 35 07 47 29
FAX: (16) 35 89 06 67
Beautiful color magazine published in France; each article is in English and French; some also in German. Lots of full-page color pictures, profiles of skaters, reports on international events and competitions.

Paul's Pro Shop
Contact: Paul Tassone, President-Owner
2300 Old Glenview Road
Wilmette, IL 60091
(708) 251-0880
FAX: (708) 251-3123
Founded: 1988. Paul's Pro Shop is owned and operated by figure skaters for figure skaters.

Peck and Goodie
Contact: Scott Kelleher, Director of Marketing
919 8th Avenue
New York, NY 10019
(212) 246-6123
FAX: (212) 807-6115
Mounting, some wholesaling, hockey equipment, retail.

Performance Coaching Inc.
Contact: Shelly Swallow, Manager
P.O. Box 119
Rockwood, Ontario, N0B 2K0 Canada
(519) 856-9064; FAX: (519) 856-9939
Founded: 1991. The *Skater's Inside Edge* is a two-tape skill-based program in basic sports psychology by Dr. Peter Jensen, Canada's Olympic performance coach. The program focuses on the mental dimension of performance with quality practice, mental preparation, relaxation and imagery exercises.

Philbrick Sports
Contact: Dan Philbrick, Owner
161 Portland Avenue
Dover, NH 03820
(603) 742-4333
FAX: (603) 742-9311
Stocks Jackson figure skates, hockey skates, skis. 1-800- FACE OFF.

Photographic Edge
Contact: Stephan Potopnyk, Photographer
P.O. Box 370
Wasaga Beach, Ontario
L0L 2P0 Canada
(705) 429-4948
FAX: (705) 429-4948
Supplier of photographs for tour programs, advertising and promotion. Also offering skating photos for editorial use, from stock or by assignment. Photo sales to skating fans (write for detailed list).

Photos On Ice
Contact: Paul & Michelle Harvarth
9087 Corunna Road
Flint, MI 48532
(313) 635-4830
Founded: 1984. Official photographers for USFSA, *Skating* magazine, and Tom Collins' *Tour of World Figure Skating Champions*. Photographs from national and international competitions/exhibitions available to competitors/exhibitors and for publications and programs. Photos not sold to general public.

Pickwick Sport Shop
Contact: Mary Spencer, Manager
1001 Riverside Drive
Burbank, CA 91506
(818) 846-8099
FAX: (818) 845-5300
Boots: Harlick, SP-Teri, Riedell, Risport. Blades: Wilson, MK. Clothes: Bodywraps, Gilda Marx, Jerry's K&C, Rebel Without a Cause, Silver Lining. Hockey equipment. Books.

Platoro Press
Contact: Lynn Copley-Graves, Owner
4481 Floyd Drive
Columbus, OH 43232-5617
(614) 837-0003
Books: *Ice Skating Fundamentals; Figure Skating History - Evolution of Dance; Sport Psychology for Skaters; How Sport Psychology Can Make You a Champion; Key to Rhythmic Ice Dancing; Origins of Ice Dance Music; Complete Dance Patterns Manual; Compulsory Dance Manual* (with overlays); *Protopopovs*. Translations in process: *Secrets of Soviet Skaters: Off-Ice Training Methods* (Tamara Moskviva); *Pages of Russian History; Patterns of Russian Ice Dance.*

Commercial videos; Skate Spinner; skate/blade necklaces; photos of skaters.

Plie Power Workshops
Contact: Rob McBrien, Co-Director, Ice Theatre of NY
c/o Sky Rink
450 W. 33rd Street
New York, NY 10001
(212) 239-4320
FAX: (212) 239-4327
Founded: 1986. Unique and acclaimed on-ice workshop featured at PSGA, LFSA Conferences '86, '91, '92, '94. Participants experience ensemble skating while learning edge and turn combinations designed to strengthen four basics of ice movement. Class taught to music and material geared to level and special interest of the class. Material designed to facilitate athletic accomplishment and provide structure for artisitic growth. Fun for all ages.

Poe, Carl
Contact: Carl M. Poe, Strength & Conditioning Coach
3100 Sweetwater Road, Apt. #314
Lawrenceville, GA 30244
(404) 381-2837; FAX: (404) 279-7267
Sport Physiologist and off-ice coach offering seminar/workshop designed to provide information pertaining to off-ice training and skating performance; sport-specific strength, conditioning and plyometrics jump training program for all levels of skating; educational material on the physiology of skating, including principles of warming-up/cooling down and edurance conditioning for skaters both on- and off-ice.

Power Play International, Inc.
Contact: Colleen Howe, President
6645 Peninsula Drive
Traverse City, MI 49684
(616) 947-1944; (616) 947-1948
FAX: (616) 947-1944
Founded: 1962. Offer services of well-known hockey players, including Gordie Howe. Design and consult for events and appearances and arrange for saleable items for these gatherings.

Pro Serve
Contact: Jerry Solomon
1101 Wilson Boulevard
Arlington, VA 22209
(703) 276-3030
Represents Nancy Kerrigan.

Pro Skating European Association
Contact: Angel Philippe, President
116 Avenue Charles de Gaulle
Neuilly/Seine, 92250 France
011-33-1-6767 8600
FAX: 011-33-1-6767 8600
Founded: 1991. Specialize in organizing skating events (professional competitions, galas, ice shows) in Europe. Plans to organize a tour in Germany, Lyon, and England in 1995.

Pro-2-Pro Services
Contact: Daryl Austman, Marketing Manager
Unit G2, 14884 North Bluff Road
White Rock, B.C., V4B 3E2 Canada
(604) 531-8007; (800) 662-1833
FAX: (604) 531-8007
Founded: 1992. Aimed toward coaches. Provides coaches with computer software to help with billing, invoicing, and tracking students, and other office supplies. Also supplies teaching aids, such as: harnesses, warm-up pants, markers for the ice, etc. Call for catalogue.

Pro-Power
Contact: Lynne Leger, Edward Apy, Power Skating Instructors
388 Milton Avenue
Oceanport, NJ 07757
(908) 571-6765
Founded: 1991. Hockey power skating instruction. Power stroking techniques for all levels focusing on edges and body alignment.

Productions East Video
Contact: Jon Cromer, Owner
20 Sunset Drive
Saratoga, NY 12866
(518) 587-4853
Founded: 1984. Video-taping ice shows, competitions and training sessions and copies of each.

Professional Skater Magazine
Professional Skaters Guild of America
P.O. Box 5904
Rochester, MN 55403
(507) 281-5122; FAX: (507) 281-5491
Bi-monthly magazine written for and by members of PSGA. Reports on rule changes, Guild activities and programs, seminars, etc. Includes Tips from the Masters, profiles of professional skaters, and historical articles.

Professional Skaters Guild of America (PSGA)
Contact: Carole Shulman, Executive Director
P.O. Box 5904
Rochester, MN 55403
(507) 281-5122; FAX: (507) 281-5491
National association for professional skaters and coaches. Publishes *Professional Skater* magazine, holds annual educational conferences and offers free fall seminars.

Proper Marketing Associates
Contact: Shep Goldberg
322 Vista Del Mar
Redondo Beach, CA 90277
(310) 378-8666
Represents Michelle Kwan.

Pumpers
Contact: Terri Fabian, Owner
300 S. Belmont
Wichita, KS 67218
(316) 683-3360
FAX: (316) 263-7636
Founded: 1968. Skating dresses, leggings, hair accessories, and skirts. Custom designing available.

R & J Video
Contact: Ron Singson
P.O. Box 70287
Stockton, CA 95267
(209) 466-3878; (209) 476-0124
Videotapes competitions; sells skating videos.

R.L.C. Skate Designs
Contact: Rhona Cantor, Manager/Director
160 Street & Viateur Street East
Montreal, Quebec, H2T 1A8 Canada
(514) 276-2000
FAX: (514) 276-0092
Founded: 1980. Manufacturer of skating apparel and accessories; skate bags, scribe and costume bags, team jackets, complete side-zip pants. Wholesale only to retail outlets.

"PLANNING A NEW RINK OR UPGRADING YOUR PRESENT FACILITY?"
Check with:

Rink-Tec International Inc.
ARENA SPECIALISTS

Let us show you what we have to offer in state-of-the-art refrigeration packages. Our computer control cross rack reduction compressor system gives you the ultimate in efficiency and ease of operation.

FOR ALL OF YOUR ARENA REQUIREMENTS, GIVE US A CALL!
RINK-TEC INTERNATIONAL, INC.
U.S.: 1-612-635-0127
CANADA: 1-807-623-1708

Racer, The
Contact: Brenda Gallagher
1600 James Naismith Drive
Suite 804
Gloucester, Ontario, K1B 5N4 Canada
ISU official-member journal of the Canadian skating federation. Deals with speed skating.

Racing Blade, The
404 Hilusi Avenue
Mt. Prospect, IL 60056
ISU official-member journal of U.S. speed-skating federation.

Rainbo Sport Shop
Contact: Cale Carvell, Owner
4836 N. Clark Street
Chicago, IL 60640
(312) 275-5500
FAX: (312) 275-5506
Founded: 1956. Toll free ordering at 800-752-8370. World-wide shipping of boots, blades, clothes, statues, books, videos, jewelry and many hard-to-find products.

Rainbow Technologies
Contact: Coola Ellestad
2353 North 120th Street
Wauwatosa, WI 53226
(414) 476-7693; FAX: (414) 476-7693
SkateMate is a hand-held ice-skate sharpener. Two knobs adjust the width of the Teflon-coated gap for optimal fit. The patented abrasive cylinder is removable and flexes under slight pressure to fit all deep-ground blades (hockey), special-ground blades (figures & freestyle), and almost all narrow flat-ground blades (speed). The result of ten years refinement and testing in Sweden.

Rebel Without A Cause/Profile
Contact: Nancy Sigel, Owner
P.O. Box 626
Sky Forest, CA 92385-0626
(909) 337-8279
FAX: (909) 337-8279
Founded: 1994. Fashion lace and velvet dresses, lycra dresses (print & solid), leotards and chiffon skirts.

Recreational Ice Skating
Contact: Justine Townsend-Smith, Editor-in-Chief
ISIA, 355 West Dundee Road
Buffalo Grove, IL 60089-3500
(708) 808-7528
Quarterly color magazine published by the Ice Skating Institute of America (ISIA) and sent to its members. Instructional articles, profiles of skaters, features on skating legends, rink and club news, plus reports on ISIA competitions and results.

Red Brick Entertainment
Contact: Rob Dustin, President
1349 Lexington Avenue
New York, NY 10128
(212) 427-4762
FAX: (212) 369-8766
Founded: 1994. Network television shows. Competitions, exhibitions, specials, video and film projects.

Red Line Sports
Contact: Vince Redford, Manager
P.O. Box 716
Soldatna, AK 99669
(907) 262-5860
FAX: (907) 262-5860
Founded: 1983. Red Line Sports is a pro shop located in an Olympic-sized ice arena (Central Penninsula Sports Center) with a capacity of 2500 people. Basically ice-hockey equipment, but also serve figure skating, in-line rollers and racquetball. We are a family/partnership.

Rice & Company
Contact: Joan Rice, Vice President
37 Franklin, #400
Buffalo, NY 14202
(800) 733-RICE; FAX: (716) 854-3346
Founded: 1974. Specialized insurance packages for skating rinks across the country - very reasonable rates.

Richardson G & A Inc.
Contact: John Gray, President
P.O. Box 1831
Exeter, NH 03833
(603) 772-0860; FAX: (603) 772-0873
Founded: 1990. Property and casualty insurance for ice or in-line skating arenas.

Ricque Sportswear
Contact: Rick Young, Vice President
24371 Catherine Industrial Rd., Suite 227
Novi, MI 48375
(800) 344-1230; FAX: (810) 344-7663
Founded: 1988. We sell a wide variety of skating clothes and accessories for both the individual skater and precision teams. This company was founded by a family that holds the sport close at heart and realizes the need for top-quality, yet affordable skating apparel and accessories: skating dresses, leotards, legs, stirrups, skirts, bike shorts, unitards, warm-ups, jackets, bags, scribes, bootcovers, etc. We handle custom orders for teams.

Riedell Skate Co.
Contact: Daniel Riegelman,
 Vice President
122 Cannon River Avenue
Red Wing, MN 55066
(612) 388-8251; FAX: (612) 388-8616
Founded: 1945. Manufacturer of Riedell custom-made and stock skating boots for figure skating, hockey and speed skating, plus boots for skate rental. Also serves as distributor for Wilson and MK blades and other skating accessories.

Rink Systems, Inc.
Contact: Stacey Overgaard, Operations
 Manager
1103 Hershey St.
Albert Lea, MN 56007
(800) 944-7930; FAX: (507) 377-1060
Founded: 1993. Design, construction, and renovation of complete ice rink systems. Manufacture, install, and provide service and accessories for refrigeration systems, concrete and sand rink floors, dasherboards, and rink maintenance equipment.

Rink-Tec International Inc.
Contact: Daryl Cox, District Manager
1751 W. County Road B, Suite 107
Roseville, MN 55113
(612) 635-0127
FAX: (612) 638-9023
Founded: 1979. We can supply all or any part of an ice arena. Refrigeration systems and floors, dehumidification, dasher boards, ice resurfacers (new and used). Ice edgers, skate sharpeners, nets, skates, etc.

Risport
Contact: Advertising Director
31035 Crocetta del Montello
Treviso, Italy
47 42 12 13; FAX: 47 42 06 07
See *Boots and Blades* chapter for U.S. distributors.

RMI Industrial Refrigeration Systems
Contact: Thomas Brenton, Sales & Engineering Manager
6790 Kitimat Road., Unit 20
Mississauga, L5N5L9 Canada
(905) 858-7969; FAX: (905) 858-7973
Design, supply and installation of refrigeration systems for ice rinks and other applications.

Roller Stop Inc.
Contact: John Petell, President
P.O. Box 219
Malden, MA 02148
(617) 324-2272; FAX: (617) 324-4449
Founded: 1992. This toe pic for in-line skates serves as a guide for forward lean without over-rotating, as well as a pic to plant in preparation for jumps. The pic provides the assurance you need to perform jumps, spins, Bauers, three-turns, etc.

Rollerblade, Inc.
Contact: Maureen O'Neill, Public Relations Manager
5101 Shady Oak Road
Minnetonka, MN 55343
(800) 232-7655; (612) 930-7000
Founded: 1980. Rollerblade, Inc. manufactures in-line skates, protective gear, and accessories. It is the pioneer of the in-line skating industry.

Rose Custom Boots, Ltd.
P.O. Box 21057
Holiday Postal Outlet
Cambridge, Ontario, N3C 4B1 Canada
(519) 622-3340
Founded: 1974. Manufactures line of custom Rose skate boots.

Rosenberg, Michael.
See MARCO Entertainment.

S.H. Stoery & Son
Contact: Jess Stoery, Chief of Operations
2139 Evert Court
Northbrook, IL 60062
(708) 205-1548
Founded: 1977. Precision sharpening and mounting of figure-skating blades. Sell SP-Teri, Harlick, Riedell boots (new and used). Waterproofing, proper balancing.

Sasaki Associates, Inc.
Contact: Roy Viklund, AIA, Principal; Director, Sports Facility Design Group
64 Pleasant Street
Watertown, MA 02172
(617) 926-3300; FAX: (617) 924-2748
Founded: 1953. Planning, programming, feasibility studies, architecture, site design and engineering for college and university athletic and recreational

Sports Shop
RAINBO

YOUR *BEST* ICE SKATING SOURCE!

OUR HUGE ICE SKATING INVENTORY IS JUST A *FREE* PHONE CALL AWAY.
FAST FRIENDLY DEPENDABLE SERVICE---
GUARANTEED!

- SP-Teri & Riedell Boots
- Harlick & Risport Boots
- Wilson & MK Blades
- Bags - Scribes - Accessories
- Artwork & Stationery
- Books & Videos
- The Kickline Collection Apparel
- Inga - Danskin - Mondor
- T-Shirts & Sweatshirts
- Beadwork Patterns & Austrian Crystals
- Fine & Novelty Jewelry
- Speed & Hockey Lines
- Christmas Ornaments & Novelties
- Ceramics - Pewter - Collectibles
- Everything for Ice Skaters

CALL TODAY FOR YOUR *FREE* 32 PAGE FULL COLOR CATALOG
1/800-752-8370

3 CHICAGOLAND LOCATIONS...

RAINBO SPORTS SHOP
4836 N. CLARK STREET
CHICAGO, IL 60640
PH 312/275-5500
FAX 312/275-5506
Toll-Free Ordering:
1-800/752-8370

RAINBO II
5920 W. DEMPSTER
MORTON GROVE, IL. 60053
708/470-0323

COMING SOON----
RAINBO III
NAPERVILLE, IL.

Serving the Skating Community with Honesty & Integrity for over 38 Years.

facilities. Recent projects include Conte Forum at Boston College, with an 8,800 seat hockey/basketball arena, and the Arena/Student Recreation Center at the University of New Hampshire (which includes a new 6,000-seat hockey arena), and the conversion of the existing Snively Hockey Arena into a three-level recreation center with gymnasium, fitness center, racquet courts and administrative offices.

Satin Stitches
Contact: Deborah J. Nelson, Owner/Designer
11894 Reisling Blvd. NW
Minneapolis, MN 55433
(612) 323-9507
FAX: (612) 323-9741
Founded: 1978. Custom designed costumes! We specialize in performance costumes for precision teams, pairs and soloists. We custom design for all sizes and shapes, men and women. Out of state, call (800) 48-SATIN.

Schaats Magazine
Postbox 1120
NL-3800 BC, Amersfoort, Netherlands
ISU official-member journal of the Netherlands' skating federation.

Sharpe Public Relations
Contact: Kathi Sharpe-Ross, President
9230 Olympic Blvd., Suite 203
Beverly Hills, CA 90212
(310) 274-3587
FAX: (310) 274-5980
Founded: 1988. Public relations and promotion for Robin Cousins. Promotion, marketing, international show production, sponsorship development.

Sherman (Keith) & Associates
Contact: Keith Sherman, President
120 West 44th St,
New York, NY 10036
(212) 764-7900
FAX: (212) 764-0344
Founded: 1989. Public relations agency whose clients include Brian Boitano, Bill Graham Presents, arena tours (Boitano/Witt, Nancy Kerrigan/Aaron Neville) and television specials (*Ice Wars, Canvas of Ice*).

Show-Off, Inc.
Contact: Tommye, President
2567 Greenleaf Avenue
Elk Grove, IL 60007
(708) 439-0206; FAX: (708) 439-0219
Founded: 1973. Manufacturer of custom-made costumes. We also carry fabrics, trims, beads, sequins and rhinestones. Can design special costumes for soloists as well as teams.

Silver Blade Tours
Contact: Barbara Cassella, President
412 Cromwell Avenue
Rocky Hill, CT 06067
(203) 721-7670
FAX: (203) 563-6717
Arrange trips for spectators to many skating tours and competitions, including World Championships and the U.S. Open.

Silver Lining, Ltd.
Contact: Shirley Banghart, President
13006 Crescent Court
Crestwood, IL 60445
Sales: (708) 458-4030; (708) 388-1485
FAX: (708) 388-9083
Founded: 1983. Customized wholesale - offering the largest selection of fabrics available. Also specializing in precision teams, gymnastic teams and ice shows.

SK Sport Shoes Ltd.
Contact: Steve Kolozsvary, President
280 Donlands Avenue
Toronto, Ontario, M4J 3R4 Canada
(416) 465-2784
FAX: (416) 465-7802
Founded: 1966. SK boots are hand-made in Canada (stock or cutom). The current World Champion (1994) wears SK boots, as do many top skaters. We make many models to suit each skater.

Skate Art Jewelry by John Albeita
Contact: John Albeita, Owner
6131 Luther Lane #224
Dallas, TX 75225
(214) 369-6191; (800) 323-2638
FAX: (214) 369-6855
Founded: 1981. Our most popular item is *The Skater* design. Available in three sizes with and without diamonds. Other designs available all in 14kt gold and sterling silver. 1-800-323-2638.

Skate Bag, The
Contact: David & Rita Lowery, Owners
251 Lakeview Drive
Oldsmar, FL 34677
(813) 855-7998
FAX: (813) 854-4031
Founded: 1992. Pro shop for figure skating and hockey equipment. Skating clothes, accessories, and bags. Memorabilia, old magazines, books and photos.

Skate Design International
Contact: Sue Lyons, Owner
50191 Mile End
Utica, MI 48317
(810) 731-2272
Founded: 1983. Fabrics: Lycra, glissinette, stretch satin & velvet, knit stretch chiffon. Patterns: Boys and mends pants, girls skirted trunks & legs, plus dresses. Custom patterns made from sketches. No ready-made apparel.

Skate Music
Contact: Nancy Varner, Music Librarian
25 Holyoke Street, Apt. #6
Boston, MA 02116
(617) 859-7844
Founded: 1990. Music research service which helps skaters find and choose instrumental versions of vocal music, out-of-print music, etc.

Skate 'N Style
Contact: Susan Lynch, Marcia Steinberg, Partners
175 Underhill Blvd.
Syosset, NY 11791
(516) 496-3448
FAX: (516) 496-4964
Founded: 1991. Skate 'N Style is the exclusive supplier of Zip-Eze Brand line of warm-up suits and sweaters, featuring pants with side seam zippers from waist to cuff allowing easy-on-easy-off without removing your skates. Hot fashion colors!

Skate Shop - IL
Contact: John Harmata, President
5505 West 127th S.
Crestwood, IL 60445
(708) 389-7849
Boots: SP-Teri, Harlick, Riedell, Risport, Dominion. Blades: MK, Wilson.

Skate Shop - NY
Contact: Joel Halpern, Manager
99 Cutter Mill Rd.
Great Neck, NY 11021
(516) 487-6948
Founded: 1940. Full-line shop which carries boots (Harlick, Riedell, Sp-Teri), blades (MK, Wilson), outfits, hockey, etc.

Skate Spinner
Contact: George Sterling, Manager
4550 Birch Bay Lynden Road
Blaine, WA 98230
(800) 661-3199; (800) 663-1774
FAX: (206) 371-3631
Founded: 1993. Skate Spinner allows the figure skater to practice spins without ice. It is portable and moves like a skate blade on floors, tile, or carpet. Place one foot on Skate Spinner, and spin. The Canadian Olympic Team uses Skate Spinner for summer training and took it to Lillehammer. Volume discounts available.

Skater's Choice Gift Boutique
Contact: Connie Anderson, Owner
370 Deerpath Deer
Winthrop Harbor, IL 60096
(708) 746-3650
FAX: (708) 746-3655
Founded: 1987. The Gift Boutique (open Saturdays only), features custom apparel, novelty sweaters and sweatshirts, jewelry, books, collectibles, artwork, antiques, unique gift items and Christmas decorations. Telephone and mail orders welcome.

Skater's Choice Pro Shop
Contact: Connie Anderson, Owner
Kenosha County Ice Arena
7727 60th Avenue
Kenosha, WI 53142
(414) 697-1615
Founded: 1987. The Pro Shop carries a full line of figure skating and hockey equipment, apparel, accessories and gift items.

Skater's Edge
Contact: Alice Berman, Publisher
Box 500
Kensington, MD 20895
(301) 946-1971; FAX: (301) 946-1971
The world's leading international 'how-to' publication, devoted to the practical aspects of ice skating. Published five times a year. Articles by top coaches and pros, including Natalia Dubova, Robin Cousins, Don Jackson, Ron Ludington, Cecily Morrow, and many others. Write/call for free brochure. Also publisher of the *Skater's Edge Sourcebook*.

Skater's Edge - NY
Contact: Phyllis Petri, Owner
174 Plaza Drive
Williamsville, NY 14221
(716) 636-3000
FAX: (716) 636-1776
Founded: 1984. Boots: Jackson, SP-Teri, Harlick, Riedell, Risport. Blades: MK, Wilson. Clothing: Danskin. Capezio, Silver Lining, trims, sequins, gifts. Hockey: Riedell, CCM, tape/mouth guards.

STAY WARM... SAVE TIME.... WITH ZIP-EZE®

Sweaters and Warm-Up Suits

Easy - On - Easy - Off Waist to Cuff Zippers

Hot Fashion Colors

For more information call:
Skate 'N Style
175 Underhill Blvd., Syosset, NY 11791
Phone: (516) 496-3448 • Fax: (516) 496-4964
Dealer inquiries welcome

---

*Skaters

show up in a show-off— quality custom-made costumes, fabric & exquisite trim!

2567 GREENLEAF
ELK GROVE, IL 60007
708/439-0206

TRIMSUITS BY
show-off inc.

Send $2.50 for color catalog

Skater's Edge - OH
Contact: Dale or Carl Merkel, Owners
16211 Lorain Avenue
Cleveland, OH 44111
(216) 252-3986
FAX: (216) 671-4222
Founded: 1978. Boots: Riedell, SP-Teri, Harlick, Risport. Blades: Wilson, MK.

Skater's Loft
Contact: Donna Doyle, Owner
203 State St.
Ogdensburg, NY 13669
(315) 393-0764
FAX: (315) 393-4212
Founded: 1992.

Skater's Paradise, Inc.
Contact: Michael Cunningham, President
1602 Belleview Blvd.
Alexandria, VA 22307
(703) 660-6525; FAX: (703) 660-2341
Founded: 1979. Full-line skate shop offering sales and service. Boots and blades by Riedell, Harlick, S-P Teri, Klingbeil, Rose, WIFA, Risport, MK and Wilson. Tights, dresses and warm-ups. Full line hockey equipment dealer and Lacross equipment. In-line skates by Rollerblade, K2, Oxygen, Roces and CCM. Related protective gear and replacement parts. Specialize in custom boots, blade mounting and sharpening.

Skater's Paradise of Delaware, Inc.
Contact: Michael Cunningham, President
University of Delaware Ice Arena
South College Avenue, DE 19716
(302) 738-2999
Founded: 1994. Full-line skate shop offering sales and service. Boots and blades by Riedell, Harlick, S-P Teri, Klingbeil, Rose, WIFA, Risport, MK and Wilson. Tights, dresses and warm-ups. Full line hockey equipment dealer and Lacross equipment. In-line skates by Rollerblade, K2, Oxygen, Roces and CCM. Related protective gear and replacement parts. Custom boots, blade mounting and sharpening.

Skater's Scribe
Contact: Jeanne Morman
4222 Melbourne Road
Indianapolis, IN 46208
(317) 297-5772
Maintains current listing of ice dance weekends by date with city, name and contact person. Send self addressed stamped envelope with request for current listing.

Skatetours
Contact: Kathy Normile Davidson, President, CTC
206 E Court Street, P.O. Box 937
Rocky Mount, VA 24151
(703) 483-3700; FAX: (703) 483-5080
Founded: 1982. Skatetours is an all-inclusive escorted journey to a major ice event which features first class/deluxe accommodations, excellent seating at the sporting event, ground transfers and transportation to the event; local sightseeing, private functions and parties, catering to all ages. Completely packaged and handled by Kathy Normile, a former U.S. National and professional pairs competitor.

Skating Association for the Blind and Handicapped (SABAH)
Contact: Elizabeth M. O'Donnell, President & Founder
c/o Kaufmann's
1255 Niagara Falls Blvd
Buffalo, NY 14226
(716) 833-2994
FAX: (716) 833-2997
Founded: 1977. We provide skating instruction for people with mental, physical or emotional challenges. Founded in 1977, we currently serve over 750 people annually. We operate at 5 rinks in the western New York area.

Skating Magazine
Contact: Jay Miller, Editor
USFSA
20 First Street
Colorado Springs, CO 80906-3697
(719) 635-5200
Magazine published by the United States Figure Skating Association (USFSA). Six issues a year are in color and include profiles of various skaters, reports on competitions. Alternating with the six color issues are six black and white issues that list results of competitions, tests, plus rule changes, and other association details. Free with membership in USFSA.

Skating News
Contact: Pete Roberts
Little over the Water, Sanday
Orkney, KWD 2BL Great Britain
01 857 60 04 65
FAX: 01 857 60 04 65
Founded: 1987. A news magazine for competitive skaters giving local, national, and international news, reports, comment, etc. Published ten times per year (monthly except Jan. & Aug.)

Skojtesport
Gogevang 4A
Postbox 176
DK-2970 Horsholm, Denmark
ISU official-member journal of the Danish skating federation.

Skoytesport
Hauger Skolevei 1
N-1341 Rud, Norway
ISU official-member journal of the Norwegian skating federation.

Skridsko-nytt
Svenska Skridskoforbundet
Eskilsgatan 67
S-63356 Eskilstuna, Sweden
ISU official member journal of the Swedish speed-skating federation.

Slap Shot Sports
Contact: Ed Krokchmal, President
560 Northfield Avenue
West Orange, NJ 07052
(201) 736-9107; FAX: (201) 736-1115
Founded: 1978. Riedell boots, Wilson blades, recreational skates, MK blades, competition dresses.

SP-Teri Company, Inc.
Contact: George Spiteri, President
436 No Canal Street, #1
South San Francisco, CA 94080
(415) 871-1715
FAX: (415) 871-9062
Founded: 1963. SP-Teri stock and custom skate boots. Wholesale to rinks and sport shops. Retail to skaters. Ice skating and roller skating boots (not mounted).

Special Olympics International
Contact: Brian McMonagle, Sport Department
1325 G Street, NW, Suite 500
Washington, DC 20005 USA
(202) 628-3630
FAX: (202) 824-0200
Founded: 1968. Created by the Joseph P. Kennedy Jr. Foundation to promote physical fitness, sports training, and athletic competition for mentally retarded children and adults. Seeks to contribute to the physical, social, and psychological development of the mentally retarded. Participants range in age from 8 years to adult and compete in track and field, swimming, gymnastics, bowling, ice skating, basketball, and other sports.

Sport Concepts
Contact: Marsh Penning, President/Owner
P.O. Box 3126
Clearwater Beach, FL 34630-8126
(813) 442-2639
FAX: (813) 442-2639
Founded: 1982. One skate bag designed specifically for skaters. Mail order only.

The Skater's Choice

New Location:
Skating Equipment, Apparel, Accessories and Gift Items, Plus Hockey Equipment
at
The Skaters Choice
Pro Shop
Kenosha County Ice Arena
7727 60th Avenue
Kenosha, WI 53142
Telephone (414) 697-1615

Skating Gift Boutique
370 Deerpath Drive
Winthrop Harbor, IL 60096
(708) 746-3650

Open Saturdays only
12 - 4 pm

Sport Consulting Centre
Contact: Shawna Palmer, Sports Psychology Consultant
P.O. Box 54135 - 1562 Lonsdale Avenue
North Vancouver, B.C. V7M 3L5 Canada
(604) 987-8488
FAX: (604) 987-8488
Founded: 1990. *Get the Edge*, by Shawna Palmer, gives skaters and coaches the psychological skills needed to compete and perform. Topics include controlling nerves, building confidence, imagery, competition preparation, goal setting, monitoring performance, and improving concentration. In addition to private consulting, Palmer conducts sports psychology seminars.

Sports Asylum, Inc.
Contact: Don Laner, President-Owner
9018 Balboa Blvd.
Northridge, CA 91325
(800) 929-2159
FAX: (818) 895-4763
Founded: 1991. We carry a complete selection of books and videos for the player, the coach, the parent and the fan. Much of our stock is brought in from Canada and is not easily found in the U.S. Special discounts are available for retailers.

Sports Jewelry Etc.
Contact: Jim Burk, President
71 River Road
Bow, NH 03304
(603) 224-2154
FAX: (603) 228-8799
14KT gold and sterling silver skaters jewelry featuring pendents, charms and earrings.

Sports Representatives Ltd.
Contact: Robert B. Haggert, President
594 Mount Pleasant Road
Toronto, Ontario, M4S 2M8 Canada
(416) 485-4189
FAX: (416) 485-8104
Founded: 1970. Event marketing and management, licensing, merchandising, publishing, public relations.

Squaw Valley USA
Contact: Bret Smith, Advertising
P.O Box 2007
Olympic Valley, CA 96146
(916) 583-6985
FAX: (916) 581-7106
The Olympic Ice Pavillion is located at High Camp Bath and Tennis Club, elevation 2,800 feet (via cable car). Open year-round. Other activities include skiing, swimming, bungee jumping.

Stan's Skate Shop
Contact: Stan Belliveau, Vice President
662 Bay 6th Street
West Islip, NY 11795
(516) 587-1658
Founded: 1974. Figure skates and hockey equipment.

ELEGANCE ON ICE

Custom-designed costumes for precision teams, figure skating soloists and pairs, and ice dancers

Satin Stitches
Satin Stitches
11894 Reisling Blvd. N.W.
Minneapolis, MN 55433
1-800-48SATIN or 612/323-9507

design and fit,
durability and style
sensational performance

Starbuck & Company, Inc.
Contact: JoJo Starbuck, President
12 John Street, 7th Floor
New York, NY 10038
(212) 437-5283
FAX: (212) 437-5285
Starbuck & Company is a special event production company specializing in producing and staging custom tailored ice shows for corporate entertainment, events, promotional events, arena shows and celebrations. Two-time Olympian, JoJo Starbuck has conducted her clinic, JoJo's *Extra Edge* Workshop, to skaters of all levels around the U.S. and abroad. After years of working with Olympic skaters and training with dance choreographers, JoJo focuses her workshops on edges, turns, and *Moves in the Field* as well as style, expression & choreography.

Steamboats/Blades
Contact: Jim Fournier, Owner/Operator
29565 W. U.S. 40
Steamboat Spring, CO 80477
(303) 879-3286
FAX: (303) 879-3286
Northwest, central, western Colorado. Southern Wyoming, Eastern Utah. Professional service, wide selection of equipment, good prices. Bring your skates when you come to ski.

Stellar Images
Contact: George Rossano, Photographer
1116 A Eighth Street, Suite #51
Manhattan Beach, CA 90266
(310) 336-6056
FAX: (310) 336-7130
Founded: 1988. On ice, still photography, studio photography, competition video.

Sterling (Michael) and Associates
Contact: Michael Sterling, President
4242 Van Nuys Blvd.
Sherman Oaks, CA 91403-3710
(818) 385-0007
FAX: (818) 385-0004
Founded: 1982. Publicity, public relations, celebrities, theatre, literary, events. Representing Scott Hamilton since 1987.

Streeter, Meg
Contact: Meg Streeter, Freelance Director
11819 Chase Lake
Houston, TX 77077
(713) 597-1193
FAX: (713) 597-1195
Freelance television director working for the networks and cable; specializes in figure skating; not a company, but hired by others.

Stretch Quest
Contact: Duke Wier, Managing Partner
P.O. Box 770 #148
Park City, UT 84060
(800) 375-7057; (801) 649-2939
FAX: (801) 649-0931
Founded: 1993. Stretch Quest is a new portable stretching aid machine which allows safe, natural full range split stretches. Lower back and upper body stretches can also be done while on the machine, resulting in increased flexibility and range of motion and decreased risk of injury. Stretch Quest telescopes from a 24-inch split to a 98-inch split, and can be increased in 1/2-inch increments with control pin settings. It weighs approximately 6 lbs and folds to 26-inches.

Style Seminars For Skaters
Contact: Ann-Margreth Frei, Creator
Magic of Style Videos
P.O. Box 2676
Vail, CO 81658
(303) 926-3345; FAX: (303) 926-5176
Founded: 1979. Goals: Develop style, awareness, performance, choreography.

Sue's Knits
Contact: Sue Andrysiak
6393 Gallery Drive
Canton, MI 48187
(313) 416-5363; FAX: (313) 207-7758
Knit shop- Dolls with skater outfits & skates.

Sulyma Productions Inc.
Contact: Michael Sulyma, President
6620 124 Street
Edmonton, Alberta, T6H 3V3 Canada
(403) 438-8316; FAX: (403) 488-0858
Founded: 1987. Touring, film, and TV production company specializing in ice skating specials. Videos of recent production, *A Midsummer Night's Ice Dream*, available.

Sun Valley Skate Shop
Contact: Daisy Layngley
Sun Valley Center
Sun Valley, ID 83353
(208) 622-2196
Chiffon skating skirts.

Sunday River Ski Resort
Contact: Skip King, Director of Communications
P.O. Box 450
Bethel, ME 04217
(207) 824-3000; FAX: (207) 824-2111
Founded: 1960. Fourteen chairlifts, 101 trails, 90% snow making coverage. Extensive slope-side lodging. Snow activities include horsedrawn sleigh rides, ice skating. Live entertainment for kids and adults. Outdoor unrefrigerated ice surface maintained by Zamboni; skating dependent upon weather conditions.

Suomen Taitoluistelu
Radiokatu 20
FIN-00240, Helsinki, Finland
ISU official-member journal of the Finnish figure-skating federation.

Svensk Konstakning
c/o Margaretha Insulander
Spelbogard
Pl 1007, S-745 93, Enkoping Sweden
ISU official-member journal of the Swedish figure-skating federation.

S.W. Fabrics
336 West Shire Road
Baltimore, MD 21229
(800) 637-9892
Fabrics: Chiffon, pearl chiffon, Lycra, satin, stretch satin, neon stretch satin, velvet, stretch velvet, stretch sequin materials, raindrop Lycras, trims, rinestones, appliques.

Swedice Inc.
Contact: Bengt Eggemar, President
431 South Dearborn Street
Chicago, IL 60605-1121
(312) 258-5820; FAX: (312) 258-5828
The phone number above is the U.S. contact for Swedice, Inc.

Swonee's Place
Contact: Henry Welch, Owner
125 North Weinbach
Evansville, IN 47711
(800) 293-6741
Founded: 1986. Boots: Riedell, Dominion, SP-Teri, Harlick, Jackson. Blades: MK, Wilson. Clothing: Capezio, Danskin, Unicorn. Dolls.

T&T Productions
Contact: Gary Todd, Owner
1141 Thayer Avenue
Cottage Grove, OR 97424
(503) 942-9387
Founded: 1990. We offer pre-edited program tapes ranging from 1 to 3 minutes. Custom editing from CD or cassette. Our catalog includes classical, movies and shows, popular and many more with custom editing from your personal library or from ours. Blank 10 and 20 minute cassettes also available.

Tana's Gold
Contact: Susan Fogt, Owner
1204 W Main Street
Troy, OH 45373
(513) 335-4698
Founded: 1987. All 14kt gold ice-skating jewelry items. Charms, bracelets, earrings, rings, etc.

That's A Wrap
Contact: Stephanie Miller, Owner
2127 Edison Hills Court
Oxford, MI 48370
(810) 628-0396
Founded: 1992. Chiffon or Georgette single or double wrap skirts. For ice dancing or for off-ice dance. Comes in various colors and prints.

Think Rink
Contact: Michael J. Carroll, Rink Facility/ Program Manager
332 Old Route 304
New York City, NY 10956
(914) 634-8996
Arena turn-key services; revenue master planning; management and programming.

Thompson & LaPointe
Contact: Paul LaPointe, President
105 Thursfield Crescent
Toronto, Ontario, M4G 2N4 Canada
(416) 467-9864
FAX: (416) 467-0256
Founded: 1991. Art consultant and publisher of the *Ice Series* and representative for original works of art by Toller Cranston.

Tip Nunn's Events, Inc.
Contact: Lynn Plage
2801 Youngfield #210
Golden, CO 80401
(303) 237-0616; FAX: (303) 237-0609
Founded: 1986. Publicist for the Discover Card *Stars on Ice Tour* and the *America Tour*. Also promotes other sports, including U.S.A Volleyball, Indy Car Racing, and Roller Hockey, plus various bowling tournaments, tennis, and other sports.

Special Event Production ∾ Workshops ∾ Choreography

JoJo Starbuck's 13-year amateur career with partner Ken Shelley incudes three U.S. pairs titles, two Olympic Games, and two World Bronze medals. As a professional, she has starred in *Ice Capades*, numerous TV specials, and partnered Olympic Champion John Curry in his critically acclaimed show on Broadway and at the Metropolitan Opera House.

In her nine years of running Starbuck & Company, Inc., JoJo has produced, staged, directed, and/or choreographed over 100 custom-tailored ice shows and special events. Clients range from Rockefeller Center to The White House, from Durasoft and GTE to *Saturday Night Live* and Radio City Music Hall.

In addition to creating special events, JoJo has conducted her *Extra Edge Workshop* for skaters of all ages and levels, in the U.S. and abroad. Drawing from her rich and diverse background—which has included work with both Olympians and dance choreographers—JoJo's workshop focuses on edges, footwork, and *Moves in the Field*, as well as style, polish, and expression.

For more information, please call **Steven Lu** at (212) 437-5283.

JoJo Starbuck

Tohaventa Holdings Inc.
Contact: Geoffrey Leboutillier, President
10022-103rd Street
Edmonton, Alberta, T5J 0X2 Canada
(403) 421-8879
FAX: (403) 426-1049
An independent film and television production company that has created a half-hour video Christmas drama (1993) entitled *The Crystal Ball* (featuring the Ice Theatre of Canada) plus *A Midsummer Night's Ice Dream*, a one-hour drama starring Liz Manley and Yuka Sato (1994).

Tom Collins Enterprises, Inc.
Contact: Tom Collins, Owner
3500 W. 80th Street, Suite 190
Minneapolis, MN 55431
(612) 831-2237
FAX: (612) 831-0566
Founded: 1972. Produces the Tom Collins Campbell's Soup *Tour of World Figure Skating Champions*.

Tomy's Skater Shop
Contact: Cindy Carew, Vice President
1209 Baker Road #404
Virginia Beach, VA 23455
(804) 464-1464
FAX: (804) 464-1157
Founded: 1991. Provides the artisitic figure skater with quality equipment and services. Proper fitting of Risport boots, mounting of ice blades and professional sharpenings are top priority.

Tournament Sports
Contact: Wayne Sehagena
145 Northfield Drive
Waterloo, Ontartio, N2L 5J3 Canada
(519) 888-6500
FAX: (519) 888-6540
Distributor of the Jackson line of boots designed by and named after Don Jackson, 1962 World Champion.

Tracings Magazine
Contact: Mary Clarke, Editor
21 Weybosset Street
N. Weymouth, MA 02191
(617) 335-9135; FAX: (617) 340-5648
Founded: 1976. News and information on competitions, shows, and skaters. Coverage national and international. Known for incisive writing of high quality.

Travel One
Contact: Elaine Shore, Manager
121 Mount Vernon Street
Boston, MA 62108
(617) 523-8161; (800) 782-7232
FAX: (617) 523-2759
Travel agent serving members of the Professional Skaters Guild of America (PSGA) and others.

Tuflex Rubber Flooring
Contact: Nancy MacNaughton, Marketing Service Representative
4521 West Crest Avenue
Tampa, FL 33614
(800) 543-0390
FAX: (813) 875-2312
Founded: 1957. 3/8-inch thick (in 27-inch squares) resilient rubber flooring by Tuflex is exceptionally durable in locker rooms, concession areas and ice rinks. Company has been producing colorful flooring of 100% recycled rubber since 1957. Catalogue available.

Turner Sports
One CNN Center
Atlanta, GA 30303
(404) 827-1735
FAX: (404) 827-1339
Turner Broadcasting System sports division.

Twizzle Designs, Inc.
Contact: Beth Queau, President
P.O. Box 721
231 Heather Drive
Dryden, Ontario, P8N 2Z4 Canada
(807) 223-4533
FAX: (807) 223-6772
Founded: 1987. Skating apparel manufacturer: practice, competition, and custom apparel and accessories. Phone 1-800-665-4363 for colour catalogue. Dealer inquiries welcome.

U.S. Figure Skating Association (USFSA)
Contact: Jerry Lace, Executive Director
20 First Street
Colorado Sprngs, CO 80906 USA
(719) 635-5200
FAX: (719) 635-9548
Figure skating member of the ISU representing the USA. The USFSA is the governing body for amateur figure skating on ice in the U.S. Since 1921, the USFSA has directed and encouraged the development of figure skating skills instruction and supervised the competitive aspects of the sport. Its national, world, and Olympic champions have made major contributions to figure skating and established outstanding international records and reputations. The USFSA has a membership of over 120,000 athletes and supporters; membership is open to anyone.

U.S. Olympic Committee (USOC)
Contact: Bob Condron, Public Relations
One Olympic Plaza
Colorado Springs, CO 80909
(719) 578-4529
FAX: (719) 578-4677

U.S. Olympic Training Center (USOTC) — CO
1750 East Boulder
Colorado Springs, CO 80909
(719) 578-4618
FAX: (719) 578-4728
Founded: 1977. Olympic training center for ten resident sports, including figure skating. Access is limited and available only to top athletes through each sport's national governing body (e.g., USFSA). Operated under the auspices of the U.S.Olympic Committee (USOC).

U.S. Olympic Training Center (USOTC) — NY
Contact: Jack Favro
Old Military Rd.
Lake Placid, NY 12946
(518) 523-2600
FAX: (518) 523-1570
Olympic training center for winter sports, including figure skating. Operated under the auspices of the U.S.Olympic Committee (USOC). Access is limited and available only to top athletes through each sport's national governing body (e.g., USFSA). Operated under the auspices of the U.S.Olympic Committee (USOC).

U.S. Olympic Training Center (USOTC) — San Diego
San Diego National Sports Training Foundation
1650 Hotel Circle North, Suite 125
San Diego, CA 92108-2817
(619) 291-8802
FAX: (619) 291-5395
Founded: 1995. New Olympic Training

Center for summer sports, scheduled to open Spring 1995. No figure skating in the present plans, but may be incorporated in the future. Access is limited and available only to top athletes through each sport's national governing body (e.g., USFSA). Operated under the auspicies of the U.S. Olympic Committee (USOC).

Udell Photo Video
Contact: Bill Udell, Owner
6066 Vantage Avenue
North Hollywood, CA 91606
(818) 985-6866
FAX: (818) 985-6867
Founded: 1948. Award photography. Videographers.

Unicorn Sport
Contact: Barbara McKendry, President
1411 North Sixth Avenue
Knoxville, TN 37917
(615) 523-3343; FAX: (615) 522-8560
Founded: 1979. Unicorn Sport manufactures practice and competitive skatewear, bootcovers, and lighted 'Foot Lites' bootcovers. Custom designed skate clothing is available to precision teams and clubs.

Unique Skating Apparel
Contact: Judy Pingatore, Owner
1101 Davitt
Sault Ste. Marie, MI 49783
(906) 632-1276
Founded: 1986. Skating apparel pattern catalog. Patterns for: dresses with overlays; 3-in-1 skirt; long-back skirt; chiffon wrap skirts; legs; basic dress; leotard.

Univ. of MI Sport Facilities Research Laboratory (SFRL)
Contact: Jack Vivian, Director
100 South State Street
Ann Arbor, MI 48109-2201
(313) 764-4599
FAX: (313) 764-4597
Founded: 1989. A research-based organization which provides information, training, and consulting for planning, designing, and managing specialized and multipurpose ice sport and recreational facilities.

Up In The Air, Inc.
Contact: Debbie Howe, Director of Administration
1245 Old Ailpharetta Rd.
Alpharetta, GA 30202
(404) 751-0913
FAX: (404) 751-0543
Founded: 1987. Up In The Air, Inc. offers a wide variety of hockey and figure skating essentials. Our quality products help skaters look their best and perform at their highest level.

USA Hockey, Inc.
Contact: Brian S. Petrovek, Assistant Executive Director
4965 North 30th Street
Colorado Springs, CO 80919 USA
(719) 599-5500; FAX: (719) 599-5899
Founded: 1937. The national governing body for the sport of ice hockey in the U.S. Its mission is to promote the growth

STRETCH QUEST
STRETCHING AID

To Order Call: 1-800-375-7057
Special Pricing
Reg. $99.95
$85
Plus shipping and handling.

STRETCH QUEST™ *Stretching Aid was developed to provide a safe stretching routine. The compactible* **STRETCH QUEST™** *folds up to 26", is remarkable lightweight at 6 lbs. and ideal for transporting to competitions, use at the training studio, ice rink or home.*

The benefits to muscles include:

- *Takes the risk out of floor and partner stretching*
- *Builds strength in the legs through isometric stretching.*
- *Helps prevent injury.*
- *Natural stretch occurs as muscle groups fatigue.*
- *Specific to the muscle tendon group.*
- *Allows muscles to contract into the stretch, resulting in a more relaxed stretch.*

Refer a friend to purchase Stretch Quest Stretching Aid and receive $20.

U.S. Pairs National Champions

STRETCH QUEST™ • P.O. Box 770 #148 • Park City, UT 84060 • 1-800-375-7057 • Fax: 801-649-0931   *One year unconditional warranty.*

of ice hockey and to provide the best possible experience for all participants in the United States by encouraging, developing, advancing and adminstering the sport. Publishes *American Hockey Magazine*. Has formed new division, USA Hockey InLine for in-line players.

Valley Skating Supplies
Contact: Pete Lemoine, Manager/Owner
11410 Burbank Blvd. #1
North Hollywood, CA 91601
(818) 980-0414
Founded: 1983. Boots: SP-Teri, Harlick, Riedell. Blades: MK, Wilson. Clothes: Danskin, Mondor. Videos, jewelry, Rollerblades.

Varese Sarabande Records
11846 Ventura Blvd., Suite 130
Studio City, CA 91604
(818) 753-4143; FAX: (818) 753-7596
Founded: 1978. CDs; Put out movie soundtracks; Instrumental.

Variety Arts
Contact: Ellen Jacob, Co-Director
140 Sherman Street, Ground Floor
Fairfield, CT 06430
(203) 259-3959; (800) 221-2154
Founded: 1982. We specialize in quality gift items with skating themes, such as coloring books, jewelry, coffee mugs, notebooks, picture frames, pens, pencils, etc. Products (sold at full-wholesale discounts) can be used as gifts or re-sold for fund-raising or profit (clubs, schools). Items designed and manufactured excusively by Variety Arts and cannot be found elsewhere.

Video Sports Productions
P.O. Box 2700
Westfield, NJ 07901-2700
(800) USA-1996
FAX: (800) 872-1996
Founded: 1980. Retail and wholesale distribution/production of figure skating video tapes. Our catalog offers over 200 titles, including Olympic, International, World, and U.S. Championship events. The catalog also features professional competitions, instructional tapes, tours, feature films, family entertainment, and vintage footage of Sonja Henie, Dick Button and many more. Catalogs are $5.00 within the U.S. or free when requested with any order.

VIEW Video
Contact: Bob Karcy, President
34 E 23rd Street
New York, NY 10010
(212) 674-5550
FAX: (212) 979-0266
Founded: 1984. Publisher of a wide variety of programs including jazz, classical, opera, dance, children's educational and special-interest videos.

VSC Sports Consultants
Contact: Bert Blanchette, Vice President
14909 Magnolia Blvd.
Sherman Oaks, CA 91403
(818) 501-7252; (800) 818-7528
FAX: (818) 501-4192
Our staff works toward planning, creation, operation, and management of recreation facilities. Provides feasibility studies, design, construction input, programming, and employee training for clients.

Wachter (Jerry) Photography Ltd.
Contact: Jerry Wachter
6109 Eastcliff Dr.
Baltimore, MD 21209
(410) 466-3866
FAX: (410) 466-4672
Founded: 1972. Professional photography for Dorothy Hamill Ice Capades Programs- 93-'94; World Professional Figure Skating Championships for past ten years; Member of American Society of Media Photographers.

Wagenhoffer, Robert
c/o MARCO Entertainment
73271 Riata Trail
Palm Desert, CA 92260
(619) 776-5500
FAX: (619) 776-5575
Choreography for skaters and ice shows, including the 1994 Nutcracker on Ice, with Oksana Baiul, Viktor Petrenko, and Brian Boitano.

Walt Disney's World on Ice
Contact: Zanna Stuart, Director of Public Relations
8607 Westwood Center Drive
Vienna, VA 22182
(703) 749-5564
FAX: (703) 448-4119
Founded: 1981. Walt Disney's World On Ice is produced by Kenneth Feld, owner and producer of Ringling Brothers and Barnum & Bailey Circus (the largest three ring circus in the world). Walt Disney's World On Ice is the largest employer of figure skaters in the world and currently has six different productions on tour around the world.

Western Skate Sales
Contact: John Nazzaro, President
189 Constitution Drive
Menlo Park, CA 94025
(415) 324-0881
FAX: (415) 323-2818
Founded: 1954. Wholesale distributor (no direct sales or mail order). Blades - MK, Wilson. Boots - Harlick, Riedell. Ice guards, polish.

Western Starlight, Inc.
Contact: Jim Harrington, President
109 W. Whittier Blvd.
Montebello, CA 90640
(800) 929-2149; (213) 724-2149
FAX: (213) 724-6477
Founded: 1988. Western Starlight, Inc. is the supplier of pro audio and special effect lighting. We have lighting packages to fit any budget and design consultation is part of our service.

Westwood Sports
Contact: Dan Tousignant, Sales Manager
9601 Garfield Avenue South
Bloomington, MN 55420
(612) 881-2222; (800) 877-6304
FAX: (612) 881-1707
Founded: 1989. Retail: Risport, Don Jackson, Riedell, SP-Teri, boots. Wilson, Mitchel & King blades. Perfect scribe. Complete line of figure skates and apparel. Also: hockey, soccer, volleyball equipment.

Where'd You Get That !?, Inc.
Contact: Michele Gietz, President/Owner
Rt. 2 - Colonial Shopping Center
Williamstown, MA 01267
(413) 458-2206
FAX: (413) 458-0991
Founded: 1991. Novelties, fun gifts, hats, T-shirts, sweatshirts. Also work in conjunction with the Bay State Games.

Wilson, Marsden Bros & Co
Contact: Roger Margereson, Managing Director
71 Greystock Street
Sheffield, S4 7WA England
011-44-742-440238
FAX: 011-44-742-729330
Manufacturer of the Wilson line of skate blades.

Winning Edge
Contact: Vicki Stach, Owner
15909 Leavenworth Circle
Omaha, NE 68118
(402) 330-8052
FAX: (402) 330-4185
Founded: 1991. Custom sweaters with designs, angora gloves (8 styles), soakers, rhinestones. Boots - Harlick, Klingbeil, Risport, SP-Teri, Jackson. Blades - MK, Wilson (70 pairs in stock). Clothing - Danskin, Mondor.

Winning Ways
Contact: Dr. Caroline Silby, Sport Psychology Consultant
10812 Pleasant Hill Drive
Potomac, MD 20854
(301) 983-6712; FAX: (301) 469-0100
Individual consultation, small group workshops and clinics for athletes, coaches and parents on better understanding themselves and the competitive environment surrounding sports. Clinic formats are flexible, with half-day to full-week sessions available. A combination of group work and individualized on-site training can be incorporated. Topic may include the following; Confidence: How to get and maintain it, Pressure: Identifying and controlling it, Worry: Changing self-destructive messages, Motivation: Finding the right balance, Perfectionism: Does it work?

Wisconsin Ice Arena Management Association (WIAMA)
Contact: Joe Kershasky, Secretary/Treasurer
4001 S. 20th Street
Milwaukee, WI 53221
(414) 281-6289
FAX: (414) 282-4821
Founded: 1991. A professional association of arena and associated personnel, dedicated to the goal of professionalizing the industry by sharing ideas and innovative techniques through newsletters, membership meetings and seminars. Stresses a close working relationship between all types of industry personnel, from maintenance to management to suppliers.

With Pipe and Book
Contact: Breck & Julia Turner, Proprietors
91 Main Street
Lake Placid, NY 12946
(518) 523-9096
Founded: 1977. Sell used, old and rare ice skating books, magazines and programs. Generally 60-80 titles in stock. No lists available, but call if you have specific wants. Also interested in buying collections of the above items.

Woodward, Steve
Contact: Steve Woodward, Consultant
4641 Central Avenue
Western Springs, IL 60558
(708) 246-2605; FAX: (708) 246-2605
Founded: 1991. Athlete image enhancement strategies/media placement; Freelance writing (books, magazine/newspaper pieces, event scripting); Narration/voice-overs (taped or live); Event concept development for TV specials, home video; Consultant to Mentor Marketing and Management; Former reporter for *USA Today* covering figure skating.

World Figure Skating Museum & Hall of Fame
Contact: Beth Davis, Curator
c/o USFSA
20 First Street
Colorado Springs, CO 80906
(719) 635-5200; FAX: (719) 635-9548
Devoted to the preservation of all aspects of the sport of figure skating. Exhibits include a look at the history of skating, and artifacts from the 17th to the 20th century. The largest collection of skating art and memorabilia, as well as tributes to the sport's most honored and celebrated personalities.

World Ice Skating Center (Thailand) Co., Ltd.
Contact: Cynthia Lee Van Valkenberg, Skating Director
7th Fl., World Trade Center Complex, Rajprasong
4 Radjdamri Rd.
Bangkok,, 10330 Thailand
(662) 225-9500
Telex: 21369 WTCB TH
FAX: (662) 253-4488
Rink divided into beginner and advanced halves. Classes in skating and ballet. Also, restaurant and coffee shop on mezzanine level.

Wright, Brian
Contact: Brian Wright, Choreographer
c/o Indiana World Skating Academy
201 S Capitol Avenue, Suite 110, Pan American Plaza
Indianapolis, IN 40625
(317) 237-5565
Freelance choreographer for many skaters, including Scott Williams, Scott Davis, Lily Lee, Damon Allen, Jerry Campbell, Jere Michael, Matthew Kessinger, Michael Weiss, and Kristi Yamaguchi. Limits traveling; most skaters travel to him.

Yontz Corporation
Contact: Donald Yontz, President
P.O. Box 795
Brandon, FL 33509-0795
(813) 324-9372
FAX: (813) 685-4495
Founded: 1990. We manufacture and rent portable ice rinks for theatrical productions, etc. Our clients include: MARCO Entertainment, Dick Foster Productions, Richard Porter Productions, Disney World Orlando, Busch Gardens Tampa, Sea World San Diego & San Antonio, World Cup Champions On Ice Tour, Bill Graham Presents, Tom Addis Productions, Larimer Square Denver.

Zamboni
Contact: Richard F. Zamboni, President
15714 Colorado Avenue
Paramount, CA 90723
(310) 633-0751
FAX: (310) 633-9365
Founded: 1950. Manufacturer and distributor of the Zamboni ice resurfacer for use indoor and outdoor ice skating rinks for over 40 years.

TURN PAGE FOR SKATER'S MARKETPLACE ☞

SKATER'S MARKETPLACE

INGA Creations

1456 San Lorenzo Road
Palm Springs, CA 92264
Tel: (619) 327-6075
Fax: (619) 327-6075

NOW
Specializing in adult and large sizes.

Quantity discounts for clubs and precision teams.

Sweaters, Pants, Dresses and Skirts made of Lycra, Knit, or Chiffon.

Champion quality
Custom Equipment Bags & Accessories

Exclusive Embroidered Designs and Monogramming.
Call or write for information
Creative Pack Works
P.O. Box 217
Salinas, CA 93902
(408) 753-6995

K-TEE ENTERPRISES
Comfort & Health Supplies

- Le Muff
- Travel Pillow
- The Zap Pack
- The Heat Wrap
- The Thermo-Band
- Hothands
- Foot Warmup
- Body Warmup
- The Heat Solution
- Handwarmer Cover

Boot Covers
Skating & Sports Accessories

KATHERINE Y. MONNIER
P.O. Box 1063 • Kenwood, CA 95452
(707) 539-6351

TANA'S GOLD
14 KARAT
BRACELET (7 or 8")
EARRINGS
CHARMS
RINGS
Starting at $20.00

1024 W. Main St.
Troy, Ohio 45373
(513) 335-4698

WIFA Distributor

MORE WORLD AND OLYMPIC CHAMPIONS SKATE ON WIFA BOOTS

The Choice of
KURT BROWNING

CAN ALPINE AGENCIES LTD.

1314 S.W. Marine Drive
Vancouver, B.C. V6P 5Z6
(604) 266-4490 Fax (604) 266-5470

The Jumpometer Co.

Maker of electronic height-indicator device for on-ice training & practice of **skating jumps**

265 Lawlor Street, Heileybury, Ont. P.O. Box 318 P0J-1K0
Canada Fax # (705) 672-jump 5867

SKATING TIPS AT YOUR FINGERTIPS

If you love to skate and want to sharpen your skills, take advice from the experts—by reading *Skater's Edge*. Each issue is filled with how-to articles and illustrated skating tips from the world's top coaches and pros. The first three years (Sept/Oct '91 thru Sum '94) are available in a binder. For free brochure, contact: *Skater's Edge*, Box 500, Dept. SB, Kensington, MD 20895; Phone/Fax: (301) 946-1971. Free bulk brochures for rinks, clubs, competitions.

SKATER'S MARKETPLACE

Rhinestones *Seed Beads*
Sequins *Rocailles*
Pearls *Bugles*

Austrian Crystals

GERRIE BALL
(714) 529-1474

310 JUNIPER STREET • BREA, CALIFORNIA 92621

ICE DANCE MANUALS

By Jeff R. Lerner, *The Complete Manual of Ice Dance Patterns* (152 patterns, 400 pages); *The Complete Manual of Compulsory Ice Dances* (32 patterns, each with transparent overlay to show tracking, 132 pages). Each book, $40.00 including freight. ($45.00 in Canada). Volume discounts available. Contact:

Lexicon Ventures, Ltd., 1685 West 61st. Ave., Vancouver, B.C. Canada V6P 2C2
Phone: (604) 261-0371 • Fax: (604) 266-7998

718-474-6850

PATRICIA BRAMWELL, M.A., M.S.
Counselor

Sports Psychology
Performance Enhancement
Decision Making

JON R. CROMER   (518) 587-4853

PRODUCTIONS EAST
VIDEO SERVICES

20 SUNSET DRIVE
SARATOGA SPRINGS, NY 12866

Skating Pins & Medals

Custom Designed Pins & Medals
for Industry, Associations, & Clubs
manufactured in the U.S.A.
For a competitive quotation please send your
logo or design with color to:

Ashworth Associates

753 East Washington Street
North Attleboro, MA 02760
or call us at:
1-800-325-1917   1-508-695-1900   fax 1-508-695-0377

TLF

The Lenzi Foundation
4228½ River Rd., NW, Suite A
Washington, D.C. 20016
Telephone (202) 363-6503

Jean Lenzi   President

IN-LINE SKATING VIDEOS!!
By Scott Cramer
World Professional Ice Skating Champion

HOW TO IN-LINE SKATE .... $49.95 TOTAL
Basic and Advanced Skills (2 tapes, 25 mins. each)
SCOTT'S 16 IN-LINE DANCES $39.95
BUY ALL 3 VIDEOS FOR ONLY $69.90

Send check to:
PHD, 3630 Citadel Dr. North, Colorado Springs, CO 80909

It's A Laurie!
ORIGINAL

CUSTOM - MADE SKATING
COSTUMES, PROM, EVENING WEAR

LAURIE J. HILL
(813) 920-3757

COMPANIES

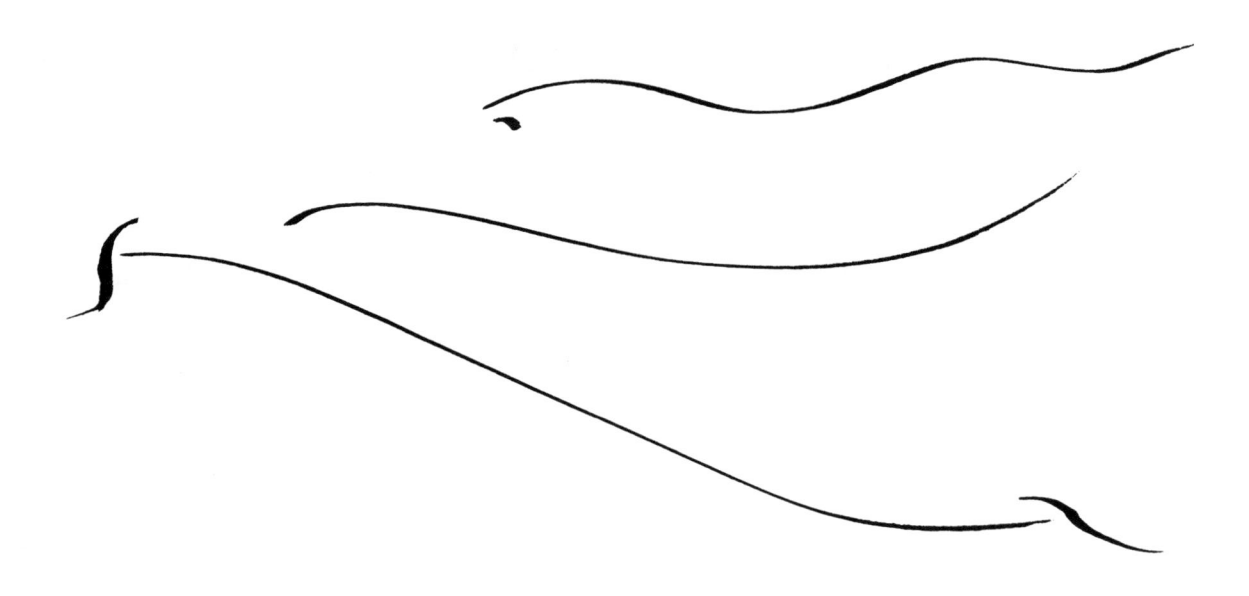

Skater's Edge
SOURCEBOOK

SKATING RINKS	VIDEOS	PUBLICATIONS
BOOTS	EQUIPMENT	RINK BUILDERS
BLADES	CLOTHING	SUMMER SCHOOLS
BOOKS	CATALOGUES	TRAINING CENTERS

Skater's Edge, the world's leading "how-to" ice skating publication, has once again broken new ground. We've created the *Skater's Edge* SOURCEBOOK, the first comprehensive resource book and directory for the skating world.

This book—released for the first time in January 1995—has quickly become an indispensable part of every skating library. **MAKES A GREAT GIFT!**

Ask for it at your favorite bookstore, or order from the publisher. Send your order with payment to *Skater's Edge* SOURCEBOOK, Box 500, Dept. SB, Kensington, MD 20895; (301) 946-1971.

❑ Yes, I want to order the *Skater's Edge* SOURCEBOOK. Please send me _____ copies at:

❑ $39.95[1] + $5 shipping[2] ($44.95 US$)[3] each

❑ I am enclosing my total payment of $_____

[1]MD RESIDENTS add 5% sales tax. [2]For U.S. & Canada; to Europe: $7—surface; $15—air; to Japan: $12—surface, $20—air. [3]U.S. $ or Canadian equivalent; int'l bank or postal orders accepted.

Name_____
Address_____
City_____ State_____ Zip_____
Phone (day) (___)_____ (eve) (___)_____

Send with payment to: *Skater's Edge* SOURCEBOOK, Box 500, Dept. SB, Kensington, MD 20895. Thank you!

ILLUSTRATION BY JOEL BERMAN

Companies by Categories

Following are abbreviated listings of companies sorted by numerous categories, ranging from *Agents and Managers* to *Workshops*. Companies providing more than one service will appear under more than one category. For more detailed information on each company, turn to the primary *Companies* listing that begins on page 71.

AGENTS AND MANGERS

Boitano (Brian) Enterprises, Los Altos, CA. (415) 948-2478. Contact: Linda Leaver.
Futerman & Futerman, Toronto, Ontario, Canada. (416) 925-4100; FAX: (416) 323-9132. *Contact:* Ed Futerman.
Ice Chalets, Inc., Los Angeles, CA. (310) 575-4466; FAX: (310) 575-4388.
International Management Group (IMG), New York, NY. (212) 772-8900; FAX: (212) 772-2617. *Contact:* Jay Ogden.
International Management Group (IMG) Canada, Toronto, Ontario, Canada. (416) 960-5312; FAX: (416) 960-0564. *Contact:* Kevin Albrecht.
Linichuk, Natalia, Newark, DE. (302) 831-2868. *Contact:* Natalia Linichuk.
MARCO Entertainment (Michael A. Rosenburg Management), Palm Desert, CA. (619) 776-5500; FAX: (619) 776-5575. *Contact:* Michael Rosenberg.
Mentor Marketing & Management, South Bend, IN. (219) 233-9601; FAX: (219) 233-9484. *Contact:* Jeanne Martin.
Mimms (Lee S.) & Associates, Glendale, CA. (818) 246-5601; FAX: (818) 246-5605. *Contact:* Lee Mimms.
Morris (William) Agency, New York, NY. (212) 586-5100; FAX: (212) 246-3583. *Contact:* Michael Carlisle.
Pro Serve, Arlington, VA. (703) 276-3030. *Contact:* Jerry Solomon.
Proper Marketing Associates, Redondo Beach, CA. (310) 378-8666. *Contact:* Shep Goldberg.

BLADE SALES

B & G Skate Supply, Ontario, CA. (909) 460-6606; FAX: (909) 460-6605. *Contact:* Barbara Johnson.
Boston Hockey Company, Dover, NH. (603) 742-4333; FAX: (603) 742-9311.
CanStar Sports, Swanton, VT. (802) 868-2711; FAX: (802) 868-4713. *Contact:* Cliff Penke.
Club Skate, San Diego, CA. (619) 965-7447; (800) CLUB SK8; FAX: (619) 589-4076. *Contact:* Sharene Eble.
Cooke's Pro Skate Shop, Wilmington, MA. (508) 657-4087; FAX: (508) 988-0000. *Contact:* Scott Cooke.
Damschroder Skate Sales, North Hollywood, CA. (818) 982-9090; FAX: (818) 982-9355. *Contact:* Jerry Damschroder.
Dante Cozzi Sports, Bellmore, NY. (516) 783-0215; FAX: (516) 783-2964. *Contact:* Dante Cozzi.
Eastern Ice Sports, Summit, NJ. (908) 277-6688; FAX: (908) 277-3957. *Contact:* Russ Depack.
Enchantment On Ice, Inc., Virginia Beach, VA. (804) 490-0676; FAX: (804) 490-0689. *Contact:* Alycia Walker-Gaynor.
Figure 8 Boutique Ltd., Ottawa, Ontario, Canada. (613) 731-4007; FAX: (613) 736-7747. *Contact:* Jasmin Simard.
Figure Skating Boutique, Willowdale, Ontario, Canada. (416) 225-1377; (416) 225-1390; FAX: (416) 225-3071. *Contact:* Laura Hallis.
Fingertips to Toepicks, Norwalk, CT. (203) 838-1203. *Contact:* Darlene Vento.
Gold Edge, The, Bloomington, MN. (612) 881-2222; (800) 877-6304; FAX: (612) 881-1707. *Contact:* Dan Tousignant.
Highland Sports Center, Seattle, WA. (206) 546-2431; FAX: (206) 546-3130. *Contact:* Rick Stewart.
Ice Chalets, Inc., Los Angeles, CA. (310) 575-4466; FAX: (310) 575-4388.
Ice Skate Conditioning Equipment Co., Littleton, CO. (303) 979-3800; FAX: (303) 979-3800. *Contact:* Sidney Broadbent.
Ice Skater's Edge, Warwick, RI. (401) 732-5252; FAX: (401) 738-4531. *Contact:* Bill Ross.
Ice Sports, Pompano Beach, FL. (305) 943-1437; FAX: (305) 781-1966. *Contact:* Robyn Levin.
J&R Skates, Skaneatles, NY. (315) 685-1048; FAX: (315) 685-7343. *Contact:* Joyce Edmonds.
Jerry's Pro Shop, Rolling Meadows, IL. (708) 398-7446; FAX: (708) 398-7452. *Contact:* Glen Busch.
Jerry's Skating World, Markham, Ontario, Canada. (905) 477-1172; FAX: (905) 477-8859. *Contact:* Jerry Zawadzki.
Lubin's Skate Supply, Inc., Nashua, NH. (603) 886-5777; FAX: (603) 883-6270. *Contact:* Brian Armbruster.
Murray Sandler Skate & Rink Supply, Belmont, MA. (617) 484-5100; FAX: (617)489-5232. *Contact:* Murray Sandler.
National Skate Distributors, Tacoma, WA. (206) 473-3636; FAX: (206) 473-3791. *Contact:* Ted Werner.
National Skate Locker, Anaheim, CA. (714) 935-9500; FAX: (714) 935-2494. *Contact:* Jim Hambas.
Oberhamer, Inc., Burnsville, MN. (612) 890-1657; FAX: (612) 890-0511. *Contact:* Kent Orwoll.

Outside Edge, Winthrop Harbor, IL. (800) SKATE 93; FAX: (708) 746-3655. *Contact:* Connie Anderson.
Paul's Pro Shop, Wilmette, IL. (708) 251-0880; FAX: (708) 251-3123. *Contact:* Paul Tassone.
Philbrick Sports, Dover, NH. (603) 742-4333; FAX: (603) 742-9311. *Contact:* Dan Philbrick.
Pickwick Sport Shop, Burbank, CA. (818) 846-8099; FAX: (818) 845-5300. *Contact:* Mary Spencer.
Rainbo Sport Shop, Chicago, IL. (312) 275-5500; FAX: (312) 275-5506. *Contact:* Cale Carvell.
Red Line Sports, Soldatna, AK. (907) 262-5860; FAX: (907) 262-5860. *Contact:* Vince Redford.
Riedell Skate Co., Red Wing, MN. (612) 388-8251; FAX: (612) 388-8616. *Contact:* Daniel Riegelman.
S.H. Stoery & Son, Northbrook, IL. (708) 205-1548. *Contact:* Jess Stoery.
Skate Bag, The, Oldsmar, FL. (813) 855-7998; FAX: (813) 854-4031. *Contact:* David & Rita Lowery.
Skate Shop - IL, Crestwood, IL. (708) 389-7849. *Contact:* John Harmata.
Skate Shop - NY, Great Neck, NY. (516) 487-6948. *Contact:* Joel Halpern.
Skater's Choice Pro Shop, Kenosha, WI. (414) 697-1615. *Contact:* Connie Anderson.
Skater's Edge - NY, Williamsville, NY. (716) 636-3000; FAX: (716) 636-1776. *Contact:* Phyllis Petri.
Skater's Edge - OH, Cleveland, OH. (216) 252-3986; FAX: (216) 671-4222. *Contact:* Dale or Carl Merkel.
Skater's Paradise, Inc., Alexandria, VA. (703) 660-6525; FAX: (703) 660-2341. *Contact:* Michael Cunningham.
Skater's Paradise of Delaware, Inc., Newark, DE. (302) 738-2999. *Contact:* Michael Cunningham.
Slap Shot Sports, West Orange, NJ. (201) 736-9107; FAX: (201) 736-1115. *Contact:* Ed Krokchmal.
Stan's Skate Shop, West Islip, NY. (516) 587-1658. *Contact:* Stan Belliveau.
Steamboats/Blades, Steamboat Spring, CO. (303) 879-3286; FAX: (303) 879-3286. *Contact:* Jim Fournier.
Swonee's Place, Evansville, IN. (800) 293-6741. *Contact:* Henry Welch.
Valley Skating Supplies, North Hollywood, CA. (818) 980-0414. *Contact:* Pete Lemoine.
Western Skate Sales, Menlo Park, CA. (415) 324-0881; FAX: (415) 323-2818. *Contact:* John Nazzaro.
Westwood Sports, Bloomington, MN. (612) 881-2222; (800) 877-6304; FAX: (612) 881-1707. *Contact:* Dan Tousignant.
Winning Edge, Omaha, NE. (402) 330-8052; FAX: (402) 330-4185. *Contact:* Vicki Stach.

BLADE MANUFACTURERS

CanStar Sports, Swanton, VT. (802) 868-2711; FAX: (802) 868-4713. *Contact:* Cliff Penke.
Mitchel & King Skates Ltd., Slough, Berkshire, England. 07-53-528-444; FAX: 07-53-528-446. *Contact:* David Whitworth.
Oberhamer, Inc., Burnsville, MN. (612) 890-1657; FAX: (612) 890-0511. *Contact:* Kent Orwoll.
Riedell Skate Co., Red Wing, MN. (612) 388-8251; FAX: (612) 388-8616. *Contact:* Daniel Riegelman.
Wilson, Marsden Bros & Co, Sheffield, England. 011-44-742-440238; FAX: 011-44-742-729330. *Contact:* Roger Margereson.

BOOKS AND BOOK SALES

American Skating World, Pittsburgh, PA. (412) 885-7600; FAX: (412) 885-7617. *Contact:* H. Kermit Jackson.
Annie's Edges, Freelton, Ontario, Canada. (905) 659-7402. *Contact:* Anne E. Schelter.
Buck's Skater's Blade Collectibles, Akron, OH. (216) 724-8972. *Contact:* Joe Mendiola.
Club Skate, San Diego, CA. (619) 965-7447; (800) CLUB SK8; FAX: (619) 589-4076. *Contact:* Sharene Eble.
Enchantment On Ice, Inc., Virginia Beach, VA. (804) 490-0676; FAX: (804) 490-0689. *Contact:* Alycia Walker-Gaynor.
Hare & Hatter Books, Inc., W. Newton, MA. (617) 928-0906. *Contact:* Susan Weindling.
Henie Onstead Art Center, Norway. (47) 67 54 30 50; FAX: (47) 67 54 32 70. *Contact:* Reidar Borjeson.
Ignel Associates, San Francisco, CA. (415) 681-5088; FAX: (415) 681-5088. *Contact:* Alina Sivorinovsky.
Kathy Barron, Simsbury, CT. (203) 658-4688. *Contact:* Kathy Barron.
Laura Stamm International Power Skating System, Tuckahoe, NY. (914) 961-7994; (800) 484-7303 x 1886; FAX: 914-961-0337. *Contact:* Bryce Leavitt McGowan.
Lexicon Ventures Limited, Vancouver, B.C., Canada. (604) 261-0371; FAX: (604) 266-7998. *Contact:* Jeff Lerner.
Morris (William) Agency, New York, NY. (212) 586-5100; FAX: (212) 246-3583. *Contact:* Michael Carlisle.
National Skate Locker, Anaheim, CA. (714) 935-9500; FAX: (714) 935-2494. *Contact:* Jim Hambas.
Outside Edge, Winthrop Harbor, IL. (800) SKATE 93; FAX: (708) 746-3655. *Contact:* Connie Anderson.
Paul's Pro Shop, Wilmette, IL. (708) 251-0880; FAX: (708) 251-3123. *Contact:* Paul Tassone.
Pickwick Sport Shop, Burbank, CA. (818) 846-8099; FAX: (818) 845-5300. *Contact:* Mary Spencer.
Platoro Press, Columbus, OH. (614) 837-0003. *Contact:* Lynn Copley-Graves.
Rainbo Sport Shop, Chicago, IL. (312) 275-5500; FAX: (312) 275-5506. *Contact:* Cale Carvell.
Skater's Choice Gift Boutique, Winthrop Harbor, IL. (708) 746-3650; FAX: (708) 746-3655. *Contact:* Connie Anderson.
Sport Consulting Centre, North Vancouver, B.C. Canada. (604) 987-8488; FAX: (604) 987-8488. *Contact:* Shawna Palmer.
Sports Asylum, Inc., Northridge, CA. (800) 929-2159; FAX: (818) 895-4763. *Contact:* Don Laner.
With Pipe and Book, Lake Placid, NY. (518) 523-9096. *Contact:* Breck & Julia Turner.
World Figure Skating Museum & Hall of Fame, Colorado Springs, CO. (719) 635-5200; FAX: (719) 635-9548. *Contact:* Beth Davis.

~ SKATER'S EDGE SOURCEBOOK ~

BOOT MANUFACTURERS

CanStar Sports, Swanton, VT. (802) 868-2711; FAX: (802) 868-4713. *Contact:* Cliff Penke.
Harlick & Company, Inc., San Carlos, CA. (415) 593-2093; FAX: (415) 593-9704. *Contact:* Sam Swartz.
Klingbeil Shoe Labs, Inc, Jamaica, NY. (718) 297-6864; FAX: (718) 658-2396. *Contact:* Donald Klingbeil.
Knebli (John) Ltd., Toronto, Ontario, Canada. (416) 368-5565. *Contact:* John Knebli.
Oberhamer, Inc., Burnsville, MN. (612) 890-1657; FAX: (612) 890-0511. *Contact:* Kent Orwoll.
Riedell Skate Co., Red Wing, MN. (612) 388-8251; FAX: (612) 388-8616. *Contact:* Daniel Riegelman.
Risport, Treviso, Italy. 47 42 12 13; FAX: 47 42 06 07.
Rose Custom Boots, Ltd., Cambridge, Ontario, Canada. (519) 622-3340.
SK Sport Shoes Ltd., Toronto, Ontario, Canada. (416) 465-2784; FAX: (416) 465-7802. *Contact:* Steve Kolozsvary.
SP-Teri Company, Inc., South San Francisco, CA. (415) 871-1715; FAX: (415) 871-9062. *Contact:* George Spiteri.

BOOT SALES

B & G Skate Supply, Ontario, CA. (909) 460-6606; FAX: (909) 460-6605. *Contact:* Barbara Johnson.
Boston Hockey Company, Dover, NH. (603) 742-4333; FAX: (603) 742-9311.
Can Alpine Agencies, Ltd., Vancouver, B.C., Canada. (604) 266-4490; FAX: (604) 266-5470. *Contact:* Hellmut May.
CanStar Sports, Swanton, VT. (802) 868-2711; FAX: (802) 868-4713. *Contact:* Cliff Penke.
Club Skate, San Diego, CA. (619) 965-7447; (800) CLUB SK8; FAX: (619) 589-4076. *Contact:* Sharene Eble.
Cooke's Pro Skate Shop, Wilmington, MA. (508) 657-4087; FAX: (508) 988-0000. *Contact:* Scott Cooke.
Damschroder Skate Sales, North Hollywood, CA. (818) 982-9090; FAX: (818) 982-9355. *Contact:* Jerry Damschroder.
Dante Cozzi Sports, Bellmore, NY. (516) 783-0215; FAX: (516) 783-2964. *Contact:* Dante Cozzi.
Eastern Ice Sports, Summit, NJ. (908) 277-6688; FAX: (908) 277-3957. *Contact:* Russ Depack.
Enchantment On Ice, Inc., Virginia Beach, VA. (804) 490-0676; FAX: (804) 490-0689. *Contact:* Alycia Walker-Gaynor.
Figure 8 Boutique Ltd., Ottawa, Ontario, Canada. (613) 731-4007; FAX: (613) 736-7747. *Contact:* Jasmin Simard.
Figure Skating Boutique, Willowdale, Ontario, Canada. (416) 225-1377; (416) 225-1390; FAX: (416) 225-3071. *Contact:* Laura Hallis.
Fingertips to Toepicks, Norwalk, CT. (203) 838-1203. *Contact:* Darlene Vento.
Gold Edge, Bloomington, MN. (612) 881-2222; (800) 877-6304; FAX: (612) 881-1707. *Contact:* Dan Tousignant.
Highland Sports Center, Seattle, WA. (206) 546-2431; FAX: (206) 546-3130. *Contact:* Rick Stewart.
Ice Chalets, Inc., Los Angeles, CA. (310) 575-4466; FAX: (310) 575-4388.
Ice Skate Conditioning Equipment Co., Littleton, CO. (303) 979-3800; FAX: (303) 979-3800. *Contact:* Sidney Broadbent.
Ice Skater's Edge, Warwick, RI. (401) 732-5252; FAX: (401) 738-4531. *Contact:* Bill Ross.
Ice Sports, Pompano Beach, FL. (305) 943-1437; FAX: (305) 781-1966. *Contact:* Robyn Levin.
J&R Skates, Skaneatles, NY. (315) 685-1048; FAX: (315) 685-7343. *Contact:* Joyce Edmonds.
Jerry's Pro Shop, Rolling Meadows, IL. (708) 398-7446; FAX: (708) 398-7452. *Contact:* Glen Busch.
Jerry's Skating World, Markham, Ontario, Canada. (905) 477-1172; FAX: (905) 477-8859. *Contact:* Jerry Zawadzki.
Klingbeil Shoe Labs, Inc, Jamaica, NY. (718) 297-6864; FAX: (718) 658-2396. *Contact:* Donald Klingbeil.
Knebli, John Ltd., Toronto, Ontario, Canada. (416) 368-5565. *Contact:* John Knebli.
Lubin's Skate Supply, Inc., Nashua, NH. (603) 886-5777; FAX: (603) 883-6270. *Contact:* Brian Armbruster.
Murray Sandler Skate & Rink Supply, Belmont, MA. (617) 484-5100; FAX: (617) 489-5232. *Contact:* Murray Sandler.
National Skate Distributors, Tacoma, WA. (206) 473-3636; FAX: (206) 473-3791. *Contact:* Ted Werner.
National Skate Locker, Anaheim, CA. (714) 935-9500; FAX: (714) 935-2494. *Contact:* Jim Hambas.
Oberhamer, Inc., Burnsville, MN. (612) 890-1657; FAX: (612) 890-0511. *Contact:* Kent Orwoll.
Outside Edge, Winthrop Harbor, IL. (800) SKATE 93; FAX: (708) 746-3655. *Contact:* Connie Anderson.
Paul's Pro Shop, Wilmette, IL. (708) 251-0880; FAX: (708) 251-3123. *Contact:* Paul Tassone.
Philbrick Sports, Dover, NH. (603) 742-4333; FAX: (603) 742-9311. *Contact:* Dan Philbrick.
Pickwick Sport Shop, Burbank, CA. (818) 846-8099; FAX: (818) 845-5300. *Contact:* Mary Spencer.
Rainbo Sport Shop, Chicago, IL. (312) 275-5500; FAX: (312) 275-5506. *Contact:* Cale Carvell.
Red Line Sports, Soldatna, AK. (907) 262-5860; FAX: (907) 262-5860. *Contact:* Vince Redford.
Riedell Skate Co., Red Wing, MN. (612) 388-8251; FAX: (612) 388-8616. *Contact:* Daniel Riegelman.
S.H. Stoery & Son, Northbrook, IL. (708) 205-1548. *Contact:* Jess Stoery.
Skate Bag, The, Oldsmar, FL. (813) 855-7998; FAX: (813) 854-4031. *Contact:* David & Rita Lowery.
Skate Shop - IL, Crestwood, IL. (708) 389-7849. *Contact:* John Harmata.
Skate Shop - NY, Great Neck, NY. (516) 487-6948. *Contact:* Joel Halpern.
Skater's Choice Gift Boutique, Winthrop Harbor, IL. (708) 746-3650; FAX: (708) 746-3655. *Contact:* Connie Anderson.

COMPANIES: CATEGORIES

111

Skater's Choice Pro Shop, Kenosha, WI. (414) 697-1615. *Contact:* Connie Anderson.

Skater's Edge - NY, Williamsville, NY. (716) 636-3000; FAX: (716) 636-1776. *Contact:* Phyllis Petri.

Skater's Edge - OH, Cleveland, OH. (216) 252-3986; FAX: (216) 671-4222. *Contact:* Dale or Carl Merkel.

Skater's Paradise, Inc., Alexandria, VA. (703) 660-6525; FAX: (703) 660-2341. *Contact:* Michael Cunningham.

Skater's Paradise of Delaware, Inc., Newark, DE. (302) 738-2999. *Contact:* Michael Cunningham.

Slap Shot Sports, West Orange, NJ. (201) 736-9107; FAX: (201) 736-1115. *Contact:* Ed Krokchmal.

Stan's Skate Shop, West Islip, NY. (516) 587-1658. *Contact:* Stan Belliveau.

Steamboats/Blades, Steamboat Spring, CO. (303) 879-3286; FAX: (303) 879-3286. *Contact:* Jim Fournier.

Swonee's Place, Evansville, IN. (800) 293-6741. *Contact:* Henry Welch.

Tomy's Skater Shop, Virginia Beach, VA. (804) 464-1464; FAX: (804) 464-1157. *Contact:* Cindy Carew.

Tournament Sports, Waterloo, Ontartio, Canada. (519) 888-6500; FAX: (519) 888-6540. *Contact:* Wayne Sehagena.

Valley Skating Supplies, North Hollywood, CA. (818) 980-0414. *Contact:* Pete Lemoine.

Western Skate Sales, Menlo Park, CA. (415) 324-0881; FAX: (415) 323-2818. *Contact:* John Nazzaro.

Westwood Sports, Bloomington, MN. (612) 881-2222 (800) 877-6304; FAX: (612) 881-1707. *Contact:* Dan Tousignant.

Winning Edge, Omaha, NE. (402) 330-8052; FAX: (402) 330-4185. *Contact:* Vicki Stach.

BOOT AND BLADE MAINTENANCE

Boston Hockey Company, Dover, NH. (603) 742-4333; FAX: (603) 742-9311.

Cag One Skate Sharpeners, Inc., White Plains, NY. (914) 949-3120; FAX: (914) 949-3132. *Contact:* Alvar Ohlsson.

CanStar Sports, Swanton, VT. (802) 868-2711; FAX: (802) 868-4713. *Contact:* Cliff Penke.

Cooke's Pro Skate Shop, Wilmington, MA. (508) 657-4087; FAX: (508) 988-0000. *Contact:* Scott Cooke.

Dante Cozzi Sports, Bellmore, NY. (516) 783-0215; FAX: (516) 783-2964. *Contact:* Dante Cozzi.

Dupliskate Jonah Ltd., Montreal, Quebec, Canada. (514) 382-1140; FAX: (514) 382-8249. *Contact:* John P. Lanfer.

Edge Specialties, Inc., Alexandria, MN. (800) 827-3343; FAX: (612) 762-5213. *Contact:* Jeff Haiskanen.

Enchantment On Ice, Inc., Virginia Beach, VA. (804) 490-0676; FAX: (804) 490-0689. *Contact:* Alycia Walker-Gaynor.

Figure 8 Boutique Ltd., Ottawa, Ontario, Canada. (613) 731-4007; FAX: (613) 736-7747. *Contact:* Jasmin Simard.

Gold Edge, Bloomington, MN. (612) 881-2222; (800) 877-6304; FAX: (612) 881-1707. *Contact:* Dan Tousignant.

Highland Sports Center, Seattle, WA. (206) 546-2431; FAX: (206) 546-3130. *Contact:* Rick Stewart.

Ice Chalets, Inc., Los Angeles, CA. (310) 575-4466; FAX: (310) 575-4388.

Ice Skater's Edge, Warwick, RI. (401) 732-5252; FAX: (401) 738-4531. *Contact:* Bill Ross.

J&R Skates, Skaneatles, NY. (315) 685-1048; FAX: (315) 685-7343. *Contact:* Joyce Edmonds.

Jerry's Pro Shop, Rolling Meadows, IL. (708) 398-7446; FAX: (708) 398-7452. *Contact:* Glen Busch.

Joe's Skate Service, Littleton, CO. (303) 798-7881; FAX: (303) 980-0356. *Contact:* P. Joseph De Lio.

Keith's Precision Skate Sharpening, Watertown, MA. (617) 924-4518. *Contact:* Keith Galgot.

Maximum Edges, Windsor, Ontario, . (519) 969-7575; FAX: (519) 969-3199. *Contact:* Doug Trudell.

Murray Sandler Skate & Rink Supply, Belmont, MA. (617) 484-5100; FAX: (617) 489-5232. *Contact:* Murray Sandler.

National Skate Locker, Anaheim, CA. (714) 935-9500; FAX: (714) 935-2494. *Contact:* Jim Hambas.

Oberhamer, Inc., Burnsville, MN. (612) 890-1657; FAX: (612) 890-0511. *Contact:* Kent Orwoll.

Ogilvie-Gutzman Blade Gauges, Ironton, MN. *Contact:* Alan Gutzman.

Paul's Pro Shop, Wilmette, IL. (708) 251-0880; FAX: (708) 251-3123. *Contact:* Paul Tassone.

THE ICESKATE SHARPENER

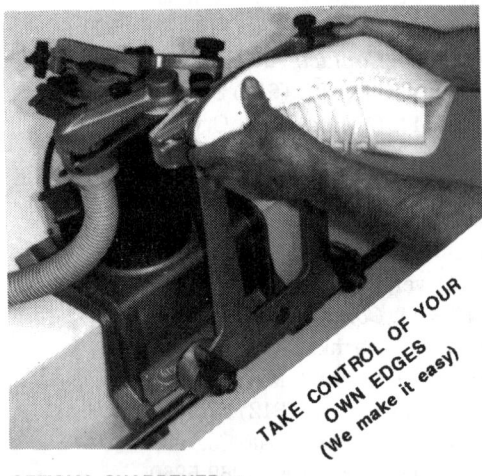

Skaters
Coaches
Skating Clubs
Sports Stores
Equipment Specialists
Skating Families
Elite Rrnks
IN
Australia
Bahrain
Belgium
Canada
China
Denmark
England
Finland
France
Germany
Hong Kong
Hungary
Japan
Mexico
New Zealand
Norway
Poland
Scotland
South Africa
South Korea
Spain
Switzerland
Thailand
Ukraine
UAR

TAKE CONTROL OF YOUR OWN EDGES (We make it easy)

OFFICIAL SHARPENER at:
1994 Olympic Winter Games, Lillehamer, Norway
1992 Olympic Winter Games, Albertville, France
1992 National Figure Skating Championships, USA
1991 World Figure Skating Championships, Germany
1991 National Figure Skating Championships, UK
1990 World Figure Skating Championships, Canada
1989 European Figure Skating Championships, UK
1989 National Figure Skating Championships, USA
1988 World Figure Skating Championships, Hungary
1987 World Figure Skating Championships, USA

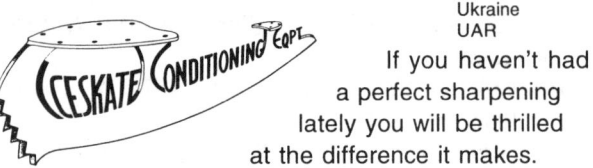

If you haven't had a perfect sharpening lately you will be thrilled at the difference it makes.

ICESKATE CONDITIONING EQUIPMENT (ICE)
5265 West Quarles Drive, Littleton, CO. 80123   Tel: & FAX 303 979 3800

Peck and Goodie, New York, NY. (212) 246-6123; FAX: (212) 807-6115. *Contact:* Scott Kelleher.
Philbrick Sports, Dover, NH. (603) 742-4333; FAX: (603) 742-9311. *Contact:* Dan Philbrick.
Pickwick Sport Shop, Burbank, CA. (818) 846-8099; FAX: (818) 845-5300. *Contact:* Mary Spencer.
Rainbo Sport Shop, Chicago, IL. (312) 275-5500; FAX: (312) 275-5506. *Contact:* Cale Carvell.
Red Line Sports, Soldatna, AK. (907) 262-5860; FAX: (907) 262-5860. *Contact:* Vince Redford.
Riedell Skate Co., Red Wing, MN. (612) 388-8251; FAX: (612) 388-8616. *Contact:* Daniel Riegelman.
Skater's Paradise, Inc., Alexandria, VA. (703) 660-6525; FAX: (703) 660-2341. *Contact:* Michael Cunningham.
Skater's Paradise of Delaware, Inc., Newark, DE. (302) 738-2999. *Contact:* Michael Cunningham.
SP-Teri Company, Inc., S. San Francisco, CA. (415) 871-1715; FAX: (415) 871-9062. *Contact:* George Spiteri.
Steamboats/Blades, Steamboat Spring, CO. (303) 879-3286; FAX: (303) 879-3286. *Contact:* Jim Fournier.
Swonee's Place, Evansville, IN. (800) 293-6741. *Contact:* Henry Welch.
Tomy's Skater Shop, Virginia Beach, VA. (804) 464-1464; FAX: (804) 464-1157. *Contact:* Cindy Carew.
Up In The Air, Inc., Alpharetta, GA. (404) 751-0913; FAX: (404) 751-0543. *Contact:* Debbie Howe.
Westwood Sports, Bloomington, MN. (612) 881-2222; (800) 877-6304; FAX: (612) 881-1707. *Contact:* Dan Tousignant.

CATALOGUE AND MAIL ORDER

Axel & Lutz Outfitters, Chicago, IL. *Contact:* Linda Khezami.
Birch Hill Designs/ Kai-Lei On Ice, Vergennes, VT. (802) 475-2327; FAX: (802) 475-2320. *Contact:* Karen Begins.
Boston Hockey Company, Dover, NH. (603) 742-4333; FAX: (603) 742-9311.
Buck's Skater's Blade Collectibles, Akron, OH. (216) 724-8972. *Contact:* Joe Mendiola.
Canada West Skating International, Ltd., Duncan, B.C., Canada. (604) 748-6619; FAX: (604) 748-1000. *Contact:* Jan Glerup.
Club Skate, San Diego, CA. (619) 965-7447; (800) CLUB SK8; FAX: (619) 589-4076. *Contact:* Sharene Eble.
Creations By Anne-Marie, Manchester, NH. (603) 645-1052. *Contact:* Anne-Marie Gamache.
Creative Pack Works, Salinas, CA. (408) 753-6995. *Contact:* Patty Martin.
Creative Pins By Lynne, Greenville, RI. (401) 949-3665; FAX: (401) 726-9688. *Contact:* Lynne Voepel-Gaudette.
Dante Cozzi Sports, Bellmore, NY. (516) 783-0215; FAX: (516) 783-2964. *Contact:* Dante Cozzi.
Enchantment On Ice, Inc., Virginia Beach, VA. (804) 490-0676; FAX: (804) 490-0689. *Contact:* Alycia Walker-Gaynor.
Figure 8 Boutique Ltd., Ottawa, Ontario, Canada. (613) 731-4007; FAX: (613) 736-7747. *Contact:* Jasmin Simard.
Figure Skating Boutique, Willowdale, Ontario, Canada. (416) 225-1377; (416) 225-1390; FAX: (416) 225-3071. *Contact:* Laura Hallis.

Figures on Ice, Manchester, NH. (603) 644-4521; FAX: (603) 644-1412. *Contact:* Christine Smith.
First Place Designs, Palm Harbor, FL. (813) 784-6418. *Contact:* Jackie McCarthy.
Free Style Designs, Woodside, CA. (415) 851-3233; FAX: (415) 851-7306. *Contact:* Susan Smith-Habelow.
Garde Sportswear, Willowdale, Ontario, Canada. (416) 225-3391; FAX: (416) 225-3391. *Contact:* Lois Gardner.
Henie Onstead Art Center, Norway. (47) 67 543050; FAX: 67 543270. *Contact:* Reidar Borjeson.
Highland Sports Center, Seattle, WA. (206) 546-2431; FAX: (206) 546-3130. *Contact:* Rick Stewart.
Ice Age, Westmont, IL. (708) 968-7921; (708) 988-3825. *Contact:* Michiko Carlson.
Ice Skater's Edge, Warwick, RI. (401) 732-5252; FAX: (401) 738-4531. *Contact:* Bill Ross.
Ice Sports, Pompano Beach, FL. (305) 943-1437; FAX: (305) 781-1966. *Contact:* Robyn Levin.
J&R Skates, Skaneatles, NY. (315) 685-1048; FAX: (315) 685-7343. *Contact:* Joyce Edmonds.
Jerry's Pro Shop, Rolling Meadows, IL. (708) 398-7446; FAX: (708) 398-7452. *Contact:* Glen Busch.
Jerry's Skating World, Markham, Ontario, Canada. (905) 477-1172; FAX: (905) 477-8859. *Contact:* Jerry Zawadzki.
K-Tee Enterprises, Kenwood, CA. (707) 539-6351. *Contact:* Katherine Monnier.
Leo's Dancewear, Inc., Chicago, IL. (312) 889-7700; FAX: (312) 889-7593. *Contact:* Kari Shannon.
Lexicon Ventures Limited, Vancouver, B.C., Canada. (604) 261-0371; FAX: (604) 266-7998. *Contact:* Jeff Lerner.
Lynch's, Dearborn, MI. (313) 565-3425; (800) 24-LYNCH; FAX: (313) 565-0590. *Contact:* Susan Lynch.
Maestro Editing Service. New Windsor, NY. (914) 691-7026. *Contact:* Mikehail A. Zverev.
Murray Sandler Skate & Rink Supply, Belmont, MA. (617) 484-5100; FAX: (617)489-5232. *Contact:* Murray Sandler.
Outside Edge, Winthrop Harbor, IL. (800) SKATE 93; FAX: (708) 746-3655. *Contact:* Connie Anderson.
Paul's Pro Shop, Wilmette, IL. (708) 251-0880; FAX: (708) 251-3123. *Contact:* Paul Tassone.
Platoro Press, Columbus, OH. (614) 837-0003. *Contact:* Lynn Copley-Graves.
Pro-2-Pro Services, White Rock, B.C., Canada. (604) 531-8007; FAX: (604) 531-8007. *Contact:* Daryl Austman.
Rainbo Sport Shop, Chicago, IL. (312) 275-5500; FAX: (312) 275-5506. *Contact:* Cale Carvell.
Show-Off, Inc., Elk Grove, IL. (708) 439-0206; FAX: 708-439-0219. *Contact:* Tommye
Skate Design International, Utica, MI. (810) 731-2272. *Contact:* Sue Lyons.
Skate 'N Style, Syosset, NY. (516) 496-3448; FAX: (516) 496-4964. *Contact:* Susan Lynch.
Skater's Edge - NY, Williamsville, NY. (716) 636-3000; FAX: (716) 636-1776. *Contact:* Phyllis Petri.
Skater's Edge - OH, Cleveland, OH. (216) 252-3986; FAX: (216) 671-4222. *Contact:* Dale or Carl Merkel.
Sport Concepts, Clearwater Beach, FL. (813) 442-2639; FAX: (813) 442-2639. *Contact:* Marsh Penning.

Sport Consulting Centre, North Vancouver, B.C.Canada. (604) 987-8488; FAX: (604) 987-8488. *Contact:* Shawna Palmer.
Sports Asylum, Inc., Northridge, CA. (800) 929-2159; FAX: (818) 895-4763. *Contact:* Don Laner.
Sports Representatives Ltd., Toronto, Ontario, Canada. (416) 485-4189; FAX: (416) 485-8104. *Contact:* Robert B. Haggert.
Sun Valley Skate Shop, Sun Valley, ID. (208) 622-2196. *Contact:* Daisy Layngley.
That's A Wrap, Oxford, MI. (810) 628-0396. *Contact:* Stephanie Miller.
Unique Skating Apparel, Sault Ste. Marie, MI. (906) 632-1276. *Contact:* Judy Pingatore.
Variety Arts, Fairfield, CT. (203) 259-3959 (800) 221-2154. *Contact:* Ellen Jacob.
Video Sports Productions, Westfield, NJ. (800) USA-1996; FAX: (800) 872-1996.
VIEW Video, New York, NY. (212) 674-5550; FAX: (212) 979-0266. *Contact:* Bob Karcy.
Western Starlight, Inc., Montebello, CA. (800) 929-2149 (213) 724-2149; FAX: (213) 724-6477. *Contact:* Jim Harrington.
Winning Edge, Omaha, NE. (402) 330-8052; FAX: (402) 330-4185. *Contact:* Vicki Stach.

CHOREOGRAPHERS

Artistry In Motion, Dallas, GA. (404) 443-0872; FAX: (404) 445-1156. *Contact:* Paula Wagener.
Bezic, Sandra, Toronto, Ontario, Canada. (416) 960-5312; FAX: (416) 960-0564. *Contact:* IMG Canada.
Cottam, Kevin, Nelson Park, Vancouver, B.C., Canada. (604) 592-6389. *Contact:* King Arthur Productions, Inc.
Cousins, Robin, Glendale, CA. (818) 246-5601; FAX: (818) 246-5605. *Contact:* Lee Mimms.
Cranston, Toller, Toronto, Ontario, Canada. (416) 467-9864; FAX: (416) 467-0256. *Contact:* Paul LaPointe.
Gardner, Randy, Palm Desert, CA. (619) 776-5500; FAX: (619) 776-5575. *Contact:* MARCO Entertainment.
Harris (Ricky) Choreography and Style, Rochester, MN. (509) 281-5122. *Contact:* PSGA.
ISIS Entertainment, Los Angeles, CA. (213) 935-3660; FAX: (213) 935-6953. *Contact:* Leslie Robinson.
Kawahara, Sarah, Palm Desert, CA. (619) 341-5174; FAX: (614) 341-5176. *Contact:* P.C.K. Enterprises.
Keszler, Uschi, Toronto, Ontario, Canada. (416) 925-4100; FAX: (416) 323-9132. *Contact:* Uschi Keszler.
Lar Lubovitch Dance Company, New York, NY. (212) 242-0633; FAX: (212) 691-8315. *Contact:* Richard Caples.
McBrien, Rob, New York, NY. (212) 239-4320; FAX: (212) 239-4327. *Contact:* Ice Theatre of New York.
Next Ice Age, Baltimore, MD. (410) 685-4977; FAX: (410) 435-5774. *Contact:* Nathan Birch.
Starbuck & Company, Inc., New York, NY. (212) 437-5283; FAX: (212) 437-5285. *Contact:* JoJo Starbuck.
Wright, Brian, Indianapolis, IN. (317) 237-5565. *Contact:* Brian Wright.

CLOTHING AND ACCESSORIES

Axel & Lutz Outfitters, Chicago, IL. *Contact:* Linda Khezami.
B & G Skate Supply, Ontario, CA. (909) 460-6606; FAX: (909) 460-6605. *Contact:* Barbara Johnson.
Beads, Etc., Brea, CA. (714) 529-1474. *Contact:* Gerrie Ball.
Birch Hill Designs/ Kai-Lei On Ice, Vergennes, VT. (802) 475-2327; FAX: (802) 475-2320. *Contact:* Karen Begins.
Blade and Roller Fashions, Waltham, MA. (617) 899-2830. *Contact:* Stephen Kanter.
Boston Skater, Brighton, MA. (617) 789-3650. *Contact:* Ann McKenna.
CanStar Sports, Swanton, VT. (802) 868-2711; FAX: (802) 868-4713. *Contact:* Penke Cliff.
Capezio/Ballet Makers, Inc., Totowa, NJ. (201) 595-9000; FAX: (201) 595-9120.
Club Skate, San Diego, CA. (619) 965-7447; (800) CLUB SK8; FAX: (619) 589-4076. *Contact:* Sharene Eble.
Competitor's Closet, Warwick, RI. (401) 737-7447. *Contact:* Angela Fusco.
Creations By Anne-Marie, Manchester, NH. (603) 645-1052. *Contact:* Anne-Marie Gamache.
Creative Pack Works, Salinas, CA. (408) 753-6995. *Contact:* Patty Martin.
Creative Pins By Lynne, Greenville, RI. (401) 949-3665; FAX: (401) 726-9688. *Contact:* Lynne Voepel-Gaudette.
D's Fashion Accents, Inc., Largo, FL. (800) 821-1603; (813) 532-6855. *Contact:* Deborah Farris.
Damschroder Skate Sales, North Hollywood, CA. (818) 982-9090; FAX: (818) 982-9355. *Contact:* Jerry Damschroder.
Dante Cozzi Sports, Bellmore, NY. (516) 783-0215; FAX: (516) 783-2964. *Contact:* Dantc Cozzi.
Del Arbour Designs, Milford, CT. (203) 882-8501; FAX: (203) 882-8503. *Contact:* Del Arbour.
Dorothy Hamill Entertainment, Scottsdale, AZ. (602) 996-1976; FAX: (602) 596-7906. *Contact:* Julie Ken Patterson.
Dreams on Ice, Amerillo, TX. (806) 352-7877. *Contact:* Sandy Mulhern.
Eastern Ice Sports, Summit, NJ. (908) 277-6688; FAX: (908) 277-3957. *Contact:* Russ Depack.
Enchantment On Ice, Inc., Virginia Beach, VA. (804) 490-0676; FAX: (804) 490-0689. *Contact:* Alycia Walker-Gaynor.
Figure 8 Boutique Ltd., Ottawa, Ontario, Canada. (613) 731-4007; FAX: (613) 736-7747. *Contact:* Jasmin Simard.
Figure Mates, E Hanover, NJ. (201) 386-9314. *Contact:* Margaret Johnson.
Figure Skating Boutique, Willowdale, Ontario, Canada. (416) 225-1377; (416) 225-1390; FAX: (416) 225-3071. *Contact:* Laura Hallis.
Figures on Ice, Manchester, NH. (603) 644-4521; FAX: (603) 644-1412. *Contact:* Christine Smith.
Fingertips to Toepicks, Norwalk, CT. (203) 838-1203. *Contact:* Darlene Vento.
First Place Designs, Palm Harbor, FL. (813) 784-6418. *Contact:* Jackie McCarthy.
Free Style Designs, Woodside, CA. (415) 851-3233; FAX: (415) 851-7306. *Contact:* Susan Smith-Habelow.

Garde Sportswear, Willowdale, Ontario, Canada. (416) 225-3391; FAX: (416) 225-3391. *Contact:* Lois Gardner.

Great Island Knits, Brunswick, ME. (800) 421-9538. *Contact:* Elisa Smith.

Highland Sports Center, Seattle, WA. (206) 546-2431; FAX: (206) 546-3130. *Contact:* Rick Stewart.

Ice Age, Westmont, IL. (708) 968-7921; (708) 988-3825. *Contact:* Michiko Carlson.

Ice Chalets, Inc., Los Angeles, CA. (310) 575-4466; FAX: (310) 575-4388.

Ice House, The, Wellesley, MA. (617) 237-6707; FAX: (617) 237-9609. *Contact:* Glen Kennis.

Ice Magic, Millersville, MD. (410) 987-5189; FAX: (410) 987-4104. *Contact:* Barbara Buchleitner.

Ice Skater's Edge, Warwick, RI. (401) 732-5252; FAX: (401) 738-4531. *Contact:* Bill Ross.

Ice Sports, Pompano Beach, FLUSA. (305) 943-1437; FAX: (305) 781-1966. *Contact:* Robyn Levin.

Impact Wear by Holjen, Inc., Ft. Collins, CO. (303) 223-8576; FAX: (303) 223-2753. *Contact:* Paul & Heidi Thibert.

INGA Creations Inc., Palm Springs, CA. (619) 327-6075; FAX: (619) 327-6075. *Contact:* Susie Holler.

It's a Laurie! Original, Odessa, FL. (813) 920-3757. *Contact:* Laurie Hill.

J&R Skates, Skaneatles, NY. (315) 685-1048; FAX: (315) 685-7343. *Contact:* Joyce Edmonds.

Jerry's Pro Shop, Rolling Meadows, IL. (708) 398-7446; FAX: (708) 398-7452. *Contact:* Glen Busch.

Jerry's Skating World, Markham, Ontario, Canada. (905) 477-1172; FAX: (905) 477-8859. *Contact:* Jerry Zawadzki.

Kathy Barron, Simsbury, CT. (203) 658-4688. *Contact:* Kathy Barron.

L.E.A. Sports, Marietta, GA. (404) 565-9536; FAX: (404) 565-9329. *Contact:* Bonnie Epstein.

Leo's Dancewear, Inc., Chicago, IL. (312) 889-7700; FAX: (312) 889-7593. *Contact:* Kari Shannon.

Lucky S Action Fashion, Stockton, CA. (800) 735-0458; FAX: (209) 946-0467. *Contact:* Sheri Hull.

Lynch's, Dearborn, MI. (313) 565-3425; (800) 24-LYNCH; FAX: (313) 565-0590. *Contact:* Susan Lynch.

M&M Trims, Wilkes Barre, PA. (717) 825-7305; FAX: (717) 825-7463. *Contact:* Myra Ward.

Michellene-Apparel, Escanada, MI. (906) 786-8032 (800) 786-8033; FAX: (906) 786-8032. *Contact:* Darlene R. McDonough.

Mondor, Iberville, Quebec, Canada. (514) 347-5321; FAX: (514) 347-5811. *Contact:* Juteau Christian.

Murray Sandler Skate & Rink Supply, Belmont, MA. (617) 484-5100; FAX: (617)489-5232. *Contact:* Murray Sandler.

National Skate Distributors, Tacoma, WA. (206) 473-3636; FAX: (206) 473-3791. *Contact:* Ted Werner.

National Skate Locker, Anaheim, CA. (714) 935-9500; FAX: (714) 935-2494. *Contact:* Jim Hambas.

Northwest Designs Ink, Bellevue, WA. (800) 925-9327; FAX: (206) 455-5778. *Contact:* Ben Smith.

Oberhamer, Inc., Burnsville, MN. (612) 890-1657; FAX: (612) 890-0511. *Contact:* Kent Orwoll.

Outside Edge, Winthrop Harbor, IL. (800) SKATE 93; FAX: (708) 746-3655. *Contact:* Connie Anderson.

Paul's Pro Shop, Wilmette, IL. (708) 251-0880; FAX: (708) 251-3123. *Contact:* Paul Tassone.

Pickwick Sport Shop, Burbank, CA. (818) 846-8099; FAX: (818) 845-5300. *Contact:* Mary Spencer.

Pumpers, Wichita, KS. (316) 683-3360; FAX: (316) 263-7636. *Contact:* Terri Fabian.

R.L.C. Skate Designs, Montreal, Quebec, Canada. (514) 276-2000; FAX: (514) 276-0092. *Contact:* Rhona Cantor.

Rainbo Sport Shop, Chicago, IL. (312) 275-5500; FAX: (312) 275-5506. *Contact:* Cale Carvell.

Rebel Without A Cause/Profile, Sky Forest, CA. (909) 337-8279; FAX: (909) 337-8279. *Contact:* Nancy Sigel.

Ricque Sportswear, Novi, MI. (800) 344-1230; FAX: (810) 344-7663. *Contact:* Rick Young.

S.W. Fabrics, Baltimore, MD. (800) 637-9892.

Satin Stitches, Minneapolis, MN. (612) 323-9507; FAX: (612) 323-9741. *Contact:* Deborah J. Nelson.

Show-Off, Inc., Elk Grove, IL. (708) 439-0206; FAX: 708-439-0219. *Contact:* Tommye

Silver Lining, Ltd., Crestwood, IL. Sales: (708) 458-4030 (708) 388-1485; FAX: (708) 388-9083. *Contact:* Shirley Banghart.

Kai Lei
ON ICE

Call or write for our free color catalog!

Dealer inquiries welcome

Quality Skating Apparel • Metallics • Velours • Cottons • Nylon Lycra & More • Beautiful Prints & Solids • Popular Styles Great Prices • Exceptional Quality & Excellent Service

BIRCH HILL DESIGNS RD3, Box 3365, Vergennes, VT 05491
(802)475-2327

Skate Design International, Utica, MI. (810) 731-2272. *Contact:* Sue Lyons.
Skate 'N Style, Syosset, NY. (516) 496-3448; FAX: (516) 496-4964. *Contact:* Susan Lynch, Marcia Steinberg.
Skate Shop - NY, Great Neck, NY. (516) 487-6948. *Contact:* Joel Halpern.
Skater's Choice Gift Boutique, Winthrop Harbor, IL. (708) 746-3650; FAX: (708) 746-3655. *Contact:* Connie Anderson.
Skater's Choice Pro Shop, Kenosha, WI. (414) 697-1615. *Contact:* Connie Anderson.
Skater's Edge - NY, Williamsville, NY. (716) 636-3000; FAX: (716) 636-1776. *Contact:* Phyllis Petri.
Skater's Edge - OH, Cleveland, OH. (216) 252-3986; FAX: (216) 671-4222. *Contact:* Dale or Carl Merkel.
Skater's Paradise, Inc., Alexandria, VA. (703) 660-6525; FAX: (703) 660-2341. *Contact:* Michael Cunningham.
Skater's Paradise of Delaware, Inc., Newark, DE. (302) 738-2999. *Contact:* Michael Cunningham.
Sue's Knits, Canton, MI. (313) 416-5363; FAX: (313) 207-7758. *Contact:* Sue Andrysiak.
Sun Valley Skate Shop, Sun Valley, ID. (208) 622-2196. *Contact:* Daisy Layngley.
Swonee's Place, Evansville, IN. (800) 293-6741. *Contact:* Henry Welch.
That's A Wrap, Oxford, MI. (810) 628-0396. *Contact:* Stephanie Miller.
Tomy's Skater Shop, Virginia Beach, VA. (804) 464-1464; FAX: (804) 464-1157. *Contact:* Cindy Carew.
Twizzle Designs, Inc., Dryden, Ontario, Canada. (807) 223-4533; FAX: (807) 223-6772. *Contact:* Beth Queau.
Unicorn Sport, Knoxville, TN. (615) 523-3343; FAX: (615) 522-8560. *Contact:* Barbara McKendry.
Up In The Air, Inc., Alpharetta, GA. (404) 751-0913; FAX: (404) 751-0543. *Contact:* Debbie Howe.
Unique Skating Apparel, Sault Ste. Marie, MI. (906) 632-1276. *Contact:* Judy Pingatore.
Valley Skating Supplies, North Hollywood, CA. (818) 980-0414. *Contact:* Pete Lemoine.
Winning Edge, Omaha, NE. (402) 330-8052; FAX: (402) 330-4185. *Contact:* Vicki Stach.

COLLECTIBLES

B & G Skate Supply, Ontario, CA. (909) 460-6606; FAX: (909) 460-6605. *Contact:* Barbara Johnson.
Buck's Skater's Blade Collectibles, Akron, OH. (216) 724-8972. *Contact:* Joe Mendiola.
Club Skate, San Diego, CA. (619) 965-7447; (800) CLUB SK8; FAX: (619) 589-4076. *Contact:* Sharene Eble.
Diamond Connection, Center Line, MI. (810) 759-2520; FAX: (810) 759-5850. *Contact:* Steven C. Graus.
Dorothy Hamill Entertainment, Scottsdale, AZ. (602) 996-1976; FAX: (602) 596-7906.
Eastern Ice Sports, Summit, NJ. (908) 277-6688; FAX: (908) 277-3957. *Contact:* Russ Depack.
Enchantment On Ice, Inc., Virginia Beach, VA. (804) 490-0676; FAX: (804) 490-0689. *Contact:* Alycia Walker-Gaynor.
Henie Onstead Art Center, Norway. (47) 67 543050; FAX: 67 543270. *Contact:* Reidar Borjeson.
Ice Skater's Edge, Warwick, RI. (401) 732-5252; FAX: (401) 738-4531. *Contact:* Bill Ross.
Jerry's Pro Shop, Rolling Meadows, IL. (708) 398-7446; FAX: (708) 398-7452. *Contact:* Glen Busch.
National Skate Locker, Anaheim, CA. (714) 935-9500; FAX: (714) 935-2494. *Contact:* Jim Hambas.
Outside Edge, Winthrop Harbor, IL. (800) SKATE 93; FAX: (708) 746-3655. *Contact:* Connie Anderson.
Paul's Pro Shop, Wilmette, IL. (708) 251-0880; FAX: (708) 251-3123. *Contact:* Paul Tassone.
Pickwick Sport Shop, Burbank, CA. (818) 846-8099; FAX: (818) 845-5300. *Contact:* Mary Spencer.
Power Play International, Inc., Traverse City, MI. (616) 947-1944; (616) 947-1948; FAX: (616) 947-1944; (616) 947-1944. *Contact:* Colleen Howe.
Rainbo Sport Shop, Chicago, IL. (312) 275-5500; FAX: (312) 275-5506. *Contact:* Cale Carvell.
Skate Bag, The, Oldsmar, FL. (813) 855-7998; FAX: (813) 854-4031. *Contact:* David & Rita Lowery.
Skater's Choice Gift Boutique, Winthrop Harbor, IL. (708) 746-3650; FAX: (708) 746-3655. *Contact:* Connie Anderson.
Swonee's Place, Evansville, IN. (800) 293-6741. *Contact:* Henry Welch.
Variety Arts, Fairfield, CT. (203) 259-3959; (800) 221-2154. *Contact:* Ellen Jacob.
VIEW Video, New York, NY. (212) 674-5550; FAX: (212) 979-0266. *Contact:* Bob Karcy.

CONSULTANTS

Anderson Ice Rinks, Inc., Roseville, MN. (612) 633-7363; FAX: (612) 633-7472. *Contact:* Joel Anderson.
Bonestroo, Rosene, Anderlik & Associates, St Paul, MN. (612) 636-4600; FAX: (612) 636-1311. *Contact:* Dave Loskota.
Burley's Rink Supply, Inc, Salix, PA. (814) 487-7666; FAX: (814) 487-5566. *Contact:* John Burley.
Coastal A.V. Inc., New Castle, DE. (302) 322-7775; FAX: (302) 322-7793. *Contact:* Kent Sponseller.
Cranston, Toller, Toronto, Ontario, Canada. (416) 467-9864; FAX: (416) 467-0256. *Contact:* Paul LaPointe.
Cutting Edge Sports Sciences, Latham, NY. (518) 785-8096. *Contact:* Dyke Naughton.
D & F Group, Washington, DC. (202) 364-8500; FAX: (202) 364-8500. *Contact:* Stephan Disson.
Devon Management Group, Inc., Little Silver, NJ. (908) 530-2677; FAX: (908) 530-2680. *Contact:* Chip Connell.
Enchantment On Ice, Inc., Virginia Beach, VA. (804) 490-0676; FAX: (804) 490-0689. *Contact:* Alycia Walker-Gaynor.
Ice Chalets, Inc., Los Angeles, CA. (310) 575-4466; FAX: (310) 575-4388.
Ice Rink Engineering, Greenville, SC. (803) 232-2591; FAX: (803) 246-4355. *Contact:* Jim Durham.
Ice Systems of America, Inc., Highlands Ranch, CO. (303) 220-1444; FAX: (303) 220-0455. *Contact:* Bob or Don May.
Independent Consulting Engineers, Inc., St Paul, MN. (612) 482-9313; FAX: (612) 482-9558. *Contact:* Bradford Lemberg.

International Ice Rink Consultants, Warwick, RI. (401) 737-8689; FAX: (401) 737-8696. *Contact:* Henry J. Coupe, Jr. P.E..
Laura Stamm International Power Skating System, Tuckahoe, NY. (914) 961-7994; (800) 484-7303 x 1886; FAX: 914-961-0337. *Contact:* Bryce Leavitt McGowan.
Marc Nelson Ice Development, White Plains, NY. (914) 428-4976. *Contact:* Marc Nelson.
Mentor Marketing & Management, South Bend, IN. (219) 233-9601; FAX: (219) 233-9484. *Contact:* Jeanne Martin.
Moletec Corporation, Tuscaloosa, AL. (800) 638-3219; (205) 553-9686; FAX: (205) 553-9726. *Contact:* Charles A. Snyder.
National Ice Skating Centers, Inc., Manhasset, NY. (516) 484-0040; FAX: (516) 484-8470. *Contact:* Peter Burrows.
Outside Edge, Winthrop Harbor, IL. (800) SKATE 93; FAX: (708) 746-3655. *Contact:* Connie Anderson.
Power Play International, Inc., Traverse City, MI. (616) 947-1944; (616) 947-1948; FAX: (616) 947-1944; (616) 947-1944. *Contact:* Colleen Howe.
Sasaki Associates, Inc., Watertown, MA. (617) 926-3300; FAX: (617) 924-2748. *Contact:* Roy Viklund, AIA.
Skate Music, Boston, MA. (617) 859-7844. *Contact:* Nancy Varner.
Sport Consulting Centre, North Vancouver, B.C.Canada. (604) 987-8488; FAX: (604) 987-8488. *Contact:* Shawna Palmer.
Sports Representatives Ltd., Toronto, Ontario, Canada. (416) 485-4189; FAX: (416) 485-8104. *Contact:* Robert Haggert.
Swedice Inc., Chicago, IL. (312) 258-5820; FAX: (312) 258-5828. *Contact:* Bengt Eggemar.
Univ. of MI Sport Facilities Research Laboratory, Ann Arbor, MI. (313) 764-4599; FAX: (313) 764-4597. *Contact:* Jack Vivian.
VSC Sports Consultants, Sherman Oaks, CA. (818) 501-7252; (800) 818-7528; FAX: (818) 501-4192. *Contact:* Bert Blanchette.
Woodward, Steve, Western Springs, IL. (708) 246-2605; FAX: (708) 246-2605. *Contact:* Steve Woodward.

DISTRIBUTORS

Alleisure Corporation, Marlboro, NJ. (908) 972-1235; FAX: (908) 972-1262. *Contact:* Stuart Bernstein.
Burley's Rink Supply, Inc, Salix, PA. (814) 487-7666; FAX: (814) 487-5566. *Contact:* John Burley.
Cag One Skate Sharpeners, Inc., White Plains, NY. (914) 949-3120; FAX: (914) 949-3132. *Contact:* Alvar Ohlsson.
Can Alpine Agencies, Ltd., Vancouver, B.C., Canada. (604) 266-4490; FAX: (604) 266-5470. *Contact:* Hellmut May.
Canada West Skating International, Ltd., Duncan, B.C., Canada. (604) 748-6619; FAX: (604) 748-1000. *Contact:* Jan Glerup.
CanStar Sports, Swanton, VT. (802) 868-2711; FAX: (802) 868-4713. *Contact:* Cliff Penke.
Competitor's Closet, Warwick, RI. (401) 737-7447. *Contact:* Angela Fusco.
Cooke's Pro Skate Shop, Wilmington, MA. (508) 657-4087; FAX: (508) 988-0000. *Contact:* Scott Cooke.
Damschroder Skate Sales, North Hollywood, CA. (818) 982-9090; FAX: (818) 982-9355. *Contact:* Jerry Damschroder.

Dick Button and Candid Productions have produced the World Professional Championships since 1980.

Enchantment On Ice, Inc., Virginia Beach, VA. (804) 490-0676; FAX: (804) 490-0689. *Contact:* Alycia Walker-Gaynor.
Figure 8 Boutique Ltd., Ottawa, Ontario, Canada. (613) 731-4007; FAX: (613) 736-7747. *Contact:* Jasmin Simard.
First Place Designs, Palm Harbor, FL. (813) 784-6418. *Contact:* Jackie McCarthy.
Gold Edge, Bloomington, MN. (612) 881-2222; (800) 877-6304; FAX: (612) 881-1707. *Contact:* Dan Tousignant.
Ice Systems of America, Inc., Highlands Ranch, CO. (303) 220-1444; FAX: (303) 220-0455. *Contact:* Bob or Don May.
Leo's Dancewear, Inc., Chicago, IL. (312) 889-7700; FAX: (312) 889-7593. *Contact:* Kari Shannon.
Lubin's Skate Supply, Inc., Nashua, NH. (603) 886-5777; FAX: (603) 883-6270. *Contact:* Brian Armbruster.
Midwest Skate Company, Farmington Hills, MI. (800) 521-0185; FAX: (810) 477-9550. *Contact:* Louis Armbruster.
Murray Sandler Skate & Rink Supply, Belmont, MA. (617) 484-5100; FAX: (617)489-5232. *Contact:* Murray Sandler.
National Skate Distributors, Tacoma, WA. (206) 473-3636; FAX: (206) 473-3791. *Contact:* Ted Werner.
Rainbo Sport Shop, Chicago, IL. (312) 275-5500; FAX: (312) 275-5506. *Contact:* Cale Carvell.
Riedell Skate Co., Red Wing, MN. (612) 388-8251; FAX: (612) 388-8616. *Contact:* Daniel Riegelman.
Skate 'N Style, Syosset, NY. (516) 496-3448; FAX: (516) 496-4964. *Contact:* Susan Lynch, Marcia Steinberg.
Tomy's Skater Shop, Virginia Beach, VA. (804) 464-1464; FAX: (804) 464-1157. *Contact:* Cindy Carew.
Tournament Sports, Waterloo, Ontartio, Canada. (519) 888-6500; FAX: (519) 888-6540. *Contact:* Wayne Sehagena.
VIEW Video, New York, NY. (212) 674-5550; FAX: (212) 979-0266. *Contact:* Bob Karcy.
Westwood Sports, Bloomington, MN. (612) 881-2222; (800) 877-6304; FAX: (612) 881-1707. *Contact:* Dan Tousignant.

EVENT PRODUCTION

Candid Productions, Inc., New York, NY. (212) 581-9450; FAX: (212) 581-9373. *Contact:* Dick Button.

Dorothy Hamill Entertainment, Scottsdale, AZ. (602) 996-1976; FAX: (602) 596-7906.
Ice Castles International Training Center, Lake Arrowhead, CA. (909) 337-0802; FAX: (909) 337-8949. *Contact:* Judith Light.
International Management Group (IMG), New York, NY. (212) 772-8900; FAX: (212) 772-2617
ISIS Entertainment, Los Angeles, CA. (213) 935-3660; FAX: (213) 935-6953. *Contact:* Leslie Robinson.
MARCO Entertainment (Michael A. Rosenburg Management), Palm Desert, CA. (619) 776-5500; FAX: (619) 776-5575. *Contact:* Michael or Nancy Rosenberg.
Pro Skating European Association, Neuilly/Seine, France. 011-33-1-6767 8600; FAX: 011-33-1-6767 8600. *Contact:* Philippe Angel.
Starbuck & Company, Inc., New York, NY. (212) 437-5283; FAX: (212) 437-5285. *Contact:* JoJo Starbuck.
Tip Nunn's Events, Inc., Golden, CO. (303) 237-0616; FAX: (303) 237-0609. *Contact:* Lynn Plage.
Tom Collins Enterprises, Inc., Minneapolis, MN. (612) 831-2237; FAX: (612) 831-0566. *Contact:* Tom Collins.

HOCKEY EQUIPMENT

B & G Skate Supply, Ontario, CA. (909) 460-6606; FAX: (909) 460-6605. *Contact:* Barbara Johnson.
Boston Hockey Company, Dover, NH. (603) 742-4333; FAX: (603) 742-9311.
CanStar Sports, Swanton, VT. (802) 868-2711; FAX: (802) 868-4713. *Contact:* Penke Cliff.
Cooke's Pro Skate Shop, Wilmington, MA. (508) 657-4087; FAX: (508) 988-0000. *Contact:* Scott Cooke.
Dante Cozzi Sports, Bellmore, NY. (516) 783-0215; FAX: (516) 783-2964. *Contact:* Dante Cozzi.
Eastern Ice Sports, Summit, NJ. (908) 277-6688; FAX: (908) 277-3957. *Contact:* Russ Depack.
Figure 8 Boutique Ltd., Ottawa, Ontario, Canada. (613) 731-4007; FAX: (613) 736-7747. *Contact:* Jasmin Simard.
Highland Sports Center, Seattle, WA. (206) 546-2431; FAX: (206) 546-3130. *Contact:* Rick Stewart.
Ice Chalets, Inc., Los Angeles, CA. (310) 575-4466; FAX: (310) 575-4388.
Ice Skater's Edge, Warwick, RI. (401) 732-5252; FAX: (401) 738-4531. *Contact:* Bill Ross.
Ice Sports, Pompano Beach, FLUSA. (305) 943-1437; FAX: (305) 781-1966. *Contact:* Robyn Levin.
International Winter Sports Museum, Lake Placid, NY. (518) 523-4100; FAX: (518) 523-3470. *Contact:* David Heim.
Jerry's Pro Shop, Rolling Meadows, IL. (708) 398-7446; FAX: (708) 398-7452. *Contact:* Glen Busch.
Lubin's Skate Supply, Inc., Nashua, NH. (603) 886-5777; FAX: (603) 883-6270. *Contact:* Brian Armbruster.
Murray Sandler Skate & Rink Supply, Belmont, MA. (617) 484-5100; FAX: (617)489-5232. *Contact:* Murray Sandler.
National Skate Locker, Anaheim, CA. (714) 935-9500; FAX: (714) 935-2494. *Contact:* Jim Hambas.
NESSI (New England Sports Sales, Inc.), Woburn, MA. (800) 878-4648; FAX: (617) 932-6695. *Contact:* Charles Gualtieri.
Paul's Pro Shop, Wilmette, IL. (708) 251-0880; FAX: (708) 251-3123. *Contact:* Paul Tassone.
Peck and Goodie, New York, NY. (212) 246-6123; FAX: (212) 807-6115. *Contact:* Scott Kelleher.
Philbrick Sports, Dover, NH. (603) 742-4333; FAX: (603) 742-9311. *Contact:* Dan Philbrick.
Pickwick Sport Shop, Burbank, CA. (818) 846-8099; FAX: (818) 845-5300. *Contact:* Mary Spencer.
Red Line Sports, Soldatna, AK. (907) 262-5860; FAX: (907) 262-5860. *Contact:* Vince Redford.
Rink Systems, Inc., Albert Lea, MN. (800) 944-7930; FAX: (507) 377-1060. *Contact:* Stacey Overgaard.
Rollerblade, Inc., Minnetonka, MN. (800) 232-7655; (612) 930-7000. *Contact:* Maureen O'Neill.
Skate Bag, The, Oldsmar, FL. (813) 855-7998; FAX: (813) 854-4031. *Contact:* David & Rita Lowery.
Skate Shop - NY, Great Neck, NY. (516) 487-6948. *Contact:* Joel Halpern.
Skater's Choice Gift Boutique, Winthrop Harbor, IL. (708) 746-3650; FAX: (708) 746-3655. *Contact:* Connie Anderson.
Skater's Edge - NY, Williamsville, NY. (716) 636-3000; FAX: (716) 636-1776. *Contact:* Phyllis Petri.
Skater's Paradise, Inc., Alexandria, VA. (703) 660-6525; FAX: (703) 660-2341. *Contact:* Michael Cunningham.
Slap Shot Sports, West Orange, NJ. (201) 736-9107; FAX: (201) 736-1115. *Contact:* Ed Krokchmal.
Sports Asylum, Inc., Northridge, CA. (800) 929-2159; FAX: (818) 895-4763. *Contact:* Don Laner.
Stan's Skate Shop, West Islip, NY. (516) 587-1658. *Contact:* Stan Belliveau.
Steamboats/Blades, Steamboat Spring, CO. (303) 879-3286; FAX: (303) 879-3286. *Contact:* Jim Fournier.
Swonee's Place, Evansville, IN. (800) 293-6741. *Contact:* Henry Welch.
Up In The Air, Inc., Alpharetta, GA. (404) 751-0913; FAX: (404) 751-0543. *Contact:* Debbie Howe.
Valley Skating Supplies, North Hollywood, CA. (818) 980-0414. *Contact:* Pete Lemoine.

INSURANCE

Allied Specialty Insurance, Treasure Island, FL. (813) 237-3355; FAX: (813) 367-1407. *Contact:* Dean Smith.
Cartier Insurance Agency, Duluth, MN. (800) 756-3346; (218) 727-5992; FAX: (218) 727-8501. *Contact:* Rob Pavlatos.
ISU Hoffman Insurance Services, Wellseley, MA. (800) 277-6052; FAX: (617) 235-6665. *Contact:* Gilbert Lincoln.
K&K Insurance Group, Inc., Fort Wayne, IN. (219) 459-5663; FAX: (219) 459-5967. *Contact:* Angie Poulos.
Karleen Insurance Agency, Schaumburg, IL. (708) 303-5070; FAX: (708) 303-5072. *Contact:* Kathleen O'Connell.
Rice & Company, Buffalo, NY. (800) 733-RICE; FAX: (716) 854-3346. *Contact:* Joan Rice.
Richardson G & A Inc., Exeter, NH. (603) 772-0860; FAX: (603) 772-0873. *Contact:* John Gray.

JEWELRY

Ashworth Associates, North Attleboro, MA. (508) 695-1900; FAX: (508) 695-0377. *Contact:* Douglas Ashworth.
Beads, Etc., Brea, CA. (714) 529-1474. *Contact:* Gerrie Ball.
Creative Pins By Lynne, Greenville, RI. (401) 949-3665; FAX: (401) 726-9688. *Contact:* Lynne Voepel-Gaudette.
D's Fashion Accents, Inc., Largo, FL. (800) 821-1603; (813) 532-6855. *Contact:* Deborah Farris.
Dreams on Ice, Amerillo, TX. (806) 352-7877. *Contact:* Sandy Mulhern.
Enchantment On Ice, Inc., Virginia Beach, VA. (804) 490-0676; FAX: (804) 490-0689. *Contact:* Alycia Walker-Gaynor.
First Place Designs, Palm Harbor, FL. (813) 784-6418. *Contact:* Jackie McCarthy.
Ice Skater's Edge, Warwick, RI. (401) 732-5252; FAX: (401) 738-4531. *Contact:* Bill Ross.
Jerry's Pro Shop, Rolling Meadows, IL. (708) 398-7446; FAX: (708) 398-7452. *Contact:* Glen Busch.
Mother Goose Imagines (MGI), Coventry, RI. (401) 828-6627; FAX: (401) 272-2560. *Contact:* Barbara Smith.
Neon 1, San Dimas, CA. (909) 592-2492. *Contact:* Don Merrell.
Outside Edge, Winthrop Harbor, IL. (800) SKATE 93; FAX: (708) 746-3655. *Contact:* Connie Anderson.
Paul's Pro Shop, Wilmette, IL. (708) 251-0880; FAX: (708) 251-3123. *Contact:* Paul Tassone.
Pickwick Sport Shop, Burbank, CA. (818) 846-8099; FAX: (818) 845-5300. *Contact:* Mary Spencer.
Rainbo Sport Shop, Chicago, IL. (312) 275-5500; FAX: (312) 275-5506. *Contact:* Cale Carvell.
Skate Art Jewelry by John Albeita, Dallas, TX. (214) 369-6191; (800) 323-2638; FAX: (214) 369-6855. *Contact:* John Albeita.
Skater's Choice Gift Boutique, Winthrop Harbor, IL. (708) 746-3650; FAX: (708) 746-3655. *Contact:* Connie Anderson.
Tana's Gold, Troy, OH. (513) 335-4698. *Contact:* Susan Fogt.
Variety Arts, Fairfield, CT. (203) 259-3959; (800) 221-2154. *Contact:* Ellen Jacob.
Winning Edge, Omaha, NE. (402) 330-8052; FAX: (402) 330-4185. *Contact:* Vicki Stach.

MUSIC AND TAPES

Annie's Edges, Freelton, Ontario, Canada. (905) 659-7402. *Contact:* Anne E. Schelter.
ASCAP, New York, NY. (212) 621-6400; FAX: (212) 873-3133. *Contact:* Patrick Collins.
B & G Skate Supply, Ontario, CA. (909) 460-6606; FAX: (909) 460-6605. *Contact:* Barbara Johnson.
Classic Cassettes, Fresno, CA. (800) 678-1127; FAX: (209) 276-8632. *Contact:* Bob Lambert.
Coastal A.V. Inc., New Castle, DE. (302) 322-7775; FAX: (302) 322-7793. *Contact:* Kent Sponseller.
First Movement Music, Co., Somerville, MA. (617) 623-0998. *Contact:* Dana Ashworth.
International Skating Union (ISU), CH-7270, Davos Platz, Switzerland. (081) 43 75 77; FAX: (081) 43 66 71. *Contact:* Beat Hasler.
Maestro Editing Service, New Windsor, NY. (914) 691-7026.

Ice Theatre of New York performing at Rockefeller Center

Manhattan Library of Dance Skating Music, New York, NY. (212) 873-2307; FAX: (212) 873-2307. *Contact:* Christian Orlov.
National Audio, Burbank, CA. (800) 777-3838. *Contact:* Kim Clark.
Performance Coaching Inc., Rockwood, Ontario, Canada. (519) 856-9064; FAX: (519) 856-9939. *Contact:* S. Swallow.
Skate Music, Boston, MA. (617) 859-7844. *Contact:* Nancy Varner.
T&T Productions, Cottage Grove, OR. (503) 942-9387. *Contact:* Gary Todd.
Varese Sarabande Records, Studio City, CA. (818) 753-4143; FAX: (818) 753-7596.
VIEW Video, New York, NY. (212) 674-5550; FAX: (212) 979-0266. *Contact:* Bob Karcy.

OFF-ICE TRAINING AND EQUIPMENT

Canada West Skating International, Ltd., Duncan, B.C., Canada. (604) 748-6619; FAX: (604) 748-1000. *Contact:* Jan Glerup.
Ice Chalets, Inc., Los Angeles, CA. (310) 575-4466; FAX: (310) 575-4388.
Laura Stamm International Power Skating System, Tuckahoe, NY. (914) 961-7994; (800) 484-7303 x 1886; FAX: 914-961-0337. *Contact:* Bryce Leavitt McGowan.
Poe, Carl, Lawrenceville, GA. (404) 381-2837; FAX: (404) 279-7267. *Contact:* Carl M. Poe.
Rainbo Sport Shop, Chicago, IL. (312) 275-5500; FAX: (312) 275-5506. *Contact:* Cale Carvell.
Roller Stop Inc., Malden, MA. (617) 324-2272; FAX: (617) 324-4449. *Contact:* John Petell.
Rollerblade, Inc., Minnetonka, MN. (800) 232-7655; (612) 930-7000. *Contact:* Maureen O'Neill.
Skate Spinner, Blaine, WA. (800) 661-3199; (800) 663-1774; FAX: (206) 371-3631. *Contact:* George Sterling.
Skater's Paradise, Inc., Alexandria, VA. (703) 660-6525; FAX: (703) 660-2341. *Contact:* Michael Cunningham.
Stretch Quest, Park City, UT. 1-800-375-7057; (801) 649-2939; FAX: (801) 649-0931. *Contact:* Duke Wier.

PHOTO BY ALICE BERMAN

ON-ICE TRAINING AND EQUIPMENT

Canada West Skating International, Ltd., Duncan, B.C., Canada. (604) 748-6619; FAX: (604) 748-1000. *Contact:* Jan Glerup.
Keszler, Uschi, Toronto, Ontario, Canada. (416) 925-4100; FAX: (416) 323-9132. *Contact:* Futerman & Futerman.

PERFORMANCE TROUPES

Dorothy Hamill Entertainment, Scottsdale, AZ. (602) 996-1976; FAX: (602) 596-7906. *Contact:* Julie Ken Patterson.
Giant On Ice, Inc., Los Angeles, CA. 310-278-5114; FAX: 310-278-5795. *Contact:* Peter Bylsma.
Ice Follies/Holiday on Ice, Sarasota, FL. (813) 377-4210; FAX: (813) 378-4591.
Ice Theatre of New York, Inc., New York, NY. (212) 239-4320; FAX: (212) 239-4327. *Contact:* Moira North.
ISIS Entertainment, Los Angeles, CA. (213) 935-3660; FAX: (213) 935-6953. *Contact:* Leslie Robinson.
National Ice Theatre of Canada, Edmonton, Alberta, Canada. (403) 421-8879; FAX: (403) 426-1049. *Contact:* Sandra Shewchuk.
Next Ice Age, Baltimore, MD. (410) 685-4977; FAX: (410) 435-5774. *Contact:* Nathan Birch.
Rollerblade, Inc., Minnetonka, MN. (800) 232-7655; (612) 930-7000. *Contact:* Maureen O'Neill.
Walt Disney's World on Ice, Vienna, VA. (703) 749-5564; FAX: (703) 448-4119. *Contact:* Zanna Stuart.

PHOTOGRAPHERS

Black (Dave) Photography, Colorado Springs, CO. (719) 636-3510. *Contact:* Dave Black.
Butt (Ingrid) Photography, Tucson, AZ. *Contact:* Ingrid Butt.
Ice Pics, San Francisco, CA. (415) 626-5289. *Contact:* Sue Pon.
Kast, Nancy L., Fresno, CA. (209) 227-0783. *Contact:* Nancy Kast.
Ledin Photo & Video, St Clair Shores, MI. (810) 778-8971. *Contact:* Noel or Alice Ledin.
Lucas (Pam) Photography, Tucson, AZ. *Contact:* Pam Lucas.
Mittan (J. Barry) Photography, Tallahasse, FL. (800) 758-7318; FAX: (904) 877-2569. *Contact:* Barry Mittan.
Newton Video Photography, Colorado Springs, CO. (719) 599-0954. *Contact:* Jim & Shelley Newton.
Photographic Edge, Wasaga Beach, Ontario, Canada. (705) 429-4948; FAX: (705) 429-4948. *Contact:* Stephan Potopnyk.
Photos On Ice, Flint, MI. (313) 635-4830. *Contact:* Paul or Michelle Harvarth.
Stellar Images, Manhattan Beach, CA. (310)336-6056; FAX: (310) 336-7130. *Contact:* George Rossano.
Udell Photo Video, North Hollywood, CA. (818) 985-6866; FAX: (818) 985-6867. *Contact:* Bill Udell.
Wachter (Jerry) Photography Ltd., Baltimore, MD. (410) 466-3866; FAX: (410) 466-4672. *Contact:* Jerry Wachter.

PUBLICATIONS

American Skating World, Pittsburgh, PA. (412) 885-7600; FAX: (412) 885-7617. *Contact:* H. Kermit Jackson.
Blades on Ice, Tucson, AZ. (602) 575-1747; FAX: (602) 575-1484. *Contact:* Gerri Walbert.
Figure Skating Historical Society, Inc., Chilmark, MA. (508) 645-3063; FAX: (508) 645-2897. *Contact:* Jilliaine Eicher.
Ice Age Magazine, Milton Keynes, Bucks, England. 09-08-366-161; FAX: 09-08-371-751. *Contact:* Alan Price.
Ice Skating Down Under, Queenland, Australia.
International Figure Skating Magazine, Worcester, MA. (508) 756-2595; FAX: (508) 792-5981. *Contact:* Mark Lund.
ISIA Newsletter, Buffalo Grove, IL. (708) 808-7528; FAX: (708) 808-8329.
Le Patinage Suisse, CH -1005, Lausanne, Switzerland.
Luistelija, FIN-00240, Helsinki, Finland.
Outside Edge, Pretoria, South Africa.
Patinage Magazine, Rouen, FRANCE. (16) 35 07 47 29; FAX: (16) 35 89 06 67. *Contact:* Vincent Guerrier.
Professional Skater Magazine, PSGA, Rochester, MN. (507) 281-5122; FAX: (507) 281-5491. *Contact:* Carole Shulman.
Racer, The (Speed Skating), Gloucester, Ontario, Canada. *Contact:* Brenda Gallagher.
Racing Blade, The, Mt. Prospect, IL.
Recreational Ice Skating, Buffalo Grove, IL. (708) 808-7528. *Contact:* Justine Townsend-Smith.
Schaats Magazine, NL-3800 BC, Amersfoort, Netherlands.
Skater's Edge, Kensington, MD. (301) 946-1971; FAX: (301) 946-1971. *Contact:* Alice Berman.
Skating Magazine, Colorado Springs, CO. (719) 635-5200. *Contact:* Jay Miller.
Skating News, Orkney, G.B. 01857 600465; FAX: 01857 600465. *Contact:* Pete Roberts.
Skojtesport, DK-2970 Horsholm, Denmark.
Skoytesport, N-1341 Rud, Norway.
Skridsko-nytt, S-63356 Eskilstuna, Sweden.
Suomen Taitoluistelu, FIN-00240, Helsinki, Finland.
Svensk Konstakning, PI 1007, S-745 93, Sweden.
Tracings Magazine, N. Weymouth, MA. (617) 335-9135; FAX: (617) 340-5648. *Contact:* Mary Clarke.

PROMOTION AND PUBLIC RELATIONS

American Video Productions, Tacoma, WA. (206) 564-4454; FAX: (206) 564-8731. *Contact:* Jim Hinte.
Giant On Ice, Inc., Los Angeles, CA. 310-278-5114; FAX: 310-278-5795. *Contact:* Peter Bylsma.
Jefferson Pilot Sports, Charlotte, NC. (704) 374-3636; FAX: (704) 374-3859. *Contact:* Michael Burg.
Lesnik Public Relations, Chicago, IL. (312) 755-3500; FAX: (312) 755-0276. *Contact:* Michael Myers.
Marc Nelson Ice Development, White Plains, NY. (914) 428-4976. *Contact:* Marc Nelson.
Mentor Marketing & Management, South Bend, IN. (219) 233-9601; FAX: (219) 233-9484. *Contact:* Jeanne Martin.
Power Play International, Inc., Traverse City, MI. (616) 947-1944; (616) 947-1948; FAX: (616) 947-1944; (616) 947-1944. *Contact:* Colleen Howe.

Pro Skating European Association, Neuilly/Seine, France. 011-33-1-6767 8600; FAX: 011-33-1-6767 8600. *Contact:* Angel Philippe.

Sharpe Public Relations, Beverly Hills, CA. (310) 274-3587; FAX: (310) 274-5980. *Contact:* Kathi Sharpe-Ross.

Sherman (Keith) & Associates, New York, NY. (212) 764-7900; FAX: (212) 764-0344. *Contact:* Keith Sherman.

Sports Representatives Ltd., Toronto, Ontario, Canada. (416) 485-4189; FAX: (416) 485-8104. *Contact:* Robert B. Haggert.

Sterling (Michael) and Associates, Sherman Oaks, CA. (818) 385-0007; FAX: (818) 385-0004. *Contact:* Michael Sterling.

Tip Nunn's Events, Inc., Golden, CO. (303) 237-0616; FAX: (303) 237-0609. *Contact:* Lynn Plage.

Tom Collins Enterprises, Inc., Minneapolis, MN. (612) 831-2237; FAX: (612) 831-0566.

RESORTS, MUSEUMS, AND VACATION SPOTS

Ice Castles International Training Center, Lake Arrowhead, CA. (909) 337-0802; FAX: (909) 337-8949. *Contact:* Judith Light.

International Winter Sports Museum, Lake Placid, NY. (518) 523-4100; FAX: (518) 523-3470. *Contact:* David Heim.

Keystone Resort, Keystone, CO. (303) 468-4208; FAX: (303) 468-4024. *Contact:* Thomas Davidson.

Lake Placid 1932 & 1980 Winter Olympic Museum, Lake Placid, NY. (518) 523-1655 x.263; FAX: (518) 523-9275. *Contact:* Jacqueline Baker.

Museum of Television and Radio, New York, NY. (212) 621-6800; FAX: (212) 621-6715.

Squaw Valley USA, Olympic Valley, CA. (916) 583-6985; FAX: (916) 581-7106. *Contact:* Bret Smith.

Sunday River Ski Resort, Bethel, ME. (207) 824-3000; FAX: (207) 824-2111. *Contact:* Skip King.

RINK BUILDING AND DESIGN

Anderson Ice Rinks, Inc., Roseville, MN. (612) 633-7363; FAX: (612) 633-7472. *Contact:* Joel Anderson.

Arena Contractors & Equipment, Inc., White Bear Lake, MN. (612) 653-4444; FAX: (612) 653-4436. *Contact:* Scott Herrick.

B.K. Mechanicals, Inc., Westchester, PA. (610) 692-7965; FAX: (610) 692-5552. *Contact:* John Krupinski.

Bonestroo, Rosene, Anderlik & Associates, St Paul, MN. (612) 636-4600; FAX: (612) 636-1311. *Contact:* Dave Loskota.

Burley's Rink Supply, Inc, Salix, PA. (814) 487-7666; FAX: (814) 487-5566. *Contact:* John Burley.

Flex-Ice, Inc., New York, NY. (212) 581-9450; FAX: (212) 581-9373. *Contact:* Kevin Kossi.

Ice Pro - C.W. Davis Supply, Inc., Syracuse, NY. (315) 453-2056; FAX: (315) 453-3852. *Contact:* Jim Hartnett.

Ice Skating Institute of America (ISIA), Buffalo Grove, IL. (708) 808-7528; FAX: (708) 808-8329. *Contact:* Justine Townsend Smith.

Ice Systems of America, Inc., Highlands Ranch, CO. (303) 220-1444; FAX: (303) 220-0455. *Contact:* Bob or Don May.

ICE SYSTEMS
OF AMERICA, INC.

Supplying Solutions
For All Your
ICE
or
REFRIGERATED SURFACE
Requirements

Ice Arenas
permanent/temporary/portable

- Bobsled/Luge Runs
- Speed Ovals
- Ski Slope Holding
- Curling Rinks
- Ski Jumps
- Toboggan Slides
- Special Applications

plus...
Solutions
For All Your
BUILDING/APPLICATION
Requirements

- Permanent Floors
- Retrofits
- Portable Floors
- ICEMAT System
- Chillers Systems
- Compressors
- Multiple Floor Coverings
- Dasher Boards *NHL Approved*
- Reheat & Dehumidification

...and much more including

- Ice Rink Design
- Operations
- Building Design
- Financing
- Business Plans
- Development

thru
Full Turn Key Projects

From Start to Skate

Call *TODAY*
(303) 220-1444
FAX (303) 220-0455

ICE SYSTEMS
of America, Inc.
6955 S. Kendall Blvd. Littleton, Colorado 80123

Independent Consulting Engineers, Inc., St Paul, MN. (612) 482-9313; FAX: (612) 482-9558. *Contact:* Bradford A. Lemberg.

International Ice Rink Consultants, Warwick, RI. (401) 737-8689; FAX: (401) 737-8696. *Contact:* Henry J. Coupe, Jr.

Jet Ice Paints Limited, Richmond Hill, Ontario, Canada. (905) 883-4204; FAX: (905) 770-3071. *Contact:* Dave Loverock.

Rink Systems, Inc., Albert Lea, MN. (800) 944-7930; FAX: (507) 377-1060. *Contact:* Stacey Overgaard.

Rink-Tec International Inc., Roseville, MN. (612) 635-0127; FAX: (612) 638-9023. *Contact:* Daryl Cox.

RMI Industrial Refrigeration Systems, Mississauga, Canada. (905) 858-7969; FAX: (905) 858-7973. *Contact:* Thomas Brenton.

Sasaki Associates, Inc., Watertown, MA. (617) 926-3300; FAX: (617) 924-2748. *Contact:* Roy Viklund, AIA.

Swedice Inc., Chicago, IL. (312) 258-5820; FAX: (312) 258-5828. *Contact:* Bengt Eggemar.

VSC Sports Consultants, Sherman Oaks, CA. (818) 501-7252; (800) 818-7528; FAX: (818) 501-4192. *Contact:* Bert Blanchette.

Western Starlight, Inc., Montebello, CA. (800) 929-2149; (213) 724-2149; FAX: (213) 724-6477. *Contact:* Jim Harrington.

RINK SUPPLIES AND EQUIPMENT

American Locker Security Systems, Jamestown, NY. (800) 828-9118; FAX: (716) 664-2949. *Contact:* David L. Henderson.

Anderson Ice Rinks, Inc., Roseville, MN. (612) 633-7363; FAX: (612) 633-7472. *Contact:* Joel Anderson.

Arena Contractors & Equipment, Inc., White Bear Lake, MN. (612) 653-4444; FAX: (612) 653-4436. *Contact:* Scott Herrick.

Becker Arena Products, Prior Lake, MN. (612) 440-8655; 800-234-5522; FAX: (612) 440-8656. *Contact:* Jim Becker.

Burley's Rink Supply, Inc, Salix, PA. (814) 487-7666; FAX: (814) 487-5566. *Contact:* John Burley.

Canada West Skating International, Ltd., Duncan, B.C., Canada. (604) 748-6619; FAX: (604) 748-1000. *Contact:* Jan Glerup.

Cimco Refrigeration, Toronto, Ontario, Canada. (416) 465-7581; FAX: (416) 465-7530. *Contact:* Steven McLeod.

Coastal A.V. Inc., New Castle, DE. (302) 322-7775; FAX: (302) 322-7793. *Contact:* Kent Sponseller.

Crystalplex, Division of Laird, Mississauga, Ontario, Canada. (905) 673-8072; (800) 665-7494; FAX: (905) 673-2696. *Contact:* Matt Broughton.

Dectron, Inc., South Burlington, VT. (802) 862-8342; FAX: (514) 334-9184. *Contact:* Eglal Homsy.

Engelhard - ICC Technologies, Philadelphia, PA. (215) 625-0700; FAX: (215) 592-8299. *Contact:* Robert Mitro.

Flex-Ice, Inc., New York, NY. (212) 581-9450; FAX: (212) 581-9373. *Contact:* Kevin Kossi.

Global Information Systems, Tampa, FL. (813) 289-3611; FAX: (813) 289-3072. *Contact:* Tim Zagorc.

Ice Pro - C.W. Davis Supply, Inc., Syracuse, NY. (315) 453-2056; FAX: (315) 453-3852. *Contact:* Jim Hartnett.

Ice Rink Engineering, Greenville, SC. (803) 232-2591; FAX: (803) 246-4355. *Contact:* Jim Durham.

Ice Skating Institute of America (ISIA), Buffalo Grove, IL. (708) 808-7528; FAX: (708) 808-8329. *Contact:* Justine Townsend Smith.

Ice Systems of America, Inc., Highlands Ranch, CO. (303) 220-1444; FAX: (303) 220-0455. *Contact:* Bob and Don May.

Ice Top International Inc, North Vancouver, B.C., Canada. (604) 924-1858; FAX: (604) 924-1878. *Contact:* Beat Aschmann.

Jet Ice Paints Limited, Richmond Hill, Ontario, Canada. (905) 883-4204; FAX: (905) 770-3071. *Contact:* Dave Loverock.

Leclair Arena Equipment Ltd., Montreal, Quebec, Canada. (514) 277-1186; FAX: (514) 277-3277. *Contact:* Cary Miller.

Lubin's Skate Supply, Inc., Nashua, NH. (603) 886-5777; FAX: (603) 883-6270. *Contact:* Brian Armbruster.

Mitchell Rubber Products, City of Industry, CA. (800) 453-7526; FAX: (818) 968-2026. *Contact:* Rachelle Mathias.

Moletec Corporation, Tuscaloosa, AL. (800) 638-3219; (205) 553-9686; FAX: (205) 553-9726. *Contact:* Charles A. Snyder.

Murray Sandler Skate & Rink Supply, Belmont, MA. (617) 484-5100; FAX: (617)489-5232. *Contact:* Murray Sandler.

Rainbo Sport Shop, Chicago, IL. (312) 275-5500; FAX: (312) 275-5506. *Contact:* Cale Carvell.

Red Line Sports, Soldatna, AK. (907) 262-5860; FAX: (907) 262-5860. *Contact:* Vince Redford.

Rink Systems, Inc., Albert Lea, MN. (800) 944-7930; FAX: (507) 377-1060. *Contact:* Stacey Overgaard.

Rink-Tec International Inc., Roseville, MN. (612) 635-0127; FAX: (612) 638-9023. *Contact:* Daryl Cox.

Think Rink, New York City, NY. (914) 634-8996. *Contact:* Michael J. Carroll.

Tuflex Rubber Flooring, Tampa, FL. (800) 543-0390; FAX: (813) 875-2312. *Contact:* Nancy MacNaughton.

VSC Sports Consultants, Sherman Oaks, CA. (818) 501-7252; (800) 818-7528; FAX: (818) 501-4192. *Contact:* Bert Blanchette.

Yontz Corporation, Brandon, FL. (813) 324-9372; FAX: (813) 685-4495. *Contact:* Donald Yontz.

Zamboni, Paramount, CA. (310) 633-0751; FAX: (310) 633-9365. *Contact:* Richard F. Zamboni.

SKATING SCHOOLS AND CAMPS

Bay State Ice Skating School, Waltham, MA. (617) 290-0556; FAX: (617) 890-1799. *Contact:* Carol Butterworth.

JAMA & Friends Skate, Livingston, NJ. (201) 992-7491. *Contact:* Jay & Amy Slatus.

National Ice Skating Centers, Inc., Manhasset, NY. (516) 484-0040; FAX: (516) 484-8470. *Contact:* Peter Burrows.

National Sports Academy, Lake Placid, NY. (518) 523-3460; FAX: (518) 523-3488. *Contact:* David Wenn.

New England Figure Skating Camp, Woodbury, NY. (516) 364-8050. *Contact:* Werner Rothchild.

Rollerblade, Inc., Minnetonka, MN. (800) 232-7655; (612) 930-7000. *Contact:* Maureen O'Neill.

SKATE SHOPS

B & G Skate Supply, Ontario, CA. (909) 460-6606; FAX: (909) 460-6605. *Contact:* Barbara Johnson.

Boston Skater, Brighton, MA. (617) 789-3650. *Contact:* Ann McKenna.

Canada West Skating International, Ltd., Duncan, B.C., Canada. (604) 748-6619; FAX: (604) 748-1000. *Contact:* Jan Glerup.

Club Skate, San Diego, CA. (619) 965-7447; (800) CLUB SK8; FAX: (619) 589-4076. *Contact:* Sharene Eble.

Cooke's Pro Skate Shop, Wilmington, MA. (508) 657-4087; FAX: (508) 988-0000. *Contact:* Scott Cooke.

Dante Cozzi Sports, Bellmore, NY. (516) 783-0215; FAX: (516) 783-2964. *Contact:* Dante Cozzi.

Eastern Ice Sports, Summit, NJ. (908) 277-6688; FAX: (908) 277-3957. *Contact:* Russ Depack.

Enchantment On Ice, Inc., Virginia Beach, VA. (804) 490-0676; FAX: (804) 490-0689. *Contact:* Alycia Walker-Gaynor.

Figure 8 Boutique Ltd., Ottawa, Ontario, Canada. (613) 731-4007; FAX: (613) 736-7747. *Contact:* Jasmin Simard.

Figure Skating Boutique, Willowdale, Ontario, Canada. (416) 225-1377; (416) 225-1390; FAX: (416) 225-3071. *Contact:* Laura Hallis.

Fingertips to Toepicks, Norwalk, CT. (203) 838-1203. *Contact:* Darlene Vento.

Gold Edge, The, Bloomington, MN. (612) 881-2222; (800) 877-6304; FAX: (612) 881-1707. *Contact:* Dan Tousignant.

Highland Sports Center, Seattle, WA. (206) 546-2431; FAX: (206) 546-3130. *Contact:* Rick Stewart.

Ice Castles International Training Center, Lake Arrowhead, CA. (909) 337-0802; FAX: (909) 337-8949. *Contact:* Judith Light.

Ice Chalets, Inc., Los Angeles, CA. (310) 575-4466; FAX: (310) 575-4388.

Ice House, The, Wellesley, MA. (617) 237-6707; FAX: (617) 237-9609. *Contact:* Glen Kennis.

Ice Skater's Edge, Warwick, RI. (401) 732-5252; FAX: (401) 738-4531. *Contact:* Bill Ross.

Ice Sports, Pompano Beach, FL. (305) 943-1437; FAX: (305) 781-1966. *Contact:* Robyn Levin.

J&R Skates, Skaneatles, NY. (315) 685-1048; FAX: (315) 685-7343. *Contact:* Joyce Edmonds.

Murray Sandler Skate & Rink Supply, Belmont, MA. (617) 484-5100; FAX: (617)489-5232. *Contact:* Murray Sandler.

National Skate Locker, Anaheim, CA. (714) 935-9500; FAX: (714) 935-2494. *Contact:* Jim Hambas.

Paul's Pro Shop, Wilmette, IL. (708) 251-0880; FAX: (708) 251-3123. *Contact:* Paul Tassone.

Peck and Goodie, New York, NY. (212) 246-6123; FAX: (212) 807-6115. *Contact:* Scott Kelleher.

Pickwick Sport Shop, Burbank, CA. (818) 846-8099; FAX: (818) 845-5300. *Contact:* Mary Spencer.

Rainbo Sport Shop, Chicago, IL. (312) 275-5500; FAX: (312) 275-5506. *Contact:* Cale Carvell.

Red Line Sports, Soldatna, AK. (907) 262-5860; FAX: (907) 262-5860. *Contact:* Vince Redford.

S.H. Stoery & Son, Northbrook, IL. (708) 205-1548. *Contact:* Jess Stoery.

Skate Bag, The, Oldsmar, FL. (813) 855-7998; FAX: (813) 854-4031. *Contact:* David & Rita Lowery.

Skate Shop - IL, Crestwood, IL. (708) 389-7849. *Contact:* John Harmata.

Skate Shop - NY, Great Neck, NY. (516) 487-6948. *Contact:* Joel Halpern.

Skater's Choice Gift Boutique, Winthrop Harbor, IL. (708) 746-3650; FAX: (708) 746-3655. *Contact:* Connie Anderson.

Skater's Choice Pro Shop, Kenosha, WI. (414) 697-1615. *Contact:* Connie Anderson.

Skater's Edge - NY, Williamsville, NY. (716) 636-3000; FAX: (716) 636-1776. *Contact:* Phyllis Petri.

Skater's Edge - OH, Cleveland, OH. (216) 252-3986; FAX: (216) 671-4222. *Contact:* Dale or Carl Merkel.

Skater's Loft, Ogdensburg, NY. (315) 393-0764; FAX: (315) 393-4212. *Contact:* Donna Doyle.

Skater's Paradise, Inc., Alexandria, VA. (703) 660-6525; FAX: (703) 660-2341. *Contact:* Michael Cunningham.

Skater's Paradise of Delaware, Inc., Newark, DE. (302) 738-2999. *Contact:* Michael Cunningham.

Slap Shot Sports, West Orange, NJ. (201) 736-9107; FAX: (201) 736-1115. *Contact:* Ed Krokchmal.

Stan's Skate Shop, West Islip, NY. (516) 587-1658. *Contact:* Stan Belliveau.

Steamboats/Blades, Steamboat Spring, CO. (303) 879-3286; FAX: (303) 879-3286. *Contact:* Jim Fournier.

WE SUPPORT ICE RINKS FROM THE GROUND UP

Burley's Rink Supply has made its name building and supplying ice rinks of all sizes. Our arenas and equipment can be found in major cities worldwide... and in small communities where tomorrow's hockey and ice skating stars are getting their start.

We support skating from the ground up with innovations that lower operating costs and extend rink life. Like TurboChiller™, refrigeration so efficient that utility companies offer rebates to users.

For rink development, rink equipment or arena maintenance, call us toll-free 24 hours a day. **1-800-4-Burley (428-7539)**

- Ice Maintenance Equipment
- Arena Products and Accessories
- Refrigeration Units
- Design-Build Services
- Complete Rink Systems
- Rinkstarter™ Community Ice Rink Packages
- Rinkmate™ Rink Management Software

Burley's Rink SUPPLY INC.

P.O. Box 250 • 1 School Street • Salix, PA 15952-0250

Sun Valley Skate Shop, Sun Valley, ID. (208) 622-2196. *Contact:* Daisy Layngley.
Tomy's Skater Shop, Virginia Beach, VA. (804) 464-1464; FAX: (804) 464-1157. *Contact:* Cindy Carew.
Valley Skating Supplies, North Hollywood, CA. (818) 980-0414. *Contact:* Pete Lemoine.
Westwood Sports, Bloomington, MN. (612) 881-2222; (800) 877-6304; FAX: (612) 881-1707. *Contact:* Dan Tousignant.
Winning Edge, Omaha, NE. (402) 330-8052; FAX: (402) 330-4185. *Contact:* Vicki Stach.

SPECIALTY ITEMS

Ashworth Associates, North Attleboro, MA. (508) 695-1900; FAX: (508) 695-0377. *Contact:* Douglas Ashworth.
Beads, Etc., Brea, CA. (714) 529-1474. *Contact:* Gerrie Ball.
Buck's Skater's Blade Collectibles, Akron, OH. (216) 724-8972. *Contact:* Joe Mendiola.
Cag One Skate Sharpeners, Inc., White Plains, NY. (914) 949-3120; FAX: (914) 949-3132. *Contact:* Alvar Ohlsson.
Canada West Skating International, Ltd., Duncan, B.C., Canada. (604) 748-6619; FAX: (604) 748-1000. *Contact:* Jan Glerup.
Club Skate, San Diego, CA. (619) 965-7447; (800) CLUB SK8; FAX: (619) 589-4076. *Contact:* Sharene Eble.
Competitor's Closet, Warwick, RI. (401) 737-7447. *Contact:* Angela Fusco.
Cosmos Software, Farmington Hills, MI. (810) 661-5881. *Contact:* Gary Garbin.
Creative Pack Works, Salinas, CA. (408) 753-6995. *Contact:* Patty Martin.
Crown Trophy, Yonkers, NY. (914) 963-0005; FAX: (914) 963-0181. *Contact:* E. Weisenfeld.
D's Fashion Accents, Inc., Largo, FL. (800) 821-1603; (813) 532-6855. *Contact:* Deborah Farris.
Eight-Mate Skating Products Co., Manassas, VA. (703) 369-6902; FAX: (703) 369-6902. *Contact:* Nicolas Perna.
Enchantment On Ice, Inc., Virginia Beach, VA. (804) 490-0676; FAX: (804) 490-0689. *Contact:* Alycia Walker-Gaynor.
Etch Design Industries, Bethel Park, PA. (412) 221-4782; FAX: (412) 833-2184. *Contact:* Lois Hill.
Figure 8 Boutique Ltd., Ottawa, Ontario, Canada. (613) 731-4007; FAX: (613) 736-7747. *Contact:* Jasmin Simard.
First Place Designs, Palm Harbor, FL. (813) 784-6418. *Contact:* Jackie McCarthy.
Foy Toys, Las Vegas, NV. (702) 454-3500. *Contact:* Teresa Foy.
Hodges Badge Company, Inc., Middletown, RI. (401) 847-2000; (800) 556-2440; FAX: (800) 292-7377. *Contact:* Wadson Eden.
Ice Chalets, Inc., Los Angeles, CA. (310) 575-4466; FAX: (310) 575-4388.
Ignel Associates, San Francisco, CA. (415) 681-5088; FAX: (415) 681-5088. *Contact:* Alina Sivorinovsky.
Jumpometer Co., Haileybury, Ontario, Canada. (705) 672-5455; FAX: (705) 672-5867. *Contact:* Allan Lee.
K-Tee Enterprises, Kenwood, CA. (707) 539-6351. *Contact:* Katherine Monnier.
Kathy Barron, Simsbury, CT. (203) 658-4688. *Contact:* Kathy Barron.
Keith's Precision Skate Sharpening, Watertown, MA. (617) 924-4518. *Contact:* Keith Galgot.
Marc Evon Enterprises, Windsor, Ontario, Canada. (519) 737-7659; FAX: (519) 737-7052. *Contact:* Marc Evon.
Murray Sandler Skate & Rink Supply, Belmont, MA. (617) 484-5100; FAX: (617)489-5232. *Contact:* Murray Sandler.
Neon 1, San Dimas, CA. (909) 592-2492. *Contact:* Don Merrell.
Northwest Designs Ink, Bellevue, WA. (800) 925-9327; FAX: (206) 455-5778. *Contact:* Ben Smith.
Ogilvie-Gutzman Blade Gauges, Ironton, MN. *Contact:* Alan Gutzman.
Outside Edge, Winthrop Harbor, IL. (800) SKATE 93; FAX: (708) 746-3655. *Contact:* Connie Anderson.
Path Editions, Toronto, Ontario, Canada. (416) 423-2271. *Contact:* Igor Mojes.
Paul's Pro Shop, Wilmette, IL. (708) 251-0880; FAX: (708) 251-3123. *Contact:* Paul Tassone.
Platoro Press, Columbus, OH. (614) 837-0003. *Contact:* Lynn Copley-Graves.
Pro-2-Pro Services, White Rock, B.C., Canada. (604) 531-8007; FAX: (604) 531-8007. *Contact:* Daryl Austman.
R.L.C. Skate Designs, Montreal, Quebec, Canada. (514) 276-2000; FAX: (514) 276-0092. *Contact:* Rhona Cantor.
Rainbo Sport Shop, Chicago, IL. (312) 275-5500; FAX: (312) 275-5506. *Contact:* Cale Carvell.
Rainbow Technologies, Wauwatosa, WI. (414) 476-7693; FAX: (414) 476-7693. *Contact:* Coola Ellestad.
Skate 'N Style, Syosset, NY. (516) 496-3448; FAX: (516) 496-4964. *Contact:* Susan Lynch, Marcia Steinberg.
Skater's Choice Gift Boutique, Winthrop Harbor, IL. (708) 746-3650; FAX: (708) 746-3655. *Contact:* Connie Anderson.
Stretch Quest, Park City, UT. 1-800-375-7057; (801) 649-2939; FAX: (801) 649-0931. *Contact:* Duke Wier.
Thompson & LaPointe, Toronto, Ontario, Canada. (416) 467-9864; FAX: (416) 467-0256. *Contact:* Paul LaPointe.
Up In The Air, Inc., Alpharetta, GA. (404) 751-0913; FAX: (404) 751-0543. *Contact:* Debbie Howe.
Variety Arts, Fairfield, CT. (203) 259-3959; (800) 221-2154. *Contact:* Ellen Jacob.
Where'd You Get That !?, Inc., Williamstown, MA. (413) 458-2206; FAX: (413) 458-0991. *Contact:* Michele Gietz.

SPORTS PSYCHOLOGY

Bramwell (Patricia) Sports Psychology, Belle Harbor, NY. (718) 474-6850. *Contact:* Patricia Bramwell.
Performance Coaching Inc., Rockwood, Ontario, Canada. (519) 856-9064; FAX: (519) 856-9939. *Contact:* Shelly Swallow.

Sport Consulting Centre, North Vancouver, B.C.Canada. (604) 987-8488; FAX: (604) 987-8488. *Contact:* Shawna Palmer.
Winning Ways, Potomac, MD. (301) 983-6712; FAX: (301) 469-0100. *Contact:* Dr. Caroline Silby.

TOUR MANAGEMENT

Giant On Ice, Inc., Los Angeles, CA. 310-278-5114; FAX: 310-278-5795. *Contact:* Peter Bylsma.
International Management Group (IMG), New York, NY. (212) 772-8900; FAX: (212) 772-2617.
MARCO Entertainment (Michael A. Rosenburg Management), Palm Desert, CA. (619) 776-5500; FAX: (619) 776-5575. *Contact:* Michael and Nancy Rosenberg.
Skatetours, Rocky Mount, VA. (703) 483-3700; FAX: (703) 483-5080. *Contact:* Kathy Normile Davidson.
Sulyma Productions Inc., Edmonton, Alberta, Canada. (403) 438-8316; FAX: (403) 488-0858. *Contact:* Michael Sulyma.
Tom Collins Enterprises, Inc., Minneapolis, MN. (612) 831-2237; FAX: (612) 831-0566.

TRAINING CENTERS

(See also chapter on Training Centers)
Dorothy Hamill Entertainment, Scottsdale, AZ. (602) 996-1976; FAX: (602) 596-7906.
Ice Castles International Training Center, Lake Arrowhead, CA. (909) 337-0802; FAX: (909) 337-8949. *Contact:* Judith Light.
Indiana/World Skating Academy Summer School, Indianapolis, IN. (317) 237-5568. *Contact:* Heidi Mallin.
Lake Placid International School of Ice Dancing, Lake Placid, NY. (518) 523-1655; FAX: (518) 523-9275. *Contact:* Natalia Dubova.
National Ice Skating Centers, Inc., Manhasset, NY. (516) 484-0040; FAX: (516) 484-8470. *Contact:* Peter Burrows.
Skating Club of Wilmington, Wilmington, DE. (302) 656-5005. *Contact:* Dot Gualtieri.
Sport-O-Rama, Monsey, NY. (914) 356-3919; FAX: (914) 356-9274. *Contact:* Glen Brawer.
Sun Valley Skating School, Sun Valley, ID. (208) 622-2193; FAX: (208) 622-2193. *Contact:* Nick Maricich.
Tony Kent Ice Arena, South Dennis, MA. (508) 760-2415. *Contact:* Dottie Larkin.
U.S. Olympic Training Center (USOTC) - CO, Colorado Springs, CO. (719) 578-4618; FAX: (719) 578-4728.
U.S. Olympic Training Center (USOTC) - NY, Lake Placid, NY. (518) 523-2600; FAX: (518) 523-1570.
U.S. Olympic Training Center (USOTC) - San Diego, San Diego, CA. (619) 291-8802; FAX: (619) 291-5395.
University of Delaware Ice Skating Science Development Center, Newark, DE. (302) 831-2868. *Contact:* Ron Ludington.
World Ice Skating Center (Thailand) Co., Ltd., Bangkok, Thailand. (662) 225-9500; Telex: 21369 WTCB TH; FAX: (662) 253-4488. *Contact:* Cynthia Lee Van Valkenberg.

TRAVEL AND EVENT PACKAGES

Bryan Sports Events, San Mateo, CA. (415) 579-0455; FAX: (415) 579-0811. *Contact:* Joan Burns.
Cartan Tours, Inc., Manhattan Beach, CA. (800) 874-1996; (310) 546-9662; FAX: (310) 546-8433. *Contact:* Don Williams.
Colonial Travel, Farmington, CT. (203) 677-0875; FAX: (203) 678-9716. *Contact:* Maria Scerrato.
Duxbury Travel Service, Inc., Duxbury, MA. (617) 934-5633; FAX: (617) 934-5739. *Contact:* Hal Gates.
Global Sports, Wellesley, MA. (617) 237-7678; FAX: (617) 431-1946. *Contact:* Laurence Chase.
Ice Castles International Training Center, Lake Arrowhead, CA. (909) 337-0802; FAX: (909) 337-8949. *Contact:* Judith Light.
Silver Blade Tours, Rocky Hill, CT. (203) 721-7670; FAX: (203) 563-6717. *Contact:* Barbara Cassella.
Skatetours, Rocky Mount, VA. (703) 483-3700; FAX: (703) 483-5080. *Contact:* Kathy Normile Davidson.
Sports Representatives Ltd., Toronto, Ontario, Canada. (416) 485-4189; FAX: (416) 485-8104. *Contact:* Robert Haggert.
Travel One, Boston, MA. (617) 523-8161; (800) 782-7232; FAX: (617) 523-2759. *Contact:* Elaine Shore.

VIDEOGRAPHERS

American Video Productions, Tacoma, WA. (206) 564-4454; FAX: (206) 564-8731. *Contact:* Jim Hinte.
BSH Video, Mystic, CT. (610) 399-0578; FAX: (203) 536-3221. *Contact:* Barry 'Hoagie' Hogenauer.
Coffey & Associates, Beaverton, OR. (503) 644-0761; FAX: (503) 644-1423. *Contact:* Michelle Coffey.
Hurd Video, Costa Mesa, CA. (714) 546-4085. *Contact:* John Hurd.
Ledin Photo & Video, St Clair Shores, MI. (810) 778-8971. *Contact:* Noel or Alice Ledin.
Newton Video Photography, Colorado Springs, CO. (719) 599-0954. *Contact:* Jim or Shelley Newton.
Productions East Video, Saratoga, NY. (518) 587-4853. *Contact:* Jon Cromer.
R & J Video, Stockton, CA. (209) 466-3878; (209) 476-0124. *Contact:* Ron Singson.
Udell Photo Video, North Hollywood, CA. (818) 985-6866; FAX: (818) 985-6867. *Contact:* Bill Udell.

VIDEO SALES

(See also chapter on Videos.)
American Video Productions, Tacoma, WA. (206) 564-4454; FAX: (206) 564-8731. *Contact:* Jim Hinte.
Annie's Edges, Freelton, Ontario, Canada. (905) 659-7402. *Contact:* Anne E. Schelter.
B & G Skate Supply, Ontario, CA. (909) 460-6606; FAX: (909) 460-6605. *Contact:* Barbara Johnson.
BSH Video, Mystic, CT. (610) 399-0578; FAX: (203) 536-3221. *Contact:* Barry 'Hoagie' Hogenauer.
Classic Cassettes, Fresno, CA. (800) 678-1127; FAX: (209) 276-8632. *Contact:* Bob Lambert.
Club Skate, San Diego, CA. (619) 965-7447; (800) CLUB SK8; FAX: (619) 589-4076. *Contact:* Sharene Eble.

Coastal A.V. Inc., New Castle, DE. (302) 322-7775; FAX: (302) 322-7793. *Contact:* Kent Sponseller.

Eastern Ice Sports, Summit, NJ. (908) 277-6688; FAX: (908) 277-3957. *Contact:* Russ Depack.

Henie Onstead Art Center, Norway. (47) 67 543050; FAX: 67 543270. *Contact:* Reidar Borjeson.

Ice Command, Easton, MD. (410) 820-5614. *Contact:* Cecily Morrow.

Laura Stamm International Power Skating System, Tuckahoe, NY. (914) 961-7994; (800) 484-7303 x 1886; FAX: 914-961-0337. *Contact:* Bryce Leavitt McGowan.

Ledin Photo & Video, St Clair Shores, MI. (810) 778-8971. *Contact:* Noel & Alice Ledin.

Lussi Technical Video, Easton, MD. (410) 820-6125. *Contact:* Cecily Morrow.

Magic of Style, Vail, CO. (303) 926-3345; FAX: (303) 926-5176. *Contact:* Ann-Margreth Frei.

National Skate Locker, Anaheim, CA. (714) 935-9500; FAX: (714) 935-2494. *Contact:* Jim Hambas.

Outside Edge, Winthrop Harbor, IL. (800) SKATE 93; FAX: (708) 746-3655. *Contact:* Connie Anderson.

P.H.D. Products, Colorado Springs, CO. (719) 591-4425. *Contact:* Wendy Pittman.

Platoro Press, Columbus, OH. (614) 837-0003. *Contact:* Lynn Copley-Graves.

Power Play International, Inc., Traverse City, MI. (616) 947-1944; (616) 947-1948; FAX: (616) 947-1944; (616) 947-1944. *Contact:* Colleen Howe.

Productions East Video, Saratoga, NY. (518) 587-4853. *Contact:* Jon Cromer.

R & J Video, Stockton, CA. (209) 466-3878; (209) 476-0124. *Contact:* Ron Singson.

Rainbo Sport Shop, Chicago, IL. (312) 275-5500; FAX: (312) 275-5506. *Contact:* Cale Carvell.

Red Brick Entertainment, New York, NY. (212) 427-4762; FAX: (212) 369-8766. *Contact:* Rob Dustin.

Rollerblade, Inc., Minnetonka, MN. (800) 232-7655; (612) 930-7000. *Contact:* Maureen O'Neill.

Skater's Edge - NY, Williamsville, NY. (716) 636-3000; FAX: (716) 636-1776. *Contact:* Phyllis Petri.

Sports Asylum, Inc., Northridge, CA. (800) 929-2159; FAX: (818) 895-4763. *Contact:* Don Laner.

Sulyma Productions Inc., Edmonton, Alberta, Canada. (403) 438-8316; FAX: (403) 488-0858. *Contact:* Michael Sulyma.

Tohaventa Holdings Inc., Edmonton, Alberta, Canada. (403) 421-8879; FAX: (403) 426-1049. *Contact:* Geoffrey Leboutillier.

Udell Photo Video, North Hollywood, CA. (818) 985-6866; FAX: (818) 985-6867. *Contact:* Bill Udell.

Valley Skating Supplies, North Hollywood, CA. (818) 980-0414. *Contact:* Pete Lemoine.

Video Sports Productions, Westfield, NJ. (800) USA-1996; FAX: (800) 872-1996.

VIEW Video, New York, NY. (212) 674-5550; FAX: (212) 979-0266. *Contact:* Bob Karcy.

WORKSHOPS

Annie's Edges, Freelton, Ontario, Canada. (905) 659-7402. *Contact:* Anne E. Schelter.

Artistry In Motion, Dallas, GA. (404) 443-0872; FAX: (404) 445-1156. *Contact:* Paula Wagener.

Have the Mental Edge, Greeley, CO. (303) 353-1098. *Contact:* Marilyn Norcross.

Ice Castles International Training Center, Lake Arrowhead, CA. (909) 337-0802; FAX: (909) 337-8949. *Contact:* Judith Light.

Ice Command Workshops, Easton, MD. (410) 820-5614. *Contact:* Cecily Morrow.

Ice Theater of New York, Inc., New York, NY. (212) 239-4320; FAX: (212) 239-4327. *Contact:* Moira North.

ISIS Entertainment, Los Angeles, CA. (213) 935-3660; FAX: (213) 935-6953. *Contact:* Leslie Robinson.

Jazz on Ice, Los Angeles, CA. (213) 936-2584; FAX: (213) 934-9571. *Contact:* G. Webster Smith.

Joe's Skate Service, Littleton, CO. (303) 798-7881; FAX: (303) 980-0356. *Contact:* P. Joseph De Lio.

Laura Stamm International Power Skating System, Tuckahoe, NY. (914) 961-7994; (800) 484-7303 x 1886; FAX: 914-961-0337. *Contact:* Bryce Leavitt McGowan.

McBrien, Rob, New York, NY. (212) 239-4320; FAX: (212) 239-4327. *Contact:* Rob McBrien.

National Ice Skating Centers, Inc., Manhasset, NY. (516) 484-0040; FAX: (516) 484-8470. *Contact:* Peter Burrows.

National Ice Theatre of Canada, Edmonton, Alberta, Canada. (403) 421-8879; FAX: (403) 426-1049. *Contact:* Sandra Shewchuk.

Plie Power Workshops, New York, NY. (212) 239-4320; FAX: (212) 239-4327. *Contact:* Rob McBrien.

Poe, Carl, Lawrenceville, GA. (404) 381-2837; FAX: (404) 279-7267. *Contact:* Carl M. Poe.

Sport Consulting Centre, North Vancouver, B.C.Canada. (604) 987-8488; FAX: (604) 987-8488. *Contact:* Shawna Palmer.

Starbuck & Company, Inc., New York, NY. (212) 437-5283; FAX: (212) 437-5285. *Contact:* JoJo Starbuck.

Style Seminars For Skaters, Vail, CO. (303) 926-3345; FAX: (303) 926-5176. *Contact:* Ann-Margreth Frei.

Winning Ways, Potomac, MD. (301) 983-6712; FAX: (301) 469-0100. *Contact:* Dr. Caroline Silby.

Fan Mail and Letters

Brian Boitano
Brian Boitano Fan Club
101 First Street, #370
Los Altos, CA 94022

Brian Boitano
Outside Edges Newsletter
85 North 750 West
Orem, UT 84057

Christopher Bowman
Christopher Bowman Fan Club
P.O. Box 725
Narragansett, RI 02882

Brasseur & Eisler
Bourne & Kraatz
Elizabeth Manley
c/o *Skating Fan Clubs*
P.O. Box 24009
Windsor, Ontario, N8Y 4V9 Canada

Kurt Browning
What A Wonderful World Newsletter
373 Saw Creek Estates
Bushkill, PA 18324

Brian Orser
The Lion Sleeps Newsletter
111 East Avenue #429
Rochester, NY 14604

Brian Orser
Orser's Endorsers Fan Club Newsletter
3634 Ash Street
Baltimore, MD 21211

Katarina Witt
Katarina Witt Fan Club
c/o Martin Kugler
Bangermannweg 1
W-3000 Hanover 72, Germany

Paul Wylie
B.J. Tritico
The Paul Wylie Update Newsletter
9250 Friendship
Houston, TX 77080

For Other U.S. Skaters:
USFSA
20 First Street
Colorado Springs, CO 80906

For Other Canadian Skaters:
CFSA
1600 James Naismith Drive
Gloucester, ON K1B 5N4 Canada

For Foreign Skaters:
International Skating Union
(Member Club Information)
Promenade 73,
Postfach CH 7270
Davos Platz, Switzerland

(Or write to the skater's home Federation; see *Federations* chapter.)

Coaches and Skating Pros
Professional Skaters Guild of America
(PSGA)
P.O. Box 5904
Rochester, MN 55903

For Other Amateur Athletes:
United States Olympic Committee
(USOC)
One Olympic Plaza
Colorado Springs, CO 80906

AGENTS and MANAGERS

Following are the agents or managers for many of the top skaters.

IMG CANADA
1 Saint Clair Ave East, #700
Toronto, Ontario, M4T 2V7 Canada

For the following skaters:
Kurt Browning
Lu Chen
Josee Chouinard
Scott Hamilton
Kristi Yamaguchi

IMG NEW YORK
22 East 71st Street
New York, NY 10021

For the following skaters:
Brasseur & Eisler
Kitty & Peter Carruthers
Isabelle & Paul Duchesnay
Gordeeva & Grinkov
Brian Orser
Jill Trenary
Paul Wylie

MARCO Entertainment
73-271 Riata Trail
Palm Desert, CA 92260

For the following skaters:
Lisa-Marie Allen
Petr Barna
Babilonia & Gardner
Bestemianova & Bulkin
Blumberg & Yorke
Surya Bonaly
Michael Chack
Tiffany Chin
Stephen Cousins
Alexander Fadeev
Gregor Filipowski
Linda Fratianne
Randy Gardner
Simone Grigorescu
Hartshorn & Sweiding
Ina & Dungjen
Caryn Kadavy
Klimova & Ponomarenko
Kovarikova & Novotny
Elizabeth Manley
McDonald & Smith
Mark Mitchell
Karen Preston
Punsalan & Swallow
Josef Sabovcik
Charlie Tickner
Urbanski & Marval
Usova & Zhulin
Valova & Vassiliev
Robert Wagenhoffer
Tracy Wainman
Elaine Zayak

1994 Olympic Silver Medalist Nancy Kerrigan

MENTOR Marketing
Societie Bank Bldg., Suite 810
South Bend, IN 46601
For the following skaters:
Ralph Burghart
Shepherd Clark
Tom Dickson
Beth Ann Duxbury
Rory Flack
Amy Jaramillo
Catarina Lindgren
David Liu
Mishkutenok & Dmitriev[1]
Pagano & Paul
Jirina Ribbens[2]
Natalie & Wayne Seybold
JoJo Starbuck
Debi Thomas
Tisha Walker
Wacholder & Sullivan
Webster & Kravette
Steve Woodward[3]
Wynne & Witherby
Zakarian & Manoukian[4]

[1] U.S. marketing projects and fan mail only.
[2] Independent producer and consultant for TV networks and Candid Productions.
[3] Freelance writer/consultant.
[4] Armenian acrobatic skaters.

Mimms & Associates
2644 East Chevy Chase Drive
Glendale, CA 91206
For: Robin Cousins

Dorothy Hamill International
15033 North 74th Street
Scottsdale, AZ 85260
For: Dorothy Hamill and the Ice Capades

Pro-Serv
1101 Wilson Blvd., Suite 1800
Arlington, VA 22209
For: Nancy Kerrigan

Futerman & Futerman
2 St. Clair Avenue East
15th Floor Colonial Tower
Toronto, ON M4T 2R1 Canada
For: Elvis Stojko

Sharpe Public Relations
922230 Olympic Blvd., #203
Beverly Hills, CA 90212
For: Robin Cousins

Debbie Turner
59, Goodwin Avenue
Swalecliffe, Nr. Whitstable
Kent, CT5 2RA, England
For: Torvill & Dean

TV STATIONS

Here's where to send your letters about broadcasting and figure skating:

ABC Sports
47 West 66th Street
13th Floor
New York, NY 10023

CBS Sports
51 West 52nd Street
30th Floor
New York, NY 10019

ESPN
ESPN Plaza
Bristol, CT 06010

FOX Broadcasting Company
P.O. Box 900
Beverly Hills, CA 90213

HTS (Home Team Sports)
1111 18th Street, NW
Washington, DC 20036

PBS
1320 Braddock Place
Alexandria, VA 22314

TBS-TNT
Turner Sports
1 CNN Center
Atlanta, GA 30348

USA (USA Network)
1230 Avenue of the Americas
New York, NY 10020

PHOTO BY ALICE BERMAN

Skating Federations

HEADQUARTERS
International Skating Union (ISU)
Founded: 1892
Beat Hasler, General Secretary
Promenade 73, Postfach
CH-7270, Davos Platz, Switzerland
Phone: (081) 43 75 77;
FAX: (081) 43 66 71
Notes: The umbrella organization and governing body for ice skating worldwide. Countries wishing to compete in the Olympics must be members of the ISU. All rules governing Olympic skating competitions are set by the ISU. The ISU also sells CDs of ice dance music; write for information.

ARM: Armenia
Armenia Skating Federation
Paul Varadian, Secretary
c/o Armenia Olympic Committee
9 Abovian St.
Yerevan, 375001, Armenia
Phone: (7885) 2 52 55 93;
FAX: (7885) 2 52 98 08
Notes: Provisional member of the ISU representing Armenia (ARM).

AUS: Australia
Australian Amateur Ice Racing Council, Inc.
James H. Hewish, Secretary
57 Charlton Ave.
Chipping Norton, N.S.W., 2170, Australia
Phone: (2) 755-2584;
FAX: (2) 755-2284
Notes: Speed skating member of the ISU representing Australia (AUS).

National Ice Skating Association of Australia Inc.
Wendy A. Langton, Secretary
P.O. Box 42
Brisbane Markets, Q. 4106, Australia
Phone: (7) 277-7563;
FAX: (7) 274-1357
Notes: Figure skating member of the ISU representing Australia (AUS).

AUT: Austria
Osterreichischer Eislaufverband
Ingrid Uthe, Secretary
Prinz Eugen Strasse 12
Haus des Sports
Vienna, A-1040, Austria
Phone: (1) 505 75 35;
FAX: (1) 505 75 35
Notes: Member of the ISU representing Austria (AUT).

AZE: Azerbaijan
Azerbaijan Figure Skating Federation
98A St. Petersburg Ave.
370072 Baku, Azerbaijan
Phone: (994412) 64 10 70;
(994412) 67 02 55;
FAX: (994412) 64 36 50
Notes: Member of the ISU representing Azerbaijan (AZE).

BLS: Belarus
Skating Union of Belarus
Oleg Krivosheev, General Secretary
Zacharova St. 30-2
Minsk, 220034, Belarus
Phone: (0172) 20 78 29;
FAX: (0172) 23 11 37
Notes: Member of the ISU representing Belarus (BLS).

BEL: Belgium
Federation Royale Belge de Patinage Artistique
Marcel Geers, Secretary
Avenue Reine Elisabeth 61
B-5000 Namur, Belgium
Phone: (81) 22 74 72;
FAX: (81) 22 74 72
Notes: Figure skating member of the ISU representing Belgium (BEL).

Federation Royale Belge de Patinage de Vitesse
Luc De Dier, General Secretary
Muilemstraat 263
B-1770 Liedekerke, Belgium
Phone: (53) 67 17 79;
FAX: (53) 67 17 79
Notes: Speed skating member of the ISU representing Belgium (BEL).

BIH: Bosnia and Herzegovina
Skating Federation of Bosnia and Herzegovina
Emir Medanhodzic, Secretary
Marsala Tita 7A/I
71000 Sarajevo, Bosnia and Herzegovina
Phone: (387) 71 663 362/(387) 71 663 514; *FAX:* (387) 71 663 362/ (387) 663 514
Notes: Member of the ISU representing Bosnia and Herzegovina (BIH).

BUL: Bulgaria
Bulgarian Skating Federation
Ivan Ivanov, General Secretary
75 Vassil Levsky Blvd.
1040 Sofia, Bulgaria
Phone: (2) 86 53 51/(2) 66 25 50;
FAX: (2) 879670/800520
Notes: Member of the ISU representing Bulgaria (BUL).

CAN: Canada
Canadian Amateur Speed Skating Association
Guy Leclair, Executive Director
1600 James Naismith Drive, Suite 312
Gloucester, Ontario, K1B 5N4, Canada
Phone: (613) 748-5669
FAX: (613) 748-5600

Notes: Speed skating member of the International Skating Union representing Canada (CAN).

Canadian Figure Skating Association (CFSA)
David M. Dore, General Director
1600 James Naismith Drive, Suite 403
Gloucester, Ontario, K1B 5N4,
Canada
Phone: (613) 748-5635;
FAX: (613) 748-5718
Notes: The governing body of figure skating for Canada (CAN), with member clubs, skaters and pros. Offers extensive training and certification program for coaches. Figure skating member of the ISU representing Canada.

CHN: China
Chinese Skating Association
Yingfu Wang, Secretary
54, Baishiqiao Road
Haidian District Beijing 10044, China
Phone: (1) 833 25 76;
FAX: (1) 835 80 83
Notes: Member of the ISU representing China (CHN).

TPE: Chinese Taipei
Chinese Taipei Skating Association
Rich K. H. Lee, General Secretary
Room #610, 6F
20, Chu Lun St.
10816, Chinese Taipei
Phone: (2) 775 8722/(2) 775 8723;
FAX: (2) 778 2778
Notes: Member of the ISU representing Chinese Taipei (TPE).

CRO: Croatia
Croatioan Skating Federation
Antica Grubisic, General Secretary
Trg sportova 11
41000 Zagreb, Croatia
Phone: (41) 339 333;
FAX: (41) 325 864/(41) 327 111
Notes: Member of the ISU representing Croatia (CRO).

CZE: Czech Republic
Czech Figure Skating Association
Frantisek Pechar, Executive Director
Mezi stadiony, P.O. Box 40
160 17 Praha 6-Strahov,
Czech Republic
Phone: (2) 357 756;
FAX: (2) 357 756/(2) 863 287
Notes: Figure skating member of the ISU representing the Czech Republic (CZE).

Czech Speed Skating Federation
Jindrich Parik, Secretary
Mezi stadiony, P.O. Box 40
160 17 Praha 6, Czech Republic
Phone: (2) 527 409;
FAX: (2) 353 007
Notes: Speed skating member of the ISU representing the Czech Republic (CZE).

DEN: Denmark
Dansk Skojte Union
Finn L. Pedersen, Secretary
Brondby Stadion 20
DK-2605 Brondby, Denmark
Phone: 42 45 71 14; FAX: 43 43 04 20
Notes: Member of the ISU representing Denmark (DEN).

PRK: DPR Korea
Skating Association of the Democratic People's Republic of Korea
Su Jang Ryu, General Secretary
Kumsong-dong 2
Manyongdae District
Pyongyang, DPR Korea
Phone: (2) 81 4164;
FAX: (2) 81 4403
Notes: Member of the ISU representing the Democratic People's Republic of Korea (PRK).

EST: Estonia
The Estonian Skating Union
Anne Saraskin, Secretary
Tallinna Linnahall
Mere puiestee 20
EE 0001 Tallinn, Estonia
Phone: (2) 601 835;
FAX: (2) 523 131
Notes: Member of the ISU representing Estonia (EST).

FIN: Finland
Suomen Luisteluliitto (Finnish Speed Skating Member)
Sauli Pollari, General Secretary
Radiokatu 20, Box 27
FIN-00240 Helsinki, Finland
Phone: (0) 158 2479;
FAX: (0) 145 237
Notes: Speed skating member of the ISU representing Finland (FIN)

Suomen Taitoluisteluliitto (Finnish Figure Skating Association)
Heikki Vuojakoski, Secretary
Radiokatu 20, Box 27
FIN-00240 Helsinki, Finland
Phone: (0) 158 2154/(0) 158 2385;
FAX: (0) 158 2095
Notes: Figure skating member of the ISU representing Finland (FIN).

FRA: France
Federation Francaise des Sports de Glace
Eugene Peizerat, Secretary
42, rue du Louvre
F-75001 Paris, France
Phone: (1) 40 26 51 38;
FAX: (1) 40 26 54 25/(1) 40 26 50 16
Notes: Member of the ISU representing France (FRA). Organizes competitions in ice skating, ice dancing, curling, bobsleigh, speed skating, ice hockey, and sled racing.

GEO: Georgia
Figure Skating Federation of Republic of Georgia
Nona Djulukhidze, Secretary
62 Chavchavadze Ave.
Tbilisi 380062, Georgia
Phone: (8832) 29 38 96;
FAX: (8832) 29 28 76
Notes: Figure skating member of the ISU representing the Republic of Georgia (GEO).

GER: Germany
Deutsche Eislauf-Union (German Figure Skating Member)
Peter Krick, Executive Director
Betzenweg 34
D-81247 Munchen, Germany

Phone: (89) 81 82 42;
FAX: (89) 81 82 46
Notes: Figure skating member of the ISU representing Germany (GER).

Deutsche Eisschnellauf-Gemeinschaft (German Speed Skating Member)
Hermann Binder, Secretary
Menzinger Strasse 68
D-80992 Munchen, Germany
Phone: (89) 811 10 55;
FAX: (89) 814 44 77
Notes: Speed skating member of the ISU representing Germany (GER).

GRB: Great Britain
National Ice Skating Association of UK Limited (NISA)
James Courtney, President
15-27 Gee Street
London, ECIV 3RE, Great Britain
Phone: (71) 253 3824/(71) 253 0910;
FAX: (71) 490 2589
Notes: Member of the ISU representing Great Britain (GRB). The National Governing body for speed, figure, precision, dance and recreational skating. Has 3700 members.

GRE: Greece
Hellenic Ice Sports Federation
Michalis Sirellis, General Secretary
272b El. Venizelou Str. (Thisseos)
GR-176 75 Kallithea Athens, Greece
Phone: (1)941 4882; (1)941 4969;
FAX: (1) 941 7939
Notes: Member of the ISU representing Greece (GRE).

HKG: Hong Kong
Hong Kong Skating Union
Dan-Dan Li, General Secretary
B8-9/F, Causeway Centre, Hong Kong
Phone: 2 827 5033; FAX: 2 827 2698
Notes: Member of the ISU representing Hong Kong (HKG).

HUN: Hungary
Hungarian National Skating Federation
Gyorgy Sallak, General Secretary
Stefania u. 2
H-1143 Budapest, Hungary
Phone: (1) 252 2369;
FAX: (1) 252 2369
Notes: Member of the ISU representing Hungary (HUN).

ISR: Israel
Israel Ice Skating Federation
Lihu Ichilov, Secretary
26, Chissin St.
Tel Aviv 64284, Israel
Phone: (3) 525 4370;
FAX: (3) 525 1349
Notes: Member of the ISU representing Israel (ISR).

ITA: Italy
Federazione Italiana Sport del Ghiaccio
Nando Buonomini, General Secretary
Via Piranesi 44/B
I-20137 Milano, Italy
Phone: (2) 701 41 331/(2) 701 41 327; FAX: (2) 701 07226-02;
(2) 701 07148-02; (2) 701 07225
Notes: Member of the ISU representing Italy (ITA).

JPN: Japan
Japan Skating Federation
Hiroichi Yano, Secretary
Kishi Memorial Hall, Room 414
1-1-1, Jinnan
Shibuya-ku, Tokyo 150-50, Japan
Phone: (3) 3481-2351/3;
FAX: (3) 3481-2350
Notes: Member of the ISU representing Japan (JPN).

KZK: Kazakhstan
Skating Federation of the Republic of Kazakhstan
Mikhail Borisov, General Secretary
Lenin St. 114
Almaty 480002, Kazakhstan
Phone: (3272) 33 46 58;
FAX: (3272) 33 04 92
Notes: Member of the ISU representing the Kazakhstan (KZK).

ROK: Korea
Korea Skating Union
Pung-Lyul Kim, Secretary
Room #412, Olympic Center,
88 Oryun-dong
Songpa-ku, Seoul, Korea
Phone: (2) 422 6165, 420 3333;
FAX: (2) 423 8097
Notes: Member of the ISU representing the Republic of Korea (ROK).

LAT: Latvia
Latvian Skating Association
Lauma Jekabsone, Secretary
Terbatas str. 4
LV 1723 Riga, Latvia
Phone: (2) 284206; FAX: (2) 284412
Notes: Member of the ISU representing Latvia (LAT).

LIT: Lithuania
Lithuanian Skating Federation
Antanas Vilcinskas, Secretary
Zemaites 6
2675 Vilnius, Lithuania
Phone: (2) 661 238; FAX: (2) 661 223
Notes: Member of the ISU representing Lithuania (LIT).

LUX: Luxembourg
Union Luxembourgeoise de Patinage
Alice Grethen, Secretary
B.P. 859
L-2018 , Luxembourg
Phone: 69213; FAX: 408764
Notes: Member of the ISU representing Luxembourg (LUX).

MEX: Mexico
Federacion Mexicana de Deportes Invernales A.C.
Ignacio Goyarzu-Gonzalez, Secretary
Via L cten 351
Jardines de Sat,lite
Naucalpan, 53129, Mexico
Phone: (5) 343 08 55;
FAX: (5) 343 08 55
Notes: Member of the ISU representing Mexico (MEX).

MGL: Mongolia
Skating Union of Mongolia
Oidov Erdene-Ulzii, Secretary
Baga Toiruu 55
Ulaanbaatar, Mongolia
Phone: (1) 320180; FAX: (1) 310011

Notes: Member of the ISU representing Mongolia (MGL).

NED: Netherlands
Koninklijke Nederlandsche Schaatsenrijders Bond
Jurjen Osinga, Executive Director
Stadsring 103
3811 HP Amersfoort, Postbox 1120
NL-3800 BC Amersfoort, Netherlands
Phone: (33) 621784;
FAX: (33) 62 08 23
Notes: Member of the ISU representing the Netherlands (NED).

NZL: New Zealand
Ice Racing Federation of New Zealand Inc. (Speed Skating Member)
Fiona H. Atkinson, Secretary
341 Eastern Terrace
Christchurch 2, New Zealand
Phone: (3) 332 6756;
FAX: (3) 332 6756; (3) 365 4404
Notes: Speed skating member of the ISU representing New Zealand (NZL).

New Zealand Ice Skating Association Inc. (Figure Skating Member)
Anne Nye Rosemarie, Secretary.
P.O. Box 15487, New Lynn
Auckland, New Zealand
Phone: (9) 376 5625;
FAX: (9) 376 2452
Notes: Figure skating member of the ISU representing New Zealand (NZL).

NOR: Norway
Norges Skoyteforbund
Arild Gjerde, General Secretary
Hauger Skolevei 1
N-1351 Rud, Norway
Phone: 67 15 46 00; FAX: 67 54 11 41
Notes: Member of the ISU representing Norway (NOR).

POL: Poland
Polish Figure Skating Association
Jacek Tascher, General Secretary
Lazienkowska 6a
00-449 Warszawa-Torwar, Poland
Phone: (22) 29 52 07;
FAX: (22) 29 52 07
Notes: Figure skating member of the ISU representing Poland (POL).

Polish Speed Skating Association
Mieczyslaw Snopinski, General Secretary
Wilcza 38a
PL-00-679 Warszawa, Poland
Phone: (2) 625 31 96;
FAX: (2) 625 31 96
Notes: Speed skating member of the ISU representing Poland (POL).

ROM: Romania
Romanian Skating Federation
Mihai Timis, Secretary
Vasile Contra Str. 16
70139 Bucharest, Romania
Phone: (1) 211 01 60; (1) 211 55 55/170; FAX: (1) 210 01 61
Notes: Member of the ISU representing Romania (ROM).

RUS: Russia
Figure Skating Federation of Russia
Alexeev Gennadi, Secretary
Luzhnetskaia nab. 8
Moscow, Russia
Phone: (095) 201 10 40; 201 13 41;
FAX: (095) 201 10 49
Notes: Figure skating member of the ISU representing Russia (RUS).

The Union of Skaters of Russia: Speed Skating Federation
Vladimir D. Komarov, Executive Director
Luzhnetskaia nab. 8
Moscow 119871, Russia
Phone: (095) 201 10 40; (095) 201 13 41; FAX: (095) 201 10 40
Notes: Speed skating member of the ISU representing Russia (RUS).

SVK: Slovak Republic
Slovak Rebublic Figure Skating Association
Jaroslava Kostialova, Secretary
Junacka 6
832 80 Bratislava, Slovak Republic
Phone: (7) 2790 244;
FAX: (7) 2790 551
Notes: Figure skating member of the ISU representing the Slovak Republic (SVK).

SLO: Slovenia
Slovene Skating Union
Marinka Jerala, Secretary
Celovska 25
61117 Ljubljana, Slovenia
Phone: (661) 1315 155 ext. 252;
FAX: (661) 126 32 32/(661)132 33 03
Notes: Member of the ISU representing Slovenia (SLO).

SAF: South Africa
South African Ice Skating Association (Figure Skating Member)
Patricia E. Norton, Secretary
P.O. Box 3366
Durban, 4000, South Africa
Phone: (31) 309 55 70;
FAX: (31) 309 55 99
Notes: Figure skating member of the ISU representing South Africa (SAF).

South African Speed Skating Association
Caroll Taylor, Secretary
19 Vlakkenberg Str.
Freeway Park
Boksburg, 1460, South Africa
Phone: (11) 893 30 22;
FAX: (11) 334 55 24
Notes: Speed skating member of the ISU representing South Africa (SAF).

SPN: Spain
Spanish Wintersport Federation
Sanchez Gregorio Lopez, Secretary
Infanta Maria Teresa, 14
28016 Madrid, Spain
Phone: (1) 344 09 44/ (1) 344 11 13;
FAX: (1) 344 18 26
Notes: Member of the ISU representing Spain (SPN).

SWE: Sweden
Svenska Konstakningsforbundet (Figure Skating)
Marianne Overby, Secretary
Idrottens Hus, S-123 87
Farsta, Sweden

Phone: (8) 605 60 00/ (8) 605 64 20/ (8) 605 64 19
FAX: (8) 605 64 29
Notes: Figure skating member of the ISU representing Sweden (SWE).

Svenska Skridskoforbundet (Speed Skating)
Anne Osterberg, Secretary
Eskilsgatan 67
S-633 56 Eskilstuna, Sweden
Phone: (16) 13 72 10;
FAX: (16) 12 53 97
Notes: Speed skating member of the ISU representing Sweden (SWE).

Stockholms Allanna Skridskoklubb
Yvonne Bergvik, Secretary
c/o M.-L. Willberg
Hagkroken 9
S-181 31 Lidingo, Sweden
Phone: (8) 23 58 25;
Notes: Club member of the ISU.

SWI: Switzerland
Schweizer Eislauf-Verband
Erika Dobler, Secretary
Maulbeerstrasse 14
CH-3011 Bern, Switzerland
Phone: (31) 382 06 60;
FAX: (31) 381 19 00
Notes: Member of the ISU representing Switzerland (SWI).

Internationaler Schlittschuh-Club Davos
Max Muller, Secretary
c/o Kur-und Verkehrsverein Davos
Promenade 67
CH-7270 Davos Platz, Switzerland
Phone: (81) 45 21 21;
FAX: (81) 45 21 01
Notes: Club member of the ISU.

THA: Thailand
Figure and Speed Skating Association of Thailand
Somporn Teasomboonkij, Secretary
7th Fl. World Trade Center Complex
Rajprasong Intersection
4 Rajdamri Rd.
Bangkok 10330, Thailand
Phone: (2) 255-9500, ext. 2740;
FAX: (2) 255-6508
Notes: Member of the ISU representing Thailand (THA).

TUR: Turkey
Turkish Ice Sports Federation
Mehmet Koc, Secretary
Sanayi Cad., Nr. 28 Kat-3
Ulus-Ankara, Turkey
Phone: (312) 310 81 67;
FAX: (312) 311 25 54
Notes: Member of the ISU representing Turkey (TUR).

UKR: Ukraine
Ukrainian Figure Skating Federation
Nina Gudimenko, Secretary
Esplanadnaya Str. 17
252023 Kiev, Ukraine
Phone: (044) 221 55 52;
FAX: (044) 221 55 52
Notes: Figure skating member of the ISU representing Ukraine (UKR).

Ukrainian Speed Skating Federation
Valery P. Khristolyubov, Secretary
Esplanadnaya Str. 42
252023 Kiev, Ukraine
Phone: (044) 220 11 32;
FAX: (044) 220 12 94
Notes: Speed skating member of the ISU representing Ukraine (UKR).

USA: United States of America
U.S. Figure Skating Association (USFSA)
Jerry Lace, Executive Director
20 First Street
Colorado Springs, CO 80906
Phone: (719) 635-5200;
FAX: (719) 635-9548
Notes: Figure skating member of the ISU representing the USA. The USFSA is the governing body for amateur figure skating on ice in the U.S. Since 1921, the USFSA has directed and encouraged the development of figure skating skills instruction and supervised the competitive aspects of the sport. Its national, world, and Olympic champions have made major contributions to figure skating and established outstanding international records and reputations. The USFSA has a membership of over 120,000 athletes and supporters; membership is open to anyone.

U.S. International Speed Skating Association
Chris Mills, Secretary
P.O. Box 16157
Rocky River, OH 44116
Phone: (216) 899-0128;
FAX: (216) 899-0109
Notes: Speed skating member of the ISU representing the United States (USA). Members are individuals interested in international speed skating. Promotes the metric or Olympic style of speed skating in the U.S. and helps U.S. skaters in international competitions, including the Olympic games. Conducts weekend seminars and summer camps. Sponsors competitions to select national champions, world competitors, and Olympic team members.

UZB: Uzbekistan
Figure Skating Federation of the Republic of Uzbekistan
Evgeni Rokhin, Secretary
Beruni Str. 41
700174 Tashkent, Uzbekistan
Phone: (3712) 46 03 19;
 (3712) 46 08 82; (3712) 46 08 25;
FAX: (3712) 45 08 52
Notes: Figure skating member of the ISU representing Uzbekistan (UZB).

YUG: Yugoslavia
Savez Klizackih I Koturaljkaskih Sportova Jugoslavije
Vojislava Popovic, General Secretary
Preradoviceva 4
11000 Belgrad, Yugoslavia
Phone: (11) 765 434; (11) 765 268;
FAX: (11) 767 668
Notes: Member of the ISU representing Yugoslavia (YUG).

~ SKATER'S EDGE SOURCEBOOK ~

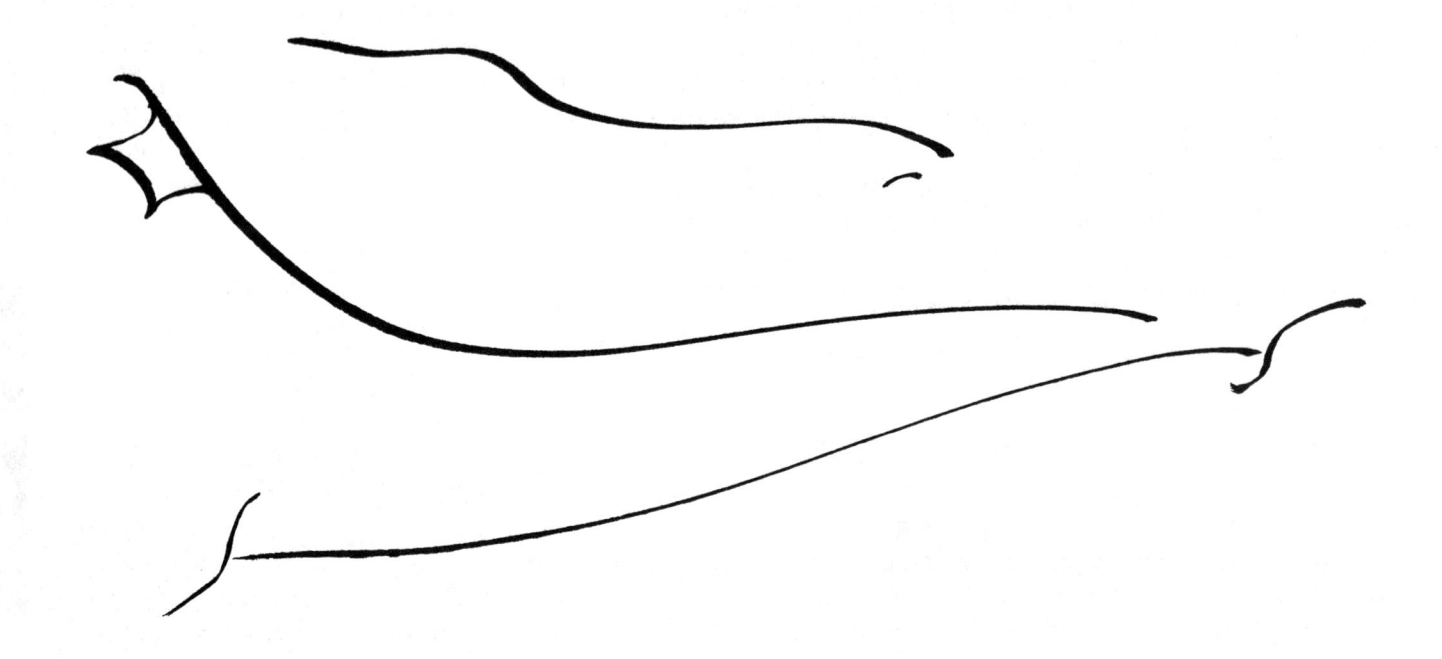

Skater's Edge
SOURCEBOOK

SKATING RINKS	VIDEOS	PUBLICATIONS
BOOTS	EQUIPMENT	RINK BUILDERS
BLADES	CLOTHING	SUMMER SCHOOLS
BOOKS	CATALOGUES	TRAINING CENTERS

Skater's Edge, the world's leading "how-to" ice skating publication, has once again broken new ground. We've created the *Skater's Edge* SOURCEBOOK, the first comprehensive resource book and directory for the skating world.

This book—released for the first time in January 1995—has quickly become an indispendable part of every skating library. **MAKES A GREAT GIFT!**

Ask for it at your favorite bookstore, or order from the publisher. Send your order with payment to *Skater's Edge* SOURCEBOOK, Box 500, Dept. SB, Kensington, MD 20895; (301) 946-1971.

❏ Yes, I want to order the *Skater's Edge* SOURCEBOOK. Please send me _____ copies at:

❏ $39.95[1] + $5 shipping[2] ($44.95 US$)[3] each

❏ I am enclosing my total payment of $_____

[1]**MD RESIDENTS** add 5% sales tax. [2]For U.S. & Canada; to Europe: $7—surface; $15—air; to Japan: $12—surface, $20—air. [3]U.S. $ or Canadian equivalent; int'l bank or postal orders accepted.

Name_____
Address_____
City_____ State_____ Zip_____
Phone (day) (___)_____ (eve) (___)_____

Send with payment to: *Skater's Edge* SOURCEBOOK, Box 500, Dept. SB, Kensington, MD 20895. Thank you!

ILLUSTRATION BY JOEL BERMAN

Rinks, Rinks, Rinks

The rinks in the following section are listed in alphabetical order first by *state abbreviation* (see *Key to State Abbreviations* below), then by *rink name*. Cross-references in later pages list the rinks (1) in order by state abbreviation, then city; (2) in order by rink name; and (3) rinks affiliated with colleges or universities.

If we are missing any rinks, please ask the manager to contact us or send the rink name and address to: *Skater's Edge Sourcebook Update*, Box 500, Kensington, MD 20895; Phone/FAX: (301) 946-1971. We'll do the rest!

APPRECIATION

We'd like to express appreciation to the following people for their hard work in surveying the rinks, entering the data, and/or verifying numerous tidbits of information: **Hannah Grisar, Joanna Wlodawer, Brenda Chu, Mike Subelsky, Arlene Lehner, Ilana Berman,** and **Carrie Casey.** In addition, we'd like to thank the **New England Ice Skating Managers Association (NEISMA),** the **Wisconsin Ice Arena Management Association,** USA Hockey, the USFSA, ISIA, the Massachusetts Metropolitan District Commission, Orrin Getz, Doris Penndorf, and many others for their assistance in helping us locate rinks. Last, but not least, thanks to **Jaya Kanal** for her invaluable expertise in designing the rink database and helping us turn the raw data into usable form!

KEY TO LISTINGS

The rink listings are set up in the following manner:
Rink name, address, phone/FAX numbers; manager and skating director (when available).
Ice Surfaces: # of ice surfaces, rink sizes, and whether the facility is enclosed or outdoor/semi-outdoor (with or without a roof, but no walls).
Open: Months open or open year round.
Ownership: Whether ownership is municipal or private.
Access: Whether rink is open to the public, or restricted to club members, school staff/students, etc.
Clubs: Affiliated skating clubs when known. FSC = figure skating club.
College/Univ: Rink affiliated with or used by college and/or university listed.
Sessions: Types of skating sessions offered, and whether the rink is available for rental.
Classes/Lessons: Types of classes and/or lessons available.
Program Affiliation: Whether the classes and/or lessons are affiliated with the Ice Skating Institute of America (ISIA) and/or the U.S. Figure Skating Association (USFSA).
Summer School: Rink offers either local, regional, or national summer school. "No" means there is no summer school.
Services: Extra services or additional facilities available. Pool/Athletic facilities means Pool and/or Athletic facilities; call ahead to confirm additional facilities and public access.
Notes: Miscellaneous details that might be of interest.

Turn page for rink listings ☞

KEY TO RINK ORDER AND STATE ABBREVIATIONS

State	Abbreviation	Page #	State	Abbr	Page	State	Abbr	Page
Alabama	AL	137	Kentucky	KY	155	Ohio	OH	200
Alaska	AK	136	Louisiana	LA	155	Oklahoma	OK	202
Arizona	AZ	137	Maine	ME	167	Oregon	OR	203
Arkansas	AR	137	Maryland	MD	166	Pennsylvania	PA	203
California	CA	138	Massachusetts	MA	155	Puerto Rico	PR	—
Colorado	CO	141	Michigan	MI	169	Rhode Island	RI	207
Connecticut	CT	143	Minnesota	MN	175	South Carolina	SC	208
Delaware	DE	146	Mississippi	MS	—	South Dakota	SD	209
District of Columbia	DC	146	Missouri	MO	183	Tennesse	TN	209
Florida	FL	147	Montana	MT	184	Texas	TX	209
Georgia	GA	148	Nebraska	NE	186	Utah	UT	210
Hawaii	HI	148	Nevada	NV	190	Vermont	VT	211
Idaho	ID	149	New Hampshire	NH	186	Virginia	VA	211
Illinois	IL	149	New Jersey	NJ	188	Washington	WA	213
Indiana	IN	153	New Mexico	NM	190	Washington, DC	DC	146
Iowa	IA	148	New York	NY	190	West Virginia	WV	218
Kansas	KS	155	North Carolina	NC	184	Wisconsin	WI	214
			North Dakota	ND	185	Wyoming	WY	218

AK: ALASKA

Anchorage Sports Center Ice Rink
University of Alaska
3211 Providence Dr.
Anchorage AK 99508
(907) 786-1232
FAX: (907) 563-4565
Mgr: Allen Picard
Ice surfaces: 1, 200x85, Enclosed. *Open:* Year Round. *Ownership:* Private. *Access:* Public. *Clubs:* Anchorage FSC. *College/Univ:* University of Alaska. *Sessions:* Rental, Hockey, Public. *Classes/Lessons:* Private, Group. *Program Affiliation:* Own. *Summer School:* Local. *Services:* Studio Rink, Snack Bar, Pool and/or Athletic Facilities, Ballet Room, Weight Room, Lockers, Dressing Rooms. *Notes:* Club offers freestyle, patch & dance; not open to public.

Big Dipper Ice Rink
1920 Lathrop St.
Fairbanks AK 99707
(907) 459-1104
Mgr: Janie West
Ice surfaces: 4, 200x85; 200x85; 200x85; 200x85, Enclosed, Outdoor/Semi Outdoor. *Open:* Year Round. *Ownership:* Municipal. *Access:* Public. *Sessions:* Public, Private/Club, Rental, Freestyle, Patch, Dance, Hockey. *Classes/Lessons:* Group, Private. *Program Affiliation:* USFSA, ISIA. *Services:* Skate Rental, Snack Bar, Pool and/or Athletic Facilities, Lockers. *Notes:* Track, aerobics mezzanine, speed skating oval.

Boeke (Ben) Ice Arena
334 E 16th Ave.
Anchorage AK 99501
(907) 274-2715
FAX: (907) 279-0617
Mgr: Annetta Powell
Ice surfaces: 2, 200x85; 200x85, Enclosed. *Open:* Year Round. *Ownership:* Municipal. *Access:* Public. *Sessions:* Public, Private/Club, Rental, Freestyle, Patch, Dance, Hockey. *Classes/Lessons:* Group, Private. *Program Affiliation:* ISIA. *Services:* Pro Shop, Skate Rental, Skate Sharpening, Snack Bar, Ballet Room, Dressing Rooms, Lockers.

Brett Memorial Ice Arena
800 Bogard Rd.
Wasilla AK 99654
(907) 376-9260
Mgr: Bruce Urban
Ice surfaces: 1, 200x85, Enclosed. *Open:* June-Apr. *Ownership:* Municipal. *Access:* Public. *Clubs:* Mat-su FSC. *Sessions:* Public, Rental, Freestyle, Patch, Hockey. *Classes/Lessons:* Group, Private. *Program Affiliation:* ISIA. *Services:* Skate Rental, Skate Sharpening, Snack Bar, Dressing Rooms. *Notes:* Vending machines.

Central Peninsula Sports Center
538 Arena Dr.
Soldotna AK 99669
(907) 262-3151
Mgr: Bob Shastany
Skating Dir: Cathy Shearer
Ice surfaces: 1, 200x85, Enclosed. *Open:* Aug.-Mar. *Ownership:* Municipal. *Access:* Public. *Sessions:* Public, Private/Club, Rental, Freestyle, Hockey. *Classes/Lessons:* Group, Private. *Program Affiliation:* ISIA. *Summer School:* No. *Services:* Pro Shop, Skate Rental, Skate Sharpening, Snack Bar, Weight Room, Lockers, Dressing Rooms.

Dempsey-Anderson Arena
1741 W. Northern Lights
Anchorage AK 99501
(907) 277-7571
Mgr: Anetta Powell
Ice surfaces: 2, 200x85; 200x85, Enclosed, Outdoor/Semi Outdoor. *Open:* Aug.-Apr. *Ownership:* Municipal. *Access:* Public. *Clubs:* Alaska Assn. FS; Anchorage FSC. *Sessions:* Public, Rental, Hockey. *Classes/Lessons:* None. *Program Affiliation:* Own. *Summer School:* No. *Services:* Studio Rink, Snack Bar, Dressing Rooms. *Notes:* Main rink is enclosed, the studio rink is outdoors.

Dimond Center Ice Capades Chalet
800 E. Dimond Blvd., Suite 3002
Anchorage AK 99515
(907) 344-1212
FAX: (907) 349-2411
Mgr: Steve Ondra
Ice surfaces: 1, 145x65, Enclosed. *Open:* Year Round. *Ownership:* Private. *Access:* Public. *Clubs:* Alaska Assn. of Figure Skaters. *Sessions:* Public, Private/Club, Rental, Hockey. *Classes/Lessons:* Group. *Program Affiliation:* USFSA. *Summer School:* Local. *Services:* Pro Shop, Skate Rental, Skate Sharpening, Ballet Room, Lockers, Dressing Rooms. *Notes:* Located in a mall.

Fire Lake Recreation Center
13701 Old Glen Hwy.
Eagle River AK 99577
(907) 696-0050
FAX: (907) 696-0092
Mgr: John Rodda
Ice surfaces: 1, 200x100, Enclosed. *Open:* June-Mar. *Ownership:* Municipal. *Access:* Public. *Sessions:* Public, Rental, Freestyle, Patch, Dance, Hockey. *Classes/Lessons:* Group, Private. *Program Affiliation:* ISIA. *Summer School:* Local. *Services:* Skate Rental, Skate Sharpening, Snack Bar, Lockers, Dressing Rooms.

Patty Center Ice Arena
University of Alaska, 410 Alatna Dr.
Fairbanks AK 99775-7440
(907) 474-6888
FAX: (907) 474-5162
Mgr: Scott Roselius
Ice surfaces: 1, 200x85, Enclosed. *Open:* July-Apr. *Access:* Public. *Clubs:* Fairbanks FSC, Fairbanks Amateur Youth Hockey. *College/Univ:* University of Alaska. *Sessions:* Public, Private/Club, Rental, Hockey. *Classes/Lessons:* Group, Private. *Program Affiliation:* Own. *Summer School:* No. *Services:* Skate Sharpening, Snack Bar, Dressing Rooms. *Notes:* Lessons, Freestyle, Patch and Dance sessions are offered through the school. Weight room and pool in adjacent recreation center. Raquetball and a gym are also offered on campus.

Peterson (Jason) Memorial Ice Rink
Mile 23.4 Spur Hwy., Pool Side Ave.
Nikiski AK 99635
(907) 776-8472
FAX: (907) 776-5122
Mgr: Karen Kester
Ice surfaces: 1, 200x85, Outdoor/Semi Outdoor. *Open:* Year Round. *Ownership:* Municipal. *Access:* Public. *Sessions:* Public, Freestyle, Hockey. *Classes/Lessons:* Group. *Program Affiliation:* Own. *Summer School:* No.

AL: ALABAMA

Alpine Ice Arena
160 Oxmoor Rd.
Birmingham AL 35209
(205) 942-0223
Mgr: Glen Grabeldinger
Ice surfaces: 1, 200x85, Enclosed.
Open: Year Round. *Ownership:* Private.
Access: Public. *Clubs:* Birm. FSC, Birm.
Youth Hockey League; Birm. Amateur
Hockey Assn., practice for Birm. Bulls.
Sessions: Public, Private/Club, Rental,
Freestyle, Patch, Dance, Hockey.
Classes/Lessons: Group, Private.
Program Affiliation: USFSA, ISIA.
Services: Pro Shop, Skate Rental, Skate
Sharpening, Snack Bar, Lockers, Dressing Rooms. *Notes:* Dance room; off-ice
training; game room; video room; upper
and lower viewing lobbies.

Eastdale Ice Palace
1000 Eastdale Mall
Montgomery AL 36117
(205) 272-7225
Mgr: Kathy Shankle
Ice surfaces: 1, 125x65, Enclosed. *Open:*
Year Round. *Ownership:* Private. *Access:*
Public. *Sessions:* Public, Private/Club,
Rental. *Classes/Lessons:* Group, Private.
Program Affiliation: ISIA. *Services:* Pro
Shop, Skate Rental, Skate Sharpening,
Lockers. *Notes:* Located in a mall.
Freestyle and dance sessions offered
through club only.

Point Mallard Ice Rink
1800 Point Mallard Dr.
Decatur AL 35601
(205) 355-9817
Mgr: Joann Cunningham
Ice surfaces: 1, 185x85, Outdoor/Semi
Outdoor. *Open:* Nov.-Mar. *Ownership:*
Municipal. *Access:* Public. *Sessions:*
Public, Private/Club, Rental, Freestyle,
Hockey. *Classes/Lessons:* Private.
Summer School: No. *Services:* Pro
Shop, Skate Rental, Skate Sharpening,
Snack Bar, Lockers, Dressing Rooms.

Wilcoxon (Benton H.) Municipal Iceplex
3185 Leeman Ferry Rd.
Huntsville AL 35801
(205) 883-3774
FAX: (205) 883-3685
Mgr: Doug Minor
Skating Dir: Marian Dotson
Ice surfaces: 2, 200x85; 200x85,
Enclosed. *Open:* Year Round. *Ownership:* Municipal. *Access:* Public. *Clubs:*
Huntsville FSC, Haha Hockey. *Sessions:*
Public, Private/Club, Rental, Hockey.
Classes/Lessons: Private, Group.
Program Affiliation: USFSA, ISIA.
Summer School: Local. *Services:* Pro
Shop, Skate Rental, Skate Sharpening,
Studio Rink, Snack Bar, Ballet Room,
Weight Room, Lockers, Dressing Rooms.
Notes: Freestyle, patch, dance and pairs
offered through club only.

AR: ARKANSAS

Little Rock Skating Arena
1311 Bowman Rd.
Little Rock AR 72221
(501) 227-4333
Mgr: Lech Matuszewski
Skating Dir: Sharon Sauders
Ice surfaces: 1, 185x85, Enclosed. *Open:*
Year Round. *Ownership:* Private. *Access:*
Public. *Clubs:* Diamond Edge FSC,
Arkansas Ice Hockey Assn. *Sessions:*
Public, Rental, Freestyle, Patch, Dance,
Hockey. *Classes/Lessons:* Group, Private.
Program Affiliation: ISIA. *Summer
School:* Regional. *Services:* Pro Shop,
Skate Rental, Skate Sharpening, Snack
Bar, Lockers, Dressing Rooms. *Notes:*
Roller rink; hospitality room.

AZ: ARIZONA

Flagstaff Municipal Ice Arena
1850 North Turquoise
Flagstaff AZ 86001
(602) 774-1051
Mgr: Greg Hunter
Ice surfaces: 1, 200x85, Enclosed.
Open: Oct.- Mar. *Ownership:* Municipal.
Access: Public. *Clubs:* Flagstaff Youth
Hockey Assn.; Flagstaff FSC. *College/
Univ:* Northern Arizona University.
Sessions: Public, Private/Club, Rental,
Freestyle, Patch, Dance, Hockey.
Classes/Lessons: Group, Private.
Program Affiliation: ISIA. *Services:* Pro
Shop, Skate Rental, Skate Sharpening,
Lockers, Dressing Rooms. *Notes:* Video
games. From May -Sept. functions as a
roller-skating rink.

Ice Palace Arena
Tower Plaza, 3853 East Thomas Rd.
Phoenix AZ 85018
(602) 267-0591
Mgr: Donna Dornan
Ice surfaces: 1, 200x85, Enclosed. *Open:*
Year Round. *Ownership:* Private. *Access:*
Public. *Clubs:* Arizona FSC, Valley of the
Sun Hockey Association. *Sessions:*
Public, Private/Club, Rental, Freestyle,
Patch, Dance, Hockey. *Classes/Lessons:*
Group, Private. *Program Affiliation:*
ISIA. *Summer School:* Local. *Services:*
Pro Shop, Skate Rental, Skate Sharpening, Lockers, Dressing Rooms. *Notes:*
Discount rates for groups; full line
hockey & pro-shop; birthday parties.

Lively (Jay) Activity Center
1850 N. Turquoise Dr.
Flagstaff AZ 86007
(602) 774-1051
Mgr: Greg Hunter
Ice surfaces: 1, 200x85. *Open:* Oct.-Apr.
Ownership: Municipal. *Access:* Public.
Clubs: Flagstaff FSC. *Sessions:* Public,
Private/Club, Rental, Freestyle, Hockey.
Classes/Lessons: Group, Private.
Program Affiliation: ISIA. *Summer
School:* No. *Services:* Pro Shop, Skate
Rental, Skate Sharpening, Snack Bar,
Lockers, Dressing Rooms. *Notes:* Hockey,
whirlpools, medical training room, books
& records room.

Oceanside Ice Arena
1520 N. McClintock Dr.
Tempe AZ 85281
(602) 941-0944
FAX: (602) 994-4749
Mgr: Greg Babicka
Ice surfaces: 1, 200x90. *Open:* Year
Round. *Ownership:* Private. *Access:*
Public. *Clubs:* Youth Hockey Assn.
Sessions: Public, Private/Club, Rental,
Freestyle, Patch, Dance, Hockey.
Classes/Lessons: Private, Group.
Program Affiliation: USFSA, ISIA.
Services: Pro Shop, Skate Rental,
Skate Sharpening, Snack Bar, Lockers,
Dressing Rooms.

CA: CALIFORNIA

Belmont Iceland
815 Old County Rd.
Belmont CA 94002
(415) 592-0532
Mgr: Chris Bryant
Skating Dir: Kay Faynor
Ice surfaces: 1, 176x50, Enclosed. *Open:* Year Round. *Ownership:* Private. *Access:* Public. *Sessions:* Public, Private/Club, Rental, Freestyle, Patch, Hockey. *Classes/Lessons:* Group, Private. *Program Affiliation:* USFSA, ISIA. *Services:* Pro Shop, Skate Rental, Skate Sharpening, Lockers, Dressing Rooms. *Notes:* Vending machines.

Berkeley Iceland
2727 Milvia St.
Berkeley CA 94703
(510) 843-8801
Mgr: Ed Peduto
Ice surfaces: 1, 200x100. *Open:* Year Round. *Ownership:* Municipal. *Access:* Public. *Clubs:* Saint Moritz Ice Skating Club. *Sessions:* Public, Private/Club, Rental, Freestyle, Patch, Hockey. *Classes/Lessons:* Group, Private. *Program Affiliation:* ISIA. *Summer School:* No. *Services:* Pro Shop, Skate Rental, Skate Sharpening, Lockers, Dressing Rooms. *Notes:* Vending machines; dance sessions offered through club only; dressing rooms for women only.

Blue Jay Ice Castles
27307 Hwy. 189
Blue Jay CA 92317-9998
(909) 336-2111
Mgr: Linda Mayes
Ice surfaces: 1, 185x85, Enclosed. *Open:* Year Round. *Ownership:* Private. *Access:* Public. *Clubs:* Rim of the World FSC. *Sessions:* Public, Rental, Hockey. *Classes/Lessons:* Group, Private. *Program Affiliation:* USFSA. *Services:* Pro Shop, Skate Rental, Skate Sharpening, Snack Bar, Lockers, Dressing Rooms, Weight Room.

Conejo Valley Ice Center
510 N. Ventu Park Rd.
Newbury Park CA 91320
(805) 498-6660
FAX: (805) 497-4493
Mgr: Betty Robinson
Skating Dir: Terry Tonius
Ice surfaces: 1, 185x85, Enclosed. *Open:* Year Round. *Ownership:* Private. *Access:* Public. *Clubs:* FSC. *Sessions:* Public, Rental, Freestyle, Patch, Hockey, Broomball. *Classes/Lessons:* Group, Private. *Program Affiliation:* ISIA. *Services:* Skate Rental, Skate Sharpening, Snack Bar, Dressing Rooms.

Costa Mesa Ice Chalet
2701 Harbor Blvd.
Costa Mesa CA 92626
(714) 979-8880
FAX: (714) 979-5929
Mgr: Steve Benson
Skating Dir: Tracy Gregory
Ice surfaces: 1, 180x80, Enclosed. *Open:* Year Round. *Ownership:* Private. *Access:* Public. *Clubs:* Orange Country FSC Calstar Hockey. *Sessions:* Public, Rental, Freestyle, Patch, Hockey. *Classes/Lessons:* Group, Private. *Program Affiliation:* Own. *Services:* Pro Shop, Skate Rental, Skate Sharpening, Ballet Room, Lockers, Dressing Rooms. *Notes:* Vending machines.

Culver Ice Arena
4545 Sepulveda Blvd.
Culver City CA 90230
(310) 398-5719
Mgr: Joe Setta
Ice surfaces: 1, 200x85, Enclosed. *Open:* Year Round. *Ownership:* Private. *Access:* Public. *Clubs:* All Year FSC Hockey Association. *Sessions:* Public, Private/Club, Rental, Freestyle, Patch, Dance, Hockey. *Classes/Lessons:* Group, Private. *Program Affiliation:* ISIA. *Services:* Pro Shop, Skate Rental, Skate Sharpening, Snack Bar, Ballet Room, Lockers, Dressing Rooms. *Notes:* Meeting room.

Dublin Iceland
7212 San Ramon Rd.
Dublin CA 94568
(510) 829-4445
FAX: (510) 829-4447
Mgr: Barry Keast
Ice surfaces: 1, 192x85, Enclosed. *Open:* Year Round. *Ownership:* Private. *Access:* Public. *Clubs:* St. Moritz. *Sessions:* Broomball, Public, Private/Club, Freestyle, Patch, Dance, Hockey. *Classes/Lessons:* Group, Private. *Program Affiliation:* USFSA. *Services:* Pro Shop, Skate Rental, Skate Sharpening, Ballet Room, Lockers, Dressing Rooms. *Notes:* Vending machines, party room.

Eastridge Ice Arena
2190 A Tully Rd.
San Jose CA 95122
(408) 238-0440
FAX: (408) 238-0796
Mgr: Ron Glasow
Ice surfaces: 1, 175x75, Enclosed. *Open:* Year Round. *Ownership:* Private. *Access:* Public. *Sessions:* Public, Rental, Freestyle, Patch, Broomball. *Classes/Lessons:* Group, Private. *Program Affiliation:* USFSA, ISIA. *Services:* Pro Shop, Skate Rental, Skate Sharpening, Lockers, Dressing Rooms. *Notes:* Vending machines.

Glacial Garden Ice Arena
1000 E Cerritos Ave
Anaheim CA 92805
(714) 502-9197
FAX: (714) 502-9025
Mgr: Chris Tetrilla
Ice surfaces: 2, 197x87; 170x72. *Open:* Year Round. *Ownership:* Private. *Access:* Public. *Sessions:* Public, Private/Club, Rental, Freestyle, Patch, Dance, Hockey. *Classes/Lessons:* Group, Private. *Program Affiliation:* USFSA, ISIA. *Services:* Pro Shop, Skate Rental, Skate Sharpening, Snack Bar, Lockers, Dressing Rooms.

Golden Gate Ice Arena
3140 Bay Rd.
Redwood City CA 94063
(415) 364-8091
FAX: (415) 364-8634
Mgr: Allen Carl
Ice surfaces: 1, 185x85, Enclosed. *Open:* Year Round. *Ownership:* Private. *Access:* Public. *Clubs:* Palomares & Peninsula FSC San Mateo City Jr. Hockey Club Pacific Hockey Association. *Sessions:* Public, Rental, Freestyle, Patch, Dance, Hockey. *Classes/Lessons:* Group, Private. *Program Affiliation:* ISIA. *Services:* Pro Shop, Skate Rental, Skate Sharpening, Ballet Room, Lockers, Dressing Rooms. *Notes:* Two pro shops, vending machines.

Ice Castles International Training Center
401 Burnt Mill Road
Lake Arrowhead, CA 92352
(909) 336-4085; FAX: (909) 336-2452
Manager: Michelle Coffey
Ice surfaces: 1, Enclosed. *Open:* Year Round. *Ownership:* Private. *Access:* Restricted. *Restrictions:* Figure skaters in training only. *Sessions:* Freestyle, Patch, Dance, Pairs. *Classes/Lessons:* Private. *Program Affiliation:* USFSA. *Summer School:* National/International. *Notes:* Ballet room, weight room, pool and other facilities located in resident camp facilities at 480 Cottage Grove Rd. Full service lodge on 10 acres.

Ice Centre of San Jose
1500 S. 10th St.
San Jose CA 95112-6410
(408) 279-6000
Mgr: David McGowan
Skating Dir: Candy Goodson
Ice surfaces: 2, 200x85; 200x85, Enclosed. *Open:* Year Round. *Ownership:* Municipal, Private. *Access:* Public. *Sessions:* Public, Freestyle, Patch, Dance, Hockey, Speed skating, Broomball. *Classes/Lessons:* Group, Private. *Program Affiliation:* ISIA. *Services:* Pro Shop, Skate Rental, Skate Sharpening, Snack Bar, Ballet Room, Weight Room, Lockers, Dressing Rooms.

Ice Chalet Palm Desert
72840 Hwy. 111, Suite A
Palm Desert CA 92260
(619) 340-4412
Mgr: Angela Harris
Ice surfaces: 1, 170x60, Enclosed. *Open:* Year Round. *Ownership:* Private. *Access:* Public. *Clubs:* Palm Desert ISC, SOCA Hockey Association. *Sessions:* Public, Rental, Freestyle, Patch, Hockey. *Classes/Lessons:* Group, Private. *Program Affiliation:* Own. *Services:* Pro Shop, Skate Rental, Lockers, Skate Sharpening. *Notes:* Meeting room.

Ice Chalet Rolling Hills
550 Deep Valley Dr., Suite 130
Rolling Hills Estates CA 90274
(310) 541-6630
Mgr: Mike Robertson
Ice surfaces: 1, 157x57, Enclosed. *Open:* Year Round. *Ownership:* Private. *Access:* Public. *Sessions:* Public, Rental, Freestyle, Patch, Dance, Hockey. *Classes/Lessons:* Private, Group. *Program Affiliation:* ISIA. *Summer School:* Local. *Services:* Skate Rental, Pro Shop, Skate Sharpening, Ballet Room, Lockers, Dressing Rooms. *Notes:* Located in a mall.

Ice Chalet San Diego
4545 LaJolla Village Dr.
San Diego CA 92122
(619) 452-9110
FAX: (619) 452-8974
Mgr: Cindi Glatfelter
Skating Dir: Cindi Glatfelter
Ice surfaces: 1, 185x85, Enclosed. *Open:* Year Round. *Ownership:* Private. *Access:* Public. *Clubs:* La Jolla FSC. *Sessions:* Public, Rental, Freestyle, Patch, Hockey. *Classes/Lessons:* Group, Private. *Program Affiliation:* ISIA, USFSA. *Summer School:* Regional. *Services:* Pro Shop, Skate Rental, Skate Sharpening, Lockers, Dressing Rooms, Ballet Room. *Notes:* Located in shopping mall.

Ice Chalet San Mateo
2202 Fashion Island
San Mateo CA 94404
(415) 574-1616
Mgr: Kyle Jacobs
Ice surfaces: 1, 185x85, Enclosed. *Open:* Year Round. *Ownership:* Private. *Access:* Public. *Sessions:* Public, Private/Club, Rental, Freestyle, Patch, Dance. *Classes/Lessons:* Group, Private. *Program Affiliation:* ISIA. *Services:* Pro Shop, Skate Rental, Skate Sharpening, Lockers.

Ice Chalet Vallco Fashion Park
10123 N. Wolf Rd.
Culpertino CA 95014
(408) 446-2908
FAX: (408) 446-1642
Mgr: Janice Vaughn
Skating Dir: Sheri Callison
Ice surfaces: 1, 175x75, Enclosed. *Open:* Year Round. *Ownership:* Private. *Access:* Public. *Clubs:* Vallco SC. *Sessions:* Public, Rental, Freestyle, Patch, Dance, Hockey. *Classes/Lessons:* Group, Private. *Program Affiliation:* Own. *Summer School:* Local. *Services:* Skate Rental, Pro Shop, Skate Sharpening, Ballet Room, Snack Bar, Lockers, Dressing Rooms. *Notes:* Located in a mall; vending machines.

Ice Floe Ice Center
555 N. Tulip
Escondido CA 92025
(619) 489-5550
Mgr: Marc Spenser
Ice surfaces: 2, 200x100; 200x100, Enclosed. *Open:* Year Round. *Ownership:* Private. *Access:* Public. *Clubs:* Ice Floe FSC, San Diego Youth Hockey. *Sessions:* Public, Private/Club, Rental, Freestyle, Patch, Dance, Hockey. *Classes/Lessons:* Group, Private. *Program Affiliation:* USFSA, ISIA. *Summer School:* Local. *Services:* Pro Shop, Skate Rental, Skate Sharpening, Snack Bar, Pool and/or Athletic Facilities, Lockers, Dressing Rooms. *Notes:* Aerobics room, fitness center.

Icelandia Fresno
2455 North Marks Ave.
Fresno CA 93722
(209) 275-1119
Mgr: Shirley Kerwin
Ice surfaces: 1, 200x85, Enclosed. *Open:* Year Round. *Ownership:* Private. *Access:* Public. *Clubs:* Fresno ISC; Fresno Falcons. *College/Univ:* California State University. *Sessions:* Public, Private/Club, Rental, Hockey. *Classes/Lessons:* Group, Private. *Program Affiliation:* USFSA, ISIA. *Summer School:* No. *Services:* Pro Shop, Skate Rental, Skate Sharpening, Snack Bar, Lockers, Dressing Rooms. *Notes:* Freestyle and patch offered through the club only.

Iceoplex Fremont
44388 Old Warm Springs Blvd.
Fremont CA 94538
(510) 490-6621
FAX: (510) 490-8115
Mgr: Bill Dobbs
Ice surfaces: 1, 200x85, Enclosed. *Open:* Year Round. *Ownership:* Private. *Access:* Public. *Sessions:* Public, Private/Club, Rental, Freestyle, Patch, Hockey, Powerskating. *Classes/Lessons:* Group, Private. *Program Affiliation:* USFSA, ISIA. *Services:* Pro Shop, Skate Rental, Skate Sharpening, Snack Bar, Ballet Room, Weight Room. *Notes:* Banquet room.

Iceoplex North Hills
8345 Havenhurst Place
North Hills CA 91343
(818) 893-1784
FAX: (818) 894-7154
Mgr: Ronnie Henry
Skating Dir: Susan Berens
Ice surfaces: 1, 200x85, Enclosed. *Open:* Year Round. *Ownership:* Private. *Access:* Public. *Sessions:* Public, Rental, Freestyle, Patch, Hockey, Dance. *Classes/Lessons:* Group, Private. *Program Affiliation:* ISIA. *Services:* Pro Shop, Skate Rental, Skate Sharpening, Snack Bar, Weight Room, Lockers, Dressing Rooms. *Notes:* Restaurant; connected to in-line roller rink.

Long Barn Ice Arena
25957 Long Barn Rd.
Long Barn CA 95335
(209) 586-0753
FAX: (209) 586-5779
Mgr: Scott Richards
Ice surfaces: 1, 110x48, Outdoor/Semi Outdoor. *Open:* Nov.-Apr. *Ownership:* Private. *Access:* Public. *Clubs:* Sierra Ice Gliders FSC. *Sessions:* Freestyle, Rental, Private/Club, Public. *Classes/Lessons:* Group, Private. *Program Affiliation:* ISIA. *Summer School:* No. *Services:* Pro Shop, Skate Rental, Skate Sharpening, Snack Bar, Pool and/or Athletic Facilities, Lockers, Dressing Rooms.

North Hollywood Ice Chalet
6100 Laurel Canyon Blvd.
N. Hollywood CA 91606
(818) 985-5555
Mgr: Mike Robertson
Ice surfaces: 1, 178x78, Enclosed. *Open:* Year Round. *Ownership:* Private. *Access:* Public. *Clubs:* San Fernando Valley FSC. *Sessions:* Public, Rental, Freestyle, Patch, Hockey. *Classes/Lessons:* Group, Private. *Program Affiliation:* ISIA. *Services:* Pro Shop, Skate Rental, Skate Sharpening, Lockers, Dressing Rooms. *Notes:* All purpose room; inside shopping mall.

Norwalk Ice Arena
14100 Shoemaker Rd.
Norwalk CA 90650
(310) 921-5391
FAX: (310) 921-5738
Mgr: Darius Madjzoub
Ice surfaces: 1, 200x85, Enclosed. *Open:* Year Round. *Ownership:* Private. *Access:* Public. *Sessions:* Public, Private/Club, Rental, Freestyle, Patch, Dance, Hockey. *Classes/Lessons:* Group, Private. *Program Affiliation:* ISIA. *Services:* Pro Shop, Skate Rental, Skate Sharpening, Snack Bar, Ballet Room, Dressing Rooms.

Oak Park Ice Arena
3545 Alvarado
Stockton CA 95204
(209) 937-7432
Mgr: Mary Richardson
Skating Dir: Barbara Wagoner
Ice surfaces: 1, 200x87, Enclosed. *Open:* Year Round. *Ownership:* Municipal. *Access:* Public. *Clubs:* Stockton FSC, SC of Sacramento. *Sessions:* Public, Private/Club, Rental, Freestyle, Patch, Dance, Hockey. *Classes/Lessons:* Group, Private. *Program Affiliation:* USFSA, ISIA. *Services:* Pro Shop, Skate Rental, Skate Sharpening, Snack Bar, Lockers, Dressing Rooms. *Notes:* Admiral's room.

Ontario Ice Skating Center
1225 West Holt Blvd.
Ontario CA 91762
(909) 986-0793
FAX: (909) 983-2663
Mgr: Don Bartleson
Ice surfaces: 1, 165x72, Enclosed. *Open:* Year Round. *Ownership:* Private. *Access:* Public. *Clubs:* Arrowhead FSC, Ontario YHA. *Sessions:* Public, Private/Club, Rental, Freestyle, Patch, Hockey. *Classes/Lessons:* Group, Private. *Program Affiliation:* ISIA. *Services:* Skate Rental, Skate Sharpening, Lockers, Dressing Rooms.

Paramount Iceland Arena
1430 Del Paso Blvd.
Sacramento CA 95815
(916) 925-3529
FAX: (916) 925-1929
Mgr: Judith Gallagher
Skating Dir: Jayne Meyer
Ice surfaces: 1, 140x70, Enclosed. *Open:* Year Round. *Ownership:* Private. *Access:* Public. *Clubs:* Arctic Blades FSC, Paramount YHA, In-house hockey league. *Sessions:* Public, Rental, Freestyle, Hockey, Private/Club, Patch, Dance. *Classes/Lessons:* Group, Private. *Program Affiliation:* USFSA. *Summer School:* Regional. *Services:* Pro Shop, Skate Rental, Skate Sharpening, Snack Bar, Lockers, Dressing Rooms, Ballet Room. *Notes:* Dressing rooms for hockey only; multi-purpose room.

Pasadena Ice Skating Center
300 East Green St.
Pasadena CA 91101
(818) 578-0801
FAX: (818) 501-4192
Mgr: Michael Paikin
Ice surfaces: 1, 150x95, Enclosed. *Open:* Year Round. *Ownership:* Private. *Access:* Public. *Clubs:* Pasadena FSC. *Sessions:* Public, Rental, Freestyle, Patch, Dance, Hockey. *Classes/Lessons:* Group, Private. *Program Affiliation:* USFSA, ISIA. *Services:* Pro Shop, Skate Rental, Skate Sharpening, Lockers, Dressing Rooms. *Notes:* Party room/all-purpose room.

Pickwick Ice Arena
1001 Riverside Dr.
Burbank CA 91506
(818) 846-0035
Mgr: Eddie Shipstad
Ice surfaces: 1, 200x85, Enclosed. *Open:* Year Round. *Ownership:* Private. *Access:* Public. *Clubs:* Los Angeles FSC, Golden Bears Hockey. *Sessions:* Public, Private/Club, Rental, Freestyle, Patch, Hockey. *Classes/Lessons:* Group, Private. *Program Affiliation:* ISIA. *Services:* Pro Shop, Skate Rental, Skate Sharpening, Snack Bar, Lockers, Dressing Rooms. *Notes:* Banquet center in complex, two party rooms in rink.

Redwood Empire Ice Arena
1667 W. Steele Lane
Santa Rosa CA 95403
(707) 546-7147
Mgr: Craig Gates
Skating Dir: Craig Gates
Ice surfaces: 1, 185x85, Enclosed. *Open:* Year Round. *Ownership:* Private. *Access:* Public. *Sessions:* Public, Private/Club, Rental, Freestyle, Patch, Dance, Hockey. *Classes/Lessons:* Group, Private. *Program Affiliation:* USFSA, ISIA. *Services:* Pro Shop, Skate Rental, Skate Sharpening, Snack Bar, Ballet Room, Lockers, Dressing Rooms. *Notes:* Dressing rooms for hockey only.

San Diego Ice Arena
11048 Ice Skate Place
San Diego CA 92126
(619) 530-1826
FAX: (619) 530-0606
Mgr: Steve Bireley
Skating Dir: Wendy Smith
Ice surfaces: 1, 200x85, Enclosed. *Open:* Year Round. *Ownership:* Private. *Access:* Public. *Clubs:* San Diego FSC. *Sessions:* Public, Private/Club, Rental, Freestyle, Patch, Dance, Hockey. *Classes/Lessons:* Group, Private. *Program Affiliation:* USFSA, ISIA. *Services:* Pro Shop, Skate Rental, Skate Sharpening, Snack Bar, Ballet Room, Weight Room, Lockers, Dressing Rooms.

Side By Side Ice Skating Rink
16091 Gothard St.
Huntington Beach CA 92647
(714) 842-9143
Mgr: Mehron Yaz
Skating Dir: Wanda Guntert
Ice surfaces: 1, 180x75, Enclosed. *Open:* Year Round. *Ownership:* Private. *Access:* Public. *College/Univ:* Long Beach State. *Sessions:* Public, Rental, Freestyle, Patch, Dance, Hockey. *Classes/Lessons:* Private, Group. *Program Affiliation:* USFSA, ISIA. *Summer School:* Local. *Services:* Pro Shop, Skate Rental, Skate Sharpening, Snack Bar, Ballet Room, Pool and/or Athletic Facilities, Dressing Rooms, Lockers. *Notes:* Roller skating rink nearby.

Skating Edge, Inc.
23770 S. Western Ave.
Harbor City CA 90710
(310) 325-4475
FAX: (310) 325-0934
Mgr: Sandra Amschler
Ice surfaces: 1, 200x85, Enclosed. *Open:* Year Round. *Ownership:* Private. *Access:* Public. *Clubs:* South Bay ISC. *Sessions:* Public, Rental, Freestyle, Patch, Hockey, Private/Club. *Classes/Lessons:* Group, Private. *Program Affiliation:* USFSA, ISIA. *Summer School:* No. *Services:* Pro Shop, Skate Rental, Skate Sharpening, Snack Bar, Lockers, Dressing Rooms. *Notes:* Dance available through club only.

Squaw Valley USA
1960 Squaw Valley Rd.
Squaw Valley CA 96146
(916) 581-5518
Ice surfaces: 1, 200x100, Outdoor/Semi Outdoor. *Open:* Year Round. *Ownership:* Private. *Access:* Public. *Clubs:* Sierra Nevada FSC. *Sessions:* Public, Private/Club, Rental, Freestyle, Hockey. *Classes/Lessons:* Group, Private. *Program Affiliation:* ISIA. *Summer School:* No. *Services:* Skate Rental, Skate Sharpening, Dressing Rooms, Lockers. *Notes:* Price for public session ($17 in '94) includes cable car ride. Also available: swimming, tennis, sand volleyball, bungee jumping, skiing.

Van Nuys Iceland
14318 Calvert St.
Van Nuys CA 91401
(818) 785-2171
Mgr: Bill Glass
Ice surfaces: 1, 150x85, Enclosed. *Open:* Year Round. *Ownership:* Private. *Access:* Public. *Sessions:* Public, Rental, Freestyle, Patch, Hockey. *Classes/Lessons:* Group, Private. *Program Affiliation:* ISIA. *Services:* Pro Shop, Skate Sharpening, Skate Rental, Snack Bar. *Notes:* All-purpose room.

Winter Lodge, The
3009 Middlefield Rd.
Palo Alto CA 94304
(415) 493-4566
Mgr: Linda Stebbins Jensen
Skating Dir: Linda Stebbins Jensen
Ice surfaces: 2, 165x85; 85x40, Enclosed, Outdoor/Semi Outdoor. *Open:* Oct.-Apr. *Ownership:* Private. *Access:* Public. *Sessions:* Public, Rental. *Classes/Lessons:* Group. *Program Affiliation:* ISIA. *Services:* Pro Shop, Skate Rental, Skate Sharpening, Lockers, Dressing Rooms.

Yosemite Concession Services Rink
Yosemite National Park
Yosemite National Park CA 95389
(209) 372-1418
FAX: (209) 372-1364
Mgr: Joe Alfano
Ice surfaces: 1, 180x65. *Open:* Nov.-Mar. *Ownership:* Municipal. *Access:* Public. *Sessions:* Public. *Program Affiliation:* ISIA. *Services:* Skate Rental, Skate Sharpening. *Notes:* All purpose room; vending machines.

CO: COLORADO

Air Force Academy Ice Arena
Field House Dr.
US Air Force Academy
Colorado Springs CO 80840
(719) 472-4032
FAX: (719) 472-3798
Mgr: Dama Hurlbutt
Ice surfaces: 1, 200x85, Enclosed. *Open:* Year Round. *Ownership:* Federal. *Access:* Restricted. *Restrictions:* Military & guests & authorized groups. *Clubs:* Broadmoor Club. *College/Univ:* U.S. Air Force Academy. *Sessions:* Private/Club. *Classes/Lessons:* Group. *Program Affiliation:* USFSA. *Notes:* Lessons are for military families only; indoor track; basketball arena.

Aspen Ice Garden
233 W. Hyman
Aspen CO 81611
(303) 920-5141
FAX: (303) 920-5197
Ice surfaces: 1, Enclosed. *Open:* June-Mar. *Ownership:* Municipal. *Access:* Public. *Sessions:* Public, Private/Club, Rental, Hockey. *Classes/Lessons:* Group, Private. *Program Affiliation:* USFSA, ISIA. *Summer School:* National/International. *Services:* Pro Shop, Skate Rental, Skate Sharpening, Snack Bar, Lockers.

Broadmoor World Arena
Colorado Springs CO
Notes: The original historic rink located in the Broadmoor Hotel was demolished in 1994. A new facility was scheduled for construction in 1995.

Crested Butte Ice Rink
620 2nd St.
Crested Butte CO 81224
(303) 349-5338
Mgr: Jerry Deverell
Ice surfaces: 1, 185x85, Outdoor/Semi Outdoor. *Open:* Dec.-Feb. *Ownership:* Municipal. *Access:* Public. *Sessions:* Public, Rental, Hockey. *Classes/Lessons:* Group, Private. *Program Affiliation:* ISIA. *Summer School:* No. *Services:* Skate Rental, Skate Sharpening.

Dobson (John A.) Arena
321 East Lionshead Circle
Vail CO 81657
(303) 479-2271
FAX: (303) 479-2197
Mgr: Jim Heber
Skating Dir: Gordon McKellen
Ice surfaces: 1, 200x85, Enclosed, Outdoor/Semi Outdoor. *Open:* Year Round. *Ownership:* Municipal. *Access:* Public. *Clubs:* SC of Vail. *Sessions:* Public, Freestyle, Patch, Hockey, Private/Club, Rental. *Classes/Lessons:* Group, Private. *Program Affiliation:* USFSA. *Summer School:* National/International. *Services:* Pro Shop, Skate Rental, Skate Sharpening, Lockers, Dressing Rooms. *Notes:* Access to golf course; gymnastics.

Edora Pool Ice Center
1801 Riverside
Ft. Collins CO 80525
(303) 221-6679
Mgr: Paul Thibert
Skating Dir: Paul Thibert
Ice surfaces: 1, 200x85, Enclosed. *Open:* Year Round. *Ownership:* Municipal. *Access:* Public. *Clubs:* ISC of Ft. Collins. *College/Univ:* Colorado State University. *Sessions:* Public, Private/Club, Rental, Freestyle, Patch, Dance, Hockey, Competitive, Learn to Skate, Youth Hockey. *Classes/Lessons:* Group, Private. *Program Affiliation:* USFSA, ISIA. *Summer School:* Local. *Services:* Pro Shop, Skate Rental, Skate Sharpening, Snack Bar, Weight Room, Pool and/or Athletic Facilities, Lockers, Dressing Rooms, Ballet Room. *Notes:* Meeting room.

Howelsen Ice Rink
243 Howelsen Pkwy.
Steamboat Springs CO 80477
(303) 879-0341
Mgr: John LeClaire
Ice surfaces: 1, 200x100, Outdoor/Semi Outdoor. *Open:* Nov.-Feb. *Ownership:* Municipal. *Access:* Public. *Clubs:* Steamboat Skaters. *Sessions:* Public, Private/Club, Rental, Hockey. *Classes/Lessons:* Group, Private. *Program Affiliation:* USFSA, ISIA. *Summer School:* No. *Services:* Skate Rental, Pro Shop, Skate Sharpening, Snack Bar, Lockers, Dressing Rooms.

Hyland Hills Ice Arena
4201 West 94th Ave.
Westminster CO 80030
(303) 650-7552
Mgr: John Gratkins
Ice surfaces: 1, 185x85, Enclosed. *Open:* Year Round. *Ownership:* Municipal. *Access:* Public. *Sessions:* Public, Rental, Freestyle, Patch, Dance, Hockey. *Classes/Lessons:* Group, Private. *Program Affiliation:* USFSA. *Services:* Pro Shop, Skate Rental, Skate Sharpening, Snack Bar, Lockers, Dressing Rooms. *Notes:* All-purpose room.

Keystone Resort Ice Rink
1254 Sodaridge Rd.
Keystone CO 80435
(303) 468-4245
FAX: (303) 468-4024
Mgr: Thomas Davidson
Ice surfaces: 1, Outdoor/Semi Outdoor. *Open:* Dec.-Mar. *Ownership:* Private. *Access:* Public. *Sessions:* Public, Hockey, Speedskating club. *Classes/Lessons:* Group, Private. *Program Affiliation:* ISIA. *Summer School:* No. *Services:* Skate Rental, Skate Sharpening, Snack Bar. *Notes:* Has no compressors, is the largest 'natural' rink in the country—a five-acre frozen lake located at Keystone Resort; restaurants surround lake.

North Jeffco Ice Arena
9101 Ralston Rd.
Arvada CO 80002
(303) 421-1786
Mgr: Bob Bebber
Ice surfaces: 1, 185x85, Enclosed. *Open:* Year Round. *Ownership:* Municipal. *Access:* Public. *Clubs:* Corumbine FSC. *Sessions:* Public, Rental, Freestyle, Patch, Hockey. *Classes/Lessons:* Group, Private. *Program Affiliation:* USFSA. *Services:* Pro Shop, Skate Rental, Skate Sharpening, Snack Bar, Pool and/or Athletic Facilities, Lockers, Dressing Rooms. *Notes:* Basketball court.

Pioneer Ice Arena
3601 S. Monaco
Denver CO 80237
(303) 758-8019
Mgr: Bob Lemon
Ice surfaces: 1, 200x85, Enclosed. *Open:* Year Round. *Ownership:* Private. *Access:* Public. *Clubs:* Alpine Skating Club; Pioneer Jr. Hockey Association. *Sessions:* Public, Private/Club, Rental, Freestyle, Patch, Dance, Hockey. *Classes/Lessons:* Group, Private. *Program Affiliation:* USFSA, ISIA. *Summer School:* National/International. *Services:* Pro Shop, Skate Rental, Skate Sharpening, Snack Bar, Lockers, Dressing Rooms.

Pueblo Plaza Ice Arena
100 N. Grand Ave.
Pueblo CO 81003
(719) 542-8784
Mgr: Karen Willson
Ice surfaces: 1, 200x85, Enclosed. *Open:* Year Round. *Ownership:* Municipal. *Access:* Public. *Clubs:* Pueblo FSC. *Sessions:* Public, Rental, Freestyle, Patch, Dance, Hockey. *Classes/Lessons:* Group, Private. *Program Affiliation:* USFSA. *Services:* Skate Rental, Skate Sharpening, Snack Bar, Lockers, Dressing Rooms. *Notes:* Six all-purpose rooms.

Sertich (Mark "Pa") Ice Center
1705 Pikes Peak
Colorado Springs CO 80909
(719) 578-6883
FAX: (719) 578-6885
Mgr: Mike Swirka
Ice surfaces: 1, 200x85, Enclosed. *Open:* Year Round. *Ownership:* Municipal. *Access:* Public. *Clubs:* Centennial Skating Club. *Sessions:* Public, Private/Club, Rental, Freestyle, Patch, Dance, Hockey. *Classes/Lessons:* Group, Private. *Program Affiliation:* USFSA, ISIA. *Summer School:* No. *Services:* Skate Rental, Skate Sharpening, Lockers, Dressing Rooms.

South Suburban Ice Arena
6580 S. Vine St.
Littleton CO 80121
(303) 798-7881
FAX: (303) 798-3030
Mgr: Tom Moriarty
Ice surfaces: 2, 200x85; 200x85, Enclosed, Outdoor/Semi Outdoor. *Open:* Year Round. *Ownership:* Municipal. *Access:* Public. *Sessions:* Public, Rental, Freestyle, Patch, Dance, Hockey, Private/Club. *Classes/Lessons:* Group, Private. *Program Affiliation:* USFSA. *Summer School:* National/International. *Services:* Pro Shop, Skate Rental, Skate Sharpening, Snack Bar, Lockers, Dressing Rooms. *Notes:* Nearby recreation center.

University of Colorado Ice Arena
Boulder CO 80309
(303) 492-7678
FAX: (303) 492-7430
Mgr: Penny Kipley
Skating Dir: Chad Richert
Ice surfaces: 1, 185x85, Enclosed. *Open:* Year Round. *Ownership:* Club. *Access:* Restricted. *Restrictions:* Students and members. *College/Univ:* University of Colorado. *Sessions:* Private/Club, Freestyle, Patch, Hockey, General. *Classes/Lessons:* Group, Private. *Program Affiliation:* USFSA. *Services:* Skate Rental, Skate Sharpening, Snack Bar, Ballet Room, Weight Room, Pool and/or Athletic Facilities, Lockers, Dressing Rooms. *Notes:* 220,000 sq. foot recreation center.

University of Denver Ice Arena
2250 E. Jewell Ave.
Denver CO 80208-0321
(303) 871-3905
FAX: (303) 871-3905
Mgr: Judd Donnelly
Ice surfaces: 1, 200x85, Enclosed. *Open:* Year Round. *Ownership:* Municipal. *Access:* Public. *College/Univ:* University of Denver. *Sessions:* Public, Rental, Freestyle, Patch, Hockey. *Classes/Lessons:* Group, Private. *Program Affiliation:* ISIA. *Services:* Pro Shop, Skate Rental, Skate Sharpening, Lockers.

CT: CONNECTICUT

Bennett (Edward L.) Skating Rink
One Circle St.
West Haven CT 06516
(203) 932-1461
Mgr: Peter Dixon
Ice surfaces: 1, 200x85, Enclosed. *Open:* Aug.-May. *Ownership:* Private. *Access:* Public. *Sessions:* Public, Private/Club, Rental, Freestyle, Patch, Dance, Hockey. *Classes/Lessons:* Group, Private. *Program Affiliation:* USFSA. *Summer School:* Local. *Services:* Skate Rental, Pro Shop, Skate Sharpening, Snack Bar, Weight Room, Lockers, Dressing Rooms. *Notes:* Precision team.

Bolton Ice Palace
145 Hop River Rd., Rte. # 6
Bolton CT 06043
(203) 646-7851
Mgr: Charles Morris
Ice surfaces: 1, 200x85, Enclosed. *Open:* Year Round. *Ownership:* Private. *Access:* Members Only. *Clubs:* Bolton FSC, Hockey leagues. *Sessions:* Private/Club, Rental. *Classes/Lessons:* Private, Group. *Program Affiliation:* USFSA. *Services:* Pro Shop, Skate Sharpening, Snack Bar, Dressing Rooms.

Brown Rink
Pomfret School
Rt. 44 & Rt. 169
Pomfret CT 06258
(203) 928-7731
Mgr: Dave Cheever
Ice surfaces: 1, 200x100, Enclosed. *Open:* Nov.-Mar. *Ownership:* Private. *Access:* Restricted. *Restrictions:* Students; limited public skating. *Clubs:* Griffin Youth Hockey. *Sessions:* Public, Rental. *Classes/Lessons:* None. *Program Affiliation:* Own. *Summer School:* No. *Services:* Skate Sharpening, Lockers, Dressing Rooms.

Choate-Rosemary Hall ice Rink
Choate-Rosemary School
333 Christian St.
Wallingford CT 06492
(203) 697-2000
Mgr: Larry Rider
Ice surfaces: 1, 200x85, Enclosed. *Open:* Nov.-Feb. *Ownership:* Private. *Access:* Public. *Clubs:* Youth Hockey League, local high schools. *Sessions:* Public, Rental, Hockey. *Classes/Lessons:* None. *Program Affiliation:* Own. *Summer School:* No. *Services:* Skate Sharpening, Snack Bar, Lockers, Dressing Rooms.

Conners (Terry) Ice Rink
Cove Island Park
Stamford CT 06902
(203) 977-4514
Mgr: Dean Pomeroy
Ice surfaces: 1, 200x85, Enclosed. *Open:* July-Apr. *Ownership:* Municipal. *Access:* Public. *Clubs:* Youth Hockey Assn. *Sessions:* Public, Private/Club, Rental, Freestyle, Patch, Dance, Hockey. *Classes/Lessons:* Group, Private. *Program Affiliation:* USFSA, ISIA. *Summer School:* Local. *Services:* Pro Shop, Skate Rental, Skate Sharpening, Snack Bar, Lockers, Dressing Rooms.

Darien Ice Rink
Old Kings Hwy. N.
Darien CT 06820
(203) 655-8251
Mgr: Doug Scott
Ice surfaces: 1, 200x85, Enclosed. *Open:* Year Round. *Ownership:* Private. *Access:* Public. *Clubs:* Darien SC of S. CT. *Sessions:* Public, Private/Club, Rental, Hockey. *Classes/Lessons:* Group, Private. *Program Affiliation:* None. *Services:* Pro Shop, Skate Rental, Skate Sharpening, Snack Bar, Ballet Room, Dressing Rooms. *Notes:* Meeting room. Freestyle, patch, and dance offered through the club only.

Dayton Arena
Connecticut College, 270 Mohegan Ave.
New London CT 06320
(203) 439-2575
Mgr: Doug Roberts
Skating Dir: Diane Rubin
Ice surfaces: 1, 200x85, Enclosed. *Open:* Oct.-Mar. *Ownership:* Private. *Access:* Public. *College/Univ:* Connecticut College. *Sessions:* Public, Rental, Freestyle, Hockey, General. *Classes/Lessons:* Group, Private. *Program Affiliation:* USFSA. *Summer School:* Local. *Services:* Skate Rental, Skate Sharpening, Snack Bar, Dressing Rooms, Pool and/or Athletic Facilities. *Notes:* Part of a large athletic complex for students.

Draddy Arena at Canterbury High School
Aspetuck Ave.
New Milford CT 06776
(203) 355-3103
Mgr: Mike Onorato
Ice surfaces: 1, 192x84, Enclosed. *Open:* Nov.-Mar. *Ownership:* Private. *Access:* Public. *Sessions:* Public, Private/Club, Rental, Freestyle, Patch, Dance, Hockey. *Classes/Lessons:* Group, Private. *Program Affiliation:* ISIA. *Summer School:* No. *Services:* Pro Shop, Skate Sharpening, Snack Bar, Dressing Rooms.

East Haven Veterans Memorial Ice Rink
71 Hudson St.
East Haven CT 06512
(203) 468-3367
Mgr: Don McGinnis
Ice surfaces: 1, 200x85, Enclosed. *Open:* Sept.-June. *Ownership:* Municipal. *Access:* Public. *Clubs:* Shoreline Figure Skaters. *Sessions:* Public, Private/Club, Rental, Hockey. *Classes/Lessons:* Group, Private. *Program Affiliation:* USFSA. *Services:* Pro Shop, Skate Rental, Skate Sharpening, Snack Bar, Dressing Rooms. *Notes:* Freestyle, patch, and dance offered through the club only.

Enfield Twin Rinks
1 Prior Rd.
Enfield CT 06082
(203) 745-2461
Mgr: John McCormack
Skating Dir: Jean Bridge
Ice surfaces: 2, 185x85; 185x85, Enclosed. *Open:* Year Round. *Ownership:* Private. *Access:* Public. *Sessions:* Public, Private/Club, Rental, Freestyle, Patch, Hockey. *Classes/Lessons:* Group, Private. *Program Affiliation:* ISIA. *Services:* Pro Shop, Skate Rental, Skate Sharpening, Snack Bar, Dressing Rooms.

Fairchild (Jennings) Rink
500 Old Farms Rd.
Avon CT 06001
(203) 673-3201
FAX: (203) 675-8369
Mgr: Walter Ullram
Ice surfaces: 1, 200x87, Enclosed. *Open:* July - Apr. *Ownership:* Private. *Access:* Restricted. *Restrictions:* Students and rentals. *Clubs:* Hartford Whalers Training Center; Youth Hockey. *Sessions:* Public, Private/Club, Rental, Hockey. *Classes/Lessons:* Group, Private. *Program Affiliation:* ISIA. *Summer School:* Local. *Services:* Skate Sharpening, Snack Bar, Lockers, Dressing Rooms.

Greenwich Skating Club
Cardinal Rd.
Greenwich CT 06836
(203) 622-9583
Mgr: Mickey Madigan
Ice surfaces: 1, 196x85, Outdoor/Semi Outdoor. *Open:* Nov.-Mar. *Ownership:* Private. *Access:* Members Only. *Sessions:* Private/Club, Freestyle, Patch, Dance, Hockey. *Classes/Lessons:* Group, Private. *Program Affiliation:* ISIA, USFSA. *Summer School:* No. *Services:* Pro Shop, Skate Rental, Skate Sharpening, Snack Bar, Lockers, Dressing Rooms.

Gunnery School
99 Greenhill Rd.
Washington CT 06793
(203) 868-2176
Mgr: Bob Ullram
Ice surfaces: 1, 200x85, Enclosed. *Open:* Oct.-Mar. *Ownership:* Private. *Access:* Restricted. *Restrictions:* School and staff. *Clubs:* Gunnery Varsity Hockey. *Sessions:* Private/Club, Rental, Hockey. *Classes/Lessons:* None. *Summer School:* No. *Services:* Skate Sharpening, Snack Bar, Dressing Rooms. *Notes:* Athletic facilities available to students and staff; skate sharpening available for teams.

Hamden Community Ice Rink
595 Mix Ave.
Hamden CT 06514
(203) 287-2610
Mgr: Rick Gentile
Ice surfaces: 1, 200x80, Enclosed. *Open:* Year Round. *Ownership:* Municipal. *Access:* Public. *Clubs:* Hamden YHA; Hamden FS Assn. *College/Univ:* Quinnitiac College. *Sessions:* Public, Private/Club, Rental, Hockey. *Classes/Lessons:* Group. *Program Affiliation:* USFSA. *Services:* Skate Rental, Snack Bar, Dressing Rooms. *Notes:* Freestyle, patch, and dance offered through the club only.

Hamill (Dorothy) Skating Rink
Sherman Ave.
Greenwich CT 06831
(203) 531-8560
Mgr: Donald Mohr
Skating Dir: Nancy Lemey
Ice surfaces: 1, 120x85, Enclosed. *Open:* Sept.-Mar. *Ownership:* Municipal. *Access:* Public, Restricted. Greenwich residents. *Clubs:* Windy Hill Skating Club. *Sessions:* Public, Private/Club, Rental, Freestyle, Patch, Hockey. *Classes/Lessons:* Private. *Program Affiliation:* USFSA, ISIA. *Summer School:* No. *Services:* Pro Shop, Skate Rental, Snack Bar, Lockers, Dressing Rooms, Skate Sharpening.

Inglass Rink
73 Sachem
New Haven CT 06520
(203) 432-0877
Mgr: George Arnaoutis
Ice surfaces: 1, 200x85, Enclosed. *Open:* Oct.-Mar. *Ownership:* Private. *Access:* Public. *Clubs:* Yale FSC. *College/Univ:* Yale University. *Sessions:* Public, Rental, Hockey. *Classes/Lessons:* None. *Program Affiliation:* USFSA. *Services:* Skate Sharpening, Weight Room, Lockers, Dressing Rooms. *Notes:* Alumni room. Freestyle, patch, and dance are offered through the club only.

International Skating Center of Connecticut
1375 Hopmeadow St.
Simsbury CT 06070
(203) 651-5400
FAX: (203) 651-5204
Mgr: Zane Collings
Skating Dir: Bob Young
Ice surfaces: 2, 200x85; 197x98, Enclosed. *Open:* Year Round. *Ownership:* Private. *Access:* Public. *Clubs:* Charter Oaks FSC. *Sessions:* Private/Club, Public, Rental, Freestyle, Patch, Dance, Hockey. *Classes/Lessons:* Private, Group. *Program Affiliation:* ISIA, USFSA. *Summer School:* National/International. *Services:* Dressing Rooms, Weight Room, Snack Bar, Ballet Room, Skate Sharpening, Pro Shop, Skate Rental. *Notes:* Summer school starting summer of 1995.

Kingswood-Oxford School Rink
170 Kingswood Rd.
West Hartford CT 06119
(203) 233-9631
FAX: (203) 232-3843
Mgr: Mike Frier
Ice surfaces: 1, 200x85, Enclosed. *Open:* Oct.-Mar. *Ownership:* Private. *Access:* Restricted. *Restrictions:* Students and faculty. *College/Univ:* Trinity College. *Sessions:* Rental, Hockey, Public. *Classes/Lessons:* None. *Summer School:* No. *Services:* Skate Sharpening, Snack Bar, Lockers, Weight Room, Dressing Rooms. *Notes:* Hockey lessons for students.

Loomis-Chaffee School Ice Rink
Island Rd.
Windsor CT 06095
(203) 688-4934
Mgr: Dave Lamenzo
Ice surfaces: 1, 200x85, Enclosed. *Open:* Nov.-Feb. *Ownership:* Private. *Access:* Restricted. *Restrictions:* Students & rentals. *Clubs:* Youth Hockey; Windsor High School. *Sessions:* Rental. *Summer School:* No. *Services:* Snack Bar, Dressing Rooms, Lockers.

Milford Ice Pavilion
291 Bic Dr.
Milford CT 06460
(203) 878-6516
Mgr: Perry Roos
Ice surfaces: 1, 200x85, Enclosed. *Open:* Year Round. *Ownership:* Private. *Clubs:* New Haven SC. *Sessions:* Public, Rental, Freestyle, Patch, Hockey. *Classes/Lessons:* Private. *Program Affiliation:* USFSA. *Services:* Pro Shop, Skate Sharpening, Snack Bar, Lockers, Dressing Rooms.

Nadal Rink
Kent School
Kent CT 06757
(203) 927-3501
Mgr: Todd Marble
Ice surfaces: 1, 200x85, Enclosed. *Open:* Nov.-Feb. *Ownership:* Private. *Access:* Restricted. *Restrictions:* Students only. *Sessions:* Private/Club, Rental, Freestyle, Hockey, General. *Classes/Lessons:* Group. *Program Affiliation:* None, Own. *Services:* Skate Sharpening, Lockers, Dressing Rooms.

New Canaan Winter Club
604 Frogtown Rd.
New Canaan CT 06840
(203) 966-4280
Mgr: Bruce Bartolo
Ice surfaces: 1, 200x85, Outdoor/Semi Outdoor. *Open:* Nov.-Mar. *Ownership:* Private. *Access:* Members Only. *Sessions:* Private/Club, Freestyle, Dance, Hockey. *Classes/Lessons:* Private, Group. *Program Affiliation:* USFSA. *Services:* Dressing Rooms.

Remson Hockey Ice Rink
333 Christian
Wallingford CT 06492
(203) 697-2000
FAX: (203) 697-2601
Mgr: Chuck Timlin
Ice surfaces: 1, 200x85, Enclosed. *Open:* Nov.-Mar. *Ownership:* Choate Rosemary. *Access:* Members Only. *Clubs:* Wallingford Hawks. *Sessions:* Private/Club, Hockey. *Classes/Lessons:* None. *Summer School:* No. *Services:* Skate Sharpening, Snack Bar.

Ridgefield Skating Center
111 Prospect Ridge Rd.
Box 636
Ridgefield CT 06877
(203) 438-5277
Mgr: A. Bessette
Ice surfaces: 1, 200x85, Outdoor/Semi Outdoor. *Open:* Oct.-Mar. *Ownership:* Private. *Access:* Public. *Clubs:* Laurel Ridge SC. *College/Univ:* Western Connecticut State University. *Sessions:* Public, Private/Club, Rental, Freestyle, Patch, Dance, Hockey. *Classes/Lessons:* Group, Private. *Program Affiliation:* USFSA. *Summer School:* No. *Services:* Pro Shop, Skate Sharpening, Snack Bar, Lockers, Dressing Rooms.

Salisbury School
251 Canaan Rd.
Salisbury CT 06068
(203) 435-9658
Ice surfaces: 1, 200x100, Enclosed. *Open:* Nov.-Mar. *Ownership:* Private. *Access:* Restricted. *Restrictions:* School use. *Sessions:* Public, Private/Club, Rental, Freestyle, Dance, Hockey. *Classes/Lessons:* None. *Program Affiliation:* Own. *Summer School:* No. *Services:* Dressing Rooms, Lockers, Pool and/or Athletic Facilities. *Notes:* Lockers for hockey teams only.

Schmidt Ice Rink
Hothchkiss School, Rt. 41
Lakeville CT 06039
(203) 435-2591
Ice surfaces: 2, 200x85; 200x85, Enclosed. *Open:* Nov.-Mar. *Ownership:* Private. *Access:* Restricted. *Restrictions:* School community. *Sessions:* Public, Private/Club, Rental, Freestyle, Hockey. *Classes/Lessons:* None. *Program Affiliation:* Own. *Summer School:* No. *Services:* Pool and/or Athletic Facilities, Skate Sharpening. *Notes:* Pool and/or Athletic facilities not open to public.

Simsbury Farms Recreation Complex Ice Rink
100 Old Farms Rd.
W. Simsbury CT 06092
(203) 658-3836
Mgr: John Thibeault
Ice surfaces: 1, Outdoor/Semi Outdoor. *Open:* Nov.-Feb. *Ownership:* Municipal. *Access:* Public. *Sessions:* Rental, Hockey, General. *Classes/Lessons:* Group. *Summer School:* No. *Services:* Snack Bar, Pool and/or Athletic Facilities, Lockers, Dressing Rooms. *Notes:* Tennis and paddle court; volleyball; 18-hole golf; picnic area; 2.5 mile fitness trail; and playground.

South Kent School Arena
40 Bulls Bridge Rd.
South Kent CT 06785
(203) 927-4896
Mgr: Sam Simmons
Ice surfaces: 1, 200x85, Enclosed. *Open:* Nov.-Mar. *Ownership:* Private. *Access:* Members Only. Students and staff. *Clubs:* South Kent Hockey; South Kent FSC. *Sessions:* Private/Club, Rental, Freestyle, Hockey. *Classes/Lessons:* None. *Summer School:* No. *Services:* Skate Sharpening, Snack Bar, Dressing Rooms. *Notes:* Weight room in school.

South Windsor Arena
585 John Fitch Rd.
South Windsor CT 06072
(208) 289-3401
Mgr: Steve Grigorian
Ice surfaces: 1, 190x85, Enclosed. *Open:* June-Apr. *Ownership:* Private. *Access:* Public. *Clubs:* SC of Hartford; Youth Hockey. *Sessions:* Private/Club, Rental, Freestyle, Patch, Dance, Hockey. *Classes/Lessons:* Group, Private. *Program Affiliation:* USFSA. *Summer School:* Regional. *Services:* Skate Sharpening, Pro Shop, Lockers, Dressing Rooms.

Taft School Mays Rink
Guerseytown Rd.
Watertown CT 06795
(203) 274-2516
Mgr: Mary Duran
Ice surfaces: 1, 190x86, Enclosed. *Open:* Nov.-Mar. *Ownership:* Private. *Access:* Restricted. *Restrictions:* Limited public skating; all else is rental time. *Sessions:* Public, Rental. *Program Affiliation:* USFSA. *Summer School:* No. *Services:* Skate Sharpening, Snack Bar, Dressing Rooms. *Notes:* Classes and lessons are offered through the club.

Tri-Town Sports Center
Box 317, Sebeths Dr.
Cromwell CT 06416
(203) 632-0323
FAX: (203) 632-0323
Mgr: Don Baldwin
Skating Dir: Kathy Sternberg
Ice surfaces: 1, 200x100, Enclosed. *Open:* Year Round. *Ownership:* Private. *Access:* Public. *Clubs:* SC of Hartford. *Sessions:* Public, Rental, Freestyle, Patch, Dance, Hockey. *Classes/Lessons:* Group, Private. *Program Affiliation:* USFSA. *Services:* Pro Shop, Skate Sharpening, Snack Bar, Weight Room, Lockers, Dressing Rooms. *Notes:* Aerobics room.

University of Connecticut Ice Rink
U/78 Athletic Building
Storrs CT 06268
(203) 486-3808
Mgr: Bruce Marshall
Skating Dir: Gloria Sykes
Ice surfaces: 1, 200x85, Outdoor/Semi Outdoor. *Open:* Oct.-Mar. *Ownership:* University. *Access:* Public. *College/Univ:* University of Connecticut. *Sessions:* Public, Rental, Hockey. *Classes/Lessons:* Private. *Program Affiliation:* USFSA. *Summer School:* No. *Services:* Skate Rental, Skate Sharpening, Lockers, Dressing Rooms. *Notes:* University athletic complex.

Veterans Memorial Skating Rink
56 Buena Vista Dr.
West Hartford CT 06107
(203) 521-1573
Mgr: John Zullo
Ice surfaces: 1, 200x85, Enclosed. *Open:* Oct.-Mar. *Ownership:* Municipal. *Access:* Public. *Clubs:* Charter Oak FSC, West Hartford Youth Hockey. *Sessions:* Public, Rental, Freestyle, Patch, Dance, Hockey. *Classes/Lessons:* Group, Private. *Program Affiliation:* None. *Services:* Pro Shop, Skate Rental, Skate Sharpening, Lockers, Dressing Rooms. *Notes:* Birthday party room; vending machines; heated.

Wesleyan Arena - Freeman Athletic Center
161 Cross St.
Middletown CT 06459
(203) 685-2927
FAX: (203) 685-2691
Mgr: Dave Snyder
Ice surfaces: 1, 200x85, Enclosed. *Open:* Oct.-Mar. *Ownership:* Private. *Access:* Restricted. *Restrictions:* Limited public sessions. *Clubs:* Middlesex Youth Hockey. *College/Univ:* Wesleyan University. *Sessions:* Public, Rental, Freestyle, Patch, Hockey, Private/Club. *Classes/Lessons:* Private, Group. *Program Affiliation:* Own. *Summer School:* No. *Services:* Pro Shop, Skate Sharpening, Snack Bar, Lockers, Dressing Rooms. *Notes:* Private, freestyle and patch sessions for the university only; located in athletic complex.

Westminster School Ice Arena
995 Hopmeadow St.
Simsbury CT 06070
(203) 658-4444
FAX: (203) 658-1378
Mgr: Peter Newman
Ice surfaces: 1, 200x85, Outdoor/Semi Outdoor. *Open:* Nov.-Mar. *Ownership:* Private. *Access:* Restricted. *Restrictions:* School use only. *Clubs:* Westminster Boys Hockey; Westminster Girls Hockey. *Sessions:* Private/Club, Rental, Hockey. *Classes/Lessons:* None. *Summer School:* No. *Services:* Skate Sharpening, Snack Bar, Weight Room, Lockers, Dressing Rooms.

Wonderland of Ice
123 Glenwood Ave.
Bridgeport CT 06610
(203) 576-8110
Mgr: Lisa Fettick
Ice surfaces: 1, 200x85, Enclosed. *Open:* Year Round. *Ownership:* Private, Municipal. *Access:* Public. *Clubs:* Bridgeport FSC, Greater Bridgeport JHYA. *Sessions:* Public, Rental, Hockey. *Classes/Lessons:* Group, Private. *Program Affiliation:* USFSA, ISIA. *Services:* Pro Shop, Skate Rental, Skate Sharpening, Snack Bar, Lockers, Dressing Rooms. *Notes:* Birthday room, meeting room; freestyle, patch and dance sessions offered through club only.

DC: DISTRICT OF COLUMBIA

Fort Dupont
3779 Ely Place, SE
Washington DC 20019
(202) 584-3040
Mgr: Jim Walton
Ice surfaces: 1, 210x185, Enclosed. *Open:* Sept.-Apr. *Ownership:* Municipal. *Access:* Public. *Sessions:* Public, Private/Club, Hockey. *Classes/Lessons:* Group, Private. *Program Affiliation:* USFSA. *Services:* Skate Rental, Skate Sharpening, Snack Bar, Lockers, Dressing Rooms.

Sculpture Garden Ice Rink
7th and Constitution Ave. NW
Washington DC 20355
(202) 371-5340
Mgr: Kirk Huserick
Ice surfaces: 1, 150x64, Outdoor/Semi Outdoor. *Open:* Nov.-Mar. *Ownership:* Private. *Access:* Public. *Clubs:* DC Sports. *Sessions:* Public. *Classes/Lessons:* Group, Private. *Program Affiliation:* USFSA, ISIA. *Summer School:* No. *Services:* Skate Rental, Skate Sharpening, Snack Bar, Lockers.

DE: DELAWARE

Skating Club of Wilmington, Inc.
1301 Carruthers Lane
Wilmington DE 19803-0307
(302) 656-5007
Mgr: Peter Bilous
Ice surfaces: 1, 200x85, Enclosed. *Open:* Year Round. *Ownership:* Club. *Access:* Members Only. Mostly members. *Clubs:* SC of Wilmington, Inc. *Sessions:* Public, Private/Club, Rental, Hockey. *Classes/Lessons:* Private, Group. *Program Affiliation:* USFSA. *Summer School:* National/International. *Services:* Pro Shop, Skate Rental, Skate Sharpening, Snack Bar, Lockers, Dressing Rooms. *Notes:* Upstairs mezzanine for ballet, functions, observing skating, etc.

Freestyle, patch, and dance offered through the club.

University of Delaware Arena
South College Ave.
Newark DE 19716
(302) 831-6038
FAX: (302) 831-3693
Mgr: Jim Gossard
Ice surfaces: 2, 200x100; 200x85, Enclosed. *Open:* Year Round. *Ownership:* Private. *Access:* Public. *College/Univ:* University of Delaware. *Sessions:* Public, Private/Club, Rental, Freestyle, Patch, Dance, Hockey. *Classes/Lessons:* Group, Private. *Program Affiliation:* ISIA. *Summer School:* National/International. *Services:* Pro Shop, Skate Rental, Skate Sharpening, Snack Bar, Ballet Room, Weight Room, Lockers, Dressing Rooms. *Notes:* VIP lounge; conference roo; viewing room.

FL: FLORIDA

Centre Ice Countryside Mall
27001 U.S. Hwy. 19N
Clearwater FL 34621
(813) 796-0586
FAX: (813) 787-8693
Mgr: Bruce Hyland
Ice surfaces: 1, 100x50. *Open:* Year Round. *Ownership:* Private. *Access:* Public. *Sessions:* Public, Private/Club, Rental, Freestyle, Patch, Dance. *Classes/Lessons:* Group, Private. *Program Affiliation:* ISIA. *Services:* Pro Shop, Skate Rental, Skate Sharpening, Lockers, Dressing Rooms.

Gold Coast Ice Arena
4601 N. Federal Hwy.
Pompano Beach FL 33064
(305) 943-1437
Mgr: Hal Jacovitz
Ice surfaces: 1, 185x80, Enclosed. *Open:* Year Round. *Ownership:* Private. *Access:* Public. *Clubs:* NHL- Florida Panthers practice rink. *Sessions:* Public, Private/Club, Rental, Freestyle, Patch, Dance, Hockey. *Classes/Lessons:* Group, Private. *Program Affiliation:* USFSA, ISIA. *Summer School:* National/International. *Services:* Pro Shop, Skate Rental, Skate Sharpening, Snack Bar, Lockers, Dressing Rooms. *Notes:* Broomball.

Ice Chateau, Inc.
1097 Tamiami Trail North
Nokomis FL 34275
(813) 484-0080
FAX: (813) 484-3160
Mgr: Marti Gaudiel
Ice surfaces: 1, 99x60, Enclosed. *Open:* Year Round. *Ownership:* Private. *Access:* Public. *Clubs:* Florida Suncoast FSC. *Sessions:* Public, Private/Club, Freestyle, Patch. *Classes/Lessons:* Group, Private. *Program Affiliation:* USFSA, ISIA. *Services:* Pro Shop, Skate Rental, Skate Sharpening, Snack Bar, Ballet Room, Lockers. *Notes:* Dance offered through club only.

Lakeland Civic Center
700 W. Lemon St.
Lakeland FL 33802
(813) 499-8110
Mgr: Allen Johnson
Ice surfaces: 1, 200x85, Enclosed. *Open:* Oct.-Mar. *Ownership:* Municipal. *Access:* Public. *Clubs:* Walt Disney World On Ice; Tampa Bay Lightning. *Sessions:* Public, Private/Club, Rental, Freestyle, Patch, Dance, Hockey. *Classes/Lessons:* None. *Program Affiliation:* ISIA. *Summer School:* No. *Services:* Skate Rental, Skate Sharpening, Lockers, Dressing Rooms.

Miami Ice Arena, Inc.
14770 Biscayne Blvd.
North Miami Beach FL 33181
(305) 940-8222
FAX: (305) 947-1993
Mgr: Joe Durning
Ice surfaces: 1, 185x85, Enclosed. *Open:* Year Round. *Ownership:* Private. *Access:* Public. *Sessions:* Public, Private/Club, Rental, Freestyle, Patch, Hockey. *Classes/Lessons:* Group, Private. *Program Affiliation:* USFSA, ISIA. *Services:* Pro Shop, Skate Rental, Skate Sharpening, Snack Bar, Ballet Room, Lockers, Dressing Rooms.

Orlando Ice Skating Palace
3123 W. Colonial Dr.
Orlando FL 32808
(407) 294-5419
Mgr: Grey Doppel
Ice surfaces: 1, 200x100, Enclosed, Outdoor/Semi Outdoor. *Open:* Year Round. *Ownership:* Private. *Access:* Public. *Clubs:* Citrus FSC. *Sessions:* Public, Private/Club, Rental, Freestyle, Patch, Hockey. *Classes/Lessons:* Group, Private. *Program Affiliation:* ISIA. *Summer School:* Local. *Services:* Skate Rental, Pro Shop, Skate Sharpening, Snack Bar, Lockers. *Notes:* Two-hour minimum to rent ice time.

Rakow (Scott) Youth Center Ice Rink
2700 Sheridan Ave.
Miami Beach FL 33140
(305) 673-7767
FAX: (305) 673-7074
Mgr: Kim Reed
Ice surfaces: 1, 60x30, Enclosed. *Open:* Year Round. *Ownership:* Municipal. *Access:* Public. *Sessions:* Public, Rental, Hockey, General. *Classes/Lessons:* Group, Private. *Program Affiliation:* ISIA. *Summer School:* Local. *Services:* Pro Shop, Skate Rental, Skate Sharpening, Snack Bar, Lockers.

Rock On Ice
7500 Canada Dr.
Orlando FL 32819
(407) 352-4043
Mgr: Brad Holland
Skating Dir: Corey Naylor
Ice surfaces: 1, 200x85, Enclosed. *Open:* Year Round. *Ownership:* Private. *Access:* Public. *Clubs:* Int'l SC of Orland; Orlando Youth Hockey Association; Rock On Ice ISIA Competitors Club, Inc. *Sessions:* Public, Rental, Freestyle, Patch, Dance, Hockey, Private/Club. *Classes/Lessons:* Group, Private. *Program Affiliation:* ISIA, USFSA. *Summer School:* National/International. *Services:* Pro Shop, Skate Rental, Skate Sharpening, Snack Bar, Ballet Room, Lockers, Dressing Rooms. *Notes:* Lighting & sound system; team room; video arcade; jump harness.

Skate World, Inc.
3605 Phillips Hwy.
Jacksonville FL 32207
(904) 399-3223
FAX: (904) 696-6768
Mgr: Bob Sabourin
Skating Dir: Leena Domoskaya
Ice surfaces: 1, 200x85, Enclosed. *Open:* Year Round. *Ownership:* Private. *Access:* Public. *Clubs:* Jacksonville FSC, North Florida Hockey Assn.; Sunshine Hockey League; Bullets minor league hockey team. *Sessions:* Public, Private/Club,

Rental, Freestyle, Patch, Dance, Hockey. *Classes/Lessons:* Group, Private. *Program Affiliation:* ISIA. *Summer School:* Local, Regional. *Services:* Pro Shop, Skate Rental, Skate Sharpening, Snack Bar, Weight Room, Lockers, Dressing Rooms. *Notes:* Large rollerblade track; arcade; state-accredited medic; medical office equipped with oxygen.

Sun Blades Ice Rink
13940 Icot Blvd.
Clearwater FL 34620
(813) 536-5843
FAX: (813) 530-3790
Mgr: Howard Buck
Ice surfaces: 1, 185x85, Enclosed. *Open:* Year Round. *Ownership:* Private. *Access:* Public. *Clubs:* Florida Suncoast FSC, Jr. Lightning Hockey Association. *Sessions:* Public, Rental, Freestyle, Patch, Dance, Hockey. *Classes/Lessons:* Group, Private. *Program Affiliation:* ISIA. *Summer School:* National/International. *Services:* Pro Shop, Skate Rental, Skate Sharpening, Snack Bar, Lockers, Dressing Rooms.

Sunrise Ice Skating Center
3363 N. Pine Island Rd.
Sunrise FL 33351
(305) 741-2366
Mgr: Rosslyn Gudino
Ice surfaces: 1, 200x85, Enclosed. *Open:* Year Round. *Ownership:* Private. *Access:* Public. *Clubs:* SC of Sunrise. *Sessions:* Public, Private/Club, Rental, Freestyle, Patch, Hockey. *Classes/Lessons:* Group, Private. *Program Affiliation:* ISIA. *Services:* Pro Shop, Skate Rental, Skate Sharpening, Snack Bar, Lockers, Dressing Rooms.

Tampa Bay Skating Academy
251 Lakeview Dr.
Oldsmar FL 34677
(813) 854-4009
FAX: (813) 854-4031
Mgr: Glenn Jones
Ice surfaces: 2, 200x85; 200x85, Enclosed. *Open:* Year Round. *Ownership:* Private. *Access:* Public. *Clubs:* Tampa Bay SC. *Sessions:* Public, Private/Club, Rental, Freestyle, Patch, Dance, Hockey. *Classes/Lessons:* Group, Private. *Program Affiliation:* ISIA. *Summer School:* Local, National/International. *Services:* Pro Shop, Skate Rental, Skate Sharpening, Snack Bar, Ballet Room, Weight Room, Lockers, Dressing Rooms. *Notes:* Lounge overlooking ice; multi-purpose room.

GA: GEORGIA

Atlanta Iceplex
2300 Satellite Blvd.
Duluth GA 30136
(404) 813-1010
FAX: (404) 495-0032
Mgr: Chuck Robinson
Skating Dir: Don Laws
Ice surfaces: 1, 200x85, Enclosed. *Open:* Year Round. *Ownership:* Private. *Access:* Public. *Clubs:* Atlanta FSC. *Sessions:* Public, Rental, Freestyle, Patch, Dance, Hockey. *Classes/Lessons:* Private, Group. *Program Affiliation:* ISIA. *Summer School:* Regional. *Services:* Pro Shop, Skate Rental, Skate Sharpening, Snack Bar, Ballet Room, Weight Room, Lockers, Dressing Rooms.

Parkaire Ice Arena
4880 Lower Rosewell Rd. NE, Suite 900
Marietta GA 30068
(404) 973-0753; FAX: (404) 973-0837
Mgr: Sharon Fischer
Skating Dir: Mindy Fischer
Ice surfaces: 1, 185x85, Enclosed. *Open:* Year Round. *Ownership:* Private. *Access:* Public. *Clubs:* Atlanta FSC, GA Amateur Hockey Assn., Atlanta Amateur Hockey Assn. *Sessions:* Public, Rental, Freestyle, Patch, Dance, Hockey. *Classes/Lessons:* Group, Private. *Program Affiliation:* USFSA, ISIA. *Services:* Pro Shop, Skate Rental, Skate Sharpening, Lockers, Dressing Rooms, Snack Bar. *Notes:* NHL Atlanta Knights practice facility.

HI: HAWAII

Ice Palace
4510 Salt Lake Blvd.
Honolulu HI 96818
(808) 487-9921
Mgr: Doug Taylor
Ice surfaces: 1, 187x85, Enclosed. *Open:* Year Round. *Ownership:* Private. *Access:* Public. *Sessions:* Public, Rental, Freestyle, Patch, Dance, Hockey. *Classes/Lessons:* Group, Private. *Program Affiliation:* USFSA, ISIA. *Services:* Pro Shop, Skate Rental, Skate Sharpening, Snack Bar, Ballet Room, Lockers, Dressing Rooms.

IA: IOWA

Ames — Iowa State University Ice Arena
1500 Gateway Hills Dr.
Ames IA 50014
(515) 292-6835
Mgr: Chris Roy
Ice surfaces: 1, 185x85, Enclosed. *Open:* Year Round. *Ownership:* Municipal. *Access:* Public. *Clubs:* Ames FSC, Ames Minor Hockey Assn. *College/Univ:* Iowa State University. *Sessions:* Public, Private/Club, Freestyle, Patch, Hockey. *Classes/Lessons:* Group, Private. *Program Affiliation:* USFSA, ISIA. *Summer School:* Local. *Services:* Pro Shop, Skate Rental, Skate Sharpening, Snack Bar, Lockers, Dressing Rooms. *Notes:* Offers inter-mural hockey, broomball, curling.

Dubuque Five Flags Center
4th & Main
Dubuque IA 52001
(319) 589-4254
Mgr: Carole Barry
Ice surfaces: 1, 185x85, Enclosed. *Open:* Oct.-Mar. *Ownership:* Municipal. *Access:* Public. *Sessions:* Public, Rental, Hockey. *Classes/Lessons:* Group. *Program Affiliation:* Own. *Summer School:* No. *Services:* Skate Rental, Snack Bar, Lockers, Dressing Rooms. *Notes:* Group lessons are for hockey only.

Metro Ice Sports Arena
7201 Hickman Rd.
Urbandale IA 50322
(515) 278—9757
Mgr: Tom Mussleman
Ice surfaces: 1, 200x85, Enclosed. *Open:* June-Apr. *Ownership:* Private. *Access:* Public. *Clubs:* DesMoine FSC, DesMoines Amateur Hockey Assn. *Sessions:* Public, Private/Club, Rental, Hockey, Freestyle. *Classes/Lessons:* Group. *Program Affiliation:* USFSA, ISIA. *Summer School:* No. *Services:* Pro Shop, Skate Rental, Skate Sharpening, Snack Bar, Dressing Rooms, Lockers. *Notes:* Club offers Learn to Skate program.

North Iowa Ice Arena
3700 4th St. SW
Mason City IA 50401
(515) 424-3547
Mgr: Ted Klemas

Ice surfaces: 1, 200x80, Enclosed. *Open:* Oct.-Mar. *Ownership:* Municipal. *Access:* Public. *Clubs:* Mason City Youth Hockey, North Iowa FSC. *Sessions:* Public, Private/Club, Rental, Freestyle, Patch, Hockey. *Classes/Lessons:* Group, Private. *Program Affiliation:* USFSA. *Services:* Skate Rental, Skate Sharpening, Snack Bar, Dressing Rooms. *Notes:* Freestyle, patch sessions and lessons are offered though the club.

Quad City Sports Center
700 West River Dr.
Davenport IA 52802
(319) 322-5220
FAX: (319) 322-5240
Mgr: Thomas Bahls
Ice surfaces: 1, 200x100, Enclosed. *Open:* Year Round. *Ownership:* Private. *Access:* Public. *Sessions:* Public, Rental, Freestyle, Patch, Hockey. *Classes/Lessons:* Group, Private. *Program Affiliation:* ISIA. *Summer School:* Local. *Services:* Pro Shop, Skate Rental, Skate Sharpening, Dressing Rooms. *Notes:* Developing a figure skating club and several hockey leagues.

Sioux City Municipal Auditorium
401 Gordon Dr.
Sioux City IA 51102
(712) 279-4800
FAX: (712) 279-4903
Mgr: Walt Johnson
Ice surfaces: 1, 165x80, Enclosed. *Open:* Sept.-Mar.; June. *Ownership:* Municipal. *Access:* Public. *Clubs:* Sioux City Musketeers. *College/Univ:* University of South Dakota. *Sessions:* Public, Rental, Hockey, Dance. *Classes/Lessons:* Group. *Program Affiliation:* USFSA. *Summer School:* Local. *Services:* Skate Rental, Skate Sharpening, Snack Bar, Lockers, Dressing Rooms, Pro Shop. *Notes:* Hockey camp offered in June.

Young Arena
Commercial St.
Waterloo IA 50701
(319) 291-4491
FAX: (319) 291-4270
Mgr: Bud Eggelston
Ice surfaces: 1, 200x100, Enclosed. *Open:* Year Round. *Ownership:* Municipal. *Access:* Public. *Clubs:* USHC Team (Blackhawks); N.E. Iowa FSC. *Sessions:* Public, Private/Club, Rental, Hockey. *Classes/Lessons:* Group, Private. *Services:* Skate Rental, Skate Sharpening, Snack Bar, Weight Room, Dressing Rooms. *Notes:* Freestyle, patch, dance and hockey sessions are offered through clubs only.

ID: IDAHO

Marmo (Joe) and Wayne Lehto Ice Arena
Tautphaus Park
Idaho Falls ID 83405
(208) 529-1479
Mgr: Sharon Johnson
Ice surfaces: 1, 200x85, Enclosed. *Open:* Nov.-Mar. *Ownership:* Municipal. *Access:* Public. *Clubs:* Youth Hockey. *Sessions:* Public, Rental, Freestyle, Patch, Hockey. *Classes/Lessons:* Group, Private. *Program Affiliation:* USFSA. *Summer School:* No. *Services:* Skate Rental, Skate Sharpening, Dressing Rooms.

Sun Valley Skating Center
Dollar Loop Rd.
Sun Valley ID 83353
(208) 622-2194
FAX: (208) 622-3700
Mgr: Nick Maricich
Ice surfaces: 2, 200x85; 180x90, Enclosed. *Open:* Year Round. *Ownership:* Private. *Access:* Public. *Clubs:* Sun Valley Skating Co. *Sessions:* Public, Private/Club, Rental, Freestyle, Patch, Dance, Hockey. *Classes/Lessons:* Private, Group. *Program Affiliation:* USFSA, ISIA. *Summer School:* National/International. *Services:* Pro Shop, Skate Rental, Skate Sharpening, Ballet Room, Weight Room, Lockers, Dressing Rooms.

IL: ILLINOIS

All Seasons Twin Ice Rinks
31 W. 330 N. Aurora Rd.
Naperville IL 60563
(708) 851-0755
Mgr: Heather Eberle
Skating Dir: Jeff Gruber
Ice surfaces: 2, 175x80; 200x85, Enclosed. *Open:* Sept.-June. *Ownership:* Private. *Access:* Public. *Sessions:* Public, Private/Club, Rental, Freestyle, Patch, Dance, Hockey. *Classes/Lessons:* Private, Group. *Program Affiliation:* ISIA. *Summer School:* No. *Services:* Pro Shop, Skate Rental, Skate Sharpening, Snack Bar, Ballet Room, Lockers. *Notes:* Indoor rollerblading and floor hockey.

Barrington Ice Arena
Commercial & Pepper Rd.
Barrington IL 60010
(708) 381-9702
Mgr: Geno Goss
Ice surfaces: 1, 185x85. *Open:* Sept.-June. *Ownership:* Municipal. *Access:* Members Only. *Clubs:* Barrington Area FSC. *Sessions:* Private/Club, Rental, Freestyle, Hockey, Patch. *Classes/Lessons:* Private, Group. *Program Affiliation:* ISIA. *Summer School:* No. *Services:* Pro Shop, Skate Rental, Skate Sharpening, Snack Bar, Lockers, Dressing Rooms. *Notes:* Precision team; ice bought 6-9 weeks at a time.

Centennial Ice Arena
3100 Trailway
Highland Park IL 60035
(708) 432-4790
FAX: (708) 831-0818
Mgr: David Harris
Ice surfaces: 1, Enclosed. *Open:* Aug.-May. *Ownership:* Municipal. *Access:* Public. *Clubs:* Highland Park FSC. *Sessions:* Public, Private/Club, Rental, Freestyle, Patch, Dance, Hockey. *Classes/Lessons:* Group, Private. *Program Affiliation:* ISIA. *Services:* Pro Shop, Skate Rental, Skate Sharpening, Lockers, Dressing Rooms, Snack Bar. *Notes:* Vending machine; gymnastics room.

Centennial Ice Rink
2300 Old Glenview Rd.
Wilmette IL 60091
(708) 256-6100
FAX: (708) 256-8776
Mgr: Terry Juliar
Skating Dir: Doddie Bova
Ice surfaces: 2, 200x85; 100x60, Enclosed. *Open:* Year Round. *Ownership:* Municipal. *Access:* Public. *Sessions:* Public, Rental, Freestyle, Patch, Hockey. *Classes/Lessons:* Group, Private. *Program Affiliation:* ISIA. *Services:* Pro Shop, Skate Rental, Skate Sharpening, Studio Rink, Snack Bar. *Notes:* Multi-purpose/party room.

Center Ice of Du Page
1 N. 450 Highland Ave.
Glen Ellyn IL 60137
(708) 790-9696
FAX: (708) 790-9695
Mgr: Ed Nickey
Ice surfaces: 2, 200x100; 200x80, Enclosed. *Open:* Year Round. *Ownership:* Private. *Access:* Public. *Sessions:* Public, Private/Club, Rental, Freestyle, Patch, Dance, Hockey. *Classes/Lessons:* Group, Private. *Program Affiliation:* USFSA, ISIA. *Services:* Pro Shop, Skate Rental, Skate Sharpening, Snack Bar, Ballet Room, Lockers, Dressing Rooms.

Crown (Robert) Ice Center
1701 Main St.
Evanston IL 60202
(708) 328-9401
Mgr: Bob Dornekor
Skating Dir: Sandra Cole
Ice surfaces: 2, 200x85; 90x65, Enclosed. *Open:* Year Round. *Ownership:* Municipal. *Access:* Public. *Clubs:* Evanston FSC. *Sessions:* Public, Rental, Freestyle, Patch, Dance, Hockey. *Classes/Lessons:* Group, Private. *Program Affiliation:* ISIA. *Services:* Skate Rental, Skate Sharpening, Studio Rink, Snack Bar, Ballet Room, Lockers, Dressing Rooms.

Crystal Ice House
320 E. Prairie St.
Crystal Lake IL 60012
(815) 356-8500
Mgr: Jeff Johnson
Skating Dir: Kim Sell
Ice surfaces: 1, 200x85, Enclosed. *Open:* Year Round. *Ownership:* Private. *Access:* Public. *Sessions:* Public, Private/Club, Rental, Freestyle, Patch, Dance, Hockey. *Classes/Lessons:* Group. *Program Affiliation:* ISIA. *Summer School:* Local. *Services:* Pro Shop, Skate Rental, Skate Sharpening, Snack Bar, Dressing Rooms.

Decatur Civic Center
1 Gary Anderson Plaza
Decatur IL 62525
(217) 422-7300
FAX: (217) 422-3220
Mgr: Ann Brunson
Ice surfaces: 1, 200x85, Enclosed. *Open:* Oct.-Mar. *Ownership:* Civic Center. *Access:* Public. *Clubs:* Decatur Youth Hockey Assn. *Sessions:* Public, Private/Club, Rental, Hockey. *Classes/Lessons:* Group. *Program Affiliation:* Own. *Summer School:* No. *Services:* Pro Shop, Skate Rental, Skate Sharpening, Snack Bar, Lockers, Dressing Rooms.

Downers Grove Ice Arena
5501 Walnut Ave.
Downers Grove IL 60515
(708) 971-3780
FAX: (708) 971-3786
Mgr: Jack Markert
Skating Dir: Barbara Wavra
Ice surfaces: 1, 200x85, Enclosed. *Open:* Year Round. *Ownership:* Private. *Access:* Public. *Sessions:* Public, Rental, Freestyle, Patch. *Classes/Lessons:* Group, Private. *Program Affiliation:* USFSA, ISIA. *Services:* Pro Shop, Skate Rental, Skate Sharpening, Snack Bar, Ballet Room.

Franklin Park Ice Arena
9711 Waveland Ave.
Franklin Park IL 60131
(708) 671-4268
Mgr: Sara Bolan
Skating Dir: Anita Healy
Ice surfaces: 2, 200x85; 80x60. *Open:* Sept.-Aug. *Ownership:* Municipal. *Access:* Public. *Sessions:* Public, Rental, Freestyle, Patch, Hockey. *Classes/Lessons:* Group, Private. *Program Affiliation:* ISIA. *Services:* Pro Shop, Skate Rental, Skate Sharpening, Studio Rink, Snack Bar, Ballet Room, Lockers, Dressing Rooms. *Notes:* Party room.

Glen Ellyn Ice Skating School
19 N. Park Blvd.
Glen Ellyn IL 60137
(708) 469-5770
Mgr: Ron Schlabach
Ice surfaces: 1, 80x40, Enclosed. *Open:* Sept.-May. *Ownership:* Private. *Access:* Public. *Sessions:* Dance. *Services:* Pro Shop, Studio Rink. *Notes:* Vending machines.

Glenview Ice Arena
1851 Landwehr Rd.
Glenview IL 60025
(708) 724-2800
FAX: (708) 657-0510
Mgr: Jim Weides
Ice surfaces: 2, 200x85; 90x60, Enclosed. *Open:* Year Round. *Ownership:* Municipal. *Access:* Public. *Clubs:* Chicago FSC, Glenview Stars Hockey. *Sessions:* Public, Private/Club, Rental, Freestyle, Patch, Dance, Hockey. *Classes/Lessons:* Group, Private. *Program Affiliation:* ISIA. *Services:* Pro Shop, Skate Rental, Skate Sharpening, Studio Rink, Snack Bar, Lockers, Dressing Rooms. *Notes:* Multi-purpose room; dance offered in the summer only.

Granite City Park Ice Rink
2900 Benton St.
Granite City IL 62040
(618) 877-2549
Mgr: Steve Chosich
Ice surfaces: 1, 200x85, Outdoor/Semi Outdoor. *Open:* Oct.-Mar. *Ownership:* Municipal. *Access:* Public. *Clubs:* Granite City HS; Granite City Amateur Hockey Assn., Madison City Hockey Club. *Sessions:* Public, Private/Club, Rental, Freestyle, Hockey. *Classes/Lessons:* Group, Private. *Program Affiliation:* ISIA. *Summer School:* No. *Services:* Skate Sharpening, Skate Rental, Snack Bar, Pool and/or Athletic Facilities, Lockers, Dressing Rooms. *Notes:* Will soon offer patch sessions.

Homewood Flossmoor Ice Arena
777 Kedzie Ave.
Homewood IL 60430
(708) 957-0100
Ice surfaces: 2, 200 x 85; 100 x 40, Enclosed. *Ownership:* Municipal. *Access:* Public. *Clubs:* Glenwood FSC. *Sessions:* Public, Private/Club, Rental, Freestyle, Patch, Hockey. *Classes/Lessons:* Group, Private. *Program Affiliation:* ISIA. *Services:* Pro Shop, Skate Rental, Skate Sharpening, Snack Bar, Lockers, Dressing Rooms.

Iceland
8435 Ballard Rd.
Niles IL 60648
(708) 297-8011
FAX: (708) 824-3415
Mgr: Joe Modrich
Skating Dir: Tom Hickey
Ice surfaces: 1, 185x85, Enclosed. *Open:* Year Round. *Ownership:* Municipal. *Access:* Public. *Clubs:* DuPage FSC, Spin FSC. *Sessions:* Public, Private/Club, Rental, Freestyle, Patch, Dance, Hockey. *Classes/Lessons:* Group, Private. *Program Affiliation:* ISIA. *Services:* Pro

Shop, Skate Rental, Skate Sharpening, Snack Bar, Ballet Room, Pool and/or Athletic Facilities, Lockers, Dressing Rooms.

Inwood Ice Arena
3000 W. Jefferson
Joliet IL 60435
(815) 741-7275
FAX: (815) 741-7280
Mgr: Amy Milewski
Ice surfaces: 1, 200x85, Enclosed. *Open:* Year Round. *Ownership:* Municipal. *Access:* Public. *Sessions:* Public, Rental, Freestyle, Patch, Dance, Hockey. *Classes/Lessons:* Group, Private. *Program Affiliation:* USFSA. *Summer School:* Regional. *Services:* Pro Shop, Skate Rental, Skate Sharpening, Snack Bar, Ballet Room, Lockers, Dressing Rooms. *Notes:* McDonald's in rink; fitness studio and tumbling room.

MacKenzie Ice Arena
Lake Forest Academy, 1800 Kennedy Rd.
Lake Forest IL 60045
(708) 234-3210
Mgr: Dubb Ansburg
Ice surfaces: 1, 200x100, Enclosed. *Open:* Aug.-May. *Ownership:* Private. *Access:* Restricted. *Restrictions:* Students & rentals. *Sessions:* Hockey. *Classes/Lessons:* None. *Program Affiliation:* Own. *Summer School:* No. *Services:* Skate Sharpening, Snack Bar, Dressing Rooms. *Notes:* Primarily a hockey rink.

McFetridge Sports Center
3843 N. California Ave.
Chicago IL 60618
(312) 478-0210
FAX: (312) 267-8525
Mgr: Bill Schultz
Ice surfaces: 1, 200x85, Enclosed. *Open:* Year Round. *Ownership:* Municipal. *Access:* Public. *Clubs:* Windy City FSC. *Sessions:* Public, Rental, Freestyle, Patch, Dance, Hockey. *Classes/Lessons:* Group, Private. *Program Affiliation:* ISIA. *Services:* Pro Shop, Skate Rental, Skate Sharpening, Snack Bar, Weight Room, Lockers, Dressing Rooms.

Memorial Arena - Pekin Park District
1701 Court St.
Pekin IL 61554
(309) 346-1240
FAX: (309) 353-1787
Mgr: Pete Zanos
Ice surfaces: 1, 200x85, Enclosed. *Open:* Oct.-Mar. *Ownership:* Municipal. *Access:* Public. *Sessions:* Public, Private/Club, Rental, Freestyle, Patch, Hockey. *Classes/Lessons:* Group, Private. *Program Affiliation:* ISIA. *Services:* Skate Rental, Skate Sharpening, Snack Bar, Lockers, Dressing Rooms. *Notes:* Connected to full gym with tennis, weights, and whirlpools.

Nelson (Franklin) Center
Springfield Park District: Lincoln Park
1601 N. 5th
Springfield IL 62702
(217) 753-2800
FAX: (217) 525-0053
Mgr: Gene Hayes
Skating Dir: Julie Alexander
Ice surfaces: 1, 200x85, Enclosed. *Open:* Year Round. *Ownership:* Springfield Park District. *Access:* Public. *Clubs:* Springfield Youth Hockey Assn.; Springfield FSC. *Sessions:* Public, Private/Club, Rental, Freestyle, Patch, Dance, Hockey. *Classes/Lessons:* Group, Private. *Program Affiliation:* ISIA. *Summer School:* No. *Services:* Skate Rental, Skate Sharpening, Snack Bar, Pool and/or Athletic Facilities, Lockers, Dressing Rooms, Pro Shop. *Notes:* Observation & all-purpose room.

Northbrook Sports Center
1730 Pfingsten Rd.
Northbrook IL 60062
(708) 291-2980
Mgr: Spiro Giotis
Skating Dir: Mary Pat Stoll
Ice surfaces: 2, 200x85; 185x85, Enclosed. *Open:* Year Round. *Ownership:* Municipal. *Access:* Public. *Clubs:* Chicago FSC, DuPage FSC. *Sessions:* Public, Private/Club, Rental, Freestyle, Patch, Hockey. *Classes/Lessons:* Group, Private. *Program Affiliation:* ISIA. *Services:* Pro Shop, Skate Rental, Skate Sharpening, Snack Bar, Ballet Room, Pool and/or Athletic Facilities, Lockers, Dressing Rooms. *Notes:* Community room; dance offered through clubs only.

Oaklawn Ice Arena
9400 S. Kenton
Oaklawn IL 60453
(708) 857-2210
FAX: (708) 636-9877
Mgr: Mike Burnard
Ice surfaces: 1, 170x73, Enclosed. *Open:* Sept.-May. *Ownership:* Municipal. *Access:* Public. *Sessions:* Public, Rental, Freestyle, Patch, Hockey, Precision. *Classes/Lessons:* Group, Private. *Program Affiliation:* ISIA. *Services:* Skate Rental, Skate Sharpening, Snack Bar, Lockers, Dressing Rooms. *Notes:* Olympic size rink to be completed in May 1995.

Oakton Ice Arena
2800 W. Oakton
Park Ridge IL 60068
(708) 692-3359
Mgr: Matt Horbas
Ice surfaces: 1, 200x85, Enclosed. *Open:* Sept.-Apr. *Ownership:* Municipal. *Access:* Public. *Sessions:* Public, Rental, Freestyle, Patch, Hockey. *Classes/Lessons:* Group, Private. *Program Affiliation:* ISIA. *Services:* Pro Shop, Skate Rental, Skate Sharpening, Lockers, Dressing Rooms.

Owens Recreation Center
1019 West Lake Ave.
Peoria IL 61614
(309) 686-3368
Mgr: Bob Jones
Ice surfaces: 2, 200 x 85; 200 x 85, Enclosed. *Open:* Year Round. *Ownership:* Municipal. *Access:* Public. *Clubs:* IL Valley FSC, Peoria Youth Hockey Assn. *Sessions:* Public, Private/Club, Rental, Freestyle, Patch, Dance, Hockey. *Classes/Lessons:* Group, Private. *Program Affiliation:* USFSA, ISIA. *Services:* Pro Shop, Skate Rental, Skate Sharpening, Snack Bar, Lockers, Dressing Rooms. *Notes:* Recreation room.

Palmer (David S.) Civic Center
100 W. Main St.
Danville IL 61832
(217) 431-2424
FAX: (217) 431-6444
Mgr: Tracy Jones
Ice surfaces: 1, 200x85, Enclosed. *Open:* Aug.-Apr. *Ownership:* Municipal. *Sessions:* Public, Private/Club, Rental, Hockey. *Classes/Lessons:* Group.

Program Affiliation: USFSA. *Summer School:* No. *Services:* Pro Shop, Skate Rental, Skate Sharpening, Snack Bar, Lockers, Dressing Rooms.

Polar Dome Ice Arena
601 Dundee Ave.
East Dundee IL 60118
(708) 426-6753
FAX: (708) 426-8163
Mgr: Don Holliman
Skating Dir: Sue Holliman
Ice surfaces: 1, 200x85, Enclosed. *Open:* Sept.-Apr. *Ownership:* Private. *Access:* Public. *Sessions:* Public, Private/Club, Rental, Freestyle, Dance, Hockey. *Classes/Lessons:* Group, Private. *Program Affiliation:* ISIA. *Summer School:* No. *Services:* Pro Shop, Skate Rental, Skate Sharpening, Snack Bar, Lockers, Dressing Rooms. *Notes:* Meeting room; Alpine lounge with bar.

Ridgeland Common
415 Lake St.
Oak Park IL 60302
(708) 848-9661
Mgr: Mike Clark
Ice surfaces: 1, 180x65, Enclosed. *Open:* Sept.-Mar. *Ownership:* Municipal. *Access:* Public. *Clubs:* Silver Blades FSC. *Sessions:* Public, Private/Club, Rental, Freestyle, Patch, Hockey. *Classes/Lessons:* Group, Private. *Program Affiliation:* ISIA. *Services:* Skate Rental, Skate Sharpening, Snack Bar. *Notes:* Multi-purpose room.

Riverview Ice House
324 N. Madison
Rockford IL 61107
(815) 963-7465
FAX: (815) 987-1597
Mgr: John Haled
Ice surfaces: 2, 200x85; 100x60, Enclosed. *Open:* Year Round. *Ownership:* Municipal. *Access:* Public. *Clubs:* FSC of Rockford; Rockford Hockey Club; Riverview Ice Angels; precision teams. *Sessions:* Public, Private/Club, Rental, Freestyle, Patch, Dance, Hockey, Broomball. *Classes/Lessons:* Group. *Program Affiliation:* Own. *Summer School:* National/International. *Services:* Pro Shop, Skate Rental, Skate Sharpening, Studio Rink, Snack Bar, Lockers, Dressing Rooms. *Notes:* Lobby with fireplace & view of river; multi-purpose room with ballet floor.

Rolling Meadows Ice Arena
3900 Owl Dr.
Rolling Meadows IL 60008
(708) 818-3210
FAX: (708) 818-3224
Mgr: Tim Mueller
Skating Dir: Carol Gohde
Ice surfaces: 1, 185x85, Enclosed. *Open:* Year Round. *Ownership:* Municipal. *Access:* Public. *Clubs:* Wagon Wheel FSC. *Sessions:* Public, Rental, Freestyle, Patch, Hockey. *Classes/Lessons:* Group, Private. *Program Affiliation:* ISIA. *Services:* Pro Shop, Skate Rental, Skate Sharpening, Snack Bar, Weight Room, Lockers, Dressing Rooms. *Notes:* Ballet room half-block away.

Saints Spectrum
9645 S. 76th Ave.
Bridgeview IL 60455
(708) 598-3738
Mgr: Willie Watson
Ice surfaces: 1, 200x85, Enclosed. *Open:* Year Round. *Ownership:* Private. *Access:* Public. *Clubs:* St. Rita High Hockey; Chicago Hawks. *Sessions:* Public, Private/Club, Rental, Freestyle, Patch, Dance, Hockey. *Classes/Lessons:* Group. *Program Affiliation:* Own. *Summer School:* Local. *Services:* Pro Shop, Skate Rental, Skate Sharpening, Snack Bar, Lockers.

Seven Bridges Ice Arena
6690 South Rt. 53
Woodridge IL 60517
(708) 271-4423
Mgr: Carl Sutton
Skating Dir: Jill Devadik
Ice surfaces: 3, 200x100; 200x85; 165x70, Enclosed. *Open:* Year Round. *Ownership:* Private. *Access:* Public. *Clubs:* Team Illinois. *Sessions:* Public, Private/Club, Rental, Freestyle, Patch, Dance, Hockey. *Classes/Lessons:* Group, Private. *Program Affiliation:* USFSA, ISIA. *Summer School:* Regional. *Services:* Pro Shop, Skate Rental, Skate Sharpening, Snack Bar, Ballet Room, Pool and/or Athletic Facilities, Weight Room, Lockers, Dressing Rooms. *Notes:* Aerobics area.

Skatium
9300 N. Bronx
Skokie IL 60077
(708) 674-1510
Mgr: Frank Gallagher
Ice surfaces: 1, 200x85, Enclosed. *Open:* Year Round. *Ownership:* Municipal. *Access:* Public. *Clubs:* Chicago FSC. *Sessions:* Public, Private/Club, Dance, Rental. *Classes/Lessons:* Group, Private. *Program Affiliation:* ISIA. *Services:* Pro Shop, Skate Rental, Studio Rink, Snack Bar, Weight Room, Pool and/or Athletic Facilities, Lockers, Dressing Rooms. *Notes:* Indoor track; dance offered through club only.

Southwest Ice Arena
5505 W. 127th St.
Crestwood IL 60445
(708) 371-1344
Mgr: Bob Nylen
Ice surfaces: 2, 200x85; 80x40, Enclosed. *Open:* Year Round. *Ownership:* Private. *Access:* Public. *Clubs:* Southwest Ice Arena FSC. *Sessions:* Public, Private/Club, Rental, Freestyle, Patch, Dance, Hockey. *Classes/Lessons:* Group, Private. *Program Affiliation:* ISIA. *Services:* Pro Shop, Skate Rental, Skate Sharpening, Studio Rink, Snack Bar, Lockers, Dressing Rooms. *Notes:* Dance offered in summer only.

Stream (Carol) Ice Rink
540 E. Gundersen Dr.
Carol Stream IL 60188
(708) 682-4480
FAX: (708) 682-4483
Mgr: Barbara Giblin
Ice surfaces: 1, 200x85, Enclosed. *Open:* Year Round. *Ownership:* Private. *Access:* Public. *Sessions:* Public, Private/Club, Rental, Freestyle, Patch, Hockey. *Classes/Lessons:* Group, Private. *Program Affiliation:* USFSA, ISIA. *Services:* Pro Shop, Skate Rental, Skate Sharpening, Snack Bar, Dressing Rooms.

University of IL at Chicago Auxiliary Practice Ice Rink
839 W. Roosevelt Road
Chicago IL 60608
(312) 413-5300
Mgr: Sal Guerrero
Ice surfaces: 1, 200x85, Enclosed. *Open:* Aug.-May. *Ownership:* Municipal. *Access:* Public. *Clubs:* Chicago Senior

Hockey League; Hockey North America. *College/Univ:* University of Illinois at Chicago. *Sessions:* Public, Rental, Private/Club. *Classes/Lessons:* Group, Private. *Program Affiliation:* ISIA. *Summer School:* No. *Services:* Skate Rental, Skate Sharpening, Lockers. *Notes:* Classes and lessons are for UIC students only.

University of Illinois Arena
406 E. Armory Dr.
Champaign IL 61820
(217) 333-2212
FAX: (217) 244-4004
Mgr: Robyn Deterding
Ice surfaces: 1, 200x115, Enclosed. *Open:* Sept.-July. *Ownership:* Private. *Access:* Public. *Clubs:* Illinois FSC. *College/Univ:* University of Illinois. *Sessions:* Public, Private/Club, Rental, Freestyle, Patch, Dance, Hockey. *Classes/Lessons:* Group, Private. *Program Affiliation:* ISIA. *Summer School:* Local. *Services:* Skate Rental, Skate Sharpening, Snack Bar, Lockers, Dressing Rooms, Pool and/or Athletic Facilities. *Notes:* Freestyle, patch, and dance sessions as well as summer school programs are offered through club only.

Watts Ice Center - Glencoe Park District
999 Green Bay Rd.
Glencoe IL 60022
(708) 835-4440
FAX: (708) 835-4942
Mgr: Will Jones
Skating Dir: Ellen Kleidon
Ice surfaces: 2, Outdoor/Semi Outdoor. *Open:* Dec-Mar. *Ownership:* Municipal. *Access:* Public. *Sessions:* Public, Private/Club, Rental, Freestyle, Patch, Hockey. *Classes/Lessons:* Group, Private. *Program Affiliation:* ISIA. *Services:* Skate Rental, Skate Sharpening, Studio Rink, Snack Bar, Lockers, Dressing Rooms. *Notes:* Recreation room with fireplace.

Winnetka Ice Arena
490 Hibbard Rd.
Winnetka IL 60093
(708) 501-2060
Mgr: Tom Gullen
Skating Dir: Angie Sopranos
Ice surfaces: 1, 200x85, Enclosed. *Open:* Sept.-June. *Ownership:* Municipal.

Access: Public. *Clubs:* Skokie Valley FSC. *Sessions:* Public, Private/Club, Rental, Freestyle, Patch, Dance, Hockey. *Classes/Lessons:* Group, Private. *Program Affiliation:* ISIA. *Services:* Skate Rental, Skate Sharpening, Snack Bar, Dressing Rooms.

Winter Club of Lake Forest
956 N. Sheridan Rd.
Lake Forest IL 60045
(708) 234-0030
Mgr: Mike Romito
Ice surfaces: 2, 185x85; 116x55, Outdoor/Semi Outdoor. *Open:* Nov.-Mar. *Ownership:* Private. *Access:* Members Only. *Clubs:* Winter Club. *Sessions:* Private/Club, Freestyle, Hockey. *Classes/Lessons:* Private, Group. *Program Affiliation:* ISIA. *Summer School:* No. *Services:* Pro Shop, Skate Sharpening, Snack Bar, Ballet Room, Pool and/or Athletic Facilities, Dressing Rooms, Lockers. *Notes:* General skating free with membership.

Zion Ice Arena
2400 Dowie Memorial Dr.
Zion IL 60099
(708) 746-5503
FAX: (708) 746-5506
Mgr: Larry Myers
Skating Dir: Denise Myers
Ice surfaces: 2, 200x85; 100x85, Enclosed. *Open:* Year Round. *Ownership:* Municipal. *Access:* Public. *Clubs:* Southport SC. *Sessions:* Public, Rental, Freestyle, Patch, Hockey. *Classes/Lessons:* Group, Private. *Program Affiliation:* ISIA. *Services:* Pro Shop, Skate Rental, Skate Sharpening, Studio Rink, Snack Bar, Ballet Room, Lockers, Dressing Rooms, Pool and/or Athletic Facilities. *Notes:* Gym.

IN: INDIANA

Allen County War Memorial Coliseum
4000 Parnell Ave.
Fort Wayne IN 46805
(219) 482-9502
FAX: (219) 484-1637
Mgr: Randy Brown
Ice surfaces: 1, 200x85, Enclosed. *Open:* Sept.-May. *Ownership:* Municipal. *Access:* Public. *Clubs:* Komets Hockey Team. *Sessions:* Private/Club, Rental,

Hockey. *Classes/Lessons:* Group, Private. *Program Affiliation:* USFSA. *Summer School:* No. *Services:* Skate Rental, Snack Bar, Lockers, Dressing Rooms.

Carmel Ice Skatium
1040 3rd Ave. SW
Carmel IN 46032
(317) 844-8889
Mgr: Whitey Guenin
Ice surfaces: 2, 200x90; 200x90, Enclosed. *Open:* Year Round. *Ownership:* Private. *Access:* Public. *Clubs:* Indianapolis Ice Skating Club. *Sessions:* Public, Private/Club, Rental, Freestyle, Patch, Dance, Hockey. *Classes/Lessons:* Group, Private. *Program Affiliation:* USFSA, ISIA. *Summer School:* Regional. *Services:* Skate Rental, Pro Shop, Skate Sharpening, Snack Bar, Dressing Rooms, Lockers. *Notes:* Freestyle, patch, and dance sessions done through the club.

Howard Park Ice Rink
219 S. Saint Louis
South Bend IN 46617
(219) 235-9451
Mgr: Melanie Trowbridge
Ice surfaces: 1, 200x85, Outdoor/Semi Outdoor. *Open:* Nov.-Mar. *Ownership:* Municipal. *Access:* Public. *Sessions:* Public, Rental, Hockey. *Classes/Lessons:* Group. *Program Affiliation:* Own. *Summer School:* No. *Services:* Skate Rental, Skate Sharpening, Snack Bar.

Ice Box
1421 S. Walnut St.
South Bend IN 46619
(219) 288-3300
Ice surfaces: 2, 200x85, Enclosed. *Open:* Year Round. *Ownership:* Private. *Access:* Public. *Sessions:* Public, Rental, Freestyle, Patch, Dance, Hockey. *Classes/Lessons:* Group, Private. *Program Affiliation:* Own. *Summer School:* No. *Services:* Pro Shop, Skate Rental, Studio Rink, Skate Sharpening, Snack Bar, Weight Room, Lockers, Dressing Rooms.

Ice Rink on the Terrace
4201 Coldwater Rd.
Ft. Wayne IN 46805
(219) 484-2014
Mgr: Karol Daron
Ice surfaces: 1, 100x50, Enclosed. *Open:* Year Round. *Ownership:* Private. *Access:*

Public. *Sessions:* Public, Rental, Freestyle, Patch, Dance. *Classes/Lessons:* Group, Private. *Program Affiliation:* ISIA. *Services:* Pro Shop, Skate Rental, Skate Sharpening, Snack Bar, Lockers. *Notes:* Located in a mall. No walk-on for freestyle, patch or dance.

Indiana State Fair Coliseum
1202 E. 38th St.
Indianapolis IN 46205
(317) 927-7622
FAX: (317) 927-7695
Mgr: Dave Hummel
Skating Dir: Sandy Lamb
Ice surfaces: 1, 200x90, Enclosed. *Open:* Oct.-Mar. *Ownership:* Municipal. *Access:* Public. *Clubs:* The Winter Club of Indianapolis. *Sessions:* Public, Hockey, Private/Club, Rental. *Classes/Lessons:* Group, Private. *Program Affiliation:* ISIA, USFSA. *Summer School:* No. *Services:* Pro Shop, Skate Rental, Skate Sharpening, Snack Bar, Dressing Rooms. *Notes:* Weight room for pro hockey team. Freestyle, patch and dance sessions are offered through the club only.

Indiana World Skating Academy
201 S. Capitol Ave. Suite 001,
PanAmerica Plaza
Indianapolis IN 40625
(317) 237-5565
Mgr: Jim Rowley
Skating Dir: Pieter Kollen
Ice surfaces: 2, 200x85; 200x100, Enclosed. *Open:* Year Round. *Ownership:* Private. *Access:* Public. *Clubs:* Indiana WSA FSC, Indianapolis Jr. Ice (NHJAL). *Sessions:* Public, Freestyle, Patch, Dance, Hockey. *Classes/Lessons:* Group, Private. *Program Affiliation:* ISIA. *Summer School:* National/International. *Services:* Pro Shop, Snack Bar, Skate Sharpening, Ballet Room, Weight Room, Lockers, Dressing Rooms, Skate Rental.

Indianapolis Pepsi Coliseum
1202 E. 38th St.
Indianapolis IN 46205
(317) 927-7536
Mgr: David Hummel
Skating Dir: Sandy Lamb
Ice surfaces: 1, 200x85, Enclosed. *Open:* Oct.1-March 30. *Ownership:* Municipal. *Access:* Public. *Clubs:* Winter Club of Indianapolis; Butler Hockey. *Sessions:* Public, Private/Club, Rental, Freestyle, Hockey. *Classes/Lessons:* Group, Private. *Program Affiliation:* USFSA, ISIA. *Summer School:* No. *Services:* Pro Shop, Skate Rental, Skate Sharpening, Snack Bar, Weight Room, Lockers, Dressing Rooms. *Notes:* A second rink is planned.

Lincoln Center Ice Arena
25th St. & Lincoln Park Dr.
Columbus IN 47201
(812) 376-2686
Mgr: Geary Baxter
Skating Dir: Elizabeth Fernandez
Ice surfaces: 2, 200x85; 72x54, Enclosed. *Open:* June-Apr. *Ownership:* Municipal. *Access:* Public. *Clubs:* Lincoln Center FSC. *Sessions:* Public, Rental, Freestyle, Patch, Dance, Hockey, Private/Club. *Classes/Lessons:* Group, Private. *Program Affiliation:* USFSA, ISIA. *Summer School:* Regional. *Services:* Pro Shop, Skate Rental, Skate Sharpening, Studio Rink, Snack Bar, Lockers, Dressing Rooms.

McMillen Ice Arena
3901 Abbott St.
Ft. Wayne IN 46806
(219) 744-0848
Mgr: Mizi Toefer
Ice surfaces: 2, 160x65; 65x40, Enclosed. *Open:* Aug.-May. *Ownership:* Municipal. *Access:* Public. *Clubs:* Ft. Wayne ISC; USA Hockey Groups. *Sessions:* Public, Private/Club, Rental, Hockey. *Classes/Lessons:* Private. *Program Affiliation:* USFSA. *Services:* Pro Shop, Skate Rental, Skate Sharpening, Studio Rink, Snack Bar, Dressing Rooms.

Merrifield Complex
1000 E. Mishawaka
Mishawaka IN 46545
(219) 258-1664
FAX: (219) 258-1736
Mgr: Peter Schmidt
Ice surfaces: 1, 205x85, Outdoor/Semi Outdoor. *Open:* Nov.-Mar. *Ownership:* Municipal. *Access:* Public. *Clubs:* Irish Youth Hockey League. *Sessions:* Public, Private/Club, Rental, Freestyle, Dance, Hockey. *Classes/Lessons:* Group, Private. *Program Affiliation:* Own. *Summer School:* No. *Services:* Skate Sharpening, Skate Rental, Pool and/or Athletic Facilities, Dressing Rooms, Lockers, Snack Bar.

Notre Dame Ice Arena
Notre Dame ACC
Notre Dame IN 46556
(219) 631-5247
Mgr: Tom Nevala
Ice surfaces: 1, 200x85. *Open:* Sept.-Mar. *Ownership:* Private. *Access:* Public. *Clubs:* Michiana FSC. *College/Univ:* University of Notre Dame. *Sessions:* Public, Private/Club, Hockey. *Classes/Lessons:* None. *Program Affiliation:* Own. *Summer School:* No. *Services:* Pro Shop, Skate Rental, Skate Sharpening, Dressing Rooms. *Notes:* Club offers lessons.

Perry Park Ice Rink
451 E. Stop 11 Rd.
Indianapolis IN 46227
(317) 888-0070
Mgr: Jamie Richardson
Skating Dir: 200x75
Ice surfaces: 1, Enclosed. *Open:* Oct.-Apr. *Ownership:* Municipal. *Access:* Public. *Clubs:* Sycamore ISC. *Sessions:* Public, Private/Club, Rental, Freestyle, Patch, Dance, Hockey. *Classes/Lessons:* Group, Private. *Program Affiliation:* Own. *Summer School:* No. *Services:* Skate Rental, Skate Sharpening, Snack Bar.

Southern (Frank) Center Ice Arena
349 S. Walnut
Bloomington IN 47401
(812) 331-6465
FAX: (812) 331-6482
Mgr: John LeClaire
Ice surfaces: 1, 185x85, Enclosed. *Open:* Oct.- March. *Ownership:* Municipal. *Access:* Public. *Sessions:* Public, Private/Club, Rental, Freestyle, Patch, Dance, Hockey. *Classes/Lessons:* Group, Private. *Program Affiliation:* USFSA, ISIA. *Services:* Pro Shop, Skate Rental, Skate Sharpening, Snack Bar, Lockers, Dressing Rooms.

Swonder Ice Rink
201 N. Boeke Rd.
Evansville IN 47711
(812) 479-0989
Mgr: Ken Knight
Ice surfaces: 1, 200x85, Enclosed. *Open:*

Sept.-May. *Ownership:* Municipal. *Access:* Public. *Clubs:* Greater Evansville FSC, Evansville Youth Hockey League. *Sessions:* Public, Private/Club, Rental, Freestyle, Patch, Hockey. *Classes/ Lessons:* Group, Private. *Program Affiliation:* ISIA. *Services:* Pro Shop, Skate Rental, Skate Sharpening, Snack Bar, Lockers, Dressing Rooms. *Notes:* Community room.

KS: KANSAS

Ice Chateau of King Louie West
8788 Metcalf
Overland Park KS 66212
(913) 648-0130
FAX: (913) 648-1846
Mgr: Randy Brilliantine
Skating Dir: Kathy Lange
Ice surfaces: 1, 185x85, Enclosed. *Open:* Year Round. *Ownership:* Private. *Access:* Public. *Clubs:* Kansas City FSC, Silver Blades FSC. *Sessions:* Public, Private/ Club, Rental, Freestyle, Patch, Dance, Hockey. *Classes/Lessons:* Private, Group. *Program Affiliation:* ISIA. *Summer School:* National/International. *Services:* Pro Shop, Skate Rental, Skate Sharpening, Snack Bar, Ballet Room, Dressing Rooms, Lockers.

Kansas Coliseum
1229 E. 85 St. N.
Valley Center
Witchita KS 67147
(316) 755-1243
Mgr: Sam Sulco
Ice surfaces: 1, 200x85, Enclosed. *Open:* Nov.-Mar. *Ownership:* Municipal. *Access:* Restricted. *Restrictions:* FSC runs intermittently as does hockey assn. *Clubs:* Witchita FSC, Witchita Thunder Central Hockey League. *Sessions:* Public, Private/Club, Hockey. *Classes/ Lessons:* Private*Notes:* Coliseum primarily puts on shows; ice time is very limited; lessons offered though the FSC.

KY: KENTUCKY

All Seasons Ice Center
2638 Crescent Springs Rd.
Crescent Springs KY 41017
(606) 344-1981
FAX: (606) 341-7239
Mgr: Cliff Brown
Skating Dir: Stephanie Miller
Ice surfaces: 2, 200x85, Enclosed. *Open:* Year Round. *Ownership:* Private. *Access:* Public. *Clubs:* Queens City FSC. *Sessions:* Public, Patch, Dance, Hockey, Freestyle. *Classes/Lessons:* Group, Private. *Program Affiliation:* USFSA. *Summer School:* Local. *Services:* Snack Bar, Skate Sharpening, Studio Rink, Skate Rental, Pro Shop, Weight Room, Pool and/or Athletic Facilities, Lockers, Dressing Rooms. *Notes:* The racquetball room is used for ballet.

Alpine Ice Arena
1825 Gardiner Ln.
Louisville KY 40205
(502) 459-9500
FAX: (502) 583-2244
Mgr: Robert Farmer
Skating Dir: Lorene Caudill
Ice surfaces: 1, 200x85, Enclosed. *Open:* Sept.-Apr. *Ownership:* Private. *Access:* Public. *Sessions:* Public, Rental, Freestyle, Hockey. *Classes/Lessons:* Group, Private. *Program Affiliation:* ISIA. *Summer School:* No. *Services:* Pro Shop, Skate Sharpening, Skate Rental, Snack Bar, Lockers. *Notes:* Multi-purpose room used for parties and dressing.

Lexington Ice Arena
560 Eureka Springs Dr.
Lexington KY 40517
(606) 269-5681
Mgr: Dennis Hyde
Ice surfaces: 1, 185x85, Enclosed. *Open:* July-Apr. *Ownership:* Private. *Access:* Public. *Clubs:* Thoroughbred FS Team. *Sessions:* Public, Private/Club, Rental, Freestyle, Patch, Dance, Hockey. *Classes/Lessons:* Group, Private. *Program Affiliation:* ISIA. *Services:* Pro Shop, Skate Rental, Skate Sharpening, Snack Bar, Weight Room, Lockers, Dressing Rooms. *Notes:* Aerobic rooms; 3 gymnasiums; meeting rooms; youth hockey leagues.

Owensboro Ice Arena
1215 Parkview Dr.
Owensboro KY 42302
(502) 687-8720
Mgr: Hal Mitchell
Skating Dir: Jennifer Ayer
Ice surfaces: 1, 200x85, Enclosed. *Open:* Oct.-Mar. *Ownership:* Municipal. *Access:* Public. *Sessions:* Public, Private/Club, Rental, Hockey. *Classes/Lessons:* Private, Group. *Program Affiliation:* ISIA. *Services:* Pro Shop, Skate Rental, Skate Sharpening, Snack Bar, Lockers, Dressing Rooms. *Notes:* Freestyle and patch sessions offered through the skating club only.

LA: LOUISIANA

Riverside Centroplex
275 S. River Rd.
Baton Rouge LA 70802
(504) 389- 3030
FAX: (504) 389-4954
Mgr: Brian Broussard
Skating Dir: Susan Hernandez
Ice surfaces: 1, 200x85, Enclosed. *Open:* public skating in Dec. only; other months for ice shows. *Ownership:* Municipal. *Access:* Public. *Sessions:* Public, Private/ Club, Hockey, General. *Classes/Lessons:* None. *Services:* Snack Bar, Lockers, Dressing Rooms. *Notes:* Ice shows throughout the year.

MA: MASSACHUSETTS

Aleixo (Theodore) Skating Rink
1 Gordon Owen River Way
Taunton MA 02780
(508) 824-4987
Mgr: Chuck Ranahan
Ice surfaces: 1, 200x85, Enclosed. *Open:* Jul. - Apr. *Ownership:* Municipal. *Access:* Public. *Clubs:* SC of Southern New England; Taunton Brewins Hockey; Tri - County Saints. *College/Univ:* Wheaton College. *Sessions:* Public, Rental, Freestyle, Patch, Dance, Hockey. *Classes/Lessons:* Private, Group. *Program Affiliation:* ISIA, USFSA. *Summer School:* Local. *Services:* Skate Rental, Pro Shop, Skate Sharpening, Snack Bar, Lockers.

Anderson Park Skating Rink
25 Newton St.
Brookline MA 02146
(617) 730-2080
Mgr: Thomas Curtain
Ice surfaces: 2, 205x90; 125x25, Outdoor/Semi Outdoor. *Open:* Dec.-Mar. *Ownership:* Municipal. *Access:* Public. *Sessions:* Public, Rental, Freestyle, Hockey. *Classes/Lessons:* Group. *Program Affiliation:* USFSA. *Summer School:* No. *Services:* Pro Shop, Skate Rental, Skate Sharpening, Studio Rink,

Snack Bar, Pool and/or Athletic Facilities, Dressing Rooms, Lockers.

Armstrong (John) Memorial Skating Rink
103 Long Pond Rd.
Plymouth MA 02360
(800) 273-7776
Mgr: John Cashman
Ice surfaces: 1, 200x85, Enclosed. *Open:* June-Apr. *Ownership:* Private. *Access:* Public. *Clubs:* Pilgrim FSC, Plymouth High School Hockey. *Sessions:* Public, Private/Club, Rental, Freestyle, Patch, Dance, Hockey. *Classes/Lessons:* Group, Private. *Program Affiliation:* ISIA, USFSA. *Summer School:* Regional. *Services:* Pro Shop, Skate Rental, Skate Sharpening, Lockers, Dressing Rooms. *Notes:* Vending machines.

Asiaf Arena
Forrest Ave.
Brockton MA 02401
(508) 583-6804
Mgr: Paul Sorji
Ice surfaces: 1, 185x85, Enclosed. *Open:* Sept.-May. *Ownership:* Private. *Access:* Public. *Clubs:* Flag Pond SC. *Sessions:* Public, Private/Club, Rental, Hockey, Patch, Dance. *Classes/Lessons:* Group, Private. *Program Affiliation:* USFSA, ISIA. *Summer School:* No. *Services:* Pro Shop, Skate Rental, Skate Sharpening, Dressing Rooms, Lockers. *Notes:* Freestyle sessions are offered through the club only.

Babson Recreation Center
150 Great Plain Ave.
Wellesley MA 02181
(617) 239-6050
FAX: (617) 235-0672
Mgr: Joan Allen
Skating Dir: Nancy Judge
Ice surfaces: 1, 200x85, Enclosed. *Open:* Year Round. *Ownership:* Private. *Access:* Public. *College/Univ:* Babson College. *Sessions:* Public, Private/Club, Rental, Freestyle, Patch, Dance, Hockey. *Classes/Lessons:* Group, Private. *Program Affiliation:* ISIA. *Services:* Pro Shop, Skate Rental, Skate Sharpening, Snack Bar, Lockers. *Notes:* Complex with weight room; dance studio for members only.

Bajko (Alexander) Memorial Skating Rink
75 Turtle Pond Park
Hyde Park MA 02136
(617) 364-9188
Mgr: Anthony Abdal-Khabir
Ice surfaces: 2, 200x85; 185x85, Enclosed. *Open:* Sept.-Mar. *Ownership:* Municipal. *Access:* Public. *Sessions:* Public, Rental. *Classes/Lessons:* Group. *Program Affiliation:* Own. *Summer School:* No. *Services:* Studio Rink, Snack Bar, Lockers, Dressing Rooms.

Belmont Skating Rink
Concord Ave.
Belmont MA 02178
(617) 489-8245
Mgr: Skip Viglirolo
Skating Dir: Sue Riberio
Ice surfaces: 1, 200x85, Enclosed. *Open:* Oct.-Mar. *Ownership:* Municipal. *Access:* Restricted. *Restrictions:* Town residents. *Sessions:* Public, Rental, Patch, Hockey. *Classes/Lessons:* Group. *Program Affiliation:* USFSA. *Summer School:* No. *Services:* Snack Bar, Dressing Rooms, Lockers.

Berkshire School
245 N. Undermountain Rd.
Sheffield MA 01257
(413) 229-8511
FAX: (413) 229-3178
Mgr: Ed Hunt
Ice surfaces: 1, 185x85, Enclosed. *Open:* Nov.-Feb. *Ownership:* Berkshire School. *Access:* Members Only. Faculty and staff only. *Sessions:* Rental. *Classes/Lessons:* None. *Summer School:* No. *Services:* Lockers.

Boston College Ice Rink
Contee Forum
Chesnut Hill MA 02167
(617) 552-8000
Mgr: Norm Reed
Skating Dir: Mary Connors-Kelly
Ice surfaces: 1, 200x85, Enclosed. *Open:* Oct.-Mar. *Ownership:* Private. *Access:* Restricted. *Restrictions:* Students, faculty, members. *Sessions:* Hockey, General. *Classes/Lessons:* Group, Private. *Program Affiliation:* USFSA. *Summer School:* No. *Services:* Weight Room, Lockers. *Notes:* Restricted access to athletic facilities.

Bright Hockey Center
79 N. Harvard St.
Cambridge MA 02138
(617) 495-7541
Ice surfaces: 1, 204x87, Enclosed. *Open:* Oct.-Apr. *Ownership:* Private. *Access:* Restricted. *Restrictions:* Students and staff. *College/Univ:* Harvard University. *Sessions:* Freestyle, Patch, Dance. *Classes/Lessons:* None. *Summer School:* No.

Brooks School Rink
1160 Great Pond Rd.
North Andover MA 01845
(508) 686-6101
Mgr: Mary Manseau
Ice surfaces: 1, 200x85, Enclosed. *Open:* Aug.-Mar. *Ownership:* Private. *Access:* Restricted. *Restrictions:* School use. *Clubs:* North Andover FSC. *Sessions:* Private/Club, Rental, Freestyle, Patch, Dance, Hockey. *Classes/Lessons:* None. *Program Affiliation:* Own. *Summer School:* No. *Services:* Lockers, Dressing Rooms.

Brown (Walter) Arena
285 Babcock St.
Boston MA 02215
(617) 353-4632
FAX: (617) 353-6428
Mgr: Alan Weinberger
Ice surfaces: 1, 200x85, Enclosed. *Open:* Year Round. *Ownership:* Private. *Access:* Members Only. Students and staff. *College/Univ:* Boston University. *Sessions:* Private/Club, Rental. *Classes/Lessons:* None. *Program Affiliation:* Own. *Summer School:* No. *Services:* Skate Rental, Skate Sharpening, Lockers, Dressing Rooms.

Browne & Nichols Skating Rink
Browne & Nichols School
Gerry's Landing Rd.
Cambridge MA 02183
(617) 864-8668
Mgr: Jack Etter
Ice surfaces: 1, 200x85, Outdoor/Semi Outdoor. *Open:* Nov.-Mar. *Ownership:* Private. *Access:* Public. *Clubs:* Cambridge SC. *Sessions:* Public, Private/Club, Rental, Freestyle, Patch, Dance, Hockey. *Classes/Lessons:* Group, Private. *Program Affiliation:* Own. *Summer School:* No. *Services:* Weight Room, Pool and/or Athletic Facilities, Lockers. *Notes:*

Limited public sessions open to students and family.

Bryan Memorial Skating Rink
VFW Pky.
West Roxbury MA 02132
(617) 323-9512
Mgr: John Bourque
Ice surfaces: 1, 185x85, Enclosed. *Open:* Oct.-Mar. *Ownership:* Municipal. *Access:* Public. *Clubs:* Parkway Youth Hockey. *Sessions:* Public, Rental, Hockey. *Classes/Lessons:* Group. *Program Affiliation:* ISIA. *Summer School:* No. *Services:* Lockers, Dressing Rooms.

Burlington Ice Palace
36 Ray Ave.
Burlington MA 01803
(617) 272-9517
Mgr: Virginia Mungillo
Skating Dir: Dave Malta
Ice surfaces: 1, 200x85, Enclosed. *Open:* Year Round. *Ownership:* Municipal. *Clubs:* Winchester FSC, Burlington Hockey & Skating Assn. *Sessions:* Public, Rental, Freestyle, Patch, Hockey. *Classes/Lessons:* Private, Group. *Services:* Pro Shop, Skate Sharpening, Lockers, Dressing Rooms.

Canton Metropolis Skating Rink
2167 Washington St.
Canton MA 02021
(617) 821-5032
Mgr: Jeff Kaylor
Ice surfaces: 1, 185x85, Enclosed. *Open:* Sept.-Apr. *Ownership:* Municipal. *Access:* Public. *College/Univ:* Curry College. *Sessions:* Public, Rental, Hockey. *Classes/Lessons:* Group. *Program Affiliation:* ISIA. *Summer School:* No. *Services:* Pro Shop, Skate Sharpening, Snack Bar, Lockers, Dressing Rooms. *Notes:* Meeting room.

Clark Athletic Center Ice Rink
University of Massachusetts, 100 Morrissey Blvd.
Boston MA 02125-3393
(617) 287-7801
FAX: (617) 287-7840
Mgr: Jack Dowling
Ice surfaces: 1, 200x85, Enclosed. *Open:* Sept.-Mar. *Ownership:* Private. *Access:* Restricted. *Restrictions:* Staff; students. *College/Univ:* University of Massachusetts, University of Boston. *Sessions:* Hockey. *Summer School:* No. *Services:* Snack Bar, Weight Room, Pool and/or Athletic Facilities, Dressing Rooms, Lockers.

Clark Memorial Arena
155 Central
Winchendon MA 01475
(508) 297-0102
Mgr: Todd O'Dea
Ice surfaces: 1, 190x85, Enclosed. *Open:* Sept.-Mar. *Ownership:* Private. *Access:* Public. *Clubs:* Winchendon Youth Hockey; Winchendon FSC. *College/Univ:* Franklin Pierce College. *Sessions:* Public, Rental, Hockey. *Classes/Lessons:* Private, Group. *Program Affiliation:* USFSA. *Services:* Pro Shop, Skate Rental, Skate Sharpening, Snack Bar, Ballet Room, Weight Room, Pool and/or Athletic Facilities, Lockers, Dressing Rooms.

Collins Moylan Memorial Skating Rink
1 Barr Ave.
Greenfield MA 01301
(413) 772-6891
Mgr: Chip Ainsworth
Ice surfaces: 1, 200x85, Enclosed. *Open:* Oct.-Apr. *Ownership:* Private. *Access:* Public. *Clubs:* Greenfield Area FSC. *Sessions:* Public, Private/Club, Rental, Freestyle, Dance, Hockey. *Classes/Lessons:* Group, Private. *Program Affiliation:* USFSA. *Summer School:* No. *Services:* Pro Shop, Skate Rental, Skate Sharpening, Snack Bar, Lockers, Dressing Rooms.

Connell Memorial Rink
220 Broad St.
Weymouth MA 02189
(617) 335-2090
Mgr: James Kelly
Ice surfaces: 1, 185x85, Enclosed. *Open:* Oct.-Mar. *Ownership:* Municipal. *Access:* Public. *Clubs:* Youth Hockey. *Sessions:* Public, Rental, Hockey. *Services:* Skate Rental, Skate Sharpening, Snack Bar, Lockers, Dressing Rooms.

Connery (Lynn) Memorial Rink
Shepard St.
Lynn MA 01902
(617) 599-9474
Mgr: Ron Albia
Ice surfaces: 1, 200x85, Enclosed. *Open:* Nov.-Mar. *Ownership:* Municipal. *Access:* Public. *Clubs:* Lynn Youth Hockey Assn.; Bay State FSC. *Sessions:* Public, Rental, Hockey. *Classes/Lessons:* Group, Private. *Program Affiliation:* USFSA, ISIA. *Summer School:* No. *Services:* Lockers, Dressing Rooms. *Notes:* Vending machines.

Cronin Memorial Rink
850 Revere Beach Pkwy.
Revere MA 02151
(617) 284-9491
Mgr: Frank Badolato
Ice surfaces: 2, 185x85, Enclosed. *Open:* Nov.-Mar. *Ownership:* Municipal. *Access:* Public. *Clubs:* Baystate FSC, Metropolitan FSC, Revere Youth Hockey. *Sessions:* Public, Rental. *Classes/Lessons:* Group, Private. *Program Affiliation:* USFSA, ISIA. *Summer School:* No. *Services:* Skate Sharpening, Studio Rink, Snack Bar, Lockers, Dressing Rooms.

CYR Arena - Forest Park
200 Trafton Rd.
Springfield MA 01108
(413) 787-6438
Mgr: John Cirelli
Ice surfaces: 1, 200x85, Enclosed. *Open:* Sept.-Apr. *Ownership:* Municipal. *Access:* Public. *Clubs:* Youth Hockey. *Sessions:* Public, Rental, Hockey. *Classes/Lessons:* None. *Summer School:* No. *Services:* Skate Rental, Pro Shop, Skate Sharpening, Snack Bar, Lockers, Dressing Rooms.

Daly Memorial Rink
Nonanton Rd.
Brighton MA 02135
(617) 527-1741
Mgr: Luke Smith
Ice surfaces: 1, 200x85, Outdoor/Semi Outdoor. *Open:* Nov.-Mar,. *Ownership:* Municipal. *Access:* Public. *Clubs:* Bay State Ice Skating School. *Sessions:* Public, Rental, Hockey. *Classes/Lessons:* None. *Summer School:* No. *Services:* Skate Rental, Skate Sharpening, Snack Bar, Lockers.

Deerfield Academy Skating Rink
7 Albany Rd.
Deerfield MA 01342
(413) 772-0241
Mgr: James Lindsay
Ice surfaces: 1, 200x85, Enclosed. *Open:*

Nov.-Mar. *Ownership:* Private. *Access:* Restricted. *Restrictions:* Students & local community. *Sessions:* Public, Rental, Hockey. *Summer School:* No. *Services:* Skate Sharpening, Weight Room, Pool and/or Athletic Facilities, Lockers, Dressing Rooms.

Devine (Robert M.) Rink
Morissey Blvd.
Neponset MA 02122
(617) 436-4356
Mgr: Robert Mahoney
Ice surfaces: 1, 200x85, Enclosed. *Open:* Oct.-Mar. *Ownership:* Municipal. *Access:* Public. *Sessions:* Public, Private/Club, Rental, Freestyle, Hockey. *Classes/Lessons:* Group. *Program Affiliation:* ISIA. *Summer School:* No. *Services:* Pro Shop, Skate Rental, Skate Sharpening, Snack Bar, Lockers, Dressing Rooms.

Dexter Rink
20 Newton St.
Brookline MA 02146
(617) 524-9377
Mgr: Rick Saul
Ice surfaces: 1, 200x85, Enclosed. *Open:* Year Round. *Ownership:* Private. *Access:* Members Only. *Sessions:* Private/Club, Rental, Hockey. *Classes/Lessons:* None. *Summer School:* No. *Services:* Skate Sharpening, Lockers, Dressing Rooms.

Driscoll (Arthur R.) Memorial Skating Rink
272 Elsbree St.
Fall River MA 02720
(508) 679-3274
Mgr: Tom Olivera
Ice surfaces: 1, 200x85, Enclosed. *Open:* July-Apr. *Ownership:* Private, Municipal. *Access:* Public. *Clubs:* SC of Southern New England. *Sessions:* Public, Private/Club, Rental, Freestyle, Patch, Hockey. *Classes/Lessons:* Group, Private. *Summer School:* No. *Services:* Pro Shop, Skate Rental, Skate Sharpening, Snack Bar, Lockers, Dressing Rooms. *Notes:* Conference room.

Falmouth Ice Arena
Skating Lane
Falmouth MA 02540
(508) 548-7080
Mgr: Edward Chicoine
Ice surfaces: 1, 185x85, Enclosed. *Open:* July-Mar. *Ownership:* Club. *Access:* Public. *Clubs:* Falmouth FSC, Falmouth Youth Hockey League. *Sessions:* Public, Private/Club, Rental, Freestyle, Patch, Hockey. *Classes/Lessons:* Group, Private. *Summer School:* No. *Services:* Pro Shop, Skate Sharpening, Snack Bar, Lockers, Dressing Rooms.

Franklin Arena
919 Panther Way
Franklin MA 02038
(508) 541-7024
Mgr: Bruce Bertoni
Ice surfaces: 1, 200x85, Enclosed. *Open:* Year Round. *Access:* Public. *Clubs:* Symmetric FSC, Franklin Blades Skating School. *Sessions:* Public, Private/Club, Rental, Freestyle, Patch, Hockey. *Classes/Lessons:* Group, Private. *Program Affiliation:* USFSA, ISIA. *Services:* Pro Shop, Skate Rental, Skate Sharpening, Snack Bar, Lockers, Dressing Rooms.

Gallo (John B.) Ice Arena
231 Sandwich Rd.
Bourne MA 02532
(508) 759-8904
Mgr: James McMorrow
Skating Dir: Diane Woodside
Ice surfaces: 1, 200x85, Enclosed. *Open:* Year Round. *Access:* Public. Army Core of Engineers, Bourne Recreation Authourity. *Clubs:* Bourne Skating Club. *Sessions:* Public, Private/Club, Freestyle, Patch, Hockey. *Classes/Lessons:* Group, Private. *Program Affiliation:* USFSA, ISIA. *Summer School:* Local. *Services:* Pro Shop, Skate Rental, Skate Sharpening, Snack Bar, Lockers, Dressing Rooms. *Notes:* Freestyle, patch only in summer.

Gardner Ice Rink
St. Marks School
25 Marlborough Rd.
Southboro MA 01772
(508) 485-0050
Mgr: Bob Eddy
Ice surfaces: 1, 200x80, Enclosed. *Open:* Nov.-Feb. *Ownership:* Private. *Access:* Restricted. *Restrictions:* Rentals, school programs, faculty and staff. *Sessions:* Rental, Hockey. *Classes/Lessons:* None. *Summer School:* No. *Services:* Dressing Rooms.

Gardner Veterans Skating Rink
45 Veterans Dr.
Gardner MA 01440
(508) 632-7329
Mgr: Anthony Gould
Ice surfaces: 1, 185x85, Enclosed. *Open:* Sept.-Apr. *Ownership:* Municipal. *Access:* Public. *Sessions:* Public, Private/Club, Rental, Freestyle, Patch, Hockey. *Classes/Lessons:* Group, Private. *Program Affiliation:* USFSA. *Services:* Pro Shop, Skate Rental, Skate Sharpening, Snack Bar, Lockers, Dressing Rooms. *Notes:* Conference room. Dance offered through the club only.

Governor Dummer Academy Rink
1 Elm St.
Byfield MA 01922
(508) 462-6643
Mgr: Bob Anderson
Ice surfaces: 1, 200x85, Outdoor/Semi Outdoor. *Open:* Nov.-Feb. *Ownership:* Private. *Access:* Restricted. *Restrictions:* School use & rental. *Clubs:* Newbury Port Iceliners. *Sessions:* Rental. *Classes/Lessons:* Group. *Summer School:* No. *Services:* Lockers, Dressing Rooms.

Graf (Henry Jr.) Rink
28 Low St.
Newburyport MA 01950
(508) 462-8112
Mgr: Phil Angelosauto
Ice surfaces: 1, 185x85, Enclosed. *Open:* Year Round. *Ownership:* Municipal. *Access:* Public. *Sessions:* Public, Rental, Patch, Hockey. *Summer School:* Local. *Services:* Pro Shop, Skate Rental, Skate Sharpening, Lockers, Dressing Rooms. *Notes:* All-purpose room.

Greenfield Skating Arena
Barr Ave.
Greenfield MA 01301
(413) 772-6891
Mgr: Bill Delia
Ice surfaces: 1, 200x85, Enclosed. *Open:* Aug.-Apr. *Ownership:* Private. *Access:* Public. *Clubs:* Greenfield Area FSC. *Sessions:* Public, Private/Club, Rental, Hockey. *Classes/Lessons:* Group, Private. *Services:* Pro Shop, Skate Rental, Skate Sharpening, Snack Bar, Lockers, Dressing Rooms.

Hallenborg Memorial Pavillion
Good St.
Billerica MA 01821
(508) 436-9300
Mgr: Roger Richard
Ice surfaces: 1, 200x85, Enclosed. *Open:* Sept.-June. *Ownership:* Municipal. *Access:* Public. *Clubs:* Shawsheen Hockey; Skatetech FSC. *Sessions:* Public, Rental, Hockey. *Classes/Lessons:* Private, Group. *Program Affiliation:* USFSA, ISIA. *Summer School:* No. *Services:* Lockers, Dressing Rooms. *Notes:* Private lessons, freestyle and patch session are offered through the club only.

Hart Recreation Center Ice Rink
1 College St.
Worcester MA 01610
(508) 793-3407
FAX: (508) 793-2229
Mgr: Peter Van Bushkirk
Ice surfaces: 1, 200x85. *Open:* Oct.-March. *Ownership:* Private. *Access:* Members Only. students and faculty. *College/Univ:* College of the Holy Cross. *Sessions:* Private/Club, Rental, Hockey. *Classes/Lessons:* None. *Summer School:* No. *Services:* Skate Sharpening, Snack Bar, Lockers, Dressing Rooms. *Notes:* Rents only to the community. Skate sharpening for the team only.

Hayden Recreation Center Ice Facility
24 Lincoln St.
Lexington MA 02173
(617) 862-5575
Mgr: Steven Hoar
Ice surfaces: 1, 185x85, Enclosed. *Open:* Sept.-May. *Ownership:* Private. *Access:* Members Only. Members of Hayden Rec Center. *Clubs:* Hayden FSC, Lexington-Bedford Youth Hockey. *Sessions:* Rental, Freestyle, Patch, Dance, Hockey, Private/Club. *Classes/Lessons:* Group, Private. *Program Affiliation:* USFSA. *Summer School:* No. *Services:* Snack Bar, Lockers, Dressing Rooms. *Notes:* Nearby rec center. Hockey camp available late August.

Hetland (Stephen) Memorial Skating Rink
310 Hathaway Blvd.
New Bedford MA 02740
(508) 999-9051
Mgr: Ken Gouveia
Ice surfaces: 1, 180x85, Enclosed. *Open:* Sept.-June. *Ownership:* Private. *Access:* Public. *Clubs:* SC of Southern New England; Southeastern Mass. SC; Hetland Youth Hockey. *College/Univ:* Univ. of Mass. - Dartmouth. *Sessions:* Public, Private/Club, Rental, Freestyle, Patch, Dance, Hockey. *Classes/Lessons:* Group, Private. *Program Affiliation:* ISIA, USFSA. *Services:* Pro Shop, Skate Rental, Skate Sharpening, Snack Bar, Lockers, Dressing Rooms. *Notes:* Conference room.

Hobomock Ice Arena
Hobomock St.
Pembroke MA 02359
(617) 294-0260
Mgr: Ron Woodworth
Ice surfaces: 2, 200x85; 200x85, Enclosed. *Open:* Year Round. *Ownership:* Private. *Access:* Restricted. *Restrictions: Clubs:* Figure skating; youth hockey. *Sessions:* Rental, Freestyle, Patch, Hockey. *Classes/Lessons:* Group, Private. *Program Affiliation:* USFSA, ISIA. *Summer School:* Local. *Services:* Pro Shop, Skate Sharpening, Snack Bar, Lockers, Dressing Rooms.

Hockeytown USA Inc.
953 Broadway
Saugus MA 01906
(617) 233-3667
FAX: (617) 233-4469
Mgr: Larry Abott
Ice surfaces: 2, 200x85; 200x85, Enclosed. *Open:* Year Round. *Ownership:* Private. *Access:* Restricted. *Restrictions:* Rentals only. *Sessions:* Private/Club, Rental, Hockey. *Services:* Pro Shop, Skate Sharpening, Snack Bar, Lockers, Dressing Rooms. *Notes:* Classes and lessons are offered through the club only.

Hogan Arena
403 Oxford St. N.
Auburn MA 01501
(508) 832-5932
Mgr: William Hughes
Ice surfaces: 1, 185x85, Enclosed. *Open:* Aug.-May. *Ownership:* Private. *Access:* Public. *Clubs:* Mid State Youth Hockey; Bay State Youth Hockey. *College/Univ:* Nichols University; Clark University. *Sessions:* Public, Rental, Freestyle, Patch, Hockey. *Classes/Lessons:* Group, Private. *Program Affiliation:* Own. *Summer School:* Local. *Services:* Pro Shop, Skate Rental, Skate Sharpening, Lockers, Dressing Rooms, Snack Bar.

Horgan (Daniel S.) Memorial Rink
403 Oxford St. North
Auburn MA 01501
(508) 832-5932
Mgr: William Hughes
Ice surfaces: 1, 185x85, Enclosed. *Open:* Aug.-June. *Ownership:* Municipal. *Access:* Public. *Sessions:* Public, Private/Club, Rental, Freestyle, Patch, Hockey. *Classes/Lessons:* Group, Private. *Program Affiliation:* ISIA. *Summer School:* No. *Services:* Pro Shop, Skate Rental, Skate Sharpening, Snack Bar, Lockers, Dressing Rooms.

Janas (John J.) Memorial Skating Rink
415 Douglas Rd.
Lowell MA 01852
(508) 454-6662
Mgr: Bill Gianis
Ice surfaces: 1, 185x85, Enclosed. *Open:* Aug.-June. *Ownership:* Municipal. *Sessions:* Public, Rental, Hockey. *Program Affiliation:* USFSA. *Summer School:* Local. *Services:* Pro Shop, Skate Rental, Skate Sharpening, Snack Bar, Lockers, Dressing Rooms. *Notes:* Classes and lessons are not offered by the rink.

Johnson (H. Alden) Rink
537 Highland St.
South Hamilton MA 01982
(508) 468-6232
Mgr: Chris Rand
Ice surfaces: 1, 200x85, Enclosed. *Open:* Year Round. *Ownership:* Private. *Access:* Restricted. *Restrictions:* Group rentals. *Clubs:* Silver Streaks FSC, Cape Anne FSC. *Sessions:* Private/Club, Rental. *Classes/Lessons:* Group. *Program*

Affiliation: USFSA, ISIA. *Summer School:* No. *Services:* Pro Shop, Skate Sharpening, Snack Bar, Dressing Rooms. *Notes:* The rink rents to hockey teams, leagues, and the two figure skating clubs.

Johnson Rink - Pingree School
537 Highland St.
S. Hamilton MA 01982
(508) 468-6232
Mgr: Christopher Rand
Ice surfaces: 1, 200x85, Enclosed. *Open:* Year Round. *Ownership:* Private. *Access:* Public. *Clubs:* Capeann FS; Silver Streaks FSC. *Sessions:* Public, Private/Club, Rental, Freestyle, Patch, Dance, Hockey. *Classes/Lessons:* Group, Private. *Program Affiliation:* Own. *Services:* Pro Shop, Skate Sharpening, Snack Bar, Lockers, Dressing Rooms.

Kasabuski Arena
201 Forest St.
Saugus MA 01906
(617) 231-4183
Mgr: Tom O'Hearn
Ice surfaces: 1, 200x85, Enclosed. *Open:* Year Round. *Ownership:* Municipal. *Access:* Public. *Clubs:* Mass. Bay FSC, Amateur Hockey League. *Sessions:* Public, Rental, Freestyle, Patch, Hockey. *Classes/Lessons:* Group, Private. *Program Affiliation:* USFSA, ISIA. *Summer School:* Regional. *Services:* Pro Shop, Skate Sharpening, Snack Bar, Lockers, Dressing Rooms. *Notes:* Lessons are offered through clubs only.

Keller Rink - Claflin Athletic Center
Belmont Hill School, 350 Prospect St.
Belmont MA 02178
(617) 484-6178
Mgr: Ken Martin
Ice surfaces: 1, 200x85, Enclosed. *Open:* Nov.-Feb. *Ownership:* Private. *Access:* Public. *Sessions:* Public, Rental, Hockey. *Classes/Lessons:* None. *Summer School:* No. *Services:* Lockers, Dressing Rooms.

Kennedy (Joseph P.) Jr. Memorial Skating Rink
141 Bassett Lane
Hyannis MA 02601
(508) 790-6346
Mgr: Patty Machado
Skating Dir: Patty Machado
Ice surfaces: 1, 215x85, Outdoor/Semi Outdoor. *Open:* Nov.-Mar. *Ownership:* Municipal. *Access:* Public. *Clubs:* Cape Cod Skating Club. *Sessions:* Public, Rental, Hockey. *Classes/Lessons:* Group. *Program Affiliation:* USFSA. *Summer School:* No. *Services:* Skate Rental, Skate Sharpening, Snack Bar, Dressing Rooms. *Notes:* Function room; warming house. Freestyle, patch and dance sessions are offered through clubs only.

Kent (Tony) Arena
8 S. Gages Way
South Dennis MA 02660
(508) 760-2415
Mgr: Dottie Larkin
Skating Dir: Dottie Larkin
Ice surfaces: 1, 185x85, Enclosed. *Open:* Year Round. *Ownership:* built from donations by people in surrounding towns; run by board of directors; non-profit. *Access:* Public. *Clubs:* Yarmouth Ice Club. *Sessions:* Public, Private/Club, Rental, Freestyle, Patch, Dance, Hockey. *Classes/Lessons:* Private. *Summer School:* National/International. *Services:* Pro Shop, Skate Rental, Skate Sharpening, Snack Bar, Ballet Room, Weight Room, Lockers, Dressing Rooms.

Larsen Ice Skating Facility
45 Puline St.
Wintrop MA 02152
(617) 846-5700
FAX: (617) 539-0891
Mgr: Mark Wallace
Ice surfaces: 1, 200x85, Enclosed. *Open:* Sept.-May. *Ownership:* Municipal. *Access:* Public. *Clubs:* Winthrop Figure Skating Assn. *Sessions:* Public, Rental, Freestyle, Patch. *Classes/Lessons:* None. *Summer School:* Local. *Services:* Pro Shop, Snack Bar, Dressing Rooms, Skate Sharpening.

Lawrence Academy Ice Rink
56 Powder House Rd.
Groton MA 01450
(508) 448-2239
Mgr: Tim Sherman
Ice surfaces: 1, 200x85, Outdoor/Semi Outdoor *Ownership:* Private. *Access:* Public. *Sessions:* Public, Private/Club, Rental, Hockey. *Classes/Lessons:* None. *Summer School:* No. *Services:* Skate Sharpening, Weight Room, Lockers, Dressing Rooms.

LoConte Memorial Skating Rink
Verterns Memorial Pkwy.
Medford MA 02155
(617) 395-9594
Mgr: Robert McNulty
Ice surfaces: 1, 200x85, Enclosed. *Open:* Oct.-Mar. *Ownership:* Municipal. *Access:* Public. *Clubs:* Medford Recreational Hockey Assn.; Medford HS; Winchester HS. *Sessions:* Public, Rental, Hockey. *Classes/Lessons:* Group, Private. *Summer School:* No. *Services:* Skate Rental, Skate Sharpening, Snack Bar, Dressing Rooms. *Notes:* Hockey through club; classes through Bay State Ice Skating School.

Loring (E. F.) Arena
Fountain St.
Framingham MA 01701-3066
(508) 620-4876
Mgr: Dick Rodenheiser
, 200x85, Enclosed. *Open:* Sept.-Mar. *Ownership:* Municipal. *Access:* Public. *Clubs:* Bay Path FSC. *Sessions:* Public, Private/Club, Rental, Freestyle, Patch, Hockey. *Classes/Lessons:* Group, Private. *Program Affiliation:* USFSA, ISIA. *Services:* Pro Shop, Skate Rental, Skate Sharpening, Snack Bar, Dressing Rooms.

Lossone Ice Rink - Williston Academy
19 Payson Ave.
East Hampton MA 01027
(413) 527-1520
Mgr: Jim Sudherland
Ice surfaces: 1, 190x85, Enclosed. *Open:* June-Apr. *Ownership:* Private. *Access:* Restricted. *Restrictions:* Students. *Sessions:* Private/Club, Rental, Freestyle, Hockey. *Classes/Lessons:* Group, Private. *Program Affiliation:* USFSA, ISIA. *Summer School:* Local. *Services:* Skate Sharpening, Ballet Room, Pool and/or Athletic Facilities, Lockers, Dressing Rooms.

Martha's Vineyard Arena
Edgartown Vineyard Haven Rd.
Oak Bluffs MA 02557
(508) 693-4438
FAX: (508) 693-4223
Mgr: Kurt Mundt
Ice surfaces: 1, 200x85, Enclosed. *Open:* July-Apr. *Ownership:* Municipal. *Access:* Public. *Clubs:* Martha's Vineyard FSC, Youth hockey. *Sessions:* Public, Private/

Club, Rental, Freestyle, Patch, Dance, Hockey. *Classes/Lessons:* Group, Private. *Program Affiliation:* USFSA. *Summer School:* Local. *Services:* Pro Shop, Skate Rental, Skate Sharpening, Snack Bar, Lockers, Dressing Rooms.

Matthews Arena at Northeastern University
238 St. Boltoph St.
Boston MA 02115
(617) 373-3377
Mgr: Mark Coates
Ice surfaces: 1, 186x85, Outdoor/Semi Outdoor. *Open:* Nov.-Apr. *Ownership:* Private. *Access:* Public. *College/Univ:* Northeastern University. *Sessions:* Public. *Classes/Lessons:* None. *Summer School:* No. *Services:* Studio Rink, Snack Bar, Weight Room, Lockers, Dressing Rooms. *Notes:* Club buys ice time from the rink.

McVann - O'Keefe Memorial Rink
511 Lowell St.
Peabody MA 01960
(508) 535-2110
Mgr: Norman Pelletier
Ice surfaces: 1, 185x60, Enclosed. *Open:* Aug.-June. *Ownership:* Municipal. *Access:* Public. *Clubs:* Silver Streaks FSC. *Sessions:* Public, Private/Club, Rental, Freestyle, Patch, Dance, Hockey. *Classes/Lessons:* Group, Private. *Services:* Pro Shop, Skate Rental, Skate Sharpening, Lockers, Dressing Rooms, Snack Bar. *Notes:* Meeting room.

Methuen High Skating Rink
1 Ranger Rd.
Methuen MA 01844
(508) 687-8008
Mgr: Wally Martin
Ice surfaces: 1, 200x85, Enclosed. *Open:* Sept.-Apr. *Ownership:* Municipal. *Access:* Public. *Clubs:* Methuen High FSC, Methuen Hockey Assn. *Sessions:* Public, Rental, Hockey. *Classes/Lessons:* Group. *Program Affiliation:* USFSA, ISIA. *Summer School:* No. *Services:* Skate Sharpening, Snack Bar, Lockers, Dressing Rooms.

Minute Man Skating School Rink
Valley Sports Arena
2320 Main St. and Rt. 62
West Concord MA 01742
(508) 649-6391
Mgr: Duncan Finch
Skating Dir: Don Cornwell
Ice surfaces: 2, 185 x 80; 185 x 80, Enclosed. *Open:* Year Round. *Ownership:* Private. *Access:* Restricted. *Clubs:* Minute Man FSC, Patriot FSC. *Sessions:* Private/Club, Hockey, Freestyle, Patch, Dance. *Classes/Lessons:* Group, Private. *Program Affiliation:* ISIA, USFSA. *Summer School:* Local. *Services:* Pro Shop, Skate Sharpening, Snack Bar, Lockers, Dressing Rooms. *Notes:* Meeting room; all-purpose room.

MIT Skating Rink - Johnson Athletic Center
77 Mass. Ave.
Cambridge MA 02146
(617) 253-4497
Ice surfaces: 1, 185x85, Enclosed. *Open:* Oct.-Mar. *Ownership:* Private. *Access:* Restricted. *Restrictions:* MIT community. *Clubs:* MIT FSC. *College/Univ:* Mass. Institute of Technology. *Sessions:* Private/Club, Freestyle, Dance, Hockey. *Classes/Lessons:* Group, Private. *Summer School:* No. *Services:* Skate Rental, Skate Sharpening, Weight Room, Lockers, Dressing Rooms.

McCollum Ice Arena - Northfield School
28 Mount Herman Rd.
Mount Herman MA 01354
(413) 498-3000
Mgr: Frank Millard
Ice surfaces: 1, 200 x 85, Enclosed. *Open:* Nov.-Mar. *Ownership:* Private. *Access:* Restricted. *Restrictions:* School community. *Sessions:* Rental, Hockey. *Summer School:* No. *Services:* Dressing Rooms.

Moore (Charles) Arena
O'Conner Rd., Box 1441
Orleans MA 02653
(508) 255-5902
Mgr: Judy Kostas
Ice surfaces: 1, 200x85, Enclosed. *Open:* Sept.-Apr. *Access:* Public. *Sessions:* Public, Rental, Freestyle, Patch, Dance, Hockey. *Classes/Lessons:* Group, Private. *Program Affiliation:* ISIA. *Summer School:* No. *Services:* Pro Shop, Skate Rental, Skate Sharpening, Snack Bar.

Mullins (William D.) Memorial Center
Mullins Center
University of Massachusetts
Amherst MA 01003
(413) 545-4770
Mgr: Ed Murphy
Ice surfaces: 2, 200x96; 200x96, Enclosed. *Open:* July—May. *Access:* Public. *Clubs:* Skating Club of Amherst. *College/Univ:* University of Massachusetts. *Sessions:* Public, Private/Club, Rental, Hockey. *Classes/Lessons:* Group, Private. *Program Affiliation:* USFSA, ISIA. *Summer School:* Local. *Services:* Skate Rental, Skate Sharpening, Snack Bar, Dressing Rooms, Lockers.

Murphy (Frances Al) Memorial Skating Rink
Day Blvd.
S. Boston MA 02127
(617) 269-7060
Mgr: James Tobin
Ice surfaces: 2, 200x85; 100x75, Enclosed. *Open:* Year Round. *Ownership:* Municipal. *Access:* Public. *Clubs:* S. Boston Youth Hockey; Special Olympics. *Sessions:* Public, Private/Club, Rental, Freestyle, Patch, Dance, Hockey. *Classes/Lessons:* None. *Program Affiliation:* USFSA, ISIA. *Summer School:* No. *Services:* Skate Rental, Skate Sharpening, Studio Rink, Snack Bar, Dressing Rooms. *Notes:* The rink only offers public skating, S. Boston Youth Hockey rents the ice and conducts their own sessions.

Nashoba Valley Olympia
34 Massachusetts Ave., Route 111
Boxborough MA 01719
(508) 263-3020
Mgr: Russ Long
Ice surfaces: 2, 200x85, Enclosed. *Open:* Year Round. *Ownership:* Private. *Access:* Public. *Clubs:* Colonial FSC. *Sessions:* Public, Private/Club, Rental, Freestyle, Patch, Dance, Hockey. *Classes/Lessons:* Group, Private. *Program Affiliation:* USFSA, ISIA. *Summer School:* National/International. *Services:* Pro Shop, Skate Rental, Skate Sharpening, Snack Bar, Ballet Room, Weight Room, Dressing Rooms.

Navin (John J.) Rink
451 Bolton St.
Marlboro MA 01572
(508) 481-5252
Ice surfaces: 1, 200x85, Enclosed. *Open:* June-Apr. *Ownership:* Club. *Access:* Public. *Clubs:* Glacier FSC. *Sessions:* Public, Rental, Freestyle, Patch, Hockey. *Classes/Lessons:* Group, Private. *Program Affiliation:* USFSA. *Services:* Pro Shop, Skate Rental, Skate Sharpening, Snack Bar, Lockers, Dressing Rooms.

Nobel & Greenough School Ice Rink
Flood Rink, 507 Bridge St.
Dedham MA 02026
(617) 326-3700
FAX: (617) 329-8118
Mgr: Tom Resor
Ice surfaces: 1, 200x85, Outdoor/Semi Outdoor. *Open:* Nov.-Mar. *Ownership:* Private. *Access:* Restricted. *Restrictions:* Students only. *Clubs:* School hockey teams. *Sessions:* Public, Hockey. *Classes/Lessons:* None. *Services:* Skate Sharpening, Lockers, Dressing Rooms.

North Star Youth Forum
15 Bridle Ln.
Westboro MA 01581
(508) 366-1562
Mgr: Dave Roy
Ice surfaces: 2, 200x85; 200x85. *Open:* Aug.-Apr. *Ownership:* Private. *Access:* Restricted. *Restrictions:* Club or rentals only. *Clubs:* North Star FSC. *Sessions:* Private/Club, Rental, Hockey. *Classes/Lessons:* Group, Private. *Program Affiliation:* ISIA. *Services:* Pro Shop, Skate Rental, Skate Sharpening, Snack Bar, Lockers. *Notes:* Freestyle, patch, and dance offered through club only.

O'Brian Ice Rink
Locust St.
Woburn MA 01801
(617) 938-1620
Mgr: Bill Holland
Ice surfaces: 1, 200x85, Enclosed. *Open:* Aug.-Apr. *Ownership:* Private. *Access:* Restricted. *Restrictions:* No public skating. *Sessions:* Private/Club, Rental, Freestyle, Patch, Hockey. *Classes/Lessons:* Group, Private. *Summer School:* No. *Services:* Pro Shop, Skate Sharpening, Snack Bar, Dressing Rooms.

O'Keefe Rink at Salem State College
225 Canal St.
Salem MA 01970
(508) 741-6560
Mgr: Bill O'Neil
Ice surfaces: 1, 200x85, Enclosed. *Open:* Aug.-Mar. *Ownership:* Private. *Access:* Public. *College/Univ:* Salem State College. *Sessions:* Public, Rental, Freestyle, Hockey. *Classes/Lessons:* None. *Summer School:* No. *Services:* Pro Shop, Skate Rental, Skate Sharpening, Ballet Room, Pool and/or Athletic Facilities, Lockers, Dressing Rooms.

O'Neill (Emmons Horrigan) Memorial Rink
46 Union St.
Charlestown MA 02129
(617) 242-9728
Mgr: James O'Donovan
Ice surfaces: 1, 200x85, Enclosed. *Open:* Oct.-Mar. *Ownership:* Municipal. *Access:* Public. *Clubs:* Charlestown Youth Hockey Association. *Sessions:* Public, Private/Club, Rental, Hockey. *Classes/Lessons:* Group. *Program Affiliation:* Own. *Summer School:* No. *Services:* Skate Sharpening, Dressing Rooms, Snack Bar.

Olympia Skate and Roller Center
125 Capital Dr.
West Springfield MA 01089
(413) 736-8100
Mgr: Vicky Sheehan
Ice surfaces: 1, 185x85, Enclosed. *Open:* Year Round. *Ownership:* Club. *Access:* Members Only, Restricted. Club members and hockey only. *Clubs:* SC of Springfield. *Sessions:* Private/Club, Hockey. *Classes/Lessons:* Group, Private. *Program Affiliation:* USFSA. *Summer School:* Local. *Services:* Pro Shop, Skate Rental, Skate Sharpening, Snack Bar, Ballet Room, Weight Room, Dressing Rooms. *Notes:* Roller rink also.

Orr Rink
Amherst College
Amherst MA 01002
(413) 542-7950
Mgr: Jack Arena
Ice surfaces: 1, 200x85, Enclosed. *Open:* Nov.-Mar. *Ownership:* Private. *Access:* Restricted. *Restrictions:* Students and staff. *College/Univ:* Amherst College.
Sessions: Private/Club, Rental, Hockey. *Classes/Lessons:* Private, Group. *Program Affiliation:* USFSA. *Summer School:* No. *Services:* Skate Sharpening, Weight Room, Lockers.

Pilgrim Skating Arena
75 Recreation Park Dr.
Hingham MA 02043
(617) 749-6660
Skating Dir: Michelle Kelley
Ice surfaces: 3, 185x85; 185x85; 145x45, Enclosed. *Open:* Year Round. *Ownership:* Private. *Access:* Restricted. *Restrictions:* Group renters. *Clubs:* SC of Hingham; Rainbow Club. *Sessions:* Public, Private/Club, Rental, Freestyle, Patch, Dance, Hockey. *Classes/Lessons:* Group, Private. *Program Affiliation:* USFSA, ISIA. *Summer School:* Local. *Services:* Pro Shop, Skate Sharpening, Studio Rink, Snack Bar, Dressing Rooms.

Pittsfield Boys & Girls Club Skating Arena
16 Melville St.
Pittsfield MA 01201
(413) 447-9380
FAX: (413) 448-8259
Mgr: Marty Martin
Ice surfaces: 1, 185x85, Enclosed. *Open:* Sept.-Mar. *Ownership:* Municipal. *Access:* Public. *Clubs:* Pittsville FSC, local high schools; Speed Skating Club. *Sessions:* Public, Rental, Hockey. *Classes/Lessons:* Group. *Program Affiliation:* Own. *Services:* Skate Rental, Skate Sharpening, Dressing Rooms, Pro Shop, Snack Bar.

Porazzo (Lt. Lewis) Skating Arena
Constitution Beach
East Boston MA 02128
(617) 567-9571
Mgr: Jack Martelli
Ice surfaces: 1, 200x85, Enclosed. *Open:* Oct. -Mar. *Ownership:* Municipal. *Access:* Public. *Clubs:* E. Boston Youth Hockey; E. Boston HS. *Sessions:* Public, Private/Club, Rental, Hockey. *Classes/Lessons:* None. *Summer School:* No. *Services:* Snack Bar, Lockers, Dressing Rooms, Pro Shop.

Pratt (Frederick) Memorial Rink
Middlesex School, 1400 Lowell Rd.
Concord MA 01742
(508) 369-2550
Mgr: Chip Vigne
Ice surfaces: 1, 200x85, Enclosed. *Open:* Nov.-Feb. *Ownership:* Private. *Access:* Restricted. *Restrictions:* Students. *Clubs:* Speed Skating. *Sessions;* Private/Club, Rental. *Classes/Lessons:* None. *Program Affiliation:* Own. *Summer School:* No. *Services:* Skate Sharpening, Ballet Room, Weight Room, Lockers, Dressing Rooms.

Pratt Rink at Groton School
Farmers Row
Groton MA 01450
(508) 448-3363
Mgr: Ralph Giles
Ice surfaces: 1, 200x85, Enclosed. *Open:* Nov.-Mar. *Ownership:* Private. *Access:* Restricted. *Restrictions:* School use. *Sessions:* Public, Private/Club, Rental, Hockey. *Classes/Lessons:* Group. *Summer School:* No. *Services:* Pro Shop, Skate Sharpening, Weight Room, Pool and/or Athletic Facilities, Dressing Rooms.

Quincy Youth Arena
60 Murphy Memorial Dr.
Quincy MA 02169
(617) 479-8371
Mgr: Beverly Reinhardt
Ice surfaces: 1, 200x85, Enclosed. *Open:* Year Round. *Ownership:* Private. *Access:* Restricted. *Restrictions:* Hockey and lessons. *Clubs:* Quincy Youth Hockey; High school hockey. *Sessions:* Rental, Hockey. *Classes/Lessons:* Group, Private. *Summer School:* Regional. *Services:* Pro Shop, Skate Sharpening, Snack Bar, Lockers, Dressing Rooms.

Randolph Ice Arena
240 North St.
Randolph MA 02368
(617) 961-4053
Mgr: Dave Theadual
Ice surfaces: 1, 170x70, Enclosed. *Open:* Year Round. *Ownership:* town. *Access:* Public. *Clubs:* Mohawks Youth Hockey; Mass. FSC. *Sessions:* Public, Private/Club, Rental, Freestyle, Patch, Dance, Hockey. *Classes/Lessons:* Group, Private. *Services:* Pool and/or Athletic Facilities, Snack Bar, Dressing Rooms. *Notes:* Summer camps are offered.

Reilly Memorial Rink
355 Chestnut Hill Ave.
Brighton MA 02135
(617) 277-7822
Mgr: Andy Yee
Ice surfaces: 1, 200x85, Enclosed. *Open:* Nov.-Mar. *Ownership:* Municipal. *Access:* Public. *Clubs:* Bay State Skating School. *Sessions:* Public, Rental, Hockey, Private/Club. *Classes/Lessons:* Group. *Summer School:* No. *Services:* Pro Shop, Skate Rental, Skate Sharpening, Snack Bar, Pool and/or Athletic Facilities, Lockers, Dressing Rooms.

Ristuccia (Eleanor M.) Memorial Arena
190 Main St.
Wilmington MA 01887
(508) 657-3976
Mgr: Arelene Reidy
Ice surfaces: 1, 200x85, Enclosed. *Open:* Year Round. *Ownership:* Private. *Access:* Public. *Clubs:* Wilmington FSC, Wilmington Youth Hockey. *Sessions:* Public, Private/Club, Rental, Freestyle, Patch, Dance, Hockey. *Classes/Lessons:* Group, Private. *Program Affiliation:* USFSA. *Summer School:* Local. *Services:* Pro Shop, Skate Sharpening, Snack Bar, Ballet Room, Dressing Rooms.

Roberts (James) Ice Rink at Milton Academy
170 Center St.
Milton MA 02186
(617) 698-7800
Mgr: Megan Brott
Ice surfaces: 1, 200x85, Outdoor/Semi Outdoor. *Open:* Nov.-Mar. *Ownership:* Private. *Access:* Restricted. *Restrictions:* School use; community. *Sessions:* Rental, Freestyle, Hockey. *Classes/Lessons:* None. *Summer School:* No. *Services:* Dressing Rooms. *Notes:* All ice time must be rented; school does not supervise sessions beyond its own use.

Rockland Rink
599 Summer St.
Rockland MA 02043
(617) 878-5591
Mgr: Robert McBride
Skating Dir: Katie Hayden
Ice surfaces: 1, 200x85, Enclosed. *Open:* Year Round. *Ownership:* Private. *Access:* Public. *Clubs:* Youth Hockey, figure skating school, Silver Blade SC, Winterland. *Sessions:* Public, Private/Club, Rental, Hockey. *Classes/Lessons:* Group, Private. *Program Affiliation:* USFSA, ISIA. *Summer School:* Regional. *Services:* Pro Shop, Skate Sharpening, Snack Bar, Lockers, Dressing Rooms. *Notes:* Freestyle, patch and dance sessions offered through the club only.

Ryan (John A.) Skating Arena
1 Paramount Place
Watertown MA 02172
(617) 972-6468
Mgr: Ted O'Leary
Ice surfaces: 1, 200x85, Enclosed. *Open:* Aug.-Apr. *Ownership:* Municipal. *Access:* Public. *College/Univ:* Bentley College. *Sessions:* Public, Private/Club, Rental, Hockey. *Classes/Lessons:* Private, Group. *Program Affiliation:* USFSA, ISIA. *Summer School:* No. *Services:* Pro Shop, Skate Rental, Skate Sharpening, Snack Bar, Lockers, Dressing Rooms.

Shea Memorial Rink
651 Willard St.
Quincy MA 02169
(617) 472-9325
Mgr: Bridget Roache
Ice surfaces: 1, 200x85, Enclosed. *Open:* Nov.-Mar. *Ownership:* Municipal. *Access:* Public. *Clubs:* Hockey teams; High schools. *Sessions:* Public, Private/Club, Rental, Freestyle, Hockey. *Classes/Lessons:* Group. *Summer School:* No.

Simoni (Romano) Skating Rink
Gore St.
Cambridge MA 02141
(617) 354-9523
Mgr: Joe Cedrone
Ice surfaces: 1, 200x80, Enclosed. *Open:* Sept.-Apr. *Ownership:* Metropolitan District Commission, Municipal. *Access:* Public. *Clubs:* Bay State Ice Skating School. *Sessions:* Public, Rental, Hockey. *Classes/Lessons:* Group, Private. *Program Affiliation:* Own. *Summer School:* No. *Services:* Pro Shop, Skate Rental, Skate Sharpening, Snack Bar, Dressing Rooms.

Skating Club of Boston
1240 Soldiers Field Rd.
Brighton MA 02135
(617) 782-5900
Mgr: Jeff Rubin
Ice surfaces: 1, 185x85, Enclosed. *Open:* Year Round. *Ownership:* Club. *Access:* Public. Limited public skating. *Clubs:* SC of Boston. *Sessions:* Public, Private/Club, Rental, Freestyle, Patch, Dance, Hockey. *Classes/Lessons:* Group, Private. *Program Affiliation:* USFSA. *Summer School:* Local. *Services:* Pro Shop, Skate Rental, Skate Sharpening, Ballet Room, Lockers, Dressing Rooms, Pool and/or Athletic Facilities.

Smead (Ray) Ice Arena
1780 Roosevelt Ave.
Springfield MA 01109
(413) 787-6453
Mgr: Tom Sirelli
Ice surfaces: 1, 200x85, Enclosed. *Open:* Sept.-Mar. *Ownership:* Municipal. *Access:* Public. *Clubs:* Little Sun Valley SC. *College/Univ:* American International College. *Sessions:* Public, Private/Club, Rental. *Classes/Lessons:* None. *Services:* Pro Shop, Skate Rental, Skate Sharpening, Snack Bar, Lockers, Dressing Rooms.

St. Sebastian's Ice Skating Rink
1191 Greendale Ave.
Needham MA 02192
(617) 449-5208
Mgr: Mickey Bell-Isle
Ice surfaces: 1, 200x90, Enclosed. *Open:* Sept.-Mar. *Ownership:* Private. *Access:* Restricted. *Restrictions:* Hockey clubs & students. *Sessions:* Rental, Freestyle, Hockey. *Classes/Lessons:* None. *Summer School:* No. *Services:* Skate Sharpening, Weight Room, Pool and/or Athletic Facilities, Dressing Rooms.

Steriti Memorial Rink
Commercial St.
Boston MA 02108
(617) 523-9327
Mgr: Joe Cedlone
Ice surfaces: 1, 195x90, Enclosed. *Open:* Nov.-Mar. *Ownership:* Municipal. *Access:* Public. *Clubs:* Youth Hockey. *College/Univ:* Suffolk University. *Sessions:* Public, Private/Club, Rental, Freestyle, Hockey. *Classes/Lessons:* None. *Services:* Lockers, Dressing Rooms.

Stoneham Arena
101 Montreal Ave.
Stoneham MA 02180
(617) 279-2628
Mgr: June Scarpe
Ice surfaces: 1, 194x85, Enclosed. *Open:* July-May. *Ownership:* Municipal. *Access:* Public. *Clubs:* Stoneham FSC, Youth Hockey; Middlesex Islanders. *College/Univ:* Tufts University. *Sessions:* Public, Private/Club, Rental, Freestyle, Patch, Dance, Hockey. *Classes/Lessons:* Group, Private. *Program Affiliation:* ISIA, USFSA. *Summer School:* National/International. *Services:* Pro Shop, Skate Rental, Skate Sharpening, Snack Bar, Lockers, Dressing Rooms. *Notes:* Vending machines.

Sumner Smith Hockey Rink
Phillips Academy, South Main St.
Andover MA 01810
(508) 475-3400
Mgr: Chuck Lane
Ice surfaces: 1, 200x100, Outdoor/Semi Outdoor. *Open:* Nov.-Mar. *Ownership:* Private. *Access:* Restricted. *Restrictions:* Students only. *Clubs:* Andover SC. *Sessions:* Private/Club. *Classes/Lessons:* None. *Program Affiliation:* Own.

Talbot (Dorothy M.) Memorial Rink
O'Malley School, Osman Babson Rd.
Gloucester MA 01930
(508) 281-9856
Mgr: J. D. MacEachern
Ice surfaces: 1, 200x85, Enclosed. *Open:* Oct.-Apr. *Ownership:* Municipal. *Access:* Public. *Clubs:* Cape Anne FSC, Cape Anne Youth Hockey; Viking Youth Hockey. *Sessions:* Public, Private/Club, Rental. *Classes/Lessons:* Group, Private. *Summer School:* No. *Services:* Pro Shop, Skate Rental, Skate Sharpening, Snack Bar, Lockers, Dressing Rooms. *Notes:* Freestyle, patch, dance and hockey offered through clubs only.

Talsor Academy Skating Rink
66 Spring St.
Marion MA 02738
(508) 748-2000
Mgr: Jerry Larson
Ice surfaces: 1, 200x90, Outdoor/Semi Outdoor. *Open:* Nov.-Mar. *Ownership:* Private. *Access:* Public. *Sessions:* Public, Private/Club, Rental, Hockey. *Classes/Lessons:* None. *Summer School:* No. *Services:* Skate Rental, Skate Sharpening, Snack Bar, Pool and/or Athletic Facilities, Dressing Rooms.

Tully Forum—University of Massachusetts, Lowell
Brick Kiln Rd.
North Billerica MA 01862
(508) 934-4987
Mgr: Donald Lampron
Ice surfaces: 1, 185x85, Enclosed. *Open:* Aug.-May. *Ownership:* Private. *Access:* Public. *Clubs:* Youth Hockey; Colonial FSC, River Hawks. *College/Univ:* University of Massachussets. *Sessions:* Private/Club, Rental, Hockey. *Classes/Lessons:* None. *Summer School:* No. *Services:* Pro Shop, Skate Sharpening, Snack Bar, Lockers, Dressing Rooms.

Ulin Memorial Rink
Unquity Rd.
Milton MA 02186
(617) 696-9869
Mgr: Albert Brown
Ice surfaces: 1, 200x85, Enclosed. *Open:* Nov.-Mar. *Ownership:* Commonwealth. *Access:* Public. *Clubs:* Milton Youth Hockey; Bay State Ice Skating School. *Sessions:* Public, Rental, Hockey. *Classes/Lessons:* Group. *Summer School:* No. *Services:* Skate Rental, Skate Sharpening, Snack Bar, Lockers, Dressing Rooms.

Veteran's Memorial Ice Rink
229 Brook St.
Haverhill MA 01832
(508) 373-9351
Mgr: Daniel Archambault
Ice surfaces: 1, 100x85, Enclosed. *Open:* Sept.-June. *Ownership:* Municipal. *Access:* Public. *Clubs:* Haverhill FSC, Youth hockey. *Sessions:* Public, Private/Club, Rental, Freestyle, Patch, Hockey. *Classes/Lessons:* Group, Private. *Program Affiliation:* USFSA. *Summer School:* No. *Services:* Pro Shop, Skate Rental, Skate Sharpening, Snack Bar, Lockers.

Veteran's Memorial Ice Rink
65 Elm St.
Everett MA 02149
(617) 389-9401
Mgr: Daniel Keese
Ice surfaces: 1, 185x100, Enclosed.

Open: Oct.-Mar. *Ownership:* Municipal. *Access:* Public. *Sessions:* Public, Private/Club, Rental, Hockey. *Classes/Lessons:* Group, Private. *Summer School:* No. *Services:* Snack Bar, Pool and/or Athletic Facilities, Dressing Rooms.

Veterans Memorial Arena
910 Panther Way
Franklin MA 02038
(508) 541- 7024
Mgr: Bruce Bertoni
Ice surfaces: 1, 165x85, Enclosed. *Open:* Apr.-May. *Access:* Public. *Clubs:* 4 Youth Hockey Programs; Franklin FSC, Franklin Blades FSC, Marian Kerrigan Figure Skating School. *Sessions:* Public, Private/Club, Freestyle, Rental, Patch, Dance, Hockey. *Classes/Lessons:* Group, Private. *Program Affiliation:* Own. *Summer School:* Local. *Services:* Pro Shop, Skate Rental, Skate Sharpening, Snack Bar, Lockers, Dressing Rooms. *Notes:* Classes and lessons are run by the club. Summer hockey schools.

Veterans Memorial Rink,
Totten Pond Rd.
Waltham MA 02154
(617) 893-9409
Mgr: Bob Hanson
Ice surfaces: 1, 185x80, Enclosed. *Open:* Oct.-Mar. *Ownership:* Municipal. *Access:* Public. *Clubs:* Bay State Skating School. *Sessions:* Public, Rental, General. *Classes/Lessons:* None. *Services:* Snack Bar, Dressing Rooms. *Notes:* Bay State Skating School uses the rink.

Veterans Memorial Rink
570 Somerville Ave.
Somerville MA 02143
(617) 623-3523
Mgr: Tom Dunn
Ice surfaces: 1, 185x85, Enclosed. *Open:* Sept.-March. *Ownership:* Federal. *Access:* Public. *Clubs:* Bay State FSC, Somerville Youth Hockey. *College/Univ:* Suffolk University. *Sessions:* Public, Rental, Hockey. *Classes/Lessons:* Group, Private. *Program Affiliation:* ISIA. *Summer School:* No. *Services:* Pro Shop, Skate Rental, Skate Sharpening, Snack Bar, Lockers, Dressing Rooms.

Veterans Memorial Rink
422 Summer St.
Arlington MA 02174
(617) 641-5492
FAX: (617) 641- 5495
Mgr: Barb McKeown
Ice surfaces: 1, 200x85, Enclosed. *Open:* Oct.-Mar. *Ownership:* Municipal. *Access:* Public. *Clubs:* Arlington Hockey Club. *Sessions:* Public, Hockey. *Classes/Lessons:* Group. *Program Affiliation:* Own. *Services:* Skate Sharpening, Weight Room, Lockers.

Vietnam Veterans Memorial Rink
S. Church St.
North Adams MA 01247
(413) 664-9474
Mgr: David Casey
Ice surfaces: 1, 185x85, Enclosed. *Open:* Aug.-Mar. *Ownership:* N. Adam State College. *Access:* Public. *Clubs:* Chris Brook Skating Club; North Berskshire Youth Hockey. *College/Univ:* North Adam State College. *Sessions:* Public, Rental, Freestyle, Patch, Hockey. *Classes/Lessons:* Group. *Summer School:* No. *Services:* Pro Shop, Skate Rental, Skate Sharpening, Snack Bar, Lockers, Dressing Rooms. *Notes:* Learn-to-Skate programs.

Volpe (St. Peter) Complex
Merrimack College, 315 Turnpike Rd.
North Andover MA 01845
(508) 837-5295
Mgr: Bob DeRigario
Ice surfaces: 1, 200x85, Enclosed. *Open:* Sept.-May. *Ownership:* Private. *Access:* Restricted. *Restrictions:* Students and staff. *College/Univ:* Merrimack College. *Sessions:* Hockey, Public, Private/Club, Rental. *Classes/Lessons:* None. *Summer School:* No. *Services:* Snack Bar, Weight Room, Lockers. *Notes:* Basketball gym.

Wallace Civic Center Complex
1000 John Fitch Hwy.
Fitchburg MA 01420
(508) 345-7593
Mgr: Benjamin Ruggles
Skating Dir: Kim Swart
Ice surfaces: 2, 200x85; 200x85, Enclosed. *Open:* Year Round. *Ownership:* Private, Municipal. *Access:* Public. *Clubs:* Wallace FSC, Pat Youth Hockey; Twin City Youth Hockey. *College/Univ:* Fitchburg College. *Sessions:* Public, Private/Club, Rental, Freestyle, Dance, Patch, Hockey. *Classes/Lessons:* Group, Private. *Program Affiliation:* USFSA, ISIA. *Summer School:* No. *Services:* Skate Rental, Pro Shop, Skate Sharpening, Snack Bar, Dressing Rooms.

West Suburban Arena
Windsor Ave.
Natick MA 01760
(508) 655-1013
Mgr: David Flood
Skating Dir: Roland Bessette
Ice surfaces: 1, 200x85, Enclosed. *Open:* Year Round. *Ownership:* Private. *Access:* Public. *Clubs:* SC of Natick. *Sessions:* Public, Private/Club, Rental, Freestyle, Patch, Dance, Hockey. *Classes/Lessons:* Group, Private. *Program Affiliation:* USFSA, ISIA. *Summer School:* Regional. *Services:* Pro Shop, Skate Sharpening, Snack Bar, Ballet Room, Lockers, Dressing Rooms. *Notes:* Public sessions are only offered in the winter.

Williams College, Lausing Chapman Rink
Latham St.
Williamstown MA 01267
(413) 597-2283
Mgr: Bill Bryce
Ice surfaces: 1, 200x85, Enclosed. *Open:* Nov.-Mar. *Ownership:* Private. *Access:* Public, Restricted. Students and staff. *Clubs:* Christmas Brook SC; Mount Graylock Hockey. *College/Univ:* Williams College. *Sessions:* Public, Rental, Hockey. *Classes/Lessons:* Group, Private. *Program Affiliation:* USFSA. *Services:* Snack Bar, Pool and/or Athletic Facilities, Dressing Rooms. *Notes:* Group and private lessons offered through club only.

Worcester State Rink
284 Lake Ave.
Worcester MA 01604
(508) 755-0582
FAX: (508) 799-6484
Mgr: Paul Ferraro
Skating Dir: Wesley Tuttle
Ice surfaces: 1, 200x85, Enclosed. *Open:* Aug.-May. *Ownership:* Private. *Access:* Public. *Clubs:* Lakers/Shewsbry; Worcester Skating Club. *Sessions:* Public, Rental, Freestyle, Patch, Hockey. *Classes/Lessons:* Group, Private. *Program Affiliation:* USFSA. *Summer School:* No. *Services:* Pro Shop, Skate

Rental, Skate Sharpening, Snack Bar, Lockers.

MD: MARYLAND

Benfield Pines Ice Rink
1031 Benfield Blvd.
Millersville MD 21108
(410) 987-5100
Mgr: Ken Milliken
Ice surfaces: 1, 185x85, Enclosed. *Open:* Year Round. *Ownership:* Private. *Access:* Public. *Sessions:* Public, Rental, Freestyle, Patch, Hockey, Dance. *Classes/Lessons:* Group, Private. *Program Affiliation:* ISIA. *Services:* Pro Shop, Skate Rental, Skate Sharpening, Snack Bar, Lockers, Dressing Rooms.

Bowie Ice Arena
3330 Northview Dr.
Bowie MD 20716
(301) 805-7990
FAX: (301) 262-1191
Ice surfaces: 1, 200x85, Outdoor/Semi Outdoor. *Open:* Oct.-Mar. *Ownership:* Municipal. *Access:* Public. *Sessions:* Public, Private/Club, Rental, Freestyle, Patch, Dance, Hockey. *Classes/Lessons:* Group, Private. *Program Affiliation:* ISIA. *Summer School:* No. *Services:* Pro Shop, Skate Rental, Skate Sharpening, Snack Bar, Lockers. *Notes:* Pick up sessions are offered through the clubs.

Cabin John Ice Rink
10610 Westlake Dr.
Rockville MD 20852
(301) 365-2246
Mgr: Bill Gillette
Skating Dir: Walter Chapman
Ice surfaces: 1, 200x85, Enclosed. *Open:* Sept.-July. *Ownership:* Municipal. *Access:* Public. *Clubs:* Washington FSC. *Sessions:* Public, Private/Club, Rental, Freestyle, Patch, Dance, Hockey. *Classes/Lessons:* Group, Private. *Program Affiliation:* USFSA. *Summer School:* Local. *Services:* Pro Shop, Skate Rental, Skate Sharpening, Studio Rink, Snack Bar, Lockers. *Notes:* Pick up hockey available.

Carousel Hotel Ice Rink
11700 Coastal Hwy.
Ocean City MD 21842
(410) 524-1000
Mgr: Keith Hitchens
Ice surfaces: 1, 90x50, Enclosed. *Open:* Year Round. *Ownership:* Private. *Access:* Public. *Clubs:* Carousel Skaters. *Sessions:* Public. *Classes/Lessons:* None. *Summer School:* No. *Services:* Snack Bar, Skate Rental.

Chevy Chase Club Inc.
6100 Conneticut Ave.
Chevy Chase MD 20815
(301) 652-4100
Mgr: Linda Wurzberger
Ice surfaces: 1, 200x85, Outdoor/Semi Outdoor. *Open:* Nov.-Mar. *Ownership:* Chevy Chase Country Club. *Access:* Members Only. *Clubs:* Chevy Chase FSC. *Sessions:* Private/Club, Freestyle, Patch, Hockey. *Classes/Lessons:* Group, Private. *Program Affiliation:* USFSA, ISIA. *Summer School:* No. *Services:* Pro Shop, Skate Rental, Skate Sharpening, Snack Bar, Pool and/or Athletic Facilities, Lockers. *Notes:* Admission fee included in club membership.

Columbia Ice Rink
5876 Thunder Hill Rd.
Columbia MD 21045
(410) 730-0322
FAX: (410) 992-0605
Mgr: Robert B. Eckhoff
Ice surfaces: 1, 200x85, Outdoor/Semi Outdoor. *Open:* Sept.-Mar. *Ownership:* Municipal. *Access:* Public. *Sessions:* Public, Rental, Freestyle, Patch, Hockey. *Classes/Lessons:* Group. *Program Affiliation:* USFSA, ISIA. *Services:* Skate Rental, Skate Sharpening, Pro Shop, Snack Bar, Lockers.

Dahlgren Hall Ice Rink
U. S. Naval Academy, 103 Fullham Ct.
Annapolis MD 21402
(410) 263-4527
FAX: (410) 267-2226
Mgr: Jackie Jessup
Ice surfaces: 1, 200x85, Enclosed. *Open:* Oct.-Mar. *Access:* Restricted. *Restrictions:* Military personnel & family, midshipmen. *College/Univ:* Naval Academy. *Sessions:* Private/Club, Rental, Hockey. *Classes/Lessons:* Group, Private. *Program Affiliation:* Own. *Summer School:* No. *Services:* Skate Rental, Skate Sharpening, Snack Bar, Lockers, Dressing Rooms.

Frederick Fort & Ice Arena
1288 Riverbend
Frederick MD 21701
(301) 662-7362
FAX: (301) 662-7361
Mgr: Byron Dyke
Ice surfaces: 1, 200x85, Enclosed. *Open:* Year Round. *Ownership:* Private. *Access:* Public. *Sessions:* Public, Private/Club, Rental, Freestyle, Patch, Dance, Hockey. *Classes/Lessons:* Private, Group. *Program Affiliation:* ISIA. *Services:* Pro Shop, Skate Rental, Skate Sharpening, Snack Bar, Lockers, Dressing Rooms. *Notes:* Fitness club to be built in fall '95.

Mt. Pleasant Ice Arena
6101 Hillen Road
Baltimore MD 21234
(410) 444-1888
Ice surfaces: 1, Enclosed. *Access:* Public. *Sessions:* Public. *Classes/Lessons:* Group, Private. *Program Affiliation:* ISIA. *Services:* Skate Rental.

Northwest Family Sports Center, Inc.
5600 Cottonworth Ave.
Baltimore MD 21209
(410) 433-4970
Mgr: Jackie Eliasberg
Ice surfaces: 1, 200x85, Enclosed. *Open:* June-May. *Access:* Public. *Clubs:* Ice Club of Baltimore. *Sessions:* Public, Private/Club, Rental, Freestyle, Patch, Dance, Hockey. *Classes/Lessons:* Group, Private. *Program Affiliation:* ISIA. *Summer School:* Local. *Services:* Pro Shop, Skate Rental, Skate Sharpening, Snack Bar, Lockers.

Piney Orchard Ice Arena
8781 Piney Orchard Pkwy.
Odenton MD 21113
(410) 621-7992
FAX: (410) 672-5202
Mgr: Kristen Walsh
Skating Dir: Patti DeLisi
Ice surfaces: 1, 200x85, Enclosed, Outdoor/Semi Outdoor. *Open:* Year Round. *Ownership:* Private. *Access:* Public. *Sessions:* Public, Rental, Freestyle, Patch, Hockey. *Classes/Lessons:* Group, Private. *Program*

Affiliation: ISIA. *Services:* Pro Shop, Skate Rental, Skate Sharpening, Snack Bar, Dressing Rooms, Lockers. *Notes:* Meeting room; 500-capacity arena; *Washington Capitals* training center (they have sauna and equipment). Public can watch the team practice.

Talbot County Community Center
10028 Ocean Gateway
Easton MD 21601
(410) 822-7070
Mgr: Karl Oesterling
Ice surfaces: 1, 200x85, Enclosed. *Open:* Oct.-Mar. *Ownership:* Municipal. *Access:* Public. *Sessions:* Public, Private/Club, Freestyle, Patch, Hockey, Rental. *Classes/Lessons:* Group, Private. *Program Affiliation:* USFSA. *Summer School:* No. *Services:* Snack Bar, Lockers.

Tucker Road Ice Arena
1771 Tucker Rd.
Fort Washington MD 20744
(301) 248-3124
Mgr: Julieanne Schrom
Ice surfaces: 1, 200x85, Outdoor/Semi Outdoor. *Open:* Oct.-Mar. *Ownership:* Municipal. *Access:* Public. *Clubs:* Capital Boys Hockey Club; Tucker Rd. FSC, Northern VA. Hockey Club. *Sessions:* Public, Rental, Freestyle, Patch, Hockey. *Classes/Lessons:* Private, Group. *Program Affiliation:* ISIA. *Summer School:* No. *Services:* Skate Rental, Skate Sharpening, Snack Bar, Lockers, Dressing Rooms.

Wells (Herbert) Ice Rink
5211 Calvert Rd
College Park MD 20740
(301) 277-3717
FAX: (301) 779-0302
Mgr: Carrye Massey
Ice surfaces: 1, 200x80, Outdoor/Semi Outdoor. *Open:* Oct.-Mar. *Ownership:* Municipal. *Access:* Public. *Sessions:* Public, Private/Club, Rental, Freestyle, Patch, Dance, Hockey. *Classes/Lessons:* Group, Private. *Program Affiliation:* ISIA. *Summer School:* No. *Services:* Pro Shop, Skate Rental, Skate Sharpening, Snack Bar, Dressing Rooms, Lockers.

Wheaton Ice Rink
Arcola Ave. & Orebaugh
Wheaton MD 20902
(301) 649-2703
Mgr: Ron Postman
Ice surfaces: 1, 200x75, Outdoor/Semi Outdoor. *Open:* Oct.-Mar. *Ownership:* Municipal. *Access:* Public. *Sessions:* Public, Rental, Freestyle, Patch, Dance, Hockey. *Classes/Lessons:* Group, Private. *Program Affiliation:* ISIA. *Summer School:* No. *Services:* Skate Sharpening, Skate Rental, Snack Bar, Lockers. *Notes:* Multi-purpose room.

ME: MAINE

Alfond Arena
4900 Mayflower Dr.
Waterville ME 04901
(207) 872-3000
Mgr: Scott Borek
Ice surfaces: 1, 200x85, Enclosed. *Open:* Oct.-Mar. *Ownership:* Private. *Access:* Public. *Clubs:* Waterville HS, Waterville Youth Hockey, Central Maine Skating Club. *College/Univ:* Colby College. *Sessions:* Public, Private/Club, Rental, Hockey. *Classes/Lessons:* Group, Private. *Program Affiliation:* USFSA. *Summer School:* No. *Services:* Skate Rental, Skate Sharpening, Weight Room, Lockers, Dressing Rooms. *Notes:* Freestyle, patch and dance sessions are offered through the club only.

Alfond Ice Arena, University of Maine at Orono
5747 College Ave.
Orono ME 04469
(207) 581-1106
Mgr: Arnold Robertson
Ice surfaces: 1, 185x85, Enclosed. *Open:* Year Round. *Ownership:* Private. *Access:* Public. *Clubs:* Univ. of Maine Blackbears. *College/Univ:* Univ. of Maine. *Sessions:* Public, Private/Club, Rental, Freestyle, Hockey. *Classes/Lessons:* None. *Summer School:* No. *Services:* Skate Rental, Skate Sharpening, Snack Bar, Ballet Room, Weight Room, Pool and/or Athletic Facilities, Lockers, Dressing Rooms.

Ashland Area Recreational Ice Rink
Ashland ME 04732
(207) 435-6893
Mgr: Lenbell Tarr
Ice surfaces: 1, 200x85, Outdoor/Semi Outdoor. *Open:* Dec.-Feb. *Ownership:* Municipal. *Access:* Public. *Sessions:* Public. *Classes/Lessons:* None. *Summer School:* No. *Services:* Skate Rental, Skate Sharpening. *Notes:* Warming hut.

Biddeford Ice Arena
Alfred St.
Biddeford ME 04005
(207) 283-0615
Mgr: Earl Goodwin
Ice surfaces: 1, 200x85, Enclosed. *Open:* Oct.-Apr.; few weeks in summer. *Ownership:* Municipal. *Access:* Public. *Clubs:* Southern Maine FSC. *Sessions:* Public, Private/Club, Rental, Hockey. *Classes/Lessons:* Group, Private. *Program Affiliation:* ISIA, USFSA. *Summer School:* Local. *Services:* Pro Shop, Skate Sharpening, Snack Bar, Dressing Rooms. *Notes:* Freestyle, patch, and dance sessions offered through club only. Game room available.

Bridgeton Academy Ice Arena
Bridgeton Academy, Rt. 37
North Bridgeton ME 04057
(207) 647-3322
Mgr: Brad Smith
Ice surfaces: 1, 200x85, Outdoor/Semi Outdoor. *Open:* Jan.-Mar. *Ownership:* Private. School, community use. *Sessions:* Hockey. *Classes/Lessons:* None. *Program Affiliation:* Own. *Services:* Skate Sharpening, Weight Room.

Central Maine Civic Center
1 Birch St. Extension
Lewiston ME 04240
(207) 783-2009
Mgr: Georgette Richard
Ice surfaces: 1, 200x85, Enclosed, Outdoor/Semi Outdoor. *Open:* Year Round. *Ownership:* Private. *Access:* Public. *Clubs:* Local high school hockey. *Sessions:* Public, Private/Club, Rental, Freestyle, Dance, Hockey. *Classes/Lessons:* Group, Private. *Program Affiliation:* USFSA. *Summer School:* No. *Services:* Pro Shop, Skate Rental, Skate Sharpening, Snack Bar, Dressing Rooms.

City of Auburn Ice Arena
Pettengill Park
Auburn ME 04210
(207) 795-6375
Ice surfaces: 1, 200*85, Enclosed. *Open:* Oct.1-March 30. *Ownership:* Municipal. *Access:* Public. *Clubs:* Local high schools. *Sessions:* Public, Private/Club, Rental, Freestyle, Patch, Dance, Hockey. *Classes/Lessons:* Group. *Program Affiliation:* USFSA. *Summer School:* No. *Services:* Pro Shop, Skate Sharpening, Snack Bar, Lockers, Dressing Rooms.

City Parks & Recreation
Bangor ME 04402
(207) 947-1018
Outdoor. *Open:* Contingent on weather conditions. *Ownership:* Municipal. *Access:* Public. *Sessions:* Public. *Classes/Lessons:* None. *Program Affiliation:* Own. *Summer School:* No. *Notes:* Parks & Rec flood 10 areas in winter. No lessons are offered & all ice is public skate. For information on location, months & hours of operation, call the Parks Department above.

City Parks & Recreation Dept.
Auburn ME 04210
(207) 784-0191
Outdoor. *Open:* Contingent on weather conditions. *Ownership:* Municipal. *Access:* Public. *Sessions:* Public. *Classes/Lessons:* None. *Program Affiliation:* Own. *Summer School:* No. *Notes:* Parks & Rec floods 5 areas in winter. No lessons are offered & all ice is public skate. For information on location, months & hours of operation, call the Parks Department above.

Cumberland County Civic Center
1 Civic Center Square
Portland ME 04101
(201) 775-3481
Mgr: Steve Crane
Ice surfaces: 1, 200x85, Enclosed. *Open:* Oct.-May. *Ownership:* Municipal. *Access:* Members Only. *Clubs:* Rocky Coast FSC. *Sessions:* Rental. *Classes/Lessons:* None. *Summer School:* No. *Services:* Dressing Rooms.

Dayton Arena
Bowdoin College
Harpswell and Bath Rd.
Brunswick ME 04011
(207) 725-3332
Mgr: Terry Meagher
Ice surfaces: 1, 200x85, Enclosed. *Open:* Oct.-Mar. *Ownership:* Private. *Access:* Restricted. *Restrictions:* College community. *Clubs:* Costal Hockey League; Brunswick FSC, Brunswick Hockey Club; Midcoast Youth Hockey. *College/Univ:* Bowdoin College. *Sessions:* Private/Club, Rental, Freestyle, Hockey. *Services:* Skate Sharpening, Lockers, Dressing Rooms. *Notes:* Lessons offered through clubs.

Forum, The
84 Mechanic St.
Presque Isle ME 04769
(207) 764-0491
FAX: (207) 764-2525
Mgr: Jim Kaiser
Ice surfaces: 1, 185x85, Enclosed. *Open:* Oct.-Mar. *Ownership:* Municipal. *Access:* Public. *Clubs:* Gentleman's Hockey League; Skating Club of Maine. *College/Univ:* Northern Maine Technical College. *Sessions:* Public, Rental, Hockey, Private/Club. *Classes/Lessons:* None. *Summer School:* No. *Services:* Pro Shop, Skate Rental, Skate Sharpening, Snack Bar, Dressing Rooms, Lockers.

Kennebec Ice Arena
Whitten Rd.
Hallowell ME 04347
(207) 622-6354
Mgr: Allan Globensky
Skating Dir: John Millier
Ice surfaces: 1, 200x85, Enclosed. *Open:* Year Round. *Ownership:* Private. *Access:* Public. *Clubs:* SC of Maine, SC of Brunswick. *Sessions:* Public, Freestyle, Patch, Dance, Hockey, Rental. *Classes/Lessons:* Private, Group. *Program Affiliation:* USFSA. *Summer School:* Local. *Services:* Pro Shop, Skate Rental, Skate Sharpening, Snack Bar, Lockers, Dressing Rooms. *Notes:* Conference and multi-purpose rooms.

North Yarmouth Academy Ice Arena
123 Main St.
Yarmouth ME 04096
(207) 846-9051
Mgr: Lee Roy
Ice surfaces: 1, 200x85, Enclosed. *Open:* July-Mar. *Ownership:* Private. *Access:* Public. *Clubs:* Casko Bay Youth Hockey; Midcoast Youth Hockey. *Sessions:* Public, Rental, Hockey. *Classes/Lessons:* None. *Program Affiliation:* Own. *Summer School:* Local. *Services:* Pro Shop, Skate Sharpening, Snack Bar, Lockers.

Portland Ice Arena
225 Park Ave.
Portland ME 04102
(207) 774-8553
Mgr: Jeffrey Bearey
Skating Dir: Lynda Hathaway
Ice surfaces: 1, 200x85, Enclosed. *Open:* July-Apr. *Ownership:* Municipal. *Access:* Public. *Clubs:* Rocky Coast FSC, SC of Maine; Rocky Coast Division; Industrial Hockey. *College/Univ:* University of Southern Maine. *Sessions:* Public, Private/Club, Rental, Freestyle, Patch, Dance, Hockey. *Classes/Lessons:* Group, Private. *Program Affiliation:* ISIA. *Summer School:* National/International. *Services:* Pro Shop, Skate Rental, Skate Sharpening, Snack Bar, Dressing Rooms. *Notes:* Vending machines; game room.

Robinson Arena at Hebron Academy
Rt. 119
Hebron ME 04238
(207) 966-2812
Mgr: Michael Toole
Ice surfaces: 1, 200x85, Enclosed. *Open:* Oct.-Mar. *Ownership:* Private. *Access:* Public. *Clubs:* New England Prep School Hockey Assn. *Sessions:* Public, Rental, Hockey. *Classes/Lessons:* Group. *Program Affiliation:* USFSA. *Summer School:* No. *Services:* Snack Bar, Lockers, Dressing Rooms. *Notes:* Will soon have summer school.

Sawyer Ice Arena
107 13th St.
Bangor ME 04401
(207) 947-0071
Mgr: Tim McDoogal
Ice surfaces: 1, 200x85, Enclosed. *Open:* Nov.-Apr. *Ownership:* Municipal. *Access:*

Public. *Clubs:* Bangor Youth Hockey and four high schools. *Sessions:* Public, Hockey, General, Rental. *Classes/Lessons:* Group. *Program Affiliation:* USFSA. *Summer School:* No. *Services:* Snack Bar, Dressing Rooms. *Notes:* Primarily a hockey rink.

Sukee Arena and Events Center
1270 Verti Dr.
Winslow ME 04901
(207) 872-5994
Mgr: Sandy McCabe
Ice surfaces: 1, 200x85, Enclosed. *Open:* Sept.-Mar. *Ownership:* Private. *Access:* Public. *Clubs:* Winslow Youth Hockey; Central Maine Skating Club. *Sessions:* Public, Private/Club, Rental, Freestyle, Hockey. *Classes/Lessons:* Group, Private. *Program Affiliation:* USFSA. *Summer School:* No. *Services:* Skate Rental, Skate Sharpening, Snack Bar, Lockers, Dressing Rooms.

Sunday River Ski Resort
Sunday River Access Rd.
Bethel ME 04217
(207) 824-3000
FAX: (207) 824-2111
Ice surfaces: 1, Outdoor/Semi Outdoor. *Open:* Dec.-Feb. *Ownership:* Private. *Access:* Restricted. *Restrictions:* Guests of the lodge. *Sessions:* Public. *Classes/Lessons:* None. *Program Affiliation:* Own. *Summer School:* No. *Notes:* Primarily a ski resort.

Thibodiau (Marc) Memorial Rink
State St.
Millinocket ME 04462
(207) 723-7013
Mgr: Jeff Ketchum
Ice surfaces: 2, 200x85; 60x50, Outdoor/Semi Outdoor. *Open:* Dec.-mid Feb. *Ownership:* Municipal. *Access:* Public. *Sessions:* Public, Private/Club, Hockey. *Classes/Lessons:* Group. *Program Affiliation:* Own. *Summer School:* No. *Services:* Studio Rink, Snack Bar, Dressing Rooms. *Notes:* Dressing rooms for hockey use only.

Van Buren Ice Rink
5 Champlain St.
Van Buren ME 04785
(207) 868-3395
Mgr: Brian Hews
Ice surfaces: 1, 185x85, Outdoor/Semi Outdoor. *Open:* Dec.-Mar. *Ownership:* Municipal. *Access:* Public. *Sessions:* Public, Hockey. *Classes/Lessons:* None. *Summer School:* No. *Services:* Snack Bar, Dressing Rooms.

MI: MICHIGAN

Adams (Jack) Arena
10500 Lindon
Detroit MI 48238
(313) 935-4510
Mgr: Earnest Hunter
Skating Dir: Earnest Hunter
Ice surfaces: 1, 200x85, Enclosed. *Open:* Aug.-May. *Ownership:* Municipal. *Access:* Public. *Clubs:* Renaissance FSC, Detroit Hockey Assn. *Sessions:* Public, Rental, Freestyle, Patch, Dance, Hockey. *Classes/Lessons:* Group, Private. *Program Affiliation:* ISIA. *Summer School:* No. *Services:* Pro Shop, Skate Rental, Skate Sharpening, Snack Bar, Pool and/or Athletic Facilities, Lockers, Dressing Rooms. *Notes:* Attached to recreation center.

Adray (Mike) Sports Arena
14900 Ford Rd.
Dearborn MI 48126
(313) 943-4098
Mgr: Kirk Young
Ice surfaces: 1, 185x85, Enclosed. *Open:* Aug.-May. *Ownership:* Municipal. *Access:* Public. *Clubs:* Dearborn Hockey Assn., Great Lakes FSC. *Sessions:* Public, Private/Club, Rental, Freestyle, Patch, Hockey. *Classes/Lessons:* Group, Private. *Program Affiliation:* ISIA. *Summer School:* No. *Services:* Snack Bar, Lockers, Dressing Rooms. *Notes:* Meeting room.

Adrian Ice Rink
Riverside Park, 631 McKinzie
Adrian MI 49221
(517) 265-8675
Mgr: Tim Kopka
Ice surfaces: 1, 200x85, Outdoor/Semi Outdoor. *Open:* Dec.-Mar. *Ownership:* Municipal. *Access:* Public. *Sessions:* Public, Private/Club, Rental, Hockey. *Classes/Lessons:* Group. *Program Affiliation:* Own. *Summer School:* No. *Services:* Pro Shop, Skate Sharpening, Snack Bar, Pool and/or Athletic Facilities, Dressing Rooms, Skate Rental.

Alger Centennial Arena
Munising MI 49862
(906) 387-9975
Mgr: John Kolbus
Ice surfaces: 1, 187x87, Enclosed. *Open:* Oct.-Mar. *Ownership:* Alger Centennial Arena Committee. *Access:* Public. *Clubs:* Munising Youth Hockey; FSC. *Sessions:* Public, Rental, Hockey. *Classes/Lessons:* None. *Summer School:* No. *Services:* Skate Rental, Skate Sharpening, Snack Bar, Dressing Rooms.

Belknap Park Arena
30 Coldbrook
Grand Rapids MI 49503
(616) 235-0503
Mgr: Ron Stack
Ice surfaces: 1, 200x85, Enclosed. *Open:* Sept-May. *Ownership:* Municipal. *Access:* Public. *Clubs:* Lake Effect FSC, Grand Rapids Hockey Assn. *Sessions:* Public, Rental. *Classes/Lessons:* Group. *Program Affiliation:* USFSA. *Summer School:* No. *Services:* Skate Rental, Pro Shop, Skate Sharpening, Snack Bar, Lockers. *Notes:* Learn-to-Skate programs offered.

Berkley Ice Arena
2300 Robina Ave.
Berkley MI 48072
(810) 546-2460
Mgr: John Allen
Skating Dir: Laurie McCormick
Ice surfaces: 1, 200x85, Enclosed. *Open:* Sept.-Apr. *Ownership:* Municipal. *Access:* Public. *Clubs:* Berkley Royal Blades FSC . *Sessions:* Public, Rental, Patch, Freestyle, Dance, Hockey. *Classes/Lessons:* Group. *Program Affiliation:* USFSA. *Services:* Pro Shop, Skate Rental, Skate Sharpening, Studio Rink, Snack Bar, Weight Room, Lockers, Dressing Rooms.

Bicentennnial Ice Arena
Laurium MI 49913
(906) 337-1881
FAX: (906) 337-4461
Mgr: Eddie Verton
Ice surfaces: 1, 180x80, Enclosed. *Open:* Dec.-Mar. *Ownership:* Municipal. *Access:* Public. *Clubs:* Calumet Jr. Hockey Assn.; Calumet FSC. *Sessions:* Public, Private/Club, Rental. *Classes/Lessons:* None. *Summer School:* No. *Services:* Dressing Rooms, Snack Bar.

Birmingham Ice Sports Arena
2300 E. Lincoln
Birmingham MI 48009
(313) 654-0731
FAX: (313) 644-5614
Mgr: Robert Fox
Ice surfaces: 1, 200x80, Enclosed. *Open:* Sept.-Apr. *Ownership:* Municipal. *Access:* Public. *Sessions:* Public, Private/Club, Rental, Freestyle, Patch, Dance, Hockey. *Classes/Lessons:* Group, Private. *Program Affiliation:* ISIA. *Services:* Pro Shop, Skate Rental, Skate Sharpening, Studio Rink, Snack Bar, Lockers, Dressing Rooms. *Notes:* Video room; conference room; handicapped access.

Buhr Park Ice Rink
2751 Packard Rd.
Ann Arbor MI 48108
(313) 994-2784
Mgr: Cynthia Jones
Ice surfaces: 1, 185x80, Outdoor/Semi Outdoor. *Open:* Nov.-Mar. *Ownership:* Municipal. *Access:* Public. *Sessions:* Public, Rental, Hockey. *Classes/Lessons:* Group. *Program Affiliation:* USFSA. *Services:* Pro Shop, Skate Rental, Skate Sharpening, Snack Bar, Lockers, Dressing Rooms.

Cheboygan Ice Rink / Pavillion
480 Seymour
Cheboygan MI 49721
(616) 627-3255
Mgr: Ralph Cantile
Skating Dir: Barb Deeter
Ice surfaces: 1, 200x85, Enclosed. *Open:* Sept.- Mar. *Ownership:* Private. *Access:* Public. *Sessions:* Public, Rental, Hockey. *Classes/Lessons:* Group. *Program Affiliation:* Own. *Summer School:* No. *Services:* Skate Rental, Skate Sharpening, Snack Bar, Weight Room, Lockers, Dressing Rooms. *Notes:* Learn-to-skate programs.

City Sports Center Ice Rink
3401 E. Lafayette
Detroit MI 48207
(313) 567-2423
Mgr: Bill Stars
Ice surfaces: 2, 200x85; 200x85, Enclosed. *Open:* Year Round. *Ownership:* Private. *Access:* Restricted. *Restrictions:* hockey; rental. *Clubs:* Redwings Hockey; Grosse Point Hockey; Wayne Chiefs Jr. Hockey. *Sessions:* Public, Private/Club, Rental, Hockey. *Classes/Lessons:* Group. *Summer School:* Local. *Services:* Pro Shop, Skate Sharpening, Snack Bar, Weight Room, Lockers, Dressing Rooms.

Compuware Oak Park Arena
13950 Oak Park Blvd.
Oak Park MI 48237
(810) 543-2338
FAX: (810) 543-2792
Mgr: Mike Vellucci
Ice surfaces: 1, 200x70, Enclosed. *Open:* Year Round. *Access:* Public. *Clubs:* Compuware Embassador Junior A Team. *Sessions:* Public, Rental, Hockey. *Classes/Lessons:* None. *Summer School:* No. *Services:* Pro Shop, Skate Rental, Skate Sharpening, Snack Bar, Lockers, Dressing Rooms.

Detroit Skating Club
888 Denison Ct.
Bloomfield Hills MI 48302
(810) 332-7133
FAX: (810) 332-9912
Mgr: Ron Holbrook
Skating Dir: Johnny Johns
Ice surfaces: 2, 200x100; 200x100, Enclosed. *Open:* Year Round. *Ownership:* Club. *Access:* Members Only. *Clubs:* Detroit SC. *Sessions:* Freestyle, Patch, Dance, Hockey, pairs. *Classes/Lessons:* Group, Private. *Program Affiliation:* USFSA. *Summer School:* National/International. *Services:* Pro Shop, Skate Sharpening, Snack Bar, Ballet Room, Weight Room, Lockers, Dressing Rooms. *Notes:* Snack bar; homemade healthy food.

Edgar (Eddie) Arena
33841 Lyndon
Livonia MI 48154
(313) 427-1280
FAX: (313) 421-1807
Mgr: Gary Gray
Ice surfaces: 1, 200x80, Enclosed. *Open:* Sept.-Mar. *Ownership:* Municipal. *Access:* Public. *Clubs:* Hockey Assn., Figure Skating Assn., Livonia Public Schools. *Sessions:* Public, Private/Club, Rental, Freestyle, Patch, Dance, Hockey. *Classes/Lessons:* Group, Private. *Program Affiliation:* ISIA. *Summer School:* No. *Services:* Snack Bar, Pool and/or Athletic Facilities, Dressing Rooms.

Ewigleben (Robert L.) Ice Arena
Ferris State University, 210 Sports Dr.
Big Rapids MI 49307
(616) 592-2881
FAX: (616) 592-2883
Mgr: Ben Mumah
Ice surfaces: 2, 1, 200x85; 110x75, Enclosed. *Open:* Year Round. *Ownership:* University. *Access:* Public. *Clubs:* Big Rapids FSC, Big Rapids Area Jr. Hockey Assn. *College/Univ:* Ferris State University. *Sessions:* Public, Private/Club, Rental, Freestyle, Patch, Dance, Hockey. *Classes/Lessons:* Group, Private. *Program Affiliation:* ISIA. *Summer School:* Local. *Services:* Pro Shop, Skate Rental, Skate Sharpening, Studio Rink, Snack Bar, Lockers, Dressing Rooms.

Flint Four Seasons Sport Center
1160 South Elms Rd.
Flint MI 48532
(313) 635-8487
FAX: (313) 635-9313
Mgr: Sam Shukary
Ice surfaces: 2, 100x85; 100x85, Enclosed. *Open:* Year Round. *Ownership:* Private. *Access:* Public. *Clubs:* Flint Four Seasons Skating Club, East MI Hockey Assn., Flint City Hockey. *Sessions:* Public, Private/Club, Rental, Freestyle, Patch, Dance, Hockey. *Classes/Lessons:* Group, Private. *Program Affiliation:* USFSA, ISIA. *Services:* Pro Shop, Skate Rental, Skate Sharpening, Snack Bar, Dressing Rooms, Lockers.

Fraser Ice Arenas
34400 Utica Rd.
Fraser MI 48026
(810) 294-8700
FAX: (810) 294-1290
Mgr: Jamie LaLonde
Skating Dir: Adrienne Leonard
Ice surfaces: 4, 200x85; 200x85; 200x85; 200x85, Enclosed. *Open:* Year Round. *Ownership:* Private. *Access:* Public. *Clubs:* Fraser FSC. *Sessions:* Public, Private/Club, Rental, Hockey. *Classes/Lessons:* Group, Private. *Program Affiliation:* ISIA. *Summer School:* Local. *Services:* Pro Shop, Skate Sharpening, Snack Bar, Ballet Room, Weight Room, Lockers, Dressing Rooms. *Notes:* Freestyle, patch and dance sessions offered through the club only.

Garden City Ice Arena
200 Log Cabin Rd.
Garden City MI 48135
(313) 261-3491
FAX: (313) 525-8881
Mgr: Tim Whitson
Ice surfaces: 1, 200x85, Enclosed. *Open:* Aug.-June. *Ownership:* Municipal. *Access:* Public. *Clubs:* Garden City FSC, Garden City Youth Athletic Assn. *Sessions:* Public, Rental, Freestyle, Patch, Hockey. *Classes/Lessons:* Group, Private. *Program Affiliation:* USFSA. *Services:* Skate Rental, Snack Bar, Pool and/or Athletic Facilities, Lockers, Dressing Rooms. *Notes:* Bleachers; meeting and kitchen facilities.

Grand Oaks Arena
970 Grand Oaks Dr.
Howell MI 48843
(517) 548-4355
Mgr: Fred Joncas
Ice surfaces: 1, 200x85, Enclosed. *Open:* July-May. *Ownership:* Private. *Access:* Public. *Clubs:* ISIA and USFSC. *Sessions:* Public, Private/Club, Hockey, Rental. *Classes/Lessons:* Group, Private. *Program Affiliation:* ISIA. *Summer School:* Local. *Services:* Pro Shop, Skate Sharpening, Snack Bar, Lockers, Dressing Rooms.

Grosse Pointe Community Rink
4831 Canyon Dr.
Detroit MI 48236
(313) 885-4100
Mgr: Ray Rivard
Ice surfaces: 1, 200x85, Enclosed. *Open:* Year Round. *Ownership:* Club. *Access:* Restricted, Members Only. Rentals . *Clubs:* Grosse Pointe Skating Club,;Grosse Pointe Hockey Assn. *Sessions:* Rental. *Classes/Lessons:* Group. *Services:* Pro Shop, Skate Sharpening, Snack Bar, Dressing Rooms.

Heilmann Recreation Center
19601 Crusade St.
Detroit MI 48205
(313) 267-7153
Mgr: Linda Murff
Ice surfaces: 1, 200x85, Outdoor/Semi Outdoor. *Open:* Jan.-May. *Ownership:* Municipal. *Access:* Public. *Sessions:* Public, Rental, Freestyle, Patch, Hockey. *Classes/Lessons:* Group, Private. *Program Affiliation:* Own. *Services:* Skate Rental, Snack Bar, Lockers, Dressing Rooms.

Howe Arena
1125 West Civic Center Dr.
Traverse City MI 49684
(616) 922-4814
FAX: (616) 922-2064
Mgr: Bob Schlitts
Ice surfaces: 1, 192x85, Enclosed. *Open:* July-Mar. *Ownership:* Municipal. *Access:* Public. *Clubs:* Twin Bay SC; Grand Traverse Hockey Assn.; high school hockey. *Sessions:* Public, Private/Club, Rental, Hockey. *Classes/Lessons:* Group, Private. *Program Affiliation:* USFSA. *Summer School:* Local. *Services:* Snack Bar, Lockers, Dressing Rooms. *Notes:* Freestyle, patch and dance sessions are offered through the club only.

I. M. A. Ice Arena
3501 Lapeer Rd.
Flint MI 48503
(810) 744-0580
Mgr: George Dellinger
Ice surfaces: 2, 200x85; 200x85, Enclosed. *Open:* Sept.-Apr. *Ownership:* Municipal. *Access:* Public. *Sessions:* Public, Rental, Hockey. *Services:* Lockers, Dressing Rooms.

Icebox Sports Arena
21902 Telegraph Rd.
Trenton MI 48183
(313) 676-6429
Mgr: Artie Norian
Ice surfaces: 2, 200x85; 200x85, Enclosed. *Open:* Year Round. *Ownership:* Private. *Access:* Restricted. *Restrictions:* No public sessions. *Sessions:* Private/Club, Rental, Freestyle, Patch, Dance, Hockey. *Classes/Lessons:* Group, Private. *Program Affiliation:* USFSA, ISIA. *Services:* Pro Shop, Skate Sharpening, Snack Bar, Ballet Room, Lockers, Dressing Rooms, Weight Room. *Notes:* All-purpose room.

Inkster Civic Arena
27077 S River Park Dr.
Inkster MI 48141
(616) 277-1001
Mgr: Eddie Roth
Ice surfaces: 1, 200x85, Enclosed. *Open:* Sept.-May. *Ownership:* Municipal. *Access:* Public. *Sessions:* Public, Private/Club, Rental, Hockey. *Program Affiliation:* Own. *Summer School:* No. *Services:* Pro Shop, Skate Sharpening, Snack Bar, Lockers, Dressing Rooms. *Notes:* Any lessons are offered by clubs that infrequently rent ice time. The rink offers no lessons.

Kennedy Ice Arena
Kennedy Recreation Center
3131 W. Road
Trenton MI 48183
(313) 676-7171
Mgr: Rocky Hibbard
Ice surfaces: 1, 190 x 85, Enclosed. *Open:* Sept.-Mar. *Ownership:* Municipal. *Access:* Public. *Sessions:* Public, Rental, Hockey, General. *Classes/Lessons:* Group. *Program Affiliation:* ISIA. *Summer School:* No. *Services:* Skate Sharpening, Pro Shop, Snack Bar, Pool and/or Athletic Facilities, Lockers, Dressing Rooms. *Notes:* Pool is not open simultaneously with ice rink.

Kentwood Ice Arena
6198 Campus Park SE
Kentwood MI 49508
(616) 698-0100
FAX: (616) 698-3013
Mgr: Todd Bell
Ice surfaces: 1, 200x85, Enclosed. *Open:* Year Round. *Ownership:* Kentwood Public School System. *Access:* Public. *Clubs:* Kentwood Amateur Hockey Assn.; Grand Rapids FSC. *Sessions:* Public, Rental, Freestyle, Patch, Dance, Hockey. *Classes/Lessons:* Group. *Program Affiliation:* USFSA, ISIA. *Summer School:* Regional. *Services:* Lockers, Dressing Rooms, Snack Bar, Skate Sharpening, Pro Shop.

L'Anse Arena
Main St.
L'Anse MI 49946
(906) 524-5707
Mgr: Al Marcot
Ice surfaces: 1, 200x85, Enclosed. *Open:* Oct.-May. *Ownership:* Municipal. *Access:* Public. *Clubs:* L'Anse FSC. *Sessions:* Public, Private/Club, Rental, Freestyle, Patch, Dance, Hockey. *Classes/Lessons:* Group, Private. *Program Affiliation:* USFSA. *Summer School:* No. *Services:* Skate Rental, Skate Sharpening, Snack Bar, Weight Room, Lockers, Dressing Rooms.

Lakeland Ice Arena
7330 Highland Rd.
Waterford MI 48327
(810) 666-1911
FAX: (810) 666-1903
Mgr: Urban Rice
Skating Dir: Hollie Head
Ice surfaces: 3, 200x85; 200x85; 200x85, Enclosed. *Open:* Year Round. *Ownership:* Private. *Access:* Public. *Clubs:* Lakeland Hockey Assn., Lakeland FSC. *Sessions:* Private/Club, Rental, Freestyle, Patch, Hockey. *Classes/Lessons:* Private, Group. *Program Affiliation:* ISIA, USFSA. *Summer School:* Local. *Services:* Pro Shop, Skate Sharpening, Snack Bar, Ballet Room, Lockers, Dressing Rooms.

Lakeview Arena
401 E. Fair Ave.
Marquette MI 49855
(906) 228-0490
Mgr: Butch Runstrom
Ice surfaces: 2, 200x85; 200x85, Enclosed. *Open:* Oct.-Mar.; June-Aug. *Ownership:* Municipal. *Access:* Public. *Clubs:* Marquette FSC, northern Michigan University Hockey Team. *College/Univ:* Northern Michigan University. *Sessions:* Public, Private/Club, Rental, Hockey. *Classes/Lessons:* Group, Private. *Program Affiliation:* Own. *Services:* Pro Shop, Skate Sharpening, Snack Bar, Dressing Rooms. *Notes:* Two conference/reception rooms.

Lansing Ice Arena
1475 Lake Lansing Rd.
Lansing MI 48912
(517) 482-1597
FAX: (517) 372-3445
Mgr: Fred Brunyate
Skating Dir: Brenda Peterson
Ice surfaces: 1, 200x85, Enclosed. *Open:* Year Round. *Ownership:* Private. *Access:* Public. *Clubs:* Lansing SC; Greater Lansing Amateur Hockey Assn. *Sessions:* Public, Private/Club, Freestyle, Rental, Patch, Dance, Hockey. *Classes/Lessons:* Group, Private. *Program Affiliation:* USFSA. *Summer School:* Local. *Services:* Skate Rental, Pro Shop, Skate Sharpening, Snack Bar, Pool and/or Athletic Facilities, Dressing Rooms, Lockers. *Notes:* On-site gym.

Lawson Ice Arena
Western Michigan University
Kalamazoo MI 49008
(616) 387-3050
Mgr: Paul Schneider
Skating Dir: Jaci Dalke
Ice surfaces: 1, 200x85, Enclosed. *Open:* Year Round. *Ownership:* Private. *Access:* Public. *Clubs:* Kalamazoo FSC. *College/Univ:* Western Michigan University. *Sessions:* Public, Private/Club, Rental, Freestyle, Patch, Hockey. *Classes/Lessons:* Group, Private. *Program Affiliation:* USFSA, ISIA. *Summer School:* Local. *Services:* Pro Shop, Skate Rental, Skate Sharpening, Snack Bar, Weight Room, Pool and/or Athletic Facilities, Lockers, Dressing Rooms.

Lincoln Park Community Center
3525 Dix Ave.
Lincoln Park MI 48146
(313) 386-4075
Mgr: Tom McPartlin
Ice surfaces: 1, 200x85, Enclosed. *Open:* Aug.-Apr. *Ownership:* Municipal. *Access:* Public. *Clubs:* Skate Company SC; Lincoln Park Hockey Assn. *Sessions:* Public, Rental, Freestyle, Patch, Dance, Hockey. *Classes/Lessons:* Group, Private. *Program Affiliation:* USFSA. *Services:* Pro Shop, Skate Rental, Skate Sharpening, Snack Bar, Lockers, Dressing Rooms.

Lindell (John) Arena
1403 Lexington Blvd.
Royal Oak MI 48073
(810) 544-6690
Mgr: Noreen Daley-Seile
Skating Dir: Noreen Daley-Seile
Ice surfaces: 2, 200x85; 200x75, Enclosed, Outdoor/Semi Outdoor. *Open:* Aug.-May. *Ownership:* Municipal. *Access:* Public. *Clubs:* North Suburban FSC, Royal Oak Hockey Assn. *Sessions:* Public, Private/Club, Rental, Hockey. *Classes/Lessons:* Group, Private. *Program Affiliation:* USFSA. *Services:* Skate Sharpening, Snack Bar, Lockers, Dressing Rooms. *Notes:* Meeting rooms. Freestyle and patch session are offered through the skating club only.

McMorran Place Arena
701 McMorran Blvd.
Port Huron MI 48060
(810) 985-6166
FAX: (313) 985-3358
Mgr: Morris Snider
Ice surfaces: 2, 185x85; 185x85, Enclosed. *Open:* Aug.-Mar.; Nov.-Feb. *Ownership:* Municipal. *Access:* Public. *Clubs:* Port Huron FSC, Port Huron Minor Hockey Assn.; Happy Blades Club. *Sessions:* Public, Private/Club, Rental, Hockey. *Classes/Lessons:* None. *Program Affiliation:* Own. *Services:* Skate Sharpening, Dressing Rooms. *Notes:* Concession stands; theatre space; banquet rooms.

Melvindale Arena
4300 S. Dearborne
Melvindale MI 48122
(313) 928-1201
Mgr: Carol Burns
Skating Dir: Mary Haskin
Ice surfaces: 1, 200x85, Enclosed. *Open:* Aug.-May. *Ownership:* Municipal. *Access:* Public. *Clubs:* Melvindale FS Boosters. *Sessions:* Public, Private/Club, Rental, Freestyle, Patch, Hockey. *Classes/Lessons:* Group, Private. *Program Affiliation:* ISIA. *Summer School:* No. *Services:* Pro Shop, Skate Sharpening, Snack Bar, Dressing Rooms.

Mich - E - Kewis Ice Rink
State Ave.
Alpena MI 49707
(517) 354-8191
Mgr: Peter Parker
Ice surfaces: 1, 200x85, Enclosed. *Open:* Oct.-Mar. *Ownership:* Municipal. *Access:* Public. *Clubs:* MAHA USA Hockey. *Sessions:* Public, Private/Club, Freestyle, Hockey. *Classes/Lessons:* Private. *Summer School:* No. *Services:* Snack Bar, Lockers, Dressing Rooms.

Michigan Tech Skating Academy Student Ice Arena
1400 Townsend Dr.
Houghton MI 49931-1295
(906) 487-2994
FAX: (906) 487-3062
Skating Dir: Cheryl DePuydt
Ice surfaces: 1, 200x85, Enclosed. *Open:* June-Mar. *Ownership:* Municipal. *Access:* Public. *Clubs:* Copper Co. Jr. Hockey Assn.; Copper Co. Skating

Academy; Portage Lake FSC. *College/ Univ:* Michigan Tech. *Sessions:* Public, Rental, Freestyle, Patch, Dance, Hockey. *Classes/Lessons:* Group, Private. *Program Affiliation:* USFSA. *Summer School:* Regional, National/International. *Services:* Pro Shop, Skate Sharpening, Snack Bar, Ballet Room, Weight Room, Lockers, Dressing Rooms. *Notes:* 200x85 gymnastics studio; summer hockey camp.

Midland Civic Arena
515 E. Collins
Midland MI 48640
(517) 832-8438
Mgr: Jim Chapman
Ice surfaces: 2, 205x90; 200x84, Enclosed. *Open:* June-Mar. *Ownership:* Municipal. *Access:* Public. *Clubs:* Midland FSC, Amateur Hockey League. *Sessions:* Public, Rental. *Classes/Lessons:* None. *Summer School:* No. *Services:* Pro Shop, Skate Sharpening, Snack Bar, Pool and/or Athletic Facilities, Lockers, Dressing Rooms. *Notes:* Lessons, freestyle, patch, dance and hockey sessions are offered through the club only.

Mountain Lions Club
Greenland & Depot St.
Greenland MI 49948
(906) 883-3208
Mgr: John Drunton
Ice surfaces: 1, 108x72, Enclosed. *Open:* Dec.-Mar. *Ownership:* Private. *Access:* Public. *Clubs:* Lions Club. *Sessions:* Public. *Classes/Lessons:* None. *Program Affiliation:* Own. *Summer School:* No. *Services:* Snack Bar. *Notes:* Rink is open on weekends only.

Mountain View Ice Arena
500 E. Hughitt St.
Iron Mountain MI 49801
(906) 774-1480
Mgr: Andy Bray
Ice surfaces: 1, 200x85, Enclosed. *Open:* Oct.-Mar. *Ownership:* Private. *Access:* Public. *Clubs:* Mountain View FSC, Veterans Hockey League. *Sessions:* Public, Rental, Hockey. *Classes/Lessons:* Group. *Summer School:* No. *Services:* Pro Shop, Skate Sharpening, Snack Bar, Lockers, Dressing Rooms. *Notes:* Special sessions are offered for beginners, teenagers, and senior citizens.

Munn Ice Arena
Michigan State University
1 Chestnut Rd.
East Lansing MI 48824
(517) 353-4698
FAX: (517) 336-1047
Mgr: Tom Campbell
Skating Dir: Tom Campbell
Ice surfaces: 1, 200x85, Enclosed. *Open:* June-Apr. *Ownership:* Private. *Access:* Public. *Clubs:* Michigan State Spartans Hockey; Lansing SC; Morning Ladies SC. *College/Univ:* Michigan State University. *Sessions:* Public, Rental, Freestyle, Hockey, Patch. *Classes/Lessons:* Group, Private. *Program Affiliation:* USFSA. *Summer School:* No. *Services:* Pro Shop, Skate Rental, Skate Sharpening, Snack Bar, Weight Room, Lockers, Dressing Rooms.

Negawnee Ice Arena
141 Rail Rd.
Negawnee MI 49866
(906) 475-7900
Ice surfaces: 1, 200x85, Enclosed. *Open:* Oct.-Mar. *Ownership:* Municipal. *Clubs:* Marquette FSC. *Sessions:* Public, Private/Club, Rental, Freestyle, Hockey. *Classes/Lessons:* Private, Group. *Summer School:* No. *Services:* Skate Rental, Skate Sharpening, Snack Bar, Ballet Room, Pool and/or Athletic Facilities, Lockers, Dressing Rooms.

Patterson Ice Center
2550 Patterson Ave. SE
Grand Rapids MI 49546
(616) 940-1423
Mgr: Don Cooley
Skating Dir: April Treadu
Ice surfaces: 2, 200x100; 200x85, Enclosed. *Open:* Year Round. *Ownership:* Private. *Access:* Public. *Clubs:* Greater Grand Rapids FSC, Greater Grand Rapids Amateur Hockey League. *College/Univ:* Calvin College. *Sessions:* Public, Private/Club, Rental, Freestyle, Patch, Dance, Hockey. *Classes/Lessons:* Group, Private. *Program Affiliation:* USFSA, ISIA. *Summer School:* Local. *Services:* Skate Rental, Pro Shop, Skate Sharpening, Snack Bar, Ballet Room, Lockers, Dressing Rooms.

Plymouth Cultural Center
525 Farmer St.
Plymouth MI 48170
(313) 455-6620
FAX: (313) 453-1132
Mgr: Steve Anderson
Ice surfaces: 1, 200 x 85, Enclosed. *Open:* Year Round. *Ownership:* Municipal. *Access:* Public. *Clubs:* Plymouth FSC, Plymouth Canton Hockey Assn. *College/Univ:* East Michigan University. *Sessions:* Public, Private/Club, Rental, Hockey. *Classes/Lessons:* Group, Private. *Program Affiliation:* ISIA. *Services:* Pro Shop, Skate Rental, Skate Sharpening, Snack Bar, Dressing Rooms. *Notes:* Freestyle and patch sessions are offered through the club only. Rink connected to the Plymouth Cultural Center.

Pullar Stadium
435 E. Portage Ave.
Sault Ste Marie MI 49783
(906) 632-6853
Mgr: Gordan Clarke
Ice surfaces: 1, 200x85, Enclosed. *Open:* Oct.-Mar. *Ownership:* Municipal. *Access:* Public. *Clubs:* Hiawatha FSC, Sault Michigan Hockey Assn. *Sessions:* Public, Rental. *Classes/Lessons:* None, Group, Private. *Program Affiliation:* USFSA, ISIA. *Summer School:* No. *Services:* Dressing Rooms, Lockers, Snack Bar, Skate Sharpening, Pro Shop, Skate Rental. *Notes:* Lessons, freestyle, patch, dance and hockey sessions are offered through the club only.

Redford Ice Arena
12400 Beach Daly
Redford MI 48239
(313) 937-0913
Mgr: Dan McManamon
Ice surfaces: 1, 200x85, Enclosed. *Open:* July-May. *Ownership:* Municipal. *Access:* Public. *Clubs:* Redford Township Hockey Assn. *Sessions:* Public, Private/Club, Rental, Freestyle, Patch, Hockey. *Classes/Lessons:* Group, Private. *Program Affiliation:* ISIA. *Summer School:* No. *Services:* Pro Shop, Skate Rental, Skate Sharpening, Snack Bar, Lockers, Dressing Rooms.

Saginaw Bay Ice Arena
6129 Bay Rd.
Saginaw MI 48604
(517) 799-8950
FAX: (517) 790-1723
Mgr: David Westner
Ice surfaces: 1, 200x85, Enclosed. *Open:* Aug.-May. *Ownership:* Private. *Access:* Public. *Clubs:* Greater Saginaw Amateur Hockey League. *Sessions:* Public, Rental, Freestyle, Patch, Dance, Hockey. *Classes/Lessons:* Group, Private. *Program Affiliation:* USFSA, ISIA. *Summer School:* No. *Services:* Pro Shop, Skate Rental, Skate Sharpening, Snack Bar, Lockers, Dressing Rooms.

Southfield Civic Center
26000 Evergreen Rd.
Southfield MI 48073
(313) 354-9357
Mgr: Dave Bayer
Skating Dir: Ron Baster
Ice surfaces: 1, 200x85, Enclosed. *Open:* Aug.-May. *Ownership:* Municipal. *Access:* Public. *Clubs:* Southfield HC. *College/Univ:* Lawrence Technical Institute. *Sessions:* Public, Private/Club, Rental, Freestyle, Patch, Dance, Hockey. *Classes/Lessons:* Group, Private. *Program Affiliation:* USFSA. *Summer School:* Local. *Services:* Pro Shop, Skate Rental, Skate Sharpening, Snack Bar, Pool and/or Athletic Facilities, Lockers, Dressing Rooms.

Southgate Civic Center Arena
14700 Reanne Pkwy.
Southgate MI 41895
(313) 246-1342
Mgr: Allen Kowalkowski
Skating Dir: Tom Caribandi
Ice surfaces: 1, 200x85, Enclosed. *Open:* Aug.-Apr. *Ownership:* Municipal. *Access:* Public. *Clubs:* Southgate Figures Boosters Club. *Sessions:* Public, Private/Club, Rental, Freestyle, Patch, Hockey. *Classes/Lessons:* Group, Private. *Program Affiliation:* USFSA, ISIA. *Summer School:* No. *Services:* Pro Shop, Skate Sharpening, Snack Bar, Lockers, Dressing Rooms.

St. Clair Shores Civic Arena
20000 Stephens
St. Clair Shores MI 48080
(313) 445-5350
Mgr: Larry Weis
Skating Dir: Jill Juegues
Ice surfaces: 2, 200x85; 200x85, Enclosed. *Open:* Year Round. *Ownership:* Municipal. *Access:* Public. *Clubs:* High schools; St. Clair Shores FSC. *Sessions:* Public, Private/Club, Rental, Freestyle, Patch, Dance, Hockey. *Classes/Lessons:* Group, Private. *Program Affiliation:* USFSA, ISIA. *Summer School:* National/International. *Services:* Pro Shop, Skate Sharpening, Snack Bar, Ballet Room, Weight Room, Lockers, Dressing Rooms.

The Rink
75 Huston St.
Battle Creek MI 49017
(616) 966-3625
FAX: (616) 966-3653
Mgr: Don Silver
Ice surfaces: 1, 200x85, Enclosed. *Open:* Aug.-June. *Ownership:* Municipal. *Access:* Public. *Sessions:* Public, Private/Club, Rental, Freestyle, Patch, Hockey. *Classes/Lessons:* Group, Private. *Program Affiliation:* ISIA. *Summer School:* No. *Services:* Pro Shop, Skate Rental, Skate Sharpening, Snack Bar, Lockers, Dressing Rooms.

University of Michigan Dearborn Arena
Field House, 4901 Evergreen Rd.
Dearborn MI 48128
(313) 593-5540
FAX: (313) 593-5436
Mgr: Mike Gibson
Ice surfaces: 1, 200x85, Enclosed. *Open:* June-Apr. *Ownership:* Private. *Access:* Restricted. *Restrictions:* Students, staff, and rentals. *College/Univ:* University of Michigan. *Sessions:* Rental. *Classes/Lessons:* Group. *Notes:* Concession stand; field house.

Veterans Ice Arena
2150 Jackson Ave.
Ann Arbor MI 48104
(313) 994-2785
Mgr: Rich Schiller
Ice surfaces: 1, 200x85, Enclosed. *Open:* Sept.-May. *Ownership:* Municipal. *Access:* Public. *Clubs:* Ann Arbor FSC, Youth Hockey. *Sessions:* Public, Private/Club, Rental, Freestyle, Patch, Dance, Hockey. *Classes/Lessons:* Group, Private. *Program Affiliation:* USFSA. *Services:* Pro Shop, Skate Rental, Skate Sharpening, Snack Bar, Weight Room, Pool and/or Athletic Facilities, Lockers. *Notes:* Fitness center.

Walker Arena
955 4th St.
Muskegon MI 49440
(616) 726-2939
FAX: (616) 726-4620
Mgr: Neil Hawryliw
Ice surfaces: 1, 200x85, Enclosed. *Open:* Sept.-Apr. *Ownership:* Municipal. *Access:* Public. *Clubs:* Muskegon SC. *Sessions:* Public, Rental, Freestyle, Hockey. *Classes/Lessons:* Group. *Program Affiliation:* ISIA. *Summer School:* Local. *Services:* Skate Rental, Skate Sharpening, Dressing Rooms. *Notes:* Open one week in July for hockey camp.

Washington Ice Rink
2700 South Washington Ave.
Lansing MI 48910
(517) 483-4230
Mgr: Don Ballard
Ice surfaces: 1, 200x85, Outdoor/Semi Outdoor. *Open:* Dec.-Feb. *Ownership:* Municipal. *Access:* Public. *Sessions:* Public, Rental. *Classes/Lessons:* Group. *Summer School:* No. *Services:* Pro Shop, Skate Rental, Skate Sharpening, Snack Bar, Lockers. *Notes:* Warming house.

Wayne Community Center
4635 Horre Rd.
Wayne MI 48184
(313) 721-7400
FAX: (313) 722-5052
Mgr: Gordy Harris
Skating Dir: Janice Rychlinski
Ice surfaces: 1, 200x85, Enclosed. *Open:* Year Round. *Ownership:* Municipal. *Access:* Public. *Clubs:* SC of Wayne, Wayne Youth Hockey Assn. *Sessions:* Public, Rental, Freestyle, Patch, Dance, Hockey. *Classes/Lessons:* Group. *Program Affiliation:* ISIA. *Services:* Pro Shop, Skate Rental, Skate Sharpening, Snack Bar, Ballet Room, Weight Room, Dressing Rooms. *Notes:* Health center; saunas.

Wells Sports Complex
1647 174 Rd.
Escanaba MI 49829
(906) 786-3995
FAX: (906) 786-0273
Mgr: Ward Johnson
Ice surfaces: 1, 200x85, Enclosed. *Open:* Nov.-Mar. *Ownership:* Municipal. *Access:* Public. *Clubs:* Escanaba FSC, Youth Hockey. *Sessions:* Public, Rental, Freestyle, Hockey. *Classes/Lessons:* Private, Group. *Program Affiliation:* ISIA, USFSA. *Summer School:* No. *Services:* Skate Rental, Skate Sharpening, Snack Bar, Lockers, Dressing Rooms.

Westland Sports Arena
6210 Wildwood
Westland MI 48185
(313) 729-4560
Mgr: Tammy Hombirg
Skating Dir: Tammy Hombirg
Ice surfaces: 1, 200x85, Enclosed. *Open:* June-May. *Ownership:* Municipal. *Access:* Public. *Clubs:* Westland FSC, Hockey Assn. *Sessions:* Public, Private/Club, Rental, Freestyle, Patch, Hockey. *Classes/Lessons:* Group, Private. *Program Affiliation:* USFSA, ISIA. *Summer School:* Local. *Services:* Pro Shop, Skate Rental, Snack Bar, Ballet Room, Dressing Rooms. *Notes:* Meeting room.

Wings Annex
3620 Van Rick Dr.
Kalamazoo MI 49002
(616) 345-1125
FAX: (616) 345-6584
Mgr: Dick Keys
Ice surfaces: 2, 200x85; 200x85, Enclosed. *Open:* Year Round. *Ownership:* Private. *Access:* Public. *Clubs:* Kalamazoo Wings Hockey Club. *Sessions:* Public, Private/Club, Rental, Hockey. *Classes/Lessons:* Group, Private. *Program Affiliation:* ISIA. *Summer School:* Local. *Services:* Skate Rental, Pro Shop, Skate Sharpening, Snack Bar, Ballet Room, Weight Room, Pool and/or Athletic Facilities, Lockers, Dressing Rooms.

Wings Stadium
3600 Van Rick
Kalamazoo MI 49902
(616) 345-1125
Mgr: Richard Keyes
Ice surfaces: 2, 200x85, Enclosed. *Open:* Sept.-July. *Ownership:* Private. *Access:* Public. *Sessions:* Public, Private/Club, Rental, Freestyle, Patch, Dance, Hockey, General. *Classes/Lessons:* Group, Private. *Program Affiliation:* USFSA. *Services:* Pro Shop, Skate Rental, Skate Sharpening, Snack Bar, Lockers, Dressing Rooms.

Yack (Benjamin F.) Arena
246 Sycamore
Wyandotte MI 48192
(313) 246-4490
FAX: (313) 246-4496
Mgr: Len Trusewicz
Skating Dir: Len Trusewicz
Ice surfaces: 1, 200x85, Enclosed. *Open:* Sept.-Mar. *Ownership:* Municipal. *Access:* Public. *Clubs:* Wyandotte FSC. *Sessions:* Public, Private/Club, Rental. *Classes/Lessons:* Group, Private. *Summer School:* No. *Services:* Snack Bar, Dressing Rooms. *Notes:* Two meeting rooms. Freestyle, patch, dance and hockey sessions offered through the clubs.

Yost Ice Arena - University of Michigan
1000 South State Street
Ann Arbor MI 48109
(313) 764-4599
FAX: (313) 764-4597
Mgr: Doug Daugherty
Ice surfaces: 1, Enclosed. *Open:* July - May. *Ownership:* Private. *Access:* Public. *College/Univ:* University of Michigan, Ann Arbor. *Sessions:* Public, Rental, Hockey. *Classes/Lessons:* Group. *Program Affiliation:* USFSA. *Services:* Skate Rental, Skate Sharpening, Snack Bar, Lockers, Dressing Rooms. *Notes:* Dept of Sports Management & Communication maintains training lab for ice rink managers.

MN: MINNESOTA

Adams (Biff) Ice Arena
743 Western Ave.
St. Paul MN 55103
(612) 488-1336
FAX: (612) 777-6519
Mgr: Jim Rolling
Ice surfaces: 1, 200x85, Enclosed. *Open:* Oct.-Mar. *Ownership:* Municipal. *Access:* Public. *Clubs:* Numerous Youth Hockey Assn.; numerous HS. *Sessions:* Public, Private/Club, Rental, Freestyle, Hockey, General. *Classes/Lessons:* None. *Summer School:* No. *Notes:* Vending machines.

Aldrich Arena
1850 White Bear Ave.
Maplewood MN 55109
(612) 777-2233
FAX: (612) 777-6519
Mgr: Gary Palfe
Ice surfaces: 1, 200x85, Enclosed. *Open:* Oct.-Mar. *Ownership:* Municipal. *Access:* Public. *Clubs:* Maplewood FSC, Skating Academy. *Sessions:* Public, Private/Club, Hockey, Longblade Sessions, Rental, Freestyle, Patch. *Classes/Lessons:* Group, Private. *Program Affiliation:* USFSA, Own. *Summer School:* No. *Services:* Snack Bar, Lockers, Skate Rental, Dressing Rooms.

All Seasons Arena
301 Monks Ave.
Mankato MN 56001
(507) 387-6552
Mgr: Mike Carrol
Ice surfaces: 1, 200x85, Enclosed. *Open:* June-Apr. *Ownership:* Municipal. *Access:* Public. *Clubs:* Mankato FSC, Mankato Area Hockey Assn. *Sessions:* Public, Private/Club, Rental, Freestyle, Patch, Hockey. *Classes/Lessons:* Group, Private. *Program Affiliation:* ISIA. *Services:* Pro Shop, Skate Rental, Skate Sharpening, Snack Bar, Dressing Rooms. *Notes:* Banquet room.

Anoka Area Ice Arena
4111 7th Ave. N.
Anoka MN 55303
(612) 427-8163
Mgr: Bill Ruckel
Ice surfaces: 2, 200x85; 200x85, Enclosed. *Open:* July-May; Oct.-Aug. *Ownership:* Private. *Access:* Public.

RINKS

Sessions: Public, Private/Club, Rental, Freestyle, Hockey. *Classes/Lessons:* Group. *Program Affiliation:* ISIA. *Services:* Pro Shop, Skate Sharpening, Snack Bar, Dressing Rooms.

Apple Valley Sports Facility
14200 Cedar Ave. S.
Apple Valley MN 55124
(612) 431-8866
Mgr: Gary Pietig
Ice surfaces: 1, 200x85, Enclosed. *Open:* Oct.-Mar. *Ownership:* Municipal. *Access:* Public. *Sessions:* Public, Rental. *Classes/Lessons:* Group. *Program Affiliation:* ISIA. *Services:* Skate Rental, Skate Sharpening, Snack Bar, Lockers, Dressing Rooms.

Arlington Ice Rink
665 E. Rose St.
St. Paul MN 55106
(612) 298-5701
Mgr: Marietta Ward
Ice surfaces: 2, 200x85; 200x85, Outdoor/Semi Outdoor. *Open:* Dec.-Feb. *Ownership:* Municipal. *Access:* Public. *Sessions:* Public, Rental, Hockey. *Classes/Lessons:* Group. *Summer School:* No. *Services:* Pool and/or Athletic Facilities, Lockers, Dressing Rooms, Weight Room.

Augsburg College Ice Arena
2323 Riverside Ave.
Minneapolis MN 55454
(612) 330-1252
FAX: (612) 330-1382
Mgr: Jim Carey
Ice surfaces: 2, 185x85; 200x85, Enclosed. *Open:* Year Round. *Ownership:* Private. *Access:* Restricted. *Restrictions: College/Univ:* Augsburg College. *Sessions:* Private/Club, Rental, Freestyle, Patch, Hockey. *Classes/Lessons:* Private, Group. *Program Affiliation:* USFSA, ISIA. *Services:* Lockers. *Notes:* Attached gym.

Babbitt Ice Arena
South Dr.
Babbitt MN 55706
unlisted phone #
FAX: (218) 827-2204
Mgr: Elaine Posadensic
Ice surfaces: 1, 200x85, Enclosed. *Open:* Nov.-Mar. *Ownership:* Municipal. *Access:* Public. *Clubs:* Babbitt FSC, Babbitt Blue Line Club. *Sessions:* Public, Private/Club, Rental, Hockey. *Classes/Lessons:* None, Group, Private. *Program Affiliation:* USFSA. *Summer School:* No. *Services:* Lockers, Snack Bar, Skate Sharpening. *Notes:* Lessons, freestyle, patch and dance sessions are offered through the club only.

Baudette Arena
County Rd. 1
Baudette MN 56623
(218) 634-1319
Ice surfaces: 1, 200x85, Enclosed. *Open:* Nov.-March; July. *Ownership:* Municipal. *Access:* Public. *Sessions:* Public, Private/Club, Rental, Freestyle, Hockey. *Classes/Lessons:* Group. *Program Affiliation:* Own. *Summer School:* No. *Services:* Pro Shop, Skate Sharpening, Snack Bar, Dressing Rooms.

Bergwall (George) Arena
306 Pioneer Rd.
Red Wing MN 55066
(612) 388-6088
Mgr: Dave Lynch
Ice surfaces: 1, 200x85, Enclosed. *Open:* Oct.-Mar. *Ownership:* Municipal. *Access:* Public. *Clubs:* Minnesota Hockey; USA Hockey. *Sessions:* Public, Private/Club, Rental, Freestyle, Hockey. *Classes/Lessons:* Group. *Program Affiliation:* ISIA. *Summer School:* No. *Services:* Skate Rental, Skate Sharpening, Snack Bar, Dressing Rooms.

Blake Ice Arena
110 Blake Rd.
Hopkins MN 55343
(612) 938-0209
Mgr: Todd Burkart
Ice surfaces: 1, 200x85, Enclosed. *Open:* Year Round. *Ownership:* Private. *Access:* Public. *Sessions:* Public, Rental, Freestyle, Patch, Hockey. *Classes/Lessons:* Group, Private. *Services:* Skate Rental, Skate Sharpening, Snack Bar, Lockers, Dressing Rooms.

Bloomington Ice Garden
3600 W. 98th St.
Bloomington MN 55431
(612) 887-9642
Mgr: Dennis May
Ice surfaces: 3, 200x85; 200x85; 200x100, Enclosed. *Open:* Year Round. *Ownership:* Municipal. *Access:* Public. *Clubs:* FSC, Bloomington Amateur Hockey Assn. *Sessions:* Public, Rental, Hockey. *Classes/Lessons:* Group, Private. *Program Affiliation:* USFSA. *Services:* Skate Rental, Skate Sharpening, Snack Bar, Dressing Rooms. *Notes:* Two all-purpose rooms. Freestyle, patch and dance sessions are offered through the club only.

Brainerd Area Civic Center
502 Jackson St.
Brainerd MN 56401
(218) 829-3351
Mgr: Mark Olsen
Ice surfaces: 1, 185x85, Enclosed. *Open:* Year Round. *Ownership:* non-profit organization. *Access:* Public. *Clubs:* Brainerd Amateur Hockey Association; Vacationland FSC. *Sessions:* Public, Private/Club, Rental. *Classes/Lessons:* None. *Program Affiliation:* USFSA, ISIA. *Summer School:* No. *Services:* Skate Sharpening, Snack Bar, Lockers, Dressing Rooms. *Notes:* Freestyle, patch and dance sessions are offered through the clubs only.

Breckenridge Skating Rink
Breckenridge MN 56520
(218) 643-3455
FAX: (218) 643-1173
Mgr: Dan Keyes
Ice surfaces: 2, 200x85; 500x250, Outdoor/Semi Outdoor. *Open:* Dec.—late March. *Ownership:* Municipal. *Access:* Public. *Clubs:* Breckenridge Blades Hockey. *Sessions:* Public, Private/Club, Rental. *Classes/Lessons:* None. *Summer School:* No. *Services:* Snack Bar.

Brick Ice Center
5800 Wayzata Blvd.
Minneapolis MN 55416
(612) 545-1614
Mgr: Red Kairies
Ice surfaces: 1, 185x85, Enclosed. *Open:* Year Round. *Ownership:* Private. *Access:* Members Only. *Clubs:* FSC of Minneapolis; Youth Hockey. *Sessions:* Private/Club, Rental, Hockey. *Classes/Lessons:* None. *Services:* Pro Shop, Skate Sharpening, Snack Bar, Dressing Rooms. *Notes:* Upper level lounge/observation room.

~ SKATER'S EDGE SOURCEBOOK ~

Bronco Arena
Falls High School, 1501 11th St.
International Falls MN 56649
(218) 283-2424
Ice surfaces: 1, 200x85, Enclosed. *Open:* Oct.-April. *Ownership:* Private. *Access:* Public. *Clubs:* International Falls FSC, International Falls Bronco Team. *College/Univ:* Rainer River Community College. *Sessions:* Public. *Classes/Lessons:* None. *Program Affiliation:* Own. *Summer School:* No. *Services:* Lockers, Dressing Rooms, Snack Bar.

Brooklyn Park Community Center
5600 85th Ave. N.
Brooklyn Park MN 55443
(612) 424-8017
Mgr: Mike Holtz
Skating Dir: Cassie Joyce
Ice surfaces: 1, 200x85, Enclosed. *Open:* Year Round. *Ownership:* Municipal. *Access:* Public. *Clubs:* FSC of Minneapolis. *Sessions:* Public, Private/Club, Rental, Freestyle, Patch, Hockey, Dance. *Classes/Lessons:* Group, Private. *Program Affiliation:* USFSA. *Summer School:* Local. *Services:* Skate Rental, Skate Sharpening, Snack Bar, Weight Room, Pool and/or Athletic Facilities, Lockers, Dressing Rooms. *Notes:* Second rink under construction.

Buffalo Community Civic Center
214 First Ave.
Buffalo MN 55313
(612) 682-4132
FAX: (612) 682-5200
Mgr: Vicky Andres
Skating Dir: Anita Underberg
Ice surfaces: 1, 200x85, Enclosed. *Open:* Oct.-Feb. *Ownership:* Municipal. *Access:* Public. *Sessions:* Public, Private/Club, Rental, Hockey. *Classes/Lessons:* Group, Private. *Program Affiliation:* USFSA, ISIA. *Services:* Pro Shop, Skate Sharpening, Snack Bar, Lockers. *Notes:* Most ice time is rented to group users.

Burnsville Ice Center
251 Civic Center Pkwy.
Burnsville MN 55337
(612) 895-4651
FAX: (612) 895-4656
Mgr: Mry Gerhardt
Ice surfaces: 2, 200x85; 200x85, Enclosed. *Open:* Year Round. *Ownership:* Municipal. *Access:* Public. *Clubs:* FSC. *Sessions:* Public, Rental, Freestyle, Patch, Hockey. *Classes/Lessons:* Group, Private. *Program Affiliation:* USFSA. *Services:* Pro Shop, Skate Rental, Skate Sharpening, Snack Bar, Ballet Room. *Notes:* Concession stand.

Butte Parks & Recreation Department
1700 Civic Center Rd.
Butte MN 59701
(406) 723-8262
Outdoor. *Open:* Contingent on weather conditions. *Ownership:* Municipal. *Access:* Public. *Sessions:* Public. *Classes/Lessons:* None. *Program Affiliation:* Own. *Summer School:* No. *Notes:* Parks & Rec. floods 10 areas in winter. No lessons are offered, and all sessions are public skate. For information on location, months & hours of operation contact the Parks Department above.

Chisago Lakes Arena
11665 Maxwell Rd.
Chisago MN 55013
(612) 257-5936
Mgr: Peter Nelson
Skating Dir: Darcy Caye
Ice surfaces: 1, Enclosed. *Open:* Aug.-Mar. *Ownership:* Municipal. *Access:* Public. *Sessions:* Public, Rental, Freestyle, Patch, Hockey, Dance. *Classes/Lessons:* Group, Private. *Program Affiliation:* ISIA. *Services:* Skate Sharpening, Snack Bar, Lockers, Dressing Rooms.

Chisholm Sports Arena
600 First St. NW
Chisholm MN 55719
(218) 254-2635
Mgr: William Podlager
Ice surfaces: 1, 195x85, Enclosed. *Open:* Oct.-Mar. *Ownership:* Municipal. *Access:* Public. *Clubs:* Chisholm FSC, Chisholm Blue Line Club. *Sessions:* Public, Private/Club, Rental, Freestyle, Patch, Dance, Hockey. *Classes/Lessons:* Private, Group. *Program Affiliation:* Own. *Summer School:* Local. *Services:* Skate Sharpening, Snack Bar, Lockers, Dressing Rooms.

City Hall
124 N. Broadway
Crookston MN 56716
(218) 281-1232
Outdoor. *Open:* Contingent on weather conditions. *Ownership:* Municipal. *Access:* Public. *Sessions:* Public. *Classes/Lessons:* None. *Program Affiliation:* Own. *Summer School:* No. *Notes:* City Hall floods 3 areas in winter. No lessons are offered and all ice is public skate. For information on locations, months and hours of operation, call City Hall above.

City of Udina Braemar Arena
7501 Highway 169
Udina MN 55439
(612) 941-1322
Mgr: Larry Thayer
Skating Dir: Joan Orvis
Ice surfaces: 2, 200x85; 200x85, Enclosed. *Open:* Year Round. *Ownership:* Municipal. *Access:* Public. *Clubs:* Braemar City of Lakes FSC, Udina Hockey Assn. *Sessions:* Public, Rental, Private/Club, Freestyle, Patch, Dance, Hockey. *Classes/Lessons:* Group, Private. *Program Affiliation:* ISIA, USFSA. *Summer School:* Local. *Services:* Skate Rental, Skate Sharpening, Snack Bar, Ballet Room, Lockers, Dressing Rooms.

City Parks & Recreation
221 E. Clark St.
Albert Lea MN 56007
(507) 377-4370
Outdoor. *Open:* Contingent on weather conditions. *Ownership:* Municipal. *Sessions:* Public. *Classes/Lessons:* None. *Program Affiliation:* Own. *Summer School:* No. *Notes:* Parks & Rec. floods a dozen areas in winter. No lessons are offered, and all ice is public skate. For information on location, months and hours of operation, call the Parks Department above.

City Parks & Recreation Department
400 Second St. S.
St. Cloud MN 56301
(612) 255-7216
Outdoor. *Open:* Contingent on weather conditions. *Ownership:* Municipal. *Access:* Public. *Sessions:* Public. *Classes/Lessons:* None. *Program Affiliation:* Own. *Summer School:* No. *Notes:* Parks & Rec. floods 20 areas in winter. No lessons are offered, and all sessions are public skate. For information on location, months and hours of operation contact the Parks Department above.

RINKS

Cook Ice Arena
11091 Mississippi Blvd.
Coon Rapids MN 55433
(612) 421-5035
Mgr: Robert Larsen
Ice surfaces: 1, 200x85, Enclosed. *Open:* Sept.-Apr. *Ownership:* Municipal. *Access:* Public. *Sessions:* Public, Freestyle, Patch, Dance, Hockey, Rental. *Classes/Lessons:* Group, Private. *Program Affiliation:* ISIA. *Services:* Pro Shop, Skate Sharpening, Snack Bar.

Cook (Joe) Memorial Arena
11091 Mississippi Blvd.
Coon Rapids MN 55433
(612) 421-5035
Mgr: Bob Larson
Skating Dir: Karen Mech
Ice surfaces: 1, 200x85, Enclosed. *Open:* Oct.-Apr.; one month in summer. *Ownership:* Municipal. *Access:* Public. *Sessions:* Public, Private/Club, Rental, Freestyle, Patch, Dance, Hockey. *Classes/Lessons:* Group, Private. *Program Affiliation:* ISIA. *Summer School:* Local. *Services:* Pro Shop, Skate Sharpening, Snack Bar, Lockers, Dressing Rooms.

Cottage Grove Ice Arena
8020 80th St. S.
Cottage Grove MN 55016
(612) 458-2845
FAX: (612) 458-2820
Mgr: Tim Johnson
Ice surfaces: 2, 200x85; 120x65, Enclosed. *Open:* June-Apr. *Ownership:* Municipal. *Access:* Public. *Sessions:* Public, Rental, Freestyle, Patch, Dance, Hockey. *Classes/Lessons:* Group, Private. *Program Affiliation:* ISIA. *Services:* Pro Shop, Skate Sharpening, Studio Rink, Snack Bar, Lockers, Dressing Rooms.

Drake Ice Arena
1712 Randolph Ave.
St. Paul MN 55105
(612) 698-2455
FAX: (612) 698-6787
Mgr: Mike Foley
Ice surfaces: 1, 200x88, Enclosed. *Open:* Oct.-Mar.; June-July. *Ownership:* Private. *Access:* Restricted. *Restrictions:* Rentals only. *Clubs:* Senior Mens Hockey. *Sessions:* Rental, Hockey. *Classes/Lessons:* None. *Program Affiliation:* Own. *Summer School:* Regional. *Services:* Pro Shop, Skate Sharpening, Lockers, Dressing Rooms. *Notes:* Rink offers summer hockey league.

Duluth Entertainment
350 S. 5th Ave. - The Deck
Duluth MN 55802
(218) 722-5573
Mgr: Walt Bruley
Ice surfaces: 2, 190x85; 190x85, Enclosed. *Open:* Sept.-Mar. *Ownership:* Municipal. *Access:* Public. *Clubs:* Duluth FSC. *College/Univ:* University of Minnesota at Duluth. *Sessions:* Public, Private/Club, Freestyle, Hockey. *Classes/Lessons:* None. *Summer School:* No. *Services:* Snack Bar, Lockers, Dressing Rooms. *Notes:* Limited public skating.

Eden Prairie Community Center
16700 Valley View Rd.
Eden Prairie MN 55346
(612) 949-8470
FAX: (612) 949-8492
Mgr: Dave Black
Ice surfaces: 2, 200x85; 200x100, Enclosed. *Open:* Year Round. *Ownership:* Municipal. *Access:* Public. *Clubs:* Eden Prairie FSC, Eden Prairie Hockey Assn. *Sessions:* Public, Private/Club, Rental, Patch, Hockey, General. *Classes/Lessons:* Group, Private. *Program Affiliation:* ISIA. *Services:* Skate Rental, Skate Sharpening, Snack Bar, Weight Room, Pool and/or Athletic Facilities, Lockers, Dressing Rooms. *Notes:* Meeting room, raquetball courts.

Farmington Ice Arena
114 W. Spruce St.
Farmington MN 55024
(612) 463-2510
Mgr: Jim Bell
Skating Dir: Judy Martin
Ice surfaces: 1, 200x85, Enclosed. *Open:* Sept.-Apr. *Ownership:* Municipal. *Access:* Public. *Clubs:* Tri - Metro FSC. *Sessions:* Public, Private/Club, Rental, Freestyle, Patch, Hockey. *Classes/Lessons:* Private. *Program Affiliation:* USFSA. *Summer School:* No. *Services:* Skate Sharpening, Snack Bar, Lockers, Dressing Rooms.

Four Seasons Civic Center
Steele County Fairgrounds
Owatonna MN 55060
(507) 451-1093
Mgr: Bill Carlson
Ice surfaces: 1, 200x85, Enclosed. *Open:* Oct.-Mar. *Ownership:* Municipal. *Access:* Public. *Clubs:* MIAMA. *Sessions:* Public, Rental, Private/Club. *Services:* Skate Sharpening, Snack Bar, Lockers. *Notes:* Freestyle, patch, dance and hockey sessions available to renters only.

Glass (John) Field House
1500 Birchmont Dr.
Bemidji MN 56601
(218) 755-4140
Mgr: Craig Stensen
Ice surfaces: 1, 185x85, Enclosed. *Open:* Oct.-Mar.; July-Aug. *Ownership:* Private. *Access:* Public. *College/Univ:* Bemidji State University. *Sessions:* Public, Rental, Hockey. *Classes/Lessons:* None. *Services:* Lockers, Dressing Rooms. *Notes:* Limited public ice time.

Gustafson - Phalen Skating Arena
1320 Walsh St.
St. Paul MN 55106
(612) 776-2554
FAX: (612) 777-6519
Mgr: Jim Rolling
Ice surfaces: 1, 200x85, Enclosed. *Open:* Apr.-Sept. *Ownership:* Municipal. *Access:* Public. *Clubs:* Maplewood FSC, Skating Academy; Youth Hockey Assn.; local High Schools. *Sessions:* Public, Private/Club, Rental, Freestyle, Patch, Hockey, General. *Classes/Lessons:* None. *Summer School:* Local. *Notes:* Vending machines.

Harding Arena
1496 E. 6th St.
St. Paul MN 55106
(612) 774-2127
FAX: (612) 777-6519
Mgr: Jim Rolling
Ice surfaces: 1, 200x85, Enclosed. *Open:* Oct.-Mar. *Ownership:* Municipal. *Access:* Public. *Clubs:* many Youth Hockey Assn.; numerous high schools. *Sessions:* Public, Private/Club, Rental, Freestyle, Hockey, General. *Classes/Lessons:* None. *Summer School:* No. *Notes:* Vending machines.

Hastings Civic Arena
2801 Redwing Blvd.
Hastings MN 55033
(612) 437-4940
FAX: (612) 437-7082
Mgr: Jim McGree
Ice surfaces: 1, 200x85, Enclosed. *Open:* Apr.-Sept. *Ownership:* Municipal. *Access:* Public. *Sessions:* Public, Private/Club, Rental. *Classes/Lessons:* Group, Private. *Program Affiliation:* ISIA. *Services:* Pro Shop, Skate Rental, Skate Sharpening, Snack Bar, Lockers. *Notes:* Freestyle, patch, dance, and hockey sessions offered through clubs only.

Hibbing Memorial Ice Arena
23rd St. & 5th Ave. E.
Hibbing MN 55746
(218) 263-4379
Mgr: Gary Stark
Skating Dir: Terry Hammer
Ice surfaces: 1, 200x90, Enclosed. *Open:* Nov.-July. *Ownership:* Municipal. *Access:* Public. *Clubs:* Hibbing FSC, youth, high school and college hockey. *Sessions:* Public, Rental, Freestyle, Patch, Hockey. *Classes/Lessons:* Group, Private. *Program Affiliation:* USFSA. *Services:* Snack Bar, Lockers, Dressing Rooms. *Notes:* Youth center; concession stand; meeting rooms.

Highland Arena
800 Snelling Ave. S.
St. Paul MN 55116
(612) 699-7156
FAX: (612) 777-6519
Mgr: Jim Rolling
Ice surfaces: 1, 200x86, Enclosed. *Open:* Oct.-Mar. *Ownership:* Municipal. *Access:* Public. *Clubs:* Youth Hockey Assn., local high schools. *Sessions:* Public, Private/Club, Rental, Freestyle, Hockey, General. *Classes/Lessons:* None. *Summer School:* No. *Notes:* Vending machines.

Hutchinson Civic Arena
900 Harrington St.
Hutchinson MN 55350
(612) 234-4227
FAX: (612) 234-4240
Mgr: Marv Haugen
Ice surfaces: 2, 200x85; 200x85, Enclosed, Outdoor/Semi Outdoor. *Open:* Oct.-Mar. *Ownership:* Municipal. *Access:* Public. *Clubs:* Hutchinson FSA. *Sessions:* Public, Private/Club, Rental, Freestyle, Broomball. *Classes/Lessons:* Group, Private. *Summer School:* No. *Services:* Skate Sharpening, Snack Bar, Pool and/or Athletic Facilities, Dressing Rooms.

IRA Civic Center Arena
14th St. & 4th Ave. NW
Grand Rapids MN 55744
(218) 326-2591
FAX: (218) 326-7608 (City Hall)
Mgr: Jeff Davey
Ice surfaces: 1, 188x85, Enclosed. *Open:* Oct.-Mar.; July. *Ownership:* Municipal. *Access:* Public. *Clubs:* Star of the North FSC, Grand Rapids Area Hockey Assn. *Sessions:* Public, Private/Club, Rental. *Classes/Lessons:* None. *Program Affiliation:* USFSA. *Summer School:* No. *Services:* Skate Sharpening, Snack Bar, Lockers, Dressing Rooms. *Notes:* Freestyle, patch, dance and hockey sessions are through the club only; fax number is for city hall.

Kristofferson (Oscar) Ice Rink
500 Maplewood Dr.
Baxter MN 56401
(218) 828-3066
Mgr: Roy Rauen
Ice surfaces: 1, 200x80, Outdoor/Semi Outdoor. *Open:* Dec.-Mar. *Ownership:* Municipal. *Access:* Public. *Clubs:* Brainerd FSC, Brainerd Hockey Assn. *Sessions:* Public, Freestyle, Hockey. *Classes/Lessons:* None. *Summer School:* No. *Services:* Lockers.

Lakes Sports Arena
1025 Roosevelt Ave.
Detroit Lakes MN 56501
(218) 847-7738
FAX: (218) 847-3557
Mgr: Roy Estes
Ice surfaces: 1, 200x85, Enclosed. *Open:* July-Mar. *Ownership:* Municipal. *Access:* Public. *Clubs:* Lakes FSC, Detroit Lakes Hockey Assn. *Sessions:* Private/Club, Rental, Precision. *Services:* Skate Sharpening, Snack Bar, Dressing Rooms. *Notes:* Frestyle, patch and dance sessions offered through the club only.

Lea (Albert) City Arena
701 Lake Chapean Dr.
Albert Lea MN 56007
(507) 377-4374
Mgr: Dean Mulse
Ice surfaces: 1, 200x85, Enclosed. *Open:* Oct.-Mar. *Ownership:* Municipal. *Access:* Public. *Sessions:* Public, Private/Club, Rental, Freestyle, Patch, Dance, Hockey. *Classes/Lessons:* Group, Private. *Program Affiliation:* ISIA. *Services:* Skate Rental, Skate Sharpening, Lockers. *Notes:* Concession stand.

Litchfield Civic Arena
900 N. Gilman Rd.
Litchfield MN 55355
(612) 693-2679
Mgr: Steve Olson
Ice surfaces: 1, 200x85, Enclosed. *Open:* Oct.-Mar. *Ownership:* Municipal. *Access:* Public. *Clubs:* Litchfield FSA. *Sessions:* Public, Private/Club, Rental, Hockey, Broomball. *Classes/Lessons:* Group. *Program Affiliation:* ISIA. *Summer School:* No. *Services:* Skate Sharpening, Snack Bar, Lockers, Dressing Rooms.

Lund Center Ice Arena
800 W. College Ave.
St. Peters MN 56082
(507) 933-7615
Mgr: Larry Moore
Ice surfaces: 1, 200x85, Enclosed. *Open:* Oct.-Mar. *Ownership:* Private. *Access:* Restricted. *Restrictions:* College use only. *College/Univ:* Gustavus Adolphus College. *Sessions:* Private/Club, Rental, Hockey. *Classes/Lessons:* Group. *Summer School:* No. *Services:* Skate Sharpening, Snack Bar, Weight Room, Lockers, Dressing Rooms. *Notes:* Lessons offered as physical education class.

Lyon County Ice Facility
Fairground Rd.
Marshall MN 56258
(507) 537-6795
Mgr: Bob Serreyn
Ice surfaces: 1, 200x85, Enclosed. *Open:* Nov.-Mar. *Ownership:* Private. *Access:* Public. *Sessions:* Public, Private/Club, Rental, Hockey, Broom Ball. *Classes/Lessons:* Group. *Summer School:* No. *Services:* Skate Rental, Skate Sharpening, Snack Bar, Dressing Rooms. *Notes:* Pro shop in planning.

Memorial Arena
707 Elk St.
Warroad MN 56763
(218) 386-9979
Mgr: Albert Hasbargen
Ice surfaces: 2, 200x100; 190x85, Enclosed. *Open:* Oct.-Apr. *Ownership:* Private. *Access:* Public. *Sessions:* Public, Freestyle, Hockey. *Classes/Lessons:* Group. *Program Affiliation:* Own. *Summer School:* No. *Services:* Skate Sharpening, Snack Bar, Weight Room, Pool and/or Athletic Facilities, Dressing Rooms.

Minneapolis Parks & Recreation Board
310 4th Ave. S.
Minneapolis MN 55415
(612) 661-4800
Outdoor. *Open:* Contingent on weather conditions. *Ownership:* Municipal. *Access:* Public. *Sessions:* Public. *Classes/Lessons:* None. *Program Affiliation:* Own. *Summer School:* No. *Notes:* Parks & Rec. flood 32 areas in winter. No lessons are offered, and all ice is public skate. For information on locations, months and hours of operation, call the Parks Department above.

Minnehaha Ice Arena
4200 West River Pkwy
Minneapolis MN 55406
(612) 729-8770
Mgr: Bruce Peterson
Ice surfaces: 1, 200x85, Enclosed. *Open:* Nov.-Mar. *Ownership:* Private. *Access:* Restricted. *Restrictions:* Owned and used by a private school. *Clubs:* Youth hockey.

Minnetonka Ice Arena
3401 Williston Rd.
Minnetonka MN 55345
(612) 939-8310
Mgr: John Hansen
Skating Dir: Carol Timm
Ice surfaces: 2, 200x85; 200x85, Enclosed. *Open:* Year Round. *Ownership:* Municipal. *Access:* Public. *Clubs:* Lake Minnetonka FSC. *Sessions:* Public, Private/Club, Rental, Freestyle, Patch, Hockey. *Classes/Lessons:* Group, Private. *Program Affiliation:* ISIA. *Summer School:* Local. *Services:* Pro Shop, Skate Sharpening, Snack Bar, Skate Rental, Dressing Rooms.

Mora Civic Center - Kanabu County Fair Grounds
Union St. - Hwy. 65
Mora MN 55051
(612) 679-2443
FAX: (612) 679-3862
Mgr: Skeeter Mason
Ice surfaces: 1, 200x85, Enclosed. *Open:* Oct.-Mar. *Ownership:* Private. *Access:* Public. *Clubs:* Cambridge High Hockey; Mora High Hockey; Pine City North Branch High Hockey; Mora FSC. *Sessions:* Public, Private/Club, Rental, Hockey. *Classes/Lessons:* Group, Private. *Summer School:* No. *Services:* Pro Shop, Skate Sharpening, Snack Bar, Lockers, Dressing Rooms.

National Hockey Center
St. Cloud State University
1204 4th Ave. S.
St. Cloud MN 56301
(612) 255-3327
Mgr: Joe Meierhofer
Skating Dir: Joe Meierhofer
Ice surfaces: 2, 200x100; 200x100, Enclosed. *Open:* Year Round. *Ownership:* Private. *Access:* Public. *Clubs:* St. Cloud FSC. *College/Univ:* St. Cloud State University. *Sessions:* Public, Private/Club, Rental, Freestyle, Patch, Dance, Hockey. *Classes/Lessons:* Private, Group. *Program Affiliation:* Own. *Summer School:* Regional. *Services:* Pro Shop, Skate Rental, Skate Sharpening, Snack Bar, Weight Room, Pool and/or Athletic Facilities, Lockers, Dressing Rooms. *Notes:* National hockey training center; summer camp is for hockey only.

New Hope Ice Arena
4949 Louisiana Ave. N.
New Hope MN 55428
(612) 531-5181
Mgr: Jim Corbett
Skating Dir: Dawn Landon
Ice surfaces: 1, 200x85, Enclosed. *Open:* Year Round. *Ownership:* Municipal. *Access:* Public. *Sessions:* Public, Private/Club, Rental, Freestyle, Patch, Dance, Hockey. *Classes/Lessons:* Private, Group. *Program Affiliation:* USFSA, ISIA. *Summer School:* Local. *Services:* Pro Shop, Skate Sharpening, Snack Bar, Ballet Room, Lockers, Dressing Rooms.

Northfield Ice Arena
1280 South Highway 3
Northfield MN 55057
(507) 645-6556
Mgr: Tom Reller
Ice surfaces: 1, 200x85, Enclosed. *Open:* Oct.-Mar. *Ownership:* Municipal. *Access:* Public. *Clubs:* Northfield FSC. *College/Univ:* St. Olaf College. *Sessions:* Public, Private/Club, Rental, Patch, Hockey. *Classes/Lessons:* Group, Private. *Program Affiliation:* ISIA. *Summer School:* No. *Services:* Pro Shop, Skate Sharpening, Snack Bar, Lockers, Dressing Rooms.

O'Leary Park VFW Arena
711 3rd St. SE
East Grand Forks MN 56721
(218) 773-9073
FAX: (218) 773-1182
Mgr: Garry Hadden
Ice surfaces: 7, 200x85; 190x85, Enclosed, Outdoor/Semi Outdoor. *Open:* Year Round. *Ownership:* Municipal. *Access:* Public. *Clubs:* Blue Line Hockey Club; Northern Lights FSC. *Sessions:* Public, Rental, Freestyle, Patch, Dance, Hockey. *Classes/Lessons:* Group, Private. *Program Affiliation:* USFSA. *Services:* Skate Sharpening, Snack Bar, Weight Room, Dressing Rooms. *Notes:* Six rinks are 200x85; the seventh is 190x85.

Olson (Huck) Memorial Civic Center
West 2nd St.
Thief River Falls MN 56701
(218) 681-2519
FAX: (218) 681-8225
Mgr: Madelyn Vigen
Ice surfaces: 2, 200x85; 185x80, Enclosed. *Open:* Oct.-Mar. *Ownership:* Municipal. *Access:* Public. *Sessions:* Public, Private/Club, Rental, Hockey. *Classes/Lessons:* Group, Private. *Program Affiliation:* USFSA. *Summer School:* Local. *Services:* Snack Bar, Lockers, Dressing Rooms. *Notes:* Summer school program in June.

Oscar Johnson Arena
1039 Decourcy Circle
St. Paul MN 55105
(612) 645-7203
FAX: (612)777-6519
Mgr: Jim Rolling
Ice surfaces: 1, 200x85, Enclosed. *Open:*

Nov.-Mar. *Access:* Public. *Clubs:* Numerous youth hockey associations and high schools. *Sessions:* Public, Private/Club, Rental, Freestyle, Hockey, General. *Classes/Lessons:* None. *Summer School:* No. *Notes:* Vending machines.

Parade Ice Arena
600 Kenwood Pkwy.
Minneapolis MN 55403
(612) 348-4853
Mgr: Nancy Kaufmann
Skating Dir: Shar Martin
Ice surfaces: 3, 200x85; 200x85; 95x45, Enclosed. *Open:* Year Round. *Ownership:* Municipal. *Access:* Public. *Clubs:* Parade FSC. *Sessions:* Public, Private/Club, Freestyle, Rental, Patch, Dance, Hockey. *Classes/Lessons:* Group, Private. *Program Affiliation:* USFSA, ISIA. *Summer School:* Local. *Services:* Pro Shop, Skate Rental, Skate Sharpening, Studio Rink, Snack Bar, Dressing Rooms.

Parks & Recreation Department
1313 E. Hwy. 13
Burnsville MN 55337
(612) 895-4500
Outdoor. *Open:* Contingent on weather conditions. *Ownership:* Municipal. *Access:* Public. *Sessions:* Public. *Classes/Lessons:* None. *Program Affiliation:* Own. *Summer School:* No. *Notes:* Parks & Rec. floods a dozen areas in winter. No lessons are offered, and all ice is public skate. For information on location, months and hours of operation, call the Parks Department above.

Parks & Recreation Department
Fergus Falls MN 56538
(218) 739-3205
Outdoor. *Open:* Contingent on weather conditions. *Ownership:* Municipal. *Access:* Public. *Sessions:* Public. *Classes/Lessons:* None. *Program Affiliation:* Own. *Summer School:* No. *Notes:* Parks & Rec floods six areas in winter. No lessons are offered & all ice is public skate. For information on location, months and hours of operation, call the Parks Department above.

Parks & Recreation Department
Box 755
Willmar MN 56201
(612) 235-1854
Outdoor. *Open:* Contingent on weather conditions. *Ownership:* Municipal. *Access:* Public. *Sessions:* Public. *Classes/Lessons:* None. *Program Affiliation:* Own. *Summer School:* No. *Notes:* Parks & Rec floods ten areas in winter. No lessons are offered & all ice is public skate. For information on locations, months and hours of operation, call the Parks Department above.

Pleasant Arena
848 Pleasant Ave.
St. Paul MN 55102
(612)228-1143
FAX: (612) 777-6519
Mgr: Jim Rolling
Ice surfaces: 1, 200x85, Enclosed. *Open:* Oct.-Mar. *Access:* Public. *Clubs:* Numerous youth hockey associations and high schools. *Sessions:* Public, Private/Club, Rental, Freestyle, Hockey, General. *Classes/Lessons:* None. *Summer School:* No. *Notes:* Vending machines.

Reise (Nielson) Arena
23rd & Ashe
Bemidji MN 56601
(218) 751-4541
FAX: (218) 751-7578
Ice surfaces: 1, 100x85, Enclosed. *Open:* Year Round. *Ownership:* Municipal. *Access:* Public. *Clubs:* Bemidji FSC, Bemidji Youth Hockey. *Sessions:* Public, Private/Club, Rental, Hockey. *Classes/Lessons:* Group, Private. *Program Affiliation:* USFSA. *Services:* Lockers, Dressing Rooms. *Notes:* Freestyle, patch and dance sessions are offered through the club only.

Riverside Arena
501 NE 2nd Ave.
Austin MN 55912
(507) 437-7676
Mgr: Dennis Maschka
Ice surfaces: 1, 200x85, Enclosed. *Open:* Oct.-Apr. *Ownership:* Municipal. *Access:* Public. *Clubs:* Riverside FSC, Austin Youth Hockey Assn. *Sessions:* Public, Rental. *Classes/Lessons:* Private. *Summer School:* No. *Services:* Pro Shop, Skate Rental, Skate Sharpening, Snack Bar, Dressing Rooms. *Notes:* Freestyle, patch, dance and hockey sessions are offered through the clubs only.

Rochester Olmstead Recreation Center
21 Elton Hills Dr. NW
Rochester MN 55901
(507) 281-6167
Mgr: Fred Fibeger
Ice surfaces: 2, 200x85; 200x85, Enclosed. *Open:* Year Round. *Ownership:* Municipal. *Access:* Public. *Clubs:* Rochester FSC. *Sessions:* Public, Private/Club, Rental, Freestyle, Hockey. *Classes/Lessons:* Group, Private. *Program Affiliation:* USFSA. *Summer School:* Local. *Services:* Pro Shop, Skate Rental, Skate Sharpening, Weight Room, Pool and/or Athletic Facilities, Dressing Rooms. *Notes:* Lessons offered through the club only.

Roseville Ice Arena
1200 Woodhill Dr.
Roseville MN 55113
(612) 484-0269
Mgr: Bill Olein
Skating Dir: Marylou Girby
Ice surfaces: 2, 200x85, Enclosed, Outdoor/Semi Outdoor. *Open:* Year Round. *Ownership:* Municipal. *Access:* Public. *Clubs:* Roseville FSC. *College/Univ:* Northwestern College. *Sessions:* Public, Private/Club, Rental, Freestyle, Patch, Hockey. *Classes/Lessons:* Group, Private. *Program Affiliation:* USFSA, ISIA. *Summer School:* Local. *Notes:* 400m speed skating oval.

Runestone Community Center
802 3rd Ave. W.
Alexandria MN 56308
(612) 763-4466
Mgr: Dale Yager
Ice surfaces: 1, 200x85. *Open:* Sept.-Apr. *Ownership:* Municipal. *Access:* Public. *Clubs:* Alexandria FSC, Hockey Club. *Sessions:* Public, Private/Club, Rental. *Classes/Lessons:* Group, Private. *Program Affiliation:* USFSA. *Summer School:* No. *Services:* Skate Sharpening, Snack Bar, Lockers, Dressing Rooms. *Notes:* Freestyle, patch and dance sessions are offered through the club only.

Shoreview Arena
877 Hwy. 96
Shoreview MN 55126
(612) 484-2400
FAX: (612) 777-6519
Mgr: Jim Rolling
Ice surfaces: 1, 200x85, Enclosed. *Open:* Oct.-Mar. *Access:* Public. *Clubs:* Numerous youth hockey associations and high schools. *Sessions:* Public, Private/Club, Rental, Freestyle, Hockey, General. *Classes/Lessons:* None. *Summer School:* No. *Notes:* Vending machines.

St. Louis Park Recreation Center
5005 W. 36th St.
St. Louis Park MN 55416
(612) 924-2545
Mgr: Craig Panning
Skating Dir: Chas Martin
Ice surfaces: 1, 200x85, Enclosed. *Open:* Year Round. *Ownership:* Municipal. *Access:* Public. *Sessions:* Public, Rental, Freestyle, Patch, Hockey. *Classes/Lessons:* Group, Private. *Program Affiliation:* ISIA. *Summer School:* No. *Services:* Skate Sharpening, Snack Bar, Lockers, Skate Rental, Pool and/or Athletic Facilities, Dressing Rooms.

St. Mary's College Ice Arena
700 Terrace Heights, P. O. Box 58
Winona MN 55987
(507) 457-1412
FAX: (507) 457-1633
Mgr: Greg Dick
Ice surfaces: 1, 200x94, Enclosed. *Open:* July-Mar. *Ownership:* Private. *Access:* Restricted. *Restrictions:* Students. *College/Univ:* St. Mary's College. *Sessions:* Hockey, Broomball. *Classes/Lessons:* Private. *Services:* Pro Shop, Snack Bar, Weight Room, Lockers, Dressing Rooms.

St. Paul Parks & Recreation
Department of Community Services
300 City Hall Annex, 25th W. 4th St.
St. Paul MN 55102
(612) 266-6400
Outdoor. *Open:* Contingent on weather conditions. *Ownership:* Municipal. *Access:* Public. *Sessions:* Public. *Classes/Lessons:* None. *Program Affiliation:* Own. *Summer School:* No. *Notes:* Parks & Rec. floods 30 areas in winter. No lessons are offered, and all sessions are public skate. For information on location, months and hours of operation, contact the Parks Department above.

Thompson (Loren) Park
Kingwood Dr.
Baxter MN 56401
(218) 829-7161
Mgr: Roy Rauen
Ice surfaces: 1, 200x80, Outdoor/Semi Outdoor. *Open:* Dec.-Mar. *Ownership:* Municipal. *Access:* Public. *Clubs:* Brainerd Hockey Assn. *Sessions:* Public, Hockey. *Classes/Lessons:* None. *Summer School:* No. *Services:* Lockers.

Victory Memorial Ice Arena
1900 42nd Ave. N.
Minneapolis MN 55412
(612) 627-2953
Mgr: Virgil Oldre
Ice surfaces: 1, 200x85, Enclosed. *Open:* Year Round. *Ownership:* Municipal. *Access:* Public. *Sessions:* Public, Rental, Hockey. *Classes/Lessons:* Group. *Program Affiliation:* ISIA. *Summer School:* Local. *Services:* Pro Shop, Skate Rental, Skate Sharpening, Lockers, Dressing Rooms.

Vogel Arena
122 S. Garden St.
New Ulm MN 56073
(507) 354-8321
FAX: (507) 359-8342
Mgr: Jim Krapf
Ice surfaces: 1, 200x85, Enclosed. *Open:* Oct.-Mar.; July-Aug. *Ownership:* Municipal. *Access:* Public. *Clubs:* New Ulm FSC, New Ulm Hockey Assn. *Sessions:* Public, Private/Club, Rental, Freestyle, Patch, Dance, Hockey. *Classes/Lessons:* Group, Private. *Program Affiliation:* USFSA, ISIA. *Summer School:* Regional. *Services:* Snack Bar, Weight Room, Pool and/or Athletic Facilities, Lockers, Dressing Rooms.

Wakota Arena
141 6th St. S.
South St Paul MN 55075
(612) 451-1727
Mgr: Ritch Rakness
Ice surfaces: 1, 200x85, Enclosed. *Open:* Sept.-Mar.; June-Aug. *Ownership:* Municipal. *Access:* Public. *Clubs:* Jump & Spin Skating School. *Sessions:* Public, Rental. *Classes/Lessons:* Group. *Program Affiliation:* Own. *Summer School:* Local. *Services:* Pro Shop, Skate Rental, Skate Sharpening, Snack Bar, Dressing Rooms. *Notes:* All lessons are offered through the skating school.

White Bear Arena
2610 Orchard Lane
White Bear Lake MN 55110
(612) 777-8255
FAX: (612) 777-6519
Mgr: Jim Rolling
Ice surfaces: 1, 200x85, Enclosed. *Open:* Oct.-Mar. *Access:* Public. *Clubs:* Numerous youth hockey associations and high schools. *Sessions:* Public, Private/Club, Rental, Freestyle, Hockey, General. *Classes/Lessons:* None. *Summer School:* No. *Notes:* Vending machines.

White Bear Lake Sports Center
1328 Hwy. 96
White Bear Lake MN 55110
(612) 429-8571
Mgr: Bruce Bates
Skating Dir: Angie Rice
Ice Surfaces: 1, 200x85, Enclosed. *Open:* June-Apr. *Ownership:* Municipal. *Access:* Public. *Clubs:* White Bear Hockey Assn. *Sessions:* Public, Private/Club, Rental, Freestyle, Patch, Dance, Hockey. *Classes/Lessons:* Group, Private. *Program Affiliation:* USFSA. *Summer School:* Local. *Services:* Skate Rental, Skate Sharpening, Snack Bar, Pool and/or Athletic Facilities, Lockers, Dressing Rooms. *Notes:* Aerobics room, racquetball court.

Willmar Civic Center
2707 Arena Dr.
Willmar MN 56201
(612) 235-1454
Mgr: Bill Abel
Skating Dir: Rachael Sunderman
Ice Surfaces: 1, 200x85, Enclosed. *Open:* Oct.-Mar.; July-Aug. *Ownership:* Municipal. *Access:* Public. *Clubs:* Willmar FSC. *Sessions:* Public, Private/Club, Rental, Freestyle, Hockey. *Classes/Lessons:* Group, Private. *Program Affiliation:* USFSA. *Summer School:* Local. *Services:* Skate Rental, Pro Shop, Skate Sharpening, Snack Bar, Lockers, Dressing Rooms. *Notes:* Dance lessons are available, but no dance sessions.

Yackel (Ken) - West Side Arena
44 East Isabel St.
St. Paul MN 55107
(612) 228-1145
FAX: (612) 777-6519
Mgr: Jim Rolling
Ice surfaces: 1, 200x85, Enclosed. *Open:* Oct.-Mar. *Access:* Public. *Clubs:* Youth Hockey Assn.; local high schools. *Sessions:* Public, Private/Club, Rental, Freestyle, Hockey, General. *Classes/Lessons:* None. *Summer School:* No. *Notes:* Vending machines.

MO: MISSOURI

Bode Ice Arena
2500 Southwest Pkwy.
St. Joseph MO 64503
(816) 271-5506
Mgr: Jean Wyatt
Ice surfaces: 1, 185x85, Enclosed. *Open:* June-Apr. *Ownership:* Municipal. *Access:* Public. *Clubs:* The Show Me Blades SC. *Sessions:* Public, Private/Club, Rental, Hockey. *Classes/Lessons:* Group, Private. *Program Affiliation:* USFSA. *Summer School:* Local. *Services:* Skate Rental, Skate Sharpening, Snack Bar, Lockers, Dressing Rooms. *Notes:* Club handles all lessons and figure skating activities.

Brentwood Ice Arena
2505 S. Brentwood Blvd.
Brentwood MO 63144
(314) 962-4806
Mgr: Sherry Olar
Skating Dir: Sherry Olar
Ice surfaces: 1, 200x80, Enclosed. *Open:* Year Round. *Ownership:* Municipal. *Access:* Public. *Clubs:* Brentwood FSC. *Sessions:* Public, Private/Club, Rental, Freestyle, Patch, Dance, Hockey. *Classes/Lessons:* Group, Private. *Program Affiliation:* ISIA, USFSA. *Summer School:* Local. *Services:* Pro Shop, Skate Rental, Skate Sharpening, Snack Bar, Lockers, Dressing Rooms.

Carriage Club Ice Rink
5301 State Line Rd.
Kansas City MO 64112
(816) 363-2733
FAX: (816) 363-2338
Mgr: Jim Mullen
Ice surfaces: 1, 146x75, Outdoor/Semi Outdoor. *Open:* Nov.-Feb. *Ownership:* Club. *Access:* Restricted, Members Only. *Sessions:* Freestyle, Hockey, Private/Club. *Classes/Lessons:* Group, Private. *Program Affiliation:* ISIA. *Summer School:* No. *Services:* Pro Shop, Skate Rental, Skate Sharpening, Snack Bar, Weight Room, Pool and/or Athletic Facilities, Lockers, Dressing Rooms.

City of Creve Coeur Ice Arena
11400 Old Cabin Rd.
Creve Coeur MO 63141
(314) 432-3960
FAX: (314) 569-5039
Mgr: Jim Wheeler
Skating Dir: Neil Peterson
Ice surfaces: 1, 185x85, Enclosed. *Open:* Year Round. *Ownership:* Municipal. *Access:* Public. *Clubs:* Creve Coeur FSC. *Sessions:* Public, Private/Club, Rental. *Classes/Lessons:* Group, Private. *Program Affiliation:* ISIA. *Summer School:* Local. *Services:* Skate Rental, Skate Sharpening, Snack Bar, Lockers, Dressing Rooms. *Notes:* Freestyle and patch sessions are offered through the club only.

Crown Center Ice Terrace
2405 Grand Ave., Suite 200
Kansas City MO 64108
(816) 274-8412
FAX: (816) 274-4567
Mgr: Terry Williams
Ice surfaces: 1, 105x105, Outdoor/Semi Outdoor. *Open:* Nov.-Mar. *Ownership:* Private. *Access:* Public. *Sessions:* Rental, Public. *Classes/Lessons:* None. *Summer School:* No. *Services:* Skate Rental, Skate Sharpening, Snack Bar. *Notes:* No sessions other than general due to small rink size.

Ice Plaza Galleria
2001 Independence St.
Cape Cirardeau MO 63701
(314) 335-4405
Mgr: Betty Talbort
Skating Dir: Tamara Niedbalski
Ice surfaces: 1, 140x70, Enclosed. *Open:* Sept.-July. *Ownership:* Private. *Clubs:* St. Joseph FSC. *Sessions:* Public, Private/Club, Rental, Hockey. *Classes/Lessons:* Group, Private. *Program Affiliation:* ISIA. *Services:* Skate Rental, Skate Sharpening, Snack Bar, Lockers. *Notes:* Freestyle, patch and dance sessions offered through the club only.

Kennedy (Wayne C.) Recreation Complex
6050 Wells Rd.
St. Louis MO 63128
(314) 894-3088
Mgr: Daina Skujins-Kinlen
Ice surfaces: 1, 200x85, Enclosed. *Open:* Oct.-Mar. *Ownership:* Municipal. *Access:* Public. *Sessions:* Public, Rental, Freestyle, Dance, Hockey. *Classes/Lessons:* Private, Group. *Program Affiliation:* ISIA. *Summer School:* No. *Services:* Skate Rental, Skate Sharpening, Snack Bar, Pool and/or Athletic Facilities, Lockers, Dressing Rooms. *Notes:* Dressing rooms for hockey only.

Marriot Tam-Tara Resort
State Rd. KK
Osage Beach MO 65065
(314) 348-3131
Mgr: Randy Hunt-Reed
Skating Dir: Randy Reed
Ice surfaces: 1, 100x40, Enclosed. *Open:* Oct.-May. *Ownership:* Private. *Access:* Public. *Sessions:* Freestyle, Public. *Classes/Lessons:* Group, Private. *Program Affiliation:* Own. *Summer School:* No. *Services:* Skate Rental, Skate Sharpening, Snack Bar, Pool and/or Athletic Facilities, Lockers, Dressing Rooms. *Notes:* Located in a hotel.

North Country Recreation Center
2577 Redman Rd.
St. Louis MO 63136
(314) 355-7374
Mgr: Gary Magg
Ice surfaces: 1, 200x100, Enclosed. *Open:* Sept.-Apr. *Ownership:* Municipal. *Access:* Public. *Clubs:* Mississippi Valley FSC, Mississippi Valley Hockey Assn. *Sessions:* Public, Private/Club, Rental, Freestyle, Patch, Hockey. *Classes/Lessons:* Group, Private. *Program Affiliation:* ISIA. *Services:* Skate Rental, Skate Sharpening, Snack Bar, Lockers, Dressing Rooms. *Notes:* Seating capacity of 600; meeting room.

St. Peters Rec-Plex
One St. Peters Center Blvd.
St. Peters MO 63376
(314) 298-2550
FAX: (314) 447-4440
Mgr: Denise Jensen
Ice surfaces: 1, 200x85, Enclosed. *Open:* Year Round. *Ownership:* Municipal.

Access: Public. *Clubs:* St. Charles County Youth Hockey Assn. *Sessions:* Public, Private/Club, Rental, Freestyle, Patch, Dance, Hockey. *Classes/Lessons:* Group, Private. *Program Affiliation:* USFSA. *Services:* Skate Sharpening, Skate Rental, Snack Bar, Ballet Room, Pool and/or Athletic Facilities, Weight Room, Lockers, Dressing Rooms.

Washington Park Ice Arena
320 E. McCarthy St.
Jefferson City Parks & Recreation
Jefferson City MO 65101
(314) 634-6482
FAX: (314) 634-6329
Mgr: Phil Stiles
Ice surfaces: 1, 185x85, Enclosed. *Open:* Oct.-Mar. *Ownership:* Municipal. *Access:* Public. *Clubs:* Jefferson City FSC. *Sessions:* Public, Private/Club, Rental, Freestyle, Patch, Dance, Hockey. *Classes/Lessons:* Group, Private. *Program Affiliation:* ISIA. *Summer School:* No. *Services:* Skate Rental, Skate Sharpening, Snack Bar, Lockers, Dressing Rooms.

MT: MONTANA

Centennial Ice Arena
427 Bench Blvd.
Billings MT 59105
(406) 256-1192
Mgr: Don Nafts
Ice surfaces: 1, 200x85, Enclosed. *Open:* July-Apr. *Ownership:* Private. *Access:* Public. *Clubs:* FSC of Billings. *Sessions:* Public, Private/Club, Rental, Hockey. *Classes/Lessons:* Private, Group. *Program Affiliation:* USFSA. *Summer School:* No. *Services:* Pro Shop, Skate Rental, Skate Sharpening, Snack Bar, Dressing Rooms. *Notes:* Freestyle, patch and dance sessions are offered through the club only.

Four Seasons Arena
403rd St. NW
Great Falls MT 59401
(406) 727-8900
Mgr: Bill Ogg
Skating Dir: Penlee Atchison
Ice surfaces: 2, 200x85; 200x76, Enclosed. *Open:* Year Round. *Ownership:* Municipal. *Access:* Public. *Clubs:* Great Falls FS Assn. *Sessions:* Public, Rental, Freestyle, Patch, Dance, Hockey. *Classes/Lessons:* Private, Group. *Program Affiliation:* USFSA. *Summer School:* Local. *Services:* Skate Rental, Pro Shop, Skate Sharpening, Snack Bar, Lockers, Dressing Rooms.

Queen City Ice Palace
400 Lola
Helena MT 59601
(406) 443-4559
Mgr: Jackie Avon
Skating Dir: Cheryl Barr
Ice surfaces: 1, 200x85, Enclosed. *Open:* Year Round. *Ownership:* Private. *Access:* Public. *Sessions:* Public, Private/Club, Rental, Freestyle, Patch, Dance, Hockey. *Classes/Lessons:* Group, Private. *Program Affiliation:* USFSA. *Services:* Pro Shop, Skate Rental, Skate Sharpening, Snack Bar, Ballet Room, Weight Room, Lockers, Dressing Rooms.

US High Altitude Sports Center
#1 Olympic Way
Butte MT 59701
(406) 723-7060
Ice surfaces: 2, 200x85; 400 meter oval, Outdoor/Semi Outdoor. *Open:* Oct.-Mar. *Ownership:* Private. *Access:* Public. *Clubs:* Butte Amateur Hockey Assn. *Sessions:* Public, Rental, Freestyle, Hockey. *Classes/Lessons:* Group. *Program Affiliation:* Own. *Summer School:* No. *Services:* Dressing Rooms. *Notes:* Facility is the Junior National Olympic training center for speed skating. Has *Learn To Skate* programs.

NC: NORTH CAROLINA

Boone (Daniel) Ice Rink
339 JA - MAX Dr.
Hillsborough NC 27278
(919) 644-8222
Mgr: Chris Smithey
Ice surfaces: 1, 185x85, Enclosed. *Open:* Oct.-Apr. *Ownership:* Private. *Access:* Public. *Sessions:* Public, Private/Club, Rental, Freestyle, Patch, Dance, Hockey. *Classes/Lessons:* Group, Private. *Program Affiliation:* ISIA. *Services:* Pro Shop, Skate Rental, Skate Sharpening, Snack Bar, Pool and/or Athletic Facilities, Dressing Rooms.

Cleland Skating Rink
Bldg. #3-1606 Reilly Rd.
Fort Bragg NC 28307
(910) 396-5127
FAX: (910) 396-6339
Mgr: Irene Hahn
Ice surfaces: 1, 200x85, Enclosed. *Open:* Year Round. *Access:* Restricted. *Restrictions:* Military personnel. *Sessions:* Public, Rental, Freestyle, Patch, Hockey. *Classes/Lessons:* Group, Private. *Program Affiliation:* ISIA. *Services:* Skate Rental, Skate Sharpening, Lockers.

Greensboro Coliseum
1921 W. Lee St.
Greensboro NC 27403
(910) 373-7400
Mgr: Larry Updike
Ice surfaces: 1, 200x90, Enclosed. *Open:* Nov.-Mar. *Ownership:* Municipal. *Access:* Public. *Clubs:* Ice Sports, Inc. *Sessions:* Public, Private/Club, Rental, Freestyle, Patch, Dance, Hockey. *Classes/Lessons:* Group, Private. *Program Affiliation:* USFSA. *Summer School:* No. *Services:* Skate Rental, Snack Bar, Ballet Room, Weight Room, Lockers, Dressing Rooms.

Ice Chalet Eastland Mall
5595 Central Ave.
Charlotte NC 28212
(704) 568-0772
Mgr: Neal Frye
Ice surfaces: 1, 180x80, Enclosed. *Open:* Year Round. *Ownership:* Private. *Access:* Public. *Sessions:* Public, Private/Club, Rental, Freestyle, Patch, Dance, Hockey. *Classes/Lessons:* Group, Private. *Program Affiliation:* Own. *Services:* Pro Shop, Skate Rental, Skate Sharpening, Lockers. *Notes:* Party room.

Ice House
1410 Buck Jones Rd.
Cary NC 27606
(919) 467-6000
Mgr: Scott Cudmore
Ice surfaces: 1, 187 x 85, Enclosed. *Open:* Year Round. *Ownership:* Private. *Access:* Public. *Clubs:* SC of North Carolina. *Sessions:* Public, Private/Club, Rental, Freestyle, Patch, Dance, Hockey. *Classes/Lessons:* Group. *Program Affiliation:* USFSA. *Summer School:* Local. *Services:* Pro Shop, Skate Rental, Snack Bar, Ballet Room, Lockers, Dressing Rooms.

Joel (Lawrence) Veterans Memorial Coliseum
300 Deacon Blvd.
Winston-Salem NC 27102
(910) 725-5635
Mgr: Kenneth Smith
Ice surfaces: 1, 200x85, Enclosed. *Open:* Oct.-Mar. *Ownership:* Municipal. *Access:* Public. *Clubs:* FSC, two amateur hockey associations. *Sessions:* Public, Private/Club, Rental, Freestyle, Patch, Hockey. *Classes/Lessons:* Group, Private. *Program Affiliation:* ISIA. *Summer School:* No. *Services:* Skate Rental, Skate Sharpening, Snack Bar, Lockers, Dressing Rooms.

Mitchell YMCA
97 Pinebridge Ave.
Spruce Pine NC 28777
(704) 765-7766
Mgr: Cindy Lindsey
Ice surfaces: 1, 200x100, Enclosed. *Open:* Sept.-Mar. *Ownership:* Private. *Access:* Public. *Sessions:* Public, Private/Club, Hockey. *Classes/Lessons:* Group, Private. *Program Affiliation:* ISIA. *Summer School:* No. *Services:* Pro Shop, Skate Sharpening, Snack Bar, Pool and/or Athletic Facilities, Lockers, Dressing Rooms.

ND: NORTH DAKOTA

All Seasons Arena
2005 Burdick Expressway E.
Minot ND 58701
(701) 857-7620
Mgr: Terry Wallace
Ice surfaces: 2, 200x85; 185x75, Enclosed. *Open:* Oct.-Mar. *Ownership:* Municipal. *Access:* Public. *Clubs:* Lake Region SC. *Sessions:* Public, Private/Club, Rental, Freestyle, Patch, Dance, Hockey. *Classes/Lessons:* Group, Private. *Program Affiliation:* Own. *Summer School:* Local. *Services:* Skate Rental, Skate Sharpening, Snack Bar, Lockers, Dressing Rooms.

Burdick Arena
Hwy. 20 N.
Devil's Lake ND 58301
(701) 662-8418
Ice surfaces: 2, 200x85; 185x75, Enclosed. *Open:* Oct.-Mar. *Ownership:* Municipal. *Access:* Public. *Clubs:* Blue Line Club; Lake Region Skating Club. *Sessions:* Public, Private/Club, Rental, Freestyle, Patch, Dance, Hockey. *Classes/Lessons:* Group, Private. *Program Affiliation:* USFSA. *Summer School:* Local. *Services:* Skate Sharpening, Skate Rental, Snack Bar, Lockers, Dressing Rooms.

Carlson (John E.) Coliseum
807 17th Ave. N.
Fargo ND 58102
(701) 241-8155
Mgr: Wayne Loeffler
Ice surfaces: 1, 185x85, Enclosed. *Open:* Oct.-Mar. *Ownership:* Municipal. *Access:* Public. *Clubs:* Fargo North Hockey; Red River Valley FSC, ND State University Hockey. *Sessions:* Public, Private/Club, Rental, Freestyle, Patch, Dance, Hockey. *Classes/Lessons:* Group, Private. *Program Affiliation:* USFSA, ISIA. *Summer School:* No. *Services:* Skate Rental, Skate Sharpening, Snack Bar, Lockers, Dressing Rooms.

Fargo Sports Arena
2001 17th Ave. S.
Fargo ND 58103
(701) 241-8152
Mgr: Wayne Loeffler
Skating Dir: Laura Jacobson
Ice surfaces: 2, 200x85; 60x30, Enclosed. *Open:* Sept.-Feb. *Ownership:* Municipal. *Access:* Public. *Clubs:* Southside Flyers; River Valley FSC, North Side Raiders. *Sessions:* Public, Rental, Freestyle, Patch, Dance, Hockey, Private/Club. *Classes/Lessons:* Private, Group. *Program Affiliation:* USFSA. *Summer School:* No. *Services:* Skate Rental, Skate Sharpening, Studio Rink, Weight Room, Dressing Rooms, Lockers. *Notes:* Indoor track.

Grafton Centennial Center
School Rd.
Grafton ND 58237
(701) 352-3874
FAX: (701) 352-2730
Mgr: Keith Lindenberg
Ice surfaces: 1, 200x85, Enclosed. *Open:* Oct.-Mar. *Ownership:* Municipal. *Access:* Public. *Clubs:* VFW Hockey; Grafton High Hockey. *Sessions:* Public, Private/Club, Rental, Freestyle, Patch, Dance, Hockey. *Classes/Lessons:* Private, Group. *Program Affiliation:* ISIA, USFSA. *Summer School:* No. *Services:* Skate Sharpening, Snack Bar, Ballet Room, Lockers, Dressing Rooms.

Grafton Winter Sports Arena
120 E. 5th St.
Grafton ND 58237
(701) 352-3707
Mgr: Todd Durand
Ice surfaces: 1, 150x75, Enclosed. *Open:* Oct.-Mar. *Ownership:* Municipal. *Access:* Public. *Clubs:* VFW Hockey; Grafton FSC. *Sessions:* Public, Private/Club, Rental, Freestyle, Patch, Dance, Hockey. *Classes/Lessons:* Private, Group. *Program Affiliation:* ISIA, USFSA. *Summer School:* No. *Services:* Skate Sharpening, Lockers, Dressing Rooms, Snack Bar.

Hill Avenue Outdoor Rink
Hill and Willow Ct.
Grafton ND 58237
(701) 352-1842
Mgr: Keith Lindenberg
Ice surfaces: 1, 125x60, Outdoor/Semi Outdoor. *Open:* Nov.-Apr. *Ownership:* Municipal. *Access:* Public. *Sessions:* Public. *Classes/Lessons:* None. *Summer School:* No. *Notes:* Adjacent to park.

Purpur Arena
1122 7th Ave. S.
Grand Forks ND 58201
(701) 746-2764
Mgr: Bill Palmiscio
Ice surfaces: 1, 190x85, Enclosed. *Open:* Nov.-Mar. *Ownership:* Municipal. *Access:* Public. *Clubs:* High school hockey. *Sessions:* Public, Private/Club, Rental, Freestyle, Patch, Dance, Hockey. *Classes/Lessons:* Private, Group. *Program Affiliation:* USFSA. *Summer School:* No. *Services:* Snack Bar, Lockers, Dressing Rooms. *Notes:* Pros rent ice for freestyle, patch and dance sessions. This is included in the session fee for skaters.

Schaumberg Ice Rink
221 Reno Ave.
Bismark ND 58504
(701) 221-6813
Mgr: Jim Peluso
Ice surfaces: 1, 200x85, Enclosed. *Open:* Nov.-Mar. *Ownership:* Municipal. *Access:* Public. *Clubs:* Bismark FSC. *Sessions:* Public, Private/Club, Rental, Hockey. *Classes/Lessons:* Group, Private.

Summer School: No. *Services:* Skate Sharpening, Snack Bar, Dressing Rooms.

VFW All Seasons Arena
1200 N. Washington
Bismarck ND 58501
(701) 221-6814
Mgr: Jim Peluso
Ice surfaces: 1, 200x85, Enclosed. *Open:* June-Apr. *Ownership:* Municipal. *Access:* Public. *Clubs:* Bismarck Hockey Boosters; Bismarck Figure Skaters; local public schools. *Sessions:* Public, Private/Club, Rental, Freestyle, Patch, Dance, Hockey. *Classes/Lessons:* Group, Private. *Program Affiliation:* USFSA. *Summer School:* Local. *Services:* Skate Sharpening, Snack Bar, Ballet Room, Lockers, Dressing Rooms.

Wilson (John L.) Arena
7th St. & 12th Ave. NE
Jamestown ND 58401
(701) 252-3939
Mgr: Doug Hogan
Ice surfaces: 2, 200x85; 200x85, Enclosed. *Open:* Oct.-Mar./June-July. *Clubs:* Jamestown FSC, Jamestown Hockey Booster Assn. *Sessions:* Public, Private/Club, Rental, Hockey. *Classes/Lessons:* Private, Group. *Program Affiliation:* USFSA. *Summer School:* Local. *Services:* Pro Shop, Skate Sharpening, Pool and/or Athletic Facilities, Lockers, Dressing Rooms. *Notes:* Freestyle, patch and dance sessions are offered through the club only.

NE: NEBRASKA

Aksarben Coliseum
63rd & Shirley St.
Omaha NE 68106
(402) 444-4031
Mgr: Kay Telford
Ice surfaces: 1, 200x85, Enclosed. *Open:* Nov.-Apr. *Ownership:* Municipal. *Access:* Restricted. *Restrictions:* Mainly rentals; infrequent public sessions. *Clubs:* Lancer Hockey Team; FSC of Omaha. *Sessions:* Public, Private/Club, Rental, Freestyle, Patch, Dance, Hockey. *Classes/Lessons:* None. *Summer School:* No. *Services:* Skate Rental, Skate Sharpening, Snack Bar, Lockers, Dressing Rooms. *Notes:* Ice is rented to groups only.

Benson Ice Arena
6920 Military Ave.
Omaha NE 68104
(402) 444-5971
Mgr: Mike Vlassakis
Ice surfaces: 1, Enclosed. *Open:* Oct.-Apr. *Ownership:* Municipal. *Access:* Public. *Sessions:* Public, Private/Club, Freestyle, Patch, Dance, Hockey. *Classes/Lessons:* Group, Private. *Program Affiliation:* USFSA, ISIA. *Services:* Skate Rental, Skate Sharpening.

Hitchcock Ice Arena
5015 S. 45th St.
Omaha NE 68127
(402) 444-4955
FAX: (402) 444-4921
Mgr: Mike Vlassakis
Ice surfaces: 1, 200x85, Enclosed. *Open:* Year Round. *Ownership:* Municipal. *Access:* Public. *Clubs:* Blade & Edge FSC of Omaha. *Sessions:* Public, Private/Club, Rental, Freestyle, Patch, Dance, Hockey. *Classes/Lessons:* Group, Private. *Program Affiliation:* USFSA, ISIA. *Services:* Skate Rental, Skate Sharpening, Snack Bar, Lockers. *Notes:* Conference center.

NH: NEW HAMPSHIRE

Campion Rink / Thompson Arena
Route 10
West Lebanon NH 03784
(603) 643-1222
Mgr: Bill McFaden
Ice surfaces: 1, 200x85, Enclosed. *Open:* Oct.-Mar. *Ownership:* Private. *Access:* Public. *Clubs:* SC at Dartmouth, Inc. *Sessions:* Public, Rental, Freestyle, Patch, Dance, Hockey. *Classes/Lessons:* Group, Private. *Summer School:* No. *Services:* Skate Sharpening, Snack Bar, Lockers.

Cardigan Mountain School Rink
Back Bay Rd.
Canaan NH 03741
(603) 523-4321
Mgr: Jim Marrion
Ice surfaces: 1, 202x87, Enclosed. *Open:* Nov.-Jan. *Ownership:* Private. *Access:* Restricted. *Restrictions:* Students and staff. *Sessions:* Public, Rental, Hockey. *Classes/Lessons:* None. *Summer School:* No. *Services:* Pro Shop, Skate Sharpening, Weight Room, Pool and/or Athletic Facilities, Lockers, Dressing Rooms.

Cheshire Fair Ice Arena
319 Monadnock Hwy.
East Swanzey NH 03469
(603) 357-4740
FAX: (603) 357-0310
Mgr: John Thurber
Skating Dir: Lorrain Damon
Ice surfaces: 1, 200x85, Enclosed. *Open:* Oct.-Mar. *Ownership:* Private. *Access:* Public. *Clubs:* Cheshire FSC, Keene Youth Hockey; Keene Men's Hockey League; Keene High School. *Sessions:* Public, Private/Club, Rental, Hockey. *Classes/Lessons:* Group. *Summer School:* No. *Services:* Pro Shop, Skate Rental, Skate Sharpening, Snack Bar, Lockers, Dressing Rooms. *Notes:* Lessons, freestyle, patch and dance sessions through club only.

Dartmouth College Thompson Arena
Park St.
Hanover NH 03755
(603) 646-1110
Mgr: Becky Rice
Ice surfaces: 1, 200x85, Enclosed. *Open:* Oct.-Mar. *Ownership:* Private. *Access:* Restricted. *Restrictions:* College use; some public sessions. *College/Univ:* Dartmouth College. *Sessions:* Public, Rental, Freestyle, Hockey. *Classes/Lessons:* None. *Summer School:* No. *Services:* Snack Bar, Lockers, Dressing Rooms.

Dover Ice Arena
110 Portland Ave.
Dover NH 03820
(603) 743-6060
Mgr: Paul Chalue
Skating Dir: Laura
Ice surfaces: 1, 200x85, Enclosed. *Open:* June-Apr. *Ownership:* Municipal. *Access:* Public. *Clubs:* Great Bay FSC, Grand State Stars Hockey; high schools. *Sessions:* Public, Private/Club, Freestyle, Patch, Hockey, Rental. *Classes/Lessons:* Group. *Program Affiliation:* USFSA. *Summer School:* Local. *Services:* Pro Shop, Skate Rental, Skate Sharpening, Snack Bar, Lockers, Dressing Rooms.

Evertt Arena
Loudon Rd.
Concord NH 03301
(603) 746-3195
Ice surfaces: 1, 190x85, Enclosed. *Open:* Year Round. *Ownership:* Municipal. *Access:* Public. *Sessions:* Public, Freestyle, Patch, Dance, Hockey. *Classes/Lessons:* Group, Private. *Program Affiliation:* USFSA. *Summer School:* National/International. *Services:* Pro Shop, Lockers, Dressing Rooms.

Gordon (Malcolm) Memorial Rink at St. Paul's School
325 Pleasant St.
Concord NH 03301
(603) 225-3341
Mgr: Elaine Castigan
Ice surfaces: 1, 200x85, Enclosed. *Open:* Nov.-Feb. *Ownership:* Private. *Access:* Restricted. *Restrictions:* School community. *Sessions:* Hockey. *Classes/Lessons:* None. *Summer School:* No. *Services:* Lockers, Dressing Rooms.

J.F.K. Memorial Rink
Dartmouth College, 303 Beech St.
Manchester NH 03755
(603) 649-2109
Ice surfaces: 1, Enclosed. *Open:* Sept.-Feb. *Ownership:* Private. *Access:* Public. *College/Univ:* Dartmouth College. *Sessions:* Public, Rental, Hockey. *Classes/Lessons:* Group, Private. *Services:* Skate Sharpening.

Kimball Union Academy Ice Arena
Main St.
Meriden NH 03770
(603) 469-3211
Mgr: Rod McLain
Ice surfaces: 1, 200x85, Enclosed. *Open:* Nov.-Mar. *Ownership:* Private. *Access:* Public. *Sessions:* Public, Private/Club, Rental, Freestyle, Patch, Hockey. *Classes/Lessons:* None. *Summer School:* No. *Services:* Skate Sharpening, Weight Room, Lockers, Dressing Rooms. *Notes:* All sessions other than public sessions are for school use or by invitation only.

La Clement Arena
New England College, 29 Bridge St.
Henniker NH 03242
(603) 428-9806
FAX: (603) 428-7230
Mgr: Tom Pratt
Ice surfaces: 1, 200x85, Enclosed. *Open:* Oct.-Mar. *Ownership:* Private. *Access:* Public. *Clubs:* Granite FSC, Skating Club of Southern NH. *College/Univ:* New England College. *Sessions:* Public, Private/Club, Rental. *Classes/Lessons:* Group, Private. *Program Affiliation:* USFSA, ISIA. *Summer School:* No. *Services:* Snack Bar, Dressing Rooms. *Notes:* Freestyle sessions are offered through the club only.

Merill-Lindsay Arena
New Hampton School, Main St.
New Hampton NH 03256
(603) 744-5401
Mgr: Bruce Paro
Ice surfaces: 1, 200x85, Outdoor/Semi Outdoor. *Open:* Nov.-Mar. *Ownership:* Private. *Access:* Restricted. *Restrictions:* School use & rentals. *College/Univ:* Plymouth State College. *Sessions:* Private/Club, Rental, Hockey. *Classes/Lessons:* None. *Summer School:* No. *Services:* Skate Sharpening, Snack Bar, Weight Room, Pool and/or Athletic Facilities, Lockers, Dressing Rooms.

New Hampshire College Ice Rink
25 N. River Rd.
Manchester NH 03106
(603) 668-2211
Mgr: Peter Tufts
Ice surfaces: 1, 190x85, Outdoor/Semi Outdoor. *Open:* Nov.-Mar. *Ownership:* Private. *Access:* Restricted. *Restrictions:* Rented by groups. *Clubs:* High schools, Special Olympics training. *College/Univ:* Daniel Webster College. *Sessions:* Hockey. *Classes/Lessons:* Group, Private. *Summer School:* No. *Services:* Skate Sharpening, Weight Room, Pool and/or Athletic Facilities, Dressing Rooms.

Notre Dame Arena Inc.
Hill Side Ave.
Berlin NH 03570
(603) 752-9846
Mgr: Michael O'Neal
Ice surfaces: 1, 185x85, Enclosed. *Open:* Sept.-Apr. *Ownership:* Private. *Access:* Public. *Sessions:* Public, Private/Club, Rental, Hockey. *Classes/Lessons:* None. *Services:* Pro Shop, Skate Sharpening, Dressing Rooms, Snack Bar.

Phillips Exeter Academy Rink
Court St.
Exeter NH 03833
(603) 772-4311
Mgr: Daniel Conner
Ice surfaces: 2, 185x85; 185x85, Enclosed. *Open:* Nov.-Mar.; June-Aug. *Ownership:* Private. *Access:* Restricted. *Restrictions:* School use. *Sessions:* Public, Private/Club, Rental, Freestyle, Patch, Hockey. *Classes/Lessons:* Group, Private. *Program Affiliation:* USFSA, ISIA. *Summer School:* Local. *Services:* Skate Sharpening, Dressing Rooms. *Notes:* Skate sharpening is for Academy use only.

Pop Whalen Rink
Rt. 109A
Wolfboro NH 03894
(603) 569-5639
Mgr: Sue Glenn
Ice surfaces: 1, 200x80, Enclosed, Outdoor/Semi Outdoor. *Open:* Oct.-Mar. *Ownership:* Municipal. *Access:* Public. *Sessions:* Public, Private/Club, Rental, Hockey. *Classes/Lessons:* Group. *Program Affiliation:* USFSA. *Summer School:* No. *Services:* Snack Bar, Lockers. *Notes:* The rink also floods an area for additional skating.

Proctor Academy Ice Arena
Box 500 Main St.
Andover NH 03216
(603) 735-6000
Mgr: Bob Dunlop
Ice surfaces: 1, 197x85, Enclosed. *Open:* Nov.-Mar. *Ownership:* Private. *Access:* Public. *Clubs:* ECAC Youth Hockey; Men's League. *Sessions:* Public, Rental, Hockey. *Classes/Lessons:* None. *Program Affiliation:* USFSA. *Summer School:* No. *Services:* Skate Sharpening, Snack Bar, Dressing Rooms.

Rochester Arena
63 A Lowell St.
Rochester NH 03867
(603) 335-6749
FAX: (603) 335-7558
Mgr: Bill Page
Skating Dir: Randy Willard
Ice surfaces: 1, 185x80, Enclosed. *Open:* Sept.-Apr. *Ownership:* Municipal. *Access:* Public. *Clubs:* Youth hockey. *Sessions:* Public, Rental, Hockey. *Classes/Lessons:* Group. *Summer*

School: No. *Services:* Skate Sharpening, Snack Bar, Lockers, Dressing Rooms. *Notes:* The snack bar is run by the Youth Hockey Association.

Tilton School Rink
30 School St.
Tilton NH 03276
(603) 286-4342
Mgr: William Saunders
Ice surfaces: 1, 200x100, Enclosed. *Open:* Nov.-Mar. *Ownership:* Private. *Access:* Restricted. *Restrictions:* Residents, rentals, and students. *Clubs:* Hockey. *Sessions:* Rental, Hockey. *Classes/Lessons:* None. *Summer School:* No. *Services:* Lockers, Dressing Rooms.

West Side Ice Arena
Electric St.
Manchester NH 03102
(603) 624-6574
Mgr: Ben Goudreau
Ice surfaces: 1, 200x85, Enclosed. *Open:* July-Apr. *Ownership:* Municipal. *Access:* Public. *Clubs:* Southern N.H. Skating Club. *College/Univ:* St. Aslem College. *Sessions:* Public, Private/Club, Rental, Hockey. *Classes/Lessons:* Group. *Program Affiliation:* Own. *Summer School:* No. *Services:* Pro Shop, Skate Rental, Skate Sharpening, Snack Bar, Lockers. *Notes:* Four locker rooms.

NJ: NEW JERSEY

American Hockey and Ice Skating Center
1215 Wyckoff Rd.
Farmingdale NJ 07727-0621
(908) 919-7070
FAX: (908) 919-0284
Mgr: Ned Doudican
Ice surfaces: 2, 200x85; 200x85, Enclosed. *Open:* Year Round. *Ownership:* Private. *Access:* Public. *Sessions:* Public, Private/Club, Rental, Freestyle, Patch, Dance, Hockey. *Program Affiliation:* USFSA, ISIA. *Services:* Skate Rental, Pro Shop, Skate Sharpening, Snack Bar, Weight Room, Dressing Rooms.

Baker Rink
Princeton University
Princeton NJ 08540
(609) 258-3000
Mgr: Jeff Graydon
Ice surfaces: 1, 200x85, Enclosed. *Open:* Year Round. *Ownership:* Private. *Access:* Restricted. *Restrictions:* University community; students; faculty. *Clubs:* Princeton FSC. *College/Univ:* Princeton University. *Sessions:* Public, Private/Club, Rental, Freestyle, Patch, Dance, Hockey. *Classes/Lessons:* Group, Private. *Program Affiliation:* Own. *Summer School:* Local. *Services:* Skate Sharpening, Snack Bar, Ballet Room, Pool and/or Athletic Facilities, Dressing Rooms. *Notes:* Very limited public sessions.

Bayonne High School
Physical Education Community
 Education Center
28th St. & Ave. A
Bayonne NJ 07002
(201) 858-5589
Mgr: Joe Broderick
Ice surfaces: 1, 200x85, Enclosed. *Open:* July-May. *Ownership:* Municipal. *Access:* Public. *Sessions:* Public, Private/Club, Rental, Hockey. *Classes/Lessons:* Private, Group. *Program Affiliation:* USFSA, ISIA. *Services:* Pro Shop, Skate Rental, Skate Sharpening, Snack Bar, Ballet Room, Pool and/or Athletic Facilities, Lockers, Dressing Rooms. *Notes:* Lessons, freestyle and patch sessions are offered through the club only; facility has a track.

Bridgewater Sports Arena
1425 Frontier Rd.
Bridgewater NJ 08807
(908) 627-0006
Mgr: Joan Mack
Skating Dir: Lisa Spitz Uliano
Ice surfaces: 2, 200x85; 200x85, Enclosed. *Open:* Year Round. *Ownership:* Private. *Access:* Public. *Sessions:* Public, Rental, Freestyle, Patch, Dance, Hockey, Private/Club. *Classes/Lessons:* Group, Private. *Summer School:* Regional. *Services:* Pro Shop, Skate Rental, Skate Sharpening, Snack Bar, Weight Room, Lockers, Dressing Rooms, Ballet Room, Pool and/or Athletic Facilities. *Notes:* Tae Kwon Do classes.

Chimney Rock
Rt 22 E. & Chimney Rock Rd., Central Jersey Industrial Park-Building 1EC
Bridgewater NJ 08807
(908) 302-9425
Mgr: Pat Messano
Skating Dir: Bill Aquilino
Ice surfaces: 1, 200x85, Enclosed. *Open:* Year Round. *Ownership:* Private. *Access:* Public. *College/Univ:* Rutger's University. *Sessions:* Public, Freestyle, Patch, Dance, Hockey. *Classes/Lessons:* Group, Private. *Program Affiliation:* USFSA. *Summer School:* Local. *Services:* Pro Shop, Skate Rental, Skate Sharpening, Snack Bar, Lockers. *Notes:* A second rink is in the planning stages.

Coliseum Rink
333 Preston Ave.
Voorhees NJ 08043
(609) 429-6908
FAX: (609) 429-2992
Mgr: Al Zurzolo
Ice surfaces: 1, 200x85, Enclosed. *Open:* Year Round. *Ownership:* Private. *Access:* Public. *Clubs:* Coliseum FSC, Philadelphia Flyers. *Sessions:* Public, Private/Club, Rental, Freestyle, Patch, Hockey. *Classes/Lessons:* Group, Private. *Program Affiliation:* USFSA, ISIA. *Summer School:* Regional. *Services:* Skate Rental, Pro Shop, Skate Sharpening, Snack Bar, Weight Room, Pool and/or Athletic Facilities, Lockers. *Notes:* Rollerblading; aerobics; volleyball.

Dietl (Fritz) Ice Rink
639 Broadway
Westwood NJ 07675
(201) 664-9812
Mgr: Corolla Dietl
Ice surfaces: 1, 150x70, Enclosed. *Open:* Year Round. *Ownership:* Private. *Access:* Public. *Clubs:* Bear Mountain FSC, NJ FSC Inc. *Sessions:* Public, Private/Club, Freestyle, Patch, Dance, Hockey. *Classes/Lessons:* Group, Private. *Services:* Snack Bar, Lockers, Dressing Rooms. *Notes:* Party room.

Essex Hunt Club
51 Holland Rd.
Peapack NJ 07977
(908) 234-0062
FAX: (908) 234-0515
Mgr: Marie Toto
Ice surfaces: 1, 180x85, Outdoor/Semi

Outdoor. *Open:* Nov.-Mar. *Ownership:* Club. *Access:* Members Only. *Sessions:* Freestyle, Patch, Hockey, Private/Club. *Classes/Lessons:* Group, Private. *Program Affiliation:* USFSA, ISIA. *Summer School:* No. *Services:* Pro Shop, Skate Sharpening, Snack Bar, Lockers.

Hollydell Ice Arena
601 Hollydell Dr.
Sewell NJ 08080-0472
(609) 589-5599
Mgr: Pat Hedenberg
Ice surfaces: 1, 200x85, Enclosed. *Open:* Year Round. *Ownership:* Private. *Access:* Public. *Clubs:* Hollydell FSC. *Sessions:* Public, Rental, Freestyle, Patch, Hockey. *Classes/Lessons:* Group, Private. *Program Affiliation:* USFSA. *Services:* Pro Shop, Skate Rental, Skate Sharpening, Dressing Rooms, Lockers. *Notes:* All-purpose rooms.

Iceland Associates
6 Tennis Ct.
Hamilton NJ 08619
(609) 588-6672
FAX: (609) 588-6969
Mgr: John Boyd
Skating Dir: Denise Cattani
Ice surfaces: 2, 200x185; 200x185, Enclosed. *Open:* Year Round. *Ownership:* Private. *Access:* Public. *Sessions:* Public, Private/Club, Rental, Freestyle, Patch, Dance, Hockey. *Classes/Lessons:* Group, Private. *Program Affiliation:* USFSA, ISIA. *Summer School:* Regional. *Services:* Pro Shop, Skate Rental, Skate Sharpening, Snack Bar, Ballet Room, Lockers, Dressing Rooms.

Lawrenceville School Rink
Main St.
Lawrenceville NJ 08648
(609) 896-0123
FAX: (609) 895-2158
Mgr: Jim Brown
Ice surfaces: 1, 185x85, Enclosed. *Open:* Year Round. *Ownership:* Private. *Access:* Public. *Sessions:* Public, Private/Club, Rental, Hockey. *Classes/Lessons:* None. *Summer School:* No. *Services:* Snack Bar, Pool and/or Athletic Facilities, Lockers, Dressing Rooms. *Notes:* Field house attached.

Mackay Ice Arena Inc.
130 W. Englewood Ave.
Englewood NJ 07631
(201) 568-3133
FAX: (201) 568-1703
Mgr: Barbara Heran
Skating Dir: Neil Rubin
Ice surfaces: 1, 200x95, Outdoor/Semi Outdoor. *Open:* Sept.-Mar. *Ownership:* Private. *Access:* Public. *Clubs:* Mavericks Hockey Club. *College/Univ:* Columbia University; Stevens Institute of Technology; NYU. *Sessions:* Rollerhockey, Public, Rental, Hockey. *Classes/Lessons:* Group, Private. *Program Affiliation:* USFSA, ISIA. *Summer School:* No. *Services:* Pro Shop, Skate Rental, Skate Sharpening, Snack Bar, Dressing Rooms, Lockers.

Mennen (William G.) Sports Arena
161 East Hanover Ave.
Morris Township NJ 07960
(201) 326-7651 973-326-7651
FAX: (201) 644-2726
Mgr: Reynold Fauci
Skating Dir: Bill Schank
Ice surfaces: 2, 200x85; 200x85, Enclosed. *Open:* Year Round. *Ownership:* Municipal. *Access:* Public. *Clubs:* Crystal Blades (ISIA), SC of Morris County (USFSA). *Sessions:* Public, Private/Club, Rental, Freestyle, Patch, Dance, Hockey. *Classes/Lessons:* Group, Private. *Program Affiliation:* USFSA, ISIA. *Summer School:* Local. *Services:* Skate Rental, Pro Shop, Skate Sharpening, Snack Bar, Ballet Room, Dressing Rooms, Lockers.

Mercer County Public Skating Center
Mercer County Park Commission
640 S. Broad St.
Trenton NJ 08650
(609) 586-8092
FAX: (609) 695-5124
Mgr: Bob Ash
Ice surfaces: 1, 185x85, Outdoor/Semi Outdoor. *Open:* Nov.-Mar. *Ownership:* Municipal. *Access:* Public. *Sessions:* Public, Private/Club, Rental, Freestyle, Patch, Dance, Hockey. *Classes/Lessons:* Group, Private. *Program Affiliation:* USFSA, ISIA. *Summer School:* No. *Services:* Skate Rental, Skate Sharpening, Snack Bar, Dressing Rooms.

Montclair Arena
41 Chestnut St.
Montclair NJ 07042
(201) 744-6088
Mgr: Bill Irving
Ice surfaces: 1, 185x85, Enclosed. *Open:* Oct.-Mar. *Ownership:* Municipal. *Access:* Public. *Clubs:* Montclair Inside Edge SC. *Sessions:* Public, Private/Club, Rental, Freestyle, Patch, Hockey. *Classes/Lessons:* Group, Private. *Program Affiliation:* USFSA, ISIA. *Summer School:* No. *Services:* Pro Shop, Skate Rental, Skate Sharpening, Snack Bar, Pool and/or Athletic Facilities, Lockers, Dressing Rooms. *Notes:* The hockey sessions are offered through the club.

Navesink Country Club
Navesink River Rd.
Middletown NJ 07748
(908) 842-3111
FAX: (908) 219-1971
Mgr: Deb Brooks
Ice surfaces: 1, Outdoor/Semi Outdoor. *Open:* Oct.-Mar. *Ownership:* Private. *Access:* Members Only. *Sessions:* Private/Club, Freestyle, Hockey. *Classes/Lessons:* Group, Private. *Program Affiliation:* ISIA. *Summer School:* No. *Services:* Pro Shop, Skate Sharpening, Snack Bar, Pool and/or Athletic Facilities, Dressing Rooms, Lockers.

Ocean Ice Palace
197 Chambers Bridge Rd.
Brick NJ 08723
(908) 477-4411
Ice surfaces: 1, 200x85, Enclosed. *Open:* Year Round. *Ownership:* Private. *Access:* Restricted. *Restrictions:* To the programs offered by the rink. *Sessions:* Private/Club, Rental, Hockey. *Classes/Lessons:* None. *Program Affiliation:* Own. *Summer School:* Regional. *Services:* Skate Rental, Pro Shop, Skate Sharpening, Snack Bar, Lockers, Dressing Rooms. *Notes:* Summer school is hockey only.

Old Bridge Arena
1 Old Bridge Plaza
Old Bridge NJ 08857
(908) 679-3100
Mgr: Frank Martinelli
Ice surfaces: 1, 200x80, Outdoor/Semi Outdoor. *Open:* Oct.-Apr. *Ownership:* Municipal. *Access:* Public. *Clubs:* Raritan

Valley FSC, Inc. *Sessions:* Public, Rental, Freestyle, Patch, Hockey, General. *Classes/Lessons:* Group, Private. *Program Affiliation:* ISIA. *Summer School:* No. *Services:* Pro Shop, Skate Sharpening, Snack Bar, Lockers. *Notes:* Small accessory shop available. Lockers for hockey players only.

South Mountain Arena
560 Northfield Ave
West Orange NJ 07052
(201) 731-3828
Mgr: Jack Sheik
Ice surfaces: 2, 200x85; 200x85, Enclosed. *Open:* Year Round. *Ownership:* Municipal. *Clubs:* New Jersey Devils; Essex SC of NJ, Inc.; South Mountain FSC, Inc. *Sessions:* Public, Private/Club, Rental, Freestyle, Patch, Dance, Hockey. *Classes/Lessons:* Group, Private. *Summer School:* Local. *Services:* Pro Shop, Skate Rental, Skate Sharpening, Snack Bar, Dressing Rooms.

Twin Rinks Ice Sports & Entertainment Center
6725 River Rd.
Pennsauken NJ 08110
(609) 488-9300
FAX: (609) 488-9307
Mgr: Jerry Domish
Skating Dir: Lynn Mooney
Ice surfaces: 2, 200x85; 200x85, Enclosed. *Open:* Year Round. *Ownership:* Private. *Access:* Public. *Clubs:* Rivers Edge FSC. *Sessions:* Public, Rental, Freestyle, Patch, Dance, Hockey. *Classes/Lessons:* Group, Private. *Summer School:* Local. *Services:* Pro Shop, Skate Rental, Skate Sharpening, Snack Bar, Lockers, Dressing Rooms. *Notes:* Multi-purpose rooms.

Ventor Ice Rink
Newport Ave. & Atlantic Ave.
Ventor NJ 08201
(609) 823-7947
Mgr: Dominic Cappela
Ice surfaces: 1, 100x80, Outdoor/Semi Outdoor. *Open:* Oct.-Apr. *Ownership:* Municipal. *Access:* Public. *Clubs:* Atlantic City FSC, Ventor FSC. *Sessions:* Public, Private/Club, Rental, Freestyle, Patch, Dance, Hockey. *Classes/Lessons:* Group, Private. *Program Affiliation:* USFSA, ISIA. *Summer School:* No. *Services:* Skate Rental, Lockers, Dressing Rooms.

Warinanco Skating Center
Warinanco Park
Roselle NJ 07207
(908) 298-7850
Ice surfaces: 1, 200x85, Outdoor/Semi Outdoor. *Open:* Oct.-Apr. *Ownership:* Municipal. *Access:* Public. *Sessions:* Public, Private/Club, Rental, Freestyle, Hockey. *Classes/Lessons:* Group, Private. *Program Affiliation:* Own. *Summer School:* No. *Services:* Pro Shop, Skate Rental, Skate Sharpening, Snack Bar, Dressing Rooms, Lockers.

Williams Arena
University of Minneapolis
1901 4th St SE
Minneapolis NJ 55455
(612) 625-5804
Ice surfaces: 1, 200x100, Enclosed. *Open:* Year Round. *Ownership:* Private. *Access:* Public. *College/Univ:* University of Minneapolis. *Sessions:* Public, Rental, Hockey. *Classes/Lessons:* None. *Program Affiliation:* Own. *Summer School:* No. *Services:* Skate Rental, Skate Sharpening, Weight Room, Dressing Rooms. *Notes:* Facility mainly used by hockey teams.

Winding River Skating Center
1211 Whitesville Rd.
Toms River NJ 08753
(908) 244-0720
Mgr: Richard Broadbelt
Ice surfaces: 1, 200x85, Outdoor/Semi Outdoor. *Open:* Oct.-Mar. *Ownership:* Municipal. *Access:* Public. *Clubs:* Toms River FSC, Garden State FSC. *Sessions:* Dance, Hockey, General, Rental. *Classes/Lessons:* Group. *Services:* Pro Shop, Skate Rental, Skate Sharpening, Snack Bar, Dressing Rooms.

NM: NEW MEXICO

Outpost Ice Arena
9530 Tramway Blvd. NE
Albuquerque NM 87122
(505) 856-7594
Mgr: Cindy Douglas
Skating Dir: Cindy Douglas
Ice surfaces: 1, 200x85, Enclosed. *Open:* Year Round. *Ownership:* Private. *Access:* Public. *Clubs:* Albuquerque FSC, Hockey Assn. *Sessions:* Public, Private/Club, Rental, Hockey. *Classes/Lessons:* Group, Private. *Program Affiliation:* USFSA. *Services:* Pro Shop, Skate Rental, Skate Sharpening, Snack Bar, Weight Room, Lockers, Dressing Rooms. *Notes:* Freestyle, patch and dance sessions are offered through the club only; Learn-to-Skate programs are offered.

NV: NEVADA

Santa Fe Ice Skating Arena
4949 N. Rancho Dr.
Las Vegas NV 89130
(702) 658-4991
Mgr: Karen Doherty
Ice surfaces: 1, 200x85, Enclosed. *Open:* Year Round. *Ownership:* Private. *Access:* Public. *Sessions:* Public, Private/Club, Rental, Freestyle, Patch, Hockey. *Classes/Lessons:* Group, Private. *Program Affiliation:* USFSA. *Summer School:* National/International. *Services:* Pro Shop, Skate Rental, Skate Sharpening, Snack Bar, Ballet Room, Lockers, Dressing Rooms. *Notes:* The rink is located in a hotel and is open 24 hours daily; casino at hotel.

NY: NEW YORK

Achilles Rink - Union College
Union College
Schenectady NY 12308-2311
(518) 388-6134
FAX: (518) 388-6134
Mgr: Dennis Flavin
Ice surfaces: 1, 200x85, Enclosed. *Open:* Sept.-Mar. *Ownership:* Private. *Access:* Restricted. *Restrictions:* Students only. *Clubs:* Achilles FSC, Inc. *College/Univ:* Union College. *Sessions:* Private/Club, Rental, Freestyle, Patch, Dance, Hockey. *Classes/Lessons:* None. *Program Affiliation:* USFSA. *Summer School:* No. *Services:* Pro Shop, Skate Sharpening, Snack Bar, Weight Room.

Alexandria Municipal Recreation Center
Bolton Ave.
Alexandria Bay NY 13607
(315) 482-9360
Mgr: Bruce Miller
Ice surfaces: 1, Enclosed. *Open:* Nov.-Apr. *Ownership:* Municipal. *Access:* Public. *Clubs:* High schools. *Sessions:* Public, Private/Club, Rental, Freestyle, Patch, Hockey. *Classes/Lessons:* Private. *Program Affiliation:* Own. *Summer*

School: No. *Services:* Lockers.

Allen Park Ice Rink
Elizabeth Ave.
Jamestown NY 14701
(716) 483-0614
Mgr: David Evanzik
Ice surfaces: 1, 200x85, Enclosed. *Open:* Year Round. *Ownership:* Municipal. *Access:* Public. *Clubs:* Youth Hockey. *Sessions:* Public, Private/Club, Rental, Freestyle, Patch, Dance, Hockey. *Classes/Lessons:* Group, Private. *Program Affiliation:* USFSA, ISIA. *Summer School:* Regional. *Services:* Skate Rental, Skate Sharpening, Snack Bar, Pool and/or Athletic Facilities, Dressing Rooms.

Allyn Arena
East Osten St. & Jordan St.
Skaneateles NY 13152
(315) 685-7757
FAX: (315) 685-0745
Mgr: Matt Major
Ice surfaces: 1, 200x85, Enclosed. *Open:* Oct.-Apr. *Ownership:* Municipal. *Access:* Public. *Clubs:* Skaneateles Youth Hockey; Skaneateles FSC. *Sessions:* Public, Private/Club, Rental, Freestyle, Hockey. *Classes/Lessons:* Group. *Program Affiliation:* USFSA. *Summer School:* No. *Services:* Pro Shop, Skate Sharpening, Snack Bar, Dressing Rooms.

Alumni Arena - State University College at Cortland
PR Facility
Cortland NY 13045
(607) 753-4961
FAX: (607) 753-4929
Mgr: Al MacCormack
Ice surfaces: 1, 190x85, Enclosed. *Open:* Sept.-Mar. *Access:* Public. *Clubs:* Corland FSC, Inc. *Sessions:* Public, Private/Club, Rental, Hockey. *Classes/Lessons:* Group, Private. *Program Affiliation:* ISIA. *Summer School:* No. *Services:* Skate Rental, Skate Sharpening, Pool and/or Athletic Facilities, Lockers. *Notes:* Freestyle, patch and dance sessions are offered through the club only.

Appleton Arena
St. Lawrence University
Miner St. & Leigh St.
Canton NY 13617
(315) 379-5696
FAX: (315) 379-5805
Mgr: Paul Flannigan
Ice surfaces: 1, 200x85, Enclosed. *Open:* Sept.-Apr. *Ownership:* Private. *Access:* Public. *College/Univ:* St. Lawrence University. *Sessions:* Public, Rental, Hockey. *Classes/Lessons:* None. *Program Affiliation:* Own. *Summer School:* No. *Services:* Weight Room, Pool and/or Athletic Facilities, Lockers, Dressing Rooms.

Audubon Recreation Center
1615 Amherst Manner Dr.
Williamsville NY 14221
(716) 631-7136
Mgr: Fran Schaab
Ice surfaces: 1, 183x84. *Open:* Sept.-Apr. *Ownership:* Municipal. *Access:* Public. *Clubs:* Amherst SC; Amherst Hockey Assn. *Sessions:* Public, Private/Club, Rental, Freestyle, Patch, Dance, Hockey. *Classes/Lessons:* Private, Group. *Program Affiliation:* USFSA. *Summer School:* No. *Services:* Skate Sharpening, Snack Bar, Pool and/or Athletic Facilities, Lockers, Dressing Rooms.

Bear Mountain State Park Ice Rink
Bear Mountain NY 10911
(914) 786-2701
Mgr: Tom Margiotta
Ice surfaces: 1, 185x85, Outdoor/Semi Outdoor. *Open:* Nov.-Mar. *Ownership:* Municipal. *Access:* Public. *Sessions:* Public, Private/Club, Freestyle, Hockey.

Bethpage Community Park Ice Rink
Stuart Ave.
Bethpage NY 11714
(516) 733-8404
Mgr: William Thau
Ice surfaces: 1, 200x80, Outdoor/Semi Outdoor. *Open:* Nov.-Mar. *Ownership:* Municipal. *Access:* Public. *Sessions:* Public, Rental, Hockey. *Classes/Lessons:* Group, Private. *Summer School:* No. *Services:* Skate Rental, Pro Shop, Snack Bar, Lockers, Dressing Rooms, Pool and/or Athletic Facilities.

Brockport Ice Rink
B 207 Tuttle North Sun
Brockport NY 14420
(716) 395-5365
Mgr: Susan Reynolds
Ice surfaces: 1, 200x85, Enclosed. *Open:* Sept.-Mar. *Ownership:* Municipal. *Access:* Public. *College/Univ:* State of New York College at Brockport. *Sessions:* Public, Private/Club, Rental, Hockey. *Classes/Lessons:* Private, Group. *Summer School:* No. *Services:* Skate Rental, Skate Sharpening, Weight Room, Pool and/or Athletic Facilities, Lockers, Dressing Rooms.

Burnet Park Arena
Avery & Coolridge Ave.
Syracuse NY 13204
(315) 473-4333
Mgr: Jerry Brown
Ice surfaces: 1, 200x85, Outdoor/Semi Outdoor. *Open:* Dec.-Mar. *Ownership:* Municipal. *Access:* Public. *Clubs:* Valley Youth Hockey. *Sessions:* Private/Club, Public, Freestyle, Hockey. *Classes/Lessons:* Group, Private. *Program Affiliation:* ISIA. *Summer School:* No. *Services:* Skate Rental, Skate Sharpening, Pool and/or Athletic Facilities.

Cantiague Park Ice Arena
W. John St.
Hicksville NY 11801
(516) 571-7056
Mgr: Mary Schroeder
Ice Surfaces: 1, 195x98, Enclosed. *Open:* Sept.-May. *Ownership:* Municipal. *Access:* Public. *Clubs:* Cantiague FSC. *Sessions:* Public, Rental, Freestyle, Patch, Hockey. *Classes/Lessons:* Private, Group. *Program Affiliation:* USFSA. *Summer School:* No. *Services:* Skate Rental, Skate Sharpening, Snack Bar, Pool and/or Athletic Facilities, Lockers, Dressing Rooms.

Casey Park
Casey Park, N. Division St.
Auburn NY 13021
(315) 253-4247
Mgr: William Cowmey
Ice surfaces: 1, 200x85, Outdoor/Semi Outdoor. *Open:* Oct.-Mar. *Ownership:* Municipal. *Access:* Public. *Clubs:* Auburn HS Hockey Club. *Sessions:* Public, Rental, Hockey. *Classes/Lessons:* Group. *Summer School:* No. *Services:* Skate

RINKS

Rental, Skate Sharpening, Snack Bar, Pool and/or Athletic Facilities, Lockers.

Cass Park Ice Rink
701 Taughannock Blvd.
Ithaca NY 14850
(607) 273-1090
FAX: (607) 273-2817
Mgr: Susie Mormile
Ice Surfaces: 1, 200x85, Outdoor/Semi Outdoor. *Open:* Oct.-Mar. *Ownership:* Municipal. *Access:* Public. *Sessions:* Public, Private/Club, Rental, Hockey. *Classes/Lessons:* Group. *Program Affiliation:* ISIA. *Summer School:* No. *Services:* Skate Rental, Pro Shop, Skate Sharpening, Snack Bar, Pool and/or Athletic Facilities.

Castle (Bonnie) Recreation Center
Rt. 12
Alexandria Bay NY 1607
(315) 482-4336
Mgr: Gary Williams
Ice surfaces: 1, 185x85, Enclosed. *Open:* Sept.-June. *Ownership:* Private. *Access:* Public. *Sessions:* Public, Private/Club, Rental, Freestyle, Patch, Dance. *Classes/Lessons:* Group, Private. *Program Affiliation:* USFSA. *Services:* Skate Rental, Pro Shop, Skate Sharpening, Snack Bar, Ballet Room, Pool and/or Athletic Facilities, Dressing Rooms, Lockers.

Center City Ice Rink
433 Stare St.
Schenectady NY 12304
(518) 382-5105
Mgr: Greg Davenport
Ice surfaces: 1, 185x85, Enclosed. *Open:* Oct.-Mar. *Ownership:* Municipal. *Access:* Public. *Sessions:* Public, Rental. *Classes/Lessons:* Group. *Program Affiliation:* ISIA. *Summer School:* No. *Services:* Skate Rental, Skate Sharpening, Snack Bar, Lockers, Dressing Rooms.

Clayton Recreation Arena
East Line Rd.
Clayton NY 13624
(315) 686-4310
Mgr: Dennis Honeywell
Ice surfaces: 1, 200x90, Enclosed. *Open:* Nov.-Mar. *Ownership:* Municipal. *Access:* Public. *Clubs:* Clayton FSC. *Sessions:* Public, Private/Club, Rental, Freestyle, Patch, Dance. *Classes/Lessons:* Group, Private. *Program Affiliation:* USFSA. *Summer School:* No. *Services:* Snack Bar, Pool and/or Athletic Facilities, Lockers, Dressing Rooms.

Clearfield Community Center
730 Hopkins Rd.
Williamsville NY 14221
(716) 689-1418
Mgr: Daniel Mathewson
, 183x84, Enclosed. *Open:* Sept.-Apr. *Ownership:* Municipal. *Access:* Public. *Sessions:* Private/Club, Public, Rental, Freestyle, Patch, Dance, Hockey. *Classes/Lessons:* Private, Group. *Program Affiliation:* USFSA. *Summer School:* No. *Services:* Skate Sharpening, Snack Bar, Pool and/or Athletic Facilities, Lockers, Dressing Rooms.

Clifton - Fine Arena
Main St.
Star Lake NY 13690
(315) 848-2578
Ice surfaces: 1, 200x85, Enclosed. *Open:* Dec.-Mar. *Ownership:* Towns of Clifton and Fine. *Access:* Public. *Clubs:* Clifton-Fine FSA, Clifton-Fine Hockey Assn. *Sessions:* Public, Club/Private, Hockey. *Classes/Lessons:* Through club only. *Program Affiliation:* USFSA. *Summer School:* No. *Services:* Snack Bar, Dressing Rooms. *Notes:* Freeestyle, Patch offered through club only; classes and lessons through club only.

Clifton Park Arena
16 Clifton Commons Blvd.
Clifton Park NY 12065
(518) 383-5440
Mgr: Tom Sheehan
Ice surfaces: 1, 200x85, Enclosed. *Open:* June-Mar. *Ownership:* Private. *Access:* Public. *Sessions:* Public, Rental, Freestyle, Patch, Dance, Hockey. *Classes/Lessons:* Private, Group. *Program Affiliation:* ISIA. *Services:* Skate Rental, Skate Sharpening, Snack Bar, Lockers.

Clinton Arena
36 Kirkland Ave.
Clinton NY 13323
(315) 853-5541
Mgr: Elaine Kane
Ice surfaces: 1, 190x87, Enclosed. *Open:* Sept.-Apr. *Ownership:* Municipal. *Access:* Public. *Clubs:* Clinton FSC.

Sessions: Public, Rental, Freestyle, Patch, Hockey. *Classes/Lessons:* Private, Group. *Summer School:* No. *Services:* Skate Rental, Pro Shop, Skate Sharpening, Snack Bar, Lockers.

Creek (Thomas) Ice Rink
80 Lyndon Rd.
Fairport NY 14450
(716) 223-2160
Mgr: Bill Lukaszonas
Ice surfaces: 1, 200x85, Enclosed. *Open:* Year Round. *Ownership:* Private. *Access:* Public. *Sessions:* Public, Rental, Freestyle, Hockey. *Classes/Lessons:* Group, Private. *Program Affiliation:* USFSA. *Summer School:* Local. *Services:* Pro Shop, Skate Rental, Skate Sharpening, Snack Bar, Ballet Room, Weight Room, Lockers, Dressing Rooms.

Crisafulli (Anthony J.) Memorial Skating Rink
East 9th St.
Oswego NY 13126
(315) 343-4054
Mgr: Anthony Ponzi
Ice surfaces: 1, 200x85, Enclosed. *Open:* Oct.-Apr. *Ownership:* Municipal. *Access:* Public. *Clubs:* Oswego FSC, Oswego Minor Hockey Assn., Senior Men's Hockey League, Broom Ball League. *Sessions:* Public. *Classes/Lessons:* None. *Program Affiliation:* Own. *Summer School:* No. *Services:* Pro Shop, Skate Sharpening, Snack Bar, Dressing Rooms. *Notes:* Classes are coordinated through clubs.

Culliman (James P.) Skating Rink
West 4th St. & Varick St.
Oswego NY 13126
(315)343-6594
Mgr: Anthony Ponzi
Ice surfaces: 1, 185x75, Enclosed. *Open:* Oct.-Apr. *Ownership:* Municipal. *Access:* Public. *Clubs:* Oswego FSC, Oswego Men's Hockey Assn. *Sessions:* Public. *Classes/Lessons:* None. *Program Affiliation:* Own. *Summer School:* No.

Dann Memorial Rink - Nichols School
1250 Amherst St.
Buffalo NY 14216
(716) 874-7174
Mgr: Frank Sacheli
Skating Dir: Frank Sacheli

Ice surfaces: 2, 185x85; 120x65, Enclosed. *Open:* Oct.-Mar. *Ownership:* Private. *Access:* Public. *Clubs:* Bisons Hockey Organization; Canisius College Hockey Team. *Sessions:* Private/Club, Rental, Hockey. *Classes/Lessons:* None. *Summer School:* No. *Services:* Studio Rink, Skate Sharpening, Snack Bar, Dressing Rooms. *Notes:* Reception room overlooks rinks.

Dix Hills Ice Rink
575 Vanderbilt Pkwy.
Dix Hills NY 11743
(516) 499-8058
Mgr: Karen O'Gara
Ice Surfaces: 1, 200x85. *Open:* Year Round. *Sessions:* Public, Rental, Freestyle, Patch, Dance. *Classes/Lessons:* Group, Private. *Program Affiliation:* ISIA. *Services:* Pro Shop, Skate Rental, Skate Sharpening, Snack Bar, Lockers, Dressing Rooms.

Ebersole Ice Rink
Lake St.
White Plains NY 10605
(914) 422-1336
FAX: (914) 422-1250
Mgr: Greg Prout
Ice surfaces: 1, 200x85, Outdoor/Semi Outdoor. *Open:* Nov.-Mar. *Ownership:* Municipal. *Access:* Public. *Sessions:* Public, Private/Club, Rental, Freestyle, Patch, Dance, Hockey. *Classes/Lessons:* Private, Group. *Program Affiliation:* ISIA. *Services:* Skate Rental, Pro Shop, Skate Sharpening, Snack Bar, Lockers, Dressing Rooms.

Freeport Recreation Center Ice Rink
130 E. Merrick Rd.
Freport NY 11520
(516) 223-8000
Mgr: John Jeffries
Ice surfaces: 1, 220x110, Enclosed. *Open:* Sept.-May. *Ownership:* Municipal. *Access:* Public. *Sessions:* Public, Private/Club, Rental, Freestyle, Patch, Dance, Hockey. *Classes/Lessons:* Private, Group. *Program Affiliation:* ISIA. *Summer School:* No. *Services:* Skate Rental, Skate Sharpening, Snack Bar, Ballet Room, Weight Room, Pool and/or Athletic Facilities, Dressing Rooms, Lockers.

Fulton Recreation Center, War Memorial
West Broadway
Fulton NY 13069
(315) 592-2474
Mgr: Barry Ostrander
Ice surfaces: 1, 200x87, Enclosed. *Open:* Oct.-Mar. *Ownership:* Municipal. *Access:* Public. *Clubs:* Fulton Youth Hockey; Fulton FSC, Men's Senior Hockey. *Sessions:* Public, Rental, Hockey. *Classes/Lessons:* None. *Program Affiliation:* Own. *Summer School:* No. *Services:* Skate Rental, Snack Bar, Pool and/or Athletic Facilities, Dressing Rooms.

Genesee Valley Park Ice Rink
131 Elmwood Ave.
Rochester NY 14611
(716) 253-3290
Mgr: Kathy Warren
Ice surfaces: 1, 200x85, Enclosed. *Open:* Oct.-Apr. *Sessions:* Public, Rental, Hockey. *Classes/Lessons:* Group. *Program Affiliation:* ISIA. *Summer School:* No. *Services:* Skate Rental, Pro Shop, Skate Sharpening, Snack Bar, Lockers, Dressing Rooms.

Granite Ice Skating Rink
Granite Hotel, Granite Rd.
Kerhonkson NY 12446
(914) 626-3141
Mgr: Jon Newson
Ice Surfaces: 1, 80x40, Enclosed. *Open:* Year Round. *Ownership:* Private. *Access:* Restricted. *Restrictions:* Club members; hotel guests. *Sessions:* Public, Private/Club, Rental, Freestyle, Hockey. *Classes/Lessons:* Private, Group. *Program Affiliation:* ISIA. *Summer School:* Local. *Services:* Skate Rental, Pro Shop, Skate Sharpening, Snack Bar, Weight Room, Pool and/or Athletic Facilities, Lockers, Dressing Rooms. *Notes:* Public sessions are only offered from Dec.-Apr.; patch and dance sessions are offered through the club only.

Grippen Park Ice Rink
Grippen Ave.
Endicott NY 13760
(617) 748-6323
Mgr: Dave Hill
Ice surfaces: 1, 200x85, Enclosed. *Open:* Nov.-Mar. *Ownership:* Municipal. *Access:* Public. *Sessions:* Public, Rental, Freestyle, Patch, Dance, Hockey. *Classes/Lessons:* Private, Group. *Program Affiliation:* USFSA. *Summer School:* No. *Services:* Skate Rental, Skate Sharpening, Snack Bar, Lockers, Dressing Rooms.

Harvey School Rink
Rt. 22
Katonah NY 10536
(914) 232-3618
Mgr: Bruce Osborne
Ice surfaces: 1, 195x85, Enclosed. *Open:* Year Round. *Ownership:* Private. *Access:* Public. *Clubs:* Hickory Hills FSC. *Sessions:* Private/Club, Freestyle, Patch, Dance, Hockey. *Classes/Lessons:* Private, Group. *Program Affiliation:* USFSA. *Summer School:* Local. *Services:* Pro Shop, Skate Sharpening, Snack Bar, Dressing Rooms, Lockers.

Holiday Twin Rinks
3465 Broadway
Buffalo NY 14227
(716) 685-3660
FAX: (716) 66802098
Mgr: Mark Grundtische
Skating Dir: Wilma Dee
Ice surfaces: 4, 200x85; 200x85; 200x85; 200x85, Enclosed. *Open:* Year Round. *Ownership:* Private. *Access:* Public. *Sessions:* Private/Club, Rental, Freestyle, Patch, Dance, Hockey. *Classes/Lessons:* Private, Group. *Program Affiliation:* ISIA. *Summer School:* Regional. *Services:* Skate Rental, Pro Shop, Skate Sharpening, Snack Bar, Lockers, Dressing Rooms.

Hommocks Park Ice Rink
740 W. Boston Post Rd.
Mamaronick NY 10548
(914) 834-1069
FAX: (914) 381-7809
Mgr: Rob Lundy
Skating Dir: Alana Kelton
Ice surfaces: 1, 200x85, Enclosed. *Open:* Sept.-Apr. *Ownership:* Municipal. *Access:* Public. *Sessions:* Public, Rental, Freestyle, Patch, Hockey. *Classes/Lessons:* Private, Group. *Program Affiliation:* ISIA. *Summer School:* No. *Services:* Skate Rental, Snack Bar, Pool and/or Athletic Facilities, Dressing Rooms, Lockers.

Houston Field House
Peoples Ave.
Troy NY 12180
(518) 276-6262
Mgr: Katherine Edick
Ice Surfaces: 1, 200x85, Enclosed. *Open:* Sept.-Mar. *Ownership:* Private. *Access:* Public. *Clubs:* Huron Mohawk FSC, Division 1 Hockey Team. *College/Univ:* Rensseler Polytechnic Institute. *Sessions:* Public, Private/Club, Rental, Freestyle, Dance, Patch, Hockey. *Classes/Lessons:* Private, Group. *Program Affiliation:* USFSA, ISIA. *Summer School:* No. *Services:* Skate Rental, Snack Bar, Lockers, Dressing Rooms.

Ice Studio, Inc.
1034 Lexington Ave.
New York NY 10021
(212) 535-0304
Mgr: Rovert La Cross
Ice surfaces: 1, 50x30, Enclosed. *Open:* Year Round. *Ownership:* Private. *Access:* Public. *Sessions:* Rental, Public, Freestyle. *Classes/Lessons:* Group, Private. *Program Affiliation:* ISIA. *Services:* Skate Rental, Pro Shop, Skate Sharpening, Dressing Rooms, Lockers.

Ice Time, Inc.
Ragnet Rd.
Newbury NY
(914) 647-4802
Mgr: Paul Lloyd
Ice surfaces: 2, 200x85; 100x50, Enclosed. *Open:* Year Round. *Ownership:* Private. *Access:* Public. *Sessions:* Public, Private/Club, Rental, Freestyle, Patch, Dance. *Classes/Lessons:* Private, Group. *Summer School:* Local. *Services:* Skate Rental, Pro Shop, Skate Sharpening, Studio Rink, Ballet Room, Snack Bar, Weight Room, Lockers, Dressing Rooms. *Notes:* Gym.

Iceland Skating Rink
3345 Hillside Ave.
New Hyde Park NY 11040
(516) 746-1100
Mgr: Ritch Roulston
Ice surfaces: 1, 200x85, Enclosed. *Open:* Year Round. *Ownership:* Private. *Access:* Public. *Clubs:* Metropolitan FSC, Long Island Goals Youth Hockey. *Sessions:* Private/Club, Public, Rental, Freestyle, Patch, Dance, Hockey. *Classes/Lessons:* Private, Group. *Program Affiliation:* USFSA. *Summer School:* Local. *Services:* Skate Rental, Pro Shop, Skate Sharpening, Snack Bar, Lockers, Dressing Rooms.

Knickerbocker Ice Arena Facility
103rd St.
Troy NY 12182
(518) 235-7761
Mgr: Irma Magee
Ice surfaces: 2, 200x85, Outdoor/Semi Outdoor, Enclosed. *Open:* Year Round. *Ownership:* Municipal. *Access:* Public. *Clubs:* Uncle Sam FSC, Uncle Sam Hockey Club. *Sessions:* Public, Private/Club, Rental, Freestyle, Patch, Hockey. *Classes/Lessons:* Group, Private. *Program Affiliation:* USFSA, ISIA. *Summer School:* Local. *Services:* Skate Rental, Pro Shop, Skate Sharpening, Snack Bar, Dressing Rooms, Lockers, Weight Room, Pool and/or Athletic Facilities.

Kutsher's Ice Rink
Monticello NY 12751
(914) 794-5621
Mgr: Celia Duffy
Ice Surfaces: 1, 100x60. *Open:* Year Round. *Ownership:* Private. *Access:* Restricted. *Restrictions: Sessions:* Private/Club, Rental, Freestyle. *Classes/Lessons:* Private. *Program Affiliation:* USFSA, ISIA. *Summer School:* Local. *Services:* Skate Rental, Pro Shop, Skate Sharpening.

Le Grange (Gerald) Feild House
Rye Country Day School, Grandview Ave.
Rye NY 10580
(914) 967-5876
FAX: (914) 921-4263
Mgr: Frank Effinger
Ice surfaces: 1, 200x85, Enclosed. *Open:* Nov.-Mar. *Ownership:* Private. *Access:* Restricted. *Restrictions:* Students, staff, club members. *Clubs:* Rye Rangers Hockey Club. *Sessions:* Private/Club, Rental, Hockey. *Classes/Lessons:* Group. *Summer School:* No. *Services:* Pro Shop, Skate Sharpening, Weight Room, Dressing Rooms, Lockers. *Notes:* Lessons are affiliated with the NCAA and USA Hockey.

Leisure Rinks Southtowns Inc.
75 Weiss Rd.
Buffalo NY 14224
(716) 675-8992
Mgr: Paul Grundtish
Skating Dir: Wilma Dee
Ice surfaces: 2, 200x85; 200x85, Enclosed. *Open:* Year Round. *Ownership:* Private. *Access:* Public. *Clubs:* W. New York FSC, Holiday and Leisure FSC. *College/Univ:* Erie Community College. *Sessions:* Rental, Hockey. *Classes/Lessons:* Group. *Program Affiliation:* USFSA. *Summer School:* Local. *Services:* Pro Shop, Skate Sharpening, Snack Bar, Dressing Rooms. *Notes:* Private lessons, freestyle and patch sessions offered through clubs only.

Long Island Skating Academy
175 Underhill Blvd.
Syosset NY 11791
(516) 496-2277
Mgr: Robert Phornton
Skating Dir: Dan Bedard
Ice surfaces: 2, 200x85; 130x85, Enclosed. *Open:* Year Round. *Ownership:* Private. *Access:* Restricted. *Restrictions:* New York Islanders; FSC, hockey groups. *Clubs:* Cantiague FSC. *Sessions:* Public, Private/Club, Rental, Freestyle, Hockey. *Classes/Lessons:* Private, Group. *Summer School:* Local. *Services:* Skate Rental, Pro Shop, Skate Sharpening, Snack Bar, Weight Room, Lockers, Dressing Rooms. *Notes:* Youth Islanders Hockey League Training Center.

Longbeach Arena, Inc.
150 W. Bay Dr.
Long Beach NY 11561
(516) 431-6501
Mgr: Lorraine Battaglini
Ice Surfaces: 1, 200x85, Enclosed. *Open:* Year Round. *Ownership:* Private. *Access:* Public. *Clubs:* NY Apple Core Hockey; Long Island FSC. *Sessions:* Hockey, Dance, Patch, Freestyle, Rental, Private/Club, Public. *Classes/Lessons:* Group, Private. *Program Affiliation:* USFSA. *Summer School:* Local. *Services:* Skate Rental, Pro Shop, Skate Sharpening, Snack Bar, Ballet Room, Lockers, Dressing Rooms, Pool and/or Athletic Facilities.

Lynah Rink
Cornell University
Campus Dr.
Ithaca NY 14850
(607) 255-3793
Mgr: Gene Beavers
Ice surfaces: 1, 200x85, Enclosed. *Open:* Oct.-Mar. *Ownership:* Private. *Access:* Restricted. *Restrictions:* Students. *College/Univ:* Cornell University. *Sessions:* Public, Hockey. *Classes/Lessons:* Group. *Services:* Skate Rental, Skate Sharpening, Lockers. *Notes:* Limited public sessions.

Lysander - Radisson Arena
2725 W. Entry Rd.
Baldwinsville NY 13027
(315) 635-1555
Mgr: Julie Taylor
Skating Dir: Lois Jenkins
Ice surfaces: 1, 200x85, Enclosed. *Open:* Year Round. *Ownership:* Private. *Access:* Public. *Clubs:* Syracuse FSC. *Sessions:* Public, Private/Club, Rental, Freestyle, Patch, Dance, Hockey. *Classes/Lessons:* Group, Private. *Program Affiliation:* ISIA. *Summer School:* Local. *Services:* Skate Rental, Pro Shop, Skate Sharpening, Snack Bar, Dressing Rooms.

Massena Arena
180 Hart Haven Plaza
Massena NY 13662
(315) 769-3161
Mgr: Paul Patterson
Ice surfaces: 1, 200x85, Enclosed. *Open:* Sept.-Apr. *Ownership:* Municipal. *Access:* Public. *Clubs:* Massena FSA; High Schools. *Sessions:* Public, Private/Club, Rental, Freestyle, Patch, Dance, Hockey, Broomball. *Classes/Lessons:* Group, Private. *Program Affiliation:* USFSA. *Summer School:* No. *Services:* Snack Bar, Lockers, Dressing Rooms.

McCann Ice Arena
14 Civic Center Plaza
Poughkeepsie NY 12601
(914) 454-5800
Mgr: Sue DuMoulin
Ice surfaces: 1, 200x85, Enclosed. *Open:* Year Round. *Ownership:* Private. *Access:* Public. *Clubs:* FSC. *Sessions:* Public, Private/Club, Rental, Freestyle, Patch, Dance, Hockey. *Classes/Lessons:* Group, Private. *Program Affiliation:* USFSA, ISIA. *Summer School:* Local. *Services:* Pro Shop, Skate Rental, Skate Sharpening, Snack Bar, Ballet Room, Lockers, Dressing Rooms.

Meachen Arena
121 W. Seneca Turnpike
Syracuse NY 13205
(315) 492-0179
FAX: (315) 428-8513
Mgr: Brian Long
Ice surfaces: 1, 200x85, Enclosed. *Open:* Year Round. *Ownership:* Municipal. *Access:* Public. *Clubs:* South City FSC, Corcoran High Hockey; Valley Youth Hockey. *Sessions:* Public, Private/Club, Freestyle, Hockey, Rental. *Classes/Lessons:* Group. *Program Affiliation:* USFSA, ISIA. *Summer School:* Local. *Services:* Skate Rental, Skate Sharpening, Snack Bar, Lockers, Dressing Rooms.

Murray (Edward J.) Memorial Skating Center
348 Tuckahoe Rd.
Yonkers NY 10710
(914) 377-6469
Mgr: Paul McInnis
Ice surfaces: 1, 200x85. *Open:* Oct.-Apr. *Ownership:* Municipal. *Access:* Public. *Clubs:* Bronxville FSC. *Sessions:* Public, Rental, Freestyle, Patch, Dance, Hockey. *Classes/Lessons:* Group, Private. *Program Affiliation:* USFSA, ISIA. *Services:* Skate Rental, Pro Shop, Skate Sharpening, Snack Bar, Dressing Rooms, Lockers.

Nasser Civic Center Ice Rink
8 Civic Center Plaza
Corning NY 14830
(607) 936-3764
Mgr: Kris Pashley
Ice surfaces: 1, 185x85, Outdoor/Semi Outdoor. *Open:* Nov.-Mar. *Ownership:* Municipal. *Access:* Public. *Sessions:* Public, Rental, Hockey. *Classes/Lessons:* Group. *Summer School:* No. *Services:* Skate Rental, Skate Sharpening, Snack Bar, Lockers.

New Hartford Recreation Center
Mill St.
New Hartford NY 13413
(315) 724-0600
Mgr: John Cunningham
Ice surfaces: 1, 185x85, Enclosed. *Open:* Sept.-Apr. *Ownership:* Municipal. *Access:* Public. *Clubs:* SC of New Hartford; New Hartford Junior Hockey. *Sessions:* Public, Private/Club, Rental, Freestyle, Patch, Dance, Hockey. *Classes/Lessons:* Group, Private. *Program Affiliation:* USFSA. *Summer School:* No. *Services:* Pro Shop, Skate Rental, Skate Sharpening, Snack Bar, Dressing Rooms. *Notes:* Freestyle, patch and dance sessions offered through club.

Newbridge Road Ice Rink
2600 Newbridge Rd.
Bellmore NY 11710
(516) 783-6181
FAX: (516) 783-6186
Mgr: Craig Lohsen
Ice surfaces: 1, 200x85, Enclosed. *Open:* Sept.-Apr. *Ownership:* Private. *Access:* Public. *Clubs:* Green Machine Hockey; Metropolitan FSC, Long Island Chiefs. *Sessions:* Public, Rental, Freestyle, Patch. *Classes/Lessons:* Private, Group. *Program Affiliation:* USFSA, ISIA. *Summer School:* No. *Services:* Pro Shop, Skate Rental, Skate Sharpening, Snack Bar, Lockers, Dressing Rooms.

Newell II (Edgar Allen) Dome
1100 State St.
Ogdensburg NY 13669
(315) 393-5320
Mgr: Chris Erickson
Ice surfaces: 1, 185x95, Enclosed. *Open:* Nov.-Mar. *Ownership:* Private. *Access:* Public. *Clubs:* Ogdensburg FSC, Ogdensburg Minor Hockey. *Sessions:* Public, Private/Club, Rental, Freestyle, Patch, Dance, Hockey. *Classes/Lessons:* None. *Summer School:* No. *Services:* Snack Bar, Weight Room, Pool and/or Athletic Facilities, Lockers, Dressing Rooms.

Olean Recreation Center
Front & East State St.
Olean NY 14760
(716) 373-7465
Mgr: Mark Cotton
Ice surfaces: 1, 200x85, Enclosed. *Open:* Oct.-Apr. *Ownership:* Municipal. *Access:* Public. *Clubs:* Olean Area Youth Hockey Assn., Olean Area SC. *Sessions:* Public, Private/Club, Rental, Freestyle, Patch, Dance, Hockey. *Classes/Lessons:* Group. *Summer School:* No. *Services:* Skate Rental, Skate Sharpening.

Olympic Regional Development Authority Olympic Center (ORDA)
216 Main St., Olympic Center
Lake Placid NY 12946
(518) 523-3325
FAX: (518) 523-9275
Mgr: Denny Allen
Ice surfaces: 4, 200x100; 200x100; 200x85; 136x81, Enclosed. *Open:* Year Round. *Ownership:* Municipal. *Access:* Restricted, Public. Limited public sessions. *Clubs:* SC of Lake Placid. *Sessions:* Public, Freestyle, Patch, Dance. *Classes/Lessons:* Group, Private. *Program Affiliation:* USFSA. *Summer School:* National/International. *Services:* Pro Shop, Skate Rental, Ballet Room, Lockers, Dressing Rooms, Weight Room.

On Center Arena
800 S. State St.
Syracuse NY 13202
(315) 435-8000
FAX: (315) 435-8099
Mgr: Paul Abe
Ice surfaces: 1, 200x87, Enclosed. *Open:* Year Round. *Ownership:* Municipal. *Access:* Restricted. *Clubs:* Jr. Crunch Hockey; Midstate Hockey; Skating Academy of Syracuse. *Sessions:* Private/Club, Rental, Freestyle, Hockey. *Classes/Lessons:* Private, Group. *Program Affiliation:* USFSA, ISIA. *Summer School:* No. *Services:* Skate Sharpening, Snack Bar, Weight Room, Lockers, Dressing Rooms.

Parkwood Ice Rink
65 Arrondale Ave.
Great Neck NY 11023
(516) 487-2976
FAX: (516) 487-6805
Mgr: Fred Ondris
Ice surfaces: 1, 200x100, Enclosed. *Open:* Oct.-Apr. *Ownership:* Municipal. *Access:* Restricted. *Clubs:* Great Neck FSC. *Sessions:* Public, Private/Club, Rental, Freestyle, Patch, Dance. *Classes/Lessons:* Group, Private. *Program Affiliation:* USFSA, ISIA. *Summer School:* No. *Services:* Pro Shop, Skate Rental, Skate Sharpening, Snack Bar, Pool and/or Athletic Facilities, Lockers, Dressing Rooms.

Pine Street Arena
Pine St.
Postdam NY 13676
(315) 265-4030
Mgr: Tim Carey
Ice surfaces: 1, 200x85, Enclosed. *Open:* Oct.-Mar. *Ownership:* Municipal. *Access:* Public. *Clubs:* Postdam Junior Hockey Assn.; Postdam FSC. *Sessions:* Public, Rental, Hockey. *Classes/Lessons:* Private. *Program Affiliation:* USFSA. *Summer School:* No. *Services:* Pro Shop, Skate Sharpening, Snack Bar, Dressing Rooms. *Notes:* Lessons, freestyle and patch sessions are offered through the club only.

Playland Ice Casino: Westchester County
Playland Pkwy.
Rye NY 10580
(914) 921-0370
Mgr: Norbert Bouchard
Skating Dir: Valerie Gomez
Ice surfaces: 3, 208x80; 150x50; 80x20, Enclosed. *Open:* Sept.-Apr. *Ownership:* Municipal. *Access:* Public. *Clubs:* Rye FSC. *Sessions:* Public, Private/Club, Rental, Freestyle, Patch, Hockey. *Classes/Lessons:* Group, Private. *Program Affiliation:* ISIA. *Services:* Pro Shop, Skate Rental, Skate Sharpening, Studio Rink, Snack Bar, Pool and/or Athletic Facilities, Lockers, Dressing Rooms. *Notes:* Dance sessions are offered through the club only. Arcade; large amusement park; beach.

Polar Cap Recreation Center
River Rd.
Chenango Bridge NY 13745
(607) 648-9888
Mgr: David Armstrong
Skating Dir: Nate Alden
Ice surfaces: 1, 200x85, Enclosed. *Open:* July-May. *Ownership:* Private. *Access:* Public. *College/Univ:* Bringham City University. *Sessions:* Public, Private/Club, Rental, Freestyle, Patch, Dance, Hockey. *Classes/Lessons:* Group, Private. *Program Affiliation:* USFSA, ISIA. *Summer School:* No. *Services:* Pro Shop, Skate Rental, Skate Sharpening, Snack Bar, Ballet Room, Lockers, Dressing Rooms.

Port Washington Family Rink
70 Seaview Blvd.
Port Washington NY 11050
(516) 484-6800
Mgr: Fred Neilsen
Ice surfaces: 1, 180x65, Enclosed. *Open:* Year Round. *Ownership:* Private. *Access:* Public. *Clubs:* Long Island Youth Hockey. *Sessions:* Public, Private/Club, Rental, Freestyle, Patch, Hockey. *Classes/Lessons:* Group, Private. *Program Affiliation:* ISIA. *Summer School:* Local. *Services:* Skate Rental, Pro Shop, Skate Sharpening, Lockers, Dressing Rooms.

Rinx, The - Hidden Pond Park
660 Terry Rd.
Hauppague NY 11788
(516) 232-5222
Mgr: Randy Nash
Skating Dir: Lynn Lynch
Ice surfaces: 2, 200x85; 200x85, Enclosed. *Open:* Year Round. *Ownership:* Private. *Access:* Public. *Sessions:* Public, Private/Club, Rental, Freestyle, Patch, Hockey. *Classes/Lessons:* Group, Private. *Program Affiliation:* USFSA, ISIA. *Summer School:* Local. *Services:* Pro Shop, Skate Rental, Skate Sharpening, Studio Rink, Snack Bar, Ballet Room, Weight Room, Pool and/or Athletic Facilities, Lockers, Dressing Rooms. *Notes:* Training center; pre-school for skating.

Ritter (Frank) Memorial Arena
51 Lomb Memorial Dr.
Rochester NY 14623
(716) 475-2222
Mgr: Neil Kromer
Ice surfaces: 1, 200x85. *Open:* June-Apr. *Ownership:* Private. *Clubs:* RIT FSC, Genesse FSC. *College/Univ:* Rochester Institute of Technology. *Sessions:* Public, Rental, Hockey. *Program Affiliation:* USFSA. *Services:* Skate Rental, Pro Shop, Skate Sharpening, Lockers. *Notes:* Freestyle, patch and dance sessions are offered through the club only.

Rivergate Ice Rink
401 E. 34th St.
New York NY 10016
(212) 689-0035
Mgr: Neil Nerich
Ice surfaces: 1, 100x65, Outdoor/Semi Outdoor. *Open:* Nov.-Mar. *Ownership:*

Municipal. *Access:* Public. *Sessions:* Public, Private/Club, Rental, Hockey. *Classes/Lessons:* Group, Private. *Program Affiliation:* ISIA. *Services:* Skate Rental, Skate Sharpening, Snack Bar.

Rockefeller Plaza Ice Rink
Rockefeller Plaza, between 49th & 50th Streets and 5th & 6th Avenues
New York NY 10020
(212) 757-5730
Mgr: Carol Olsen
Ice surfaces: 1, 125x65, Outdoor/Semi Outdoor. *Open:* Oct.-Apr. *Ownership:* Private. *Access:* Public. *Sessions:* Public, Rental. *Classes/Lessons:* Private. *Summer School:* No. *Services:* Skate Rental. *Notes:* Located outdoors in center of Rockefeller Plaza. Several restaurants with view of rink (American Festival Cafe, Sea Grill, Savories). JoJo Starbuck is head pro, and teaches early morning adult beginner classes for local professionals. The rink and restaurants can be rented for private parties; call (212) 757-5731. Annual Christmas tree lit at night.

Rouses Point Recreation Center
Lake St.
Rouses Point NY 19279
(518) 297-6776
Mgr: Mike O'Brian
Ice surfaces: 1, 200x85, Enclosed. *Open:* Oct.-Apr. *Ownership:* Municipal. *Access:* Public. *Clubs:* North Country FSC. *Sessions:* Public, Private/Club, Rental. *Classes/Lessons:* None. *Program Affiliation:* USFSA. *Summer School:* No. *Services:* Pro Shop, Skate Sharpening, Snack Bar, Lockers, Dressing Rooms. *Notes:* Freestyle sessions and lessons offered through skating club only.

Salmon River Central Skating Arena
Bombay Rd.
Ft. Covington NY 12937
(518) 358-2215
FAX: (518) 358-3492
Mgr: Carl Cross
Ice surfaces: 1, 200x85, Enclosed. *Open:* Nov.-Mar. *Ownership:* School District. *Access:* Public. *Clubs:* Shamrock FS; North Franklin Sports FS; North Franklin Sports Hockey. *Summer School:* No. *Services:* Snack Bar, Lockers, Dressing Rooms.

Saranac Lake Civic Center
Ampersand Ave.
Saranac Lake NY 12983
(518) 891-3800
FAX: (518) 891-3547
Mgr: Mike Ritchie
Ice surfaces: 1, 200x85, Enclosed. *Open:* Nov.-Apr. *Ownership:* Private. *Access:* Public. *College/Univ:* North County Community Collge. *Sessions:* Public, Private/Club, Rental, Freestyle, Patch, Hockey. *Classes/Lessons:* Group. *Program Affiliation:* ISIA. *Summer School:* No. *Services:* Skate Sharpening, Snack Bar, Dressing Rooms.

Saratoga Springs Ice Rink - Weibel Ave.
Saratoga Springs NY 12866
(518) 583-3462
Mgr: Linda Terricola
Skating Dir: Becky DeWitt
Ice surfaces: 1, 200x100. *Open:* Year Round. *Ownership:* Municipal. *Access:* Public. *Clubs:* Speed skating; Youth hockey; FSC. *Sessions:* Public, Private/Club, Rental, Hockey, General, Tots, Adult, Family Skate. *Classes/Lessons:* Group, Private. *Summer School:* Local. *Services:* Pro Shop, Skate Rental, Skate Sharpening, Snack Bar, Lockers, Dressing

SKY RINK

Manhattan's only indoor ice arena offers year-round figure skating programs for skaters of all ages and ability levels. Our sessions are tailored to fit your needs whether you aspire to be an Olympian or are skating purely for the fun of it.

Programs include Summer Skating School, Special Events, Patch/Freestyle/Dance/*Moves in the Field* sessions, Skating Club of New York, and Ice Theatre of New York.

For more information, call:

**Darlene Parent
(212) 239-8385**

In the summer of 1995, Sky Rink will move to the **Chelsea Piers Sports and Entertainment Complex** located on Pier 61, overlooking the Hudson River. In its new home on Pier 61, Sky Rink will be a 160,000 square foot Olympic Village with **two** ice rinks and seating capacity for over 2000.

Rooms. *Notes:* Boxing on premises.

Saratoga Springs Ice Rink - Excelsior Ave.
Saratoga Springs NY 12866
(518) 587-3550
Mgr: Linda Terricola
Skating Dir: Becky DeWitt
Ice surfaces: 1, 200x80, Outdoor/Semi Outdoor. *Open:* Nov.-Mar. *Ownership:* Municipal. *Access:* Public. *Clubs:* Speed skating; Youth hockey; FSC. *Sessions:* Public, Private/Club, Rental, Hockey, General, Tots, Adult, Family Skate. *Classes/Lessons:* Group. *Summer School:* No. *Services:* Pro Shop, Skate Rental, Skate Sharpening, Snack Bar, Lockers, Dressing Rooms.

Scottsville Ice Arena
1800 Scottsville & Schili Rd.
Scottsville NY 14546
(716) 889-1817
Mgr: Dan Farwley
Ice surfaces: 1, 200x85, Enclosed. *Open:* Year Round. *Ownership:* Private. *Access:* Public. *Clubs:* Scottsville FSC. *Sessions:* Public, Private/Club, Rental, Freestyle, Hockey. *Classes/Lessons:* Group, Private. *Program Affiliation:* ISIA. *Summer School:* Local. *Services:* Pro Shop, Skate Rental, Skate Sharpening, Snack Bar, Lockers, Dressing Rooms.

Shove Park Recreation Center
Shove Park, Slawson Dr.
Chamillus NY 13031
(315) 487-5068
Mgr: Maureen Sheedy
Ice surfaces: 1, 185x85, Enclosed. *Open:* Oct.-Mar. *Ownership:* Municipal. *Access:* Public. *Clubs:* Camillus FSC, Camillus Youth Hockey. *College/Univ:* Lemoin College. *Sessions:* Public, Private/Club, Rental, Freestyle, Hockey. *Classes/Lessons:* Private, Group. *Summer School:* No. *Services:* Pro Shop, Skate Rental, Skate Sharpening, Snack Bar, Lockers, Dressing Rooms.

Skating Institute of Rochester
1 Boys Club Place
Rochester NY 14608
(716) 325-2216
FAX: (716) 325-2216
Mgr: Al Viverberg
Ice surfaces: 1, 185x85, Enclosed. *Open:* July-May. *Ownership:* Private. *Access:* Public. *Sessions:* Public, Hockey. *Classes/Lessons:* Group, Private. *Summer School:* Local. *Services:* Skate Sharpening, Snack Bar, Lockers, Dressing Rooms.

Sky Rink
450 W. 33rd St.
New York NY 10001
(212) 239-8385
Mgr: Ron Kraut
Ice surfaces: 1, 185x85, Enclosed. *Open:* Year Round. *Ownership:* Private. *Access:* Public. *Clubs:* Skating Club of New York; Rangers Hockey Team. *Sessions:* Public, Private/Club, Rental, Freestyle, Patch, Dance, Hockey. *Classes/Lessons:* Group, Private. *Program Affiliation:* USFSA, ISIA. *Summer School:* Regional. *Services:* Pro Shop, Skate Rental, Skate Sharpening, Studio Rink, Snack Bar, Ballet Room, Lockers, Dressing Rooms. Moving to Chelsea Piers in Summer of 1995.

Sport-O-Rama
18 College Rd.
Monsey NY 10952
(914) 356-3919
Mgr: Robert Tweedy
Ice surfaces: 2, 200x90; 200x90, Enclosed. *Open:* Year Round. *Ownership:* Private. *Access:* Public. *Sessions:* Public, Rental, Freestyle, Patch, Dance, Hockey. *Classes/Lessons:* Group, Private. *Program Affiliation:* USFSA, ISIA. *Summer School:* National/International. *Services:* Pro Shop, Skate Rental, Skate Sharpening, Snack Bar, Ballet Room, Weight Room, Lockers, Dressing Rooms. *Notes:* Health club.

Sports Park, The
8695 S. Sandy Pkwy.
Sandy NY 84070
(801) 562-4444
Mgr: Karen Snyder
Ice surfaces: 1, 90x90, Outdoor/Semi Outdoor. *Open:* Oct.-Mar. *Ownership:* Private. *Access:* Public. *Sessions:* Public, Rental, Freestyle. *Classes/Lessons:* None. *Program Affiliation:* Own. *Summer School:* No. *Services:* Skate Rental, Skate Sharpening, Snack Bar, Lockers.

Starr Rink - Reid Athletic Center
Colgate University, 13 Oak Dr.
Hamilton NY 13346
(315) 824-7570
Mgr: Dick Brantis
Ice surfaces: 1, 200x85, Enclosed. *Open:* Oct.-Mar. *Ownership:* Private. *Access:* Public. *Sessions:* Private/Club, Public, Rental, Hockey. *Classes/Lessons:* Group. *Services:* Snack Bar, Weight Room, Lockers, Dressing Rooms. *Notes:* Bowling alley; basketball arena.

Staten Island War Memorial Ice Rink
Clove Rd. and Victory Blvd.
Staten Island NY 10301
(718) 720-1010
Ice surfaces: 2, 200x85, Enclosed. *Open:* Oct.-May. *Ownership:* Municipal. *Access:* Public. *Sessions:* Public, Hockey. *Classes/Lessons:* Group. *Program Affiliation:* ISIA. *Summer School:* No. *Services:* Skate Rental, Studio Rink, Snack Bar, Lockers, Dressing Rooms.

Sunnycrest Arena
Robinson St.
Syracuse NY
(315) 473-4333
Mgr: Jerry Brown
Ice surfaces: 1, 200x85, Enclosed. *Open:* Nov.-Mar. *Ownership:* Municipal. *Access:* Public. *Clubs:* South City FSC, Syracuse Speed Skaters; Valley Youth Hockey. *Sessions:* Public, Private/Club, Freestyle, Hockey. *Classes/Lessons:* Private, Group. *Program Affiliation:* USFSA. *Services:* Skate Rental, Skate Sharpening, Lockers, Dressing Rooms. *Notes:* The listed phone number is for parks and recreation; call for information.

SUNY Field House
Rugar St.
Plattsburgh NY 12901
(518) 564-3060
Mgr: Mark Christiansen
Skating Dir: Mark Christiansen
Ice surfaces: 1, 185x85, Enclosed. *Open:* June-Mar. *Ownership:* Municipal. *Access:* Public. *Clubs:* SC of the Adirondacks. *College/Univ:* SUNY; Plattsburgh. *Sessions:* Public, Rental, Hockey. *Classes/Lessons:* Group, Private. *Program Affiliation:* USFSA. *Summer School:* National/International. *Services:* Skate Rental, Snack Bar, Weight Room,

Lockers, Dressing Rooms, Pool and/or Athletic Facilities. *Notes:* Freestyle, patch and dance sessions are offered through the club only.

Superior Ice Rink
270 Indianhead Rd.
Kings Park NY 11754
(516) 269-3904
Mgr: Norm Rider
Skating Dir: Donna Capolino
Ice surfaces: 1, 200x85, Enclosed. *Open:* Year Round. *Ownership:* Private. *Access:* Public. *Sessions:* Public, Private/Club, Freestyle, Rental, Patch, Hockey. *Classes/Lessons:* Group, Private. *Program Affiliation:* USFSA, ISIA. *Summer School:* Local. *Services:* Pro Shop, Skate Rental, Skate Sharpening, Snack Bar, Lockers, Dressing Rooms. *Notes:* Roller hockey programs.

Tate Rink at West Point
Holleder Center at
U. S. Military Academy, Bldg. 714
West Point NY 10996
(914) 938-4011
FAX: (914) 446-6805
Mgr: Louis Federico
Ice surfaces: 1, 200x90, Enclosed. *Open:* Year Round. *Ownership:* Municipal, Federal. *Access:* Public. *Sessions:* Public, Rental. *Classes/Lessons:* None. *Program Affiliation:* Own. *Summer School:* No. *Services:* Skate Rental, Skate Sharpening, Snack Bar, Weight Room, Lockers, Dressing Rooms. *Notes:* Weight room for military only.

Trinity-Pawling School Rink
300 Rt. 22
Pawling NY 12564
(914) 855-3100
Mgr: Miles Hubbard
Ice surfaces: 1, 200x85, Enclosed. *Open:* Nov.-Mar. *Ownership:* Private. *Access:* Public. *Sessions:* Public, Rental, Hockey. *Classes/Lessons:* None. *Summer School:* No. *Services:* Pro Shop, Weight Room, Pool and/or Athletic Facilities, Lockers, Dressing Rooms, Skate Sharpening.

Utica Memorial Auditorium
Oriskany Blvd.
Utica NY 13502
(315) 853-6147
Mgr: Murray Sislen
Ice surfaces: 1, 200x85. *Open:* Sept.-Mar. *Ownership:* Municipal. *Access:* Restricted. *Clubs:* SC of Utica. *Sessions:* Freestyle, Patch, Hockey. *Classes/Lessons:* Private. *Program Affiliation:* USFSA. *Services:* Pro Shop, Lockers, Dressing Rooms.

Wallman (Kate) Prospect Park
95 Prospect Park
Brooklyn NY 11215
(718) 282-1226
Mgr: Violet Eagan
Ice surfaces: 1, 150x100, Outdoor/Semi Outdoor. *Open:* Nov.-Mar. *Ownership:* Municipal. *Access:* Public. *Clubs:* Prospect Park FSC, Prospect Park Hockey. *Sessions:* Public, Private/Club, Rental, Freestyle, Patch, Hockey. *Classes/Lessons:* Private, Group. *Program Affiliation:* ISIA, USFSA. *Summer School:* No. *Services:* Skate Sharpening, Skate Rental, Snack Bar, Lockers.

Watertown Fairgrounds Arena
William T. Field Dr.
Watertown NY 13601
(315) 785-7836
Mgr: Jayme St. Croix
Ice surfaces: 1, 200x85, Enclosed. *Open:* Sept.-Apr. *Ownership:* Municipal. *Access:* Public. *Clubs:* High schools. *Sessions:* Public, Private/Club, Rental, Freestyle, Patch, Dance, Hockey. *Classes/Lessons:* Group, Private. *Program Affiliation:* USFSA. *Summer School:* No. *Services:* Skate Rental, Skate Sharpening, Snack Bar, Pool and/or Athletic Facilities, Lockers, Dressing Rooms.

Whitestown Community Center
Westmoreland Rd.
Whitestown NY 13492
(315) 853-6147
Mgr: Robert Creslak
Ice surfaces: 1, 185x85, Enclosed. *Open:* Year Round. *Ownership:* Municipal. *Access:* Public. *Clubs:* SC of Utica. *Sessions:* Public, Freestyle, Patch, Dance, Hockey. *Classes/Lessons:* Private, Group. *Program Affiliation:* USFSA, ISIA. *Services:* Pro Shop, Skate Rental, Studio Rink, Snack Bar, Lockers, Dressing Rooms.

Wilson (Ira S.) Ice Arena
State University of New York
SUNY - Geneseo
Geneseo NY 14654
(716) 245-5356
FAX: (716) 245-5347
Mgr: Paul Duffy
Ice surfaces: 1, 195x85, Enclosed. *Open:* Oct.-March. *Ownership:* Private. *Access:* Public. *Clubs:* Finger Lakes FSC, Geneseo Valley Youth Hockey League. *College/Univ:* State University of New York. *Sessions:* Public, Rental, Hockey. *Classes/Lessons:* None. *Summer School:* No. *Services:* Skate Sharpening, Ballet Room, Weight Room, Pool and/or Athletic Facilities, Lockers, Dressing Rooms. *Notes:* Lessons offered through club.

Winter Club, The,
West Main St.,
Huntington NY 11743
(516) 421-3889
Mgr: Tom Fehrs
Ice surfaces: 1, 180x80, Outdoor/Semi Outdoor. *Open:* Nov.-Mar. *Ownership:* Private. *Access:* Members Only. *Clubs:* Winter Club FSC, Youth Hockey. *Sessions:* Private/Club, Hockey. *Classes/Lessons:* Private, Group. *Program Affiliation:* Own. *Summer School:* No. *Services:* Skate Sharpening, Snack Bar, Lockers, Dressing Rooms. *Notes:* Skating is free for members of the club.

Wollman Rink - Central Park Ice Chalet
830 5th Ave.
New York NY 10021
(212) 517-4800
Mgr: LuAnne Schleicher
Ice surfaces: 1, 33,000 sq. ft., Outdoor/Semi Outdoor. *Open:* Oct.-Apr. *Ownership:* Municipal. *Access:* Public. *Sessions:* Hockey, Dance, Patch, Freestyle, Rental, Private/Club, Public. *Classes/Lessons:* Private, Group. *Program Affiliation:* ISIA. *Summer School:* No. *Services:* Skate Rental, Pro Shop, Skate Sharpening, Snack Bar, Dressing Rooms, Lockers.

Woodbury Community Park Ice Rink
9800 Jericho Turnpike
Woodbury NY 11797
(516) 677-5990
Mgr: Don Calemmo
Ice surfaces: 1, 200x85, Outdoor/Semi Outdoor. *Open:* Nov.-Mar. *Ownership:* Municipal. *Access:* Public. *Sessions:* Public, Rental, Hockey. *Classes/Lessons:* Group, Private. *Summer School:* No. *Services:* Skate Rental, Snack Bar.

World's Fair Ice Skating Rink
Flushing Meadows Corona Park
Flushing NY 11368
(718) 699-4215
Skating Dir: Morico Nishiura
Ice surfaces: 1, 190x90, Enclosed. *Open:* Oct.-Apr. *Ownership:* Municipal. *Access:* Public. *Clubs:* Parks FSC. *Sessions:* Speed skating, Public, Private/Club, Hockey. *Classes/Lessons:* Group, Private. *Program Affiliation:* ISIA. *Summer School:* No. *Services:* Skate Rental, Snack Bar, Lockers, Dressing Rooms.

YMCA Albany County Hockey Training Facility
830 Albany Shaker Rd.
Loudenville NY 12211
(518) 452-7396
Mgr: Matt Clark
Skating Dir: Lolita Anthos
Ice surfaces: 1, 200x100, Enclosed. *Open:* Year Round. *Ownership:* Municipal. *Access:* Public. *Sessions:* Public, Rental, Freestyle, Hockey. *Classes/Lessons:* Group, Private. *Program Affiliation:* ISIA. *Summer School:* No. *Services:* Skate Rental, Snack Bar, Weight Room, Lockers, Dressing Rooms.

OH: OHIO

Bowling Green State University Ice Arena
Mercer Rd.
Bowling Green OH 43403
(419) 372-2264
FAX: (419) 372-0303
Mgr: Randy Sokoll
Ice surfaces: 3, 200x85; 80x40; 150x57, Enclosed. *Open:* June-Apr.; studio rink - only to March. *Ownership:* Bowling Green State U. *Access:* Public. *College/Univ:* Bowling Green State University. *Sessions:* Public, Private/Club, Rental, Freestyle, Patch, Dance, Hockey, Curling, Precision. *Classes/Lessons:* Group, Private. *Program Affiliation:* USFSA. *Summer School:* National/International. *Services:* Pro Shop, Skate Sharpening, Skate Rental, Studio Rink, Dressing Rooms, Lockers.

Brooklyn Indoor Recreation Center
7600 Memphis Ave.
Brooklyn OH 44144
(216) 351-2111
FAX: (216) 351-7601
Mgr: James Coyne
Ice surfaces: 1, 200x90, Enclosed. *Open:* Aug.-May. *Ownership:* Municipal. *Access:* Public. *Clubs:* Brooklyn FSC of Ohio. *Sessions:* Public, Private/Club, Rental, Freestyle, Patch, Hockey, General, Speed Skating. *Classes/Lessons:* Group, Private. *Program Affiliation:* USFSA. *Services:* Skate Rental, Skate Sharpening, Snack Bar, Ballet Room, Weight Room, Pool and/or Athletic Facilities, Lockers, Dressing Rooms. *Notes:* Whirlpool; steam room; sauna.

Chiller, Central Ohio Ice Rinks Inc.
7001 Dublin Park Dr.
Dublin OH 43017
(614) 791-9999
Mgr: Gene Lesinski
Skating Dir: Todd Bell
Ice surfaces: 2, 200x85; 200x85, Enclosed. *Open:* Year Round. *Ownership:* Private. *Access:* Public. *Sessions:* Public, Rental, Freestyle, Patch, Dance, Hockey. *Classes/Lessons:* Group, Private. *Program Affiliation:* ISIA. *Services:* Pro Shop, Skate Rental, Skate Sharpening, Snack Bar, Lockers, Dressing Rooms.

Cleveland Skating Club
Skating Office, 2500 Kemper Rd.
Shaker Heights OH 44120
(216) 791-2800
FAX: (216) 791-9501
Mgr: Clifford Parke
Skating Dir: Diane Murphy
Ice surfaces: 1, 185x85, Enclosed. *Open:* Year Round. *Ownership:* Private. *Access:* Members Only. *Clubs:* Cleveland SC. *Sessions:* Freestyle, Patch, Dance, Hockey, Private/Club. *Classes/Lessons:* Group, Private. *Program Affiliation:* USFSA. *Summer School:* Local. *Services:* Skate Rental, Snack Bar, Pool and/or Athletic Facilities, Lockers, Dressing Rooms. *Notes:* Tennis courts.

Goggin Ice Arena
Miami University, High St.
Oxford OH 45056
(513) 529-3343
FAX: (513) 529-6988
Mgr: Mitch Korn
Skating Dir: Vicki Korn
Ice surfaces: 2, 200 x 85; 150 x 65. *Open:* June-Apr. *Ownership:* Municipal. *Access:* Public. *Clubs:* Oxford SC; Miami SC. *College/Univ:* Miami University. *Sessions:* Public, Private/Club, Rental, Freestyle, Patch, Dance, Hockey. *Classes/Lessons:* Group, Private. *Program Affiliation:* USFSA, ISIA. *Summer School:* Regional, National/International. *Services:* Pro Shop, Skate Rental, Skate Sharpening, Lockers, Dressing Rooms. *Notes:* Vending machines.

Hamilton Sports Arena
1600 Beck Blvd.
Hamilton OH 45011
(513) 868-5992
Mgr: Bob Alston
Ice surfaces: 1, 200x85, Outdoor/Semi Outdoor. *Open:* Oct.-Mar. *Ownership:* Municipal. *Access:* Public. *Clubs:* Golden Triangle Hockey. *Sessions:* Public, Rental, Hockey. *Classes/Lessons:* Private, Group. *Program Affiliation:* ISIA. *Summer School:* No. *Services:* Skate Rental, Skate Sharpening, Snack Bar, Dressing Rooms.

Hancock Recreation Center
3430 N. Main St.
Findlay OH 45840
(419) 423-8534
Mgr: Bob Coslett
Ice surfaces: 1, 200x80, Enclosed. *Open:* Oct.-Mar. *Ownership:* Municipal. *Access:* Public. *Clubs:* Silber Blades FSC. *Sessions:* Public, Private/Club, Rental, Hockey. *Classes/Lessons:* Group. *Program Affiliation:* USFSA, ISIA. *Summer School:* No. *Services:* Pro Shop, Skate Rental, Skate Sharpening, Snack Bar, Lockers. *Notes:* Freestyle, patch and dance sessions are offered through the club only.

Hobart Arena
255 Adams
Troy OH 45373
(513) 339-2911
Mgr: Charles Sharett
Ice surfaces: 1, 180x92, Enclosed. *Open:* Sept.-July. *Ownership:* Municipal. *Access:* Public. *Clubs:* Troy SC. *Sessions:* Public, Private/Club, Rental, Freestyle, Patch, Dance, Hockey. *Classes/Lessons:* Private, Group. *Program Affiliation:* USFSA, ISIA. *Summer School:* Regional. *Services:* Skate Rental, Pro Shop, Skate Sharpening, Snack Bar, Pool and/or Athletic Facilities, Lockers, Dressing Rooms.

Icelands
10765 Reading Rd.
Evendale OH 45241
(513) 769-0004
Mgr: John Stadler
Ice surfaces: 2, 200x85; 200x85, Enclosed. *Open:* Year Round. *Ownership:* Municipal. *Access:* Public. *Clubs:* Moller Crusaders Hockey. *Sessions:* Public, Private/Club, Rental, Freestyle, Patch, Hockey. *Classes/Lessons:* Group, Private. *Program Affiliation:* USFSA. *Summer School:* No. *Services:* Pro Shop, Skate Rental, Skate Sharpening, Lockers, Snack Bar.

Kent State University Ice Arena
Loop Rd.
Kent OH 44242
(216) 672-2415
Mgr: Rich Mest
Ice surfaces: 2, 200x85; 150x80, Enclosed. *Open:* July-May. *Ownership:* Private. *Access:* Public. *Clubs:* Kent SC; Tri County Youth Hockey; Youngstown Youth Program. *College/Univ:* Kent State University. *Sessions:* Public, Private/Club, Freestyle, Rental, Patch, Dance, Hockey. *Classes/Lessons:* Group, Private. *Program Affiliation:* ISIA. *Summer School:* National/International. *Services:* Skate Rental, Pro Shop, Skate Sharpening, Snack Bar, Dressing Rooms, Lockers.

Kettering Ice Arena
2900 Glengarry Dr.
Kettering OH 45420
(513) 296-2587
Mgr: Kevin Swartz
Ice surfaces: 1, 200x85, Enclosed. *Open:* Sept.-Mar. *Ownership:* Municipal. *Access:* Public. *Sessions:* Public, Private/Club, Rental, Freestyle, Patch, Hockey. *Classes/Lessons:* Group, Private. *Program Affiliation:* ISIA. *Summer School:* No. *Services:* Pro Shop, Skate Rental, Skate Sharpening, Snack Bar, Ballet Room, Weight Room, Pool and/or Athletic Facilities, Lockers, Dressing Rooms. *Notes:* Athletic complex and water park.

Kostel (Dan) Recreation Center
5411 Turney Rd.
Garfield Heights OH 44125
(216) 475-7272
Mgr: James Bukac
Ice surfaces: 1, 185x85, Enclosed. *Open:* Sept.-Apr. *Ownership:* Municipal. *Access:* Public. *Clubs:* FSC. *Sessions:* Public, Private/Club, Hockey. *Classes/Lessons:* Group, Private. *Program Affiliation:* ISIA. *Services:* Skate Rental, Skate Sharpening, Snack Bar, Lockers, Dressing Rooms. *Notes:* Freestyle and patch sessions offered through club only.

Mentor Civic Ice Arena
8600 Munson Rd.
Mentor OH 44060
(216) 255-1777
Mgr: Gene Elkin
Skating Dir: Mary Jo Hanson
Ice surfaces: 2, 200x85, Enclosed. *Open:* Year Round. *Ownership:* Municipal. *Access:* Public. *Clubs:* Mentor FSC. *Sessions:* Public, Private/Club, Rental, Freestyle, Patch, Dance, Hockey. *Classes/Lessons:* Group, Private. *Program Affiliation:* USFSA. *Summer School:* Local. *Services:* Pro Shop, Skate Rental, Skate Sharpening, Studio Rink, Snack Bar, Ballet Room, Lockers, Dressing Rooms.

Mill Creek Park Ice Rink
816 Glenwood Ave.
Youngstown OH 44502
(216) 740-7114
FAX: (216) 740-7132
Mgr: Tom Bresko
Ice surfaces: 1, 200x85, Outdoor/Semi Outdoor. *Open:* Dec.-Feb. *Ownership:* Municipal. *Access:* Public. *Sessions:* Public, Rental, Hockey. *Classes/Lessons:* Group, Private. *Program Affiliation:* ISIA. *Services:* Pro Shop, Skate Rental, Skate Sharpening, Snack Bar, Lockers.

North Olmstead Recreation Complex
26000 Lorain Rd.
North Olmstead OH 44070
(216) 734-8200
Mgr: Ginna Crea
Ice surfaces: 2, 200x85; 85x50, Enclosed. *Open:* Sept.-May. *Ownership:* Municipal. *Access:* Public. *Clubs:* West Shore FSC. *Sessions:* Public, Private/Club, Rental, Freestyle, Patch, Hockey. *Classes/Lessons:* Group, Private. *Services:* Pro Shop, Skate Rental, Skate Sharpening, Studio Rink, Snack Bar, Pool and/or Athletic Facilities.

Northland Ice Center
10400 Redding Rd.
Cincinnati OH 45421
(513) 563-0001
Mgr: Tim Holland
Skating Dir: Linda Comberger-Martin
Ice surfaces: 1, 200x85, Enclosed. *Open:* Year Round. *Ownership:* Private. *Access:* Public. *Clubs:* Queen City FSC, Cincinnati FSC, NSA FSC. *Sessions:* Public, Private/Club, Rental, Freestyle, Patch, Dance, Hockey. *Classes/Lessons:* Group, Private. *Program Affiliation:* ISIA. *Summer School:* Regional. *Services:* Pro Shop, Skate Rental, Skate Sharpening, Snack Bar, Dressing Rooms.

Ohio State University Ice Rink
390 Woody Hayes Dr.
Columbus OH 43210
(614) 292-4154
Mgr: George Burke
Skating Dir: Duke Johnson
Ice surfaces: 1, 185x85, Enclosed. *Open:* Sept.-Aug. *Ownership:* University. *Access:* Public. *Clubs:* Columbus FSC. *College/Univ:* Ohio State University. *Sessions:* Public, Private/Club, Rental, Hockey. *Classes/Lessons:* Group, Private. *Program Affiliation:* USFSA, ISIA. *Summer School:* Regional, National/International. *Services:* Pro Shop, Skate Rental, Skate Sharpening, Lockers, Dressing Rooms. *Notes:* Vending machines; freestyle, patch and dance sessions offered through club only.

Orr (Clifford E.) Arena
22550 Milton Dr.
Euclid OH 44123
(216) 289-8649
Mgr: Jeff Beall
Skating Dir: Beth Mckinley
Ice surfaces: 1, 200x75, Enclosed. *Open:* Sept.-Apr. *Ownership:* Municipal. *Access:* Public. *Clubs:* Euclid Blade & Edge Club, Inc. *Sessions:* Public, Private/Club, Rental, Freestyle, Patch, Hockey. *Classes/Lessons:* Group, Private. *Program Affiliation:* USFSA. *Services:* Skate Rental, Pro Shop, Skate Sharpening, Snack Bar, Pool and/or Athletic Facilities, Lockers, Dressing Rooms.

Parma Heights Municipal Ice Rink
6200 Pearl Rd.
Parma Heights OH 44130
(216) 842-5005
Mgr: Lynda Blalock
Skating Dir: Lynda Blalock
Ice surfaces: 1, 150x85, Enclosed. *Open:* July-May. *Ownership:* Municipal. *Access:* Public. *Clubs:* Greenbriar FSC. *Sessions:* Public, Private/Club, Rental, Freestyle, Patch, Dance, Hockey. *Classes/Lessons:* Group, Private. *Program Affiliation:* USFSA, ISIA. *Summer School:* Regional. *Services:* Skate Rental, Skate Sharpening, Snack Bar, Ballet Room, Pool and/or Athletic Facilities, Lockers, Dressing Rooms.

Pavillion Recreation Center
1 Monticello Blvd.
Cleveland Heights OH 44118
(216) 321-2090
Mgr: Mike Rezac
Ice surfaces: 1, 185x85, Enclosed. *Open:* Sept.-Apr. *Ownership:* Municipal. *Access:* Public. *Clubs:* Pavillion SC. *Sessions:* Public, Private/Club, Rental, Freestyle, Patch, Hockey. *Classes/Lessons:* Group, Private. *Program Affiliation:* USFSA. *Summer School:* No. *Services:* Skate Rental, Skate Sharpening, Snack Bar, Ballet Room, Lockers, Dressing Rooms. *Notes:* Fitness room with bikes and stair climbers.

Reis Ice Rink
5000 Forestwood Dr.
Parma OH 44134
(216) 885-8870
Mgr: Ralph Kolesar
Ice surfaces: 1, 200x85, Enclosed. *Open:* July-Apr. *Ownership:* Municipal. *Access:* Public. *Clubs:* Parma Hockey Assn.; Forestwood FSC of Parma. *Sessions:* Public, Private/Club, Rental, Freestyle, Patch, Dance, Hockey. *Classes/Lessons:* Private, Group. *Program Affiliation:* USFSA. *Summer School:* Local. *Services:* Skate Rental, Snack Bar, Lockers, Dressing Rooms.

Rocky River Recreation Center
21018 Hillird Blvd.
Rocky River OH 44116
(216) 356-5658
FAX: (216) 356-5663
Mgr: Charmaine Aerni
Ice surfaces: 1, 200x85, Enclosed. *Open:* Sept.-Mar. *Ownership:* Municipal. *Clubs:* West Shore FSC. *Sessions:* Public, Private/Club, Rental, Freestyle, Patch, Dance, Hockey. *Classes/Lessons:* Group. *Program Affiliation:* USFSA. *Services:* Skate Rental, Skate Sharpening, Snack Bar, Lockers, Dressing Rooms. *Notes:* Freestyle, patch and dance sessions are offered through the club only.

Tam O'Shanter Ice Rink
7060 Sylvania Ave.
Sylvania OH 43560
(419) 885-1167
FAX: (419) 885-2479
Mgr: Tom Cline
Ice surfaces: 3, 200x85; 200x85, Enclosed. *Open:* Year Round. *Ownership:* County. *Access:* Public. *Clubs:* Sylvania Metro Amateur Hockey. *Sessions:* Public, Rental, Freestyle, Patch, Hockey. *Classes/Lessons:* Group, Private. *Program Affiliation:* USFSA. *Services:* Skate Rental, Pro Shop, Skate Sharpening, Studio Rink, Snack Bar, Lockers, Dressing Rooms. *Notes:* Restaurant and lounge overlook ice rink.

Thornton Park Ice Rink
20701 Farnsleigh Rd.
Shaker Heights OH 44122
(216) 491-1290
FAX: (216) 991-4219
Mgr: Bill Murray
Ice surfaces: 1, 185x85, Enclosed. *Open:* Year Round. *Ownership:* Municipal. *Access:* Public. *Clubs:* Shaker Heights FSC. *Sessions:* Public, Private/Club, Rental, Freestyle, Patch, Dance, Hockey. *Classes/Lessons:* Group, Private. *Program Affiliation:* USFSA. *Services:* Skate Rental, Skate Sharpening, Snack Bar, Ballet Room, Lockers, Dressing Rooms.

Winterhurst Ice Rink
14740 Lakewood Heights Blvd.
Lakewood OH 44107
(216) 529-4400
Mgr: Bill Needham
Ice surfaces: 2, 200x85; 200x85, Enclosed. *Open:* June-Apr. *Ownership:* Municipal. *Access:* Public. *Clubs:* Winterhurst FSC. *Sessions:* Public, Private/Club, Rental, Hockey, Speed Skating. *Classes/Lessons:* Group, Private. *Summer School:* National/International. *Services:* Skate Rental, Skate Sharpening, Ballet Room, Lockers, Dressing Rooms. *Notes:* Freestyle, patch and dance sessions are offered through the club only.

OK: OKLAHOMA

Iceland Sports Centre
3200 N. Rockwell
Bethany OK 73008
(405) 789-2090
Mgr: Bobby Burkett
Ice surfaces: 1, 185x85, Enclosed. *Open:* Year Round. *Ownership:* Private. *Access:* Public. *Clubs:* Oklahoma City FSC, Oklahoma Junior Hockey. *Sessions:* Public, Private/Club, Rental, Freestyle, Patch, Dance, Hockey. *Classes/Lessons:* Group, Private. *Program Affiliation:* USFSA, ISIA. *Summer School:* Regional. *Services:* Pro Shop, Skate Rental, Skate Sharpening, Snack Bar, Ballet Room, Lockers, Dressing Rooms. *Notes:* Vending machines; arcade.

Tulsa Ice Arena
6910 S. 101 East Ave.
Tulsa OK 74133
(918) 254-7272
FAX: (918)254-4676
Mgr: Kathy Pasco
Skating Dir: Shane Douglas
Ice surfaces: 1, 200x85, Enclosed. *Open:* Year Round. *Ownership:* Private. *Access:* Public. *Clubs:* Tulsa FSC. *Sessions:* Public, Private/Club, Rental, Freestyle, Patch, Dance, Hockey. *Classes/Lessons:* Group, Private. *Program Affiliation:* USFSA, ISIA. *Summer School:* Local. *Services:* Pro Shop, Skate Rental, Skate Sharpening, Snack Bar, Ballet Room,

Weight Room, Lockers, Dressing Rooms. *Notes:* Hockey camps in summer; broom ball available.

OR: OREGON

Hamill (Dorothy) Ice Chalet
Clackamas Town Center
12000 SE 82nd Ave.
Portland OR 97266
(503) 654-7733
Mgr: Bob Sacken
Ice surfaces: 1, 185x85, Enclosed. *Open:* Year Round. *Ownership:* Private. *Access:* Public. *Sessions:* Public, Rental, Freestyle, Patch, Hockey. *Classes/Lessons:* Group, Private. *Program Affiliation:* ISIA. *Services:* Pro Shop, Skate Rental, Skate Sharpening, Lockers. *Notes:* Party room.

Inn of the Seventh Mountain
18575 S. Century Dr.
Bend OR 97702
(503) 382-8711
Mgr: Barry Norton
Ice surfaces: 1, 100x50, Outdoor/Semi Outdoor. *Open:* Oct.-Apr. *Ownership:* Private. *Access:* Public. *Sessions:* Public, Freestyle, Hockey. *Classes/Lessons:* Group, Private. *Program Affiliation:* USFSA. *Summer School:* No. *Services:* Skate Rental, Skate Sharpening, Snack Bar, Lockers.

Lane County Ice
796 W. 13th Ave.
Eugene OR 97402
(503) 687-3615
Mgr: John Crosson
Ice surfaces: 1, 192x85, Enclosed. *Open:* Year Round. *Ownership:* Municipal. *Access:* Public. *Clubs:* Eugene FSC. *Sessions:* Public, Private/Club, Rental, Freestyle, Patch, Hockey, Speed Skating. *Classes/Lessons:* Group, Private. *Program Affiliation:* ISIA. *Summer School:* Regional. *Services:* Pro Shop, Skate Rental, Skate Sharpening, Snack Bar, Ballet Room, Lockers, Dressing Rooms. *Notes:* Dance and conditioning taught; dance sessions are offered through the club only.

Lloyd Center Ice Pavillion
2201 Lloyd Center
Portland OR 97232
(503) 288-4599
FAX: (503) 280-9407
Mgr: Larry Sperling
Skating Dir: Delores Mezyk
Ice surfaces: 1, 176x76, Enclosed. *Open:* Year Round. *Ownership:* Private. *Access:* Public. *Clubs:* Lloyd Center ISC. *Sessions:* Public, Private/Club, Rental, Freestyle, Patch, Dance. *Classes/Lessons:* Group, Private. *Program Affiliation:* ISIA. *Summer School:* National/International. *Services:* Pro Shop, Skate Rental, Skate Sharpening, Snack Bar, Lockers. *Notes:* Power skating and precision. Athletic club next door.

Valley Ice Arena
9250 SW Beaverton Hwy.
Beaverton OR 97005
(503) 297-2521
Mgr: John McBride
Skating Dir: Susie Sermon
Ice surfaces: 1, 200x85, Enclosed. *Open:* Year Round. *Ownership:* Private. *Access:* Public. *Clubs:* Carousel FSC. *Sessions:* Public, Private/Club, Rental, Freestyle, Patch, Hockey. *Classes/Lessons:* Private, Group. *Program Affiliation:* ISIA, USFSA. *Summer School:* Local. *Services:* Skate Rental, Skate Sharpening, Snack Bar, Ballet Room, Lockers, Dressing Rooms.

PA: PENNSYLVANIA

Beaver County Ice Arena
Rd. 1 Box 526,
Beaver Falls PA 15010
(412) 846-5600
Mgr: Jay Francona
Ice surfaces: 1, 200x85, Enclosed. *Open:* May-Aug. *Ownership:* Municipal. *Access:* Public. *Clubs:* American Hockey Assn.; Beaver Falls FSC. *Sessions:* Public, Private/Club, Rental, Hockey. *Classes/Lessons:* Private, Group. *Program Affiliation:* ISIA. *Services:* Pro Shop, Skate Rental, Skate Sharpening, Snack Bar, Lockers, Dressing Rooms. *Notes:* Freestyle, patch and dance sessions are for club members only.

Belmont Complex Armstrong County Recreation Authority
415 Butler Rd.
Kittaning PA 16201
(412) 548-1067
FAX: (412) 548-3285
Mgr: Suzanne Ault Boarts
Skating Dir: Carrie Richardson
Ice surfaces: 1, 200x85, Enclosed. *Open:* July-Apr. *Ownership:* Municipal. *Access:* Public. *Clubs:* Belmont Blaze FSC, Armstrong Amateur Hockey League. *Sessions:* Private/Club, Public, Rental, Hockey. *Classes/Lessons:* Group, Private. *Program Affiliation:* USFSA, ISIA. *Summer School:* No. *Services:* Pro Shop, Skate Rental, Skate Sharpening, Snack Bar, Dressing Rooms, Lockers. *Notes:* Freestyle, patch and dance sessions offered through the club only.

Bethlehem Municipal Ice Rink
Illicks Mill Rd.
Bethlehem PA 18018
(215) 865-7104
Mgr: Norm Stark
Ice surfaces: 1, 200x100, Outdoor/Semi Outdoor. *Open:* Dec.-Mar. *Ownership:* Municipal. *Access:* Public. *Clubs:* Comets Hockey. *Sessions:* Public, Rental, Freestyle, Hockey. *Classes/Lessons:* Group. *Summer School:* No. *Services:* Skate Rental, Skate Sharpening, Snack Bar.

Blade Runners Ice Complex
66 Alpha Dr.
Pittsburgh PA 15238
(412) 826-0800
FAX: (412) 826-1278
Mgr: Dale Rossetti
Ice surfaces: 2, 200x85; 200x85, Enclosed. *Open:* Year Round. *Ownership:* Private. *Access:* Public. *Sessions:* Public, Private/Club, Rental, Freestyle, Patch, Dance, Hockey. *Classes/Lessons:* Group, Private. *Program Affiliation:* USFSA, ISIA. *Summer School:* National/International, Regional. *Services:* Pro Shop, Skate Rental, Skate Sharpening, Snack Bar, Lockers, Dressing Rooms. *Notes:* Party room.

Cambria County War Memorial
326 Napolean St.
Johnstown PA 15901
(814) 536-5156
Mgr: Jim Vauter
Ice surfaces: 1, 200x85, Enclosed. *Open:* July-Apr. *Ownership:* Municipal. *Access:* Public. *Clubs:* Johnstown FSC. *College/Univ:* University of Pittsburgh at Johnstown; Indian University of PA. *Sessions:* Public, Private/Club, Rental, Freestyle, Patch, Dance, Hockey. *Classes/Lessons:* Group, Private. *Program Affiliation:* ISIA. *Summer School:* Regional. *Services:* Skate Rental, Pro Shop, Skate Sharpening, Snack Bar, Lockers, Dressing Rooms. *Notes:* Lessons, freestyle, patch and dance sessions offered through club only.

Class of 1923 Ice Rink
3130 Walnut St.
Philadelphia PA 19104
(215) 898-1923
Mgr: Det Pappenfuss
Ice surfaces: 1, 200x85, Enclosed. *Open:* Sept.-Apr. *Ownership:* Private. *Access:* Public. *College/Univ:* University of Pennsylvania, Drexell University. *Sessions:* Public, Private/Club, Rental, Freestyle, Patch, Dance, Hockey. *Classes/Lessons:* Group, Private. *Program Affiliation:* Own. *Summer School:* No. *Services:* Skate Rental, Skate Sharpening, Snack Bar, Lockers, Dressing Rooms.

Cleveland (John M.) Rink
420 West Street Rd.
Kennett Square PA 19348
(610) 444-5119
FAX: (610) 444-4932
Mgr: Nick Basilio
Skating Dir: Nick Basilio
Ice surfaces: 1, 200x85, Enclosed. *Open:* Oct.-Mar. *Ownership:* Private. *Access:* Members Only. *Clubs:* Chester County Skating Club. *Sessions:* Private/Club, Rental, Freestyle, Hockey. *Classes/Lessons:* Group, Private. *Summer School:* No. *Services:* Pro Shop, Skate Sharpening, Snack Bar, Lockers, Dressing Rooms. *Notes:* Affiliated with USA Hockey.

Cochran (Jim) Memorial Ice Rink
38th & Cherry St.
Erie PA 16508
(814) 868-3652
FAX: (814) 864-6272
Mgr: Scott Mitchell
Ice surfaces: 1, 185x85, Enclosed. *Open:* Sept.-Mar. *Ownership:* Erie 200. *Access:* Public. *Clubs:* FSC of Erie; Westminster Figure Skating Club. *Sessions:* Public, Private/Club, Rental, Hockey. *Classes/Lessons:* Private, Group. *Program Affiliation:* USFSA. *Summer School:* No. *Services:* Lockers, Dressing Rooms, Snack Bar, Skate Sharpening, Pro Shop, Skate Rental. *Notes:* Freestyle, patch and dance sessions are offered through the club only.

Face Off Circle, Inc.
1185 York Rd.
Warminster PA 18974
(215) 674-1345
FAX: (215) 674-0382
Mgr: Ken Reddy
Ice surfaces: 1, 200x85, Enclosed. *Open:* Year Round. *Ownership:* Private. *Access:* Public. *Clubs:* SC of Bucks City. *Sessions:* Public, Private/Club, Rental, Freestyle, Patch, Dance, Hockey, General. *Program Affiliation:* USFSA. *Services:* Pro Shop, Skate Sharpening, Skate Rental, Snack Bar, Lockers, Dressing Rooms.

Golden Mile Ice Center
4650 Old Franktown Rd.
Pittsburgh PA 15239
(412) 327-7465
Mgr: Alex Reyes
Ice surfaces: 1, 180x85, Enclosed. *Open:* Year Round. *Ownership:* Private. *Access:* Public. *Clubs:* Alleghany Hockey Assn.; Western PA Interscholastic League. *College/Univ:* Western PA College; University of Pittsburgh; Carnegie Mellon University. *Sessions:* Public, Private/Club, Rental, Freestyle, Patch, Hockey. *Classes/Lessons:* Group. *Program Affiliation:* USFSA. *Summer School:* Regional. *Services:* Skate Rental, Pro Shop, Skate Sharpening, Snack Bar, Lockers, Dressing Rooms.

Grundy Ice Center
700 Jefferson Ave.
Bristol PA 19007
(215) 788-3312
Skating Dir: Gail Gomez
Ice surfaces: 1, 185x85, Enclosed. *Open:* June-May. *Ownership:* Municipal. *Access:* Public. *Clubs:* Colonial SC. *Sessions:* Public, Rental, Freestyle, Patch, Hockey. *Classes/Lessons:* Group. *Program Affiliation:* ISIA. *Services:* Pro Shop, Skate Rental, Skate Sharpening, Snack Bar, Dressing Rooms.

Havertown Skatium
Darby and Manoa Rds.
Havertown PA 19083
(610) 853-2226
Mgr: Dave Schultz
Skating Dir: Sandra Loflin
Ice surfaces: 1, 200x85, Enclosed. *Open:* Year Round. *Ownership:* Municipal. *Access:* Public. *Clubs:* Hawks Hockey Club; Philadelphia SC. *Sessions:* Public, Rental, Freestyle, Patch, Dance, Hockey. *Classes/Lessons:* Private, Group. *Program Affiliation:* ISIA. *Summer School:* National/International. *Services:* Pro Shop, Skate Rental, Skate Sharpening, Snack Bar, Ballet Room, Lockers. *Notes:* Lockers for hockey. Offers 'Moves in the Field' sessions.

Hershey Park Arena
100 W. Hershey Park Dr.
Hershey PA 17033
(717) 534-3911
Mgr: Tom Stevens
Skating Dir: Marjorie Thorpe
Ice surfaces: 2, 200x85; 70x50, Enclosed, Outdoor/Semi Outdoor. *Open:* Sept.-May; June-Aug. *Ownership:* Private. *Access:* Public. *Clubs:* Hershey FSC. *Sessions:* Public, Private/Club, Rental, Hockey, Freestyle. *Classes/Lessons:* Group. *Program Affiliation:* USFSA. *Summer School:* Regional. *Services:* Skate Rental, Skate Sharpening, Snack Bar, Lockers, Dressing Rooms.

Hess Ice Rinks
3131 Mercer Rd.
New Castle PA 16105
(412) 658-6332
FAX: (412) 658-4014
Mgr: Chris Nevarra
Ice surfaces: 1, 75x75, Enclosed. *Open:* Oct.- May. *Ownership:* Municipal.

Access: Public. *Clubs:* Lawrence County Amateur Hockey. *Sessions:* Public, Private/Club, Rental, Freestyle, Hockey. *Classes/Lessons:* Group, Private. *Program Affiliation:* ISIA. *Summer School:* No. *Services:* Pro Shop, Skate Rental, Skate Sharpening, Snack Bar, Lockers, Dressing Rooms.

Ice Connection
136 Dorothy Dr.
Pittsburgh PA 15235
(412) 898-2440
FAX: (412) 856-7545
Mgr: Jill Simpson
Ice surfaces: 1, 200x85, Enclosed. *Open:* June-Apr. *Ownership:* Private. *Access:* Public. *Sessions:* Public, Rental, Freestyle, Patch, Hockey. *Classes/Lessons:* Group, Private. *Program Affiliation:* ISIA. *Summer School:* No. *Services:* Pro Shop, Skate Rental, Skate Sharpening, Snack Bar, Dressing Rooms.

Ice Garden, Inc.
Rd. #2 & Rt. 51
Belle Vernon PA 15012
(412) 379-7100
Mgr: Jim Murphy
Ice surfaces: 1, 200x85, Enclosed. *Open:* Year Round. *Ownership:* Private. *Access:* Public. *Sessions:* Public, Private/Club, Rental, Freestyle, Patch, Dance, Hockey. *Classes/Lessons:* Group, Private. *Program Affiliation:* ISIA. *Services:* Pro Shop, Skate Rental, Skate Sharpening, Snack Bar, Lockers, Dressing Rooms. *Notes:* Two banquet rooms.

Ice Palace
623 Hanover Ave.
Allentown PA 18103
(610) 435-3031
FAX: (610) 435-4453
Mgr: Rik McKinnon
Ice surfaces: 1, 185x85, Enclosed. *Open:* Year Round. *Ownership:* Private. *Access:* Public. *Sessions:* Public, Private/Club, Rental, Freestyle, Patch, Dance, Hockey. *Classes/Lessons:* Group, Private. *Program Affiliation:* USFSA, ISIA. *Services:* Pro Shop, Skate Rental, Skate Sharpening, Snack Bar, Dressing Rooms.

Indiana Ice Center, East Pike Recreational Complex
497 East Pike
Indiana PA 15701
(412) 465-2665
Mgr: Sam Kelly
Ice surfaces: 2, 200x85; 200x100, Enclosed. *Open:* Year Round. *Ownership:* Private. *Access:* Public. *Sessions:* Public, Rental, Freestyle, Patch, Dance, Hockey. *Classes/Lessons:* Private, Group. *Program Affiliation:* ISIA. *Summer School:* No. *Services:* Pro Shop, Skate Rental, Skate Sharpening, Snack Bar, Lockers, Dressing Rooms. *Notes:* Meeting rooms.

Lancaster Ice Arena
371 Carrera Dr.
Lancaster PA 17601
(717) 581-0274
FAX: (717) 581-5825
Mgr: Mark Panassow
Skating Dir: Ross Buettner
Ice surfaces: 1, 200x85, Enclosed. *Open:* Year Round. *Ownership:* Club. *Access:* Public. *Clubs:* Lancaster FSC, Lady Firebirds; Adult Hockey League; Old Timers League. *Sessions:* Public, Private/Club, Rental, Freestyle, Patch, Dance, Hockey. *Classes/Lessons:* Group, Private. *Program Affiliation:* USFSA. *Summer School:* Regional. *Services:* Skate Rental, Pro Shop, Skate Sharpening, Snack Bar, Lockers, Dressing Rooms.

Lehigh Valley Ice Arena
3323 7th St.
Whitehall PA 18052
(610) 434-6899
Mgr: Steve Camaro
Skating Dir: Sandra Camarano
Ice surfaces: 1, 200x85, Enclosed. *Open:* Year Round. *Ownership:* Private. *Access:* Public. *Clubs:* Lehigh Valley SC; Lehigh Hockey Club. *College/Univ:* Lehigh Univ.; Kutztown Univ.; E. Stroudsburg Univ.; Layfayett Univ. *Sessions:* Public, Private/Club, Rental, Freestyle, Patch, Hockey. *Classes/Lessons:* Group, Private. *Program Affiliation:* USFSA. *Summer School:* Regional. *Services:* Pro Shop, Skate Rental, Skate Sharpening, Snack Bar, Dressing Rooms.

Meadville Area, Recreation Complex
800 Thurston Rd.
Meadville PA 16335
(814) 724-6006
Mgr: Michael Fisher
Skating Dir: Marie Koman
Ice surfaces: 1, 200x85, Outdoor/Semi Outdoor. *Open:* Sept.-Apr. *Ownership:* Municipal. *Access:* Public. *Clubs:* Meadville FSC, FSC of Erie. *College/Univ:* Allegheny; Slippery Rock; Edinborough. *Sessions:* Public, Private/Club, Rental, Hockey. *Classes/Lessons:* Group. *Program Affiliation:* USFSA, ISIA. *Summer School:* No. *Services:* Pro Shop, Skate Rental, Skate Sharpening, Snack Bar, Pool and/or Athletic Facilities, Lockers, Dressing Rooms. *Notes:* Rink is being enclosed; freestyle sessions offered through the club only.

Melody Brook Ice Rink
Rt. 309 and Lenhart Rd.
Colmar PA 18915
(215) 822-3613
Mgr: Walt Yeutler
Ice surfaces: 1, 185x80, Enclosed. *Open:* Sept.-Apr. *Ownership:* Private. *Access:* Public. *Clubs:* Lasers Hockey Team; Youth Hockey. *Sessions:* Public, Private/Club, Rental, Freestyle, Patch, Hockey. *Classes/Lessons:* Private, Group. *Summer School:* No. *Services:* Lockers, Snack Bar, Skate Sharpening, Pro Shop, Skate Rental.

Mercyhurst College Ice Rink
501 E. 38th St.
Erie PA 16546
(814) 824-2142
Ice surfaces: 1, 200x85, Enclosed. *Open:* Oct.-Aug. *Ownership:* Private. *Access:* Restricted. *Restrictions: Clubs:* Erie Youth Hockey; Westminster FSC, SC of Erie. *College/Univ:* Mercyhurst College. *Sessions:* Rental, Freestyle, Hockey. *Classes/Lessons:* Group, Private. *Program Affiliation:* USFSA. *Summer School:* Local. *Services:* Skate Rental, Skate Sharpening, Snack Bar, Lockers, Dressing Rooms. *Notes:* There are no public sessions; all ice time is rented out.

Mt. Lebanon Recreation Center
900 Cedar Blvd.
Mt. Lebanon PA 15228
(412) 561-4363
Mgr: Bob Hlbinski
Skating Dir: Carolyn Thayer
Ice surfaces: 1, 200x85, Enclosed. *Open:* Year Round. *Ownership:* Municipal. *Access:* Restricted. *Restrictions:* Local residents. *Clubs:* SC of Mt. Lebanon. *Sessions:* Public, Private/Club, Rental, Freestyle, Patch, Dance, Hockey. *Classes/Lessons:* Group, Private. *Program Affiliation:* USFSA. *Summer School:* Regional. *Services:* Pro Shop, Skate Rental, Skate Sharpening, Studio Rink, Snack Bar, Ballet Room, Weight Room, Pool and/or Athletic Facilities, Lockers, Dressing Rooms.

Neville Ice Arena
220 S. 21st St.
Pittsburgh PA 15203
(412) 481-3351
Mgr: Paul Shuttleworth
Skating Dir: Bob Mock
Ice surfaces: 1, 200x85, Enclosed. *Open:* Year Round. *Ownership:* Private. *Access:* Public. *Clubs:* Mt. Lebanon FSC. *Sessions:* Public, Rental, Freestyle, Dance, Patch, Hockey. *Classes/Lessons:* Group, Private. *Program Affiliation:* USFSA, ISIA. *Summer School:* Regional. *Services:* Skate Rental, Pro Shop, Skate Sharpening, Snack Bar, Lockers, Dressing Rooms.

Nevin (Kirk) Ice Arena
Rt. 119 N.
Greensburg PA 15601
(412) 834-4880
Mgr: Tom Sphon
Skating Dir: Bob Mock
Ice surfaces: 1, 200x85, Enclosed. *Open:* Aug.-May. *Ownership:* Municipal. *Access:* Public. *Sessions:* Public, Private/Club, Rental, Freestyle, Patch, Dance, Hockey, General. *Classes/Lessons:* Group, Private. *Program Affiliation:* ISIA. *Summer School:* Regional. *Services:* Pro Shop, Skate Rental, Skate Sharpening, Snack Bar, Pool and/or Athletic Facilities, Dressing Rooms, Lockers.

North Park Ice Rink
303 Pearce Mill Rd.
Allison Park PA 15101
(412) 935-1280
Mgr: John Long
Skating Dir: Margaret Kalmeyer
Ice surfaces: 1, 200x85, Outdoor/Semi Outdoor. *Open:* Nov.-Mar. *Access:* Public. *Sessions:* Public, Rental, Hockey. *Classes/Lessons:* Group. *Program Affiliation:* ISIA. *Summer School:* No. *Services:* Skate Rental, Skate Sharpening.

Old York Rd. Skating Club
Church and Old York Rd.
Elkins Park PA 19117
(215) 635-2770
Mgr: Frank Finn
Ice surfaces: 1, 200x85, Outdoor/Semi Outdoor. *Open:* Oct.-Apr. *Ownership:* Private. *Access:* Public, Members Only. *Clubs:* Old York Rd. SC; Old York Rd. Raiders; Old York Rd. FSC. *Sessions:* Public, Private/Club, Rental, Freestyle, Patch, Dance, Hockey. *Classes/Lessons:* Private, Group. *Program Affiliation:* USFSA. *Summer School:* No. *Services:* Pro Shop, Skate Rental, Skate Sharpening, Snack Bar, Lockers, Dressing Rooms.

Penn State Ice Pavillion
Penn State University
Pollock & McKean Rds.
University Park PA 16803
(814) 863-2039
FAX: (814) 863-7906
Mgr: Larry Fies
Skating Dir: Dena Yeagley
Ice surfaces: 2, 200x85; 56x53, Enclosed. *Open:* Year Round. *Ownership:* Private. *Access:* Public. *Clubs:* Penn State FSC. *College/Univ:* Penn State. *Sessions:* Public, Private/Club, Rental, Freestyle, Patch, Dance, Hockey. *Classes/Lessons:* Group, Private. *Program Affiliation:* USFSA, ISIA. *Summer School:* National/International. *Services:* Pro Shop, Skate Rental, Skate Sharpening, Studio Rink, Snack Bar, Weight Room, Lockers, Dressing Rooms. *Notes:* Adjoining indoor field house.

Philadelphia Skating Club and Humane Society
220 Holland Ave.
Ardmore PA 19003
(610) 642-8700
Mgr: Fran Mycek
Ice surfaces: 1, 200 x 100, Enclosed. *Open:* Sept.- May. *Ownership:* Private. *Access:* Public. *Sessions:* Public, Rental, Freestyle, Patch, Dance. *Classes/Lessons:* Group, Private. *Program Affiliation:* USFSA. *Summer School:* No. *Services:* Pro Shop, Skate Rental, Snack Bar, Ballet Room, Lockers, Dressing Rooms, Skate Sharpening.

Rizzo Ice Rink
Front St. & Washington Ave.
Philadelphia PA 19147
(215) 685-1593
Mgr: Tony Nazzario
Skating Dir: Lynn Pastor
Ice surfaces: 1, 155x78, Outdoor/Semi Outdoor. *Open:* Nov.-Mar. *Ownership:* Municipal. *Access:* Public. *Sessions:* Public, Hockey. *Classes/Lessons:* Group, Private. *Program Affiliation:* ISIA. *Summer School:* No. *Services:* Skate Rental, Snack Bar, Pool and/or Athletic Facilities, Lockers. *Notes:* Limited private sessions are offered; facility also has an outdoor roller skating rink.

Schenley Park Ice Arena
Schenley Park, Overlook Dr.
Pittsburgh PA 15207
(412) 422-6523
FAX: (412) 422-6571
Mgr: Tom Driscoll
Ice surfaces: 1, 200x80, Outdoor/Semi Outdoor. *Open:* Nov.-Mar. *Ownership:* Municipal. *Access:* Public. *Sessions:* Public, Private/Club, Hockey. *Classes/Lessons:* Group, Private. *Program Affiliation:* Own. *Summer School:* No. *Services:* Snack Bar, Lockers, Skate Sharpening. *Notes:* Party room.

Timberline Ice Arena
530 Old Pricetown Rd.
Reading PA 19612
(610) 929-0808
Mgr: James Sincavage
Ice surfaces: 1, 185x85, Enclosed. *Open:* July-Apr. *Ownership:* Private. *Access:* Public. *Clubs:* Timberline Wolfpack Youth Hockey; Boyertown HS; Timberline Sr. League. *Sessions:* Public, Private/Club,

Rental. *Services:* Pro Shop, Skate Rental, Skate Sharpening, Snack Bar, Lockers, Dressing Rooms. *Notes:* Freestyle, patch, dance through FSC, hockey through clubs; group/private lesson through club; power skating through rink; local hockey summer school through camps; local summer school through FSC.

Twin Ponds, Inc.
3904 Corey Rd.
Harrisburg PA 17109
(717) 558-7663
Mgr: Steve Baun
Skating Dir: Cindy Berr
Ice surfaces: 2, 200x85; 200x85, Enclosed. *Open:* Year Round. *Ownership:* Private. *Access:* Public. *Clubs:* York FSC, Hershey FSC. *Sessions:* Public, Private/Club, Rental, Freestyle, Patch, Dance, Hockey. *Classes/Lessons:* Group, Private. *Program Affiliation:* Own. *Services:* Skate Rental, Pro Shop, Skate Sharpening, Snack Bar, Weight Room, Lockers, Dressing Rooms.

Twin Rinks
6725 River Rd.
Pensaulkin PA 08110
(609) 488-9300
Mgr: Jerry Domish
Ice surfaces: 2, 200x85; 200x85, Enclosed. *Open:* Year Round. *Ownership:* Private. *Access:* Public. *Sessions:* Public, Private/Club, Rental, Freestyle, Patch, Dance, Hockey. *Classes/Lessons:* Group, Private. *Program Affiliation:* ISIA. *Summer School:* National/International. *Services:* Pro Shop, Skate Rental, Skate Sharpening, Snack Bar, Lockers, Dressing Rooms.

Wilkes Barre Ice-A-Rama
Newsherman St. and Cole St.
Wilkes Barre PA 18702
(717) 821-1167
FAX: (717) 821-1168
Mgr: Marc Murphy
Ice surfaces: 1, 200x85, Enclosed. *Open:* Oct.-Mar. *Ownership:* Municipal. *Clubs:* Wyoming Valley ISC. *College/Univ:* Scranton University; Bloomsburg University. *Sessions:* Public, Rental, Freestyle, Patch, Dance, Hockey. *Classes/Lessons:* Group, Private. *Program Affiliation:* USFSA, ISIA. *Summer School:* No. *Services:* Skate Rental, Skate Sharpening, Snack Bar, Pool and/or Athletic Facilities, Lockers, Dressing Rooms. *Notes:* Freestyle, patch and dance sessions through club only.

Willow Grove Ice Rink, Inc.
551 North York Rd.
Willow Grove PA 19090
(215) 659-4253
Mgr: Ed Fino
Ice surfaces: 1, 190x85, Enclosed. *Open:* Year Round. *Ownership:* Private. *Access:* Public. *Clubs:* Hockey clubs. *Sessions:* Public, Rental, Hockey. *Classes/Lessons:* Group, Private. *Program Affiliation:* ISIA. *Summer School:* Regional. *Services:* Skate Rental, Pro Shop, Skate Sharpening, Lockers, Dressing Rooms. *Notes:* Summer hockey camps only.

Wissahickon Skating Club
550 W. Willow Grove Ave.
Philadelphia PA 19118
(215) 247-1759
Mgr: Ken Class
Ice surfaces: 1, 185x85, Enclosed. *Open:* Year Round. *Ownership:* Club. *Access:* Members Only. Oct.-March for use of club only. *Sessions:* Public, Private/Club, Freestyle, Rental, Patch, Dance, Hockey. *Classes/Lessons:* Group, Private. *Program Affiliation:* USFSA. *Summer School:* Local. *Services:* Skate Rental, Pro Shop, Skate Sharpening, Lockers, Dressing Rooms. *Notes:* Limited public sessions.

York City Ice Rink
Rockdale and Vander
York PA 17403
(717) 843-3959
FAX: (717) 845 7457
Mgr: Marie Malandro
Ice surfaces: 1, 184x85, Enclosed. *Open:* Oct. - Mar. *Ownership:* Municipal. *Access:* Public. *Clubs:* White Rose FSC, York Ice Hockey League. *College/Univ:* York College. *Sessions:* Public, Private/Club, Rental, Freestyle, Patch, Hockey. *Classes/Lessons:* Group, Private. *Program Affiliation:* USFSA, ISIA. *Summer School:* No. *Services:* Pro Shop, Skate Rental, Skate Sharpening, Snack Bar, Dressing Rooms. *Notes:* Summer school planned.

RI: RHODE ISLAND

Adelard Arena
800 Logee St.
Woonsocket RI 02895
(401) 769-7727
Mgr: Bill Bellisle
Ice surfaces: 1, 194x85, Enclosed. *Open:* June-March. *Ownership:* Private. *Access:* Public. *Clubs:* Woonsocket Youth FSC, King Philip Hockey; Tri-Valley Hockey. *Sessions:* Private/Club, Rental, Hockey. *Classes/Lessons:* Group, Private. *Summer School:* Regional. *Services:* Pro Shop, Snack Bar, Lockers, Dressing Rooms.

Cabot Memorial Rink
St. George's School
372 Purgatory Rd.
Middletown RI 02842-5984
(401) 849-3620
Mgr: Dolly Howard
Skating Dir: Skip Howard
Ice surfaces: 1, 200x85, Enclosed. *Open:* Oct.-Feb. *Ownership:* Private. *Access:* Restricted. *Restrictions:* Students and faculty of St. George's. *Clubs:* Sachuest SC; Newport CT Youth Hockey Assn. *College/Univ:* Salve Regina University. *Sessions:* Private/Club, Rental, Hockey. *Classes/Lessons:* Group. *Program Affiliation:* USFSA. *Summer School:* No. *Services:* Snack Bar, Dressing Rooms, Lockers. *Notes:* Group lessons are for adults only.

Cranston Veterans Memorial Rink
900 Phoenix Ave.
Cranston RI 02921
(401) 944-8690
Mgr: Patrick Grenier
Ice surfaces: 1, 200x85, Enclosed. *Open:* Year Round. *Ownership:* Private. *Access:* Public. *Clubs:* Rhode Island Saints; Cranston FSC, Youth Hockey. *Sessions:* Public, Private/Club, Rental, Freestyle, Patch, Dance, Hockey. *Classes/Lessons:* Group, Private. *Summer School:* Regional. *Services:* Pro Shop, Skate Rental, Skate Sharpening, Snack Bar, Lockers, Dressing Rooms.

Dennis Lynch Arena
25 Veatty St.
Pawtucket RI 02860
(401) 728-7420
Mgr: Ray Mello
Ice surfaces: 1, 200x85, Enclosed. *Open:* Year Round. *Ownership:* Municipal. *Access:* Public. *Clubs:* Pawtucket Providence FSC, Pawtucket Youth Hockey Assn. *Sessions:* Public, Rental, Hockey. *Classes/Lessons:* Group, Private. *Program Affiliation:* USFSA. *Summer School:* Regional. *Services:* Snack Bar, Lockers, Dressing Rooms. *Notes:* Freestyle, patch and dance sessions are offered through the club only.

Levy Community Ice Rink
425 East Ave.
Harrisville RI 02830
(401) 568-8615
Mgr: Dennis Courtemanche
Ice surfaces: 1, 215x85, Enclosed. *Open:* Sept.-May. *Ownership:* Municipal. *Access:* Public. *Clubs:* Burrillville FS Assn.; Mens Hockey League, Junior Hockey League. *Sessions:* Public, Rental, Freestyle, Hockey. *Classes/Lessons:* Group. *Program Affiliation:* Own. *Summer School:* No. *Services:* Pro Shop, Skate Sharpening, Snack Bar, Weight Room, Dressing Rooms.

Meehan (George) Auditorium
Brown University, 235 Hope St.
Providence RI 02912
(401) 863-2236
FAX: (401) 863-3409
Mgr: Bob Gaudet
Ice surfaces: 1, 200x85, Enclosed. *Open:* Oct.-Mar. *Ownership:* Private. *Access:* Restricted. *Restrictions:* Students and faculty. *Clubs:* Brown Men's & Women's hockey. *College/Univ:* Brown University. *Sessions:* Public, Private/Club, Rental, Hockey. *Classes/Lessons:* Group. *Program Affiliation:* Own. *Summer School:* No. *Services:* Skate Sharpening, Weight Room, Lockers, Dressing Rooms. *Notes:* Skate sharpening for hockey teams only.

Portsmouth Abbey School Rink
285 Cory's Lane
Portsmouth RI 02871
(401) 683-0621
Mgr: Mitch Klerner
Ice surfaces: 1, 200x85, Enclosed. *Open:* Oct.-Mar. *Ownership:* Private. *Access:* Public. *Clubs:* Newport YH; Eastbay Club. *College/Univ:* Roger Williams University. *Sessions:* Public, Rental, Hockey. *Classes/Lessons:* Private, Group. *Program Affiliation:* USFSA. *Summer School:* No. *Services:* Pro Shop, Skate Rental, Skate Sharpening, Snack Bar, Lockers, Dressing Rooms.

Rhode Island Sports Center
1186 Eddie Dowling Hwy.
North Smithfield RI 02895
(401) 762-1588
FAX: (401) 765-4726
Mgr: Frank Robinson
Ice surfaces: 1, 200x85, Enclosed. *Open:* Year Round. *Ownership:* Private. *Access:* Public. *Clubs:* Rhode Island FSC, Rhode Island Junior Sharks. *Sessions:* Public, Private/Club, Rental. *Classes/Lessons:* None. *Summer School:* No. *Services:* Dressing Rooms, Snack Bar, Skate Sharpening, Pro Shop, Skate Rental.

Schneider Arena
Huxley Ave.
Providence RI 02918
(401) 865-2168
Mgr: Jeff Goggin
Ice surfaces: 1, 200x85, Enclosed. *Open:* Year Round. *Ownership:* Private. *Access:* Public. *College/Univ:* Providence College. *Sessions:* Public, Rental, Hockey. *Classes/Lessons:* None. *Program Affiliation:* Own. *Summer School:* Regional. *Services:* Pro Shop, Skate Sharpening, Snack Bar, Dressing Rooms.

Smithfield Municipal Ice Rink
109 Pleasant View Ave.
Smithfield RI 02917
(401) 231-7677
Mgr: Bob Summerville
Ice surfaces: 1, 200x85, Enclosed. *Open:* Year Round. *Ownership:* Municipal. *Access:* Public. *Clubs:* Smithfield FSC, Northern RI Vikings. *Sessions:* Public, Private/Club, Rental. *Classes/Lessons:* Group, Private. *Program Affiliation:* USFSA, ISIA. *Summer School:* Regional. *Services:* Skate Sharpening, Snack Bar, Lockers, Dressing Rooms. *Notes:* Freestyle, patch, dance, group and private lessons are offered through the club only.

Thayer (William H.) Arena and Warburton (Joe) Arena
Mickey Stevens Sports Complex
975 Sandy Lane
Warwick RI 02889
(401) 738-2000
FAX: (401) 738-2000
Mgr: Bobby Anderson
Ice surfaces: 2, 200x85; 200x85, Enclosed. *Open:* July-April; Oct.-Apr. *Ownership:* Municipal. *Access:* Public. *Clubs:* Warwick FSC. *Sessions:* Public, Freestyle, Patch, Dance, Hockey. *Classes/Lessons:* None. *Summer School:* No. *Services:* Skate Sharpening, Snack Bar, Dressing Rooms.

West Warwick Civic Center Arena
Factory St.
West Warwick RI 02893
(401) 822-9260
FAX: (410) 822-9212
Mgr: Ray LaFerriere
Ice surfaces: 1, 185x85, Enclosed. *Open:* Sept.-Mar. *Ownership:* Municipal. *Access:* Public. *College/Univ:* University of Rhode Island. *Sessions:* Public, Rental, Hockey. *Classes/Lessons:* None. *Program Affiliation:* Own. *Summer School:* No. *Services:* Lockers, Dressing Rooms, Snack Bar, Skate Sharpening, Pro Shop, Skate Rental.

SC: SOUTH CAROLINA

Greenville Pavillion
400 Scottswood Rd.
Greenville SC 29650
(803) 322-7529
Mgr: Bob Faber
Skating Dir: Jimmy Crocket
Ice surfaces: 1, 185x85, Enclosed. *Open:* Year Round. *Ownership:* Municipal. *Access:* Public. *Sessions:* Public, Private/Club, Rental, Freestyle, Patch, Dance, Hockey. *Classes/Lessons:* Group, Private. *Program Affiliation:* USFSA. *Summer School:* Local. *Services:* Skate Rental, Skate Sharpening, Snack Bar, Pool and/or Athletic Facilities, Dressing Rooms, Lockers. *Notes:* Facility has indoor/outdoor tennis courts, soccer field, game room, meeting rooms, showers, karate and dance lessons.

Rockbridge Skating Club
4135 Rockbridge Rd.
Columbia SC 29206
(803) 782-3425
Mgr: Melinda Mowdy
Skating Dir: Melinda Mowdy
Ice surfaces: 1, 70x40, Enclosed. *Open:* Oct.-Apr. *Ownership:* Private. *Access:* Members Only. *Clubs:* Rockbridge FSC. *Sessions:* Private/Club, Rental. *Classes/Lessons:* Group, Private. *Program Affiliation:* ISIA. *Summer School:* No. *Services:* Pool and/or Athletic Facilities, Skate Rental, Snack Bar, Lockers, Dressing Rooms. *Notes:* Sunday rentals only.

SD: SOUTH DAKOTA

Brookings Ice Arena
221 Main Ave.
Brookings SD 57006
(605) 692-6090
Mgr: David Karolczak
Ice surfaces: 1, 200x85, Enclosed. *Open:* Nov.-Mar. *Ownership:* Municipal. *Access:* Public. *Clubs:* Brookings Assn. *Sessions:* Public, Rental. *Classes/Lessons:* None. *Services:* Skate Rental, Skate Sharpening, Snack Bar, Dressing Rooms. *Notes:* Freestyle, patch, dance, and hockey offered through the association.

TN: TENNESSEE

Centennial Sportsplex Ice Arena
222 25th Ave.
Nashville TN 37201
(615) 862-8480
Mgr: John Holmes
Ice surfaces: 1, 200x85, Enclosed. *Open:* Year Round. *Ownership:* Municipal. *Clubs:* Nashville FSC. *Sessions:* Public, Rental, Freestyle, Patch, Dance, Hockey. *Classes/Lessons:* Group, Private. *Program Affiliation:* ISIA. *Services:* Pro Shop, Skate Rental, Skate Sharpening, Snack Bar, Pool and/or Athletic Facilities, Lockers, Dressing Rooms.

Gatlinburg (Ober) Ice Rink
1001 Pky.
Gatlinburg TN 37738
(615) 436-5423
Mgr: Bill Ford
Ice surfaces: 1, 140x75, Enclosed. *Open:* Year Round. *Ownership:* Private. *Access:* Public. *Sessions:* Public, Rental. *Classes/Lessons:* Group, Private. *Program Affiliation:* ISIA. *Summer School:* No. *Services:* Skate Rental, Pro Shop, Skate Sharpening, Snack Bar, Lockers, Dressing Rooms.

Ice Chalet Knoxville
100 Lebanon St
Knoxville TN 37939
(615) 588-1858
Mgr: Robert Unger
Ice surfaces: 1, 175x75, Enclosed. *Open:* Oct.-Apr.; June-Aug. *Ownership:* Private. *Access:* Public. *College/Univ:* University of Tennessee. *Sessions:* Public, Private/Club, Rental, Freestyle, Patch, Dance, Hockey. *Classes/Lessons:* Group, Private. *Program Affiliation:* ISIA. *Summer School:* Regional. *Services:* Skate Rental, Pro Shop, Skate Sharpening, Lockers, Dressing Rooms.

Ice Chalet Memphis
4451 American Way
Memphis TN 38118
(901) 362-8877
FAX: (901) 360-0078
Mgr: Marvin Frederick
Skating Dir: Beverly Baker
Ice surfaces: 1, 175x85, Enclosed. *Open:* Year Round. *Ownership:* Private. *Access:* Public. *Sessions:* Public, Rental, Freestyle, Patch, Dance, Hockey. *Classes/Lessons:* Group. *Program Affiliation:* ISIA, USFSA. *Summer School:* Local. *Services:* Skate Rental, Skate Sharpening, Ballet Room. *Notes:* Ballet room owned by Mall of Memphis.

TX: TEXAS

Aerodrome Ice Skating Complex
16225 Lexington Blvd.
Sugar Land TX 77479
(713) 265-7465
FAX: (713) 265-7464
Mgr: Patrick Ferrick
Ice surfaces: 1, 200x85, Enclosed. *Open:* Year Round. *Ownership:* Private. *Access:* Public. *Clubs:* Houston Aeros. *Sessions:* Public, Private/Club, Rental, Freestyle, Patch, Dance, Hockey. *Classes/Lessons:* Private, Group. *Program Affiliation:* ISIA. *Summer School:* No. *Services:* Pro Shop, Skate Rental, Skate Sharpening, Snack Bar, Weight Room, Lockers, Dressing Rooms. *Notes:* Restaurant at rink.

America's Ice Garden
700 N. Pearl St.
Dallas TX 75201
(214) 922-9800
FAX: (214) 969-1081
Mgr: Adrea Meier
Ice surfaces: 1, 85x50, Enclosed. *Open:* Year Round. *Ownership:* Private. *Access:* Public. *Sessions:* Public, Freestyle, Rental, Patch. *Classes/Lessons:* Group, Private. *Program Affiliation:* ISIA. *Services:* Pro Shop, Skate Rental, Skate Sharpening. *Notes:* Athletic club upstairs.

Crystal Ice Palace
12332 IH-10 West
San Antonio TX 78230
(210) 690-4525
Mgr: Julie McSwain
Ice surfaces: 1, 165x70, Enclosed. *Open:* Year Round. *Ownership:* Private. *Access:* Public. *Clubs:* San Antonio FSC. *Sessions:* Public, Rental, Freestyle, Patch, Dance, Hockey. *Classes/Lessons:* Group, Private. *Program Affiliation:* USFSA, ISIA. *Services:* Skate Rental, Pro Shop, Skate Sharpening, Snack Bar, Dressing Rooms, Lockers.

Dallas Stars Ice Arena
211 Cowboys Pkwy.
Irving TX 75063
(214) 831-2480
FAX: (214) 831-2485
Mgr: Alex Lafave
Ice surfaces: 2, 200x85; 200x85, Enclosed. *Open:* Year Round. *Ownership:* Private. *Access:* Public. *Clubs:* Dallas Jr. Hockey; Dallas FSC. *Sessions:* Public, Private/Club, Rental, Freestyle, Patch, Dance, Hockey. *Classes/Lessons:* Private, Group. *Program Affiliation:* USFSA, ISIA. *Summer School:* National/International. *Services:* Pro Shop, Skate Rental, Skate Sharpening, Snack Bar, Ballet Room, Weight Room, Lockers, Dressing Rooms.

Galleria Ice Skating Center
5015 Westheimer Rd.
Houston TX 77056
(713) 621-7609
FAX: (713) 621-3215
Mgr: Jay Bennett
Skating Dir: Laura McDonald
Ice surfaces: 1, 185x75, Enclosed. *Open:* Year Round. *Ownership:* Private. *Access:* Public. *Clubs:* Galleria Houston ISC.

Sessions: Public, Private/Club, Rental, Freestyle, Patch, Dance, Hockey. *Classes/Lessons:* Private, Group. *Program Affiliation:* ISIA. *Summer School:* Local. *Services:* Pro Shop, Skate Sharpening, Ballet Room, Lockers, Skate Rental, Dressing Rooms. *Notes:* Located in a mall; vending machines.

Galleria Ice Skating Center
13350 Dallas Pkwy., Suite # 50
Dallas TX 75240
(214) 392-3363
Mgr: Holly Kirby
Skating Dir: Ms. Chris Castaneda
Ice surfaces: 1, 170x85, Enclosed. *Open:* Year Round. *Ownership:* Private. *Access:* Public. *Clubs:* Galleria Dallas FSC. *Sessions:* Public, Private/Club, Freestyle, Patch, Dance, Hockey. *Classes/Lessons:* Group, Private. *Program Affiliation:* USFSA, ISIA. *Summer School:* No. *Services:* Pro Shop, Skate Rental, Skate Sharpening, Snack Bar, Ballet Room, Lockers. *Notes:* In a shopping mall.

Ice Chalet Northcross
2525 W. Anderson Lane
Austin TX 78757
(512) 451-5102
Mgr: Brian Hill
Skating Dir: Kathy Goeke
Ice surfaces: 1, 160x65, Enclosed. *Open:* Year Round. *Ownership:* Private. *Access:* Public. *Clubs:* Austin FSC. *Sessions:* Public, Private/Club, Rental, Freestyle, Patch, Dance, Hockey. *Classes/Lessons:* Private, Group. *Program Affiliation:* ISIA. *Services:* Pro Shop, Skate Rental, Skate Sharpening, Lockers.

Prestonwood Ice Chalet
5301 Belt Line Rd.
Dallas TX 75240
(214) 980-8988
FAX: (214) 980-4909
Mgr: Patti Feeney
Skating Dir: Michelin Gaudin
Ice surfaces: 1, 180x80, Enclosed. *Open:* Year Round. *Ownership:* Private. *Access:* Public. *Clubs:* Lone Star FSC. *Sessions:* Public, Private/Club, Rental, Freestyle, Patch, Dance, Hockey. *Classes/Lessons:* Group, Private. *Program Affiliation:* ISIA, USFSA. *Summer School:* Local. *Services:* Pro Shop, Skate Rental, Skate Sharpening, Lockers, Snack Bar.

Sharpstown Ice Center
7300 Belleride
Houston TX 77036
(713) 784-2971
Mgr: Kathy Vackar
Ice surfaces: 1, 200x85, Enclosed. *Open:* Year Round. *Ownership:* Private. *Access:* Public. *Clubs:* Iceland FSC, Houston FSC. *Sessions:* Public, Private/Club, Rental, Freestyle, Patch, Dance, Hockey. *Classes/Lessons:* Group, Private. *Program Affiliation:* USFSA, ISIA. *Summer School:* Local. *Services:* Skate Rental, Pro Shop, Skate Sharpening, Snack Bar, Ballet Room, Lockers, Dressing Rooms.

Tandy Center Ice Rink
One Tandy Center
Fort Worth TX 76102
(817) 878-4848
Mgr: Ron Becker
Skating Dir: Kim Lytle
Ice surfaces: 1, 128x56, Enclosed. *Open:* Year Round. *Ownership:* Private. *Access:* Public. *Sessions:* Public, Private/Club, Rental, Freestyle, Patch, Dance. *Classes/Lessons:* Private. *Program Affiliation:* ISIA. *Summer School:* No. *Services:* Skate Rental, Pro Shop, Skate Sharpening, Snack Bar, Lockers, Dressing Rooms.

United Skates
115 St. S. Indiana
Lubbock TX 79423
(806) 745-3600
Mgr: James Baker
Ice surfaces: 1, 85x50, Enclosed. *Open:* Oct.-Feb. *Ownership:* Private. *Access:* Public. *Sessions:* Public, Private/Club, Rental. *Classes/Lessons:* Group, Private. *Program Affiliation:* ISIA. *Summer School:* No. *Services:* Pro Shop, Skate Rental, Skate Sharpening, Snack Bar, Pool and/or Athletic Facilities, Lockers, Dressing Rooms. *Notes:* Freestyle, patch, and dance sessions planned.

UT: UTAH

Bountiful Recreation Center
790 S. 100 East
Bountiful UT 84010
(801) 298-6220
Mgr: John Miller
Ice surfaces: 1, 200x85, Enclosed. *Open:* Year Round. *Ownership:* Municipal. *Access:* Public. *Sessions:* Public, Private/Club, Rental, Freestyle, Patch, Dance, Hockey. *Classes/Lessons:* Group, Private. *Program Affiliation:* USFSA, ISIA. *Services:* Pro Shop, Skate Rental, Skate Sharpening, Snack Bar, Ballet Room, Weight Room, Pool and/or Athletic Facilities, Lockers, Dressing Rooms. *Notes:* Racquetball.

Cottonwood Heights Ice Arena
7500 S. 2700 East
Salt Lake City UT 84121
(801) 943-3190
FAX: (801) 943-3595
Mgr: Richard Guthrie
Ice surfaces: 1, 200x85, Enclosed. *Open:* Year Round. *Ownership:* Municipal. *Access:* Public. *Clubs:* Cottonwood Heights FSC. *Sessions:* Public, Freestyle, Patch, Dance, Hockey. *Classes/Lessons:* Group, Private. *Program Affiliation:* ISIA, USFSA. *Services:* Skate Rental, Skate Sharpening, Snack Bar, Ballet Room, Lockers, Dressing Rooms, Weight Room.

Ice Sheet, The
4390 Harrison Blvd.
Ogden UT 84403
(801) 399-8750
FAX: (801) 625-3699
Mgr: Jim Schreiber
Ice surfaces: 1, 200x100, Enclosed. *Open:* July-Apr. *Ownership:* Municipal. *Access:* Public. *Clubs:* Wasatch FSC, Golden Spike Youth Hockey; Northern UT Speed Skating Club. *College/Univ:* Weber State University. *Sessions:* Public, Private/Club, Rental, Freestyle, Patch, Dance, Hockey. *Classes/Lessons:* Group, Private. *Program Affiliation:* USFSA. *Summer School:* Local. *Services:* Skate Rental, Pro Shop, Skate Sharpening, Snack Bar, Lockers, Dressing Rooms.

Resort Center Skating Rink
1415 Lowell Ave.
Park City UT 84060
(801) 649-0468
FAX: (801) 649-1464
Mgr: Junior Severs
Ice surfaces: 1, 110x55, Outdoor/Semi Outdoor. *Open:* Nov.-Mar. *Ownership:* Private. *Access:* Public. *Sessions:* Public. *Classes/Lessons:* Group, Private. *Summer School:* No. *Services:* Skate Rental.

Seven Peaks Ice Rink
1350 E. 300 North
Provo UT 84604
(801) 373-8777
Mgr: David Pincock
Skating Dir: David Pincock
Ice surfaces: 1, 300x100, Outdoor/Semi Outdoor. *Open:* Nov.-Mar. *Ownership:* Municipal. *Access:* Public. *Sessions:* Freestyle, Rental, Private/Club, Public. *Program Affiliation:* USFSA. *Summer School:* No. *Services:* Skate Rental, Pro Shop, Skate Sharpening, Snack Bar, Dressing Rooms, Lockers. *Notes:* Rink is kidney shaped; it is 22,000 square feet.

VA: VIRGINIA

Fairfax Ice Arena
3779 Pickett Rd.
Fairfax VA 22031
(703) 323-1133
Mgr: Melanie Emerick
Ice surfaces: 1, 200x85, Enclosed. *Open:* Year Round. *Ownership:* Private. *Access:* Public. *Clubs:* SC of Nova. *Sessions:* Public, Private/Club, Rental, Freestyle, Patch, Dance, Hockey. *Classes/Lessons:* Group, Private. *Program Affiliation:* USFSA, ISIA. *Services:* Pro Shop, Skate Rental, Skate Sharpening, Lockers, Dressing Rooms.

Fountain Square Ice Arena
1830 Discovery St.
Reston VA 22090
(703) 318-7541
FAX: (703) 709-6908
Mgr: David Yoder
Ice surfaces: 1, 100x60, Outdoor/Semi Outdoor. *Open:* Nov.-Mar. *Ownership:* Private. *Access:* Public. *Sessions:* Public, Private/Club, Rental, Freestyle. *Classes/Lessons:* Private, Group. *Program Affiliation:* USFSA. *Summer School:* No. *Services:* Skate Rental, Skate Sharpening.

Homestead Skating Rink
Rt. 2
Hot Springs VA 24445
(703) 839-7721
FAX: (703) 839-5954
Mgr: Sepp Kober
Ice surfaces: 1, 200x100, Outdoor/Semi Outdoor. *Open:* Nov.-Feb. *Ownership:* Private. *Access:* Public. *Sessions:* Public, Hockey. *Classes/Lessons:* Group, Private. *Program Affiliation:* ISIA. *Summer School:* No. *Services:* Pro Shop, Skate Rental, Skate Sharpening, Snack Bar, Lockers, Dressing Rooms. *Notes:* Ski shop.

Ice Palace, The
636 Johnston Willis Dr.
Richmond VA 23236
(804) 378-7465
FAX: (804) 378-0641
Mgr: Terry Brand
Ice surfaces: 1, 200x85, Enclosed. *Open:* Year Round. *Ownership:* Private. *Access:* Public. *Sessions:* Public, Rental, Freestyle, Hockey. *Classes/Lessons:* Group, Private. *Program Affiliation:* ISIA. *Summer School:* Local. *Services:* Pro Shop, Skate Rental, Skate Sharpening, Snack Bar, Lockers, Dressing Rooms, Pool and/or Athletic Facilities.

Iceland - Virginia Beach
4915 Broad St
Virginia Beach VA 23462
(804) 490-3907
Mgr: David Fies
Skating Dir: Mary Hutchinson
Ice surfaces: 1, 182x71, Enclosed. *Open:* Year Round. *Ownership:* Private. *Access:* Public. *Clubs:* Tidewater FSC. *College/Univ:* William & Mary; Old Dominion College; VA Wessleyan; Tidewater Community College. *Sessions:* Public, Private/Club, Rental, Freestyle, Patch, Dance, Hockey. *Classes/Lessons:* Group, Private. *Program Affiliation:* USFSA, ISIA. *Summer School:* Regional. *Services:* Skate Rental, Skate Sharpening, Snack Bar, Lockers, Dressing Rooms. *Notes:* Summer hockey camp for 2 weeks; figure skating camp for 8 weeks.

Mt. Vernon Recreation Center
2017 Bellview Blvd.
Alexandria VA 22307
(703) 768-3224
FAX: (703) 765-0467
Mgr: Maria Dewing
Ice surfaces: 1, 200x85. *Open:* Year Round. *Ownership:* Municipal. *Sessions:* Public, Rental, Freestyle, Patch, Dance, Hockey. *Classes/Lessons:* Group, Private. *Program Affiliation:* ISIA. *Services:* Skate Rental, Skate Sharpening, Pool and/or Athletic Facilities, Weight Room, Lockers, Dressing Rooms. *Notes:* All purpose room for dance classes.

Reston Ice Forum
1800 Michael Faraday Ct.
Reston VA 22090
(703) 709-1010
FAX: (703) 709-7916
Mgr: Brian Rienke
Ice surfaces: 2, 200x85; 200x100, Enclosed. *Open:* Year Round. *Ownership:* Private. *Access:* Public. *College/Univ:* George Mason University. *Sessions:* Public, Rental, Freestyle, Patch, Dance, Hockey. *Classes/Lessons:* Group. *Program Affiliation:* USFSA. *Summer School:* Regional. *Services:* Skate Rental, Pro Shop, Skate Sharpening, Snack Bar, Lockers, Dressing Rooms. *Notes:* A third rink is in planning; proposed size is 180x80.

Roanoke Civic Center
710 Williamson Rd.
Roanoke VA 24016
(703) 981-2241
Mgr: Christine Powell
Ice surfaces: 1, 185x90. *Open:* Oct.-Mar. *Ownership:* Municipal. *Access:* Members Only. Limited to club affiliation. *Sessions:* Private/Club, Dance, Hockey. *Classes/Lessons:* Private. *Program Affiliation:* Own. *Summer School:* No. *Services:* Lockers. *Notes:* Freestyle, patch and dance sessions are offered by the club only.

VT: VERMONT

Barre City B.O.R Rink
Seminary Hill
Barre VT 05641
(802) 476-0258
FAX: (802) 476-0257
Mgr: Stephanie Quaranta
Ice surfaces: 1, 185x85, Enclosed. *Open:* Oct.-Mar. *Ownership:* Municipal. *Access:* Public. *Clubs:* Barre FSC. *Sessions:* Public, Rental, Freestyle, Patch, Dance, Hockey. *Classes/Lessons:* Private, Group. *Program Affiliation:* ISIA, USFSA. *Summer School:* No. *Services:* Snack Bar, Dressing Rooms. *Notes:* Pro shop, skate rental and skate sharpening are very close to the rink.

Choukas (Michael) Ice Rink
Vermont Academy, Pleasant St.
Saxton's River VT 05154
(802) 869-6219
FAX: (802) 869-2115
Mgr: Jim Peters
Ice surfaces: 1, 200x85, Enclosed. *Open:* Nov.-Mar. *Ownership:* Private. *Access:* Public. *Clubs:* Springfield Youth Hockey; Pleasant Valley Youth Hockey. *Sessions:* Public, Rental, Hockey. *Classes/Lessons:* None. *Program Affiliation:* Own. *Summer School:* No. *Services:* Skate Sharpening, Dressing Rooms.

Collins-Perley Sport Center Skating Arena
71 South Main St.
St. Albans VT 05478
(802) 527-1202
Mgr: Liz Ambuhl
Ice surfaces: 1, 200x85, Enclosed. *Open:* Oct.-Mar. *Ownership:* Private. *Access:* Public. *Sessions:* Public, Freestyle, Hockey. *Classes/Lessons:* Group. *Summer School:* No. *Services:* Skate Sharpening, Snack Bar, Lockers, Dressing Rooms.

Essex Junction Skating Facility
2 Educational Dr.
Essex Junction VT 05452
(802) 878-1394
FAX: (802) 878-1370
Mgr: Bruce Murdough
Ice surfaces: 1, 200x85, Enclosed. *Open:* Sept.-Apr. *Ownership:* Municipal. *Access:* Public. *Sessions:* Public, Private/Club, Rental, Freestyle, Patch, Hockey. *Classes/Lessons:* Group, Private. *Services:* Pro Shop, Skate Rental, Skate Sharpening, Snack Bar, Lockers, Dressing Rooms.

Fenton West Chester Arena
Vale Hill Rd.
Lyndon Center VT 05850
(802) 626-9361
Ice surfaces: 1, 200x85, Enclosed. *Open:* Oct.-Mar. *Ownership:* Municipal. *Access:* Public. *Clubs:* Northeast Kingdom SC. *Sessions:* Private/Club, Rental, Freestyle, Patch, Dance, Hockey. *Classes/Lessons:* Group, Private. *Program Affiliation:* ISIA. *Summer School:* No. *Services:* Pro Shop, Skate Rental, Skate Sharpening, Snack Bar, Lockers, Dressing Rooms.

Giorgetti Ice Arena
86 Center St.
Rutland VT 05701
(802) 775-7976
Mgr: Leif Dahlin
Ice surfaces: 1, 200x85, Outdoor/Semi Outdoor. *Open:* Dec.-Apr. *Ownership:* Municipal. *Access:* Public. *Sessions:* Public, Private/Club, Freestyle. *Classes/Lessons:* Group. *Program Affiliation:* Own. *Summer School:* No. *Services:* Dressing Rooms.

Guttersonn Field House
University of Vermont
Patrick Gym, Spear St.
Burlington VT 05405
(802) 656-3074
Mgr: Donald Lacross
Ice surfaces: 1, 200x90, Enclosed. *Open:* Sept.-Mar. *Ownership:* Private. *Access:* Restricted. *Restrictions:* Faculty, staff, students. *Sessions:* Private/Club, Freestyle, Hockey. *Classes/Lessons:* Group. *Program Affiliation:* Own. *Summer School:* No. *Services:* Weight Room, Lockers, Dressing Rooms.

Highgate Sports Arena
Gore Rd.
Highgate Center VT 05459
(802) 868-4406
Mgr: Walter Medor
Ice surfaces: 1, 185x85, Enclosed. *Open:* Oct.-Mar. *Ownership:* Municipal. *Access:* Public. *Clubs:* MVU Hockey; MAHA Hockey; Highgate FSC. *Sessions:* Public, Private/Club, Rental, Hockey. *Classes/Lessons:* Private. *Program Affiliation:* ISIA. *Summer School:* No. *Services:* Pro Shop, Skate Sharpening, Snack Bar, Lockers, Dressing Rooms.

Jackson Arena
Park St.
Stowe VT 05672
(802) 253-6148
FAX: (802) 253-6137
Mgr: Bruce Godin
Ice surfaces: 1, 200x85, Outdoor/Semi Outdoor. *Open:* Nov.-Mar. *Ownership:* Municipal. *Access:* Public. *Clubs:* Stowe FSC, Stowe Youth Hockey. *Sessions:* Public, Rental. *Classes/Lessons:* Group, Private. *Program Affiliation:* USFSA, ISIA. *Summer School:* No. *Services:* Skate Rental, Skate Sharpening, Snack Bar, Dressing Rooms. *Notes:* Freestyle, patch, dance, hockey sessions and lessons offered through clubs only.

Mandigo (Royce) Arena
Rutland VT 05701
(802) 773-9416
Mgr: Leonard Clard
Ice surfaces: 1, 190x85, Enclosed. *Open:* Oct.-Mar. *Ownership:* Private. *Access:* Public. *Clubs:* Rutland Amateur Hockey Assn.; Rutland SC. *Sessions:* Public, Rental, Freestyle, Patch, Dance, Hockey. *Classes/Lessons:* Group. *Program Affiliation:* USFSA. *Summer School:* No. *Services:* Lockers, Snack Bar, Skate Sharpening, Pro Shop. *Notes:* Speed skating.

Nelson Arena at Middlebury College
Rt. 30
Middlebury VT 05753
(802) 388 3711 Ext. 5411
Mgr: Butch Atkins
Ice surfaces: 1, 200x85, Enclosed. *Open:* Nov.-Apr. *Ownership:* Private. *Access:* Restricted. *Restrictions:* Limited public sessions; primarily college use. *College/Univ:* Middlebury College. *Sessions:* Public, Patch, Hockey. *Classes/Lessons:* None. *Summer School:* No. *Services:* Weight Room, Pool and/or Athletic Facilities, Lockers, Dressing Rooms.

Northshire Civic Center
Union St.
Manchester VT 05255
(802) 362-0150
Mgr: Jeff Chaimberland
Ice surfaces: 1, 200x85, Enclosed. *Open:* Oct.-Apr. *Ownership:* Private. *Access:* Public. *Sessions:* Public. *Summer School:* No. *Services:* Pro Shop, Skate Rental, Skate Sharpening, Snack Bar, Lockers, Dressing Rooms. *Notes:* Construction scheduled for late 1994.

Paquette (Gordon H.) Municipal Arena
Leddy Park, 216 Leddy Rd.
Burlington VT 05401
(802) 864-0123
Mgr: Robert L'Ecuyer
Skating Dir: Kathy Knauer
Ice surfaces: 2, 200x100, Enclosed. *Open:* June-Apr. *Ownership:* Municipal. *Access:* Public. *Clubs:* Champions FSC. *Sessions:* Public, Private/Club, Rental,

Freestyle, Patch, Dance, Hockey. *Classes/Lessons:* Group, Private. *Program Affiliation:* USFSA, ISIA. *Summer School:* Regional, National/International. *Services:* Pro Shop, Skate Rental, Skate Sharpening, Studio Rink, Snack Bar, Pool and/or Athletic Facilities, Lockers, Dressing Rooms. *Notes:* Ice is sold monthly for freestyle.

Taylor Arena
Norwich University, S. Main St.
Northfield VT 05663
(802) 485-2567
Mgr: Bill Cahill
Ice surfaces: 1, 185x80, Enclosed. *Open:* Oct.-Mar. *Ownership:* Private. *Access:* Public, Restricted. Students and staff. *Clubs:* Northfield Amateur Youth Hockey; Northfield HS Hockey; Harwood Regional HS Hockey. *College/Univ:* Norwich University. *Sessions:* Public, Rental, Freestyle, Hockey. *Classes/Lessons:* Group. *Summer School:* No. *Services:* Skate Sharpening, Snack Bar, Pool and/or Athletic Facilities, Weight Room, Lockers, Dressing Rooms.

Town of Hartford BOR Rink
Highland Ave.
White River Junction VT 05001
(802) 295-3236
FAX: (802) 295-6382
Mgr: David Dean
Ice surfaces: 1, 200x80, Outdoor/Semi Outdoor. *Open:* Dec.-Mar. *Ownership:* Municipal. *Access:* Public. *Clubs:* Hartford Youth Hockey. *Sessions:* Public, Rental, Freestyle, Hockey. *Classes/Lessons:* Group. *Summer School:* No. *Services:* Snack Bar, Dressing Rooms.

Withington (Nelson) Arena
Guilford St.
Brattleboro VT 05301
(802) 257-2311
FAX: (802) 257-2322
Mgr: Steve Pritchard
Ice surfaces: 1, 185x85, Outdoor/Semi Outdoor. *Open:* Nov.-Mar. *Ownership:* Municipal. *Access:* Public. *Clubs:* Brattleboro FSC, Brattleboro Hockey Assn. *Sessions:* Public, Private/Club, Rental, Hockey. *Classes/Lessons:* Group, Private. *Program Affiliation:* USFSA, ISIA. *Summer School:* No. *Services:* Skate Rental, Snack Bar, Dressing Rooms, Pool and/or Athletic Facilities.

Notes: Freestyle, patch and dance sessions offered through club only.

WA: WASHINGTON

Eagles-Ice A-Rena
6321 N. Addison
Spokane WA 99208
(509) 489-9295
FAX: (509) 483-6905
Mgr: Tim Everson
Ice surfaces: 2, 200x95; 185x85, Enclosed. *Open:* Year Round. *Ownership:* Private. *Access:* Public. *Clubs:* Lilac City FSC. *Sessions:* Public, Private/Club, Rental, Freestyle, Patch, Hockey. *Classes/Lessons:* Group, Private. *Program Affiliation:* USFSA, ISIA. *Services:* Pro Shop, Skate Sharpening, Skate Rental, Snack Bar, Ballet Room, Lockers, Dressing Rooms.

Highland Ice Arena
18005 Aurora Ave. N.
Seattle WA 98133
(206) 546-2431
Mgr: Rick Stephens
Skating Dir: Jerry Greene
Ice surfaces: 2, 175x85; 150x65, Enclosed. *Open:* Year Round. *Ownership:* Private. *Access:* Public. *Clubs:* Highland SC. *Sessions:* Public, Private/Club, Rental, Freestyle, Patch, Hockey, Dance. *Classes/Lessons:* Group, Private. *Program Affiliation:* USFSA, ISIA. *Summer School:* Local. *Services:* Pro Shop, Skate Rental, Skate Sharpening, Lockers, Dressing Rooms.

Moses Lake Municipal Ice Rink
Balsan & 4th Ave.
Moses Lake WA 98837
(509) 766-9240
Mgr: Spencer Grigg
Ice surfaces: 1, 150x50, Outdoor/Semi Outdoor. *Open:* Nov.-Feb. *Ownership:* Municipal. *Access:* Public. *Sessions:* Public. *Classes/Lessons:* Group. *Program Affiliation:* ISIA.

Olympic View Ice Arena
22202 70th Ave. W.
Mt. Lake Terrace WA 98043
(206) 672-9012
Mgr: Rod Chiupka
Ice surfaces: 1, 200x100, Enclosed. *Open:* Year Round. *Ownership:* Private. *Access:* Restricted. *Restrictions:* Clubs; hockey leagues. *Clubs:* Seattle SC; Junior Hockey Assn. *Sessions:* Private/Club, Freestyle, Patch, Dance, Hockey. *Classes/Lessons:* Group, Private. *Program Affiliation:* USFSA, ISIA. *Summer School:* No. *Services:* Pro Shop, Skate Sharpening, Snack Bar, Ballet Room, Weight Room, Lockers, Dressing Rooms. *Notes:* Skating club and hockey assn. use all ice time; no public sessions. Physical therapy clinic.

Puget Sound Hockey Center
1918 Stewart St.
Tacoma WA 98421
(206) 272-1785
Mgr: Ian Burnett
Ice surfaces: 1, 200x86, Enclosed. *Open:* Year Round. *Ownership:* Private. *Access:* Restricted. *Restrictions:* Amateur hockey. *Clubs:* Susan English Ice Skating Academy; Tacoma Amateur Hockey Assn. *Sessions:* Rental, Freestyle, Hockey. *Classes/Lessons:* Group, Private. *Program Affiliation:* USFSA, ISIA. *Services:* Pro Shop, Skate Rental, Skate Sharpening, Dressing Rooms. *Notes:* Stick & Puck pro shop.

Riverfront Park
25th St.
Wenatchee WA 98801
(509) 664-5994
FAX: (509) 664-5986
Mgr: Dick Lyons
Ice surfaces: 2, 200x85; 185x85, Enclosed, Outdoor/Semi Outdoor. *Open:* Oct.-Apr. *Ownership:* Municipal. *Access:* Public. *Clubs:* Wenatchee FSC. *Sessions:* Public, Private/Club, Rental, Hockey. *Classes/Lessons:* Private, Group. *Program Affiliation:* ISIA. *Services:* Pro Shop, Skate Rental, Skate Sharpening, Snack Bar, Dressing Rooms, Lockers. *Notes:* Freestyle and patch sessions are offered through the club only.

Riverfront Park Ice Palace
507 N. Howard
Spokane WA 99201
(509) 625-6687
Mgr: Craig Butz
Skating Dir: Kimbre Dowd-Vega
Ice surfaces: 1, 185x85, Outdoor/Semi Outdoor. *Open:* Oct.-Mar. *Ownership:* Municipal. *Access:* Public. *Clubs:* Spokane FSC. *Sessions:* Public, Private/Club, Rental, Dance, Hockey, Freestyle.

Classes/Lessons: Group, Private. *Program Affiliation:* ISIA. *Summer School:* No. *Services:* Pro Shop, Skate Rental, Skate Sharpening, Snack Bar, Lockers, Dressing Rooms. *Notes:* IMAX Theatre; season passes to park, rink and theatre available.

Seattle Center Arena
365 Mercer St.
Seattle WA 98109
(206) 728-9124
Mgr: Rick Ranish
Ice surfaces: 1, 192x80, Enclosed. *Open:* Sept.-April. *Ownership:* Municipal. *Access:* Restricted. *Restrictions:* Junior hockey. *Clubs:* Seattle Thunderbirds. *Sessions:* Rental, Hockey. *Classes/Lessons:* None. *Program Affiliation:* Own. *Summer School:* No. *Services:* Snack Bar, Weight Room, Lockers, Dressing Rooms.

Sno-King Ice Arena
19803 68th Ave. W.
Lynnwood WA 98036
(206) 775-7512
FAX: (206) 776-2670
Mgr: Les Grauer
Ice surfaces: 1, 200x85, Enclosed. *Open:* Year Round. *Ownership:* Private. *Access:* Public. *Clubs:* Seattle SC; Seattle Jr. Hockey Assn.; NW Amateur Hockey Assn.; Cascade Hockey League. *Sessions:* Public, Private/Club, Rental, Freestyle, Patch, Hockey. *Classes/Lessons:* Private, Group. *Program Affiliation:* ISIA. *Summer School:* Local, Regional. *Services:* Pro Shop, Skate Rental, Skate Sharpening, Snack Bar, Ballet Room, Lockers, Dressing Rooms.

Sprinker (Harry) Recreation Center
14824 South C St., Suite 107
Tacoma WA 98444
(206) 537-2600
FAX: (206) 535-3246
Mgr: Marc Blau
Ice surfaces: 1, 200x85, Enclosed. *Open:* Year Round. *Ownership:* Municipal. *Access:* Public. *Clubs:* Blakewood Winter Club. *Sessions:* Public, Private/Club, Rental, Freestyle, Patch, Dance, Hockey. *Classes/Lessons:* Private, Group. *Program Affiliation:* USFSA, ISIA. *Services:* Pro Shop, Skate Rental, Skate Sharpening, Snack Bar, Ballet Room, Pool and/or Athletic Facilities, Dressing Rooms, Lockers. *Notes:* Broomball; 4 indoor tennis courts; 5 raquetball courts; track and field; 4 multi-purpose rooms.

Tri-Cities Coliseum
700 W. Quinalt
Kennewick WA 99336
(509) 783-8824
FAX: (509) 735-4699
Mgr: Chris Werner
Ice surfaces: 1, 185x85, Enclosed. *Open:* Aug.-Mar. *Ownership:* Municipal. *Access:* Public. *Clubs:* Tri-City FSC, Youth Hockey. *Sessions:* Public, Private/Club, Rental, Hockey. *Classes/Lessons:* Group, Private. *Program Affiliation:* USFSA. *Summer School:* No. *Services:* Skate Rental, Pro Shop, Skate Sharpening, Snack Bar, Lockers, Dressing Rooms.

Whatcom County Sports Arena
1803 W. Bakerview Rd.
Bellingham WA 98226
(206) 676-7305
Mgr: Jim McKain
Ice surfaces: 1, 200x85, Enclosed. *Open:* Sept.-Apr. *Ownership:* Private. *Access:* Public. *Clubs:* Bellingham FSC, Bellingham Ice Hawks; Whatcom Speed Skating. *College/Univ:* Western Washington Universtiy. *Sessions:* Public, Private/Club, Rental, Dance, Hockey. *Classes/Lessons:* Group, Private. *Program Affiliation:* USFSA. *Summer School:* No. *Services:* Pro Shop, Skate Rental, Skate Sharpening, Snack Bar, Dressing Rooms. *Notes:* Freestyle and patch sessions offered through club only.

Yakima Ice Arena
1700 E. Beech
Yakima WA 98901
(509) 248-6315
Mgr: Don Eastridge
Skating Dir: Anne Eastridge
Ice surfaces: 1, 150x75, Enclosed. *Open:* Oct.-Apr. *Ownership:* Private. *Access:* Public. *Clubs:* Yakima FSC, Slice of Ice SC. *Sessions:* Public, Private/Club, Rental, Freestyle, Patch, Dance, Hockey. *Classes/Lessons:* Group, Private. *Program Affiliation:* USFSA, ISIA. *Summer School:* No. *Services:* Skate Rental, Pro Shop, Skate Sharpening, Snack Bar, Lockers, Dressing Rooms.

YWCA Ice Chalet
213 South 1st Ave.
Walla Walla WA 99362
(509) 525-2575
Mgr: Leon Armstrong
Ice surfaces: 1, 65 x 90, Enclosed. *Open:* Sept.—April. *Ownership:* Private. *Access:* Public. *Clubs:* YWCA; ISIA FSC, ISIA Hockey Club. *Sessions:* Public, Private/Club, Rental, Freestyle, Patch, Hockey. *Classes/Lessons:* Group, Private. *Program Affiliation:* ISIA. *Summer School:* No. *Services:* Skate Rental, Skate Sharpening, Snack Bar, Dressing Rooms.

WASHINGTON, DC: SEE DC

WI: WISCONSIN

Blue Line Hockey Rink
225 S. Royal Ave.
Fond du Lac WI 54935
(414) 929-9664
Mgr: Nancy Braun
Ice surfaces: 1, 200x85, Enclosed. *Open:* Oct.-Mar. *Ownership:* Municipal. *Access:* Public. *Sessions:* Public, Freestyle, Patch, Hockey. *Classes/Lessons:* Private, Group. *Program Affiliation:* ISIA. *Services:* Snack Bar, Lockers, Dressing Rooms.

Brown County Youth Ice Center
875 Packard Dr.
Green Bay WI 54304
(414) 499-7222
Mgr: Keith Buzdis
Ice surfaces: 1, 178x80, Enclosed. *Open:* Oct.-Mar. *Ownership:* Municipal. *Access:* Public. *Clubs:* Notre Dame HS Hockey; Bay Area Hockey. *Sessions:* Public, Private/Club, Rental, Hockey. *Classes/Lessons:* Group. *Summer School:* No. *Services:* Pro Shop, Skate Sharpening, Snack Bar, Lockers, Dressing Rooms.

Camp Randall Memorial Sports Center
1430 Monroe St.
Madison WI 53711
(608) 263-6565
Mgr: Denny Carey
Ice surfaces: 1, 197x85, Enclosed. *Open:* Sept.-May. *Ownership:* Private. *Access:* Public. *College/Univ:* University of Wisconsin. *Sessions:* Public, Rental, Hockey. *Classes/Lessons:* None.

Program Affiliation: Own. *Summer School:* No. *Services:* Skate Rental, Pro Shop, Skate Sharpening, Weight Room, Lockers, Dressing Rooms.

Chippewa Falls Arena
Chippewa Falls WI 54729
(715) 723-4403
Mgr: Wade Hutton
Ice surfaces: 2, 200x85; 200x85, Enclosed, Outdoor/Semi Outdoor. *Open:* Sept.-Apr. *Ownership:* Chippewa Youth Hockey Assn. *Access:* Public. *Clubs:* Chippewa Youth Hockey; Chippewa FSC. *Sessions:* Public, Private/Club, Rental, Freestyle, Hockey. *Classes/Lessons:* Private, Group. *Program Affiliation:* USFSA. *Summer School:* No. *Services:* Pro Shop, Skate Sharpening, Snack Bar, Lockers, Dressing Rooms.

Dane County EXPO Center
1881 Expo Mall E.
Madison WI 53713
(608) 267-3976
FAX: (608) 267-0146
Mgr: Ray Ritari
Ice surfaces: 2, 200x97; 200x97, Enclosed. *Open:* Oct.-Mar. *Ownership:* Municipal. *Access:* Restricted. *Restrictions:* Rentals and games. *Clubs:* University of Wisconsin Badgers. *College/Univ:* University of Wisconsin. *Sessions:* Private/Club, Rental, Hockey. *Classes/Lessons:* None. *Summer School:* No. *Services:* Skate Sharpening, Lockers, Dressing Rooms.

De Pere Ice Recreation Center
1450 Fort Howard Ave.
De Pere WI 54115
(414) 339-4097
Mgr: Rod Herlache
Ice surfaces: 1, 200x85, Enclosed. *Open:* Year Round. *Ownership:* Municipal. *Access:* Public. *Clubs:* De Pere FSC. *Sessions:* Public, Rental, Hockey. *Classes/Lessons:* Group, Private. *Program Affiliation:* USFSA, ISIA. *Services:* Pro Shop, Skate Sharpening, Snack Bar, Skate Rental, Lockers, Dressing Rooms. *Notes:* Freestyle, patch, and dance sessions are offered through the club only.

Eagle River Recreation Association
4149 Hwy. 70 E.
Eagle River WI 54521
(715) 479-4858
Mgr: Gina Grigus
Ice surfaces: 2, 87x85; 190x90, Enclosed, Outdoor/Semi Outdoor. *Open:* Nov.-Mar.; June-July. *Ownership:* Private. *Access:* Public. *Clubs:* Eagle River FSC. *Sessions:* Public, Private/Club, Rental, Freestyle, Patch, Dance, Hockey. *Classes/Lessons:* Private, Group. *Program Affiliation:* USFSA. *Summer School:* No. *Services:* Pro Shop, Snack Bar, Lockers, Dressing Rooms.

Eble Park Arena
19400 W. Bluemound Rd.
Brookefield WI 53045-5942
(414) 784-7512
Mgr: Marv Bednar
Ice surfaces: 1, 200x85, Enclosed. *Open:* June-Apr. *Ownership:* Municipal. *Access:* Public. *Clubs:* Greater Milwaukee FSC, Waukesha County Youth Hockey; Marquette HS; Catholic Memorial HS; St. John's Military Academy. *College/Univ:* Milwaukee School of Engineering (MSOE). *Sessions:* Public, Private/Club, Rental, Hockey. *Classes/Lessons:* Private, Group. *Summer School:* Local. *Services:* Skate Rental, Skate Sharpening, Snack Bar, Lockers, Dressing Rooms.

Family Center Ice Arena
609 Gould
Beaver Dam WI 53916
(414) 885-9816
Mgr: Greg Nelson
Ice surfaces: 1, 200x97, Enclosed. *Open:* Sept.-Mar. *Ownership:* Private. *Access:* Public. *Clubs:* Beaver Dam Hockey Assn.; Savan City FSC. *Sessions:* Public, Private/Club, Rental, Hockey. *Classes/Lessons:* Private, Group. *Program Affiliation:* USFSA. *Summer School:* No. *Services:* Pro Shop, Skate Rental, Skate Sharpening, Snack Bar, Lockers, Dressing Rooms. *Notes:* Freestyle and patch sessions offered through club only.

Green Island Ice Arena
2312 S. 7th St.
Lacrosse WI 54601
(608) 789-7199
Mgr: Steve Reigstad
Ice surfaces: 1, 189x85, Enclosed. *Open:* Nov.-Mar. *Ownership:* Municipal. *Access:* Public. *Clubs:* River City Youth Hockey; The FSC. *Sessions:* Public, Private/Club, Rental, Hockey. *Classes/Lessons:* Private, Group. *Program Affiliation:* USFSA. *Summer School:* No. *Services:* Pro Shop, Skate Rental, Skate Sharpening, Snack Bar, Lockers, Dressing Rooms.

Hartmeyer Ice Arena
1834 Commercial Ave.
Madison WI 53704
(608) 246-4512
FAX: (608) 246-5800
Mgr: Dave Gilvin
Ice surfaces: 1, 100x60, Enclosed. *Open:* June-Mar.

Hobbs Altoona Sports Center
2300 Spooner Ave.
Altoona WI 54720
(715) 839-5188
Mgr: David Soddy
Ice surfaces: 1, 200x85, Enclosed. *Open:* Nov.-Mar. *Ownership:* Municipal. *Access:* Public. *Clubs:* Altoona Youth Hockey. *Sessions:* Public, Rental. *Classes/Lessons:* Group. *Summer School:* No. *Services:* Pro Shop, Skate Sharpening, Snack Bar, Lockers. *Notes:* Learn-to-Skate programs offered.

Hobbs Municipal Ice Arena
915 Menomonie St.
Eau Claire WI, 54703
(715) 839-5040
Mgr: Stu Taylor
Ice surfaces: 2, 200x85; 200x85, Enclosed. *Open:* June-Mar. *Ownership:* Municipal. *Access:* Public. *Clubs:* Eau Claire FSC, University of Wisconsin Hockey League. *College/Univ:* University of Wisconsin, Eau Claire. *Sessions:* Public, Private/Club, Rental, Freestyle, Hockey. *Classes/Lessons:* Private, Group. *Program Affiliation:* USFSA. *Summer School:* Local. *Services:* Skate Rental, Snack Bar, Lockers, Dressing Rooms.

Janesville Ice Arena
812 Beloit Ave.
Janesville WI 53545
(608) 755-3014
Mgr: Jane Meyers
Ice surfaces: 1, 200x85, Enclosed. *Open:* Year Round. *Ownership:* Municipal. *Access:* Public. *Clubs:* Janesville FSC. *Sessions:* Public, Private/Club, Rental,

Freestyle, Patch, Dance, Hockey. *Classes/Lessons:* Group, Private. *Program Affiliation:* USFSA. *Summer School:* Regional, National/International. *Services:* Pro Shop, Skate Rental, Skate Sharpening, Snack Bar, Lockers, Dressing Rooms.

Kenosha County Ice Arena
7727 60th Ave
Kenosha WI 53142
(414) 694-8011
Mgr: John Burke
Skating Dir: Pam Lechler
Ice surfaces: 1, 200x85, Enclosed. *Open:* Year Round. *Ownership:* Private. *Access:* Public. *Sessions:* Public, Private/Club, Rental, Freestyle, Patch, Hockey. *Classes/Lessons:* Group, Private. *Program Affiliation:* ISIA. *Summer School:* Local. *Services:* Skate Rental, Pro Shop, Skate Sharpening, Snack Bar, Dressing Rooms.

Kettle Moraine Ice Center
2330 S. Main St.
West Bend WI 53095
(414) 335-0876
Ice surfaces: 2, 200x85; 200x85, Enclosed, Outdoor/Semi Outdoor. *Open:* Sept.-Apr. *Ownership:* Private. *Access:* Public. *Sessions:* Public, Private/Club, Rental, Freestyle, Patch, Dance, Hockey. *Classes/Lessons:* Group, Private. *Program Affiliation:* ISIA. *Summer School:* No. *Services:* Skate Rental, Skate Sharpening, Snack Bar, Weight Room, Dressing Rooms.

Kingsgate Skating Club
14326 124 Ave
Kirkland WI 98034
(206) 823-1242
Ice surfaces: 1, 200x85, Enclosed. *Open:* Year Round. *Ownership:* Club. *Access:* Members Only. *Sessions:* Private/Club, Rental. *Classes/Lessons:* Group, Private. *Program Affiliation:* ISIA. *Services:* Pro Shop, Skate Rental, Skate Sharpening, Dressing Rooms. *Notes:* Meeting room.

Madison Ice Arena
725 Forward Dr.
Madison WI 53711
(608) 246-4513
Mgr: Ken Grauvogl
Ice surfaces: 2, 100x80; 50x40, Enclosed. *Open:* Oct.-Mar. *Ownership:* Municipal. *Access:* Public. *Clubs:* FSC of Madison. *Sessions:* Public, Private/Club, Rental, Hockey. *Classes/Lessons:* Private, Group. *Program Affiliation:* ISIA, USFSA. *Summer School:* No. *Services:* Pro Shop, Skate Rental, Studio Rink, Snack Bar, Lockers, Dressing Rooms.

Manitowoc Ice Center
1010 S. 8th St.
Manitowoc WI 54220
(414) 683-4530
Mgr: Jeff Beyer
Ice surfaces: 1, 200x85, Enclosed. *Open:* Oct.-Apr. *Ownership:* Municipal. *Access:* Public. *Clubs:* FSC, Youth Hockey. *Sessions:* Public, Private/Club, Rental, Freestyle, Patch, Dance, Hockey. *Classes/Lessons:* Group. *Program Affiliation:* USFSA. *Summer School:* No. *Services:* Pro Shop, Skate Rental, Snack Bar, Dressing Rooms.

Marathon County Multi-Purpose Building Ice Rink
Marathon Park
Wausau WI 54401
(715) 847-5364
Mgr: Al Opall
Ice surfaces: 2, 200x85; 196x83, Enclosed. *Open:* Nov.-Mar. *Ownership:* Municipal. *Access:* Public. *Clubs:* Timberline FSC, Cyclones Hockey Team. *Sessions:* Public, Private/Club, Rental. *Classes/Lessons:* None. *Program Affiliation:* USFSA. *Summer School:* No. *Services:* Skate Rental, Snack Bar, Lockers, Dressing Rooms. *Notes:* Freestyle, group lessons offered through FS club.

Marinette Civic Center
2000 Alice Lane
Marinette WI 54143
(715) 732-0558
Mgr: Kevin Casper
Ice surfaces: 1, 200x100, Enclosed. *Open:* Oct.-Mar. *Ownership:* Municipal. *Access:* Public. *Clubs:* Marinette Menomine Youth Hockey Assn. *Sessions:* Public, Rental, Hockey. *Classes/Lessons:* Group. *Program Affiliation:* USFSA. *Summer School:* No. *Services:* Skate Rental, Skate Sharpening, Snack Bar, Pool and/or Athletic Facilities, Lockers, Dressing Rooms. *Notes:* Indoor tennis court.

Marshfield Youth Ice and Recreation Center
17th St.
Marshfield WI 54449
(715) 384-0025
Mgr: Bruce Lautenschlager
Ice surfaces: 1, 185x85, Enclosed. *Open:* Oct.-Mar. *Ownership:* Youth Hockey Assn. *Access:* Public. *Clubs:* Marshfield Tigers; Marshfield Blades. *Sessions:* Public, Private/Club, Rental, Freestyle, Hockey. *Classes/Lessons:* Private, Group. *Program Affiliation:* Own. *Summer School:* No. *Services:* Snack Bar, Dressing Rooms.

Onalaska Omni Center
255 Riders Club St.
Onalaska WI 54650
(608) 781-9566
FAX: (608) 781-9567
Mgr: Julie Goyette
Ice surfaces: 2, 200x85; 200x85, Outdoor/Semi Outdoor, Enclosed. *Open:* Oct.-Mar. *Ownership:* Municipal. *Access:* Public. *Clubs:* Onalaska Youth Hockey; West Youth Hockey; Lacresent Youth Hockey. *Sessions:* Public, Rental, Hockey. *Classes/Lessons:* None. *Summer School:* No. *Services:* Pro Shop, Skate Rental, Skate Sharpening, Snack Bar, Dressing Rooms.

Petit National Ice Center
500 S. 84th St.
Milwaukee WI 53214
(414) 266-0100
Mgr: Jim Gukzynsai
Skating Dir: Bill Grienke
Ice surfaces: 3, 200x100; 200x100; 400m oval, Enclosed. *Open:* Year Round; oval closed Aug.-Sept. *Ownership:* Municipal. *Access:* Public. *Clubs:* U.S. Olympic training for speed skating; WI FSC. *Sessions:* Public, Private/Club, Rental, Freestyle, Patch, Dance, Hockey. *Classes/Lessons:* Group, Private. *Program Affiliation:* USFSA. *Summer School:* National/International. *Services:* Pro Shop, Skate Rental, Skate Sharpening, Snack Bar, Ballet Room, Weight Room, Lockers, Dressing Rooms.

Reedsburg Ice Arena
1700 8th St.
Reedsburg WI 53959
(608) 524-3037
Mgr: John Brey

Ice surfaces: 1, 190x90, Enclosed. *Open:* Nov.-Mar. *Ownership:* Municipal. *Access:* Public. *Clubs:* Reedsburg Youth Hockey. *Sessions:* Public, Private/Club, Rental, Hockey. *Classes/Lessons:* Group. *Summer School:* No. *Services:* Skate Sharpening, Snack Bar, Dressing Rooms.

Rhinelander Ice Arena
Rhinelander WI 54501
(715) 369-1416
Mgr: Linda Biegel
Ice surfaces: 1, 200x85, Enclosed. *Open:* Oct.-April, 6 weeks in summer. *Ownership:* Private. *Access:* Public. *Clubs:* Rhinelander FSC, Youth Hockey. *Sessions:* Public, Private/Club, Rental, Freestyle, Patch, Dance, Hockey. *Classes/Lessons:* Group, Private. *Program Affiliation:* USFSA. *Services:* Skate Rental, Skate Sharpening, Snack Bar, Lockers, Dressing Rooms.

S.A.R.A. Park Recreation Center
900 Somo Ave.
Tomahawk WI 54487
(715) 453-4040
FAX: (715) 453-2717
Mgr: Paul Garder
Ice surfaces: 1, 200x85, Enclosed. *Open:* Oct.-Mar. *Ownership:* Municipal. *Access:* Public. *Clubs:* Youth Hockey; Tomahawk FSC. *Sessions:* Public, Rental. *Classes/Lessons:* None. *Summer School:* No. *Services:* Skate Sharpening, Snack Bar, Lockers, Dressing Rooms.

Simek Recreation Center
1037 W. Broadway St.
Medford WI 54451
(715) 748-6655; FAX: (715) 748-6658
Mgr: Mike Eckland
Ice surfaces: 1, 200x85, Enclosed. *Open:* Oct.-Mar. *Ownership:* Private. *Access:* Public. *Clubs:* Medford Area Youth Hockey; Medford Area FS Assn. *Sessions:* Public, Private/Club, Rental. *Classes/Lessons:* None. *Summer School:* No. *Services:* Pro Shop, Skate Rental, Skate Sharpening, Snack Bar, Lockers, Dressing Rooms. *Notes:* Freestyle, patch, dance and hockey sessions offered through clubs only.

Sun Prairie Ice Arena
1010 N. Bird St.
Sun Prairie WI 53590
(608) 837-4434
FAX: (608) 825-6674
Mgr: Tony Scheid
Ice surfaces: 1, 190x85, Enclosed. *Open:* June-Mar. *Ownership:* Private. *Access:* Public. *Clubs:* Sun Prairie Youth Hockey. *Sessions:* Public, Rental, Freestyle. *Classes/Lessons:* Group, Private. *Summer School:* National/International. *Services:* Pro Shop, Skate Rental, Skate Sharpening, Snack Bar, Lockers, Dressing Rooms. *Notes:* Summer school is for hockey only.

Telfer Park Sports and Activity Center
2101 Cranston Rd.
Beloit WI 53511
(608) 364-2890
Mgr: Lori Jones
Ice surfaces: 1, 200x85, Outdoor/Semi Outdoor. *Open:* Oct.-Apr. *Ownership:* Municipal. *Access:* Public. *Clubs:* Beloit Youth Hockey Assn. *Sessions:* Public, Private/Club, Rental, Hockey. *Classes/Lessons:* Private, Group. *Summer School:* No. *Services:* Skate Rental, Dressing Rooms, Lockers, Snack Bar.

Tri-County Ice Arena
700 E. Shady Lane Rd.
Neenah WI 54956
(414) 731-9731
Mgr: Searl Packet
Ice surfaces: 2, 200x85; 185x85, Enclosed. *Open:* Oct.-Mar. *Ownership:* Municipal. *Access:* Public. *Clubs:* Fox Valley FSC, Fox Valley Youth Hockey. *Sessions:* Public, Private/Club, Rental, Freestyle, Patch, Hockey. *Classes/Lessons:* Group, Private. *Program Affiliation:* USFSA. *Summer School:* Regional. *Services:* Pro Shop, Skate Rental, Skate Sharpening, Studio Rink, Snack Bar, Lockers.

University of Wisconsin W.H. Hunt Arena
1072 S. Main St.
River Falls WI 54022
(715) 425-3381
Mgr: James Schmidt
Ice surfaces: 1, 200x85, Enclosed. *Open:* Oct.-Mar. *Ownership:* University owned. *Access:* Public. *College/Univ:* University of Wisconsin. *Sessions:* Public, Private/Club, Rental, Hockey. *Classes/Lessons:* Group. *Program Affiliation:* ISIA. *Summer School:* No. *Services:* Skate Rental, Skate Sharpening, Weight Room, Pool and/or Athletic Facilities, Snack Bar, Lockers, Dressing Rooms.

University School of Milwaukee Fieldhouse
2100 W. Fairy Chasm Rd.
Milwaukee WI 53217
(414) 352-6000
FAX: (414) 352-8076
Mgr: Lowell MacDonald
Ice surfaces: 1, 200x95, Enclosed. *Open:* Nov.-Mar. *Ownership:* Private. *Access:* Members Only. School and members of Winter Club. *Clubs:* Winter Club; Youth Hockey; University School of Milwaukee Hockey. *College/Univ:* University School of Milwaukee. *Sessions:* Private/Club, Freestyle, Hockey. *Classes/Lessons:* Group, Private. *Services:* Pro Shop, Skate Sharpening, Snack Bar, Dressing Rooms.

Viroqua Community Arena
856 Nelson Pkwy.
Viroqua WI 54665
(608) 637-8661
Mgr: Brad Tullberg
Ice surfaces: 1, 200x85. *Open:* Oct.-Mar. *Ownership:* Private. *Access:* Public. *Clubs:* Viroqua Ringette Assn.; Viroqua Hockey Assn. *Sessions:* Public, Private/Club, Rental, Freestyle, Hockey. *Classes/Lessons:* Private. *Summer School:* No. *Services:* Skate Rental, Pro Shop, Skate Sharpening, Snack Bar, Lockers, Dressing Rooms.

Waupun Community Center
E. Spring St.
Waupun WI 53963
(414) 324-9918
Mgr: Al Deming
Ice surfaces: 1, 200x85, Enclosed. *Open:* Oct.-March. *Ownership:* Municipal. *Access:* Public. *Clubs:* Waupun FSC, Waupun Hockey Assn. *Sessions:* Public, Private/Club, Freestyle, Patch, Dance, Hockey. *Classes/Lessons:* Private, Group. *Program Affiliation:* USFSA. *Summer School:* No. *Services:* Snack Bar, Lockers, Dressing Rooms.

Wessman Arena
University of Wisconsin at Superior
2701 Catlin Ave.
Superior WI 54880
(715) 394-8361

Mgr: Ed Notner
Ice surfaces: 1, 195x85, Enclosed. *Open:* Oct.-Mar. *Ownership:* Private. *Access:* Public. *Clubs:* Superior FSC. *College/Univ:* University of Wisconsin, Superior. *Sessions:* Public, Private/Club, Rental, Freestyle, Patch, Hockey. *Classes/Lessons:* Group, Private. *Program Affiliation:* USFSA. *Summer School:* No. *Services:* Skate Rental, Snack Bar, Weight Room, Lockers, Dressing Rooms. *Notes:* Outdoor track.

Willett (K. B.) Arena
1000 Minnesota Ave
Stevens Point WI 54481
(715) 346-1576
Mgr: Don Butkowski
Skating Dir: Lynda Schrader
Ice surfaces: 1, 200x85, Enclosed. *Open:* Oct.-June. *Ownership:* Municipal. *Access:* Public. *Clubs:* Crystal Ice FSC, Grand Masters Silver Blades. *College/Univ:* University of Wisconsin, Stevens Point. *Sessions:* Public, Private/Club, Rental, Freestyle, Patch, Hockey. *Classes/Lessons:* Group, Private. *Program Affiliation:* ISIA. *Summer School:* No. *Services:* Skate Rental, Pro Shop, Skate Sharpening, Snack Bar, Weight Room, Lockers, Dressing Rooms, Ballet Room.

Wilson Park Recreation Center
4001 S. 20th St.
Milwaukee WI 53221
(414) 281-6289
Mgr: Joe Kershasky
Ice surfaces: 1, 200x85, Enclosed. *Open:* Year Round. *Ownership:* Municipal. *Access:* Public. *Clubs:* Greater Milwaukee FSC. *College/Univ:* Markette Univ. *Sessions:* Public, Private/Club, Rental, Freestyle. *Classes/Lessons:* Private, Group. *Program Affiliation:* USFSA. *Summer School:* Local. *Services:* Skate Sharpening, Snack Bar, Lockers, Dressing Rooms, Pool and/or Athletic Facilities, Skate Rental.

WV: WEST VIRGINIA

Charleston Civic Center Ice Arena
200 Civic Center Dr.
Charleston WV 25301
(304) 345-1500
Mgr: Doug Carte
Ice surfaces: 1, 164x59, Enclosed. *Open:* Sept.-Apr. *Ownership:* Municipal. *Access:* Public. *Clubs:* Charleston FSC. *Sessions:* Public, Private/Club, Rental, Freestyle, Patch, Dance, Hockey. *Classes/Lessons:* Group, Private. *Program Affiliation:* USFSA, ISIA. *Summer School:* No. *Services:* Skate Rental, Skate Sharpening, Snack Bar.

Greenbriar Resort
Rt. 60 West
White Sulphur Springs WV 24986
(304) 536-1110
Mgr: Cyndi Bennet
Ice surfaces: 1, 100x40, Outdoor/Semi Outdoor. *Open:* Nov.-Mar. *Ownership:* Private. *Access:* Restricted. *Restrictions:* Guests and members only. *Sessions:* Private/Club. *Classes/Lessons:* Group. *Program Affiliation:* Own. *Services:* Skate Rental, Snack Bar, Weight Room, Pool and/or Athletic Facilities, Lockers, Dressing Rooms.

Morgantown Municipal Rink
Mississippi St.
Morgantown WV 26505
(304) 292-6865
Mgr: Mark Wise
Ice surfaces: 1, 200x85, Outdoor/Semi Outdoor. *Open:* Sept.-Mar. *Ownership:* Municipal. *Access:* Public. *Clubs:* Mason Dixon FSC. *College/Univ:* West Virginia University. *Sessions:* Public, Private/Club, Rental, Hockey. *Program Affiliation:* USFSA, ISIA. *Summer School:* No. *Services:* Pro Shop, Skate Rental, Skate Sharpening, Snack Bar, Dressing Rooms, Lockers. *Notes:* Freestyle sessions are offered through the club only.

Wheeling Park Memorial Ice Rink
1801 National Rd.
Wheeling WV 26003
(304) 242-3770
Mgr: Rico Coville
Ice surfaces: 1, 200x85, Outdoor/Semi Outdoor. *Open:* Nov.-Feb. *Ownership:* Municipal. *Access:* Public. *Clubs:* Wheeling Amateur Hockey Assn.; Wheeling FSC. *Sessions:* Public, Private/Club, Freestyle, Hockey. *Classes/Lessons:* Private, Group. *Program Affiliation:* ISIA, USFSA. *Summer School:* No. *Services:* Pro Shop, Skate Rental, Skate Sharpening, Snack Bar, Pool and/or Athletic Facilities, Dressing Rooms, Lockers.

WY: WYOMING

Casper Ice Arena
1801 E. 4th St.
Casper WY 82601
(307) 235-8484
FAX: (307) 235-8386
Mgr: Mark Mann
Ice surfaces: 1, 200x85, Enclosed. *Open:* Aug.-June. *Ownership:* Municipal. *Access:* Public. *Clubs:* Casper FSC, Capser Amateur Hockey Assn. *Sessions:* Public, Private/Club, Rental, Freestyle, Patch, Hockey. *Classes/Lessons:* Group, Private. *Program Affiliation:* USFSA, ISIA. *Summer School:* Local. *Services:* Pro Shop, Skate Rental, Skate Sharpening, Snack Bar, Ballet Room, Weight Room, Lockers, Dressing Rooms.

Family Recreation Center
3900 Sweetwater Dr.
Rock Springs WY 82901
(307) 382-3265
Mgr: Ken Reed
Ice surfaces: 1, 185x85, Enclosed. *Open:* Sept.-Apr. *Ownership:* Municipal. *Access:* Public. *Clubs:* Sweetwater FSC. *Sessions:* Public, Private/Club, Rental, Patch, Freestyle, Dance, Hockey. *Classes/Lessons:* Group, Private. *Program Affiliation:* ISIA. *Summer School:* No. *Services:* Pro Shop, Skate Rental, Skate Sharpening, Snack Bar, Ballet Room, Weight Room, Pool and/or Athletic Facilities, Lockers, Dressing Rooms.

Snow King Center at Snow King Resort
100 E. Snow King Ave.
Jackson WY 83001
(307) 733-5200
Mgr: Robert Carrenth
Skating Dir: Ron & Julie Barnett
Ice surfaces: 1, 200x85, Enclosed. *Open:* Oct.-May. *Ownership:* Private. *Access:* Public. *Clubs:* Jackson FSC. *Sessions:* Public, Private/Club, Rental, Freestyle, Patch, Dance, Hockey. *Classes/Lessons:* Group, Private. *Program Affiliation:* USFSA, ISIA. *Summer School:* No. *Services:* Skate Rental, Pro Shop, Skate Sharpening, Snack Bar, Lockers, Dressing Rooms.

Finding Rinks in Canada

While we are unable to include Canadian rinks in the *Skater's Edge Sourcebook*, we thought it might be helpful to include information on how to reach the section offices of the Canadian Figure Skating Association (CFSA). If you are interested in skating in Canada, contact the office nearest to where you will be staying; they should be able to help you find an ice rink.

For information on skating rinks in other countries, contact the skating association or federation for that country. (See the *Associations* and *Federations* chapters.)

HEADQUARTERS:

CANADIAN FIGURE SKATING ASSOCIATION
1600 James Naismith Drive
Gloucester, Ontario
K1B 5N4 Canada
(613) 748-5635
FAX: (613) 748-5718

SECTION OFFICES:

ALBERTA
Jennifer Byrne
AB Section Office
11759 Groat Road
Edmonton, AB
T5M 3K6
(403) 453-8505
FAX: (403) 427-1734

BRITISH COLUMBIA
Wendy Martin
BC Section Office
#206-1367 West Broadway Street
Vancouver, BC
(604) 737-3095
FAX: (604) 737-6832

MANITOBA
Jamie McGrigor
MB Section Office
200 Main Street
Winnipeg, MB
R3C 4M2
(204) 985-4064
FAX: (204) 985-4028

NEW BRUNSWICK
André Bourgeois
NB Section Office
P.O. Box 1297
Station A
Fredericton, NB
E3B 1K3
(506) 451-1321
FAX: (506) 451-1325

NEWFOUNDLAND
Marion Jeans
NF Section Office
P.O. Box 21029
St. John's, NF
A1A 5B2
(709) 576-0509
FAX: (709) 576-8787

NOVA SCOTIA
Michele Dorman
NS Section Office
Box 3010
S. Halifax, NS
B3J 3G6
(902) 425-5450
FAX: (902) 425-5606

ONTARIO FIGURE SKATING ASSOCIATION
Danielle Caldana
Program Coordinator
1185 Eglinton Ave East, Suite 302
North York, Ontario
M3C 3C6
(416) 426-7017
FAX: (416) 426-7389

PRINCE EDWARD ISLAND
Julie McNeil
Day's Corner
Wellington, PEI
C0B 2E0
(902) 854-2073

QUEBEC
Diane Choquet
QC Section Office
4545 Pierre de Coubertin
Montreal, QC
H1V 3R2
(514) 252-3073
FAX: (514) 252-3170

SASKATCHEWAN
Susan Patryluk
SK Section Office
2205 Victoria Avenue
Regina, SK
S4P 0S4
(306) 780-9423
FAX: (306) 525-4009

Rinks: Cross Reference
by State and City

Following is a cross-reference listing of rinks, in alphabetical order first by state, then by city. For complete rink information, look up the rink in the main listings section, page 135.

AK: ALASKA

Anchorage: *Anchorage Sports Center Ice Rink*, (907) 786-1232.

Anchorage: *Boeke (Ben) Ice Arena*, (907) 274-2715.

Anchorage: *Dempsey-Anderson Arena*, (907) 277-7571.

Anchorage: *Dimond Center Ice Capades Chalet*, (907) 344-1212.

Eagle River: *Fire Lake Recreation Center*, (907) 696-0050.

Fairbanks: *Big Dipper Ice Rink*, (907) 459-1104.

Fairbanks: *Patty Center Ice Arena*, (907) 474-6888.

Nikiski: *Peterson (Jason) Memorial Ice Rink*, (907) 776-8472.

Soldotna: *Central Peninsula Sports Center*, (907) 262-3151.

Wasilla: *Brett Memorial Ice Arena*, (907) 376-9260.

AL: ALABAMA

Birmingham: *Alpine Ice Arena*, (205) 942-0223.

Decatur: *Point Mallard Ice Rink*, (205) 355-9817.

Huntsville: *Wilcoxon (Benton H.) Municipal Iceplex*, (205) 883-3774.

Montgomery: *Eastdale Ice Palace*, (205) 272-7225.

AR: ARKANSAS

Little Rock: *Little Rock Skating Arena*, (501) 227-4333.

AZ: ARIZONA

Flagstaff: *Flagstaff Municipal Ice Arena*, (602) 774-1051.

Flagstaff: *Lively (Jay) Activity Center*, (602) 774-1051.

Phoenix: *Ice Palace Arena*, (602) 267-0591.

Tempe: *Oceanside Ice Arena*, (602) 941-0944.

CA: CALIFORNIA

Anaheim: *Glacial Garden Ice Arena*, (714) 502-9197.

Belmont: *Belmont Iceland*, (415) 592-0532.

Berkeley: *Berkeley Iceland*, (510) 843-8801.

Blue Jay: *Blue Jay Ice Castles*, (909) 336-2111.

Burbank: *Pickwick Ice Arena*, (818) 846-0035.

Costa Mesa: *Costa Mesa Ice Chalet*, (714) 979-8880.

Culpertino: *Ice Chalet Vallco Fashion Park*, (408) 446-2908.

Culver City: *Culver Ice Arena*, (310) 398-5719.

Dublin: *Dublin Iceland*, (510) 829-4445.

Escondido: *Ice Floe Ice Center*, (619) 489-5550.

Fremont: *Iceoplex Fremont*, (510) 490-6621.

Fresno: *Icelandia Fresno*, (209) 275-1119.

Harbor City: *Skating Edge, Inc.*, (310) 325-4475.

Huntington Beach: *Side By Side Ice Skating Rink*, (714) 842-9143.

Lake Arrowhead: *Ice Castles International Training Center*, (909) 336-4085.

Long Barn: *Long Barn Ice Arena*, (209) 586-0753.

N. Hollywood: *North Hollywood Ice Chalet*, (818) 985-5555.

Newbury Park: *Conejo Valley Ice Center*, (805) 498-6660.

North Hills: *Iceoplex North Hills*, (818) 893-1784.

Norwalk: *Norwalk Ice Arena*, (310) 921-5391.

Ontario: *Ontario Ice Skating Center*, (909) 986-0793.

Palm Desert: *Ice Chalet Palm Desert*, (619) 340-4412.

Palo Alto: *Winter Lodge, The*, (415) 493-4566.

Pasadena: *Pasadena Ice Skating Center*, (818) 578-0801.

Redwood City: *Golden Gate Ice Arena*, (415) 364-8091.

Rolling Hills Estates: *Ice Chalet Rolling Hills*, (310) 541-6630.

Sacramento: *Paramount Iceland Arena*, (916) 925-3529.

San Diego: *Ice Chalet San Diego*, (619) 452-9110.

San Diego: *San Diego Ice Arena*, (619) 530-1826.

San Jose: *Eastridge Ice Arena*, (408) 238-0440.

San Jose: *Ice Centre of San Jose*, (408) 279-6000.

San Mateo: *Ice Chalet San Mateo*, (415) 574-1616.

Santa Rosa: *Redwood Empire Ice Arena*, (707) 546-7147.

Squaw Valley: *Squaw Valley USA*, (916) 581-5518.

Stockton: *Oak Park Ice Arena*, (209) 937-7432.

Van Nuys: *Van Nuys Iceland*, (818) 785-2171.

Yosemite National Park: *Yosemite Concession Services Rink*, (209) 372-1418.

CO: COLORADO

Arvada: *North Jeffco Ice Arena*, (303) 421-1786.

CO: COLORADO (Continued)

Aspen: *Aspen Ice Garden* , (303) 920-5141.

Boulder: *University of Colorado Ice Arena*, (303) 492-7678.

Colorado Springs: *Air Force Academy Ice Arena*, (719) 472-4032.

Colorado Springs: *Broadmoor World Arena*. Demolished 4/94; new rink under construction.

Colorado Springs: *Sertich (Mark "Pa") Ice Center*, (719) 578-6883.

Crested Butte: *Crested Butte Ice Rink*, (303) 349-5338.

Denver: *Pioneer Ice Arena*, (303) 758-8019.

Denver: *University of Denver Ice Arena*, (303) 871-3905.

Ft. Collins: *Edora Pool Ice Center*, (303) 221-6679.

Keystone: *Keystone Resort Ice Rink*, (303) 468-4245.

Littleton: *South Suburban Ice Arena*, (303) 798-7881.

Pueblo: *Pueblo Plaza Ice Arena*, (719) 542-8784.

Steamboat Springs: *Howelsen Ice Rink*, (303) 879-0341.

Vail: *Dobson (John A.) Arena*, (303) 479-2271.

Westminster: *Hyland Hills Ice Arena*, (303) 650-7552.

CT: CONNECTICUT

Avon: *Fairchild (Jennings) Rink*, (203) 673-3201.

Bolton: *Bolton Ice Palace*, (203) 646-7851.

Bridgeport: *Wonderland of Ice*, (203) 576-8110.

Cromwell: *Tri-Town Sports Center*, (203) 632-0323.

Darien: *Darien Ice Rink*, (203) 655-8251.

East Haven: *East Haven Veterans Memorial Ice Rink*, (203) 468-3367.

Enfield: *Enfield Twin Rinks*, (203) 745-2461.

Greenwich: *Greenwich Skating Club*, (203) 622-9583.

Greenwich: *Hamill (Dorothy) Skating Rink*, (203) 531-8560.

Hamden: *Hamden Community Ice Rink*, (203) 287-2610.

Kent: *Nadal Rink*, (203) 927-3501.

Lakeville: *Schmidt Ice Rink*, (203) 435-2591.

Middletown: *Wesleyan Arena-Freeman Athletic Center*, (203) 685-2927.

Milford: *Milford Ice Pavilion*, (203) 878-6516.

New Canaan: *New Canaan Winter Club*, (203) 966-4280.

New Haven: *Inglass Rink*, (203) 432-0877.

New London: *Dayton Arena*, (203) 439-2575.

New Milford: *Draddy Arena at Canterbury High School*, (203) 355-3103.

Pomfret: *Brown Rink*, (203) 928-7731.

Ridgefield: *Ridgefield Skating Center*, (203) 438-5277.

Salisbury: *Salisbury School*, (203) 435-9658.

Simsbury: *International Skating Center of Connecticut*, (203) 651-5400.

Simsbury: *Westminster School Ice Arena*, (203) 658-4444.

South Kent: *South Kent School Arena*, (203) 927-4896.

South Windsor: *South Windsor Arena*, (208) 289-3401.

Stanford: *Conners (Terry) Ice Rink*, (203) 977-4514.

Storrs: *University of Connecticut Ice Rink*, (203) 486-3808.

W. Simsbury: *Simsbury Farms Recreation Complex Ice Rink*, (203) 658-3836.

Wallingford: *Choate-Rosemary Hall ice Rink*, (203) 697-2000.

Wallingford: *Remson Hockey Ice Rink*, (203) 697-2000.

Washington: *Gunnery School*, (203) 868-2176.

Watertown: *Taft SchoolMays Rink*, (203) 274-2516.

West Hartford: *Kingswood-Oxford School Rink*, (203) 233-9631.

West Hartford: *Veterans Memorial Skating Rink*, (203) 521-1573.

West Haven: *Bennett (Edward L.) Skating Rink*, (203) 932-1461.

Windsor: *Loomis-Chaffee School Ice Rink*, (203) 688-4934.

DC: DISTRICT OF COLUMBIA

Washington, DC: *Fort Dupont*, (202) 584-3040.

Washington, DC: *Sculpture Garden Ice Rink*, (202) 371-5340.

DE: DELAWARE

Newark: *University of Delaware Arena*, (302) 831-6038.

Wilmington: *Skating Club of Wilmington, Inc.*, (302) 656-5007.

FL: FLORIDA

Clearwater: *Centre Ice Countryside Mall*, (813) 796-0586.

Clearwater: *Sun Blades Ice Rink*, (813) 536-5843.

Jacksonville: *Skate World, Inc.*, (904) 399-3223.

Lakeland: *Lakeland Civic Center*, (813) 499-8110.

Miami Beach: *Rakow (Scott) Youth Center Ice Rink*, (305) 673-7767.

Nokomis: *Ice Chateau, Inc.*, (813) 484-0080.

North Miami Beach: *Miami Ice Arena, Inc.*, (305) 940-8222.

Oldsmar: *Tampa Bay Skating Academy*, (813) 854-4009.

Orlando: *Orlando Ice Skating Palace*, (407) 294-5419.

Orlando: *Rock On Ice*, (407) 352-4043.

Pompano Beach: *Gold Coast Ice Arena*, (305) 943-1437.

Sunrise: *Sunrise Ice Skating Center*, (305) 741-2366.

GA: GEORGIA

Duluth: *Atlanta Iceplex*, (404) 813-1010.

Marietta: *Parkaire Ice Arena*, (404) 973-0753.

HI: HAWAII
Honolulu: *Ice Palace*, (808) 487-9921.

IA: IOWA
Ames: *Ames/Iowa State University Ice Arena*, (515) 292-6835.
Davenport: *Quad City Sports Center*, (319) 322-5220.
Dubuque: *Dubuque Five Flags Center*, (319) 589-4254.
Mason City: *North Iowa Ice Arena*, (515) 424-3547.
Sioux City: *Sioux City Municipal Auditorium*, (712) 279-4800.
Urbandale: *Metro Ice Sports Arena*, (515) 278-9757.
Waterloo: *Young Arena*, (319) 291-4491.

ID: IDAHO
Idaho Falls: *Marmo (Joe) and Wayne Lehto Ice Arena*, (208) 529-1479.
Sun Valley: *Sun Valley Skating Center*, (208) 622-2194.

IL: ILLINOIS
Barrington: *Barrington Ice Arena*, (708) 381-9702.
Bridgeview: *Saints Spectrum*, (708) 598-3738.
Carol Stream: *Stream (Carol) Ice Rink*, (708) 682-4480.
Champaign: *University of Illinois Arena*, (217) 333-2212.
Chicago: *McFetridge Sports Center*, (312) 478-0210.
Chicago: *University of IL at Chicago Auxiliary Practice Ice Rink*, (312) 413-5300.
Crestwood: *Southwest Ice Arena*, (708) 371-1344.
Crystal Lake: *Crystal Ice House*, (815) 356-8500.
Danville: *Palmer (David S.) Civic Center*, (217) 431-2424.
Decatur: *Decatur Civic Center*, (217) 422-7300.
Downers Grove: *Downers Grove Ice Arena*, (708) 971-3780.
East Dundee: *Polar Dome Ice Arena*, (708) 426-6753.
Evanston: *Crown (Robert) Ice Center*, (708) 328-9401.
Franklin Park: *Franklin Park Ice Arena*, (708) 671-4268.
Glen Ellyn: *Center Ice of Du Page*, (708) 790-9696.
Glen Ellyn: *Glen Ellyn Ice Skating School*, (708) 469-5770.
Glencoe: *Watts Ice Center - Glencoe Park District*, (708) 835-4440.
Glenview: *Glenview Ice Arena*, (708) 724-2800.
Granite City: *Granite City Park Ice Rink*, (618) 877-2549.
Highland Park: *Centennial Ice Arena*, (708) 432-4790.
Homewood: *Homewood Flossmoor Ice Arena*, (708) 957-0100.
Joliet: *Inwood Ice Arena*, (815) 741-7275.
Lake Forest: *MacKenzie Ice Arena*, (708) 234-3210.
Lake Forest: *Winter Club of Lake Forest*, (708) 234-0030.
Naperville: *All Seasons Twin Ice Rinks*, (708) 851-0755.
Niles: *Iceland*, (708) 297-8011.
Northbrook: *Northbrook Sports Center*, (708) 291-2980.
Oak Park: *Ridgeland Common*, (708) 848-9661.
Oaklawn: *Oaklawn Ice Arena*, (708) 857-2210.
Park Ridge: *Oakton Ice Arena*, (708) 692-3359.
Pekin: *Memorial Arena - Pekin Park District*, (309) 346-1240.
Peoria: *Owens Recreation Center*, (309) 686-3368.
Rockford: *Riverview Ice House*, (815) 963-7465.
Rolling Meadows: *Rolling Meadows Ice Arena*, (708) 818-3210.
Skokie: *Skatium*, (708) 674-1510.
Springfield: *Nelson (Franklin) Center*, (217) 753-2800.
Wilmette: *Centennial Ice Rink*, (708) 256-6100.
Winnetka: *Winnetka Ice Arena*, (708) 501-2060.
Woodridge: *Seven Bridges Ice Arena*, (708) 271-4423.
Zion: *Zion Ice Arena*, (708) 746-5503.

IN: INDIANA
Bloomington: *Southern (Frank) Center Ice Arena*, (812) 331-6465.
Carmel: *Carmel Ice Skatium*, (317) 844-8889.
Columbus: *Lincoln Center Ice Arena*, (812) 376-2686.
Evansville: *Swonder Ice Rink*, (812) 479-0989.
Fort Wayne: *Allen County War Memorial Coliseum*, (219) 482-9502.
Ft. Wayne: *Ice Rink on the Terrace*, (219) 484-2014.
Ft. Wayne: *McMillen Ice Arena*, (219) 744-0848.
Indianapolis: *Indiana State Fair Coliseum*, (317) 927-7622.
Indianapolis: *Indiana World Skating Academy*, (317) 237-5565.
Indianapolis: *Indianapolis Pepsi Coliseum*, (317) 927-7536.
Indianapolis: *Perry Park Ice Rink*, (317) 888-0070.
Mishawaka: *Merrifield Complex*, (219) 258-1664.
Notre Dame: *Notre Dame Ice Arena*, (219) 631-5247.
South Bend: *Howard Park Ice Rink*, (219) 235-9451.
South Bend: *Ice Box*, (219) 288-3300.

KS: KANSAS
Overland Park: *Ice Chateau of King Louie West*, (913) 648-0130.
Witchita: *Kansas Coliseum*, (316) 755-1243.

KY: KENTUCKY
Crescent Springs: *All Seasons Ice Center*, (606) 344-1981.
Lexington: *Lexington Ice Arena*, (606) 269-5681.
Louisville: *Alpine Ice Arena*, (502) 459-9500.

KY: KENTUCKY (Continued)
Owensboro: *Owensboro Ice Arena*, (502) 687-8720.

LA: LOUISIANA
Baton Rouge: *Riverside Centroplex*, (504) 389- 3030.

MA: MASSACHUSETTS
Amherst: *Mullens (William D.) Memorial Center*, (413) 545-4770.

Amherst: *Orr Rink*, (413) 542-7950.

Andover: *Sumner Smith Hockey Rink*, (508) 475-3400.

Arlington: *Veterans Memorial Rink*, (617) 641-5492.

Auburn: *Hogan Arena*, (508) 832-5932.

Auburn: *Horgan (Daniel S.) Memorial Rink*, (508) 832-5932.

Belmont: *Belmont Skating Rink*, (617) 489-8245.

Belmont: *Keller Rink - Claflin Athletic Center*, (617) 484-6178.

Billerica: *Hallenborg Memorial Pavillion*, (508) 436-9300.

Boston: *Brown (Walter) Arena*, (617) 353-4632.

Boston: *Clark Athletic Center Ice Rink*, (617) 287-7801.

Boston: *Matthews Arena at Northeastern University*, (617) 373-3377.

Boston: *Steriti Memorial Rink*, (617) 523-9327.

Bourne: *Gallo (John B.) Ice Arena*, (508) 759-8904.

Boxborough: *Nashoba Valley Olympia*, (508) 263-3020.

Brighton: *Daly Memorial Rink*, (617) 527-1741.

Brighton: *Reilly Memorial Rink*, (617) 277-7822.

Brighton: *Skating Club of Boston*, (617) 782-5900.

Brockton: *Asiaf Arena*, (508) 583-6804.

Brookline: *Anderson Park Skating Rink*, (617) 730-2080.

Brookline: *Dexter Rink*, (617) 524-9377.

Burlington: *Burlington Ice Palace*, (617) 272-9517.

Byfield: *Governor Dummer Academy Rink*, (508) 462-6643.

Cambridge: *Bright Hockey Center*, (617) 495-7541.

Cambridge: *Browne & Nichols Skating Rink*, (617) 864-8668.

Cambridge: *MIT Skating Rink - Johnson Athletic Center*, (617) 253-4497.

Cambridge: *Simoni (Romano) Skating Rink*, (617) 354-9523.

Canton: *Canton Metropolis Skating Rink*, (617) 821-5032.

Charlestown: *O'Neill (Emmons Horrigan) Memorial Rink*, (617) 242-9728.

Chesnut Hill: *Boston College Ice Rink*, (617) 552-8000.

Concord: *Pratt (Frederick) Memorial Rink*, (508) 369-2550.

Dedham: *Nobel & Greenough School Ice Rink*, (617) 326-3700.

Deerfield: *Deerfield Academy Skating Rink*, (413) 772-0241.

East Hampton: *Lossone Ice Rink - Williston Academy*, (413) 527-1520.

East Boston: *Porazzo (Lt. Lewis) Skating Arena*, (617) 567-9571.

Everett: *Veteran's Memorial Ice Rink*, (617) 389-9401.

Fall River: *Driscoll (Arthur R.) Memorial Skating Rink*, (508) 679-3274.

Falmouth: *Falmouth Ice Arena*, (508) 548-7080.

Fitchburg: *Wallace Civic Center Complex*, (508) 345-7593.

Framingham: *Loring (E. F.) Arena*, (508) 620-4876.

Franklin: *Franklin Arena*, (508) 541-7024.

Franklin: *Veterans Memorial Arena*, (508) 541- 7024.

Gardner: *Gardner Veterans Skating Rink*, (508) 632-7329.

Gloucester: *Talbot (Dorothy M.) Memorial Rink*, (508) 281-9856.

Greenfield: *Collins Moylan Memorial Skating Rink*, (413) 772-6891.

Greenfield: *Greenfield Skating Arena*, (413) 772-6891.

Groton: *Lawrence Academy Ice Rink*, (508) 448-2239.

Groton: *Pratt Rink at Groton School*, (508) 448-3363.

Haverhill: *Veteran's Memorial Ice Rink*, (508) 373-9351.

Hingham: *Pilgrim Skating Arena*, (617) 749-6660.

Hyannis: *Kennedy (Joseph P.) Jr. Memorial Skating Rink*, (508) 790-6346.

Hyde Park: *Bajko (Alexander) Memorial Skating Rink*, (617) 364-9188.

Lexington: *Hayden Recreation Center Ice Facility*, (617) 862-5575.

Lowell: *Janas (John J.) Memorial Skating Rink*, (508) 454-6662.

Lynn: *Connery (Lynn) Memorial Rink*, (617) 599-9474.

Marion: *Talsor Academy Skating Rink*, (508) 748-2000.

Marlboro: *Navin (John J.) Rink*, (508) 481-5252.

Medford: *LoConte Memorial SkatingRink*, (617) 395-9594.

Methuen: *Methuen High Skating Rink*, (508) 687-8008.

Milton: *Roberts (James) Ice Rink at Milton Academy*, (617) 698-7800.

Milton: *Ulin Memorial Rink*, (617) 696-9869.

Mount Herman: *McCollum Ice Arena - Northfield School*, (413) 498-3000.

Natick: *West Suburban Arena*, (508) 655-1013.

Needham: *St. Sebastian's Ice Skating Rink*, (617) 449-5208.

Neponset: *Devine (Robert M.) Rink*, (617) 436-4356.

New Bedford: *Hetland (Stephen) Memorial Skating Rink*, (508) 999-9051.

Newburyport: *Graf (Henry Jr.) Rink*, (508) 462-8112.

North Adams: *Vietnam Veterans Memorial Rink*, (413) 664-9474.

North Andover: *Brooks School Rink*, (508) 686-6101.

North Andover: *Volpe (St. Peter) Complex*, (508) 837-5295.

North Billerica: *Tully Forum - University of Massachusetts, Lowell*, (508) 934-4987.

Oak Bluffs: *Martha's Vineyard Arena*, (508) 693-4438.

Orleans: *Moore (Charles) Arena*, (508) 255-5902.

Peabody: *McVann - O'Keefe Memorial Rink*, (508) 535-2110.

Pembroke: *Hobomock Ice Arena*, (617) 294-0260.

Pittsfield: *Pittsfield Boys & Girls Club Skating Arena*, (413) 447-9380.

Plymouth: *Armstrong (John) Memorial Skating Rink*, (800) 273-7776.

Quincy: *Quincy Youth Arena*, (617) 479-8371.

Quincy: *Shea Memorial Rink*, (617) 472-9325.

Randolph: *Randolph Ice Arena*, (617) 961-4053.

Revere: *Cronin Memorial Rink*, (617) 284-9491.

Rockland: *Rockland Rink*, (617) 878-5591.

Salem: *O'Keefe Rink at Salem State College*, (508) 741-6560.

Saugus: *Hockeytown USA Inc.*, (617) 233-3667.

Saugus: *Kasabuski Arena*, (617) 231-4183.

Sheffield: *Berkshire School*, (413) 229-8511.

Somerville: *Veterans Memorial Rink*, (617) 623-3523.

South Boston: *Murphy (Frances Al) Memorial Skating Rink*, (617) 269-7060.

South Dennis: *Kent (Tony) Arena*, (508) 760-2415.

South Hamilton: *Johnson (H. Alden) Rink*, (508) 468-6232.

South Hamilton: *Johnson Rink - Pingree School*, (508) 468-6232.

Southboro: *Gardner Ice Rink*, (508) 485-0050.

Springfield: *CYR Arena - Forest Park*, (413) 787-6438.

Springfield: *Smead (Ray) Ice Arena*, (413) 787-6453.

Stoneham: *Stoneham Arena*, (617) 279-2628.

Taunton: *Aleixo (Theodore) Skating Rink*, (508) 824-4987.

Waltham: *Veterans Memorial Rink*, (617) 893-9409.

Watertown: *Ryan (John A.) Skating Arena*, (617) 972-6468.

Wellesley: *Babson Recreation Center*, (617) 239-6050.

West Concord: *Minute Man School Skating Rink*, (508) 649-6391.

West Roxbury: *Bryan Memorial Skating Rink*, (617) 323-9512.

West Springfield: *Olympia Skate and Roller Center*, (413) 736-8100.

Westboro: *North Star Youth Forum*, (508) 366-1562.

Weymouth: *Connell Memorial Rink*, (617) 335-2090.

Williamstown: *Williams College, Lausing Chapman Rink*, (413) 597-2283.

Wilmington: *Ristuccia (Eleanor M.) Memorial Arena*, (508) 657-3976.

Winchendon: *Clark Memorial Arena*, (508) 297-0102.

Wintrop: *Larsen Ice Skating Facility*, (617) 846-5700.

Woburn: *O'Brian Ice Rink*, (617) 938-1620.

Worcester: *Hart Recreation Center Ice Rink*, (508) 793-3407.

Worcester: *Worcester State Rink*, (508) 755-0582.

MD: MARYLAND

Annapolis: *Dahlgren Hall Ice Rink*, (410) 263-4527.

Baltimore: *Mt. Pleasant Ice Arena*, (410) 444-1888.

Baltimore: *Northwest Family Sports Center, Inc.*, (410) 433-4970.

Bowie: *Bowie Ice Arena*, (301) 805-7990.

Chevy Chase: *Chevy Chase Club Inc.*, (301) 652-4100.

College Park: *Wells (Herbert) Ice Rink*, (301) 277-3717.

Columbia: *Columbia Ice Rink*, (410) 730-0322.

Easton: *Talbot County Community Center*, (410) 822-7070.

Fort Washington: *Tucker Road Ice Arena*, (301) 248-3124.

Frederick: *Frederick Fort & Ice Arena*, (301) 662-7362.

Millersville: *Benfield Pines Ice Rink*, (410) 987-5100.

Ocean City: *Carousel Hotel Ice Rink*, (410) 524-1000.

Odenton: *Piney Orchard Ice Arena*, (410) 621-7992.

Rockville: *Cabin John Ice Rink*, (301) 365-2246.

Wheaton: *Wheaton Ice Rink*, (301) 649-2703.

ME: MAINE

Ashland: *Ashland Area Recreational Ice Rink*, (207) 435-6893.

Auburn: *City of Auburn Ice Arena*, (207) 795-6375.

Auburn: *City Parks & Recreation Dept.*, (207) 784-0191.

Bangor: *City Parks & Recreation*, (207) 947-1018.

Bangor: *Sawyer Ice Arena*, (207) 947-0071.

Bethel: *Sunday River Ski Resort*, (207) 824-3000.

Biddeford: *Biddeford Ice Arena*, (207) 283-0615.

Brunswick: *Dayton Arena*, (207) 725-3332.

Hallowell: *Kennebec Ice Arena*, (207) 622-6354.

Hebron: *Robinson Arena at Hebron Academy*, (207) 966-2812.

Lewiston: *Central Maine Civic Center*, (207) 783-2009.

Millinocket: *Thibodiau (Marc) Memorial Rink*, (207) 723-7013.

North Bridgeton: *Bridgeton Academy Ice Arena*, (207) 647-3322.

Orono: *Alfond Ice Arena, University of Maine - Orono*, (207) 581-1106.

Portland: *Cumberland County Civic Center*, (201) 775-3481.

Portland: *Portland Ice Arena*, (207) 774-8553.

Presque Isle: *Forum, The*, (207) 764-0491.

Van Buren: *Van Buren Ice Rink*, (207) 868-3395.

Waterville: *Alfond Arena*, (207) 872-3000.

ME: MAINE (Continued)

Winslow: *Sukee Arena and Events Center*, (207) 872-5994.

Yarmouth: *North Yarmouth Academy Ice Arena*, (207) 846-9051.

MI: MICHIGAN

Adrian: *Adrian Ice Rink*, (517) 265-8675.

Alpena: *Mich - E - Kewis Ice Rink*, (517) 354-8191.

Ann Arbor: *Buhr Park Ice Rink*, (313) 994-2784.

Ann Arbor: *Veterans Ice Arena*, (313) 994-2785.

Ann Arbor: *Yost Ice Arena - University of Michigan*, (313) 764-4599.

Battle Creek: *The Rink*, (616) 966-3625.

Berkley: *Berkley Ice Arena*, (810) 546-2460.

Big Rapids: *Ewigleben (Robert L.) Ice Arena*, (616) 592-2881.

Birmingham: *Birmingham Ice Sports Arena*, (313) 654-0731.

Bloomfield Hills: *Detroit Skating Club*, (810) 332-7133.

Cheboygan: *Cheboygan Ice Rink/Pavillion*, (616) 627-3255.

Dearborn: *Adray (Mike) Sports Arena*, (313) 943-4098.

Dearborn: *University of Michigan Dearborn Arena*, (313) 593-5540.

Detroit: *Adams (Jack) Arena*, (313) 935-4510.

Detroit: *City Sports Center Ice Rink*, (313) 567-2423.

Detroit: *Grosse Pointe Community Rink*, (313) 885-4100.

Detroit: *Heilmann Recreation Center*, (313) 267-7153.

East Lansing: *Munn Ice Arena*, (517) 353-4698.

Escanaba: *Wells Sports Complex*, (906) 786-3995.

Flint: *Flint Four Seasons Sport Center*, (313) 635-8487.

Flint: *I. M. A. Ice Arena*, (810) 744-0580.

Fraser: *Fraser Ice Arenas*, (810) 294-8700.

Garden City: *Garden City Ice Arena*, (313) 261-3491.

Grand Rapids: *Belknap Park Arena*, (616) 235-0503.

Grand Rapids: *Patterson Ice Center*, (616) 940-1423.

Greenland: *Mountain Lions Club*, (906) 883-3208.

Houghton: *Michigan Tech Skating Academy Student Ice Arena*, (906) 487-2994.

Howell: *Grand Oaks Arena*, (517) 548-4355.

Inkster: *Inkster Civic Arena*, (616) 277-1001.

Iron Mountain: *Mountain View Ice Arena*, (906) 774-1480.

Kalamazoo: *Lawson Ice Arena*, (616) 387-3050.

Kalamazoo: *Wings Annex*, (616) 345-1125.

Kalamazoo: *Wings Stadium*, (616) 345-1125.

Kentwood: *Kentwood Ice Arena*, (616) 698-0100.

L'Anse: *L'Anse Arena*, (906) 524-5707.

Lansing: *Lansing Ice Arena*, (517) 482-1597.

Lansing: *Washington Ice Rink*, (517) 483-4230.

Laurium: *Bicentennnial Ice Arena*, (906) 337-1881.

Lincoln Park: *Lincoln Park Community Center*, (313) 386-4075.

Livonia: *Edgar (Eddie) Arena*, (313) 427-1280.

Marquette: *Lakeview Arena*, (906) 228-0490.

Melvindale: *Melvindale Arena*, (313) 928-1201.

Midland: *Midland Civic Arena*, (517) 832-8438.

Munising: *Alger Centennial Arena*, (906) 387-9975.

Muskegon: *Walker Arena*, (616) 726-2939.

Negawnee: *Negawnee Ice Arena*, (906) 475-7900.

Oak Park: *Compuware Oak Park Arena*, (810) 543-2338.

Plymouth: *Plymouth Cultural Center*, (313) 455-6620.

Port Huron: *McMorran Place Arena*, (810) 985-6166.

Redford: *Redford Ice Arena*, (313) 937-0913.

Royal Oak: *Lindell (John) Arena*, (810) 544-6690.

Saginaw: *Saginaw Bay Ice Arena*, (517) 799-8950.

Sault Ste Marie: *Pullar Stadium*, (906) 632-6853.

Southfield: *Southfield Civic Center*, (313) 354-9357.

Southgate: *Southgate Civic Center Arena*, (313) 246-1342.

St. Clair Shores: *St. Clair Shores Civic Arena*, (313) 445-5350.

Traverse City: *Howe Arena*, (616) 922-4814.

Trenton: *Icebox Sports Arena*, (313) 676-6429.

Trenton: *Kennedy Ice Arena*, (313) 676-7171.

Waterford: *Lakeland Ice Arena*, (810) 666-1911.

Wayne: *Wayne Community Center*, (313) 721-7400.

Westland: *Westland Sports Arena*, (313) 729-4560.

Wyandotte: *Yack (Benjamin F.) Arena*, (313) 246-4490.

MN: MINNESOTA

Albert Lea: *City Parks & Recreation*, (507) 377-4370.

Albert Lea: *Lea (Albert) City Arena*, (507) 377-4374.

Alexandria: *Runestone Community Center*, (612) 763-4466.

Anoka: *Anoka Area Ice Arena*, (612) 427-8163.

Apple Valley: *Apple Valley Sports Facility*, (612) 431-8866.

Austin: *Riverside Arena*, (507) 437-7676.

Babbitt: *Babbitt Ice Arena*, unlisted.

Baudette: *Baudette Arena*, (218) 634-1319.

Baxter: *Kristofferson (Oscar) Ice Rink*, (218) 828-3066.

Baxter: *Thompson (Loren) Park*, (218) 829-7161.

Bemidji: *Glass (John) Field House*, (218) 755-4140.

Bemidji: *Reise (Nielson) Arena*, (218) 751-4541.

Bloomington: *Bloomington Ice Garden*, (612) 887-9642.

Brainerd: *Brainerd Area Civic Center*, (218) 829-3351.

Breckenridge: *Breckenridge Skating Rink*, (218) 643-3455.

Brooklyn Park: *Brooklyn Park Community Center*, (612) 424-8017.

Buffalo: *Buffalo Community Civic Center*, (612) 682-4132.

Burnsville: *Burnsville Ice Center*, (612) 895-4651.
Burnsville: *Parks & Recreation Department*, (612) 895-4500.
Butte: *Butte Parks & Recreation Department*, (406) 723-8262.
Chisago: *Chisago Lakes Arena*, (612) 257-5936.
Chisholm: *Chisholm Sports Arena*, (218) 254-2635.
Coon Rapids: *Cook (Joe) Memorial Arena*, (612) 421-5035.
Cottage Grove: *Cottage Grove Ice Arena*, (612) 458-2845.
Crookston: *City Hall*, (218) 281-1232.
Detroit Lakes: *Lakes Sports Arena*, (218) 847-7738.
Duluth: *Duluth Entertainment*, (218) 722-5573.
East Grand Forks: *O'Leary Park VFW Arena*, (218) 773-9073.
Eden Prairie: *Eden Prairie Community Center*, (612) 949-8470.
Farmington: *Farmington Ice Arena*, (612) 463-2510.
Fergus Falls: *Parks & Recreation Department*, (218) 739-3205.
Grand Rapids: *IRA Civic Center Arena*, (218) 326-2591.
Hastings: *Hastings Civic Arena*, (612) 437-4940.
Hibbing: *Hibbing Memorial Ice Arena*, (218) 263-4379.
Hopkins: *Blake Ice Arena*, (612) 938-0209.
Hutchinson: *Hutchinson Civic Arena*, (612) 234-4227.
International Falls: *Bronco Arena*, (218) 283-2424.
Litchfield: *Litchfield Civic Arena*, (612) 693-2679.
Mankato: *All Seasons Arena*, (507) 387-6552.
Maplewood: *Aldrich Arena*, (612) 777-2233.
Marshall: *Lyon County Ice Facility*, (507) 537-6795.
Minneapolis: *Augsburg College Ice Arena*, (612) 330-1252.
Minneapolis: *Brick Ice Center*, (612) 545-1614.
Minneapolis: *Minneapolis Parks & Recreation Board*, (612) 661-4800.
Minneapolis: *Minnehaha Ice Arena*, (612) 729-8770.
Minneapolis: *Parade Ice Arena*, (612) 348-4853.
Minneapolis: *Victory Memorial Ice Arena*, (612) 627-2953.
Minnetonka: *Minnetonka Ice Arena*, (612) 939-8310.
Mora: *Mora Civic Center - Kanabu County Fair Grounds*, (612) 679-2443.
New Hope: *New Hope Ice Arena*, (612) 531-5181.
New Ulm: *Vogel Arena*, (507) 354-8321.
Northfield: *Northfield Ice Arena*, (507) 645-6556.
Owatonna: *Four Seasons Civic Center*, (507) 451-1093.
Red Wing: *Bergwall (George) Arena*, (612) 388-6088.
Rochester: *Rochester Olmstead Recreation Center*, (507) 281-6167.
Roseville: *Roseville Ice Arena*, (612) 484-0269.
Shoreview: *Shoreview Arena*, (612) 484-2400.
South St Paul: *Wakota Arena*, (612) 451-1727.

St. Cloud: *City Parks & Recreation Department*, (612) 255-7216.
St. Cloud: *National Hockey Center*, (612) 255-3327.
St. Louis Park: *St. Louis Park Recreation Center*, (612) 924-2545.
St. Paul: *Adams (Biff) Ice Arena*, (612) 488-1336.
St. Paul: *Arlington Ice Rink*, (612) 298-5701.
St. Paul: *Drake Ice Arena*, (612) 698-2455.
St. Paul: *Gustafson - Phalen Skating Arena*, (612) 776-2554.
St. Paul: *Harding Arena*, (612) 774-2127.
St. Paul: *Highland Arena*, (612) 699-7156.
St. Paul: *Oscar Johnson Arena*, (612) 645-7203.
St. Paul: *Pleasant Arena*, (612) 228-1143.
St. Paul: *St. Paul Parks & Recreation* , (612) 266-6400.
St. Paul: *Yackel (Ken) - West Side Arena*, (612) 228-1145.
St. Peters: *Lund Center Ice Arena*, (507) 933-7615.
Thief River Falls: *Olson (Huck) Memorial Civic Center*, (218) 681-2519.
Udina: *City of Udina Braemar Arena*, (612) 941-1322.
Warroad: *Memorial Arena*, (218) 386-9979.
White Bear Lake: *White Bear Arena*, (612) 777-8255.
White Bear Lake: *White Bear Lake Sports Center*, (612) 429-8571.
Willmar: *Parks & Recreation Department*, (612) 235-1854.
Willmar: *Willmar Civic Center*, (612) 235-1454.
Winona: *St. Mary's College Ice Arena*, (507) 457-1412.

MO: MISSOURI

Brentwood: *Brentwood Ice Arena*, (314) 962-4806.
Cape Cirardeau: *Ice Plaza Galleria*, (314) 335-4405.
Creve Coeur: *City of Creve Coeur Ice Arena*, (314) 432-3960.
Jefferson City: *Washington Park Ice Arena*, (314) 634-6482.
Kansas City: *Carriage Club Ice Rink*, (816) 363-2733.
Kansas City: *Crown Center Ice Terrace*, (816) 274-8412.
Osage Beach: *Marriot Tam-Tara Resort*, (314) 348-3131.
St. Joseph: *Bode Ice Arena*, (816) 271-5506.
St. Louis: *Kennedy (Wayne C.) Recreation Complex*, (314) 894-3088.
St. Louis: *North Country Recreation Center*, (314) 355-7374.
St. Peters: *St. Peters Rec-Plex*, (314) 298-2550.

MT: MONTANA

Billings: *Centennial Ice Arena*, (406) 256-1192.
Butte: *U.S. High Altitude Sports Center*, (406) 723-7060.
Great Falls: *Four Seasons Arena*, (406) 727-8900.
Helena: *Queen City Ice Palace*, (406) 443-4559.

NC: NORTH CAROLINA

Cary: *Ice House*, (919) 467-6000.
Charlotte: *Ice Chalet Eastland Mall*, (704) 568-0772.
Fort Bragg: *Cleland Skating Rink*, (910) 396-5127.
Greensboro: *Greensboro Coliseum*, (910) 373-7400.
Hillsborough: *Boone (Daniel) Ice Rink*, (919) 644-8222.
Spruce Pine: *Mitchell YMCA*, (704) 765-7766.
Winston-Salem: *Joel (Lawrence) Veterans Memorial Coliseum*, (910) 725-5635.

ND: NORTH DAKOTA

Bismarck: *VFW All Seasons Arena*, (701) 221-6814.
Bismarck: *Schaumberg Ice Rink*, (701) 221-6813.
Devil's Lake: *Burdick Arena*, (701) 662-8418.
Fargo: *Carlson (John E.) Coliseum*, (701) 241-8155.
Fargo: *Fargo Sports Arena*, (701) 241-8152.
Grafton: *Grafton Centennial Center*, (701) 352-3874.
Grafton: *Grafton Winter Sports Arena*, (701) 352-3707.
Grafton: *Hill Avenue Outdoor Rink*, (701) 352-1842.
Grand Forks: *Purpur Arena*, (701) 746-2764.
Jamestown: *Wilson (John L.) Arena*, (701) 252-3939.
Minot: *All Seasons Arena*, (701) 857-7620.

NE: NEBRASKA

Omaha: *Aksarben Coliseum*, (402) 444-4031.
Omaha: *Benson Ice Arena*, (402) 444-5971.
Omaha: *Hitchcock Ice Arena*, (402) 444-4955.

NH: NEW HAMPSHIRE

Andover: *Proctor Academy Ice Arena*, (603) 735-6000.
Berlin: *Notre Dame Arena Inc.*, (603) 752-9846.
Canaan: *Cardigan Mountain School Rink*, (603) 523-4321.
Concord: *Evertt Arena*, (603) 746-3195.
Concord: *Gordon (Malcolm) Memorial Rink - St. Paul's School*, (603) 225-3341.
Dover: *Dover Ice Arena*, (603) 743-6060.
East Swanzey: *Cheshire Fair Ice Arena*, (603) 357-4740.
Exeter: *Phillips Exeter Academy Rink*, (603) 772-4311.
Hanover: *Dartmouth College Thompson Arena*, (603) 646-1110.
Henniker: *La Clement Arena*, (603) 428-9806.
Manchester: *J.F.K. Memorial Rink*, (603) 649-2109.
Manchester: *New Hampshire College Ice Rink*, (603) 668-2211.
Manchester: *West Side Ice Arena*, (603) 624-6574.
Meriden: *Kimball Union Academy Ice Arena*, (603) 469-3211.
New Hampton: *Merill-Lindsay Arena*, (603) 744-5401.
Rochester: *Rochester Arena*, (603) 335-6749.
Tilton: *Tilton School Rink*, (603) 286-4342.
West Lebanon: *Campion Rink/Thompson Arena*, (603) 643-1222.
Wolfboro: *Pop Whalen Rink*, (603) 569-5639.

NJ: NEW JERSEY

Bayonne: *Bayonne High School*, (201) 858-5589.
Brick: *Ocean Ice Palace*, (908) 477-4411.
Bridgewater: *Bridgewater Sports Arena*, (908) 627-0006.
Bridgewater: *Chimney Rock*, (908) 302-9425.
Englewood: *Mackay Ice Arena Inc.*, (201) 568-3133.
Farmingdale: *American Hockey & Ice Skating Center*, (908) 919-7070.
Hamilton: *Iceland Associates*, (609) 588-6672.
Lawrenceville: *Lawrenceville School Rink*, (609) 896-0123.
Middletown: *Navesink Country Club*, (908) 842-3111.
Minneapolis: *Williams Arena*, (612) 625-5804.
Montclair: *Montclair Arena*, (201) 744-6088.
Morris Township: *Mennen (William G.) Sports Arena*, (201) 326-7650.
Old Bridge: *Old Bridge Arena*, (908) 679-3100.
Peapack: *Essex Hunt Club*, (908) 234-0062.
Pennsauken: *Twin Rinks Ice Sports & Entertainment Center*, (609) 488-9300.
Princeton: *Baker Rink*, (609) 258-3000.
Roselle: *Warinanco Skating Center*, (908) 298-7850.
Sewell: *Hollydell Ice Arena*, (609) 589-5599.
Toms River: *Winding River Skating Center*, (908) 244-0720.
Trenton: *Mercer County Public Skating Center*, (609) 586-8092.
Ventor: *Ventor Ice Rink*, (609) 823-7947.
Voorhes: *Coliseum Rink*, (609) 429-6908.
West Orange: *South Mountain Arena*, (201) 731-3828.
Westwood: *Dietl (Fritz) Ice Rink*, (201) 664-9812.

NM: NEW MEXICO

Albuquerque: *Outpost Ice Arena*, (505) 856-7594.

NV: NEVADA

Las Vegas: *Santa Fe Ice Skating Arena*, (702) 658-4991.

NY: NEW YORK

Alexandria Bay: *Alexandria Municipal Recreation Center*, (315) 482-9360.
Alexandria Bay: *Castle (Bonnie) Recreation Center*, (315) 482-4336.
Auburn: *Casey Park*, (315) 253-4247.

~ SKATER'S EDGE SOURCEBOOK ~

Baldwinsville: *Lysander - Radisson Arena*, (315) 635-1555.

Bear Mountain: *Bear Mountain State Park Ice Rink*, (914) 786-2701.

Bellmore: *Newbridge Road Ice Rink*, (516) 783-6181.

Bethpage: *Bethpage Community Park Ice Rink*, (516) 733-8404.

Brockport: *Brockport Ice Rink*, (716) 395-5365.

Brooklyn: *Wallman (Kate) Prospect Park*, (718) 282-1226.

Buffalo: *Dann Memorial Rink - Nichols School*, (716) 874-7174.

Buffalo: *Holiday Twin Rinks*, (716) 685-3660.

Buffalo: *Leisure Rinks Southtowns Inc.*, (716) 675-8992.

Canton: *Appleton Arena*, (315) 379-5696.

Chamillus: *Shove Park Recreation Center*, (315) 487-5068.

Chenango Bridge: *Polar Cap Recreation Center*, (607) 648-9888.

Clayton: *Clayton Recreation Arena*, (315) 686-4310.

Clifton Park: *Clifton Park Arena*, (518) 383-5440.

Clinton: *Clinton Arena*, (315) 853-5541.

Corning: *Nasser Civic Center Ice Rink*, (607) 936-3764.

Cortland: *Alumni Arena - State University College at Cortland*, (607) 753-4961.

Dix Hills: *Dix Hills Ice Rink*, (516) 499-8058.

Endicott: *Grippen Park Ice Rink*, (617) 748-6323.

Fairport: *Creek (Thomas) Ice Rink*, (716) 223-2160.

Flushing: *World's Fair Ice Skating Rink*, (718) 699-4215.

Freport: *Freeport Recreation Center IceRink*, (516) 223-8000.

Ft. Covington: *Salmon River Central Skating Arena*, (518) 358-2215.

Fulton: *Fulton Recreation Center, War Memorial*, (315) 592-2474.

Geneseo: *Wilson (Ira S.) Ice Arena*, (716) 245-5356.

Great Neck: *Parkwood Ice Rink*, (516) 487-2976.

Hamilton: *Starr Rink - Reid Athletic Center*, (315) 824-7570.

Hauppague: *Rinx, The - Hidden Pond Park*, (516) 232-5222.

Hicksville: *Cantiague Park Ice Arena*, (516) 571-7056.

Huntington: *Winter Club, The*, (516) 421-3889.

Ithaca: *Cass Park Ice Rink*, (607) 273-1090.

Ithaca: *Lynah Rink*, (607) 255-3793.

Jamestown: *Allen Park Ice Rink*, (716) 483-0614.

Katonah: *Harvey School Rink*, (914) 232-3618.

Kerhonkson: *Granite Ice Skating Rink*, (914) 626-3141.

Kings Park: *Superior Ice Rink*, (516) 269-3904.

Lake Placid: *Olympic Regional Development Authority Olympic Center (ORDA)*, (518) 523-3325.

Long Beach: *Longbeach Arena, Inc.*, (516) 431-6501.

Loudenville: *YMCA Albany County Hockey Training Facility*, (518) 452-7396.

Mamaronick: *Hommocks Park Ice Rink*, (914) 834-1069.

Massena: *Massena Arena*, (315) 769-3161.

Monsey: *Sport-O-Rama*, (914) 356-3919.

Monticello: *Kutsher's Ice Rink*, (914) 794-5621.

New Hartford: *New Hartford Recreation Center*, (315) 724-0600.

New Hyde Park: *Iceland Skating Rink*, (516) 746-1100.

New York: *Ice Studio, Inc.*, (212) 535-0304.

New York: *Rivergate Ice Rink*, (212) 689-0035.

New York: *Rockefeller Plaza Ice Rink*, (212) 757-5730.

New York: *Sky Rink*, (212) 239-8385.

New York: *Wollman Rink - Central Park Ice Chalet*, (212) 517-4800.

Newbury: *Ice Time, Inc.*, (914) 647-4802.

Ogdensburg: *Newell II (Edgar Allen) Dome*, (315) 393-5320.

Olean: *Olean Recreation Center*, (716) 373-7465.

Oswego: *Crisafulli (Anthony J.) Memorial Skating Rink*, (315) 343-4054.

Oswego: *Culliman (James P.) Skating Rink*, (315)343-6594.

Pawling: *Trinity-Pawling School Rink*, (914) 855-3100.

Plattsburgh: *SUNY Field House*, (518) 564-3060.

Port Washington: *Port Washington Family Rink*, (516) 484-6800.

Postdam: *Pine Street Arena*, (315) 265-4030.

Poughkeepsie: *McCann Ice Arena*, (914) 454-5800.

Rochester: *Genesee Valley Park Ice Rink*, (716) 253-3290.

Rochester: *Ritter (Frank) Memorial Arena*, (716) 475-2222.

Rochester: *Skating Institute of Rochester*, (716) 325-2216.

Rouses Point: *Rouses Point Recreation Center*, (518) 297-6776.

Rye: *Le Grange (Gerald) Field House*, (914) 967-5876.

Rye: *Playland Ice Casino: Westchester County*, (914) 921-0370.

Sandy: *Sports Park, The*, (801) 562-4444.

Saranac Lake: *Saranac Lake Civic Center*, (518) 891-3800.

Saratoga Springs: *Saratoga Springs Excelsior Avenue Ice Rink*, (518) 587-3550.

Saratoga Springs: *Saratoga Springs Weibel Avenue Ice Rink*, (518) 583-3462.

Schenectady: *Achilles Rink - Union College*, (518) 388-6134.

Schenectady: *Center City Ice Rink*, (518) 382-5105.

Scottsville: *Scottsville Ice Arena*, (716) 889-1817.

Skaneateles: *Allyn Arena*, (315) 685-7757.

Star Lake: *Clifton - Fine Arena*, (315) 848-2578.

Staten Island: *Staten Island War Memorial Ice Rink*, (718) 720-1010.

RINKS BY CITY

NY: NEW YORK (Continued)

Syosset: *Long Island Skating Academy*, (516) 496-2277.
Syracuse: *Burnet Park Arena*, (315) 473-4333.
Syracuse: *Meachen Arena*, (315) 492-0179.
Syracuse: *On Center Arena*, (315) 435-8000.
Syracuse: *Sunnycrest Arena*, (315) 473-4333.
Troy: *Houston Field House*, (518) 276-6262.
Troy: *Knickerbocker Ice Arena Facility*, (518) 235-7761.
Utica: *Utica Memorial Auditorium*, (315) 853-6147.
Watertown: *Watertown Fairgrounds Arena*, (315) 785-7836.
West Point: *Tate Rink at West Point*, (914) 938-4011.
White Plains: *Ebersole Ice Rink*, (914) 422-1336.
Whitestown: *Whitestown Community Center*, (315) 853-6147.
Williamsville: *Audubon Recreation Center*, (716) 631-7136.
Williamsville: *Clearfield Community Center*, (716) 689-1418.
Woodbury: *Woodbury Community Park Ice Rink*, (516) 677-5990.
Yonkers: *Murray (Edward J.) Memorial Skating Center*. (914) 377-6469.

OH: OHIO

Bowling Green: *Bowling Green State University Ice Arena*, (419) 372-2264.
Brooklyn: *Brooklyn Indoor Recreation Center*, (216) 351-2111.
Cincinnati: *Northland Ice Center*, (513) 563-0001.
Cleveland Heights: *Pavillion Recreation Center*, (216) 321-2090.
Columbus: *Ohio State University Ice Rink*, (614) 292-4154.
Dublin: *Chiller, The Central Ohio Ice Rinks Inc.*, (614) 791-9999.
Euclid: *Orr (Clifford E.) Arena*, (216) 289-8649.
Evendale: *Icelands*, (513) 769-0004.
Findlay: *Hancock Recreation Center*, (419) 423-8534.
Garfield Heights: *Kostel (Dan) Recreation Center*, (216) 475-7272.
Hamilton: *Hamilton Sports Arena*, (513) 868-5992.
Kent: *Kent State University Ice Arena*, (216) 672-2415.
Kettering: *Kettering Ice Arena*, (513) 296-2587.
Lakewood: *Winterhurst Ice Rink*, (216) 529-4400.
Mentor: *Mentor Civic Ice Arena*, (216) 255-1777.
North Olmstead: *North Olmstead Recreation Complex*, (216) 734-8200.
Oxford: *Goggin Ice Arena at Miami Univ.*, (513) 529-3343.
Parma: *Reis Ice Rink*, (216) 885-8870.
Parma Heights: *Parma Heights Municipal Ice Rink*, (216) 842-5005.
Rocky River: *Rocky River Recreation Center*, (216) 356-5658.

Shaker Heights: *Cleveland Skating Club*, (216) 791-2800.
Shaker Heights: *Thornton Park Ice Rink*, (216) 491-1290.
Sylvania: *Tam O'Shanter Ice Rink*, (419) 885-1167.
Troy: *Hobart Arena*, (513) 339-2911.
Youngstown: *Mill Creek Park Ice Rink*, (216) 740-7114.

OK: OKLAHOMA

Bethany: *Iceland Sports Centre*, (405) 789-2090.
Tulsa: *Tulsa Ice Arena*, (918) 254-7272.

OR: OREGON

Beaverton: *Valley Ice Arena*, (503) 297-2521.
Bend: *Inn of the Seventh Mountain*, (503) 382-8711.
Eugene: *Lane County Ice*, (503) 687-3615.
Portland: *Hamill (Dorothy) Ice Chalet*, (503) 654-7733.
Portland: *Lloyd Center Ice Pavillion*, (503) 288-4599.

PA: PENNSYLVANIA

Allentown: *Ice Palace*, (610) 435-3031.
Allison Park: *North Park Ice Rink*, (412) 935-1280.
Ardmore: *Philadelphia Skating Club and Humane Society*, (610) 642-8700.
Beaver Falls: *Beaver County Ice Arena*, (412) 846-5600.
Belle Vernon: *Ice Garden, Inc.*, (412) 379-7100.
Bethlehem: *Bethlehem Municipal Ice Rink*, (215) 865-7104.
Bristol: *Grundy Ice Center*, (215) 788-3312.
Colmar: *Melody Brook Ice Rink*, (215) 822-3613.
Elkins Park: *Old York Road Skating Club*, (215) 635-2770.
Erie: *Cochran (Jim) Memorial Ice Rink*, (814) 868-3652.
Erie: *Mercyhurst College Ice Rink*, (814) 824-2142.
Greensburg: *Nevin (Kirk) Ice Arena*, (412) 834-4880.
Harrisburg: *Twin Ponds, Inc.*, (717) 558-7663.
Havertown: *Havertown Skatium*, (610) 853-2226.
Hershey: *Hershey Park Arena*, (717) 534-3911.
Indiana: *Indiana Ice Center, East Pike Recreational Complex*, (412) 465-2665.
Johnstown: *Cambria County War Memorial*, (814) 536-5156.
Kennett Square: *Cleveland (John M.) Rink*, (610) 444-5119.
Kittaning: *Belmont Complex Armstrong County Recreation Authority*, (412) 548-1067.
Lancaster: *Lancaster Ice Arena*, (717) 581-0274.
Meadville: *Meadville Area, Recreation Complex*, (814) 724-6006.
Mt. Lebanon: *Mt. Lebanon Recreation Center*, (412) 561-4363.
New Castle: *Hess Ice Rinks*, (412) 658-6332.
Pensaulkin: *Twin Rinks*, (609) 488-9300.

Philadelphia: *Class of 1923 Ice Rink*, (215) 898-1923.
Philadelphia: *Rizzo Ice Rink*, (215) 685-1593.
Philadelphia: *Wissahickon Skating Club*, (215) 247-1759.
Pittsburgh: *Blade Runners Ice Complex*, (412) 826-0800.
Pittsburgh: *Golden Mile Ice Center*, (412) 327-7465.
Pittsburgh: *Ice Connection*, (412) 898-2440.
Pittsburgh: *Neville Ice Arena*, (412) 481-3351.
Pittsburgh: *Schenley Park Ice Arena*, (412) 422-6523.
Reading: *Timberline Ice Arena*, (610) 929-0808.
University Park: *Penn State Ice Pavillion*, (814) 863-2039.
Warminster: *Face Off Circle, Inc.*, (215) 674-1345.
Whitehall: *Lehigh Valley Ice Arena*, (610) 434-6899.
Wilkes Barre: *Wilkes Barre Ice-A-Rama*, (717) 821-1167.
Willow Grove: *Willow Grove Ice Rink, Inc.*, (215) 659-4253.
York: *York City Ice Rink*, (717) 843-3959.

RI: RHODE ISLAND

Cranston: *Cranston Veterans Memorial Rink*, (401) 944-8690.
Harrisville: *Levy Community Ice Rink*, (401) 568-8615.
Middletown: *Cabot Memorial Rink*, (401) 849-3620.
North Smithfield: *Rhode Island Sports Center*, (401) 762-1588.
Pawtucket: *Dennis Lynch Arena*, (401) 728-7420.
Portsmouth: *Portsmouth Abbey School Rink*, (401) 683-0621.
Providence: *Meehan (George) Auditorium*, (401) 863-2236.
Providence: *Schneider Arena*, (401) 865-2168.
Smithfield: *Smithfield Municipal Ice Rink*, (401) 231-7677.
Warwick: *Thayer (William H.) Arena and Warburton (Joe) Arena*, (401) 738-2000.
West Warwick: *West Warwick Civic Center Arena*, (401) 822-9260.
Woonsocket: *Adelard Arena*, (401) 769-7727.

SC: SOUTH CAROLINA

Columbia: *Rockbridge Skating Club*, (803) 782-3425.
Greenville: *Greenville Pavillion*, (803) 322-7529.

SD: SOUTH DAKOTA

Brookings: *Brookings Ice Arena*, (605) 692-6090.

TN: TENNESSEE

Gatlinburg: *Gatlinburg (Ober) Ice Rink*, (615) 436-5423.
Knoxville: *Ice Chalet Knoxville*, (615) 588-1858.
Memphis: *Ice Chalet Memphis*, (901) 362-8877.
Nashville: *Centennial Sportsplex Ice Arena*, (615) 862-8480.

TX: TEXAS

Austin: *Ice Chalet Northcross*, (512) 451-5102.
Dallas: *America's Ice Garden*, (214) 922-9800.
Dallas: *Galleria Ice Skating Center*, (214) 392-3363.
Dallas: *Prestonwood Ice Chalet*, (214) 980-8988.
Fort Worth: *Tandy Center Ice Rink*, (817) 878-4848.
Houston: *Galleria Ice Skating Center*, (713) 621-7609.
Houston: *Sharpstown Ice Center*, (713) 784-2971.
Irving: *Dallas Stars Ice Arena*, (214) 831-2480.
Lubbock: *United Skates*, (806) 745-3600.
San Antonio: *Crystal Ice Palace*, (210) 690-4525.
Sugar Land: *Aerodrome Ice Skating Complex*, (713) 265-7465.

UT: UTAH

Bountiful: *Bountiful Recreation Center*, (801) 298-6220.
Ogden: *Ice Sheet, The*, (801) 399-8750.
Park City: *Resort Center Skating Rink*, (801) 649-0468.
Provo: *Seven Peaks Ice Rink*, (801) 373-8777.
Salt Lake City: *Cottonwood Heights Ice Arena*, (801) 943-3190.

VA: VIRGINIA

Alexandria: *Mt. Vernon Recreation Center*, (703) 768-3224.
Fairfax: *Fairfax Ice Arena*, (703) 323-1133.
Hot Springs: *Homestead Skating Rink*, (703) 839-7721.
Reston: *Fountain Square Ice Arena*, (703) 318-7541.
Reston: *Reston Ice Forum*, (703) 709-1010.
Richmond: *Ice Palace*, (804) 378-7465.
Roanoke: *Roanoke Civic Center*, (703) 981-2241.
Virginia Beach: *Iceland -Virginia Beach*, (804) 490-3907.

VT: VERMONT

Barre: *Barre City B.O.R Rink*, (802) 476-0258.
Brattleboro: *Withington (Nelson) Arena*, (802) 257-2311.
Burlington: *Guttersonn Field House*, (802) 656-3074.
Burlington: *Paquette (Gordon H.) Municipal Arena*, (802) 864-0123.
Essex Junction: *Essex Junction Skating Facility*, (802) 878-1394.
Highgate Center: *Highgate Sports Arena*, (802) 868-4406.
Lyndon Center: *Fenton West Chester Arena*, (802) 626-9361.
Manchester: *Northshire Civic Center*, (802) 362-0150.
Middlebury: *Nelson Arena at Middlebury College*, (802) 388-3711 Ext. 5411.
Northfield: *Taylor Arena*, (802) 485-2567.
Rutland: *Giorgetti Ice Arena*, (802) 775-7976.

VT: VERMONT (Continued)

Rutland: *Mandigo (Royce) Arena*, (802) 773-9416.

Saxton's River: *Choukas (Michael) Ice Rink*, (802) 869-6219.

St. Albans: *Collins-Perley Sport Center Skating Arena*, (802) 527-1202.

Stowe: *Jackson Arena*, (802) 253-6148.

White River Junction: *Town of Hartford B.O.R Rink*, (802) 295-3236.

WA: WASHINGTON

Bellingham: *Whatcom County Sports Arena*, (206) 676-7305.

Kennewick: *Tri-Cities Coliseum*, (509) 783-8824.

Lynnwood: *Sno-King Ice Arena*, (206) 775-7512.

Moses Lake: *Moses Lake Municipal Ice Rink*, (509) 766-9240.

Mt. Lake Terrace: *Olympic View Ice Arena*, (206) 672-9012.

Seattle: *Highland Ice Arena*, (206) 546-2431.

Seattle: *Seattle Center Arena*, (206) 728-9124.

Spokane: *Eagles-Ice A-Rena*, (509) 489-9295.

Spokane: *Riverfront Park Ice Palace*, (509) 625-6687.

Tacoma: *Puget Sound Hockey Center*, (206) 272-1785.

Tacoma: *Sprinker (Harry) Recreation Center*, (206) 537-2600.

Walla Walla: *YWCA Ice Chalet*, (509) 525-2575.

Wenatchee: *Riverfront Park*, (509) 664-5994.

Yakima: *Yakima Ice Arena*, (509) 248-6315.

WI: WISCONSIN

Altoona: *Hobbs Altoona Sports Center*, (715) 839-5188.

Beaver Dam: *Family Center Ice Arena*, (414) 885-9816.

Beloit: *Telfer Park Sports and Activity Center*, (608) 364-2890.

Brookefield: *Eble Park Arena*, (414) 784-7512.

Chippewa Falls: *Chippewa Falls Arena*, (715) 723-4403.

De Pere: *De Pere Ice Recreation Center*, (414) 339-4097.

Eagle River: *Eagle River Recreation Association*, (715) 479-4858.

Eau Claire: *Hobbs Municipal Ice Arena*, (715) 839-5040.

Fond du Lac: *Blue Line Hockey Rink*, (414) 929-9664.

Green Bay: *Brown County Youth Ice Center*, (414) 499-7222.

Janesville: *Janesville Ice Arena*, (608) 755-3014.

Kenosha: *Kenosha County Ice Arena*, (414) 694-8011.

Kirkland: *Kingsgate Skating Club*, (206) 823-1242.

Lacrosse: *Green Island Ice Arena*, (608) 789-7199.

Madison: *Camp Randall Memorial Sports Center*, (608) 263-6565.

Madison: *Dane County EXPO Center*, (608) 267-3976.

Madison: *Hartmeyer Ice Arena*, (608) 246-4512.

Madison: *Madison Ice Arena*, (608) 246-4513.

Manitowoc: *Manitowoc Ice Center*, (414) 683-4530.

Marinette: *Marinette Civic Center*, (715) 732-0558.

Marshfield: *Marshfield Youth Ice and Recreation Center*, (715) 384-0025.

Medford: *Simek Recreation Center*, (715) 748-6655.

Milwaukee: *Petit National Ice Center*, (414) 266-0100.

Milwaukee: *University School of Milwaukee Fieldhouse*, (414) 352-6000.

Milwaukee: *Wilson Park Recreation Center*, (414) 281-6289.

Neenah: *Tri-County Ice Arena*, (414) 731-9731.

Onalaska: *Onalaska Omni Center*, (608) 781-9566.

Reedsburg: *Reedsburg Ice Arena*, (608) 524-3037.

Rhinelander: *Rhinelander Ice Arena*, (715) 369-1416.

River Falls: *University of Wisconsin WH Hunt Arena*, (715) 425-3381.

Stevens Point: *Willett (K. B.) Arena*, (715) 346-1576.

Sun Prairie: *Sun Prairie Ice Arena*, (608) 837-4434.

Superior: *Wessman Arena*, (715) 394-8361.

Tomahawk: *S. A. R. A. Park Recreation Center*, (715) 453-4040.

Viroqua: *Viroqua Community Arena*, (608) 637-8661.

Waupun: *Waupun Community Center*, (414) 324-9918.

Wausau: *Marathon County Multi-Purpose Building*, (715) 847-5364.

West Bend: *Kettle Moraine Ice Center*, (414) 335-0876.

WV: WEST VIRGINIA

Charleston: *Charleston Civic Center Ice Arena*, (304) 345-1500.

Morgantown: *Morgantown Municipal Rink*, (304) 292-6865.

Wheeling: *Wheeling Park Memorial Ice Rink*, (304) 242-3770.

White Sulphur Springs: *Greenbriar Resort*, (304) 536-1110.

WY: WYOMING

Casper: *Casper Ice Arena*, (307) 235-8484.

Jackson: *Snow King Center at Snow King Resort*, (307) 733-5200.

Rock Springs: *Family Recreation Center*, (307) 382-3265.

Rinks: Cross-Reference
by Rink Name

Following is a cross-reference listing of rinks in alphabetical order by rink name. For complete rink information, look up the rink in the main listings section beginning on page 135.

Achilles Rink - Union College, Schenectady, NY. (518) 388-6134.

Adams (Biff) Ice Arena, St. Paul, MN. (612) 488-1336.

Adams (Jack) Arena, Detroit, MI. (313) 935-4510.

Adelard Arena, Woonsocket, RI. (401) 769-7727.

Adray (Mike) Sports Arena, Dearborn, MI. (313) 943-4098.

Adrian Ice Rink, Adrian, MI. (517) 265-8675.

Aerodrome Ice Skating Complex, Sugar Land, TX. (713) 265-7465.

Air Force Academy Ice Arena, Colorado Springs, CO. (719) 472-4032.

Aksarben Coliseum, Omaha, NE. (402) 444-4031.

Aldrich Arena, Maplewood, MN. (612) 777-2233.

Aleixo (Theodore) Skating Rink, Taunton, MA. (508) 824-4987.

Alexandria Municipal Recreation Center, Alexandria Bay, NY. (315) 482-9360.

Alfond Arena, Waterville, ME. (207) 872-3000.

Alfond Ice Arena, University of Maine - Orono, Orono, ME. (207) 581-1106.

Alger Centennial Arena, Munising, MI. (906) 387-9975.

All Seasons Arena, Mankato, MN. (507) 387-6552.

All Seasons Arena, Minot, ND. (701) 857-7620.

All Seasons Ice Center, Crescent Springs, KY. (606) 344-1981.

All Seasons Twin Ice Rinks, Naperville, IL. (708) 851-0755.

Allen County War Memorial Coliseum, Fort Wayne, IN. (219) 482-9502.

Allen Park Ice Rink, Jamestown, NY. (716) 483-0614.

Allyn Arena, Skaneateles, NY. (315) 685-7757.

Alpine Ice Arena, Louisville, KY. (502) 459-9500.

Alpine Ice Arena, Birmingham, AL. (205) 942-0223.

Alumni Arena - State University College at Cortland, Cortland, NY. (607) 753-4961.

America's Ice Garden, Dallas, TX. (214) 922-9800.

American Hockey & Ice Skating Center, Farmingdale, NJ. (908) 919-7070.

Ames - Iowa State University Ice Arena, Ames, IA. (515) 292-6835.

Anchorage Sports Center Ice Rink, Anchorage, AK. (907) 786-1232.

Anderson Park Skating Rink, Brookline, MA. (617) 730-2080.

Anoka Area Ice Arena, Anoka, MN. (612) 427-8163.

Apple Valley Sports Facility, Apple Valley, MN. (612) 431-8866.

Appleton Arena, Canton, NY. (315) 379-5696.

Arlington Ice Rink, St. Paul, MN. (612) 298-5701.

Armstrong (John) Memorial Skating Rink, Plymouth, MA. (800) 273-7776.

Ashland Area Recreational Ice Rink, Ashland, ME. (207) 435-6893.

Asiaf Arena, Brockton, MA. (508) 583-6804.

Aspen Ice Garden, Aspen, CO. (303) 920-5141.

Atlanta Iceplex, Duluth, GA. (404) 813-1010.

Audubon Recreation Center, Williamsville, NY. (716) 631-7136.

Augsburg College Ice Arena, Minneapolis, MN. (612) 330-1252.

Babbitt Ice Arena, Babbitt, MN. unlisted.

Babson Recreation Center, Wellesley, MA. (617) 239-6050.

Bajko (Alexander) Memorial Skating Rink, Hyde Park, MA. (617) 364-9188.

Baker Rink, Princeton, NJ. (609) 258-3000.

Barre City B.O.R Rink, Barre, VT. (802) 476-0258.

Barrington Ice Arena, Barrington, IL. (708) 381-9702.

Baudette Arena, Baudette, MN. (218) 634-1319.

Bayonne High School, Bayonne, NJ. (201) 858-5589.

Bear Mountain State Park Ice Rink, Bear Mountain, NY. (914) 786-2701.

Beaver County Ice Arena, Beaver Falls, PA. (412) 846-5600.

Belknap Park Arena, Grand Rapids, MI. (616) 235-0503.

Belmont Complex Armstrong County Recreation Authority, Kittaning, PA. (412) 548-1067.

Belmont Iceland, Belmont, CA. (415) 592-0532.

Belmont Skating Rink, Belmont, MA. (617) 489-8245.

Benfield Pines Ice Rink, Millersville, MD. (410) 987-5100.

Bennett (Edward L.) Skating Rink, West Haven, CT. (203) 932-1461.

Benson Ice Arena, Omaha, NE. (402) 444-5971.

Bergwall (George) Arena, Red Wing, MN. (612) 388-6088.

Berkeley Iceland, Berkeley, CA. (510) 843-8801.

Berkley Ice Arena, Berkley, MI. (810) 546-2460.

Berkshire School, Sheffield, MA. (413) 229-8511.

Bethlehem Municipal Ice Rink, Bethlehem, PA. (215) 865-7104.

Bethpage Community Park Ice Rink, Bethpage, NY. (516) 733-8404.

Bicentennnial Ice Arena, Laurium, MI. (906) 337-1881.

Biddeford Ice Arena, Biddeford, ME. (207) 283-0615.

Big Dipper Ice Rink, Fairbanks, AK. (907) 459-1104.

Birmingham Ice Sports Arena, Birmingham, MI. (313) 654-0731.

Blade Runners Ice Complex, Pittsburgh, PA. (412) 826-0800.

Blake Ice Arena, Hopkins, MN. (612) 938-0209.

Bloomington Ice Garden, Bloomington, MN. (612) 887-9642.

Blue Jay Ice Castles, Blue Jay, CA. (909) 336-2111.

Blue Line Hockey Rink, Fond du Lac, WI. (414) 929-9664.

Bode Ice Arena, St. Joseph, MO. (816) 271-5506.

Boeke (Ben) Ice Arena, Anchorage, AK. (907) 274-2715.

Bolton Ice Palace, Bolton, CT. (203) 646-7851.

Boone (Daniel) Ice Rink, Hillsborough, NC. (919) 644-8222.

Boston College Ice Rink, Chesnut Hill, MA. (617) 552-8000.

Bountiful Recreation Center, Bountiful, UT. (801) 298-6220.

Bowie Ice Arena, Bowie, MD. (301) 805-7990.

Bowling Green State University Ice Arena, Bowling Green, OH. (419) 372-2264.

Brainerd Area Civic Center, Brainerd, MN. (218) 829-3351.

Breckenridge Skating Rink, Breckenridge, MN. (218) 643-3455.

Brentwood Ice Arena, Brentwood, MO. (314) 962-4806.

Brett Memorial Ice Arena, Wasilla, AK. (907) 376-9260.

Brick Ice Center, Minneapolis, MN. (612) 545-1614.

Bridgeton Academy Ice Arena, North Bridgeton, ME. (207) 647-3322.

Bridgewater Sports Arena, Bridgewater, NJ. (908) 627-0006.

Bright Hockey Center, Cambridge, MA. (617) 495-7541.

Broadmoor World Arena, Colorado Springs, CO. *Brockport Ice Rink*, Brockport, NY. (716) 395-5365.

Bronco Arena, International Falls, MN. (218) 283-2424.

Brookings Ice Arena, Brookings, SD. (605) 692-6090.

Brooklyn Indoor Recreation Center, Brooklyn, OH. (216) 351-2111.

Brooklyn Park Community Center, Brooklyn Park, MN. (612) 424-8017.

Brooks School Rink, North Andover, MA. (508) 686-6101.

Brown County Youth Ice Center, Green Bay, WI. (414) 499-7222.

Brown Rink, Pomfret, CT. (203) 928-7731.

Brown (Walter) Arena, Boston, MA. (617) 353-4632.

Browne & Nichols Skating Rink, Cambridge, MA. (617) 864-8668.

Bryan Memorial Skating Rink, West Roxbury, MA. (617) 323-9512.

Buffalo Community Civic Center, Buffalo, MN. (612) 682-4132.

Buhr Park Ice Rink, Ann Arbor, MI. (313) 994-2784.

Burdick Arena, Devil's Lake, ND. (701) 662-8418.

Burlington Ice Palace, Burlington, MA. (617) 272-9517.

Burnet Park Arena, Syracuse, NY. (315) 473-4333.

Burnsville Ice Center, Burnsville, MN. (612) 895-4651.

Butte Parks & Recreation Department, Butte, MN. (406) 723-8262.

Cabin John Ice Rink, Rockville, MD. (301) 365-2246.

Cabot Memorial Rink, Middletown, RI. (401) 849-3620.

Cambria County War Memorial, Johnstown, PA. (814) 536-5156.

Camp Randall Memorial Sports Center, Madison, WI. (608) 263-6565.

Campion Rink / Thompson Arena, West Lebanon, NH. (603) 643-1222.

Cantiague Park Ice Arena, Hicksville, NY. (516) 571-7056.

Canton Metropolis Skating Rink, Canton, MA. (617) 821-5032.

Cardigan Mountain School Rink, Canaan, NH. (603) 523-4321.

Carlson (John E.) Coliseum, Fargo, ND. (701) 241-8155.

Carmel Ice Skatium, Carmel, IN. (317) 844-8889.

Carousel Hotel Ice Rink, Ocean City, MD. (410) 524-1000.

Carriage Club Ice Rink, Kansas City, MO. (816) 363-2733.

Casey Park, Auburn, NY. (315) 253-4247.

Casper Ice Arena, Casper, WY. (307) 235-8484.

Cass Park Ice Rink, Ithaca, NY. (607) 273-1090.

Castle (Bonnie) Recreation Center, Alexandria Bay, NY. (315) 482-4336.

Centennial Ice Arena, Highland Park, IL. (708) 432-4790.

Centennial Ice Arena, Billings, MT. (406) 256-1192.

Centennial Ice Rink, Wilmette, IL. (708) 256-6100.

Centennial Sportsplex Ice Arena, Nashville, TN. (615) 862-8480.

Center City Ice Rink, Schenectady, NY. (518) 382-5105.

Center Ice of Du Page, Glen Ellyn, IL. (708) 790-9696.

Central Maine Civic Center, Lewiston, ME. (207) 783-2009.

Central Peninsula Sports Center, Soldotna, AK. (907) 262-3151.

Centre Ice Countryside Mall, Clearwater, FL. (813) 796-0586.

Charleston Civic Center Ice Arena, Charleston, WV. (304) 345-1500.

Cheboygan Ice Rink/Pavillion, Cheboygan, MI. (616) 627-3255.

Cheshire Fair Ice Arena, East Swanzey, NH. (603) 357-4740.

Chevy Chase Club Inc., Chevy Chase, MD. (301) 652-4100.

Chiller, The Central Ohio Ice Rinks Inc., Dublin, OH. (614) 791-9999.

Chimney Rock, Bridgewater, NJ. (908) 302-9425.

Chippewa Falls Arena, Chippewa Falls, WI. (715) 723-4403.

Chisago Lakes Arena, Chisago, MN. (612) 257-5936.

Chisholm Sports Arena, Chisholm, MN. (218) 254-2635.

Choate-Rosemary Hall ice Rink, Wallingford, CT. (203) 697-2000.

Choukas (Michael) Ice Rink, Saxton's River, VT. (802) 869-6219.

City Hall, Crookston, MN. (218) 281-1232.

City of Auburn Ice Arena, Auburn, ME. (207) 795-6375.

City of Creve Coeur Ice Arena, Creve Coeur, MO. (314) 432-3960.

City of Udina Braemar Arena, Udina, MN. (612) 941-1322.

City Parks & Recreation, Albert Lea, MN. (507) 377-4370.

City Parks & Recreation, Bangor, ME. (207) 947-1018.

City Parks & Recreation Department, St. Cloud, MN. (612) 255-7216.

City Parks & Recreation Dept., Auburn, ME. (207) 784-0191.

City Sports Center Ice Rink, Detroit, MI. (313) 567-2423.

Clark Athletic Center Ice Rink, Boston, MA. (617) 287-7801.

Clark Memorial Arena, Winchendon, MA. (508) 297-0102.

Class of 1923 Ice Rink, Philadelphia, PA. (215) 898-1923.

Clayton Recreation Arena, Clayton, NY. (315) 686-4310.

Clearfield Community Center, Williamsville, NY. (716) 689-1418.

Cleland Skating Rink, Fort Bragg, NC. (910) 396-5127.

Cleveland (John M.) Rink, Kennett Square, PA. (610) 444-5119.

Cleveland Skating Club, Shaker Heights, OH. (216) 791-2800.

Clifton - Fine Arena, Star Lake, NY. (315) 848-2578.

Clifton Park Arena, Clifton Park, NY. (518) 383-5440.

Clinton Arena, Clinton, NY. (315) 853-5541.

Cochran (Jim) Memorial Ice Rink, Erie, PA. (814) 868-3652.

Coliseum Rink, Voorhes, NJ. (609) 429-6908.

Collins Moylan Memorial Skating Rink, Greenfield, MA. (413) 772-6891.

Collins-Perley Sport Center Skating Arena, St. Albans, VT. (802) 527-1202.

Columbia Ice Rink, Columbia, MD. (410) 730-0322.

Compuware Oak Park Arena, Oak Park, MI. (810) 543-2338.

Conejo Valley Ice Center, Newbury Park, CA. (805) 498-6660.

Connell Memorial Rink, Weymouth, MA. (617) 335-2090.

Conners (Terry) Ice Rink, Stanford, CT. (203) 977-4514.

Connery (Lynn) Memorial Rink, Lynn, MA. (617) 599-9474.

Cook (Joe) Memorial Arena, Coon Rapids, MN. (612) 421-5035.

Costa Mesa Ice Chalet, Costa Mesa, CA. (714) 979-8880.

Cottage Grove Ice Arena, Cottage Grove, MN. (612) 458-2845.

Cottonwood Heights Ice Arena, Salt Lake City, UT. (801) 943-3190.

Cranston Veterans Memorial Rink, Cranston, RI. (401) 944-8690.

Creek (Thomas) Ice Rink, Fairport, NY. (716) 223-2160.

Crested Butte Ice Rink, Crested Butte, CO. (303) 349-5338.

Crisafulli (Anthony J.) Memorial Skating Rink, Oswego, NY. (315) 343-4054.

Cronin Memorial Rink, Revere, MA. (617) 284-9491.

Crown Center Ice Terrace, Kansas City, MO. (816) 274-8412.

Crown (Robert) Ice Center, Evanston, IL. (708) 328-9401.

Crystal Ice House, Crystal Lake, IL. (815) 356-8500.

Crystal Ice Palace, San Antonio, TX. (210) 690-4525.

Culliman (James P.) Skating Rink, Oswego, NY. (315)343-6594.

Culver Ice Arena, Culver City, CA. (310) 398-5719.

Cumberland County Civic Center, Portland, ME. (201) 775-3481.

CYR Arena - Forest Park, Springfield, MA. (413) 787-6438.

Dahlgren Hall Ice Rink, Annapolis, MD. (410) 263-4527.

Dallas Stars Ice Arena, Irving, TX. (214) 831-2480.

Daly Memorial Rink, Brighton, MA. (617) 527-1741.

Dane County EXPO Center, Madison, WI. (608) 267-3976.

Dann Memorial Rink - Nichols School, Buffalo, NY. (716) 874-7174.

Darien Ice Rink, Darien, CT. (203) 655-8251.

Dartmouth College Thompson Arena, Hanover, NH. (603) 646-1110.

Dayton Arena, New London, CT. (203) 439-2575.

Dayton Arena, Brunswick, ME. (207) 725-3332.

De Pere Ice Recreation Center, De Pere, WI. (414) 339-4097.

Decatur Civic Center, Decatur, IL. (217) 422-7300.

Deerfield Academy Skating Rink, Deerfield, MA. (413) 772-0241.

Dempsey-Anderson Arena, Anchorage, AK. (907) 277-7571.

Dennis Lynch Arena, Pawtucket, RI. (401) 728-7420.

Detroit Skating Club, Bloomfield Hills, MI. (810) 332-7133.

Devine (Robert M.) Rink, Neponset, MA. (617) 436-4356.

Dexter Rink, Brookline, MA. (617) 524-9377.

Dietl (Fritz) Ice Rink, Westwood, NJ. (201) 664-9812.

Dimond Center Ice Capades Chalet, Anchorage, AK. (907) 344-1212.

Dix Hills Ice Rink, Dix Hills, NY. (516) 499-8058.

Dobson (John A.) Arena, Vail, CO. (303) 479-2271.

Dover Ice Arena, Dover, NH. (603) 743-6060.

Downers Grove Ice Arena, Downers Grove, IL. (708) 971-3780.

Draddy Arena at Canterbury High School, New Milford, CT. (203) 355-3103.

Drake Ice Arena, St. Paul, MN. (612) 698-2455.

Driscoll (Arthur R.) Memorial Skating Rink, Fall River, MA. (508) 679-3274.

Dublin Iceland, Dublin, CA. (510) 829-4445.

Dubuque Five Flags Center, Dubuque, IA. (319) 589-4254.

Duluth Entertainment, Duluth, MN. (218) 722-5573.

Eagle River Recreation Association, Eagle River, WI. (715) 479-4858.

Eagles-Ice A-Rena, Spokane, WA. (509) 489-9295.

East Haven Veterans Memorial Ice Rink, East Haven, CT. (203) 468-3367.

Eastdale Ice Palace, Montgomery, AL. (205) 272-7225.

Eastridge Ice Arena, San Jose, CA. (408) 238-0440.

Ebersole Ice Rink, White Plains, NY. (914) 422-1336.

Eble Park Arena, Brookefield, WI. (414) 784-7512.

Eden Prairie Community Center, Eden Prairie, MN. (612) 949-8470.

Edgar (Eddie) Arena, Livonia, MI. (313) 427-1280.

Edora Pool Ice Center, Ft. Collins, CO. (303) 221-6679.

Enfield Twin Rinks, Enfield, CT. (203) 745-2461.

Essex Hunt Club, Peapack, NJ. (908) 234-0062.

Essex Junction Skating Facility, Essex Junction, VT. (802) 878-1394.

Evertt Arena, Concord, NH. (603) 746-3195.

Ewigleben (Robert L.) Ice Arena, Big Rapids, MI. (616) 592-2881.

Face Off Circle, Inc., Warminster, PA. (215) 674-1345.

Fairchild (Jennings) Rink, Avon, CT. (203) 673-3201.

Fairfax Ice Arena, Fairfax, VA. (703) 323-1133.

Falmouth Ice Arena, Falmouth, MA. (508) 548-7080.

Family Center Ice Arena, Beaver Dam, WI. (414) 885-9816.

Family Recreation Center, Rock Springs, WY. (307) 382-3265.

Fargo Sports Arena, Fargo, ND. (701) 241-8152.

Farmington Ice Arena, Farmington, MN. (612) 463-2510.

Fenton West Chester Arena, Lyndon Center, VT. (802) 626-9361.

Fire Lake Recreation Center, Eagle River, AK. (907) 696-0050.

Flagstaff Municipal Ice Arena, Flagstaff, AZ. (602) 774-1051.

Flint Four Seasons Sport Center, Flint, MI. (313) 635-8487.

Fort Dupont, Washington, DC. (202) 584-3040.

Forum, The, Presque Isle, ME. (207) 764-0491.

Fountain Square Ice Arena, Reston, VA. (703) 318-7541.

Four Seasons Arena, Great Falls, MT. (406) 727-8900.

Four Seasons Civic Center, Owatonna, MN. (507) 451-1093.

Franklin Arena, Franklin, MA. (508) 541-7024.

Franklin Park Ice Arena, Franklin Park, IL. (708) 671-4268.

Fraser Ice Arenas, Fraser, MI. (810) 294-8700.

Frederick Fort & Ice Arena, Frederick, MD. (301) 662-7362.

Freeport Recreation Center IceRink, Freport, NY. (516) 223-8000.

Fulton Recreation Center, War Memorial, Fulton, NY. (315) 592-2474.

Galleria Ice Skating Center, Houston, TX. (713) 621-7609.

Galleria Ice Skating Center, Dallas, TX. (214) 392-3363.

Gallo (John B.) Ice Arena, Bourne, MA. (508) 759-8904.

Garden City Ice Arena, Garden City, MI. (313) 261-3491.

Gardner Ice Rink, Southboro, MA. (508) 485-0050.

Gardner Veterans Skating Rink, Gardner, MA. (508) 632-7329.

Gatlinburg (Ober) Ice Rink, Gatlinburg, TN. (615) 436-5423.

Genesee Valley Park Ice Rink, Rochester, NY. (716) 253-3290.

Giorgetti Ice Arena, Rutland, VT. (802) 775-7976.

Glacial Garden Ice Arena, Anaheim, CA. (714) 502-9197.

Glass (John) Field House, Bemidji, MN. (218) 755-4140.

Glen Ellyn Ice Skating School, Glen Ellyn, IL. (708) 469-5770.

Glenview Ice Arena, Glenview, IL. (708) 724-2800.

Goggin Ice Arena, Oxford, OH. (513) 529-3343.

Gold Coast Ice Arena, Pompano Beach, FL. (305) 943-1437.

Golden Gate Ice Arena, Redwood City, CA. (415) 364-8091.

Golden Mile Ice Center, Pittsburgh, PA. (412) 327-7465.

Gordon (Malcolm) Memorial Rink - St. Paul's School, Concord, NH. (603) 225-3341.

Governor Dummer Academy Rink, Byfield, MA. (508) 462-6643.

Graf (Henry Jr.) Rink, Newburyport, MA. (508) 462-8112.

Grafton Centennial Center, Grafton, ND. (701) 352-3874.

Grafton Winter Sports Arena, Grafton, ND. (701) 352-3707.

Grand Oaks Arena, Howell, MI. (517) 548-4355.

Granite City Park Ice Rink, Granite City, IL. (618) 877-2549.

Granite Ice Skating Rink, Kerhonkson, NY. (914) 626-3141.

Green Island Ice Arena, Lacrosse, WI. (608) 789-7199.

Greenbriar Resort, White Sulphur Springs, WV. (304) 536-1110.

Greenfield Skating Arena, Greenfield, MA. (413) 772-6891.

Greensboro Coliseum, Greensboro, NC. (910) 373-7400.

Greenville Pavillion, Greenville, SC. (803) 322-7529.

Greenwich Skating Club, Greenwich, CT. (203) 622-9583.

Grippen Park Ice Rink, Endicott, NY. (617) 748-6323.

Grosse Pointe Community Rink, Detroit, MI. (313) 885-4100.

Grundy Ice Center, Bristol, PA. (215) 788-3312.

Gunnery School, Washington, CT. (203) 868-2176.

Gustafson - Phalen Skating Arena, St. Paul, MN. (612) 776-2554.

Guttersonn Field House, Burlington, VT. (802) 656-3074.

Hallenborg Memorial Pavillion, Billerica, MA. (508) 436-9300.

Hamden Community Ice Rink, Hamden, CT. (203) 287-2610.

Hamill (Dorothy) Ice Chalet, Portland, OR. (503) 654-7733.

Hamill (Dorothy) Skating Rink, Greenwich, CT. (203) 531-8560.

Hamilton Sports Arena, Hamilton, OH. (513) 868-5992.

Hancock Recreation Center, Findlay, OH. (419) 423-8534.

Harding Arena, St. Paul, MN. (612) 774-2127.

Hart Recreation Center Ice Rink, Worcester, MA. (508) 793-3407.

Hartmeyer Ice Arena, Madison, WI. (608) 246-4512.

Harvey School Rink, Katonah, NY. (914) 232-3618.

Hastings Civic Arena, Hastings, MN. (612) 437-4940.

Havertown Skatium, Havertown, PA. (610) 853-2226.

Hayden Recreation Center Ice Facility, Lexington, MA. (617) 862-5575.

Heilmann Recreation Center, Detroit, MI. (313) 267-7153.

Hershey Park Arena, Hershey, PA. (717) 534-3911.

Hess Ice Rinks, New Castle, PA. (412) 658-6332.

Hetland (Stephen) Memorial Skating Rink, New Bedford, MA. (508) 999-9051.

Hibbing Memorial Ice Arena, Hibbing, MN. (218) 263-4379.

Highgate Sports Arena, Highgate Center, VT. (802) 868-4406.

Highland Arena, St. Paul, MN. (612) 699-7156.

Highland Ice Arena, Seattle, WA. (206) 546-2431.

Hill Avenue Outdoor Rink, Grafton, ND. (701) 352-1842.

Hitchcock Ice Arena, Omaha, NE. (402) 444-4955.

Hobart Arena, Troy, OH. (513) 339-2911.

Hobbs Altoona Sports Center, Altoona, WI. (715) 839-5188.

Hobbs Municipal Ice Arena, Eau Claire, WI. (715) 839-5040.

Hobomock Ice Arena, Pembroke, MA. (617) 294-0260.

Hockeytown USA Inc., Saugus, MA. (617) 233-3667.

Hogan Arena, Auburn, MA. (508) 832-5932.

Holiday Twin Rinks, Buffalo, NY. (716) 685-3660.

Hollydell Ice Arena, Sewell, NJ. (609) 589-5599.

Homestead Skating Rink, Hot Springs, VA. (703) 839-7721.

Homewood Flossmoor Ice Arena, Homewood, IL. (708) 957-0100.

Hommocks Park Ice Rink, Mamaronick, NY. (914) 834-1069.

Horgan (Daniel S.) Memorial Rink, Auburn, MA. (508) 832-5932.

Houston Field House, Troy, NY. (518) 276-6262.

Howard Park Ice Rink, South Bend, IN. (219) 235-9451.

Howe Arena, Traverse City, MI. (616) 922-4814.

Howelsen Ice Rink, Steamboat Springs, CO. (303) 879-0341.

Hutchinson Civic Arena, Hutchinson, MN. (612) 234-4227.

Hyland Hills Ice Arena, Westminster, CO. (303) 650-7552.

I. M. A. Ice Arena, Flint, MI. (810) 744-0580.

Ice Box, South Bend, IN. (219) 288-3300.

Ice Castles International Training Center, Lake Arrowhead, CA. (909) 336-4085; (909) 337-0802.

Ice Centre of San Jose, San Jose, CA. (408) 279-6000.

Ice Chalet Eastland Mall, Charlotte, NC. (704) 568-0772.

Ice Chalet Knoxville, Knoxville, TN. (615) 588-1858.

Ice Chalet Memphis, Memphis, TN. (901) 362-8877.

Ice Chalet Northcross, Austin, TX. (512) 451-5102.

Ice Chalet Palm Desert, Palm Desert, CA. (619) 340-4412.

Ice Chalet Rolling Hills, Rolling Hills Estates, CA. (310) 541-6630.

Ice Chalet San Diego, San Diego, CA. (619) 452-9110.

Ice Chalet San Mateo, San Mateo, CA. (415) 574-1616.

Ice Chalet Vallco Fashion Park, Culpertino, CA. (408) 446-2908.

Ice Chateau, Inc., Nokomis, FL. (813) 484-0080.

Ice Chateau of King Louie West, Overland Park, KS. (913) 648-0130.

Ice Connection, Pittsburgh, PA. (412) 898-2440.

Ice Floe Ice Center, Escondido, CA. (619) 489-5550.

Ice Garden, Inc., Belle Vernon, PA. (412) 379-7100.

Ice House, Cary, NC. (919) 467-6000.

Ice Palace, Honolulu, HI. (808) 487-9921.

Ice Palace, Allentown, PA. (610) 435-3031.

Ice Palace, Richmond, VA. (804) 378-7465.

Ice Palace Arena, Phoenix, AZ. (602) 267-0591.

Ice Plaza Galleria, Cape Cirardeau, MO. (314) 335-4405.

Ice Rink on the Terrace, Ft. Wayne, IN. (219) 484-2014.

Ice Sheet, The, Ogden, UT. (801) 399-8750.

Ice Studio, Inc., New York, NY. (212) 535-0304.

Ice Time, Inc., Newbury, NY. (914) 647-4802.

Icebox Sports Arena, Trenton, MI. (313) 676-6429.

Iceland, Niles, IL. (708) 297-8011.

Iceland Associates, Hamilton, NJ. (609) 588-6672.

Iceland Skating Rink, New Hyde Park, NY. (516) 746-1100.

Iceland Sports Centre, Bethany, OK. (405) 789-2090.

Iceland -Virginia Beach, Virginia Beach, VA. (804) 490-3907.

Icelandia Fresno, Fresno, CA. (209) 275-1119.

Icelands, Evendale, OH. (513) 769-0004.

Iceoplex Fremont, Fremont, CA. (510) 490-6621.

Iceoplex North Hills, North Hills, CA. (818) 893-1784.

Indiana Ice Center, East Pike Recreational Complex, Indiana, PA. (412) 465-2665.

Indiana State Fair Coliseum, Indianapolis, IN. (317) 927-7622.

Indiana World Skating Academy, Indianapolis, IN. (317) 237-5565.

Indianapolis Pepsi Coliseum, Indianapolis, IN. (317) 927-7536.

Inglass Rink, New Haven, CT. (203) 432-0877.

Inkster Civic Arena, Inkster, MI. (616) 277-1001.

Inn of the Seventh Mountain, Bend, OR. (503) 382-8711.

International Skating Center of Connecticut, Simsbury, CT. (203) 651-5400.

Inwood Ice Arena, Joliet, IL. (815) 741-7275.

IRA Civic Center Arena, Grand Rapids, MN. (218) 326-2591.

J.F.K. Memorial Rink, Manchester, NH. (603) 649-2109.

Jackson Arena, Stowe, VT. (802) 253-6148.

Janas (John J.) Memorial Skating Rink, Lowell, MA. (508) 454-6662.

Janesville Ice Arena, Janesville, WI. (608) 755-3014.

Joel (Lawrence) Veterans Memorial Coliseum, Winston-Salem, NC. (910) 725-5635.

Johnson (H. Alden) Rink, South Hamilton, MA. (508) 468-6232.

Johnson Rink - Pingree School, S. Hamilton, MA. (508) 468-6232.

Kansas Coliseum, Witchita, KS. (316) 755-1243.

Kasabuski Arena, Saugus, MA. (617) 231-4183.

Keller Rink - Claflin Athletic Center, Belmont, MA. (617) 484-6178.

Kennebec Ice Arena, Hallowell, ME. (207) 622-6354.

Kennedy Ice Arena, Trenton, MI. (313) 676-7171.

Kennedy (Joseph P.) Jr. Memorial Skating Rink, Hyannis, MA. (508) 790-6346.

Kennedy (Wayne C.) Recreation Complex, St. Louis, MO. (314) 894-3088.

Kenosha County Ice Arena, Kenosha, WI. (414) 694-8011.

Kent State University Ice Arena, Kent, OH. (216) 672-2415.

Kent (Tony) Arena, South Dennis, MA. (508) 760-2415.

Kentwood Ice Arena, Kentwood, MI. (616) 698-0100.

Kettering Ice Arena, Kettering, OH. (513) 296-2587.

Kettle Moraine Ice Center, West Bend, WI. (414) 335-0876.

Keystone Resort Ice Rink, Keystone, CO. (303) 468-4245.

Kimball Union Academy Ice Arena, Meriden, NH. (603) 469-3211.

Kingsgate Skating Club, Kirkland, WI. (206) 823-1242.

Kingswood-Oxford School Rink, West Hartford, CT. (203) 233-9631.

Knickerbocker Ice Arena Facility, Troy, NY. (518) 235-7761.

Kostel (Dan) Recreation Center, Garfield Heights, OH. (216) 475-7272.

Kristofferson (Oscar) Ice Rink, Baxter, MN. (218) 828-3066.

Kutsher's Ice Rink, Monticello, NY. (914) 794-5621.

L'Anse Arena, L'Anse, MI. (906) 524-5707.

La Clement Arena, Henniker, NH. (603) 428-9806.

Lakeland Civic Center, Lakeland, FL. (813) 499-8110.

Lakeland Ice Arena, Waterford, MI. (810) 666-1911.

Lakes Sports Arena, Detroit Lakes, MN. (218) 847-7738.

Lakeview Arena, Marquette, MI. (906) 228-0490.

Lancaster Ice Arena, Lancaster, PA. (717) 581-0274.

Lane County Ice, Eugene, OR. (503) 687-3615.

Lansing Ice Arena, Lansing, MI. (517) 482-1597.

Larsen Ice Skating Facility, Wintrop, MA. (617) 846-5700.

Lawrence Academy Ice Rink, Groton, MA. (508) 448-2239.

Lawrenceville School Rink, Lawrenceville, NJ. (609) 896-0123.

Lawson Ice Arena, Kalamazoo, MI. (616) 387-3050.

Le Grange (Gerald) Feild House, Rye, NY. (914) 967-5876.

Lea (Albert) City Arena, Albert Lea, MN. (507) 377-4374.

Lehigh Valley Ice Arena, Whitehall, PA. (610) 434-6899.

Leisure Rinks Southtowns Inc., Buffalo, NY. (716) 675-8992.

Levy Community Ice Rink, Harrisville, RI. (401) 568-8615.

Lexington Ice Arena, Lexington, KY. (606) 269-5681.

Lincoln Center Ice Arena, Columbus, IN. (812) 376-2686.

Lincoln Park Community Center, Lincoln Park, MI. (313) 386-4075.

Lindell (John) Arena, Royal Oak, MI. (810) 544-6690.

Litchfield Civic Arena, Litchfield, MN. (612) 693-2679.

Little Rock Skating Arena, Little Rock, AR. (501) 227-4333.

Lively (Jay) Activity Center, Flagstaff, AZ. (602) 774-1051.

Lloyd Center Ice Pavillion, Portland, OR. (503) 288-4599.

LoConte Memorial SkatingRink, Medford, MA. (617) 395-9594.

Long Barn Ice Arena, Long Barn, CA. (209) 586-0753.

Long Island Skating Academy, Syosset, NY. (516) 496-2277.

Longbeach Arena, Inc., Long Beach, NY. (516) 431-6501.

Loomis-Chaffee School Ice Rink, Windsor, CT. (203) 688-4934.

Loring (E. F.) Arena, Framingham, MA. (508) 620-4876.

Lossone Ice Rink - Williston Academy, East Hampton, MA. (413) 527-1520.

Lund Center Ice Arena, St. Peters, MN. (507) 933-7615.

Lynah Rink, Ithaca, NY. (607) 255-3793.

Lyon County Ice Facility, Marshall, MN. (507) 537-6795.

Lysander - Radisson Arena, Baldwinsville, NY. (315) 635-1555.

Mackay Ice Arena Inc., Englewood, NJ. (201) 568-3133.

MacKenzie Ice Arena, Lake Forest, IL. (708) 234-3210.

Madison Ice Arena, Madison, WI. (608) 246-4513.

Mandigo (Royce) Arena, Rutland, VT. (802) 773-9416.

Manitowoc Ice Center, Manitowoc, WI. (414) 683-4530.

Marathon County Multi-Purpose Building, Wausau, WI. (715) 847-5364.

Marinette Civic Center, Marinette, WI. (715) 732-0558.

Marmo (Joe) and Wayne Lehto Ice Arena, Idaho Falls, ID. (208) 529-1479.

Marriot Tam-Tara Resort, Osage Beach, MO. (314) 348-3131.

Marshfield Youth Ice and Recreation Center, Marshfield, WI. (715) 384-0025.

Martha's Vineyard Arena, Oak Bluffs, MA. (508) 693-4438.

Massena Arena, Massena, NY. (315) 769-3161.

Matthews Arena at Northeastern University, Boston, MA. (617) 373-3377.

McCann Ice Arena, Poughkeepsie, NY. (914) 454-5800.

McCollum Ice Arena - Northfield School, Mount Herman, MA. (413) 498-3000.

McFetridge Sports Center, Chicago, IL. (312) 478-0210.

McMillen Ice Arena, Ft. Wayne, IN. (219) 744-0848.

McMorran Place Arena, Port Huron, MI. (810) 985-6166.

McVann - O'Keefe Memorial Rink, Peabody, MA. (508) 535-2110.

Meachen Arena, Syracuse, NY. (315) 492-0179.

Meadville Area, Recreation Complex, Meadville, PA. (814) 724-6006.

Meehan (George) Auditorium, Providence, RI. (401) 863-2236.

Melody Brook Ice Rink, Colmar, PA. (215) 822-3613.

Melvindale Arena, Melvindale, MI. (313) 928-1201.

Memorial Arena, Warroad, MN. (218) 386-9979.

Memorial Arena - Pekin Park District, Pekin, IL. (309) 346-1240.

Mennen (William G.) Sports Arena, Morris Township, NJ. (201) 326-7651.

Mentor Civic Ice Arena, Mentor, OH. (216) 255-1777.

Mercer County Public Skating Center, Trenton, NJ. (609) 586-8092.

Mercyhurst College Ice Rink, Erie, PA. (814) 824-2142.

Merill-Lindsay Arena, New Hampton, NH. (603) 744-5401.

Merrifield Complex, Mishawaka, IN. (219) 258-1664.

Methuen High Skating Rink, Methuen, MA. (508) 687-8008.

Metro Ice Sports Arena, Urbandale, IA. (515) 278-9757.

Miami Ice Arena, Inc., North Miami Beach, FL. (305) 940-8222.

Mich - E - Kewis Ice Rink, Alpena, MI. (517) 354-8191.

Michigan Tech Skating Academy Student Ice Arena, Houghton, MI. (906) 487-2994.

Midland Civic Arena, Midland, MI. (517) 832-8438.

Milford Ice Pavilion, Milford, CT. (203) 878-6516.

Mill Creek Park Ice Rink, Youngstown, OH. (216) 740-7114.

Minneapolis Parks & Recreation Board, Minneapolis, MN. (612) 661-4800.

Minnehaha Ice Arena, Minneapolis, MN. (612) 729-8770.

Minnetonka Ice Arena, Minnetonka, MN. (612) 939-8310.

Minute Man Skating School Rink, West Concord, MA. (508) 649-6391.

MIT Skating Rink - Johnson Athletic Center, Cambridge, MA. (617) 253-4497.

Mitchell YMCA, Spruce Pine, NC. (704) 765-7766.

Montclair Arena, Montclair, NJ. (201) 744-6088.

Moore (Charles) Arena, Orleans, MA. (508) 255-5902.

Mora Civic Center - Kanabu County Fair Grounds, Mora, MN. (612) 679-2443.

Morgantown Municipal Rink, Morgantown, WV. (304) 292-6865.

Moses Lake Municipal Ice Rink, Moses Lake, WA. (509) 766-9240.

Mountain Lions Club, Greenland, MI. (906) 883-3208.

Mountain View Ice Arena, Iron Mountain, MI. (906) 774-1480.

Mt. Lebanon Recreation Center, Mt. Lebanon, PA. (412) 561-4363.

Mt. Pleasant Ice Arena, Baltimore, MD. (410) 444-1888.

Mt. Vernon Recreation Center, Alexandria, VA. (703) 768-3224.

Mullins (William D.) Memorial Center, Amherst, MA. (413) 545-4770.

Munn Ice Arena, East Lansing, MI. (517) 353-4698.

Murphy (Frances Al) Memorial Skating Rink, S. Boston, MA. (617) 269-7060.

Murray (Edward J.) Memorial Skating Center, Yonkers, NY. (914) 377-6469.

Nadal Rink, Kent, CT. (203) 927-3501.

Nashoba Valley Olympia, Boxborough, MA. (508) 263-3020.

Nasser Civic Center Ice Rink, Corning, NY. (607) 936-3764.

National Hockey Center, St. Cloud, MN. (612) 255-3327.

Navesink Country Club, Middletown, NJ. (908) 842-3111.

Navin (John J.) Rink, Marlboro, MA. (508) 481-5252.

Negawnee Ice Arena, Negawnee, MI. (906) 475-7900.

Nelson Arena at Middlebury College, Middlebury, VT. (802) 388 3711 Ext. 5411.

Nelson (Franklin) Center, Springfield, IL. (217) 753-2800.

Neville Ice Arena, Pittsburgh, PA. (412) 481-3351.

Nevin (Kirk) Ice Arena, Greensburg, PA. (412) 834-4880.

New Canaan Winter Club, New Canaan, CT. (203) 966-4280.

New Hampshire College Ice Rink, Manchester, NH. (603) 668-2211.

New Hartford Recreation Center, New Hartford, NY. (315) 724-0600.

New Hope Ice Arena, New Hope, MN. (612) 531-5181.

Newbridge Road Ice Rink, Bellmore, NY. (516) 783-6181.

Newell II (Edgar Allen) Dome, Ogdensburg, NY. (315) 393-5320.

Nobel & Greenough School Ice Rink, Dedham, MA. (617) 326-3700.

North Country Recreation Center, St. Louis, MO. (314) 355-7374.

North Hollywood Ice Chalet, N. Hollywood, CA. (818) 985-5555.

North Iowa Ice Arena, Mason City, IA. (515) 424-3547.

North Jeffco Ice Arena, Arvada, CO. (303) 421-1786.

North Olmstead Recreation Complex, North Olmstead, OH. (216) 734-8200.

North Park Ice Rink, Allison Park, PA. (412) 935-1280.

North Star Youth Forum, Westboro, MA. (508) 366-1562.

North Yarmouth Academy Ice Arena, Yarmouth, ME. (207) 846-9051.

Northbrook Sports Center, Northbrook, IL. (708) 291-2980.

Northfield Ice Arena, Northfield, MN. (507) 645-6556.

Northland Ice Center, Cincinnati, OH. (513) 563-0001.

Northshire Civic Center, Manchester, VT. (802) 362-0150.

Northwest Family Sports Center, Inc., Baltimore, MD. (410) 433-4970.

Norwalk Ice Arena, Norwalk, CA. (310) 921-5391.

Notre Dame Arena Inc., Berlin, NH. (603) 752-9846.

Notre Dame Ice Arena, Notre Dame, IN. (219) 631-5247.

O'Brian Ice Rink, Woburn, MA. (617) 938-1620.

O'Keefe Rink at Salem State College, Salem, MA. (508) 741-6560.

O'Leary Park VFW Arena, East Grand Forks, MN. (218) 773-9073.

O'Neill (Emmons Horrigan) Memorial Rink, Charlestown, MA. (617) 242-9728.

Oak Park Ice Arena, Stockton, CA. (209) 937-7432.

Oaklawn Ice Arena, Oaklawn, IL. (708) 857-2210.

Oakton Ice Arena, Park Ridge, IL. (708) 692-3359.

Ocean Ice Palace, Brick, NJ. (908) 477-4411.

Oceanside Ice Arena, Tempe, AZ. (602) 941-0944.

Ohio State University Ice Rink, Columbus, OH. (614) 292-4154.

Old Bridge Arena, Old Bridge, NJ. (908) 679-3100.

Old York Rd. Skating Club, Elkins Park, PA. (215) 635-2770.

Olean Recreation Center, Olean, NY. (716) 373-7465.

Olson (Huck) Memorial Civic Center, Thief River Falls, MN. (218) 681-2519.

Olympia Skate and Roller Center, West Springfield, MA. (413) 736-8100.

Olympic Regional Development Authority Olympic Center (ORDA), Lake Placid, NY. (518) 523-3325.

Olympic View Ice Arena, Mt. Lake Terrace, WA. (206) 672-9012.

On Center Arena, Syracuse, NY. (315) 435-8000.

Onalaska Omni Center, Onalaska, WI. (608) 781-9566.

Ontario Ice Skating Center, Ontario, CA. (909) 986-0793.

Orlando Ice Skating Palace, Orlando, FL. (407) 294-5419.

Orr (Clifford E.) Arena, Euclid, OH. (216) 289-8649.

Orr Rink, Amherst, MA. (413) 542-7950.

Oscar Johnson Arena, St. Paul, MN. (612) 645-7203.

Outpost Ice Arena, Albuquerque, NM. (505) 856-7594.

Owens Recreation Center, Peoria, IL. (309) 686-3368.

Owensboro Ice Arena, Owensboro, KY. (502) 687-8720.

Palmer (David S.) Civic Center, Danville, IL. (217) 431-2424.

Paquette (Gordon H.) Municipal Arena, Burlington, VT. (802) 864-0123.

Parade Ice Arena, Minneapolis, MN. (612) 348-4853.

Paramount Iceland Arena, Sacramento, CA. (916) 925-3529.

Parkaire Ice Arena, Marietta, GA. (404) 973-0753.

Parks & Recreation Department, Burnsville, MN. (612) 895-4500.

Parks & Recreation Department, Fergus Falls, MN. (218) 739-3205.

Parks & Recreation Department, Willmar, MN. (612) 235-1854.

Parkwood Ice Rink, Great Neck, NY. (516) 487-2976.

Parma Heights Municipal Ice Rink, Parma Heights, OH. (216) 842-5005.

Pasadena Ice Skating Center, Pasadena, CA. (818) 578-0801.

Patterson Ice Center, Grand Rapids, MI. (616) 940-1423.

Patty Center Ice Arena, Fairbanks, AK. (907) 474-6888.

Pavillion Recreation Center, Cleveland Heights, OH. (216) 321-2090.

Penn State Ice Pavillion, University Park, PA. (814) 863-2039.

Perry Park Ice Rink, Indianapolis, IN. (317) 888-0070.

Peterson (Jason) Memorial Ice Rink, Nikiski, AK. (907) 776-8472.

Petit National Ice Center, Milwaukee, WI. (414) 266-0100.

Philadelphia Skating Club and Humane Society, Ardmore, PA. (610) 642- 8700.

Phillips Exeter Academy Rink, Exeter, NH. (603) 772-4311.

Pickwick Ice Arena, Burbank, CA. (818) 846-0035.

Pilgrim Skating Arena, Hingham, MA. (617) 749-6660.

Pine Street Arena, Postdam, NY. (315) 265-4030.

Piney Orchard Ice Arena, Odenton, MD. (410) 621-7992.

Pioneer Ice Arena, Denver, CO. (303) 758-8019.

Pittsfield Boys & Girls Club Skating Arena, Pittsfield, MA. (413) 447-9380.

Playland Ice Casino: Westchester County, Rye, NY. (914) 921-0370.

Pleasant Arena, St. Paul, MN. (612) 228-1143.

Plymouth Cultural Center, Plymouth, MI. (313) 455-6620.

Point Mallard Ice Rink, Decatur, AL. (205) 355-9817.

Polar Cap Recreation Center, Chenango Bridge, NY. (607) 648-9888.

Polar Dome Ice Arena, East Dundee, IL. (708) 426-6753.

Pop Whalen Rink, Wolfboro, NH. (603) 569-5639.

Porazzo (Lt. Lewis) Skating Arena, East Boston, MA. (617) 567-9571.

Port Washington Family Rink, Port Washington, NY. (516) 484-6800.

Portland Ice Arena, Portland, ME. (207) 774-8553.

Portsmouth Abbey School Rink, Portsmouth, RI. (401) 683-0621.

Pratt (Frederick) Memorial Rink, Concord, MA. (508) 369-2550.

Pratt Rink at Groton School, Groton, MA. (508) 448-3363.

Prestonwood Ice Chalet, Dallas, TX. (214) 980-8988.

Proctor Academy Ice Arena, Andover, NH. (603) 735-6000.

Pueblo Plaza Ice Arena, Pueblo, CO. (719) 542-8784.

Puget Sound Hockey Center, Tacoma, WA. (206) 272-1785.

Pullar Stadium, Sault Ste Marie, MI. (906) 632-6853.

Purpur Arena, Grand Forks, ND. (701) 746-2764.

Quad City Sports Center, Davenport, IA. (319) 322-5220.

Queen City Ice Palace, Helena, MT. (406) 443-4559.

Quincy Youth Arena, Quincy, MA. (617) 479-8371.

Rakow (Scott) Youth Center Ice Rink, Miami Beach, FL. (305) 673-7767.

Randolph Ice Arena, Randolph, MA. (617) 961-4053.

Redford Ice Arena, Redford, MI. (313) 937-0913.

Redwood Empire Ice Arena, Santa Rosa, CA. (707) 546-7147.

Reedsburg Ice Arena, Reedsburg, WI. (608) 524-3037.

Reilly Memorial Rink, Brighton, MA. (617) 277-7822.

Reis Ice Rink, Parma, OH. (216) 885-8870.

Reise (Nielson) Arena, Bemidji, MN. (218) 751-4541.

Remson Hockey Ice Rink, Wallingford, CT. (203) 697-2000.

Resort Center Skating Rink, Park City, UT. (801) 649-0468.

Reston Ice Forum, Reston, VA. (703) 709-1010.

Rhinelander Ice Arena, Rhinelander, WI. (715) 369-1416.

Rhode Island Sports Center, North Smithfield, RI. (401) 762-1588.

Ridgefield Skating Center, Ridgefield, CT. (203) 438-5277.

Ridgeland Common, Oak Park, IL. (708) 848-9661.

Rinx, The - Hidden Pond Park, Hauppague, NY. (516) 232-5222.

Ristuccia (Eleanor M.) Memorial Arena, Wilmington, MA. (508) 657-3976.

Ritter (Frank) Memorial Arena, Rochester, NY. (716) 475-2222.

Riverfront Park, Wenatchee, WA. (509) 664-5994.

Riverfront Park Ice Palace, Spokane, WA. (509) 625-6687.

Rivergate Ice Rink, New York, NY. (212) 689-0035.

Riverside Arena, Austin, MN. (507) 437-7676.

Riverside Centroplex, Baton Rouge, LA. (504) 389-3030.

Riverview Ice House, Rockford, IL. (815) 963-7465.

Rizzo Ice Rink, Philadelphia, PA. (215) 685-1593.

Roanoke Civic Center, Roanoke, VA. (703) 981-2241.

Roberts (James) Ice Rink at Milton Academy, Milton, MA. (617) 698-7800.

Robinson Arena at Hebron Academy, Hebron, ME. (207) 966-2812.

Rochester Arena, Rochester, NH. (603) 335-6749.

Rochester Olmstead Recreation Center, Rochester, MN. (507) 281-6167.

Rock On Ice, Orlando, FL. (407) 352-4043.

Rockbridge Skating Club, Columbia, SC. (803) 782-3425.

Rockefeller Plaza Ice Rink, New York, NY. (212) 757-5730.

Rockland Rink, Rockland, MA. (617) 878-5591.

Rocky River Recreation Center, Rocky River, OH. (216) 356-5658.

Rolling Meadows Ice Arena, Rolling Meadows, IL. (708) 818-3210.

Roseville Ice Arena, Roseville, MN. (612) 484-0269.

Rouses Point Recreation Center, Rouses Point, NY. (518) 297-6776.

Runestone Community Center, Alexandria, MN. (612) 763-4466.

Ryan (John A.) Skating Arena, Watertown, MA. (617) 972-6468.

S.A.R.A. Park Recreation Center, Tomahawk, WI. (715) 453-4040.

Saginaw Bay Ice Arena, Saginaw, MI. (517) 799-8950.

Saints Spectrum, Bridgeview, IL. (708) 598-3738.

Salisbury School, Salisbury, CT. (203) 435-9658.

Salmon River Central Skating Arena, Ft. Covington, NY. (518) 358-2215.

San Diego Ice Arena, San Diego, CA. (619) 530-1826.

Santa Fe Ice Skating Arena, Las Vegas, NV. (702) 658-4991.

Saranac Lake Civic Center, Saranac Lake, NY. (518) 891-3800.

Saratoga Springs Ice Rink, Saratoga Springs, NY. (518) 583-3462.

Saratoga Springs Ice Rink, Saratoga Springs, NY. (518) 587-3550.

Sawyer Ice Arena, Bangor, ME. (207) 947-0071.

Schaumberg Ice Rink, Bismarck, ND. (701) 221-6813.

Schenley Park Ice Arena, Pittsburgh, PA. (412) 422-6523.

Schmidt Ice Rink, Lakeville, CT. (203) 435-2591.

Schneider Arena, Providence, RI. (401) 865-2168.

Scottsville Ice Arena, Scottsville, NY. (716) 889-1817.

Sculpture Garden Ice Rink, Washington, DC. (202) 371-5340.

Seattle Center Arena, Seattle, WA. (206) 728-9124.

Sertich (Mark "Pa") Ice Center, Colorado Springs, CO. (719) 578-6883.

Seven Bridges Ice Arena, Woodridge, IL. (708) 271-4423.

Seven Peaks Ice Rink, Provo, UT. (801) 373-8777.

Sharpstown Ice Center, Houston, TX. (713) 784-2971.

Shea Memorial Rink, Quincy, MA. (617) 472-9325.

Shoreview Arena, Shoreview, MN. (612) 484-2400.

Shove Park Recreation Center, Chamillus, NY. (315) 487-5068.

Side By Side Ice Skating Rink, Huntington Beach, CA. (714) 842-9143.

Simek Recreation Center, Medford, WI. (715) 748-6655.

Simoni (Romano) Skating Rink, Cambridge, MA. (617) 354-9523.

Simsbury Farms Recreation Complex Ice Rink, W. Simsbury, CT. (203) 658-3836.

Sioux City Municipal Auditorium, Sioux City, IA. (712) 279-4800.

Skate World, Inc., Jacksonville, FL. (904) 399-3223.

Skating Club of Boston, Brighton, MA. (617) 782-5900.

Skating Club of Wilmington, Inc., Wilmington, DE. (302) 656-5007.

Skating Edge, Inc., Harbor City, CA. (310) 325-4475.

Skating Institute of Rochester, Rochester, NY. (716) 325-2216.

Skatium, Skokie, IL. (708) 674-1510.

Sky Rink, New York, NY. (212) 239-8385.

Smead (Ray) Ice Arena, Springfield, MA. (413) 787-6453.

Smithfield Municipal Ice Rink, Smithfield, RI. (401) 231-7677.

Sno-King Ice Arena, Lynnwood, WA. (206) 775-7512.

Snow King Center at Snow King Resort, Jackson, WY. (307) 733-5200.

South Kent School Arena, South Kent, CT. (203) 927-4896.

South Mountain Arena, West Orange, NJ. (201) 731-3828.

South Suburban Ice Arena, Littleton, CO. (303) 798-7881.

South Windsor Arena, South Windsor, CT. (208) 289-3401.

Southern (Frank) Center Ice Arena, Bloomington, IN. (812) 331-6465.

Southfield Civic Center, Southfield, MI. (313) 354-9357.

Southgate Civic Center Arena, Southgate, MI. (313) 246-1342.

Southwest Ice Arena, Crestwood, IL. (708) 371-1344.

Sport-O-Rama, Monsey, NY. (914) 356-3919.

Sports Park, The, Sandy, NY. (801) 562-4444.

Sprinker (Harry) Recreation Center, Tacoma, WA. (206) 537-2600.

Squaw Valley USA, Squaw Valley, CA. (916) 581-5518.

St. Clair Shores Civic Arena, St. Clair Shores, MI. (313) 445-5350.

St. Louis Park Recreation Center, St. Louis Park, MN. (612) 924-2545.

St. Mary's College Ice Arena, Winona, MN. (507) 457-1412.

St. Paul Parks & Recreation, St. Paul, MN. (612) 266-6400.

St. Peters Rec-Plex, St. Peters, MO. (314) 298-2550.

St. Sebastian's Ice Skating Rink, Needham, MA. (617) 449-5208.

Starr Rink - Reid Athletic Center, Hamilton, NY. (315) 824-7570.

Staten Island War Memorial Ice Rink, Staten Island, NY. (718) 720-1010.

Steriti Memorial Rink, Boston, MA. (617) 523-9327.

Stoneham Arena, Stoneham, MA. (617) 279-2628.

Stream (Carol) Ice Rink, Carol Stream, IL. (708) 682-4480.

Sukee Arena and Events Center, Winslow, ME. (207) 872-5994.

Sumner Smith Hockey Rink, Andover, MA. (508) 475-3400.

Sun Blades Ice Rink, Clearwater, FL. (813) 536-5843.

Sun Prairie Ice Arena, Sun Prairie, WI. (608) 837-4434.
Sun Valley Skating Center, Sun Valley, ID. (208) 622-2194.
Sunday River Ski Resort, Bethel, ME. (207) 824-3000.
Sunnycrest Arena, Syracuse, NY. (315) 473-4333.
Sunrise Ice Skating Center, Sunrise, FL. (305) 741-2366.
SUNY Field House, Plattsburgh, NY. (518) 564-3060.
Superior Ice Rink, Kings Park, NY. (516) 269-3904.
Swonder Ice Rink, Evansville, IN. (812) 479-0989.

Taft SchoolMays Rink, Watertown, CT. (203) 274-2516.
Talbot County Community Center, Easton, MD. (410) 822-7070.
Talbot (Dorothy M.) Memorial Rink, Gloucester, MA. (508) 281-9856.
Talsor Academy Skating Rink, Marion, MA. (508) 748-2000.
Tam O'Shanter Ice Rink, Sylvania, OH. (419) 885-1167.
Tampa Bay Skating Academy, Oldsmar, FL. (813) 854-4009.
Tandy Center Ice Rink, Fort Worth, TX. (817) 878-4848.
Tate Rink at West Point, West Point, NY. (914) 938-4011.
Taylor Arena, Northfield, VT. (802) 485-2567.
Telfer Park Sports and Activity Center, Beloit, WI. (608) 364-2890.
Thayer (William H.) Arena and Warburton (Joe) Arena, Warwick, RI. (401) 738-2000.
The Rink, Battle Creek, MI. (616) 966-3625.
Thibodiau (Marc) Memorial Rink, Millinocket, ME. (207) 723-7013.
Thompson (Loren) Park, Baxter, MN. (218) 829-7161.
Thornton Park Ice Rink, Shaker Heights, OH. (216) 491-1290.
Tilton School Rink, Tilton, NH. (603) 286-4342.
Timberline Ice Arena, Reading, PA. (610) 929-0808.
Town of Hartford BOR Rink, White River Junction, VT. (802) 295-3236.
Tri -County Ice Arena, Neenah, WI. (414) 731-9731.
Tri-Cities Coliseum, Kennewick, WA. (509) 783-8824.
Tri-Town Sports Center, Cromwell, CT. (203) 632-0323.
Trinity-Pawling School Rink, Pawling, NY. (914) 855-3100.
Tucker Road Ice Arena, Fort Washington, MD. (301) 248-3124.
Tully Forum - University of Massachusetts, Lowell, North Billerica, MA. (508) 934-4987.
Tulsa Ice Arena, Tulsa, OK. (918) 254-7272.
Twin Ponds, Inc., Harrisburg, PA. (717) 558-7663.
Twin Rinks, Pensaulkin, PA. (609) 488-9300.
Twin Rinks Ice Sports & Entertainment Center, Pennsauken, NJ. (609) 488-9300.
Ulin Memorial Rink, Milton, MA. (617) 696-9869.
United Skates, Lubbock, TX. (806) 745-3600.

University of Colorado Ice Arena, Boulder, CO. (303) 492-7678.
University of Connecticut Ice Rink, Storrs, CT. (203) 486-3808.
University of Delaware Arena, Newark, DE. (302) 831-6038.
University of Denver Ice Arena, Denver, CO. (303) 871-3905.
University of IL at Chicago Auxiliary Practice Ice Rink, Chicago, IL. (312) 413-5300.
University of Illinois Arena, Champaign, IL. (217) 333-2212.
University of Michigan Dearborn Arena, Dearborn, MI. (313) 593-5540.
University of Wisconsin WH Hunt Arena, River Falls, WI. (715) 425-3381.
University School of Milwaukee Fieldhouse, Milwaukee, WI. (414) 352-6000.
US High Altitude Sports Center, Butte, MT. (406) 723-7060.
Utica Memorial Auditorium, Utica, NY. (315) 853-6147.

Valley Ice Arena, Beaverton, OR. (503) 297-2521.
Van Buren Ice Rink, Van Buren, ME. (207) 868-3395.
Van Nuys Iceland, Van Nuys, CA. (818) 785-2171.
Ventor Ice Rink, Ventor, NJ. (609) 823-7947.
Veteran's Memorial Ice Rink, Haverhill, MA. (508) 373-9351.
Veteran's Memorial Ice Rink, Everett, MA. (617) 389-9401.
Veterans Ice Arena, Ann Arbor, MI. (313) 994-2785.
Veterans Memorial Arena, Franklin, MA. (508) 541-7024.
Veterans Memorial Rink, Waltham, MA. (617) 893-9409.
Veterans Memorial Rink, Somerville, MA. (617) 623-3523.
Veterans Memorial Rink, Arlington, MA. (617) 641-5492.
Veterans Memorial Skating Rink, West Hartford, CT. (203) 521-1573.
VFW All Seasons Arena, Bismarck, ND. (701) 221-6814.
Victory Memorial Ice Arena, Minneapolis, MN. (612) 627-2953.
Vietnam Veterans Memorial Rink, North Adams, MA. (413) 664-9474.
Viroqua Community Arena, Viroqua, WI. (608) 637-8661.
Vogel Arena, New Ulm, MN. (507) 354-8321.
Volpe (St. Peter) Complex, North Andover, MA. (508) 837-5295.

Wakota Arena, South St Paul, MN. (612) 451-1727.
Walker Arena, Muskegon, MI. (616) 726-2939.
Wallace Civic Center Complex, Fitchburg, MA. (508) 345-7593.
Wallman (Kate) Prospect Park, Brooklyn, NY. (718) 282-1226.
Warinanco Skating Center, Roselle, NJ. (908) 298-7850.
Washington Ice Rink, Lansing, MI. (517) 483-4230.

Washington Park Ice Arena, Jefferson City, MO. (314) 634-6482.

Watertown Fairgrounds Arena, Watertown, NY. (315) 785-7836.

Watts Ice Center - Glencoe Park District, Glencoe, IL. (708) 835-4440.

Waupun Community Center, Waupun, WI. (414) 324-9918.

Wayne Community Center, Wayne, MI. (313) 721-7400.

Wells (Herbert) Ice Rink, College Park, MD. (301) 277-3717.

Wells Sports Complex, Escanaba, MI. (906) 786-3995.

Wesleyan Arena-Freeman Athletic Center, Middletown, CT. (203) 685-2927.

Wessman Arena, Superior, WI. (715) 394-8361.

West Side Ice Arena, Manchester, NH. (603) 624-6574.

West Suburban Arena, Natick, MA. (508) 655-1013.

West Warwick Civic Center Arena, West Warwick, RI. (401) 822-9260.

Westland Sports Arena, Westland, MI. (313) 729-4560.

Westminster School Ice Arena, Simsbury, CT. (203) 658-4444.

Whatcom County Sports Arena, Bellingham, WA. (206) 676-7305.

Wheaton Ice Rink, Wheaton, MD. (301) 649-2703.

Wheeling Park Memorial Ice Rink, Wheeling, WV. (304) 242-3770.

White Bear Arena, White Bear Lake, MN. (612) 777-8255.

White Bear Lake Sports Center, White Bear Lake, MN. (612) 429-8571.

Whitestown Community Center, Whitestown, NY. (315) 853-6147.

Wilcoxon (Benton H.) Municipal Iceplex, Huntsville, AL. (205) 883-3774.

Wilkes Barre Ice-A-Rama, Wilkes Barre, PA. (717) 821-1167.

Willett (K.B.) Arena, Stevens Point, WI. (715) 346-1576.

Williams Arena, Minneapolis, NJ. (612) 625-5804.

Williams College, Lausing Chapman Rink, Williamstown, MA. (413) 597-2283.

Willmar Civic Center, Willmar, MN. (612) 235-1454.

Willow Grove Ice Rink, Inc., Willow Grove, PA. (215) 659-4253.

Wilson (Ira S.) Ice Arena, Geneseo, NY. (716) 245-5356.

Wilson (John L.) Arena, Jamestown, ND. (701) 252-3939.

Wilson Park Recreation Center, Milwaukee, WI. (414) 281-6289.

Winding River Skating Center, Toms River, NJ. (908) 244-0720.

Wings Annex, Kalamazoo, MI. (616) 345-1125.

Wings Stadium, Kalamazoo, MI. (616) 345-1125.

Winnetka Ice Arena, Winnetka, IL. (708) 501-2060.

Winter Club of Lake Forest, Lake Forest, IL. (708) 234-0030.

Winter Club, The, Huntington, NY. (516) 421-3889.

Winter Lodge, The, Palo Alto, CA. (415) 493-4566.

Winterhurst Ice Rink, Lakewood, OH. (216) 529-4400.

Wissahickon Skating Club, Philadelphia, PA. (215) 247-1759.

Withington (Nelson) Arena, Brattleboro, VT. (802) 257-2311.

Wollman Rink - Central Park Ice Chalet, New York, NY. (212) 517-4800.

Wonderland of Ice, Bridgeport, CT. (203) 576-8110.

Woodbury Community Park Ice Rink, Woodbury, NY. (516) 677-5990.

Worcester State Rink, Worcester, MA. (508) 755-0582.

World's Fair Ice Skating Rink, Flushing, NY. (718) 699-4215.

Yack (Benjamin F.) Arena, Wyandotte, MI. (313) 246-4490.

Yackel (Ken) - West Side Arena, St. Paul, MN. (612) 228-1145.

Yakima Ice Arena, Yakima, WA. (509) 248-6315.

YMCA Albany County Hockey Training Facility, Loudenville, NY. (518) 452-7396.

York City Ice Rink, York, PA. (717) 843-3959.

Yosemite Concession Services Rink, Yosemite National Park, CA. (209) 372-1418.

Yost Ice Arena - University of Michigan, Ann Arbor, MI. (313) 764-4599.

Young Arena, Waterloo, IA. (319) 291-4491.

YWCA Ice Chalet, Walla Walla, WA. (509) 525-2575.

Zion Ice Arena, Zion, IL. (708) 746-5503.

ILLUSTRATION BY WILLIAM CASEY

Rinks Affiliated with Colleges or Universities Listed by State

Following is a listing of colleges and universities that are affiliated with ice skating rinks. In some cases, the college owns and operates the rink; in other cases, the students have access to the ice through other arrangements. The listing below is in order by state and city. The second listing (page 248) is in alphabetical order by the name of the college or university affiliated with the rink. For more detailed information on the rinks, turn to the primary rink listing that starts on page 135.

AK: ALASKA
Anchorage, AK: University of Alaska, *Anchorage Sports Center Ice Rink*, (907) 786-1232.
Fairbanks, AK: University of Alaska, *Patty Center Ice Arena*, (907) 474- 6888.

AZ: ARIZONA
Flagstaff, AZ: Northern Arizona University, *Flagstaff Municipal Ice Arena*, (602) 774-1051.

CALIFORNIA
Fresno, CA: California State University, *Icelandia Fresno*, (209) 275-1119.
Huntington Beach, CA: Long Beach State, *Side By Side Ice Skating Rink*, (714) 842-9143.

COLORADO
Boulder, CO: University of Colorado, *University of Colorado Ice Arena*, (303) 492-7678.
Colorado Springs, CO: U.S. Air Force Academy, *Air Force Academy Ice Arena*, (719) 472-4032.
Denver, CO: University of Denver, *University of Denver Ice Arena*, (303) 871-3905.
Ft. Collins, CO: Colorado State University, *Edora Pool Ice Center*, (303) 221-6679.

CONNECTICUT
Hamden, CT: Quinnitiac College, *Hamden Community Ice Rink*, (203) 287-2610.
Middletown, CT: Wesleyan University, *Wesleyan Arena-Freeman Athletic Center*, (203) 685-2927.
New Haven, CT: Yale University, *Inglass Rink*, (203) 432-0877.
New London, CT: Connecticut College, *Dayton Arena*, (203) 439-2575.
Ridgefield, CT: Western Connecticut State University, *Ridgefield Skating Center*, (203) 438-5277.
Storrs, CT: University of Connecticut, *University of Connecticut Ice Rink*, (203) 486-3808.
West Hartford, CT: Trinity College, *Kingswood-Oxford School Rink*, (203) 233-9631.

DELAWARE
Newark, DE: University of Delaware, *University of Delaware Arena*, (302) 831-6038.

IOWA
Ames, IA: Iowa State University, *Ames/Iowa State University Ice Arena*, (515) 292-6835.
Sioux City, IA: Univerity of South Dakota, *Sioux City Municipal Auditorium*, (712) 279-4800.

ILLINOIS
Champaign, IL: University of Illinois, *University of Illinois Arena*, (217) 333-2212.
Chicago, IL: University of Illinois at Chicago, *University of IL at Chicago Auxiliary Practice Ice Rink*, (312) 413-5300.

INDIANA
Notre Dame, IN: University of Notre Dame, *Notre Dame Ice Arena*, (219) 631-5247.

MASSACHUSETTS
Amherst, MA: Amherst College, *Orr Rink*, (413) 542-7950.
Amherst, MA: University of Massachusetts, *Mullins (William D.) Memorial Center*, (413) 545-4770.
Auburn, MA: Nichols University; Clark University, *Hogan Arena*, (508) 832-5932.
Boston, MA: Boston University, *Brown (Walter) Arena*, (617) 353-4632.
Boston, MA: Northeastern University, *Matthews Arena at Northeastern University*, (617) 373-3377.
Boston, MA: Suffolk University, *Steriti Memorial Rink*, (617) 523-9327.
Boston, MA: University of Massachusetts, University of Boston, *Clark Athletic Center Ice Rink*, (617) 287-7801.
Cambridge, MA: Harvard University, *Bright Hockey Center*, (617) 495-7541.
Cambridge, MA: Mass. Institute of Technology, *MIT Skating Rink - Johnson Athletic Center*, (617) 253-4497.
Canton, MA: Curry College, *Canton Metropolis Skating Rink*, (617) 821-5032.
Fitchburg, MA: Fitchburg College, *Wallace Civic Center Complex*, (508) 345-7593.
New Bedford, MA: Univ. of Mass. - Dartmouth, *Hetland (Stephen) Memorial Skating Rink*, (508) 999-9051.
North Adams, MA: North Adam State College, *Vietnam*

Veterans Memorial Rink, (413) 664-9474.
North Andover, MA: Merrimack College, *Volpe (St. Peter) Complex*, (508) 837-5295.
North Billerica, MA: University of Massachussets, *Tully Forum - University of Massachusetts, Lowell*, (508) 934-4987.
Salem, MA: Salem State College, *O'Keefe Rink at Salem State College*, (508) 741-6560.
Somerville, MA: Suffolk University, *Veterans Memorial Rink*, (617) 623-3523.
Springfield, MA: American International College, *Smead (Ray) Ice Arena*, (413) 787-6453.
Stoneham, MA: Tufts University, *Stoneham Arena*, (617) 279-2628.
Taunton, MA: Wheaton College, *Aleixo (Theodore) Skating Rink*, (508) 824-4987.
Watertown, MA: Bentley College, *Ryan (John A.) Skating Arena*, (617) 972-6468.
Wellesley, MA: Babson College, *Babson Recreation Center*, (617) 239-6050.
Williamstown, MA: Williams College, *Williams College, Lausing Chapman Rink*, (413) 597-2283.
Winchendon, MA: Franklin Pierce College, *Clark Memorial Arena*, (508) 297-0102.
Worcester, MA: College of the Holy Cross, *Hart Recreation Center Ice Rink*, (508) 793-3407.

MD: MARYLAND

Annapolis, MD: Naval Academy, *Dahlgren Hall Ice Rink*, (410) 263-4527.

ME: MAINE

Brunswick, ME: Bowdoin College, *Dayton Arena*, (207) 725-3332.
Orono, ME: Univ. of Maine, *Alfond Ice Arena, University of Maine - Orono*, (207) 581-1106.
Portland, ME: University of Southern Maine, *Portland Ice Arena*, (207) 774-8553.
Presque Isle, ME: Northern Maine Technical College, *Forum, The*, (207) 764-0491.
Waterville, ME: Colby College, *Alfond Arena*, (207) 872-3000.

MI: MICHIGAN

Ann Arbor, MI: University of Michigan, Ann Arbor, *Yost Ice Arena - University of Michigan*, (313) 764-4599.
Big Rapids, MI: Ferris State University, *Ewigleben (Robert L.) Ice Arena*, (616) 592-2881.
Dearborn, MI: University of Michigan, *University of Michigan Dearborn Arena*, (313) 593-5540.
East Lansing, MI: Michigan State University, *Munn Ice Arena*, (517) 353-4698.
Grand Rapids, MI: Calvin College, *Patterson Ice Center*, (616) 940-1423.
Houghton, MI: Michigan Tech, *Michigan Tech Skating Academy Student Ice Arena*, (906) 487-2994.
Kalamazoo, MI: Western Michigan University, *Lawson Ice Arena*, (616) 387-3050.
Marquette, MI: Northern Michigan University, *Lakeview Arena*, (906) 228-0490.
Plymouth, MI: East Michigan University, *Plymouth Cultural Center*, (313) 455-6620.
Southfield, MI: Lawrence Technical Institute, *Southfield Civic Center*, (313) 354-9357.

MN: MINNESOTA

Bemidji, MN: Bemidji State University, *Glass (John) Field House*, (218) 755-4140.
Duluth, MN: University of Minnesota at Duluth, *Duluth Entertainment*, (218) 722-5573.
International Falls, MN: Rainer River Community College, *Bronco Arena*, (218) 283-2424.
Minneapolis, MN: Augsburg College, *Augsburg College Ice Arena*, (612) 330-1252.
Northfield, MN: St. Olaf College, *Northfield Ice Arena*, (507) 645-6556.
Roseville, MN: Northwestern College, *Roseville Ice Arena*, (612) 484-0269.
St. Cloud, MN: St. Cloud State University, *National Hockey Center*, (612) 255-3327.
St. Peters, MN: Gustavus Adolphus College, *Lund Center Ice Arena*, (507) 933-7615.
Winona, MN: St. Mary's College, *St. Mary's College Ice Arena*, (507) 457-1412.

NH: NEW HAMPSHIRE

Hanover, NH: Dartmouth College, *Dartmouth College Thompson Arena*, (603) 646-1110.
Henniker, NH: New England College, *La Clement Arena*, (603) 428-9806.
Manchester, NH: Daniel Webster College, *New Hampshire College Ice Rink*, (603) 668-2211.
Manchester, NH: Dartmouth College, *J.F.K. Memorial Rink*, (603) 649-2109.
Manchester, NH: St. Aslem College, *West Side Ice Arena*, (603) 624-6574.
New Hampton, NH: Plymouth State College, *Merill-Lindsay Arena*, (603) 744-5401.

NJ: NEW JERSEY

Bridgewater, NJ: Rutger's Univeristy, *Chimney Rock*, (908) 302-9425.
Englewood, NJ: Columbia University ; Stevens Institute of Technology ; NYU, *Mackay Ice Arena Inc.*, (201) 568-3133.
Minneapolis, NJ: University of Minneapolis, *Williams Arena*, (612) 625-5804.
Princeton, NJ: Princeton University, *Baker Rink*, (609) 258-3000.

NY: NEW YORK

Brockport, NY: State of New York College at Brockport, *Brockport Ice Rink*, (716) 395-5365.
Buffalo, NY: Erie Community College, *Leisure Rinks Southtowns Inc.*, (716) 675-8992.
Canton, NY: St. Lawrence University, *Appleton Arena*, (315) 379-5696.
Chamillus, NY: Lemoin College, *Shove Park Recreation Center*, (315) 487-5068.

Chenango Bridge, NY: Bringham City University, *Polar Cap Recreation Center*, (607) 648-9888.
Geneseo, NY: State University of New York, *Wilson (Ira S.) Ice Arena*, (716) 245-5356.
Ithaca, NY: Cornell University, *Lynah Rink*, (607) 255-3793.
Plattsburgh, NY: SUNY; Plattsburgh, *SUNY Field House*, (518) 564-3060.
Rochester, NY: Rochester Institute of Technology, *Ritter (Frank) Memorial Arena*, (716) 475-2222.
Saranac Lake, NY: North County Community Collge, *Saranac Lake Civic Center*, (518) 891-3800.
Schenectady, NY: Union College, *Achilles Rink - Union College*, (518) 388-6134.
Troy, NY: Rensseler Polytechnic Institute, *Houston Field House*, (518) 276-6262.

OH: OHIO

Bowling Green, OH: Bowling Green State University, *Bowling Green State University Ice Arena*, (419) 372-2264.
Columbus, OH: Ohio State University, *Ohio State University Ice Rink*, (614) 292-4154.
Kent, OH: Kent State University, *Kent State University Ice Arena*, (216) 672-2415.
Oxford, OH: Miami University, *Goggin Ice Arena*, (513) 529-3343.

PA: PENNSYLVANIA

Erie, PA: Mercyhurst College, *Mercyhurst College Ice Rink*, (814) 824-2142.
Johnstown, PA: University of Pittsburg at Johnstown; Indian University of PA, *Cambria County War Memorial*, (814) 536-5156.
Meadville, PA: Allegheny; Slippery Rock; Edinborough, *Meadville Area, Recreation Complex*, (814) 724-6006.
Philadelphia, PA: University of Pennsylvania, Drexell University, *Class of 1923 Ice Rink*, (215) 898-1923.
Pittsburgh, PA: Western PA College; University of Pittsburgh; Carnegie Mellon University, *Golden Mile Ice Center*, (412) 327-7465.
University Park, PA: Penn State, *Penn State Ice Pavillion*, (814) 863-2039.
Whitehall, PA: Lehigh Univ.; Kutztown Univ.; E. Stroudsburg Univ.; Layfayett Univ., *Lehigh Valley Ice Arena*, (610) 434-6899.
Wilkes Barre, PA: Scranton University; Bloomsburg University, *Wilkes Barre Ice-A-Rama*, (717) 821-1167.
York, PA: York College, *York City Ice Rink*, (717) 843-3959.

RI: RHODE ISLAND

Middletown, RI: Salve Regina University, *Cabot Memorial Rink*, (401) 849-3620.
Portsmouth, RI: Roger Williams University, *Portsmouth Abbey School Rink*, (401) 683-0621.
Providence, RI: Brown University, *Meehan (George) Auditorium*, (401) 863-2236.
Providence, RI: Providence College, *Schneider Arena*, (401) 865-2168.
West Warwick, RI: Univiversity of Rhode Island, *West Warwick Civic Center Arena*, (401) 822-9260.

TN: TENNESSEE

Knoxville, TN: University of Tennessee, *Ice Chalet Knoxville*, (615) 588-1858.

UT: UTAH

Ogden, UT: Weber State University, *Ice Sheet, The*, (801) 399-8750.

VA: VIRGINIA

Reston, VA: George Mason University, *Reston Ice Forum*, (703) 709-1010.
Virginia Beach, VA: William & Mary; Old Dominion College; VA Wessleyan; Tidewater Community College, *Iceland - Virginia Beach*, (804) 490-3907.

VT: VERMONT

Middlebury, VT: Middlebury College, *Nelson Arena at Middlebury College*, (802) 388 3711 Ext. 5411.
Northfield, VT: Norwich University, *Taylor Arena*, (802) 485-2567.

WA: WASHINGTON

Bellingham, WA: Western Washington Universtiy, *Whatcom County Sports Arena*, (206) 676-7305.

WI: WISCONSIN

Brookefield, WI: Milwaukee School of Engineering (MSOE), *Eble Park Arena*, (414) 784-7512.
Eau Claire, WI: University of Wisconsin, Eau Claire, *Hobbs Municipal Ice Arena*, (715) 839-5040.
Madison, WI: University of Wisconsin, *Camp Randall Memorial Sports Center*, (608) 263-6565.
Madison, WI: University of Wisconsin, *Dane County EXPO Center*, (608) 267-3976.
Milwaukee, WI: Markette Univ., *Wilson Park Recreation Center*, (414) 281-6289.
Milwaukee, WI: University School of Milwaukee, *University School of Milwaukee Fieldhouse*, (414) 352-6000.
River Falls, WI: University of Wisconsin, *University of Wisconsin WH Hunt Arena*, (715) 425-3381.
Stevens Point, WI: University of Wisconsin, Stevens Point, *Willett (K. B.) Arena*, (715) 346-1576.
Superior, WI: University of Wisconsin, Superior, *Wessman Arena*, (715) 394-8361.

WV: WEST VIRGINIA

Morgantown, WV: West Virginia University, *Morgantown Municipal Rink*, (304) 292-6865.

Turn page for cross-reference of rinks listed by school affiliation

Rinks Affiliated With Colleges or Universities Listed by School Affiliation

The following colleges and universities were listed by the rinks that were surveyed as affiliated in some manner with the rink and its programs. In some cases, the rink is owned by the college. In other cases, the students have access to the rink through other arrangements. The following listing is in alphabetical order by the name of the affiliated college or university. For more details on the rinks, turn to the primary rink listing that begins on page 135.

Allegheny; Slippery Rock; Edinborough: *Meadville Area, Recreation Complex*, Meadville, PA. (814) 724-6006.

American International College: *Smead (Ray) Ice Arena*, Springfield, MA. (413) 787-6453.

Amherst College: *Orr Rink*, Amherst, MA. (413) 542-7950.

Augsburg College: *Augsburg College Ice Arena*, Minneapolis, MN. (612) 330-1252.

Babson College: *Babson Recreation Center*, Wellesley, MA. (617) 239-6050.

Bemidji State University: *Glass (John) Field House*, Bemidji, MN. (218) 755-4140.

Bentley College: *Ryan (John A.) Skating Arena*, Watertown, MA. (617) 972-6468.

Boston University: *Brown (Walter) Arena*, Boston, MA. (617) 353-4632.

Bowdoin College: *Dayton Arena*, Brunswick, ME. (207) 725-3332.

Bowling Green State University: *Bowling Green State University Ice Arena*, Bowling Green, OH. (419) 372-2264.

Bringham City University: *Polar Cap Recreation Center*, Chenango Bridge, NY. (607) 648-9888.

Brown University: *Meehan (George) Auditorium*, Providence, RI. (401) 863-2236.

California State University: *Icelandia Fresno*, Fresno, CA. (209) 275-1119.

Calvin College: *Patterson Ice Center*, Grand Rapids, MI. (616) 940-1423.

Colby College: *Alfond Arena*, Waterville, ME. (207) 872-3000.

College of the Holy Cross: *Hart Recreation Center Ice Rink*, Worcester, MA. (508) 793-3407.

Colorado State University: *Edora Pool Ice Center*, Ft. Collins, CO. (303) 221-6679.

Columbia University ; Stevens Institute of Technology ; NYU: *Mackay Ice Arena Inc.*, Englewood, NJ. (201) 568-3133.

Connecticut College: *Dayton Arena*, New London, CT. (203) 439-2575.

Cornell University: *Lynah Rink*, Ithaca, NY. (607) 255-3793.

Curry College: *Canton Metropolis Skating Rink*, Canton, MA. (617) 821-5032.

Daniel Webster College: *New Hampshire College Ice Rink*, Manchester , NH. (603) 668-2211.

Dartmouth College: *Dartmouth College Thompson Arena*, Hanover, NH. (603) 646-1110.

Dartmouth College: *J.F.K. Memorial Rink*, Manchester, NH. (603) 649-2109.

East Michigan University : *Plymouth Cultural Center*, Plymouth, MI. (313) 455-6620.

Erie Community College: *Leisure Rinks Southtowns Inc.*, Buffalo, NY. (716) 675-8992.

Ferris State University: *Ewigleben (Robert L.) Ice Arena*, Big Rapids, MI. (616) 592-2881.

Fitchburg College: *Wallace Civic Center Complex*, Fitchburg, MA. (508) 345-7593.

Franklin Pierce College: *Clark Memorial Arena*, Winchendon, MA. (508) 297-0102.

George Mason University: *Reston Ice Forum*, Reston, VA. (703) 709-1010.

Gustavus Adolphus College: *Lund Center Ice Arena*, St. Peters, MN. (507) 933-7615.

Harvard University: *Bright Hockey Center*, Cambridge, MA. (617) 495-7541.

Iowa State University: *Ames/Iowa State University Ice Arena*, Ames, IA. (515) 292-6835.

Kent State University: *Kent State University Ice Arena*, Kent, OH. (216) 672-2415.

Lawrence Technical Institute: *Southfield Civic Center*, Southfield, MI. (313) 354-9357.

Lehigh Univ.; Kutztown Univ.; E. Stroudsburg Univ.; Layfayette Univ.; *Lehigh Valley Ice Arena*, Whitehall, PA. (610) 434-6899.

Lemoin College: *Shove Park Recreation Center*, Chamillus, NY. (315) 487-5068.

Long Beach State: *Side By Side Ice Skating Rink*, Huntington Beach, CA. (714) 842-9143.

Markette Univ.: *Wilson Park Recreation Center*, Milwaukee, WI. (414) 281-6289.

Mass. Institute of Technology: *MIT Skating Rink - Johnson Athletic Center*, Cambridge, MA. (617) 253-4497.
Mercyhurst College: *Mercyhurst College Ice Rink*, Erie, PA. (814) 824-2142.
Merrimack College: *Volpe (St. Peter) Complex*, North Andover, MA. (508) 837-5295.
Miami University: *Goggin Ice Arena*, Oxford, OH. (513) 529-3343.
Michigan State University: *Munn Ice Arena*, East Lansing, MI. (517) 353-4698.
Michigan Tech: *Michigan Tech Skating Academy Student Ice Arena*, Houghton, MI. (906) 487-2994.
Middlebury College: *Nelson Arena at Middlebury College*, Middlebury, VT. (802) 388 3711 Ext. 5411.
Milwaukee School of Engineering (MSOE): *Eble Park Arena*, Brookefield, WI. (414) 784-7512.

Naval Academy: *Dahlgren Hall Ice Rink*, Annapolis, MD. (410) 263-4527.
New England College: *La Clement Arena*, Henniker, NH. (603) 428-9806.
Nichols University; Clark University: *Hogan Arena*, Auburn, MA. (508) 832-5932.
North Adam State College: *Vietnam Veterans Memorial Rink*, North Adams, MA. (413) 664-9474.
North County Community Collge: *Saranac Lake Civic Center*, Saranac Lake, NY. (518) 891-3800.
Northeastern University: *Matthews Arena at Northeastern University*, Boston, MA. (617) 373-3377.
Northern Arizona University: *Flagstaff Municipal Ice Arena*, Flagstaff, AZ. (602) 774-1051.
Northern Maine Technical College: *Forum, The*, Presque Isle, ME. (207) 764-0491.
Northern Michigan University: *Lakeview Arena*, Marquette, MI. (906) 228-0490.
Northwestern College: *Roseville Ice Arena*, Roseville, MN. (612) 484-0269.
Norwich University: *Taylor Arena*, Northfield, VT. (802) 485-2567.

Ohio State University: *Ohio State University Ice Rink*, Columbus, OH. (614) 292-4154.

Penn State: *Penn State Ice Pavillion*, University Park, PA. (814) 863-2039.
Plymouth State College: *Merill-Lindsay Arena*, New Hampton, NH. (603) 744-5401.
Princeton University: *Baker Rink*, Princeton, NJ. (609) 258-3000.
Providence College: *Schneider Arena*, Providence, RI. (401) 865-2168.

Quinnitiac College: *Hamden Community Ice Rink*, Hamden, CT. (203) 287-2610.

Rainer River Community College: *Bronco Arena*, International Falls, MN. (218) 283-2424.

Paul Wylie attended Harvard while training.

Rensseler Polytechnic Institute: *Houston Field House*, Troy, NY. (518) 276-6262.
Rochester Institute of Technology: *Ritter (Frank) Memorial Arena*, Rochester, NY. (716) 475-2222.
Roger Williams University: *Portsmouth Abbey School Rink*, Portsmouth, RI. (401) 683-0621.
Rutger's Univeristy: *Chimney Rock*, Bridgewater, NJ. (908) 302-9425.

Salem State College: *O'Keefe Rink at Salem State College*, Salem, MA. (508) 741-6560.
Salve Regina University: *Cabot Memorial Rink*, Middletown, RI. (401) 849-3620.
Scranton University; Bloomsburg University: *Wilkes Barre Ice-A-Rama*, Wilkes Barre, PA. (717) 821-1167.
St. Aslem College: *West Side Ice Arena*, Manchester, NH. (603) 624-6574.
St. Cloud State University: *National Hockey Center*, St. Cloud, MN. (612) 255-3327.
St. Lawrence University: *Appleton Arena*, Canton, NY. (315) 379-5696.
St. Mary's College: *St. Mary's College Ice Arena*, Winona, MN. (507) 457-1412.
St. Olaf College: *Northfield Ice Arena*, Northfield, MN. (507) 645-6556.
State of New York College at Brockport: *Brockport Ice Rink*, Brockport, NY. (716) 395-5365.
State University of New York: *Wilson (Ira S.) Ice Arena*, Geneseo, NY. (716) 245-5356.
Suffolk University: *Steriti Memorial Rink*, Boston, MA. (617) 523-9327.
Suffolk University: *Veterans Memorial Rink*, Somerville, MA. (617) 623-3523.
SUNY; Plattsburgh: *SUNY Field House*, Plattsburgh, NY. (518) 564-3060.

Trinity College: *Kingswood-Oxford School Rink*, West Hartford, CT. (203) 233-9631.

PHOTO BY ALICE BERMAN

Tufts University: *Stoneham Arena*, Stoneham, MA. (617) 279-2628.

U.S. Air Force Academy: *Air Force Academy Ice Arena*, Colorado Springs, CO. (719) 472-4032.

Union College: *Achilles Rink - Union College*, Schenectady, NY. (518) 388-6134.

Univ. of Maine: *Alfond Ice Arena, University of Maine - Orono*, Orono, ME. (207) 581-1106.

Univ. of Mass. - Dartmouth: *Hetland (Stephen) Memorial Skating Rink*, New Bedford, MA. (508) 999-9051.

Univerity of South Dakota: *Sioux City Municipal Auditorium*, Sioux City, IA. (712) 279-4800.

University of Alaska: *Anchorage Sports Center Ice Rink*, Anchorage, AK. (907) 786-1232.

University of Alaska: *Patty Center Ice Arena*, Fairbanks, AK. (907) 474- 6888.

University of Colorado: *University of Colorado Ice Arena*, Boulder, CO. (303) 492-7678.

University of Connecticut: *University of Connecticut Ice Rink*, Storrs, CT. (203) 486-3808.

University of Delaware: *University of Delaware Arena*, Newark, DE. (302) 831-6038.

University of Denver: *University of Denver Ice Arena*, Denver, CO. (303) 871-3905.

University of Illinois: *University of Illinois Arena*, Champaign, IL. (217) 333-2212.

University of Illinois at Chicago: *University of IL at Chicago Auxiliary Practice Ice Rink*, Chicago, IL. (312) 413-5300.

University of Massachusetts: *Mullens (William D.) Memorial Center*, Amherst, MA. (413) 545-4770.

University of Massachusetts, University of Boston: *Clark Athletic Center Ice Rink*, Boston, MA. (617) 287-7801.

University of Massachussets: *Tully Forum, U Mass - Lowell*, North Billerica, MA. (508) 934-4987.

University of Michigan: *University of Michigan - Dearborn Arena*, Dearborn, MI. (313) 593-5540.

University of Michigan, Ann Arbor: *Yost Ice Arena - University of Michigan*, Ann Arbor, MI. (313) 764-4599.

University of Minneapolis: *Williams Arena*, Minneapolis, NJ. (612) 625-5804.

University of Minnesota at Duluth: *Duluth Entertainment*, Duluth, MN. (218) 722-5573.

University of Notre Dame: *Notre Dame Ice Arena*, Notre Dame, IN. (219) 631-5247.

University of Pennsylvania, Drexell University: *Class of 1923 Ice Rink*, Philadelphia, PA. (215) 898-1923.

University of Pittsburg at Johnstown; Indian University of PA: *Cambria County War Memorial*, Johnstown, PA. (814) 536-5156.

University of Southern Maine: *Portland Ice Arena*, Portland, ME. (207) 774-8553.

University of Tennessee: *Ice Chalet Knoxville*, Knoxville, TN. (615) 588-1858.

University of Wisconsin: *Camp Randall Memorial Sports Center*, Madison, WI. (608) 263-6565.

University of Wisconsin: *Dane County EXPO Center*, Madison, WI. (608) 267-3976.

University of Wisconsin, Eau Claire: *Hobbs Municipal Ice Arena*, Eau Claire, WI. (715) 839-5040.

University of Wisconsin, Stevens Point: *Willett (K. B.) Arena*, Stevens Point, WI. (715) 346-1576.

University of Wisconsin, Superior: *Wessman Arena*, Superior, WI. (715) 394-8361.

University of Wisonsin: *University of Wisconsin WH Hunt Arena*, River Falls, WI. (715) 425-3381.

University School of Milwaukee: *University School of Milwaukee Fieldhouse*, Milwaukee, WI. (414) 352-6000.

Univiversity of Rhode Island: *West Warwick Civic Center Arena*, West Warwick, RI. (401) 822-9260.

Weber State University: *Ice Sheet, The*, Ogden, UT. (801) 399-8750.

Wesleyan University: *Wesleyan Arena-Freeman Athletic Center*, Middletown, CT. (203) 685-2927.

West Virginia University: *Morgantown Municipal Rink*, Morgantown, WV. (304) 292-6865.

Western Connecticut State University: *Ridgefield Skating Center*, Ridgefield, CT. (203) 438-5277.

Western Michigan University: *Lawson Ice Arena*, Kalamazoo, MI. (616) 387-3050.

Western PA College; University of Pittsburgh; Carnegie Mellon University: *Golden Mile Ice Center*, Pittsburgh, PA. (412) 327-7465.

Western Washington Universtiy: *Whatcom County Sports Arena*, Bellingham, WA. (206) 676-7305.

Wheaton College: *Aleixo (Theodore) Skating Rink*, Taunton, MA. (508) 824-4987.

William & Mary; Old Dominion College; VA Wessleyan; Tidewater Community College: *Iceland -Virginia Beach*, Virginia Beach, VA. (804) 490-3907.

Williams College: *Williams College, Lausing Chapman Rink*, Williamstown, MA. (413) 597-2283.

Yale University: *Inglass Rink*, New Haven, CT. (203) 432-0877.

York College: *York City Ice Rink*, York, PA. (717) 843-3959.

Summer Skating Schools

Following is a listing of summer school programs we were able to survey for inclusion in this book. We chose to survey only the larger programs; please keep in mind that many rinks offer local and regional summer schools as well. There are far more summer school programs than the few listed here. We did not in any way attempt to rate or evaluate the programs.

The listings are set up in the following manner:

State, name of summer school, name and address of affiliated rink, person to contact.

Season: what months the program is typically offered; this will vary from year to year.

Sessions Offered: types of sessions offered; whether they are separated by test levels.

Lessons Available: types of lessons and classes available.

Lesson Arrangements: whether lessons need to be arranged through the rink or between the teacher and skater, or can be done either way.

Off-Ice Training: types of supplemental off-ice training offered.

Ages: whether the skating school is geared towards kids only (to 18), all ages, and/or offers adult programs.

Housing: whether available housing is supervised or unsupervised; or if you are on your own, whether a list of potential housing is available.

Ice Purchased: whether ice may be purchased on a monthly, weekly, daily or by-the-session basis.

Test Sessions: if test sessions are offered, and for what organizations.

Competitions: if competitions are held, and for what organizations.

Ice Shows: whether the school offers ice shows on a regular basis.

ILLUSTRATION BY WILLIAM CASEY

CALIFORNIA
Ice Castle International Training Center Summer School
Ice Castles International Training Center
401 Burnt Mill Road, P.O. Box 939
Lake Arrowhead, CA 92352
(909) 336-4085; (909) 337-0802
Contact: Michelle Coffey.
Season: June through August.
Sessions Offered: Patch, Free (low & high test), Dance (all levels), Pairs.
Lessons Available: Private, Power Stroking, Harness.
Lesson Arrangements: Scheduled through Rink.
Off-Ice Training: Ballet, Jazz, Stretching, Strength/Weight Training, Nutrition.
Ages: All Ages. *Housing:* Supervised.
Ice Purchased: Weekly.
Test Sessions: USFSA, ISIA.
Competitions: USFSA.

COLORADO
Aspen Summer Figure Skating School
Aspen Ice Garden
233 W. Hyman
Aspen CO 81611
(303) 920-5141
Contact: Lisa Warner.
Season: June through July.
Sessions Offered: Patch, Free (low & high test), Dance (low & high test), Hockey, Public.
Lessons Available: Private, Group, Edge Class, Power Stroking, Harness, 3-day seminar with *Annie's Edges*.
Lesson Arrangements: Scheduled through Rink, Between Teacher and Skater.
Off-Ice Training: Stretching, Plyometrics, Off-ice jump class.
Ages: All Ages.
Housing: On your own (no list).
Ice Purchased: By the session.
Test Sessions: USFSA.

Vail Summer Skating School
Dobson (John A.) Arena
321 East Lionshead Circle
Vail CO 81657
(303) 479-2271
Contact: Jim Heber.
Season: June through August.
Sessions Offered: Patch, Free (low & high test), Public.
Lessons Available: Private, Harness.
Off-Ice Training: karate.
Ages: All Ages. *Housing:* On your own (List Available).
Ice Purchased: Weekly.
Test Sessions: USFSA.
Competitions: USFSA.
Ice Shows: Yes.

South Suburban Summer Skating School
South Suburban Ice Arena
6580 S. Vine St.
Littleton CO 80121
(303) 798-7881
Contact: Gerry Lane.
Season: June through August.
Sessions Offered: Patch, Free (all levels), Dance (all levels), Pairs, Hockey, Public.
Lessons Available: Private, Group, Harness.
Lesson Arrangements: Between Teacher and Skater.
Off-Ice Training: Ballet, Stretching, Strength/Weight Training, Plyometrics, Nutrition, Gymnastics, Aerobics, Jogging, Walking, Racquetball, Slideboards, Jumpboxes, Dynabands, Video analysis.
Ages: All Ages.
Housing: On your own (List Available).
Ice Purchased: Weekly, By the session.
Test Sessions: USFSA.
Competitions: USFSA.
Ice Shows: Yes.

CONNECTICUT
International Skating Center of CT Summer School
International Skating Center of Connecticut
1375 Hopmeadow St.
Simsbury CT 06070
(203) 651-5400
Contact: Bob Young.
Season: June through August
Sessions Offered: Patch, Free (all levels), Free (low & high test), Dance (all levels), Dance (low & high test), Pairs, Hockey, Public.
Lessons Available: Power Stroking, Group, Private, *Moves in the Field.*
Lesson Arrangements: Scheduled through Rink.
Off-Ice Training: Ballet, Strength/Weight Training.
Ages: All Ages.
Housing: Supervised, On your own (List Available).
Ice Purchased: Monthly, Weekly, Daily, By the session.
Test Sessions: USFSA, ISIA.
Competitions: None. *Ice Shows:* No.

DELAWARE:
Skating Club of Wilmington Summer School
Skating Club of Wilmington, Inc.
1301 Carruthers Lane
Wilmington DE 19803-0307
(302) 656-5007
Contact: Dot Gualtieri.
Season: June through August.
Sessions Offered: Patch, Free (low & high test), Dance (low & high test), Team ice.
Lessons Available: Private, Group, Edge Class, Power Stroking, Harness.
Lesson Arrangements: Between Teacher and Skater.
Off-Ice Training: Ballet, Jazz, Strength/Weight Training.
Ages: All Ages.
Housing: Supervised, On your own (List Available).
Ice Purchased: Monthly, Weekly, Daily, By the session.
Test Sessions: USFSA.
Competitions: USFSA. *Ice Shows:* No.

University of Delaware Ice Skating Science Development Center Summer School
University of Delaware Arena
South College Ave.
Newark DE 19716
(302) 831-6038
Contact: Ron Ludington.
Season: June through August.
Sessions Offered: Patch, Free (all levels), Dance (all levels), Pairs (low & high test), Hockey, Public.
Lessons Available: Private, Team, Power Stroking, Harness.
Lesson Arrangements: Scheduled through Rink, Between Teacher and Skater.
Off-Ice Training: Jazz, Ballet, Stretching, Strength/Weight Training, Plyometrics.
Ages: All Ages.
Housing: Supervised.
Ice Purchased: Monthly, Weekly, Daily.
Test Sessions: USFSA, ISIA.
Competitions: None.

FLORIDA
Gold Coast Ice Arena Summer Program
Gold Coast Ice Arena
4601 N. Federal Hwy.
Pompano Beach FL 33064
(305) 943-1437
Contact: Jennifer Borell.
Season: June through August
Sessions Offered: Patch, Free (all levels), Dance (all levels), Hockey.
Lessons Available: Private, Group, Team, Power Stroking, Harness.
Lesson Arrangements: Between Teacher and Skater.
Off-Ice Training: Ballet.
Ages: All Ages.
Housing: On your own (no list).
Ice Purchased: Monthly, Weekly, By the session.
Test Sessions: USFSA.
Competitions: ISIA, USFSA.
Ice Shows: Yes.

Sun Blades Summer Skate
Sun Blades Ice Rink
13940 Icot Blvd.
Clearwater FL 34620
(813) 536-5843
Contact: Carol Wasilewski.
Season: June through August.
Sessions Offered: Patch, Free (all levels), Dance (all levels), Hockey, Public.
Lessons Available: Private, Edge Class, Power Stroking, Harness, Footwork, Choreography.
Lesson Arrangements: Scheduled through Rink.
Off-Ice Training: Strength/Weight Training, Endurance and Conditioning six days a week.
Ages: All Ages.
Housing: On your own (no list).

Ice Purchased: Monthly, Weekly, By the session, Daily.
Test Sessions: USFSA, ISIA.
Competitions: USFSA, ISIA.

IDAHO
Sun Valley Skating School
Sun Valley Skating Center
Dollar Loop Rd.
Sun Valley ID 83353
(208) 622-2194
Contact: Nick Maricich.
Season: June through August.
Sessions Offered: Patch, Free (low & high test), Dance (low & high test), Hockey, Public.
Lessons Available: Private, Group, Edge Class, Power Stroking, Harness.
Off-Ice Training: Ballet, Jazz, Stretching, Structural re-aligning.
Ages: All Ages.
Housing: On your own (List Available).
Ice Purchased: Monthly, Weekly, Daily, By the session.
Test Sessions: USFSA.
Competitions: USFSA.
Ice Shows: Yes.

ILLINOIS
Riverview Ice House Summer Figure Skating School
Riverview Ice House
324 N. Madison,
Rockford IL 61107
(815) 963-7465
Contact: Ried Tennant.
Season: June through August.
Sessions Offered: Patch, Free (low & high test), Dance (all levels), Pairs, Hockey, Public.
Lessons Available: Private, Group, Edge Class, Harness.
Lesson Arrangements: Between Teacher and Skater.
Off-Ice Training: Strength/Weight Training.
Ages: All Ages.
Housing: On your own (no list).
Ice Purchased: Monthly, Weekly, Daily, By the session.
Test Sessions: USFSA.
Competitions: None.
Ice Shows: Yes.

INDIANA
Indiana/World Skating Academy Summer School
Indiana World Skating Academy
201 S. Capitol Ave., Suite 001
Pan American Plaza
Indianapolis IN 40625
(317) 237-5565.
Contact: Heidi Mallin.
Season: June through August.
Sessions Offered: Patch, Free (low & high test), Dance (low & high test), Pairs (low & high test), Public.
Lessons Available: Private, Group, Edge Class, Power Stroking, Harness.
Lesson Arrangements: Between Teacher and Skater.
Off-Ice Training: Ballet, Jazz, Stretching, Strength/Weight Training.
Ages: All Ages.
Housing: Supervised, On your own (List Available).
Ice Purchased: Weekly, Daily, By the session.
Test Sessions: USFSA.
Competitions: USFSA.

KANSAS
Ice Chateau Summer School
Ice Chateau of King Louie West
8788 Metcalf
Overland Park KS 66212
(913) 648-0130
Contact: Randy Briliantine.
Season: June through August
Sessions Offered: Patch, Free (all levels), Free (low & high test), Dance (all levels), Dance (low & high test), Pairs, Hockey.
Lessons Available: Private, Group, Team, Harness.
Lesson Arrangements: Between Teacher and Skater.
Ages: All Ages.
Housing: On your own (List Available).
Ice Purchased: By the session.
Test Sessions: USFSA, ISIA.
Competitions: ISIA, USFSA.
Ice Shows: Yes.

MASSACHUSETTS
Cape Cod Summer School
Tony Kent Arena
8 S. Gages Way
South Dennis MA 02660
(508) 760-2415
Contact: Dottie Larkin.
Season: June through August.
Sessions Offered: Patch, Free (low & high test), Dance (low & high test).
Lessons Available: Private, Edge Class, Power Stroking, On-ice ballet.
Off-Ice Training: Ballet, Jazz, Strength/Weight Training, Nutrition, Aerobics, Cindy Adams - Sports Psychchology seminar.
Ages: All Ages.
Housing: Supervised.
Ice Purchased: By the session, Weekly, Monthly.
Test Sessions: USFSA.
Competitions: USFSA.

Summer Skate
Nashoba Valley Olympia
34 Massachusetts Ave., Route 111
Boxborough MA 01719
(508) 263-3020
Contact: Lynne Quinn.
Season: June through September.
Sessions Offered: Patch, Free (low & high test), Dance (low & high test), Pairs (low & high test).
Lessons Available: Private, Group, Team, Power Stroking, Harness.
Lesson Arrangements: Between Teacher and Skater.
Off-Ice Training: Ballet, Jazz, Strength/Weight Training, Nutrition.
Ages: All Ages.
Housing: On your own (List Available).
Ice Purchased: Monthly, Weekly, Daily, By the session.
Test Sessions: USFSA, ISIA.
Competitions: USFSA, ISIA.
Ice Shows: Yes.

Stoneham Arena Summer School
Stoneham Arena
101 Montreal Ave.
Stoneham MA 02180
(617) 279-2628
Contact: June Scarpe.
Season: July through September.
Sessions Offered: Patch, Free (all levels), Dance (low & high test), Hockey.
Lessons Available: Private.
Lesson Arrangements: Between Teacher and Skater.
Ages: All Ages.
Housing: On your own (no list).
Ice Purchased: By the session, Daily, Weekly, Monthly.
Test Sessions: USFSA.
Ice Shows: Yes.

MAINE
Portland Ice Arena Summer School
Portland Ice Arena
225 Park Ave.
Portland ME 04102
(207) 774-8553
Contact: Sharon Ingalls.
Season: July through August.
Sessions Offered: Patch, Free (all levels), Dance (all levels), Hockey.
Lessons Available: Group, Private.
Lesson Arrangements: Between Teacher and Skater.
Ages: All Ages.
Housing: On your own (no list).
Ice Purchased: Monthly, Weekly, Daily, By the session.
Test Sessions: ISIA, USFSA.
Competitions: USFSA, ISIA.
Ice Shows: Yes.

MICHIGAN
Detroit FSC Summer F.S. School
Detroit Skating Club
888 Denison Ct.
Bloomfield Hills MI 48302
(810) 332-7133
Contact: Debbie Johns.
Season: June through August.
Sessions Offered: Patch, Free (low & high test), Dance (low & high test), Pairs (low & high test), Hockey.
Lessons Available: Private, Group, Power Stroking, Harness, Dance Stroking.
Lesson Arrangements: Between Teacher and Skater.
Off-Ice Training: Ballet, Jazz, Stretching, Strength/Weight Training, Plyometrics, Nutrition, Jump Technique, Ballroom, Drama.
Ages: All Ages.
Housing: On your own (List Available).
Ice Purchased: By the session.
Test Sessions: USFSA.
Competitions: USFSA.

Michigan Technological University Summer Figure Skating School
Michigan Tech Skating Academy Student Ice Arena
1400 Townsend Dr.
Houghton MI 49931-1295
(906) 487-2994
Contact: Cheryl DePuydt.
Season: August through August.
Sessions Offered: Patch, Free (low & high test), Dance (low & high test).
Lessons Available: Private, Group, Edge Class, Power Stroking, Harness, Moves In The Field.
Off-Ice Training: Ballet, Jazz, Stretching, Strength/Weight Training, Plyometrics, Nutrition, Off-Ice Harness, Gymnasium.
Ages: All Ages.
Housing: Unsupervised, On your own (List Available).
Ice Purchased: Weekly, Daily, By the session.
Test Sessions: USFSA.
Competitions: None.
Ice Shows: Yes.

NEW HAMPSHIRE
New England Skating Camp
Evertt Arena
Loudon Rd.
Concord NH 03301
(603) 746-3195
Contact: Mr. Rothchild.
Season: June through August.
Sessions Offered: Patch, Free (low & high test), Dance (all levels).
Lessons Available: Private, Group, Edge Class.
Lesson Arrangements: Between Teacher and Skater.
Ages: Kids Only (to 18). *Housing*: Supervised.
Ice Purchased: Weekly.
Test Sessions: None. *Ice Shows*: Yes.

NEW YORK
Lake Placid Summer School
Olympic Regional Development Authority Olympic Center (ORDA)
216 Main St., Olympic Center
Lake Placid NY 12946
(518) 523-3325
Contact: Denny Allen.
Season: June through September.
Sessions Offered: Patch, Free (low & high test), Dance (low & high test), Pairs, Hockey, Public.
Lessons Available: Private, Team, Power Stroking, Harness.
Lesson Arrangements: Between Teacher and Skater.
Off-Ice Training: Ballet, Strength/Weight Training.
Ages: All Ages.
Housing: On your own (List Available).
Test Sessions: USFSA.
Competitions: USFSA.
Ice Shows: Yes.

Sport-O-Rama Summer Skating School
Sport-O-Rama
18 College Rd.
Monsey NY 10952;
(914) 356-3919
Contact: Glen Brawer.
Season: June through September.
Sessions Offered: Patch, Free (low & high test), Dance (all levels), Pairs.
Lessons Available: Private, Edge Class, Power Stroking, Harness.
Lesson Arrangements: Scheduled through Rink, Between Teacher and Skater.
Off-Ice Training: Jazz, Stretching, Strength/Weight Training, Aerobics, Health Club next door.
Ages: All Ages.
Housing: Supervised.
Test Sessions: USFSA, ISIA.
Competitions: USFSA.
Ice Shows: Yes.

Plattsburgh State Summer Skate
SUNY Field House, Rugar St.
Plattsburgh NY 12901
(518) 564-3060
Contact: Mark Christiansen.
Season: Late June through mid-Aug.
Sessions Offered: Patch, Free (low & high test), Dance (low & high test), Pairs, Hockey, Public.

Lessons Available: Private, Group.
Lesson Arrangements: Scheduled through Rink.
Off-Ice Training: Ballet, Jazz, Stretching, Strength/Weight Training, Choreography, Mind-training (sports psychology).
Ages: All Ages.
Housing: Supervised.
Test Sessions: USFSA.

OHIO
Bowling Green State University Arena Summer Skating School
Bowling Green State University Ice Arena
Mercer Rd.
Bowling Green OH 43403
(419) 372-2264
Contact: Randy Sokoll.
Season: June through August.
Sessions Offered: Patch, Free (low & high test), Dance (low & high test), Hockey, Public.
Lessons Available: Private, Group, Power Stroking, Harness.
Lesson Arrangements: Between Teacher and Skater.
Ages: All Ages.
Housing: Unsupervised.
Ice Purchased: By the session.
Test Sessions: USFSA.
Competitions: None.
Ice Shows: No.

Miami University Summer Figure Skating School
Goggin Ice Arena
Miami University, High St.
Oxford OH 45056
(513) 529-3343
Contact: Vicki Korn.
Season: July through August.
Sessions Offered: Patch, Free (all levels), Dance (low & high test), Hockey, Public.
Lessons Available: Private, Group, Edge Class, Power Stroking, Harness, Jump & Spin Class.
Lesson Arrangements: Scheduled through Rink.
Off-Ice Training: Ballet, Jazz, Nutrition, Psychology, Gymanstics, Aerobics, Physical Testing.
Ages: All Ages.
Housing: Supervised.
Test Sessions: USFSA, ISIA.
Competitions: USFSA. *Ice Shows*: Yes.

Columbus F.S.C. Summer School
Ohio State University Ice Rink
390 Woody Hayes Dr.
Columbus OH 43210
(614) 292-4154
Contact: Mary Haiser.
Season: June through August.
Sessions Offered: Patch, Free (all levels), Dance (all levels).
Lessons Available: Edge Class, Power Stroking, Dance Edge Class, *Annie's Edges.*
Lesson Arrangements: Between Teacher and Skater.
Off-Ice Training: Strength/Weight Training, John Kilbourne's *Movement Classes* for skaters.
Ages: All Ages.
Housing: On your own (List Available).
Ice Purchased: Monthly, Weekly, Daily, By the session.
Test Sessions: USFSA.
Competitions: None.
Ice Shows: Yes.

Winterhurst Summer Program
Winterhurst Ice Rink
14740 Lakewood Heights Blvd.
Lakewood OH 44107
(216) 529-4400
Contact: Joanne Toth.
Season: June through August.
Sessions Offered: Patch, Free (all levels), Dance (all levels), Hockey, Public.
Lessons Available: Harness, Group, Private.
Lesson Arrangements: Between Teacher and Skater.
Off-Ice Training: Ballet, Stretching.
Ages: All Ages.
Housing: On your own (no list).
Ice Purchased: Monthly.
Test Sessions: USFSA.
Competitions: USFSA.
Ice Shows: No.

OREGON
Ice Pavillion at Lloyd Center Summer School
Lloyd Center Ice Pavillion
2201 Lloyd Center
Portland OR 97232;
503) 288-4599
Contact: Delores Mezyk.
Season: June through September.
Sessions Offered: Patch, Free (all

You're Invited...
To:	Figure-skating camp
When:	July/August
Why:	Have a wonderful time and improve your skating
Where:	Philadelphia, PA Wissahickon Skating Club

JAMA & Friends, a great summer sleep-away camp for figure skaters, includes patch, freestyle, dance, and *Moves in the Field* as part of the on-ice curriculum. Off-ice activities include conditioning, dance, swimming, tennis, and more.

Skaters live in a local college dorm and skate at Wissahickon. JAMA is under the direction of **Amy and Jay Slatus**, PSGA-rated. Professional inquiries welcome.

JAMA & FRIENDS
(201) 992-7491

---

levels), Dance (all levels), Pairs (low & high test).
Lessons Available: Harness, Power Stroking, Edge Class, Team, Group, Private.
Lesson Arrangements: Between Teacher and Skater.
Off-Ice Training: Ballet, Jazz, Stretching, Strength/Weight Training.
Ages: All Ages.
Housing: Supervised.
Ice Purchased: Monthly, Weekly, Daily, By the session.
Test Sessions: USFSA, ISIA.
Competitions: USFSA, ISIA.
Ice Shows: Yes.

PENNSYLVANIA
Blade Runners Ice Complex Summer Figure Skating School
Blade Runners Ice Complex
66 Alpha Dr.
Pittsburgh PA 15238
(412) 826-0800
Contact: Barbara Kuchtsa.
Season: June through August.
Sessions Offered: Patch, Free (low &

high test), Dance (low & high test), Hockey, Public.
Lessons Available: Private, Edge Class, Power Stroking.
Lesson Arrangements: Between Teacher and Skater.
Off-Ice Training: Ballet, Jazz, Stretching, Strength/Weight Training, Plyometrics, Nutrition, Aerobics, Running, Combo dance-drama class with all phases of dance.
Ages: All Ages. *Housing*: On your own (List Available).
Ice Purchased: Monthly, Weekly, Daily, By the session.
Test Sessions: USFSA, ISIA. *Competitions*: None. *Ice Shows*: No.

Skatium Ice Program
Havertown Skatium
Darby and Manoa Rds.
Havertown PA 19083
(610) 853-2226
Contact: Sandra Loflin.
Season: June through September.
Sessions Offered: Patch, Free (all levels), Hockey.
Lessons Available: Private, Group.
Lesson Arrangements: Between Teacher and Skater.
Off-Ice Training: Ballet, Stretching.
Ages: All Ages.
Housing: On your own (no list).
Ice Purchased: By the session, Daily, Weekly, Monthly.
Test Sessions: ISIA. *Ice Shows*: Yes.

Penn State Ice Skating Camp
Penn State Ice Pavillion
Penn State University
Pollock & McKean Rds.
University Park PA 16803
(814) 863-2039
Contact: Dena Yeagley.
Season: June through July.
Sessions Offered: Patch, Free (low & high test), Dance (low & high test), Hockey, Public.
Lessons Available: Private, Group, Edge Class, Power Stroking.
Lesson Arrangements: Between Teacher and Skater.
Off-Ice Training: Ballet, Jazz, Jumping.
Ages: Kids Only (to 18).
Housing: Supervised.
Ice Purchased: Weekly.
Test Sessions: ISIA.
Competitions: None. *Ice Shows*: Yes.

Twin Rinks Summer School
Twin Rinks
6725 River Rd.
Pensaulkin PA 08110
(609) 488-9300
Contact: Lynn Mooney.
Season: June through August.
Sessions Offered: Patch, Free (all levels), Dance (all levels), Hockey.
Lessons Available: Private, Group, Power Stroking.
Lesson Arrangements: Between Teacher and Skater.
Off-Ice Training: Ballet, Stretching.
Ages: All Ages.
Housing: On your own (List Available).
Ice Purchased: Monthly, Weekly, Daily, By the session.
Test Sessions: USFSA.
Competitions: None. *Ice Shows*: Yes.

VERMONT
Gordon H. Paquette Arena Summer Figure Skating School
Paquette (Gordon H.) Municipal Arena
Leddy Park, 216 Leddy Rd.
Burlington VT 05401
(802) 864-0123
Contact: Kathy Knuaer.
Season: June through August.
Sessions Offered: Patch, Free (all levels), Free (low & high test), Dance (all levels), Dance (low & high test), Public.
Lessons Available: Private, Group, Dancers have edge class with the dance pros.
Lesson Arrangements: Between Teacher and Skater.
Off-Ice Training: Ballet.
Ages: All Ages.
Housing: Unsupervised, On your own (List Available).
Ice Purchased: Monthly, Weekly, By the session.
Test Sessions: USFSA.
Competitions: USFSA.
Ice Shows: Yes.

WISCONSIN
Janesville Ice Arena Summer School
Janesville Ice Arena
812 Beloit Ave.
Janesville WI 53545
(608) 755-3014
Contact: Jane Meyers.
Season: June through August.
Sessions Offered: Patch, Free (all levels), Dance (all levels), Public, Hockey.
Lessons Available: Private, Group, Team, Edge Class, Power Stroking, Harness.
Lesson Arrangements: Between Teacher and Skater.
Ages: All Ages.
Housing: On your own (List Available).
Test Sessions: USFSA.
Competitions: None.
Ice Shows: No.

Ice Hot Summer Skate
Petit National Ice Center
500 S. 84th St.
Milwaukee WI 53214
(414) 266-0100
Contact: Mary Dracca.
Season: June through August.
Sessions Offered: Patch, Free (low & high test), Dance (all levels), Public.
Lessons Available: Edge Class, Power Stroking, Artistry In Motion taught by Paula Wagner three times/week.
Off-Ice Training: Ballet, Jazz, Strength/Weight Training, Stretching, Plyometrics, Nutrition, Drama, Indoor track.
Ages: All Ages.
Housing: Supervised, On your own (List Available).
Ice Purchased: By the session.
Test Sessions: USFSA.
Competitions: None.
Ice Shows: Yes.

Training Centers: Where Top Skaters Train

While there is no true system for ranking the top training centers in the country, we thought it would be useful to look at where the top-ranking skaters have trained in the last few years. We've included the top six places in U.S. Mens, Ladies, Pairs and Dance for 1993 and 1994 U.S. Nationals, plus the Championship competitors (Senior level) scheduled for the 1995 season. In addition, we added some of the top Russian teams now training at various facilities in the U.S.

Please keep in mind that skaters often change partners, coaches, and training centers. Information that was current when this book was published (1/95) may well change within a season.

Here are where some of the top skaters trained from 1993 to 1995:

Rink/Training Center

| Year | Skaters Training | Coaches |

Air Force Academy Ice Arena, Colorado Springs, CO

| 1993-95 | Renee Roca
Gorsha Sur | Sandra Hess
Darlene Gilbert |

Babson Recreation Center, Wellesley, MA

| 1994-5 | Tamara Kuchiki
Neale Smull | Keith Lichtman |

Belmont Iceland, Belmont, CA

| 1993-94 | Rudy Galindo | Richard Inglesi |

Broadmoor Arena, Colorado Springs, CO
(now demolished; new rink under construction)

1993-95	Scott Davis	Kathy Casey
1993-94	Nicole Bobek	Kathy Casey
1993	Elizabeth Punsalan Jerod Swallow	Sandra Hess Igor Shpilband
1993	Rachel Mayer Peter Breen	Sandra Hess

Costa Mesa Ice Chalet, Costa Mesa, CA

| 1994-95 | Michelle Cho | John Nicks |
| 1993-95 | Jenni Meno
Todd Sand | John Nicks |

Detroit Skating Club, Bloomfield Hills, MI

1995	Nicole Bobek	Richard Callaghan
1993-5	Todd Eldredge	Richard Callaghan
1994-5	Elizabeth Punsalan Jerod Swallow	Igor Shpilband Elizabeth Coates

Dublin Iceland, Dublin, CA

| 1993-95 | Brian Boitano | Linda Leaver |

Fairfax Ice Arena, Fairfax, VA

| 1993-95 | Michael Weiss | Audrey Weisiger |

Ice Castles International Training Center, Lake Arrowhead, CA

1993-95	Michelle Kwan	Frank Carroll
1994-95	Mark Mitchell	Carlo Fassi Christa Fassi
1994-95	Stephanie Stiegler Lance Travis	Peter Oppegard

Ice Centre of San Jose, San Jose, CA

| 1994-95 | Rudy Galindo | Kevin Peeks
John Brancato
Laura Galindo |

International Skating Center of Connecticut, Simsbury, CT

1995	Oksana Baiul	Galina Zmievskaya
	Viktor Petrenko	Galina Zmievskaya
	Ekaterina Gordeeva Sergei Grinkov	

Training Centers: Where Top Skaters Train

Lake Placid Olympic Center, Lake Placid, NY

1993	Tamara Kuchiki Neale Smull	David Owen
1993-95	Maia Usova Alexandr Zhulin	Natalia Dubova

Nashoba Valley Olympia, Boxborough, MA

1995	Wendy Millette Jason Tebo	Natalia Annenko Genrick Sretenski Robbie Kaine

Skating Club of Boston, Brighton, MA

1994	Wendy Millette Jason Tebo	Barrett Brown Tom Lescinski Karen Cullinan
1993-94	Mark Mitchell	Ronna Gladstone
1993-94	Amy Webster Ron Kravette	Barrett Brown Tom Lescinski Karen Cullinan

Sport-O-Rama, Monsey, NY

1993-95	Michael Chack	Peter Burrows Marylynn Gelderman
1993-95	Kyoko Ina Jason Dungjen	Peter Burrows
1994	Natasha Kuchiki Rocky Marval	Peter Burrows
1994-95	Elaine Zayak	Peter Burrows Marylynn Gelderman

Tony Kent Arena, Cape Cod, MA

1994-95	Shepherd Clark	Laura Edmunds
1995	Lisa Ervin	Evy Scotvold Mary Scotvold
1993	Nancy Kerrigan	Evy Scotvold Mary Scotvold

Oksana Baiul and Viktor Petrenko train in Connecticut.

University of Delaware Arena, Newark, DE

1993-94	Karen Courtland Todd Reynolds	Ron Ludington Bob Young
1993-94	Galit Chait Maxim Sevostianov	Karen Ludington Ron Ludington (1993) Edward Samohin (1994)
1995	Oksana Gritschuk Evgeni Platov	Natalia Linichuk
1992-93	Calla Urbanski Rocky Marval	Ron Ludington Bob Young
1993-94	Tristen Vega Joel McKeever	Ron Ludington Bob Young
1995	Amy Webster Ron Kravette	Natalia Linichuk

Winterhurst Ice Rink, Lakewood, OH

1993	Lisa Ervin	Carol Heiss Jenkins
1993-95	Tonia Kwiatkowski	Carol Heiss Jenkins Glyn Watts
1993-95	Aren Nielsen	Carol Heiss Jenkins Glyn Watts

PHOTO BY ALICE BERMAN

Rinks and Training Centers

Following are the names and addresses of the rinks and training centers listed on the previous pages. For more information on the rink facilities and programs, refer to the main *Rinks* chapter earlier in this book.

BABSON RECREATION CENTER
150 Great Plain Avenue
Wellesley, MA 02181
(617) 239-6050
FAX: (617) 235-0672
Manager: Joan Allen
Skating Director: Nancy Judge

BROADMOOR ARENA
(demolished 4/94; new rink under construction)

BELMONT ICELAND
815 Old County Road
Belmont, CA 94002
(415) 592-0532
Manager: Chris Bryant
Skating Director: Kay Faynor

COSTA MESA ICE CHALET
2701 Harbor Blvd.
Costa Mesa, CA 92626
(714) 979-8880
FAX: (714) 979-5929
Manager: Willy Kall
Skating Director: John Nicks

DETROIT SKATING CLUB
888 Denison Court
Bloomfield Hills, MI 48302
(810) 332-7133
FAX: (810) 332-9912
Manager: Ron Holbrook
Executive Director: Johnny Johns

DUBLIN ICELAND
7212 San Ramon Road
Dublin, CA 94568
(510) 829-4445
FAX: (510) 829-4447
Manager: Barry Keast

FAIRFAX ICE ARENA
3779 Pickett Road
Fairfax, VA 22031
(703) 323-1133
Skating Director: Audrey Weisiger
Manager: Henry Weisiger

ICE CASTLES INTERNATIONAL TRAINING CENTER
401 Burnt Mill Road, P.O. Box 939
Lake Arrowhead, CA 92352
(909) 337-0802; (907) 336-4085
FAX: (909) 337-8949; (907) 336-2452
Skating Director: Frank Carroll
Manager: Michelle Coffey

ICE CENTRE OF SAN JOSE
1500 South 10th Street
San Jose, CA 95112
(408) 279-6000
Manager: David McGowan
Skating Director: Candy Goodson

INTERNATIONAL SKATING CENTER OF CONNECTICUT
1375 Hopmeadow Street
Simsbury, CT 06070
(203) 651-5400
FAX: (203) 651-5204
Skating Director: Bob Young
Manager: Bob Young

NASHOBA VALLEY OLYMPIA
34 Massachusetts Avenue
Route 111
Boxborough, MA 01719
(508) 263-3020
Manager: Russ Long

LAKE PLACID INTERNATIONAL SCHOOL OF ICE DANCE
Contact: Natalia Dubova
ORDA
Olympic Center
Lake Placid, NY 12946
(518) 523-2655
FAX: (518) 523-9275
Manager: Denny Allen

SKATING CLUB OF BOSTON
1240 Soldiers Field Road
Brighton, MA 02135
(617) 782-5900
Manager: Theodore Clark

TONY KENT ICE ARENA
P.O. Box 646
South Dennis, MA 02660
(508) 760-2415
Manager: Dottie Larkin

SPORT-O-RAMA
18 College Rd
Monsey, NY 10952
(914) 356-3919
FAX: (914) 356-9274
Skating Director: Peter Burrows
Manager: Robert Tweedy

UNIVERSITY OF DELAWARE
Ice Skating Science Development Center
Blue Ice Arena
Newark, DE 19716
(302) 831-2868
Skating Director: Ron Ludington
Manager: Jim Gossard

WINTERHURST ICE RINK
14740 Lakewood Heights Blvd.
Lakewood, OH 44107
(216) 529-4400
Manager: Bill Needham

TURN PAGE FOR SHOOTING GALLERY

~ SKATER'S EDGE SOURCEBOOK ~

Shooting Gallery

Renee Roca and Gorsha Sur train in Colorado.

Calla Urbanski and Rocky Marval trained in Delaware.

Nicole Bobek currently trains in Michigan.

Jenni Meno and Todd Sand train in California.

PHOTOS BY ALICE BERMAN

Videos, Videos, Videos

COMPILED BY MAGGIE RANGE
AND ALICE BERMAN

The following list of videotapes consists of three sections: (1) Tapes of competitions and championships; (2) Documentaries, highlights and medleys; and (3) Instructional videos. Following each title is a brief description (when available) and the name of companies that were selling the video at the time this book was published (see *Video Sources*).

In most cases, videos offered by television networks have not been included because their 800 numbers are specialized for a particular tape advertised for a limited period. However, these tapes are often eventually distributed through the main video sources listed.

Note: Tapes are sometimes available for both U.S. and European (PAL) systems. In addition, some of the videographers (Ledin, R & J, Udell, Video Sports) may have tapes of local competitions or of individual skaters.

If you know of videotapes commercially available that have not been included in this listing, please send us the following information: title, year made, length, description, and potential sources. We'll gather the information for future revisions of the *Sourcebook*.

COMPETITIONS

U.S. Figure Skating Championships; Skate America; U.S. National Precision Championships. Taping rights vary from year to year. Contact one of the videographers listed in the *Video Sources* box (Ledin, R & J Video, Bill Udell) or distributor Video Sports.

World Championships. In general, world championship tapes are not available except for 21 tapes from the 1981 and 1987 Worlds, distributed by Video Sports.

1994 Winter Olympics: Lillehammer. Two tapes. *Tape I* includes uninterrupted competition performances of the Olympic champions. *Tape II* is the Exhibition of Champions. Hosted by Tracy Wilson and Scott Hamilton, CBS Sports. Two hours. Video Sports.

1992 Winter Olympics: Albertville. Two tapes; can be bought individually or in a two-tape collector's edition. *Tape I* features competition performances and highlights of most medal winners, including Wylie, Petrenko, Yamaguchi, Kerrigan, Ito, Mishkutenok & Dmitriev, Hough & Ladret, the Duchesnays, and Klimova & Ponomerenko, plus Wylie-Kerrigan exhibition performance. *Tape II* offers highlights of other sports only. 65 mins. Rainbo Sports, Video Sports.

1988 Winter Olympics: Calgary. Features Boitano, Orser, Ito, Witt, Manley, Thomas, Gordeeva & Grinkov, Watson & Oppegard, the Duchesnays, Semanick & Gregory, and Bestemianova & Bukin. Produced by ABC Sports. 150 mins. Rainbo Sports, Video Sports.

Great Moments at the Winter Games. Features rare competition footage and personal recollections from Albright, Heiss, Graftstrom, Schafer, Henie, and the Brunets. Produced by Bud Greenspan (1979). 47 mins. Video Sports.

1992 U.S. Open Competitions (Professional): 1981, 1988-1993. Features both Challenge Cup (men's and women's events only) and Master Cup, plus individual performances. PSGA, Video Sports.

DOCUMENTARIES, FILMS, HIGHLIGHTS, AND MEDLEYS

Artistry on Ice. Compilation of top skaters brought together for Olympic size figure skating gala. Includes Kerrigan, Boitano, Baiul, Gordeeva & Grinkov, Bonaly, Lu, Stojko, Petrenko, Meno & Sand, Usova & Zhulin, Mishkutenok & Dmitriev, and the Duchesnays. 1994. Video Sports.

Blades of Courage. Full-length film about a teenage skater and pressures at the Winter Olympics (1987). Skating executed by Lynn Nightingale. 98 mins. Limited availability. Rainbo Sports, Video Sports.

The Crystal Ball. Story of a runaway teenager who tries to gain acceptance into a street gang when she meets a street person with a magic crystal ball; Christmas drama. Features Danish champion Anisette Torp-Lind with the National Ice Theatre of Canada. Choreography by Kevin Cottam. 30 mins. Tohaventa Holdings, Video Sports.

The Cutting Edge. Full-length romantic comedy about competitive skating (1992), starring D.B. Sweeney and Moira Kelly, with skating executed by Susan Carz and John Denton. Cameo appearances by Jojo Starbuck and Robin Cousins; choreography by Robin Cousins. Video Sports.

Devastating Hits of Hockey. Harry Neal hosts five decades of thrashers and bashers. 30 mins. Rainbo Sports.

ILLUSTRATION BY BILL CASEY

Don Cherry's Rock-Em Sock-Em Hockey. Action film on hockey, including great saves, best goals, and funny incidents during games. Five volumes. 30-40 mins. each. Rainbo Sports.

Dynamite on Ice. Hockey checks, one-on-one break-aways, penalty shots, behind-the-scenes of the All-Star weekend, and explosive endings. 35 mins.

Everything Happens at Night. Sonja Henie skates her way into all kinds of trouble in this light-hearted drama of international intrigue and romance. Two rival reporters (Ray Miland and Robert Cummings) compete for the same story and fall in love with the same woman (Henie). 77 mins, B&W, 1939. Video Sports.

Fantastic Hockey Fights. Some of hardest hitting, rock 'em, sock 'em fights on record. 30 min. Rainbo Sports.

Great Plays from Great Games. Great moments from Soviet/NHL games, NHL All-Star games, Stanley Cup finals, classic overtimes, and great comebacks. 45 minutes.

Happy Landing. Olympic Champion Sonja Henie plays a naive Norwegian girl who follows a womanizing bandleader (Cesar Romero) to America. When she catches him with another woman, she turns to his manager (Don Ameche) for comfort, who in turn launches her career as a skating star. 75 mins, B&W, 1938. Video Sports.

Hilarious Hockey Highlights. Crazy goals, wacky fans, amazing collisions, fighting coaches and more. 30 mins. Rainbo Sports.

Hockey: The Lighter Side. Shows a combination of bone-crunching checks, silly slips, and strange circumstances on the ice, players' pranks and gags. 30 mins.

Hockey's All Time All Stars. The great hockey players. 60 mins. Rainbo Sports.

Hockey's Hardest Hitters. Shows moments from Soviet/NHL games, NHL All-Star games, Stanley Cup finals, classic overtimes, and great comebacks. 45 mins.

Hockey, The Off Side. Comical collisions, embarrassing spills, amusing antics, and Zamboni drivers. 45 mins. Rainbo Sports.

Ice Castles. Full-length feature film about competitive figure skating and a 16-year-old skater who is blinded in an accident (1978). With Robby Benson, Colleen Dewhurst, Tom Skeritt, Lynn-Holly Johnson. 109 mins. Rainbo Sports, Video Sports.

Ice Follies. Hockey bloopers from 1991. Half-hour of goofs, gaffs, and mishaps in the National Hockey League. Rainbo Sports.

Ice Skating All-Stars: Carmen & Tango. Two performances by World and Olympic champions of Russia, choreographed by Tatyana Tarasova. 57 mins. Color. Platoro Press, Rainbo Sports, USFSA, VIEW, Video Sports.

Ice Skating All-Stars: Russian Fair. Rarely-seen World and Olympic champions of Russia in solo, pairs and ensemble performances at the Moscow Ice Theatre. Choreography by Tatyana Tarasova. 52 mins. Color. Platoro Press, Rainbo Sports, USFSA, VIEW, Video Sports.

Ice Skating Showcase: Great Routines of the 1980s (1985-89). Features 14 routines from the 1980s World Professional Championships (Landover, MD), including Hamill, Torvill & Dean, the Carruthers, the Protopopovs, Cousins, Hamilton, Cranston, Tickner, and Fratianne. Boitano and Thomas not included. 60 mins. Color. Platoro Press, Rainbo Sports, USFSA, VIEW, Video Sports.

Iceland. Unaware of Icelandic customs, a flirtatious marine (John Payne) finds that his romantic sweet talk to a native beauty (Sonja Henie) is taken as a marriage proposal. Efforts to get out of the situation lead him straight into a matrimonial trap. 79 mins, B&W, 1942. Video Sports.

The Immortals. Features Winter Olympic Champions, including rare footage of Sonja Henie. Produced by Bud Greenspan (1980). 47 mins. Video Sports.

Jump! Video biography of four-time world champion Kurt Browning, including his 1989 and 1990 World Champion programs, '88 Olympics, and super-slow-motion his quadruple jump. 56 mins. 1990. Video Sports.

Magic Memories on Ice: I. Reviews ABC Sports-televised skating since 1962. Hosted by Peggy Fleming and Dick Button. Features Curry, Lynn, Hamill, Babilonia & Gardner, Torvill & Dean, Orser, Boitano, Fleming, Hamilton, and others. 90 mins. Rainbo Sports, Signals, USFSA, Video Sports.

Magic Memories on Ice: II. Features Hamilton, Torvill & Dean, Curry, Yamaguchi, Orser, Boitano, Rodnina & Zaitsev, Fleming, Carruthers, Wylie, Lynn, Cousins, Gordeeva & Grinkov, Cranston, Hamill, Underhill & Martini, Klimova & Ponomarenko, Witt, and others. 78 mins. Rainbo Sports, Signals, USFSA, Video Sports.

Midsummer Night's Ice Dream. TV special based on Shakespeare's famous comedy; stars Liz Manley, Jozef Sabovcik, Yuka Sato, Cam Medhurst and the National Ice Theatre of Canada. 1994. 60 mins. Tohaventa Holdings.

My Lucky Star. The son of a department store tycoon (Cesar Romero) tries to impress his father with the business proposal of sending a young package wrapper (Sonja Henie) to college to wear the store's fashions on campus. She gets expelled when Romero involves her in his scandalous divorce, so it's up to her boyfriend (Richard Greene) to make things right. 84 mins, B&W, 1938. Video Sports.

The Nutcracker: A Fantasy on Ice. Features Dorothy Hamill and Robin Cousins in Tschaikovsky's ballet with The National Philharmonic Orchestra. Produced by Roy Krost (1983). 85 mins. Rainbo Sports, Video Sports.

One in a Million. Sonja Henie's first feature film. She's a young Swiss woman who dreams of winning a gold medal for her father. When the leader of a travelling theatrical troupe observes her on the ice, he senses a fortune and hustles her off to star in a skating exhibition, unaware it would change her amateur status and end her Olympic dream. A visiting American reporter (Don Ameche) stops them before it's too late. 94 mins, B&W, 1936. Video Sports.

100 Thunderous Hits. Memorable hits and checks from recent NHL seasons. 45 mins.

Rhythm Hits the Ice. Feature film (1940) about a girl who inherits an ice

~ SKATER'S EDGE SOURCEBOOK ~

CHOOSE FROM OVER
200 FIGURE SKATING VIDEOTAPES!

Here's your chance to order
the *NEW VIDEO SPORTS CATALOG*

- Olympics & Worlds
- U.S. Championships
- Skate America International
- Instructional Tapes
- All B&W Sonja Henie Movies
- Pro Tours & Competitions

*To order your catalog, send check or money order for $5.00
(Canada $8.00, Others $10.00) with your return address to:*

VIDEO SPORTS CATALOG
P.O. Box 2700
Westfield, New Jersey 07091-2700
800-USA-1996

Ice Skating Showcase/NutraSweet World Pro

This exciting video includes selected technical and artistic programs from the 1985-89 *NutraSweet® World Professional Figure Skating Championships* in Landover, Maryland. Only $19.95 (plus $5 shipping*). Call 800-USA-1996 to order and receive a *free* catalog when you mention this ad. *Ice Skating Showcase* features:

Torvill & Dean	Scott Hamilton
Robin Cousin	The Protopopovs
Charlie Tickner	Linda Fratianne
Dorothy Hamill	The Carruthers
Toller Cranston	Roslyn Sumners

The Fine Print: *Ice Skating Showcase/NutraSweet World Pro*, Catalog #441020, approx. 58 min., Color, Hi-Fi Stereo. Also available in **PAL** and **SECAM** formats (add $5.00/tape). *Shipping to Alaska, Hawaii & Canada $8.00, Foreign orders $24.00. Return Policy - Video Sports will exchange any defective tape for the identical title if still in print when returned post-paid to VSP, Inc. within 30 days of receipt.

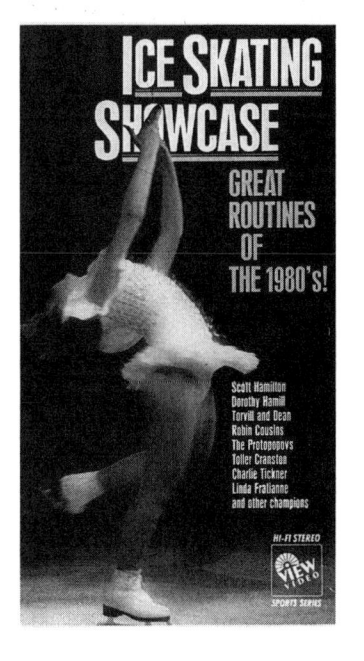

show in bankruptcy. Features Ice Capades ensemble. 80 mins. Video Sports.

Second Fiddle. A Hollywood publicity (Tyrone Power) contrives a romance between an innocent skating teacher (Sonja Henie) and a movie star (Rudy Vallee), only to fall in love with her himself. Score by Irving Berlin. 87 mins, B&W, 1939. Video Sports.

Seventy-Five Years of NHL Heroes and History. A history for hockey enthusiasts. 90 mins. Rainbo Sports.

She's A Good Skate, Charlie Brown. Animated film (1980) with Peppermint Patty and Coach Snoopy with the Peanuts crew. 30 mins. Video Sports.

Skating and Gymnastics Spectacular. Great skaters and gymnasts performing together in Vail, CO. Skaters include Boitano, Fleming, Cousins, Sumners, Martini & Underhill. Gymnasts include Comaneci, Conner, Pagano, Paul. 50 mins. Rainbo Sports, Video Sports.

Sleeping Beauty. Features Robin Cousins and Rosalyn Sumners in an ice spectacular with 16 other recognized artistic skaters (1987). 65 mins. Rainbo Sports, Video Sports.

Snow White and The Three Stooges. Features Snow White (Carol Heiss) and the Seven Dwarfs (Three Stooges) with two skating sequences (1961). 108 mins. Video Sports.

The Sonja Henie Collection. Nine black and white videotapes, including *Iceland, Thin Ice, Wintertime, My Lucky Star, Second Fiddle, Happy Landings, One in a Million, Sun Valley Serenade,* and *Everything Happens at Night.* See individual listings for descriptions. Video Sports.

Sun Valley Serenade. Sonja Henie, Milton Berle, and John Payne star in a lighthearted romantic comedy that features the Glenn Miller Orchestra as a struggling band. Nominated for three Oscars, including best song (*Chattanooga Choo Choo*). 86 mins, B&W, 1941. Soundtrack remastered. Video Sports.

Toller. Features tribute to career of Toller Cranston, champion skater and acclaimed painter and illustrator. Produced by Pen Densham & John Watson of Insight Productions (1977). 26 mins. Video Sports.

Thin Ice. Sonja Henie stars as a skating instructor at a Swiss hotel who falls in love with a shy man (Tyrone Power) with whom she skis each morning. She is unaware that he is actually Prince Rudolph and their affair is front page news around the world. 78 mins, B&W, 1937. Video Sports.

Top 50 Payoff Goals. Dramatic and unforgettable playoff moments in NHL history. 60 mins. Rainbo Sports.

Torvill & Dean Highlights. A glimpse into Torvill & Dean's feelings about skating, performing, and their careers. Includes four performances and four compulsory dances along with interviews and memories. 47 mins. Rainbo Sports.

Torvill & Dean: Path to Perfection. Describes Torvill & Dean's career, including interviews with the skaters, their coaches, parents, and friends. Features eight performances, including *Bolero* and *Barnum*. 1984. 52 mins. Rainbo Sports, Video Sports.

Torvill & Dean with the Russian All-Stars. Features Torvill & Dean's tour in the United States. 75 mins. Video Sports.

1987 Tour of Champions. Features Olympic & World Champions, including Witt, Thomas, Kadavy, Trenary, Manley, Boitano, Fadeev, Bowman, Kotin, Bestemianova & Bukin, Gordeeva & Grinkov, Valova & Vasiliev, Wilson & McCall, Watson & Oppegard. 95 mins. Video Sports.

USSR - USA Ice Skating Exhibition. Features local skaters and world champions (Klimova & Ponomarenko, Usova & Zhulin, Gordeeva & Grinkov, Petrenko, Yamaguchi, Rudi Galindo, Steven Smith) in Peninsula Figure Skating Club program, Redwood City, CA. (1990). 150 mins. (full exhibition) or 105 mins (world class skaters). R&J Video.

Wintertime. Sonja Henie stars in a romantic comedy featuring dazzling skating routines and a musical score played by the Woody Herman Orchestra. Henie falls in love with the owner of a nearly bankrupt hotel (played by Cornel Wilde) and convinces her millionaire uncle to finance the hotel's restoration. 82 mins, B&W, 1943. Video Sports.

World Champions on Ice - I. Performances from 1991-93 Worlds, with Browning, Baiul, Kerrigan, Bowman, Yamaguchi, Eldredge, Ito, Petrenko, Bonaly, the Duchesnays, and others. NBC Sports. 47 mins. Rainbo Sports, Video Sports.

World Champions on Ice - II. 1994. Overview of '94 World Championships, with performances by Baiul, Stojko, Candeloro, Bonaly, Brasseur & Eisler, Kwan, Gritschuk & Platov, Meno & Sand and others. Hosted by Kurt Browning. 55 mins. Rainbo Sports, Video Sports.

World Cup Figure Skating Champions. 1994. Exhibition performances of Klimova & Ponomarenko, Manley, Kadavy, Valova & Vasiliev, Barna, Tickner, Fadeev, Lisa Marie Allen and others. Hosted by Tai Babilonia and Randy Gardner. 45 min. Video Sports.

INSTRUCTIONAL TAPES: FIGURE SKATING

Canadian Figure Skating Association (CFSA). The CFSA offers a variety of tapes, including Competitive Update, Primary Standards, Intermediate Standards, CanPowerSkate, NCCP Level 1, NCCP Level 2, NCCP Level 2 Precision, NCCP Level 2 Singles Skating, NCCP Level 2 Ice Dance, NCCP Level 3 Technical, Hall of Fame, and Jump! (with Kurt Browning). Contact CFSA for catalogue.

Eighteen Compulsory Dances. Designed for judges. Available from the International Skating Union, Beat Hassler, General Secretary, Postfach CH-7270, Davos Platz, Switzerland.

Harmony on Ice. Promotional tape of precision teams in action. USFSA, Video Sports.

How To Ice Skate. Offers very basic look at how to improve ice skating ability. Features Tai Babilonia and Randy Gardner with coach John Nicks (1986). 60 mins. Video Sports.

How To In-Line Skate. Two tapes, *Basic* and *Advanced Skills*, 25 mins each. In-line demonstration by professional ice-skating champion Scott Cramer. *From:* PHD, 3630 Citadel Drive North, Colorado Springs, CO 80909.

Ice Skating for Everyone: The Beginner's Guide to a Lifetime Sport. A three-part series. Volume I includes tips on choosing equipment, lacing skates, plus step-by-step instruction for first steps on ice, beginning edges, pushing, gliding, backward skating, skating on one foot, and more. 60 mins. 1995. *From:* Ice Command, 207 Earle Ave., Easton, MD 21601; (410) 820-5614.

Intermediate & Novice Pair Demonstration Video. Designed for judges. Packet includes videotape, Trial Judging Forms and Evaluation Forms for each level. Directed by William Smith. 65 mins. USFSA, Video Sports.

International Dances Video. Designed for judges. Directed by Jim Disbrow. USFSA, Video Sports.

Junior & Senior Pairs Tests Demonstration Video. Designed for judges. Packet includes videotape, Trial Judging Forms and Evaluation Forms for each level. Produced by USFSA JETS Committee (1991). USFSA, Video Sports.

Learn From The Experts: 1992 CFSA/PSGA Coaches' Conference. Seven tapes. *Tape 1:* Trends in Sport: Implications for Coaches Dr. Geoff Gowan), and Directions in Choreography (Sandra Bezic). *Tape 2:* Celebrity Fashion Show--Past, Present and Future, plus Association Luncheons. *Tape 3:* Lessons to be Learned from our Past (Wally Distelmeyer, Barbara Ann Scott, Sheldon Galbraith, Dick Button). *Tape 4:* Professionalization of Coaching (Dr. Gaston Marcotte). *Tape 5:* The Stresses of Coaching (Dr. Peter Jensen). *Tape 6*: International Panel Discussion. *Tape 7:* Summary of Rap Sessions. Tapes range in length from 75 to 90 mins. CFSA.

Learn to Dance. Discussion and demonstration of compulsory dances. Produced for NISA (Nat'l Ice Skating Association of UK); demonstrated by British dance champions Sharon Jones & Paul Askham. *Vol. I* includes Dutch Waltz, Canasta Tango, Rhythm Blues, Swing Dance, Fiesta Tango and the Golden Skaters Waltz. *Vol. II* includes Willow Waltz, Ten Fox, Fourteen Step, European Waltz, and the Twenty-Two Step (14-Step social pattern). Video Sports.

Magic of Style: Volumes I, II & III. Designed for skaters of all levels and for coaches. Teaches step-by-step how to improve the style and flexibility of any skater. *Volume I* demonstrates 38 exercises and connecting steps from easy to advanced. *Volume II* focuses on flexibility, with extensions, spirals, stretching, and step-by-step technique of butterflies, split jumps, and off-ice "tune up" exercises. *Volume III* develops easy to intricate footwork, connecting steps, and Moves in the Field. Produced by Ann-Margreth Frei, PSGA Master teacher, former Olympic competitor. 60 mins each. Magic of Style Video, Rainbo Sports, Video Sports.

Moves in the Field. New USFSA test structure, which completely replaced the existing test structure as of 10/1/94. The new tests consist of progressively more difficult exercises involving edgework, turns and stroking while moving, plus corresponding levels of a *Freestyle Program with Music*. Video plus handbook detail and demonstrate new tests and compulsory moves. USFSA.

My First Skates. Describes 15 basic skills. Gives children and first-time skaters skills, confidence, and safety tips. Features instructor Leslie Heffron, students, and Maxmillan, the skating St. Bernard. 30 mins. Rainbo Sports.

Novice Original. Designed for judges. Packet includes a deduction sheet, Judging Form, examples of Original Program deductions as guidelines for judges, required elements for men's and women's singles. Directed by Janet Allen. USFSA, Video Sports.

Pre-Pair Test and Video. Designed for judges. Packet includes videotape with recommended elements, capsule guideline for judging the Preliminary Pair Test, trial Judging Forms, Preliminary Pair Information, and Judging Committee Test Sheet. Directed by William Smith (1990). 23 mins. USFSA, Video Sports.

Precision Video. Designed for clubs, coaches, and judges. Demonstrates how to develop a Precision routine, including musical selection, choreography, and team presentation. Also has an analysis of a complete national junior team routine and detailed

---

You are reading the one and only *Skater's Edge Sourcebook*.

If you don't own a copy, you can order it from the publisher for $44.95 in U.S. dollars ($39.95 plus $5 shipping in the U.S.)

Contact: *Skater's Edge* Box 500 Kensington, MD 20895 Phone/Fax: 301-946-1971

"Magic of Style" Skating Training Videos Volumes I - II and III

Vol I - 38 Exercises to Develop artistry, the winning look of the skating champions

Vol II - Flexibility / Strength for the skating athlete with 25 variations in Spirals, Extensions, Butterflies and Supersplit jump techniques, Stretching and Tone-up.

Vol III - Develop easy to intricate footwork - connecting steps and moves in the field.

Write to:
Ann-Margreth Frei
Magic of Style Skating Videos
P.O. Box 2676
Vail, CO 81658
Fax: 303/926-5176

- 1 Tape $49.95, 2 tapes $90.00 or 3 tapes $130.00 USA shipping $2.00 per tape Canada shipping $3.50 per tape
- On ice video manual - each volume
- $8.00 USA/CAN. • $10.00 Oversees
- European P.A.L. - 1 Tape $59.95, 2 tapes $110.00 or 3 tapes $160.00
- Overseas shipping $6.50 per tape
- USA checks / Mastercard / Visa

New!! Volume III

Step by Step Choreography and Style Fitness and Techniques

Produced by Ann-Margreth Frei - Former Olympian

VIDEO SOURCES

Canadian Figure Skating Association (CFSA)
1600 James Naismith Drive
Gloucester, Ontario, K1B 5N4 Canada
(613) 748-5635
FAX: (613) 748-5718

Ledin Photo & Video
22495 Madison
St. Clair Shores, Michigan 48081
(313) 778-8971
FAX: (313) 778-8971

Lussi Technical Video
207 Earle Avenue
Easton, MD 21601
(410) 820-6125

Magic of Style Videos
P.O. Box 2676
Vail, CO 81658
FAX: (303) 926-5176

Professional Skaters Guild of America (PSGA)
P.O. Box 5904
Rochester, Minnesota 55903
(507) 281-5122
FAX: (507) 281-5122

R & J Video
Ron Singson
P.O. Box 70287
Stockton, California 95267
(209) 476-0124 or (209) 466-3878

Rainbo Sports Shop
4836 North Clark Street
Chicago, Illinois 60640
(312) 275-5500
FAX: (312) 275-5506

The Sports Asylum, Inc.
9018 Balboa Blvd., Suite 575
Northridge, CA 91325
(800) 929-2159
(818) 893-9970
FAX: (818) 895-4763

Tohaventa Holdings, Inc.
1022 103rd Street
Edmonton, Alberta T5J 0X2, Canada
(403) 421-8879
FAX: (403) 426-1049

Udell Photo & Video
6006 Vantage Avenue
North Hollywood, CA 91606
(818) 985-6866
FAX: (818) 985-6867

USA Hockey, Inc.
4965 North 30th Street
Colorado Springs, CO 80919
(719) 599-5500
(800) 643-8557 (USA orders only)
FAX: (719) 599-5994

U.S. Figure Skating Association (USFSA)
20 First Street
Colorado Springs, CO 80906
(719) 635-5200
FAX: (719) 635-95

Video Sports Productions
P.O. Box 2700
Westfield, NJ 07091
(800) USA-1996; (800) 872-1996
FAX: (800) 872-1996

VIEW Video, Inc.
34 E. 23rd Street
New York City, NY 10010
(800) 843-9843 or (212) 674-5550
FAX: (212) 979-0266

OTHER SOURCES
Following are other catalogues and companies that have occasional skating videos. See also the company listing section of the *Sourcebook*.

Platoro Press
4481 Floyd Drive
Columbus, Ohio 43232
(614) 837-0003

Signals (Public Television)
P.O. Box 64428
St. Paul, MN 55164
(800) 669-9696
FAX: (612) 659-4320

Critic's Choice Video
P.O. Box 749
Itasca, IL 60143
(800) 367-7765
FAX: (708) 775-3355

---

photographs of hand grips. Produced by USFSA Precision Skating Committee. 19 mins. USFSA, Video Sports.

Professional Skaters Guild of America Educational Conferences. From the 1960s to present. Unprofessional, unedited tapes of many coaches from around the world. Good for technical research. Some video, some audio. PSGA.

Scott's 16 In-Line Dances. In-line demonstration by professional ice skating champion Scott Cramer. *From:* PHD, 3630 Citadel Dr North, Colorado Springs, CO 80909.

Senior Pair & Junior Pair Original and Long Program. Designed for judges. Displays Original Program elements individually and incorporated into the program, other lifts for Long Program, and three complete Long Programs. Produced by USFSA JETS Committee, directed by Margaret Wier and Christine Pozanac, and narrated by pairs coach John Nicks (1990). 33 mins. USFSA, Video Sports.

Skating Beautifully. Demonstrates five-part program on how to achieve grace and style on ice, warm-up, stretch, movements, warm-up and stretch on ice, and movements and proper position while skating. 60 mins. Limited or no availability.

Soviet-American Ice Dancing School & Workshop. Features full school and workshops (1989) with demonstrations by USSR Team members, including Klimova & Ponomarenko and Usova & Zhulin. Little/no editing. Six tapes, 10-11 hrs. R & J Video.

Sports Psyching for Figure Skaters. Helps young skaters improve concentration and self-confidence for competitions. Illustrated separately for novice and senior levels. Written/produced by psychologist Dr. Garry Martin of the University of Manitoba. 1989. 36 mins. Communication Systems, Educational Support Services, Univ of Manitoba, Winnipeg, Manitoba, R3T 2N2 Canada; (204) 474-6439. Also, Video Sports.

Systematic Figure Skating: The Spin and Jump Techniques of Gustave Lussi. Volume I: Spins. Step-by-step instructions from Mr. Lussi on sit spin, forward scratch, back scratch, and steps into and out of spins. Featuring Paul Wylie and others. Film footage of Albright, Button, Curry, Hamill, Jackson, Jelineks, McKellen, and Robertson. *Volume II: Advanced Spins.* Step-by-step instructions from Mr. Lussi on the camel, flying camel, flying sit and combination spins. Part of a four-volume series. Hosted by Dick Button and produced by Cecily Morrow. 60 mins each. Lussi Technical Video, Rainbo Sports, Video Sports.

Torvill & Dean Ice Dancing Seminar. Features Jayne Torvill and Christopher Dean talking about their ice dancing principles, practices, and philosophies at a Sun Valley seminar. Includes performance footage from 1990 U.S. tour, plus specific instruction and demonstration of required dances. Demonstrates weight, balancing, and positions for new skaters. Shorter version also available. Rainbo Sports.

INSTRUCTIONAL TAPES: HOCKEY

Advanced Power Skating. Introduces more complex maneuvers and proper techniques for mastering them. Includes pivot turns, backward turns, crossunder starts, backward power starts, and step-out turns. 20 mins. USA Hockey.

Beginning Checking. Introduces skill/tactic of checking through use of skating, angling, use of stick, and pinning. 30 mins. Sports Asylum, USA Hockey.

Body Checking. Continuation of techniques taught in *Beginning Checking*; includes overviews of checking, advanced contact confidence drills, body checking in three zones, and how to receive and avoid a check. 22 mins. Sports Asylum, USA Hockey.

Breakouts. With Dave Siciliano. Support, speed, agility and quick puck movement lead to a successful breakout. 30 mins. Sports Asylum, USA Hockey.

Checking. Proper skills of checking and techniques used in teaching them. 20 mins. USA Hockey.

Defensive Concepts. With George Kingston; discusses pressure/patience, triangulation, defensive side positioning, support, angling and pinning. 40 mins. Sports Asylum, USA Hockey.

Defensive Skills. Skills and drills needed to be complete defenseman. 25 mins. USA Hockey.

Designing a Practice. How to plan practice sessions. 30 mins. USA Hockey.

Emergency Response to Head and Neck Injuries. Begins with short anatomical description, followed by planned approach to dealing with both conscious and unconscious injured player. 25 mins. Sports Asylum, USA Hockey.

Emergency Response to Soft Tissue Injuries. Deals with recognizing and treating soft tissue injuries of hockey players. 30 mins. Sports Asylum, USA Hockey.

Face-Offs. With Guy Charron; discusses role of defense, wingers and centermen for all face-offs. Offensive, defensive, neutral zone, power play and penalty killing alignments described and illustrated with Olympic highlights. 40 mins. Sports Asylum, USA Hockey.

Fun and Games on Ice 1 and 2. Variety of games to add fun, skill development and motivation to practice. Games progress from beginning to advanced player. 30 mins each. Sports Asylum, USA Hockey.

Fundamentals of Power Skating. Introductory level video dealing with basic skating skills and techniques. 20 mins. USA Hockey.

Get the Edge. Power skating technique training video with Audrey Bakewell and NHL star Joe Nieuwendyk. Covers warm-up, flat-footed skating, edges, crossovers, turns, agility and more. 30 mins. Sports Asylum.

Goals I and II. With Dave King. *Goals I* demonstrates (1) read and react, the importance of on-ice thinking processes; (2) offensive support, the role of offensive players without the puck; and (3) puck protection. 35 mins. *Goals II* demonstrates (1) timing, the key to offensive support, and (2) read and react for defensemen in their own end. 25 mins. Sports Asylum, USA Hockey.

SYSTEMATIC FIGURE SKATING
The Spin and Jump Techniques of Gustave Lussi

hosted by Dick Button   produced by Cecily Morrow

"His really is the foundation of technique...no one will ever, *ever* be able to get away from it, because it's based on sound, fundamental concepts." - John Misha Petkevich

A four-volume video series which shows Mr. Lussi, coach of 16 World and Olympic champions, instructing skaters, step-by-step, in his innovative freestyle methods.

For purchasing information call 410-820-6125, VISA/MC accepted, or write to: **Lussi Technical Video**, 207 Earle Ave., Easton, MD 21601

ICE COMMAND VIDEOS

Cecily Alexandra Morrow and Cecily Hogg Morrow present

ICE SKATING FOR EVERYONE
The Beginner's Guide to a Lifetime Sport

Learn skating basics from highly qualified, experienced professionals.

•••••••••••• and ••••••••••••

STROKING EXERCISES ON ICE
The Dance Training Methods of Natalia Dubova

Renowned ice dance coach reveals basic training methods on-ice, featuring her students Elizaveta Stekolnikova and Dmitri Kazarlyga.

For purchasing information call 410-820-5614, VISA/MC accepted, or write to: **ICE COMMAND**, 207 Earle Ave., Easton, MD 21601

Goalkeeping, Parts I and II. Part I (17 mins) covers basic stance, movement and balance. Part II (20 mins) deals with playing angles, blockage and more advanced situations. USA Hockey.

Goaltending Today. Introduces ideas of positioning, anticipating and concentration for goaltenders only. USA Hockey.

Gordie Howe Instructional Tapes. For individuals or coaches. *Forwards*, 55 mins; *Defense*, 55 mins; *Stick Handling & Passing*, 35 mins; *Shooting*, 35 mins; *Power Skating*, 51 mins; *Goal Tending*, 35 mins; and *Conditioning & Coaching*, 55 mins. Rainbo Sports, Sports Asylum.

Hockey From Oates to Neely to You. With Paul Vincent, Adam Oates, Cam Neely. Teaches basics of power skating, stickhandling, passing fundamentals, and techniques for shooting and scoring. 40 mins. Sports Asylum.

Hockey Parents Make the Difference. Focuses on role of parents in minor hockey; has 25 scenarios on how good parents can make the difference. 30 mins. Sports Asylum, USA Hockey.

Laura Stamm's Power Stroking. 1994. An overview of her book by the same title. Segments include crossover, turning, forward stride, backward stride, lateral movement, starts, and stops. 28 minutes. Laura Stamm Enterprises: (914) 961-7994. Also, Sports Asylum.

Offensive Attack Options. With Dave King; emphasizes tactics available to team with possession; stresses importance of support, pressure, read and attack, and transition in execution of attack options. 30 mins. Sports Asylum, USA Hockey.

Passing and Receiving. Covers fundamentals of passing and receiving. 23 mins. USA Hockey.

Principles of Conditioning for Youth Hockey. Fundamentals of training on and off the ice to enhance speed, agility, coordination and balance. 21 mins. USA Hockey.

Puck Control. Demonstrates simple to complex stick-handling techniques. 23 mins. USA Hockey.

Puck Control and Deking. Dave King leads a group of hockey players through on-ice progressional drills; he also highlights key technical and teaching cues. 40 mins. Sports Asylum, USA Hockey.

Puckhandling for Goaltenders. With Dale Henwood. Puck control skills for goaltenders encompasses setting the puck up for a teammate, clearing the zone, or passing to a teammate. Discusses theory and technical components of each of these drills for pucks. 35 mins. Sports Asylum, USA Hockey.

Regroups. With Wayne Fleming; 23 drills to illustrate individual responsibilities of defense and forwards along with coordinated team movement in various regroup situations. 40 mins. Sports Asylum, USA Hockey.

Search for the Lost Art. Real Turcotte's stickhandling drills and techniques demonstrated with emphasis on attacking the goal. 25 mins. Sports Asylum.

The Shooter's Edge. Russ and Geoff Courtnall show techniques that can develop goal scorers. Nine segments analyzing breakaways, one-timers, rebounds, and more. 57 mins. Sports Asylum.

Shooting and Scoring. Illustrates techniques involved in performing wrist shot, snap shot, slap shot, backhand shot and flip shot. 24 mins. USA Hockey.

Skating--Balance and Power. Kozak illustrates off-ice exercises to develop balance, power, flexibility. Tuff presents on-ice drills pertaining to starting, stopping, balance, and developing stride. 40 mins. Sports Asylum, USA Hockey.

Skating Dynamics for Officials. Presents basic skating skills for officials. 30 mins. USA Hockey.

Smart Hockey. Designed to make hockey players and coaches aware of dangers of checking or pushing another player from behind. 20 mins. Sports Asylum.

Strength Training for Hockey. Highlights specifics of strength training for hockey. 18 mins. USA Hockey.

Teaching Techniques. With Dave King; ideas for coaches including communication keys, player-coach relationship and interaction, key teaching points and drill progressions, planning and organizing. 30 mins. Sports Asylum, USA Hockey.

Training for Leg Power and Quickness. On-ice and off-ice training techniques designed to improve quickness and leg power. 20 mins. USA Hockey.

Transition: Defense to Offense. With Slavomir Lener, former Czech Olympic coach. Introduces transition from defense to offense; on- and off-ice training methods presented. 30 mins. Sports Asylum, USA Hockey.

Winning In-Line Hockey. Explains how to polish skating skills with explosive starts, power turns, quick stops, smooth transitions and agile backwards skating, plus stick-handling techniques and choosing the right equipment. 32 mins. Sports Asylum.

ARE WE MISSING ANY VIDEOS?

If you know of any ice skating videos that we're missing, please send us the following information:

Title
Brief description
   (including skaters)
Length
Year made
Who made it
Where it can be obtained

Also, if you can add any of the above details that are missing in the video listings already included in this book, please share that information with us.

Send any available information to:

Skater's Edge Sourcebook
Video Update Information
Box 500
Kensington, MD 20895
Phone/FAX: (301) 946-1971

Thank you!

Advertiser Index

Anderson Ice Rinks, Inc.	73	Lexicon Ventures Limited	107
Ashworth & Associates	107	Lussi Technical Video	267
Beads, Etc.	107	Magic of Style	265
Birch Hill Designs/Kai-Lei on Ice	115	National Ice Skating Centers, Inc.	91
Bramwell (Patricia) Sports Psychology	107	Outside Edge	89
Burley's Rink Supply, Inc.	123	P.H.D. Products	107
Cag One Skatesharpeners, Inc.	75	Platoro Press	21
Can Alpine Agencies	106	Productions East Video	107
Club Skate	42	Rainbo Sport Shop	95
Coastal A.V.	77	Riedell Skate, Co.	44
Creative Pack Works	106	Rink-Tec International, Inc.	93
Creative Pins by Lynne	75	Satin Stitches	99
Enchantment on Ice	79	Show-Off, Inc.	97
Foy Toys	80	Skate 'N Style	97
Freestyle Designs	81	Skate Spinner	Back Cover
Harlick & Company	43	Skater's Choice Gift Boutique	99
K-Tee Enterprises	106	*Skater's Edge*	36
Ice Command	267	*Skater's Edge* SOURCEBOOK	108
Ice Skate Conditioning Equipment Co.	112	Skater's Paradise, Inc.	41
Ice Systems of America	121	Sky Rink	197
Impact Wear by Holjen, Inc.	83	Sport Consulting Centre	25
Inga Creations	106	Starbuck & Company	101
It's a Laurie! Original	107	Stretch Quest	103
JAMA and Friends Skate	255	Tana's Gold	106
Jumpometer Co.	106	Video Sports Productions	263
Lenzi Foundation, The	107	Walt Disney's World on Ice	79

Notes

Notes

Notes